ENGLISH TRAVELLERS TO VENICE 1450–1600

THIRD SERIES
NO. 39

# INTERNATIONAL REPRESENTATIVES OF THE HAKLUYT SOCIETY

Giovanni Bellini, portrait of Doge Leonardo Loredan. Oil on panel, *c.*1501. National Gallery, London. Bridgeman Images.

# ENGLISH TRAVELLERS TO VENICE
## 1450–1600

Edited by

## MICHAEL G. BRENNAN

*Published by*
*Routledge*
*for*
THE HAKLUYT SOCIETY
LONDON
2022

First published 2022 for the Hakluyt Society by Routledge
2 Park Square, Milton Park, Abingdon, Oxon OX14 4RN

and by Routledge
605 Third Avenue, New York, NY 10158

*Routledge is an imprint of the Taylor & Francis Group, an informa business*

*British Library Cataloguing-in-Publication Data*
A catalogue record for this book is available from the British Library

*Library of Congress Cataloging-in-Publication Data*
A catalog record has been requested for this book

ISBN: 978-1-032-17054-1 (hbk)
ISBN: 978-1-003-25157-6 (ebk)

DOI: 10.4324/9781003251576

Typeset in Garamond Premier Pro
by Waveney Typesetters, Wymondham, Norfolk

Routledge website: http://www.routledge.com

Hakuyt Society website: http://www.hakluyt.com

For Geraldine, Christina and Alice

# CONTENTS

# LIST OF MAPS AND ILLUSTRATIONS

## Maps

## Colour Plates

**Figures**

[1] Images from Giacomo Franco, *Habiti d'huomeni et donne venetiane con la processione della ser[enissi]ma. Signoria et altri particolari, cioè trionfi, feste et cerimonie publiche della nobilissima città di Venetia*, Venice: 1610; and his *La Città di Venetia con l'origine e governo di quella ... Estratte dall'opere di Gioan Nicolò Doglioni. Parte seconda*. Venice: 1614, are taken from a facsimile of the Biblioteca Marciana copy, Venice: F. Ongania, 1876. By permission of Special Collections, Brotherton Library, University of Leeds (Large Modern History F-3 FRA).

# ABBREVIATIONS AND CONVENTIONS

| | |
|---|---|
| BHO | British History Online |
| BL | British Library |
| *CSP Venice* | *Calendar of State Papers Venice ... 1202-1603* |
| HMC | *Historical Manuscripts Commission* |
| LP | *Letters and Papers, Foreign and Domestic, of the Reign of Henry VIII* |
| ODNB | *Oxford Dictionary of National Biography* |
| OED | *Oxford English Dictionary* |
| STC | *Short-Title Catalogue* |
| TNA | The National Archives, Kew, UK |

Full titles of all works cited are given in the Bibliography with abbreviated titles in the footnotes. For works printed in Britain before 1640 *Short-Title Catalogue* references are also supplied.

The most commonly traversed regions are described as 'Western Europe' and 'the continent'. In the introduction and annotations modern-day geographical delineations of specific regions (e.g. Germany, Austria, Switzerland and so on) are used rather than the less familiar territorial divisions of the 1450–1600 period.

In the edited texts, the spellings, accenting of foreign words, Middle English and proper and place names in the original manuscripts and printed texts have generally been retained with, if necessary, explanatory footnotes. The use of 'i'/'j', 'u'/'v', and long 's' has been standardized and 'yᵉ', 'yᵗ', 'yᵉˢᵉ', and 'yᵉʳᵉ' to *'the'*, *'that'*, *'these'*, and *'there'*. Other standard contractions have been expanded, such as 'wᶜʰ'/'wh*ich*' and 'yʳ'/'y*our*', indicated by italic. In some manuscript and printed texts, the use of upper-case letters is problematic because it is not always clear (especially with letters such as 's', 'p', 'm', and 'n') whether an upper-case letter was intended. In other cases, upper-case letters (or lower-case letters at the beginning of sentences) are randomly deployed. Apart from ambiguous instances, where it has been necessary to make an editorial decision for clarity, the use of capitals or lower-case letters in the original texts has been generally retained. Where translations or glosses of original texts (usually Middle English, Latin and Italian) have been provided, the translations aim to be as faithful as possible to the tone and style of original text so that the voice and thought processes of the original writer are not obliterated.

To assist the modern reader, the punctuation and paragraphing of the original manuscript and printed texts, which sometimes range from the erratic to the non-existent, have been lightly modernized. However, this kind of editorial intervention has been cautiously applied and it is noted when, to assist the reader, the original has been paragraphed. Full stops and initial capital letters for new sentences have only been supplied when essential for clarity. In both manuscript and printed texts, catchwords at the foot of pages have been omitted since they are used irregularly. Folio or page references within square brackets indicate the folios or pages of the original text. All marginal annotations included in the original texts have been recorded within square brackets in the text, preceded by '*margin:*'. Square brackets are employed in the conventional manner to enclose editorial comments or additions and all other substantive matters of scribal commission and omission are recorded in the footnotes.

When abroad after 1582, English travellers generally used the new-style (NS) Gregorian calendar, as opposed to the old-style (OS) Julian calendar, still followed in Protestant Britain (except Scotland). The new-style continental system, adopted by all other European countries (except Russia), was ten days in advance of the old-style. Under the Julian calendar, 25 March (Lady Day) was regarded as the first day of the New Year.

Finally, to avoid repetitious footnotes, an Appendix provides factual information about key Venetian locations, institutions and ceremonies, such as the Arsenal, Ghetto, Grand Canal, Ducal Palace, Marriage of the Sea, and Rialto, as well as the city's major churches, schools (*scuole*) and civic institutions mentioned in the texts. These entries are indicated in the footnotes by *.

# ACKNOWLEDGEMENTS

I have incurred many debts during the compilation of this volume. I owe special thanks to Jim Bennett, former President of the Hakluyt Society, and to my Hakluyt Society Series Editors, Janet Hartley and Joyce Lorimer, for their encouragement, support and meticulous work on this volume. I am grateful to many past and present members of the Council of the Hakluyt Society for their generously given advice, especially the series editor of my two earlier volumes for the society, Will Ryan (who has also advised on this volume), and Anthony Payne for invaluable bibliographical guidance. The efficiency and helpfulness of the Society's Administrator, Melanie Vasilescu, and its Administrative Editor, Katherine Parker, have been much appreciated. I am also indebted to David Cox (cartographer), Mary Murphy (copy-editor) and Barrie Fairhead (typesetter), and the team at Routledge.

I have been interested in early travellers to Venice for over forty years, especially the extended stay at Venice in 1573–74 of Sir Philip Sidney (1554–86), whose presence lies at the heart of this volume. I am especially grateful to the late Viscount De L'Isle, VC, KG, Viscount De L'Isle, CVO, MBE, and his son, the Hon. Philip Sidney, for their generous support of my work on Sir Philip and the Sidney family of Penshurst Place, Kent. I also owe much to L. Glenn Black who first introduced me to the writings of Sir Philip Sidney and to Alicia Black who kindly sent to me review copies of books relevant to this volume. My work on the Sidneys over many years has been supported and stimulated by my long-time collaborators, the late Margaret P. Hannay, the late Noel J. Kinnamon, and Mary Ellen Lamb, as well as Joe Black, Hannibal Hamlin, John Pitcher, Germaine Warkentin and the many contributors to the two-volume *Ashgate Research Companion to the Sidneys, 1500–1770* (2015) which I co-edited with Margaret P. Hannay and Mary Ellen Lamb.

My compilation of this volume was more recently guided by conversations with my colleague at the University of Leeds, Alexandra Bamji, whose extensive knowledge of Venice's history and writings about the city, always so generously shared, has been a source of welcome guidance. Her invitation in 2017 to address the annual interdisciplinary Venetian Seminar on 'Philip Sidney, Venice and Veronese in 1574' supported my initial plans for this volume. My colleague in Art History and Museum Studies at the University of Leeds, Mark Westgarth, has been a reliable source of advice and guidance on a wide variety of collections relating to the visual arts. I have also received much help and expert advice from Gary Baker, Anthony Bale, Bernadette Barnett, Mark Bland (in genealogical matters), Molly Bourne, Mary Boyle (who generously granted me access to the typescript of her book on the Jerusalem pilgrimage), Martin Butler, Daniel Carey, John Gallagher, Elizabeth Goldring, Paul Hammond, Claire Jowitt, Marie-Louise Leonard, David Lindley, Domenico Lovascio, Rob Lutton, P. B. Oursin, and Cathy Shrank.

I owe much to all the staff of the Brotherton Library, Leeds, and especially to Joanne Fitton (Head of Special Collections and Galleries), Oliver Pickering, Richard High and all their colleagues in Special Collections. I also owe a special debt to the late Christopher D. W. Sheppard (former Head of Special Collections) who first introduced me to the rich collections of travel literature held by the library. Much of my research, especially relating to travel writings, has been focused for over thirty-five years on these collections, created through the manuscript and book collections of Edward Allan Brotherton (1856–1930), first Baron Brotherton. Two library colleagues have been especially supportive of the compilation of this volume which draws extensively for its illustrations on the library's holdings. Rhiannon Lawrence-Francis (Collections and Engagement Manager, Rare Books and Maps) has been generous with her time and expertise in arranging for me to examine rare and valuable items from the Brotherton Collection. Ken Kajoranta (Digitisation Studio Manager) has provided his photographic expertise to produce digital images of the Breydenbach and Nuremberg Chronicle maps of Venice, the Venetian engravings of Giacomo Franco and other items from the Brotherton Library included in this volume. I am also indebted to Siân Phillips at Bridgeman Images for her assistance in obtaining many of the colour illustrations included in this volume.

I have received considerable help from the librarians and staff of the libraries, record offices and archives listed in the Bibliography, including: the Bodleian Library, Oxford; British Library, London; Canterbury Cathedral Archives (especially Cressida Williams and Toby Hultson); Chatsworth House, Derbyshire (especially Aidan Haley); Corpus Christi College, Oxford; Gallerie dell'Accademia, Venice; John Rylands Library, Manchester (especially John McCrory); Lambeth Palace Library, London; The Leeds Library, Leeds; Magdalen College Library, Oxford (especially Daryl Green); Magdalen College Library, Oxford; Museo Correr, Venice; The National Archives, Kew; New College Library and Archives, Oxford (especially Christopher Skelton-Foord); Palazzo Ducale, Venice; Rijksmuseum, Amsterdam; University of St Andrew's, Special Collections (especially Catriona Foote); Wellcome Library, University of London (especially Edward Bishop and Kate Symonds); Victoria and Albert Museum, London; and West Sussex Record Office.

It would be impossible to list and quantify my debts to the numerous individuals whose publications about Venice, its inhabitants and visitors have so helpfully informed and supported my researches. The bibliography to this volume goes some way towards recording these debts but I would also wish to confirm here my admiration for works on Venice and its residents, especially its artists, institutions and buildings, by Alexandra Bamji, David Chambers, John Garton, Deborah Howard, Ioanna Iordanou, Marion Kaminski, Francesco da Mosto, Tom Nichols, John Julius Norwich, Brian Pullan, W. R. Rearick, Carlo Ridolfi, David Rosand, Elizabeth Ross, Xavier F. Salomon and John Steer. I am also indebted to scholars and editors who have worked on individuals and locations included in this volume, especially Anthony Bale, Mary Boyle, Susan Brigden, Edward Chaney, Francis Davey, Thomas Frank, John Gallagher, Rachel Hammerton, Graham David Kew, Carole Levin, Rob Lutton, Brian Mac Cuarta, Noemi Magri, R, J. Mitchell, M. Anne Overell, Carol C. Rutter, Sebastian Sobecki and Jonathan Woolfson.

My greatest personal debt is to my wife, Geraldine, and our daughters, Christina and Alice. Geraldine has been my guide in working on materials in Latin, Italian, French and Spanish and has read complete drafts of this work. All three have enjoyed and endured over many years and during our visits to Venice my fascination with the city's history, literature, architecture, institutions, works of art and religious devotions.

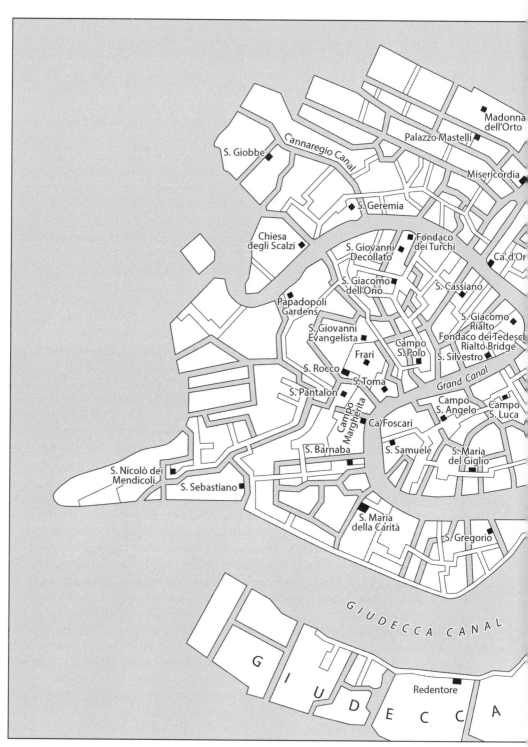

Map 1.    Venice in the fifteenth and sixteenth centuries.

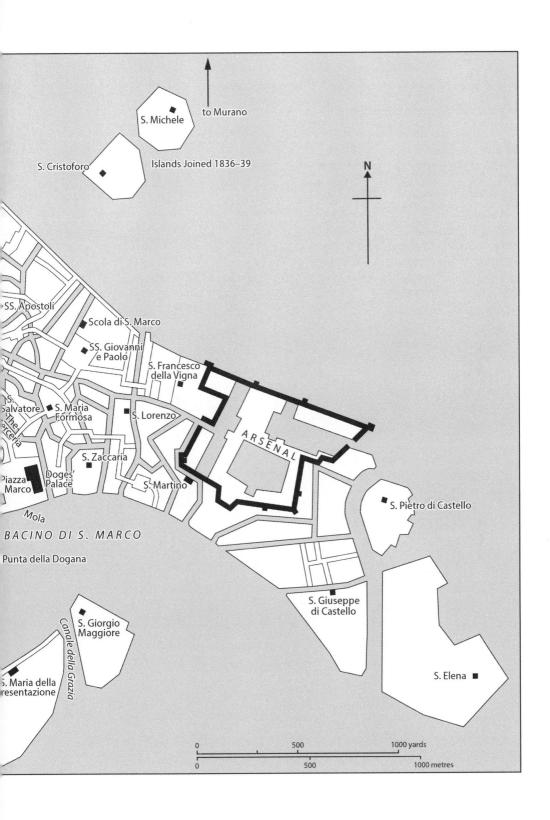

to Murano

S. Michele

S. Cristoforo

Islands Joined 1836–39

N

SS. Apostoli

Scola di S. Marco

SS. Giovanni
e Paolo

S. Francesco
della Vigna

SS.
Salvatore

S. Maria
Formosa

S. Lorenzo

ARSENAL

La
Zecceria

S. Zaccaria

Piazza
Marco

Doges'
Palace

S. Martino

S. Pietro di Castello

Mola

BACINO DI S. MARCO

Punta della Dogana

S. Giuseppe
di Castello

S. Giorgio
Maggiore

Canale della Grazia

S. Maria della
Presentazione

S. Elena

| 0 | | 500 | | 1000 yards |

| 0 | | 500 | | 1000 metres |

Map 2. The eastern Mediterranean and Venetian possessions during the fifteenth and sixteenth centuries.

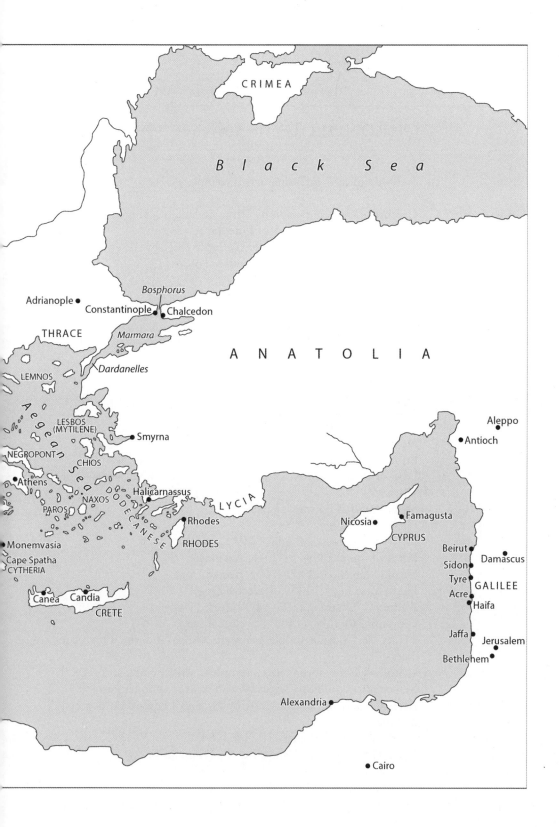

CRIMEA

*Black Sea*

Adrianople ●

*Bosphorus*
Constantinople ● ● Chalcedon

THRACE

*Marmara*

*Dardanelles*

LEMNOS

A N A T O L I A

LESBOS
(MYTILENE)

*Aegean Sea*

● Smyrna

Aleppo
●

● Antioch

NEGROPONT

CHIOS

● Athens

Halicarnassus

NAXOS

L Y C I A

Nicosia
●

● Famagusta

PAROS

DODECANESE

CYPRUS

● Monemvasia

Cape Spatha
CYTHERIA

Rhodes
●

RHODES

Beirut ●

Damascus
●

Sidon ●

Tyre ●

GALILEE

Canea  Candia

Acre ●

● Haifa

CRETE

Jaffa ●

● Jerusalem

Bethlehem ●

Alexandria ●

● Cairo

**Bold** indicates inclusion in this volume.

| | |
|---|---|
| 1453 | Capture of Constantinople by Ottoman Sultan Mehmed II |
| *c.*1454 | **Richard 'Esty'** or **Richard 'of Lincoln'** at Venice |
| 1457 | Pasquale Malipiero (1392–1462) elected Doge by the enemies of the family of his predecessor, Francesco Foscari (1373–1457), Doge 1423–57. |
| **1458** | **William Wey,** first visit to Venice |
| | **John Tiptoft, Earl of Worcester**, first visit to Venice |
| **1460** | **John Tiptoft, Earl of Worcester**, second visit to Venice |
| 1460 | King Henry VI (1422–71) imprisoned by Yorkist lords (10 July 1460–17 Feb. 1461); deposed 4 Mar. 1461 |
| 1461 (4 Mar.) | Accession of King Edward IV (1442–83) |
| 1462 | Cristoforo Moro (1390–1471) elected Doge |
| | **William Wey**, second visit to Venice (**Figure 13**) |
| 1463 | Outbreak of First Ottoman-Venetian War (1463–79) |
| 1465 | Henry VI imprisoned (until 1471) by Edward IV |
| 1469 | Printing press in operation at Venice |
| 1469 | Edward IV imprisoned (Aug.–Sept.) by Richard Neville, Earl of Warwick |
| **1460s or 70s** | **Sir Edmund Wighton** at Venice |
| 1470 (3 Oct.) | Henry VI restored |
| 1471 (11 Apr.) | Henry VI deposed and Edward IV restored |
| | Nicolo Tron (*c.*1399–1471) elected Doge |
| 1473 | Nicolo Marcello (*c.*1399–1474) elected Doge |
| 1474 | Pietro Mocenigo (1406–76) elected Doge |
| 1476 | Andrea Vendramin (1393–1478) elected Doge |
| 1478 | Giovanni Mocenigo (1409–85) elected Doge |
| 1479 (24 Jan.) | Treaty of Constantinople between Venice and the Ottoman Turks |
| (Sept.) | Gentile Bellini sent to Constantinople as artistic ambassador |
| 1482 | Venice allies with Pope Sixtus IV who seeks to conquer Ferrara |
| 1483 (9 Apr.) | Accession of King Edward V (1470–83), son of Edward IV; deposed 23 June |
| (26 June) | Accession of King Richard III (1452–85) |
| 1484 | Peace Treaty between Venice and the Ottoman Turks |
| 1485 (22 Aug.) | Accession of King Henry VII (1457–1509) |
| 1485 | Marco Barbarigo (*c.*1413–86) elected Doge |

| | |
|---|---|
| 1486 (18 Jan.) | Princess Elizabeth, daughter of Edward IV, marries Henry VII |
| | Agostino Barbarigo (1419-1501) elected Doge |
| 1486 | Publication of Bernard von Breydenbach, *Peregrinatio in Terram Sanctam*, including a fold-out woodcut map of Venice (**Maps 3-8**) |
| 1487 | Christopher Urswick (*c*.1448-1522), Henry VII's chaplain and confessor, sent as English Ambassador Extraordinary to Venice; accompanied by Dr Thomas West; Venice again in 1502; previously at Rome in 1480, 1486 and again in 1493 |
| 1488 | Portuguese explorer Bartolomeu Dias (1450-1500) rounds Cape of Good Hope, providing Venetian trade with a sea route to the Indian Ocean |
| 1489 (Feb.) | Cyprus is ceded to Venice by Catherine Cornaro (1454-1510), widow of its last king, James II (*c*.1438/40-73); their infant son James III (1473-4) accedes with his mother as regent who, after her son's suspicious death, reigns as Queen of Cyprus until 1489 |
| 1491 | Giacomo Venier, Captain of the Flanders Galleys, in England |
| 1492 | Christopher Columbus (1451-1506) discovers the Americas |
| **1492/3-97** | **Thomas Linacre** at Venice and Padua (**Plate 15**) |
| 1493 | Publication of Hartmann Schedel, *Liber chronicarum* [Nuremberg Chronicle] (Nuremberg, 1493), including the woodcut map of Venice from Bernard von Breydenbach, *Peregrinatio in Terram Sanctam* (1483) (**Maps 9-10**) |
| 1495 (July) | Francesco II Gonzaga, Marquess of Mantua, appointed Captain-General by the Venetians |
| (summer) | Syphilis first identified in northern Italy by the Venetian military surgeon Marcello Cumano and caught by the Marquess of Mantua |
| | Printer Aldus Manutius in business at Venice |
| *c*.1496 | Gentile Bellini, *Procession in St Mark's Square*, representing the procession in 1444 (**Plate 2**) |
| | Vittore Carpaccio, *Miracle of the Cross at the Ponte di Rialto* (**Plate 2**) |
| 1496-8 | Andrea Trevisan in England |
| 1497 | Pietro Contarini and Luca Valaresso in England |
| 1498 | Portuguese explorer Vasco da Gama (*c*.1460s-1524) reaches India, ending Venice's land route monopoly over Eastern trade |
| **1498/1500** | Publication of ***Informacon for pylgrymes unto the holy londe*** (rpt 1515, 1524) |
| 1499 | Venice allies with King Louis XII of France against Milan, gaining Cremona; outbreak of Second Ottoman-Venetian War; Venetian fleet defeated in Battle of Zonchio |
| 1500 | Gentile Bellini, *The Miracle of the Cross on San Lorenzo Bridge* (**Plate 3**) |
| 1500 | Jacopo de' Barbari, Aerial View of Map of Venice (**Maps 11-14**) |
| 1501 | Leonardo Loredan (1436-1521) elected Doge (**Frontispiece**) |
| 1501-2 | Francesco Capello in England |
| 1502 (2 Apr.) | Death of Prince Arthur (b. 1486), eldest son of Henry VII |

| 1504 | Richard Pace delivers at Venice an oration on the study of Greek; again in the Veneto in 1522 and 1525 |
|---|---|
| **1506 (12 June)** | **Sir Richard Guildford** and **Thomas Larke** leave Venice on pilgrimage to the Holy Land |
| 1506 | Vincent Querini in England |
| 1508–9 | Andrea Badoer in England |
| 1508–17 | War of the League of Cambrai, led by Pope Julius II, hostile to Venice |
| 1508 (28 July) | Death of Robert Blackadder, Archbishop of Glasgow, while sailing from Venice to Jaffa on pilgrimage; he died with twenty-six other pilgrims, probably from typhoid or cholera, and was buried at sea; he had previously made his will at Venice |
| 1508 (10 Dec.) | League of Cambrai agreed between the Papacy, France, the Holy Roman Empire and Spain against the Venetian Republic |
| 1509 (22 Apr.) | Accession of King Henry VIII (1491–1547) |
| (14 May) | Venice defeated at the Battle of Agnadello |
| (11 June) | Henry VIII marries Catherine of Aragon (1485–1536) |
| (Aug.) | Francesco II Gonzaga, Marquess of Mantua, taken prisoner by the Venetians; his spouse Isabella d'Este (1474–1539) negotiates for his release and his son Federico (1500–40) is sent to Rome as hostage Spain and the Pope end alliance with France and Venice Population of Venice c.102,000 |
| 1510 (14 July) | Francesco II Gonzaga, Marquess of Mantua, released from captivity Venetian/Papal alliance against Louis XII of France |
| 1513 | **Sir Thomas Newport** and **Sir Thomas Sheffield**, Knights of Rhodes, present letters from Henry VIII to Doge Leonardo Loredan at Venice (**Frontispiece**) |
| 1514 (10 Jan.) | Fire in the Rialto |
| c.1514 | **Robert Langton** at Venice, where his portrait is painted (**Plate 5**) |
| 1515 | Venice in alliance with France; victors at Battle of Marignano Andrea Badoer, Pietro Pasqualigo and Sebastian Giustinian in England |
| 1516 | Jewish Ghetto established in Cannaregio *sestiere* |
| **1517** | **Sir Richard Torkington** at Venice |
| 1518 | Hieronimo Molins appointed Venetian Consul in London |
| 1519 | Sebastian Giustinian and Antonio Surian in England |
| 1520 | Antonio Surian (until 1523) and Francesco Corner in England |
| 1520 (7–24 June) | Field of the Cloth of Gold; a summit between Henry VIII and King François I of France |
| 1521 | Antonio Grimani (1434–1523) elected Doge |
| c.1521–c.1526 | **Reginald Pole** at Venice and Padua (**Plate 6**) |
| 1522 | Gasparo Contarini in England |
| 1522–5 | Richard Pace, Ambassador Lieger to Venice; his *Plutarchi* reprinted at Venice (1522), with Plutarch's *De garrulitate* and *De avaritia*; obtained permission from Senate for printing of Nicolo Tomeo's |

edition of Aristotle's *Parva naturalia* (1523); supporting Cardinal Wolsey's attempts (1521–3) to be elected Pope

| | |
|---|---|
| 1523 | Andrea Gritti (1455–1538) elected Doge (**Plate 4**) |
| 1524 | Wooden Rialto Bridge collapses (**Plate 2** and **Map 12**) |
| 1525 (24 Feb.) | Battle of Pavia, defeat of the French army by Imperial-Spanish forces |
| 1525–6 | Lorenzo Orio in England |
| 1525–8 | Marc'Antonio Venier in England |
| 1525–*c.*1533 | Vincent Cassalis, Ambassador in Ordinary to Venice |
| 1526 | Gasparo Spinelli in England |
| 1527 | Sir Gregory Cassalis, Ambassador Extraordinary to Venice |
| 1527 | Forces of Emperor Charles V sack Rome; Medici Pope Clement VII flees the city |
| 1527 | Jacopo Sansovino (1486–1570) appointed public architect |
| 1528 | Marc'Antonio Venier and Lodovico Falier (until 1531) in England |
| 1530 | Bishops Richard Croke (*c.*1489–1558) and John Stokesley (*c.*1475–1539), Ambassadors Extraordinary to Venice |
| 1531–2 | Mario Savorgnano (1517–74), a wealthy Venetian nobleman, visits England in August and meets Henry VIII, Catherine of Aragon, Princess Mary and Anne Boleyn; describes Dover, Canterbury and London in his letters to the Signoria |
| 1531–5 | Carlo Capello in England |
| 1532 | Hieronimo Molins, friend of Edmund Harvell, again appointed Venetian Consul in London |
| 1532–6 | **Reginald Pole** at Venice and Padua (**Plate 6**) |
| 1533 (25 Jan.) | Henry VIII marries Anne Boleyn (*c.*1501–36) |
| (23 May) | Henry VIII's marriage to Catherine of Aragon declared null and void |
| 1534 | Act of Supremacy established Henry VIII as head of the Church in England |
| 1535 | Carlo Capello, Ambassador to England, recalled to Venice |
| 1535–44 | Girolamo Zuccato, Venetian First Secretary, in England |
| 1535–49 | Edmund Harvell, English Agent and Ambassador (from 1539) at Venice until his death (Jan. 1549) |
| 1536 (19 May) | Anne Boleyn executed within the precincts of the Tower of London |
| (30 May) | Henry VIII marries Jane Seymour (*c.*1508–37) |
| 1537 | Outbreak of Third Ottoman-Venetian War (1537–40) |
| **1538** | **Andrew Boorde** at Venice |
| 1538 | Pietro Lando (1462–1545) elected Doge |
| **1539** | **Edmund Harvell** formally appointed as English Ambassador to Venice |
| 1540 (6 Jan.) | Henry VIII marries Anne of Cleves (1515–57); marriage annulled 9 July 1540 |
| (28 July) | Henry VIII marries Catherine Howard (1523–42) |
| 1540–51 | Daniele Barbaro in England |
| 1542 (13 Feb.) | Catherine Howard executed |
| 1543 (12 July) | Henry VIII marries Catherine Parr (1512–48) |

| | |
|---|---|
| 1544–7 | Giacomo Zambon, Venetian First Secretary, in England |
| 1545 | Sinking of the *Mary Rose* (**Plate 7**), drowning of its commander Sir George Carew (**Plate 8**) and Venetian salvage attempts |
| 1545 | Francesco Donato (1468–1553) elected Doge |
| *c.*1545–8 | **William Thomas** at Venice |
| 1546 | **Lodovico Dall'Armi**, English Agent Extraordinary to Venice |
| *c.*1546–8 | Titian (Tiziano Vecellio) paints posthumous portrait of Doge Andrea Gritti (**Plate 4**) |
| 1547 (28 Jan.) | Death of Henry VIII; accession of King Edward VI (1537–53) |
| 1547–9 | Domenico Bollani, Venetian Ambassador, in England |
| **1548/1550** | **(1554/5) Sir Thomas Hoby** at Venice |
| 1549 | Book of Common Prayer introduced in England |
| **1550–56** | **Peter Vannes**, English Agent at Venice |
| 1551 | Alvise Agostini in England |
| **1552** | **Roger Ascham** at Venice |
| 1553 (6 July) | Death of Edward VI and accession of Lady Jane Grey (1537–54); deposed 19 July; executed 12 Feb. 1554 |
| (19 July) | Accession of Mary I (1516–58) |
| | Marcantonio Trivisan (*c.*1475–1554) elected Doge |
| 1554 (25 July) | Queen Mary I marries Philip of Spain (1527–98) at Winchester Cathedral; revives Heresy Acts, leading to persecution of Protestant reformers, many of whom go into European exile |
| 1554 | Francesco Venier (1489–1556) elected Doge |
| 1554 | Giacomo Soranzo in England |
| 1554–7 | Giovanni Michiel in England as Venetian Ambassador |
| 1555 | Anthony Browne, Viscount Montague, Ambassador Extraordinary to Venice |
| 1556 (16 Jan.) | Mary I's consort, Philip of Spain, accedes as Philip II of Spain, following abdication of his father, Charles V |
| 1556 | Lorenzo Priuli (1489–1559) elected Doge |
| 1557 | Michiel Surian in England |
| 1558 (17 Nov.) | Death of Mary I and accession of Elizabeth I (1533–1603) |
| 1559 | Act of Uniformity and Act of Supremacy re-establish Protestant Church of England |
| | Girolamo Priuli (1486–1567) elected Doge |
| 1563 | Population of Venice *c.*168,000 |
| **1564** | **Richard Smith** and **Sir Edward Unton** at Venice |
| 1567 | Mary Queen of Scots imprisoned, suspected of murdering her husband, Lord Darnley; her son James (1566–1625) is crowned as James VI of Scotland |
| | Pietro Loredan (1482–1570) elected Doge |
| 1569 (13 Sept.) | Fire at the Venice Arsenal (**Plate 12**) |
| | Publication of Gerardus Mercator's world map |
| **1570** | **Henry Cavendish** and **Gilbert Talbot** at Venice |
| | Publication of Abraham Ortelius's *Theatrum orbis terrarum*, the first modern atlas |

|  |  |
|---|---|
|  | Alvise I Mocenigo (1507–77) elected Doge |
|  | Outbreak of Fourth Ottoman-Venetian War (1570–73) |
|  | Hand-tinted Map of Venice, dated erroneously 1570 (**Map 16**) |
| (9 Sept.) | Venetian-controlled city of Nicosia, Cyprus, falls to the Ottomans |
| 1571 (1 Aug.) | After a prolonged siege, Famagusta surrenders to the Ottomans; its Venetian defender Marcantonio Bragadin flayed alive and his skin stuffed with straw |
| (7 Oct.) | Christian fleet of the Holy League defeats Turks at Battle of Lepanto; Sebastiano Venier (1496–1578) commands the Venetian naval contingent (**Plate 13**). |
|  | The Thirty-Nine Articles, defining the doctrine of the Church of England, made a legal requirement by the English Parliament |
| 1572–1617 | Plan of Venice, from Georg Braun and Frans Hogenberg, *Civitates orbis terrarum* (from engravings by Bolognino Zaltieri) (**Map 15**) |
| 1573 | Loss of Cyprus confirmed |
| **1573–4** | **Philip Sidney** (**Plate 17** and **Figure 17**) at Venice, with **Griffin Madox**, **Harry Whyte**, **John Fisher**, **Thomas Coningsby** (**Plate 18**), **Lodowick Bryskett** and **Edward, Lord Windsor** |
| 1574 (July) | King Henri III of France at Venice (**Plate 9**) |
| 1575 | Fondaco dei Turchi established |
| **1575–6** | **Edward de Vere, Earl of Oxford**, at Venice |
| **1575/7** | **Sir John North** and **Hugh Lochard** at Venice |
| *c.*1575 | **Sir Henry Unton** at Venice (**Plate 25**) |
| 1575–7 | Plague kills 25 per cent of Venice's population |
| 1577 | Sebastiano Venier (*c.*1496–1578) elected Doge |
| 1578 | Nicolò da Ponte (1491–1585) elected Doge |
| 1580 | A Jesuit mission to England established to reconvert the nation to Catholicism |
| **1581** | **Arthur Throckmorton** at Venice |
| (Sept.) | Queen Elizabeth charters the Turkey Company |
| **1581** | **Laurence Aldersey** at Venice |
| 1581 | Population of Venice *c.*124,000 |
| 1583 | Queen Elizabeth charters the Venice Company for seven years |
| 1585 | Pasqual Cicogna (1509–95) elected Doge (**Plate 22**) |
| 1586 | Cesare Vecellio, *Procession of the Doge and his Entourage in Piazza San Marco* (**Plate 10**) |
| 1587 (8 Feb.) | Mary Queen of Scots executed at Fotheringhay Castle |
| (Apr.–May) | Sir Francis Drake raids the port of Cadiz, destroying Spanish vessels, popularly known as 'The Singeing of the King of Spain's Beard' |
| **1587–8** | **Stephen Powle** at Venice |
| **1588** | **Edward Webbe** at Venice |
| (July–Aug.) | Defeat by the English fleet of the Spanish Armada |
| 1588 (9 June) | Stone Rialto bridge begun; completed 1591 |
| **1589** | **Henry Cavendish** and **Fox**, his servant, at Venice |
| (20 Aug.) | James VI of Scotland marries Anne of Denmark by proxy |

| | |
|---|---|
| 1591 (4 Nov.) | Sir Henry Wotton at Venice (**Plate 26**) |
| 1592 (Jan.) | The English Venice Company merges with the Turkey Company to become the Levant Company |
| 1593 | Outbreak of Anglo-Irish Nine Years' War |
| **1593–7** | **Fynes Moryson** at Venice |
| **1595** | **Henry Piers** at Venice |
| 1595 | Marino Grimani (1532–1605) elected Doge |
| **1595–6** | **Roger Manners, Earl of Rutland**, **Francis Manners**, **Richard Cecil** and **Edward Cecil** at Venice |
| **1596** | **Sir Robert Dallington** at Venice |
| c.1595–1600 | Vittore Carpaccio (1472–1526), *The Ambassadors Return to the English Court* (Galleria dell'Accademia, Venice), recording the return home of Venetian Ambassadors to England |
| 1598 (Apr.) | Henri IV of France signs Edict of Nantes, ending France's religious wars and allowing toleration for Protestants |
| 1600 | Bridge of Sighs built |
| (Dec.) | Queen Elizabeth charters the East India Company |

Piazza di S. Marco

In questo habito si vede il Ser.^{mo} Doge di Venetia, nelle cerimonie et feste
principali; il qual habito fuori chel corno, che è proprio ornamento, nel
rimanente è tutto regale. Franco forma con Priuilegio

Figure 1.    Giacomo Franco, *Habiti d'huomeni et donne venetiane* (1610). The official ceremonial
and festival dress of the Doge of Venice, seated facing left, with a view of the Piazza San Marco in
upper right. By permission of Special Collections, Brotherton Library, University of Leeds.

# INTRODUCTION

## 1. Early Modern Anglo-Venetian Contacts

By focusing on the experiences of English travellers to Venice between 1450 and 1600 this volume explores the importance to England of the city and the Veneto region as a political, trading and cultural crossroads between Christian Europe and the Turkish-dominated eastern Mediterranean and Ottoman Empire. It demonstrates the diversity of English travellers to Venice at this period, including pilgrims, merchants, diplomats, religious exiles, sailors, soldiers, students and cultural tourists. Their narratives highlight key areas of interest at the time, including pre- and post-Reformation religious devotions and conflicts, political diplomacy, the visual arts and architecture, humanist learning, printing, boatbuilding and language acquisition. This collection of accounts also traces how from long-established pilgrimage, diplomatic and trade routes developed the earliest elements of what later became known as the European Grand Tour undertaken mainly by privileged young men to broaden their academic education and personal knowledge of international diplomacy, politics, cultures and foreign languages.

During this period there was a growing fascination on the part of English travellers with the workings of Venetian republicanism and its various councils, the city's Jewish and cosmopolitan communities, and its reputation for religious toleration. Numerous Englishmen also visited nearby Padua and studied at its renowned university, regarded as the Venetian Republic's primary centre of learning. Many of these individuals would have visited Venice which was accessible within a day's easy travelling. Although this study focuses primarily on surviving accounts of Venice by Englishmen (and the Welshman William Thomas, the Scotsman James Crichton and the Anglo-Irishman Henry Piers) frequent reference will also be made to the intellectual, political and religious significance of the English communities at the University of Padua.

It is now impossible to estimate accurately the number of English citizens who visited northern Italy between 1450 and 1600, although there were certainly many thousands, including pilgrims, members of religious orders, diplomats, merchants, sailors, soldiers, students, political exiles, criminals and other dubious characters fleeing English justice. There were also significant numbers of Venetian merchants, craftsmen and artisans who traded with London, some of whom established bases in southern England, just as English merchants resided at Venice for extended periods. Furthermore, the travels of many other nationals took them to both England and Venice, resulting in the steady dissemination of information and intelligence about each location.

However, very few of these individuals left written accounts of their experiences and it seems that only a small number of such documents have survived to the present day.

1

Nor has it been possible to locate any accounts of Venice by Englishwomen at this period. Hence, this volume does not aspire to offer a comprehensive assessment of the experiences and views of English travellers to Venice between 1450 and 1600. Such an assessment is now impossible. Instead, it is primarily based – as is so much documentary history relating to travels from over four and five centuries ago – upon the fragmentary and chance survival of evidence drawn from manuscripts, printed books, diplomatic and political records, private correspondence and other miscellaneous sources, such as handwritten memoranda, casual jottings and even paintings. These narratives are drawn together in this volume for the first time to provide a selection of diverse and often intriguing perspectives on how English travellers to Venice prepared for their journeys to northern Italy, routes followed by land and sea and their observations of Venice as one of the most important trading, commercial, cultural and (with Padua) educational cities of the early modern period.

The chronological span of this collection of travel narratives covers a tumultuous period in English history when, between 1450 and the 1534 Act of Supremacy, the country was still an integral part of Western-European Christendom. This affiliation was shattered by the religious and civil upheavals of Henry VIII's iconoclastic Reformation, triggered by his dynastic need for a divorce from Queen Catherine of Aragon. Consequently, the latter two-thirds of the sixteenth century experienced an often strained and mutually suspicious relationship between the constitutionally Protestant monarchy of England and the Catholic republicanism and multi-denominational diversity of Venice. Significantly, during the reign of Elizabeth I (1558–1603) there was no official Venetian ambassador or diplomatic representative resident in England; nor was there any Englishman of equivalent diplomatic status resident at Venice.

Fortunately, the self-imposed isolationism from much of Western Europe occasioned by the Henrician Reformation did not end all contacts between English citizens and Venetians. Merchant ships from Venice continued to arrive at London and other docks, carrying a diversity of produce and luxury goods from Italy, the Mediterranean and Ottoman Empire. Venice remained one of the pre-eminent centres of the continental book trade and books from its printing presses were regularly imported for English buyers, either directly or via established trading locations, such as Frankfurt and Antwerp.[1] In addition to merchants and traders, other communities of Venetians worked and thrived in England. For example, this volume contains an account of how in 1545, when Henry VIII's flagship, the *Mary Rose* (**Plate 7**), sank in the Solent, it was Venetian salvage experts, then resident on the south coast of England, who were first called upon to attempt to raise the vessel (**item 15**). During the reign of Edward VI, a group of glass-blowers from the Venetian island of Murano, renowned for its exquisite glassware, came to England to work. Unfortunately, they attracted the attention of the Venetian Council of Ten (*Consiglio dei Dieci*) and were suspected of revealing secrets of Venetian glass making which could have threatened Murano's lucrative international trade. They were recalled to Venice to unknown fates. During Elizabeth's reign, a Venetian called Sebastian Orlanden became a partner in the establishment of a glassworks at Beckley, Sussex; and

---

[1] During the 16th century there were over 450 printers, stationers and booksellers in the Veneto. Wilson, *World in Venice*, III, pp. 267–8.

another Venetian craftsman, James Vasselyn, set up a glass furnace in 1575 at Crutched Friars in London.[1]

This volume also provides a survey of intelligence reports gathered by Venetian ambassadors across the continent (preserved in Venetian State Papers), concerning the progress of both Spanish and English preparations for the 1588 Armada invasion (**item 30**). These reports confirm just how dangerously isolated England had become from international news gathering because of its termination in the 1550s of formal diplomatic relations with Venice. This predicament was regretted by the Venetians themselves since they were deeply suspicious of the imperialistic ambitions of Philip II of Spain. If formal channels of information exchange (or even those covert networks which tended to surround official embassies) had been possible during 1588 between Venice and London, it seems likely that the Venetians, driven by the most powerful of political motives – defence of their own state and commercial interests – would have been willing to brief Secretary of State, William Cecil, Lord Burghley, Sir Francis Walsingham (**Plate 24**), who ran the Elizabethan international intelligence gathering networks, and Charles Howard, Lord Howard of Effingham, a trusted ally of Walsingham and commander of the victorious English fleet during the Armada invasion, with a steady flow of information about the Spanish which they were regularly receiving from their ambassadors, intelligence gatherers and spies based in Spain, Rome and France. Indeed, the Venetian Ambassador at Paris once privately expressed this view to the English Ambassador, Sir Edward Stafford – although such collaboration might well have proved double-edged since Stafford was also then under suspicion of acting as a double agent for Spain.

These narratives of travel to Venice also illustrate the growth of interest in the Italian language between 1450 and 1600. The earlier accounts reveal little knowledge of the spoken tongue other than for the practical purposes of diplomacy or trade or for acquiring essential provisions and understanding basic information about routes, currency and transportation. However, several of the later ones confirm that one of the central purposes of travel during the second half of the sixteenth century, especially for young men, was to enhance their abilities in spoken and written languages. While some of these early travellers were clearly willing to master at least enough of the language to assist their own purposes (such as the young diplomat Thomas Wyatt in 1527, **item 13** and **Plate 16**), expertise in the Italian language was not seen as either especially desirable or fashionable until the mid-sixteenth century. Mary Partridge explains:

> In the early 1550s, the number of scholars known primarily for their proficiency in this particular area was still somewhat limited. Italian was a newly fashionable language, only recently elevated to the status of an essential accomplishment for members of the political and cultural elite. The publication of the first Anglo-Italian dictionary in 1550 testifies both to the growing enthusiasm for the tongue and to the need for basic aids to its acquisition. Italian translation was a specialist skill; according to George B. Parks: 'we do not find any translations direct from Italian published in England until Thomas Wyatt's *Certain Penitential Psalms* (1549)'.[2]

---

[1] East Sussex Record Office, RYE/47/20, 'Depositions ... in the suit of John Smyth, citizen and glazier of London, against Sebastian Orlanden of Venice', 24 Mar. 1579. Wyatt, *Italian Encounter*, p. 146.

[2] Partridge, 'Thomas Hoby', p. 775. Thomas, *History of Italy*, ed. Parks, p. xii. See also Gallagher, *Learning Languages*, pp. 14–16, 25–6, 63–6, for the rise of interest in the Italian language during the 16th century.

## 2.   English Travellers to Venice 1450–1548

The earliest accounts of Venice in this collection were most often motivated by religious pilgrimage to the Holy Land and in some cases by a desire to escape complex political conditions back home in England. There is no certainty over the identity of the first traveller who has been named as either **Richard 'of Lincoln'** or a London physician, **Richard 'Esty'**, depending on how some now barely legible lettering on the manuscript is interpreted (**item 1**). This document, primarily a medical and astrological compendium begun in 1454, contains an account of its author's pilgrimage to Jerusalem and details his route there via a short stay at Venice before his departure on a pilgrim galley. Although brief and focused largely on devotional locations and objects, his description of the city is important because it remains the earliest account by an Englishman present in the city following the fall of Constantinople to the Turks in 1453.

In contrast, the next account (**item 2**) is one of the most substantial in this collection. **William Wey** was a fellow of Exeter College, Oxford, and bursar of Eton College, Windsor. His 'Itineraries' or 'The Matter of Jerusalem' include English and Latin accounts of three separate pilgrimages to Santiago de Compostela (1456), Rome and Jerusalem (1457–8) and again to Jerusalem (1462). Wey drew on a wide variety of material for his information, including his major (but unacknowledged) source, the *Book of Marvels and Travels*, reputedly by Sir John Mandeville. Probably a Lancastrian supporter, Wey may also have been seeking to avoid the recent outbreak of conflicts between the houses of Plantagenet and Lancaster which led to the Wars of the Roses (1455–85). Whatever his personal reasons for such extensive travel between 1456 and 1562, Wey visited Venice twice (in 1458 and 1462) and offered his readers a wealth of practical information on currency, essential personal effects and provisions, medications and how to negotiate with the *patronus* (commander) of a Venetian pilgrim galley for a safe, reasonably priced, and comfortable (or at least tolerable) sea journey from Venice to Jaffa and the Holy Land. His meticulous accounts were compiled not only as a personal memoir but also as a guide for other prospective religious pilgrims travelling via Venice.

One later reader of Wey's accounts was the anonymous author of a guidebook printed by Wynkyn de Worde, *Informacon for pylgrymes unto the holy londe* (*c*.1498/1500), recounting the earlier experiences of a group of forty-six pilgrims who sailed in a 'shippe of a marchaunte of Venyse' called 'John Moreson', captained by 'Luke Mantell' (**item 6**). Much of the practical information in this small manual was drawn either directly from Wey or from an intermediary copy and was probably intended for pilgrims to purchase in England and then carry with them during the journey to the Holy Land.

Wey's account of Venice is also of importance because of his informative account of the grand procession of the recently deceased Doge Pasquale Malipiero to St Mark's on the eve of the saint's feast day (25 April 1462), followed by his funeral in the following May and interment at the Dominican basilica of Santi Giovanni e Paolo where his ornate monument by Pietro Lombardo may still be seen. He then details the procedures for the election of the next doge, Cristoforo Moro, as well as providing a brief history of Venice, an account of the city's major religious buildings and relics and an informative description of boatbuilding and armaments at the Arsenal (**Plate 12**).

**John Tiptoft, Earl of Worcester**, visited Venice twice (1458 and 1460), although no personal account of his experiences seems to have survived (**item 3**). However, his inclusion in this collection is of importance for three reasons. First, Tiptoft had harboured a desire to make a pilgrimage to the Holy Land from as early as his student days during the early 1440s at University College, Oxford, when he was advised by a friend to take an artist with him to record the sights and experiences of his travels. Secondly, he later became a prominent courtier, appointed as Henry VI's Lord Treasurer, Privy Councillor and Joint Keeper of the Sea which probably entailed contacts with Venetian vessels at London. He also served on the King's Council of Edward IV and as his Constable of England. However, after the king's flight to Flanders he was executed on Tower Hill in October 1470. Thirdly, and most significantly, Tiptoft travelled from Venice to the Holy Land in the same two-galley expedition of 197 pilgrims as William Wey, with Tiptoft aboard the *Loredana* and Wey in the *Morosina*. Antonio Loredano, *patronus* of the *Loredana*, acted as Tiptoft's personal guide and courier. No less than seven accounts of this voyage have survived, compiled by three Italians, a Dutchman, a German, William Wey and another Englishman, William Denys. Tiptoft was probably the highest-status Englishman to participate in this pilgrimage and he travelled with twenty-eight retainers and valuable personal goods. Consequently, during the voyages to and from the Holy Land he was at risk of capture for ransom from Mediterranean pirates. On the outward journey his galley was harassed by the notorious Genoese-Greek pirate Giuliano Cataluxus and so, on his return to Venice, Tiptoft and his party disembarked at Corfu and commissioned a fast-moving, armed Venetian patrol boat to ferry them back to Venice, with their fellow pilgrims continuing their journey aboard the two galleys.

The London legal attorney **Sir Edmund Wighton** travelled to the Holy Land via Venice sometime during the 1460s or 1470s (**item 4**). He is of interest for this collection because of personal jottings made at the back of a fifteenth-century Middle English manuscript text of Mandeville's *Book of Marvels and Travels* which, it seems, he took with him on his pilgrimage. As noted, William Wey made extensive use of Mandeville's account and it was regarded as a useful reference work for mid-fifteenth-century travellers in the Mediterranean. Wighton added details of his itinerary 'from venys by the sea callyd mare medeteranneo' with a list of locations. He also referred to a 'trafigo' (*trafego*), a Venetian commercial galley, implying that he may have travelled both in a galley and with merchants trading between Venice, Alexandria and other eastern Mediterranean locations.

**Thomas Linacre** (**Plate 15**), one of the leading figures in the development of humanist Greek scholarship, was based in Venice and Padua from about 1492/93 until 1497 (**item 5**). He worked and lived with the city's most renowned printer, Aldus Manutius Romanus (1449/52–1515), the founder of the Aldine Press and a learned academy called the Neakademia. During his later career Linacre served as tutor to Henry VII's eldest son Prince Arthur and Henry VIII's eldest daughter Princess Mary. He also taught Greek to Sir Thomas More and pioneered the publication of works compiled by the Greek physician Galen (AD 129–*c*.210) who served in the Roman Empire, utilizing books and manuscripts acquired during his time at Venice and Padua. Linacre provided an inspiring example of pioneering scholarship for later generations of English scholars who travelled to Italy during the first half of the sixteenth century to study and work at Venice and Padua.

**Sir Richard Guildford** performed distinguished public service at the courts of Henry VII and Henry VIII but throughout his career he was dogged by serious financial problems. In June 1505 he was incarcerated in the Fleet Prison for unpaid debts and, although released by royal pardon in April 1506, he may have chosen to undertake a pilgrimage to the Holy Land partly as a means of escaping from personal issues. Guildford was then in his mid-fifties and was accompanied by John Whitby, Prior of Gisburn (Gisborough). Sadly, the expedition proved too perilous for both men when their party was hit by a severe sickness, probably dysentery. They managed to reach Jerusalem but Whitby died there on 5 September and Guildford on the following day. A record of their party's travels was penned by Guildford's chaplain and confessor, **Thomas Larke**, the brother of Joan Larke, the mistress of Thomas (later Cardinal) Wolsey and mother of his two children (**item 7**). Larke's manuscript is now lost but his account was published by Richard Pynson in about 1511 as *This is the begynnynge, and contynuance of the Pylgrymage of Sir Richarde Guylforde Knight*, presumably to commemorate Guildford and, like Wey's manuscript and the printed *Informacon for pylgrymes*, to offer useful advice to other English pilgrims. Guildford's party spent almost one month at Venice in May/June 1506 before embarking for the Holy Land and Larke's narrative is especially informative about their experiences in a pilgrim galley. Their return journey from the Holy Land to Venice, again by galley, proved traumatic and was fraught with problems. Having left Jaffa on 19 September, they did not arrive back at Venice until the night of 25 January 1507.

**Robert Langton** was a senior churchman whose uncle Thomas Langton, Archbishop-elect of Canterbury, had studied at Padua during the 1460s (**item 8**). He was licensed in October 1511 by his cousin, the firmly pro-Venetian and anti-French Cardinal Christopher Bainbridge, to undertake a pilgrimage to Santiago de Compostela, Rome and other places in France and Italy. In 1522 an account of his extensive pilgrimage, which lasted almost two and a half years, was published as *The Pylgrimage of M. Robert Langton Clerke to Saynt James in Compostell and in Other Holy Places of Crystendome*. It included a description of Venice and, intended as a guidebook for other pilgrims, also referred its readers to Thomas Larke's account of Sir Richard Guildford's pilgrimage (**item 7**). While at Venice, Langton had his portrait painted as a pilgrim (**Plate 5**). This painting (*c*.1514), last recorded in 1858 but then lost until it resurfaced in a 2014 London sale, has been attributed to the Venetian School which, if correct, makes it the only surviving portrait of an English pilgrim to be painted at Venice at this period.

**Sir Thomas Newport** and **Sir Thomas Sheffield** were knights of the Hospital of St John of Jerusalem and both had extensive experience of Mediterranean affairs, especially concerning the island of Rhodes, dating back to the late 1470s (**item 9**). They knew Venice well from these travels and were appointed in 1513 to carry diplomatic letters from Henry VIII to the doge and Senate. Their experiences at Venice were recorded by the Venetian historian, senator and diarist Marin Sanudo who described not only their formal audience with the doge and Senate and their presence at Mass at St Mark's but also their informal conversations with Troian Bolani about English and continental political affairs. The response of Doge Leonardo Loredan (**Frontispiece**) to Henry VIII and Thomas Wolsey also survives, assuring Newport and Sheffield of their safe passage to Rhodes and the Venetian state's 'extreme and ancient good will' towards England and Henry VIII.

Another account of Venice by an English pilgrim again demonstrates how information from earlier travellers was freely utilized. **Sir Richard Torkington** was a Norfolk priest who left Rye in Sussex in March 1517 to undertake a pilgrimage to the Holy Land (**item

10). He spent from 29 April until 14 June at Venice before boarding one of the pilgrimage galleys. It is clear from his manuscript account that he had access to a copy of the 1511 edition of Larke's account of Guildford's pilgrimage and to a 1515 edition of *Informacon for Pylgrymes*. He derived much of his information about Venice from Larke's description, although he also added some personal details of his experiences there. Torkington met and joined the party of Federico Gonzaga, the young son and heir of Francesco II Gonzaga, Marquess of Mantua. Francesco was a distinguished soldier with close associations with Venice but was then unable to travel and terminally ill with one of the earliest documented cases of tertiary syphilis in Western Europe. Torkington's journey home proved extremely problematic and after being detained for one month in Cyprus he was taken ill, possibly with gastric problems, and had to disembark at Rhodes where he thanked the Knights of St John, especially Sir Thomas Newport (**item 9**), for their kindness during his recuperation.

Most of these early accounts emphasize the centrality of pilgrimage to the history of English travellers to Venice and colour plates included in this volume illustrate the importance of Venice as a centre of Christian worship and devotion. Robert Langton's portrait as a pilgrim (**Plate 5**), including his pilgrim's staff, badges, and (presumably) devotional volume, conveys an impression of how English pilgrims presented themselves at Venice. Gentile Bellini's *Procession in St Mark's Square* (**Plate 1**) records the traditional procession of pilgrims before they set out for the Holy Land. Vittore Carpaccio's *Miracle of the Cross at the Ponte di Rialto* (**Plate 2**) depicts in *c.*1496 the wooden bridge which collapsed in 1524 (see **Map 12**), a predecessor to Antonio da Ponte's renowned stone bridge (completed in 1591). This painting was commissioned for the Great Hall of the Scuola Grande di San Giovanni Evangelista and records the healing of a lunatic in the loggia (open upper gallery) of a palazzo by the relic of the True Cross which was held by Francesco Querini (*c.*1320–72), the Patriarch of Grado. The painting also illustrates the German trading house, the Fondaco dei Tedeschi (although this building was destroyed by fire in 1505); the portico of Ca' da Mosto; the bell towers of San Giovanni Crisostomo and Santi Apostoli (rebuilt in the late-seventeenth century); foreign dignitaries in eastern clothing and the city's gondolas.

Bellini's *The Miracle of the Cross on San Lorenzo Bridge*, 1500 (**Plate 3**) illustrates a renowned moment in Venetian devotional history. This painting was also one of nine canvases commissioned for the Grand Hall of the Scuola Grande di San Giovanni Evangelista. It records a miracle related to Venice's fragment of the True Cross, donated in 1369 by Filippo Maser (Philippe de Mézières), Chancellor of the Kingdom of Cyprus and Jerusalem. The painting represents how the relic had fallen into the canal and could only be retrieved by Andrea Vendramin, the Gran Guardiano of the School. It also provides a clear representation of the bridge and surrounding buildings at this period and represents Caterina Cornaro (1454–1510), Queen of Cyprus, standing on the extreme left of the picture with a small girl to her left. On the extreme right a woman is urging a black slave to dive into the water, an interesting precursor to the Venetian salvage team's leading African diver during the attempted raising of the *Mary Rose* in 1545 (**item 15** and **Plate 7**). It has even been suggested that the prominent group of gentlemen includes Bellini and his brother Giovanni.

One of the most prominent English residents at Venice and Padua during Henry VIII's reign was **Reginald Pole**, later Cardinal and Archbishop of Canterbury (**item 11**).

Figure 2. Giacomo Franco, *La Città di Venetia* (1614). Racing of gondolas and rowing boats in Venice by men. By permission of Special Collections, Brotherton Library, University of Leeds.

Figure 3. Giacomo Franco, *La Città di Venetia* (1614). Racing of gondolas and rowing boats in Venice by women. By permission of Special Collections, Brotherton Library, University of Leeds.

Although he has usually been associated primarily with Padua, it has recently been established that his activities were no less centred on Venice where he often resided. Pole was in Venice and Padua for two separate periods, between *c*.1521–*c*.1526 and 1532–6. Numerous other English scholars were associated with his circle in Italy, including Thomas Starkey, George Lily, Richard Morison, John Friar (Wolsey's illegitimate son), Thomas Winter, Thomas Lupset and Michael Throckmorton. Pole knew many of the Veneto's most distinguished scholars and his closest friend and life-long companion was Alvise Priuli (d. 1560), a member of the wealthy Venetian banking family and brother of two future doges of Venice, Lorenzo and Girolamo Priuli. Pole also had his portrait painted (**Plate 6**) by the noted Venetian artist Sebastiano del Piombo.

During the mid-1530s Pole had briefly stayed at the house of the merchant and English representative at Venice **Edmund Harvell** who had been resident there since the 1520s (**item 12**). While Pole provided a welcoming academic and religious focus for Englishmen at Venice and Padua, Harvell offered a more secular environment and a reliable source of practical advice for new arrivals. He accommodated a wide range of young English visitors in his own house. He was also involved in important matters of state, for example, soliciting from the University of Padua a favourable response to Henry VIII's intended royal divorce from Catherine of Aragon. As a reward for such services, Thomas Cromwell formally appointed him in 1539 as English Ambassador to Venice. Unlike Pole, Harvell was happy to liaise with Protestant circles, especially the Germans and visitors to their Venetian trading house, the Fondaco dei Tedeschi. Similarly, he cultivated the friendship of Italian writers and scholars at Venice, most notably Pietro Aretino who in 1542 dedicated a collection of letters to Henry VIII, with Harvell making the arrangements for the king's presentation copy to be carried to England. Also recorded are Harvell's problematic dealings with a lawless Bolognese adventurer, Ludovico dall'Armi, who had ingratiated himself with the English court but proved an unwelcome visitor to Venice and was eventually executed on the order of the Council of Ten.

The embassy to Venice of the politician and poet **Thomas Wyatt** (**Plate 16**) and **Sir John Russell** exemplifies the physical perils and political dangers of travel to the Veneto at this period (**item 13**). They were sent in January 1527 to attend the court of Pope Clement VII at Rome. When the Pope agreed a three-year truce with imperial forces, the Venetian Senate became concerned that it would generate another war which could threaten the security of northern Italy and Venice in particular. Russell and Wyatt set out from Rome to Venice to consult with the Signoria, despite the threat from imperial troops and brigands. However, on the way Russell's horse stumbled and caused Russell to break his leg, requiring Wyatt to press on alone. He arrived at Venice on 1 March 1527 where he met Sir Gregorio (Gregory) Casale, English Envoy at Rome, and (probably) Edmund Harvell. With Casale, Wyatt appeared on 2 March before the Republic's Collegio and on the following day they were permitted an interview with Doge Andrea Gritti (**Plate 4**). Wyatt and Casale left Venice for Ferrara but Wyatt was captured outside Bologna by imperial forces and held for ransom. He was only freed through the influence of the Duke of Ferrara, with two members of the Gonzaga family of Mantua acting as intermediaries. As a more lasting memorial to Wyatt's time in Venice, he probably acquired there a copy of Alessandro Vellutello's 1525 edition of Petrarch's poetry. He is known to have consulted it when drafting his own lyric poetry which played a major role in importing Italian influences into Tudor verse.

The final text compiled before 1548 is by **Andrew Bo(o)rde**, a former Carthusian monk and physician (**item 14**). He travelled extensively in Western Europe on behalf of Thomas Cromwell, assessing continental responses to Henry VIII's divorce from Catherine of Aragon in 1533. He wrote a manuscript account of these experiences, 'The Itinerary of Europe', but claimed that it had been given to Cromwell and then lost by him. In either late 1537 or early 1538 Boorde left England to undertake a pilgrimage to the Holy Land, travelling there via Venice and, on his return journey, via Naples and Rome. He then lived in France and in 1542 dedicated to Princess Mary *The Fyrst Boke of the Introduction of Knowledge*, intended as a medical treatise but written in prose, verse and dialect with crude woodcut illustrations. He was back in England by 1547 but, having been charged with keeping prostitutes in his chamber at Winchester, he died in the Fleet prison in April 1549. His brief and eccentric account of Venice in doggerel verse survives in a 1555 printed edition (although references to earlier lost editions of *c.*1542 and *c.*1547 are included in his other works).

## 3. English Travellers to Venice 1548–1600

The year 1549 saw the publication of the most influential book on Italy and Venice published in English during the mid-sixteenth century. The author, **William Thomas**, was an unlikely figure – a renegade exile who escaped abroad in 1545 to evade justice for theft (**item 16**). He was probably a Welshman of unknown ancestry and had been in the service of Sir Anthony Browne, Henry VIII's Master of the Horse. Accused of embezzlement from his employer, Thomas fled to Venice but was detained by **Edmund Harvell** (**item 12**) until the stolen funds were repaid. After being freed, Thomas visited Bologna and Florence before returning to Venice and then travelling to Rome. He immersed himself in the Italian language and its history, producing the first major Italian dictionary, *Principall Rules of the Italian Grammar ...* (1550), and a compendious survey of the Italian states, *The Historie of Italie* (1549). These works, influential for the next fifty years, stimulated interest in the acquisition of spoken and written Italian among both English men and women, as exemplified by Sir Henry and Lady Mary Sidney of Penshurst Place, Kent, who employed Italian-speaking tutors for their children, including their eldest son **Philip Sidney** (**item 22**, **Plate 17** and **Figure 17**). Thomas's *Historie* also facilitated a growing interest in Italian politics and the democratic republican structures supporting the administration of Venice and its territories. Having returned to England in 1548, Thomas gained lucrative court patronage but his involvement in the Wyatt Rebellion against Queen Mary in 1554 led to his demise. He was hanged, drawn and quartered at Tyburn and his head displayed on London Bridge.

Despite his gory end, William Thomas's pioneering scholarship and publications remain key landmarks in early Anglo-Italian studies, even though the next ten years proved challenging times for Englishmen who may have wished to visit Italy or enhance their knowledge of its various states, language and dialects. **Thomas Hoby**, the half-brother of the noted diplomat Sir Philip Hoby, first visited Venice and Padua in autumn 1548 and, as a firm Protestant, spent much of Queen Mary's reign on the continent (**item 17**). He was there again in 1554 and 1555, sharing a house with other Englishmen and purchasing books to take back to England, including a Venetian edition of Dante and

Benedetto Bordone's *Isolario*, a study of ancient and modern islands, which included a striking perspective of the Venetian lagoon. Hoby was a member of an extended community of exiled Protestant Englishmen who were resident in Venice and Padua during Queen Mary's reign and later formed a substantial presence in Queen Elizabeth's later parliaments. At this period the Italian households of Edward Courtenay, Earl of Devon – a claimant to the English throne as the great-grandson of Edward IV – and Francis Russell, second Earl of Bedford, also provided important political centres for Protestant English exiles living at Venice and Padua.

**Peter Vannes** (or **Pietro Vanni**), although a native-born Italian, had lived in England since 1513 and undertook diplomatic duties abroad for Henry VIII relating to his divorce from Catherine of Aragon, as well as serving as his Latin Secretary. In 1550 Vannes was appointed by Edward VI as Ambassador to Venice (**item 18**). He was required to monitor both Protestant Englishmen in northern Italy and those thought to have Catholic sympathies, especially if they were known to have contacts with Cardinal Pole (**item 11**). His learning attracted the flattering attention of Italian scholars at Venice but he also had to deal with difficult English visitors to the city, especially Sir Robert Stafford who became notorious in Italy and France for his quarrelsome behaviour. Vannes managed to negotiate successfully his transition into Queen Mary's ardently Catholic regime and reported to the doge and College on the suppression of the Wyatt Rebellion (1554). Although a naturally cautious individual unsuited to the machinations of diplomacy, he had to deal with rumours of a plot to assassinate Queen Mary, the presence at Venice of the Protestant rebel Peter Carew and an application from the Earl of Bedford for his men to bear arms when in Venetian territories. Much to his own relief, Vannes was finally recalled back to England in 1556.

The scholar and royal tutor **Roger Ascham** only visited Venice briefly in 1552 but his angry diatribe against the city, published in his educational manual *The Scholemaster* (1570), remains one of the most frequently quoted condemnations of the moral laxity and sexual profligacy of Venice. He claimed to have seen there in nine days 'more liberty to sin than ever I heard tell of our noble city of London in nine year' (**item 19**). As continental travel began to develop during Queen Elizabeth's reign, other Englishmen also expressed their reservations over Venice's reputation as an unhealthy environment and its reputed licentiousness. **Sir Edward Unton** visited the city in 1564 and his servant **Richard Smith** compiled a brief account of his impressions (**item 20**). He was clearly familiar with the *Historie of Italie*, tartly noting, with reference to Venice, that Thomas 'speketh more in prayse of itt than it dothe deserve'.

**Henry Cavendish**, the feckless son of Elizabeth Cavendish, Countess of Shrewsbury (known as 'Bess of Hardwick'), offers a rare example of a privileged Elizabethan gentleman who made two separate trips to Venice almost twenty years apart. He was first there in 1570 in the company of **Gilbert Talbot** who had recently become a relative through his mother's complex dynastic ambitions (**item 21**). 'Bess' had married George Talbot, Earl of Shrewsbury, and in 1568 her son Henry, then aged seventeen, was married to his stepsister, the eight-year-old Grace Talbot, while Bess's daughter Mary, aged twelve, was married to Shrewsbury's heir, Gilbert, aged fifteen. Hence, Henry Cavendish and Gilbert Talbot travelled abroad together as stepbrothers. In late March 1589 Cavendish again left England to travel to Constantinople, either in a spirit of independent adventure or through commercial ambitions. He arrived at Venice in early May where his servant, known only as **Fox** recorded his impressions of the city which were very much in keeping with those of Roger Ascham and Richard Smith. Alienated by its overt sexual freedoms, Fox described it as 'a pryson of so much liberty and a plac of all maner of abomynacyon'.

One of the most prominent and erudite English visitors to Venice during Queen Elizabeth's reign was **Philip Sidney** (**Plate 17** and **Figure 17**), whose father, Sir Henry, served as Queen Elizabeth's Lord Deputy of Ireland and President of the Council in the Marches of Wales. Philip was undertaking a continental grand tour between 1572 and 1575 to familiarize himself with international politics, the courts of Western Europe and a wide range of distinguished politicians and scholars (**item 22**). He travelled with **Lodowick Bryskett**, a fluent Italian speaker whose father was a naturalized Genoese merchant resident in London and whose brother Sebastian lived periodically at Venice. Sidney was also accompanied to Venice by three trusted family servants and another young Englishman, **Thomas Coningsby** (**Plate 18**), whom he had met at Vienna and whose portrait proudly records his time in Italy. Sidney and his party arrived at Venice in early November 1573 and remained there until early August 1574. Sidney, and probably Coningsby and Bryskett, seem to have stayed as guests at the French embassy and at the private residence of a high-ranking English recusant, **Edward, Lord Windsor**. Sidney moved frequently between Venice and Padua, socializing with the dynamic, multi-national community of young scholars, noblemen and politicians. The survival of an unusually extensive selection of his personal correspondence demonstrates the many challenges and rewards encountered by a young Englishman in Italy at this period. His correspondence with his older friend and mentor Hubert Languet also records how, responding to Languet's request for a portrait, Sidney considered the respective skills of Tintoretto (**Plate 19**) and Veronese (**Plate 20**) before he decided on commissioning his portrait from the latter's workshop where he attended for his first sitting on 26 February 1574. The completed portrait was carried to Languet at Vienna by two of Sidney's friends in the following April. Its present location, if it has survived, is unknown – one of the major losses of portraiture from the Elizabethan period.

The next English traveller of note to visit Venice was **Edward de Vere, Earl of Oxford**, who arrived there in mid-May 1575 after passing through Paris where the resident Venetian Ambassador provided him with letters of introduction to the Doge Alvise I Mocenigo and his own associates at Venice (**item 23**). As with Sidney, surviving documents relating to Oxford's time in Italy demonstrate how a steady flow of information and letters circulated to and from Venice via numerous continental locations. This account of Oxford's time at Venice also corrects the long-established error that he built himself at house in the city. Instead, it is clear that he merely rented a comfortably furnished palazzo for the duration of his stay there. With Venice as a base, he visited other cities such as Genoa and Milan, and only finally left Venice in March 1576. On his return home as a dandified Italianate Englishmen, Oxford was dogged by accusations of scandalous behaviour in Italy. It was suggested by **Stephen Powle** (**item 29**) that he had associated with the renowned courtesan Virginia Padoana, and it was rumoured that he had developed a personal adherence to Catholicism. Suspicions were also aroused by him bringing back to England a young Venetian choirboy, Orazio Cuoco, who, in turn, was interrogated by the Inquisition when he returned to Venice.

An incomplete personal journal of continental travels between September 1575 and November 1577 was kept by **Sir John North** who is distinctive for having recorded his observations from the latter part of his travels in Italian (**item 24**). Long after his return to England, North maintained his facility in the Italian language and correspondence with his Venetian contacts. He probably shipped books from Venice and continued to purchase other Venetian imprints at London. His nephew, also named John North, became a close associate of Robert Dudley, Earl of Leicester (**Plate 23**) (Philip Sidney's uncle). Leicester became one of the most important patrons of Italian émigrés and refugees living in London and his household became a centre for Anglo-Italian academics and courtiers during the 1570s and 1580s. During the mid-1590s North's former servant, **Hugh Lochard**, brought a range of legal complaints against North. These included the accusation that, while North took up residence in relative safety at Piove di Sacco (about 25km south-west of Venice), Lochard was sent three times into the plague-ridden city to obtain money from his banker, Pasquale Spinola. Lochard's testimony, vividly describing the dead bodies taken away in carts, provides the only known first-hand account by an English visitor of the 1575–7 outbreak of the plague at Venice which eventually claimed some 50,000 of its citizens.

**Sir Henry Unton** (**Plate 25**), another of Leicester's clients, was at Venice and Padua with his elder brother Edward during the mid-1570s – and encountered Lochard after he was callously dismissed from North's service – but little would have been known about this visit except for the survival of a large 'narrative' oil painting recording various scenes from his life. It was probably first displayed after his death in 1596 as a temporary memorial over his grave in Faringdon Church, Berkshire, until a grand stone memorial commissioned by his widow was completed in 1606 (**item 25**). Ten scenes from Unton's life are shown, beginning with him in about 1558 as an infant in the arms of his mother Anne Seymour, formerly Countess of Warwick, and concluding in 1596 with his funeral in progress at Faringdon Church. The painting's third scene depicts Unton travelling via the Alps to visit Venice and Padua.

The young Scotsman **James ('the Admirable') Crichton**, comparable to Philip Sidney (**Plate 17** and **Figure 17**) in his precocious reputation for scholarship and personal accomplishments, arrived at Venice during summer 1580 (**item 26**). He became the protégé of the printer and publisher Aldus Manutius the Younger (1547–97) who promulgated his talents through print. He was also extravagantly praised in an anonymous handbill, *Lo scozzese, detto Giacomo Crionio* (Venice, 1580) and acclaimed for his public disputations with Venetian scholars. Having spent the winter of 1580–81 in a villa on the River Brenta, recovering from an unspecified illness, he resumed his debating at Venice, Padua and Mantua where he was killed in May 1582 in a street brawl with the Duke's son and heir, Vincenzo Gonzaga. Crichton's responses to his first encounter with Venice were preserved in a long Latin poem, 'In suum ad urbem Venetam appulsum' (On his Arrival at the City of Venice), published over fifty years later in *Delitiæ poetarum scotorum huius aevi illustrium* (Amsterdam, 1637).

**Arthur Throckmorton** was a loyal Protestant but had several recusant cousins, including those who led the 'Throckmorton Plot' (1583) to assassinate Queen Elizabeth. He travelled on the continent for two years between 1580 and 1582, meeting at Nuremberg Robert Sidney, the younger brother of Sir Philip (**item 22**). Between late July and mid-September 1581 he stayed at both Venice and Padua which had earlier been visited by other Throckmorton family members. Arthur recorded his experiences there in a personal diary into which he often jotted down his miscellaneous observations and records of his purchases of books, clothing and music, calligraphy and Italian language lessons (**item 27**). He was the brother-in-law of Sir Walter Ralegh and retained a keen interest in travel and exploration throughout his life. When he died in 1626 one of the overseers of his will was **Sir Henry Wotton** (**item 32** and **Plate 26**) who served three terms as English ambassador to Venice between 1604 and 1624. Throckmorton bequeathed to Magdalen College, Oxford, his personal library of about 220 books, many of which were purchased during his continental tour, with thirty bearing Venice imprints, including copies of Boccaccio, Castiglione, Dante, Contarini and Ramusio.

**Laurence Aldersey** was a merchant, sea captain and traveller who visited Venice in 1581 on the way to Cyprus, Jaffa and Jerusalem, following the traditional pilgrimage route to the Holy Land. His description of Venice provides an interesting perspective on the city's Jewish community and the vicissitudes of travelling across the Alps to Venice and beyond (**item 28**). When seeking a passage from Venice to Cyprus he was fortunate in deciding not to board one vessel which soon afterwards foundered in the Adriatic with the loss of many passengers. However, his own vessel was harassed by a Turkish galley and only a sudden uplift of favourable winds saved Aldersey, his fellow travellers and the crew from captivity and probably slavery.

**Stephen Powle**, a friend of Sir Walter Ralegh from when they roomed together as students at the Middle Temple, was resident in Venice from spring 1587 until late 1588 from where he sent back to England a series of detailed intelligence reports (**item 29**). Like Arthur Throckmorton, Powle had met Robert Sidney on the continent and in March 1587 Sir Francis Walsingham (**Plate 24**), Sir Philip Sidney's father-in-law, dispatched Powle to Venice with a brief to gather interesting continental news and, especially, any information or rumours about possible threats to the English state or Queen Elizabeth herself. Powle often wrote uncontroversial information in Italian and more politically sensitive intelligence in English, presumably hoping that any Italians intercepting his correspondence would not bother to translate the English sections. Powle's bi-weekly reports were especially valuable in communicating up-to-date Venetian intelligence about Spanish preparations for the 'Enterprise of England', namely, the Armada expedition of July–August 1588. He also commented on Venetian attitudes to the execution (February 1587) of Mary Queen of Scots and news of other English residents at Venice and Padua. Less formally, Powle wrote chatty letters to his friend John Chamberlain, discussing various aspects of Venetian life, including his visits to the Arsenal, St Mark's and his residence in a neighbourhood populated by noted courtesans. In later life Powle became one of the original council members of the Virginia Company and invested in Sir Walter Ralegh's second expedition to Guiana (1617).

**Edward Webbe** was an ordinary English sailor about whom little is known except for a sensational printed account of his life, *The Rare and Most Wonderfull Thinges Which Edw. Webbe an Englishman Borne, Hath Seene* (1590). This narrative – if its often lurid and astonishing incidents are true – provides a rare insight into the brutal life of a mariner and gunner who had sailed with Anthony Jenkinson to Russia and William Borough to the Gulf of Finland. Webbe was in Moscow in May 1571 when it was burnt by Crimean Tartars and was taken prisoner with other English captives to Kaffa in the Crimea and enslaved for five years. After the payment of a ransom, he was freed and made his way back to England. At about this time he was in Sicily where he claimed to have met Edward de Vere, Earl of Oxford (**item 23**). He joined another voyage to the Levant but was

Figure 4. Giacomo Franco, *Habiti d'huomeni et donne venetiane* (1610). The dress of principal courtesans, playing music with a singer. By permission of Special Collections, Brotherton Library, University of Leeds.

captured by the Turks and taken to Constantinople where he was once more enslaved, this time in the Turkish galleys. He was ransomed again through a public subscription in London and the efforts of the English Ambassador to Turkey, William Harborne. After his release, Webbe made his way to Venice and Padua where he mingled with English students but was brought before the church authorities after being accused by another Englishman (residing there in the guise of a friar) of being a Protestant heretic (**item 31**). Having managed to clear his name, he travelled to Rome where Cardinal William Allen, an active supporter of Philip II of Spain's Armada invasion of England, also accused him of heresy. A lengthy interrogation by the Inquisition eventually cleared him but at Naples he was accused of being an English spy and viciously tortured with the strappado and the threat of being quartered alive by four horses attached to his arms and legs. Webbe finally arrived back in England in May 1589 and served Henri IV of France as a master gunner at the Battle of Ivry (March 1590).

**Sir Henry Wotton** (**Plate 26**) has already been mentioned as King James I's long-serving Ambassador at Venice during the first quarter of the seventeenth century. However, he also made a short visit to Venice, arriving there on 4 November 1591 for four days before making his way to Padua, describing in a letter to a friend, Hugo Blotius,

Figure 5.    A Venetian courtesan, from Thomas Coryate, *Crudities*, London: 1611. Special Collections, Brotherton Library, Trv COR By permission of Special Collections, Brotherton Library, University of Leeds.

16

how the climate of Venice was unhealthy and how he feared that he would not be able to resist the temptations of the city's alluring courtesans (**item 32**).

This visit, although brief, remains of significance in providing Wotton with his first taste of a city which became the central focus of his later life as a diplomat, courtier and scholar. When living at Geneva in 1593 he also wrote a long essay on international affairs, 'The State of Christendom' (first printed, 1657), detailing informative material on the political relations of Venice with its Italian neighbours and other countries, its potent internal security systems and the Venetian authorities' tolerations of Jews. Wotton became so fluent in Italian during the 1590s that he was able to travel to Scotland in May 1601 as an agent of Ferdinand I (1549–1609), Grand Duke of Tuscany, disguised as an Italian merchant named 'Ottavio Baldi', to warn King James VI of a possible plot to poison him.

One of the most substantial sections in this volume focuses on the detailed descriptions of Venice, its institutions and treasures by **Fynes Moryson**. They were first published in 1617 but based upon his experiences in the city between 1593 and 1597 (**item 33**). His accounts provide informed analyses of the geographical location of the city, its history, islands, canals, and districts (*sestieri*), as well as its numerous churches, holy relics, treasury, buildings surrounding St Mark's Square, ducal palace, Rialto, Jewish ghetto and Arsenal (**Plate 12**). Moryson also collects together information on currencies used in the city, its international trade, styles of male and female clothing, its navy and the rapid building and deployment of Venetian galleys, its judiciary and annual ceremonies, civic and domestic marriages and funerals and popular forms of entertainment at Venice. Moryson's extensive record keeping and his consistent use of authoritative printed sources, renders his account of Venice in the *Itinerary* (1617) – coupled with a later unpublished manuscript completed *c*.1626 – the most notable successor in print to William Thomas's *The Historie of Italy* (1549).

**Henry Piers**, an Anglo-Irishman from a Protestant English family settled in Ulster, travelled from Dublin in June 1595 to Rome where he arrived on 25 September with a young Catholic Englishman, Philip Draycott, who wished to become a missionary priest. Piers had also developed strong Catholic sympathies but the mid-1590s was a dangerous time to be associated with Roman Catholicism and its religious orders. Therefore, while traversing England Draycott posed as Piers's servant until they could present themselves more openly as two gentlemen travelling companions on the continent (**item 34**). Piers converted to Catholicism at Rome, having first being obliged to convince the Inquisition of his sincerity. His manuscript diary of his travels was probably compiled sometime between 1604 and his death in 1623 and recorded his impressions of the city of Venice, its ducal palace, treasury, armoury, galleys and selected religious relics. He also included a detailed account of the Battle of Lepanto (1571), drawing substantially on Richard Knolles's *The General History of the Turks* (1603) and he was perhaps also inspired by Veronese's magnificent painting *Allegory of the Battle of Lepanto* in the Council Hall of the Doge's Palace (**Plate 13**). Its central image represents the Venetian Admiral Sebastiano Venier who had been appointed as Capitano Generale da Mar of the Venetian fleet in December 1570 and was elected doge in 1577. Piers's account also gives prominence to the achievements of Venier, whom he names as 'Venerius'.

This volume concludes with a survey of English attitudes to Venice by 1600. It briefly outlines the Republic's gradual political and military decline during the latter half of the

Figure 6.   Giacomo Franco, *La Città di Venetia* (1614). Theatre and gondolas, with Morosina Morosini-Grimani (1545–1614), Dogaressa of Venice (1595–1606), engraving dated 1597. By permission of Special Collections, Brotherton Library, University of Leeds.

I Capitani G.nali dell'armata Venetiana, sogliono vestire questo habito, e tale su visto
già il Ser.mo Sebastiano Veniero, quando fracasso l'armata Turca a i Curzolari l'anno 1571.
Franco forma con Privilegio

Figure 7.    Giacomo Franco, *Habiti d'huomeni et donne venetiane* (1610). The dress of captain-generals of the Venetian army with Sebastiano Venier, seated in parade armour, with a view of Lepanto through the window behind him. By permission of Special Collections, Brotherton Library, University of Leeds.

sixteenth century. In terms of the continuing flow of English visitors, it focuses upon time spent there during the 1590s by four young members of the Manners and Cecil families, as well as Inigo Jones, the most renowned architect and theatrical set designer during the reigns of James I and Charles I. It also offers brief consideration of starkly polarized depictions of Venice in English popular drama by William Shakespeare in *The Merchant of Venice* (*c.*1596–8) and by John Marston in his two plays *Antonio and Mellida* (*c.*1599) and *Antonio's Revenge* (*c.*1600–1601). Shakespeare's play – for many readers and theatregoers today the most culturally familiar sixteenth-century English representation of Venice – illustrates how Venice was viewed from a London perspective as a still dynamic trading nation which, nevertheless, cruelly exploited for financial gain its Jewish community.

In contrast, Marston's two plays provide, at first sight, a puzzling context for his Venetian settings. He adopts a member of the Sforzas (once the leading family of Milan, a city often at enmity with Venice) as the Venetian doge and depicts the position of doge as a hereditary and monarchic one rather than an office chosen by election under the city's renowned republican and democratic processes. It seems that Marston (whose mother was of Italian heritage) was deliberately blurring the factual contexts of the Venetian state to provide an implicit (and perhaps subversive) commentary on the late-Elizabethan succession question which by 1599–1601 was escalating into a constitutional crisis, culminating in the February 1601 abortive rebellion of Robert Devereux, Earl of Essex. Finally, the publication in 1599 of Lewis Lewkenor's large folio translation of Gasparo Contarini's *The Common-Wealth and Government of Venice* – extensively used by Fynes Moryson – marked the culmination of sixteenth-century English interest in Venice through a richly-informative printed volume which matched the historical, political and cultural importance of William Thomas's *The Historie of Italie* from the preceding mid-century period.

## 4.   Giacomo Franco's Engravings of Venice

This volume also includes a diverse selection of images from two volumes by the Venetian engraver, Giacomo Franco (1550–1620): *Habiti d'huomeni et donne venetiane con la processione della ser[enissima]ma Signoria et altri particolari, cioè trionfi, feste et cerimonie publiche della nobilissima Città di Venetia* (Venice: 1610); and *La Città di Venetia con l'Origine e Governo di Quella ... Estratte dall'opere di Gioan Nicolò Doglioni. Parte seconda* (Venice: 1614).[1] Giacomo was the illegitimate son of a painter, Giovanni Battista Franco (1510–61), and began training with his father as a child. He studied in Bologna with Agostino Carracci (1557–1602), the brother of Annibale (1560–1609) and cousin of Lodovico (1555–1619), and developed a wide range of artistic skills, working variously as a painter, engraver, woodcutter and commercial dealer in books and images. Giacomo

---

[1] The mathematician Giovanni Nicolò Doglioni (1548–1629) was a member of a family from Belluno, about 100 km north of Venice. He was educated at Venice and Padua and spent most of his working life at Venice, employed as a notary and chancellor in the Office of Mines. During the major outbreak of the plague in 1575–6, he lost his wife and two children and was himself taken to the Lazzaretto where he barely survived. He later remarried and had two sons and two daughters. He wrote works on historiography, cosmography and the calendar reforms proposed by Pope Gregory XIII.

Questar la real Sala del Collegio, doue ogni giorno si riduce la mattina il
Serenissimo Prencipe con la Signoria per dare udienza ai Legati del Pontefice
e à gli Ambasciatori di Rè, et d'altri Prencipi grandi, si trattano moltecose
importanti intorno al gouerno dello stato Serenissimo

Figure 8.    Giacomo Franco, *Habiti d'huomeni et donne venetiane* (1610). The Sala del Collegio in the Palazzo Ducale, with the Doge and Signoria in audience with papal legates and ambassadors, with secretaries. By permission of Special Collections, Brotherton Library, University of Leeds.

took over his father's workshop in 1595 and, although a member of the painters' guild, also ran a successful bookshop.[1]

Giacomo Franco's engravings depict typical scenes from Venetian life at the end of the sixteenth and beginning of the seventeenth centuries, although the only text in these two collections are short descriptive sentences at the bottom of each engraving.[2] They include the regalia of the doge of Venice (**Figure 1**); costumes of Venetian officials, gentlemen and ladies (**Figures 7, 27, 31–2**); formal processions (**Figures 30, 38, 40, 42**); the carnival, festivities, formal entertainments and popular games (**Figures 18, 20, 23, 28, 33–5**); the Bucentaur, gondolas and canal traffic (**Figures 2–3, 6, 9, 43**); important buildings and locations, such as the Palazzo Ducale, Piazza San Marco, Arsenal and Loggetta (**Figures 8, 29, 30, 36–7, 39, 41, 44**); and courtesans and Venetian ladies (**Figures 4, 19, 22**). The collection also includes an image of the doge and Signoria in the Sala del Collegio (**Figure 8**); and a meeting of the Gran Consiglio (**Figure 39**).

The engraving of the Sala del Collegio shows a large painting immediately above the doge's throne. However, it clearly does not correspond to the painting now in that position, Veronese's votive portrait (1581–82) of Doge Sebastiano Venier giving thanks for the victory at the Battle of Lepanto (1571) (**Plate 13** and **Figure 24**). Veronese was commissioned to paint this picture after the major fire of 1574 which destroyed much of the room's decoration, including works by Titian. Nor do the two statues on either side of the painting match those now there. Franco's engraving may have been merely impressionistic and not intended to represent accurately the specific art works in the Sala del Collegio. Alternatively, the question may be posed whether Franco's image was derived from an older engraving or woodcut, representing the Sala del Collegio before this fire.[3]

## 5. Maps of Venice

The illustrations in this volume offer a selection of some of the most important maps of Venice from this period, including, as mentioned above, the two maps included on the title pages of Giacomo's Franco's collections of engravings (**Figures 10 and 11**). Before

---

[1] Franco inherited some of his father's plates and acquired others which previously bore the address of Orazio and Luca Bertelli (e.g. Agostino Carracci's engravings of works by Veronese and Tintoretto). His engraved bird's-eye view of Venice and the lagoon, based on an earlier map published by Paolo Forlani in 1565, was published by Giovanni Orlandi, Rome, 1602. He also provided engravings for the first illustrated edition of Torquato Tasso, *Gerusalemme liberata*, Genoa, 1590. His *Effiggie naturali degli maggiori principi*, Venice, 1596, included a portrait of Queen Elizabeth I, Royal Collection Trust, London, RCIN 601228.

[2] These images are taken from a facsimile of copy of the 1610 edition at the Biblioteca nazionale Marciana, Venice: F. Ongania, 1876, by permission of Special Collections, Brotherton Library, University of Leeds, Large Modern History F-3 FRA.

[3] Titian is reputed to have painted for the Sala del Collegio commemorative portraits of Doge Leonardo Loredan (**Frontispiece** – but a different portrait), Antonio Grimani and Andrea Gritti (**Plate 4**); and a large historical painting commemorating *The Battle of Spoleto* (also known as *The Battle of Cadore*) (1537–9) located between the two windows on the south side of the state room. This painting is known only from some preparatory sketches and an etching (*c.*1569–70) by Giulio Fontana. Rosand, *Titian*, pp. 18–19. Nichols, *Titian*, pp. 30, 122, 157–8, and **Figure 98**. Ridolfi, *Titian*, pp. 74–5, writing in the 1640s, also provides an interesting account of Titian's paintings in this room (with some corrections by his modern editors).

La ser.ᵐᵃ Dogareſa dal ſuo Palazzo aſcende nel Buccintoro et accompagnata da nobiliſ.ᵐᵒ ſchiera
di gentildonne pompoſam.ᵗᵉ ueſtite et da infinito numero di Bregantini in uarie e diuerſe forme dalli
arti acconciati et adobbati uanel Ducol Palazzo
Franco Forma co̍ Priuilegio

Figure 9.   Giacomo Franco, *La Città di Venetia* (1614), The Dogaressa and noble ladies in the
Bucintoro with accompanying vessels. By permission of Special Collections, Brotherton Library,
University of Leeds.

Figure 10.    Title page of Giacomo Franco, *Habiti d'huomeni et donne venetiane* (1610), with a map of Venice and the 'new' Rialto Bridge (il Novo Ponte di Rialto). By permission of Special Collections, Brotherton Library, University of Leeds.

# LA CITTÀ
# DI VENETIA
## CON L'ORIGINE
### E GOVERNO DI QVELLA,

Et i Dogi che vi fono ftati, con tutti le cofe notabili, che di tempo
in tempo vi fono auuenute dal principio della fua
edificatione, fino à quefti tempi,

*Col reale intaglio in Rame de' più nobili Edificij, & lunghi notabili, & da Solennità,*
*& da piaceri, che in effa vi fiano.*

Eftratte dall' Opere di Gioan Nicolò Doglioni.

### PARTE SECONDA.

## IN VENETIA, MDCXIIII.

Appreffo Antonio Turini, Ad Iftanza di Giacomo Franco.

CON LICENTIA DE' SVPERIORI, ET PRIVILEGIO.

Figure 11.    Title page of Giacomo Franco, *La Città di Venetia con l'origine e governo di quella …*
*Estratte dall'opere di Gioan Nicolò Doglioni. Parte seconda*, Venice (1614). By permission of Special
Collections, Brotherton Library, University of Leeds.

1570 more maps were printed in Italy than in any other country in Europe. David Woodward explains:

> from 1480–1570, the engravers, printers, and publishers of maps in Florence, Rome, and Venice dominated the printed map trade. More maps were printed in Italy during that period than in any other country in Europe. After 1570, a period of stagnation set in, and the Venetian and Roman sellers could no longer compete with the trade in Antwerp and Amsterdam.[1]

*a.   Woodcut Map of Venice, from Bernard von Breydenbach, Peregrinatio in Terram Sanctam, (Mainz: Erhard Reuwich, 1486; from the 1502 Latin edition, Speyer: Peter Drach) (Maps 3–8)*

However, the earliest map of Venice of significance to this study was compiled by a German artist rather than a Venetian specialist. The German pilgrim, Bernard von Breydenbach (*c.*1434/5–97), was a canon of Mainz cathedral. He compiled an extensive account of his journey from April 1483 until January 1484 to the Holy Land, Jerusalem and St Catherine's Monastery, Sinai, printed in Latin as *Peregrinatio in Terram Sanctam* (1486), with a High German edition published in the same year. He took with him a skilled Dutch artist, Erhard Reuwich of Utrecht (fl. 1480s), who recorded many of the major sights visited.[2] These included a panoramic landscape of Venice in the form of a large fold-out woodcut (160 cm × 30 cm) (**Maps 5–8**). Breydenbach's small party visited the city twice, staying for three weeks before setting out from there to the Holy Land and then returning home via Venice where they arrived on 8 January 1484. Reuwich was also a designer of woodcuts and printer and he produced the first edition in Latin at Mainz, using the moveable type of a local printer, Peter Schöffer. Latin, German and Dutch editions were published between 1486 and 1488 (with *c.*380 of these copies surviving) and other printers published translations in Flemish, French, Spanish and Czech before 1500. Thirteen editions appeared before 1522, with the original woodcuts utilized in Lyons, Speyer and Zaragoza through Schöffer's connections with printers there.[3]

Breydenbach and Reuwich visited Venice when Ottoman aggressive expansionism still threatened to destabilize, or even overwhelm, Italian Christendom. Following the fall in 1453 of Constantinople to Sultan Mehmed II, Ottoman forces continued to capture Venetian territories. War was formally declared in 1463 but the loss of Negroponte (the Greek island of Euboea) in 1470 was a serious blow to the Venetians, leading ultimately to them suing for peace in 1479. The Ottoman siege of Rhodes followed in 1480 and the

---

[1] Woodward, 'Map Trade', p. 773. Numerous other maps of Venice were compiled in the 16th century. Some of the most notable include *Libro de Benedetto Bordone, nel qual si ragiona di tutte l'isole del mondo* (1528) – Thomas Hoby's copy of this work (1547 edition) is in Louisiana State University Library (see **item 17**); Cristoforo Sabbadino, map of Venice, MS 138.c.180.XVIIb, Biblioteca nazionale Marciana, Venice; and Giacomo Franco, *Viaggio da Venetia a Constantinopoli per mare*, Venice, 1597. See also Cosgrove, 'Mapping', pp. 65–89.

[2] A scholar, Martin Rath (Roth), was also appointed to work on the text of the *Peregrinatio*, probably compiling the Latin version from Breydenbach's travel notes. Boyle, *To Be a Pilgrim*, p. v (typescript).

[3] Breydenbach travelled with an 18-year-old nobleman, Count Johann von Solms-Lich (who died at Alexandria); a knight from the count's household, Philipp von Bicken; and two domestic assistants and a cook called Johannes. His party travelled from Jerusalem to Egypt with two other German pilgrims, Felix Fabri, a Dominican from Ulm, and Paul Walther von Guglingen, an Observant Franciscan. Fabri shared Breydenbach's galley back to Venice. Ross, *Breydenbach*, pp. 2–13, 56–60.

seizure of Otranto in the Kingdom of Naples. Understandably, Breydenbach and his party travelled under the expectation that the Turk, as he wrote in the *Peregrinatio*, had 'set his heart and mind against Italy, even against Rome, in order to throw down the highest seat of the Christian faith' (f. 179v).[1] His account of his visit to the Holy Land, therefore, was intended to blend together spiritual devotion and a strident call for crusade, with Venice positioned as the central but liminal place between the worlds of Christianity and Islam – an inspirational 'role model of Christian engagement with the forces of Islam'. As Elizabeth Ross explains:

> The overarching organization of the volume, word and image, supports the work's textual appeal for greater resistance to Islam. The *Peregrinatio* team has composed the book so that the pilgrim's journey from Venice to the Levant is framed as the reader's progress from a stronghold that defends Latin Christendom to a foothold for the Islamic heresy.[2]

The frontispiece to Breydenbach's book (**Maps 3 and 4**), designed by Reuwich, features a lavishly dressed Venetian woman who, encapsulating the grandeur and exotic magnificence of the city, presides over their journey to the Holy Land. She points on her right towards the shield, helm, crest and title of Breydenbach beneath which a cartouche details his social position as dean and chamberlain of Mainz Cathedral. On her left are depicted the arms of his young fellow pilgrim, Count Johann von Solms-Lich. Lower on the pedestal, as befits his status, are the arms of the count's companion, Philipp von Bicken. Her dress, jewellery and coiffure are precisely drawn to represent both the wealth of the city and the exotic appearance of its high-ranking women in the 1480s.

The text of Breydenbach's book, as in William Wey's account (**item 2**), provides extensive practical information for other pilgrims, including details of their seafaring contracts, the major sites of relics and effusive praise of Venice's wealth, mercantile reputation and – probably drawing on contemporary Italian documents – its pivotal role in defending Christendom.[3] The 180° panoramic view of Venice, the largest in the volume and printed over eight leaves, complemented Breydenbach's prose commendation of the city. It incorporated impressions of its maritime trade and commerce and Venice's major buildings and landmarks, as well as those locations centred on St Mark's piazza where pilgrims were able to buy necessities for the galley journey to the Holy Land.

*b.* *Woodcut Map of Venice from Hartmann Schedel,* Liber chronicarum *[known as the* Nuremberg Chronicle*] (Nuremberg, 1493)* (**Maps 9 and 10**)
The Breydenbach and Reuwich map of Venice was adapted for inclusion in a universal history of the Christian world from earliest times to the early 1490s. It was written in Latin by the Nuremberg physician and historian Hartmann Schedel (1440–1514) and titled *Liber chronicarum* (1493), although it is commonly referred to as the *Nuremberg Chronicle*.[4] It was commissioned by two Nuremberg merchants, Sebald Schreyer (1446–1520), and his son-in-law, Sebastian Kammermeister (1446–1503); and they also paid

---

[1] Quoted in Ross, *Breydenbach*, p. 57.

[2] Ibid., pp. 60, 66.

[3] Thomas Larke (**item 7**) appears to have utilized passages from Breydenbach's publication. Boyle, *To Be a Pilgrim*, pp. 234–40.

[4] Schedel derived his information from numerous sources, including Bede, Vincent of Beauvais, Martin of Tropau, Flavius Blondus, Bartolomeo Platina and Philippus de Bergamo (Iacopo Filippo Foresta). See Cambridge University Library Catalogue: https://cudl.lib.cam.ac.uk/view/PR-INC-00000-A-00007-00002-00888/1.

George Alt (*c.*1450–1510), a scribe at the Nuremberg Treasury, to translate it into German as *Schedelsche Weltchronik*.

Many of the *Nuremberg Chronicle*'s illustrations and maps were adapted by the Nuremberg artist and cutter of woodblocks, Michael Wolgemut (1434–1519), to whom the young Albrecht Dürer was apprenticed between 1486 and 1489.[1] The Latin and German editions were both printed in Nuremberg by Anton Koberger, the owner of Germany's then largest printing house and Dürer's godfather. Schedel was familiar with Venice from when he had gained in 1466 a doctorate in medicine from the University of Padua. His volume's map of Venice, although clearly derived from that in Breydenbach's volume, contained numerous distinctive details in both its cityscape and the background geography, as may be seen from the two comparable details from each map.

*c.   Jacopo de' Barbari, Aerial View of Map of Venice (1500), Woodcut from Six Blocks* **(Maps 11–14)**

Hartmann Schedel was a notable manuscript and book collector, and his library once contained an album with engravings by the print-maker and painter Jacopo de' Barbari (*c.*1450–*c.*1511) who moved in 1500 from Venice to Nuremberg where he stayed for one year. His earliest documented work is his huge (135 × 282 cm) woodcut from six blocks of an aerial view of Venice from the south-west (perhaps partly from the area of the bell tower of *San Giorgio Maggiore), including the islands of Murano, Forcello, Burano and Mazzorbo, with the Alps in the distance. It reputedly took three years to compile, probably with the technical assistance of other mapmakers or surveyors. It is remarkable for the sharpness of its images, as shown in the details from the map included in this volume, illustrating the wooden Rialto Bridge (**Map 12**), the Doge's Palace and Campanile (**Map 13**) and the Arsenal (**Map 14**). It was published by Anton Kolb, a native of Nuremberg, who was employed by the Emperor Maximilian I between 1500 and 1504. He petitioned the Venetian Senate in autumn 1500 for sole publication rights for the print and exemption from export duties.[2] Although a series of cartographical woodcuts, Jacopo's image of Venice was also prized as a work of art, comparable to murals or oil paintings, rather than only as a map intended for use as a means of finding one's way around the city. Its purpose was not merely to guide visitors and armchair travellers who had never been to Italy but also to celebrate the reputation and glory of the city and the Most Serene Republic of Venice, 'La Serenissima'.

*d.   Plan of Venice (Venetia), from Georg Braun and Frans Hogenberg,* Civitates orbis terrarum *[from engravings by Bolognino Zaltieri], Part 2, Engraving 4. Köln, 1572–1617* **(Map 15)**

Georg Braun (1541–1622) was born at Cologne and was a canon and dean of the church of St Maria ad Gradus in the city. Inspired by Sebastian Münster's *Cosmographia* (1544)

---

[1] The contracts (December 1491–March 1492) for the volume's composition and printing are preserved in Nuremberg City Archives. Both volumes were completed by December 1493. Numerous copies of both the Latin and German editions of the *Nuremberg Chronicle* still survive.

[2] Schulz, 'Barbari', pp. 427–41, discusses the possible methods used in compiling this map, concluding that it is 'neither a giant landscape drawing made in the field, nor a carefully compiled, foreshortened plan, it can only be a studio fabrication. It must have been assembled mosaic-fashion at the drawing table from a myriad of small view drawings made from heights, throughout the city' (pp. 439–40).

and Abraham Ortelius's *Theatrum orbis terrarum* (1570), he edited in six volumes *Civitates orbis terrarum*, which contained numerous bird's-eye views and maps of the world's cities. Frans Hogenberg (1535–90), who had worked for Ortelius, created many of the engravings contained in the first four volumes, with those in the last two by Simon van den Neuwel. These images were often based on the work of earlier artists and cartographers. Its key, with over 150 placenames, made it one of the most highly prized maps of Venice during the late-sixteenth and seventeenth centuries.

*e.  Hand-tinted Map of Venice by Matteo Florimi, dated 1570 but post 1591* (**Map 16**)
This hand-tinted map is comparable to the work of Braun and Hogenberg but with different ornamental details. The shipping has been diversified, an image added for the procession of the pilgrims on Corpus Christi and the tables of locations replaced by images of the Piazza San Marco and the stone Rialto Bridge. Matteo Florimi (*c.*1540–*c.*1613), possibly from Reggio Calabria, was a publisher and book and print dealer who arrived in Siena in about 1581 and established a shop there. He published books on lace patterns (1591) and a life of St Catherine (1597) and employed a wide range of talented engravers, including Agostino Carracci, Cornelis Galle and Pieter de Jode. Many of his engravings and maps were copies and this map represents Venice in about 1570 but updates its appeal by adding an image of the newly built stone Rialto Bridge (completed 1591).[1]

[1] Woodward, 'Map Trade', pp. 791–3.

PART I

ENGLISH TRAVELLERS TO VENICE
1450–1548

# 1.  *c*.1454 – 'THE PHYSICIAN'S HANDBOOK' OF RICHARD 'ESTY' OR RICHARD 'OF LINCOLN'

This Wellcome Library manuscript, MS 8004, is primarily a medical and astrological compendium, opening with a calendar stating that it was begun in 1454. It also provides an account of its author's pilgrimage to Jerusalem (ff. 76r–84v), comprising about one tenth of the manuscript, which includes a description of his route to Venice and a brief stay there before he boarded one of the city's pilgrimage galleys to the Holy Land. Although this author's record of Venice is brief, it remains significant in that it is the earliest known account by an Englishman of a pilgrimage to the Holy Land following the fall of Constantinople to the Turks in May 1453. Dispossessed refugees from that

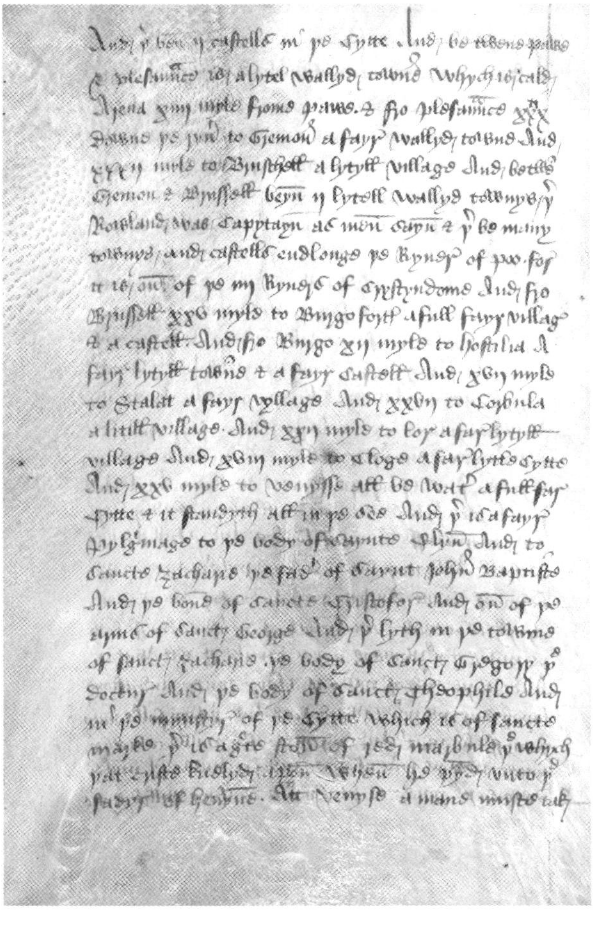

Figure 12. Page from 'The Physician's Handbook' (*c*.1454), of Richard 'Esty' or Richard 'of Lincoln'. Wellcome Library, MS 8004, f. 77r. By permission of the Wellcome Library, London.

city, including Byzantine and Greek scholars and survivors from its small Venetian colony, had recently arrived back at Venice and would still have been there during Richard's stay.[1]

**Richard 'Esty' or Richard 'of Lincoln' (fl. 1450s):** There is no certainly over the identity of the Richard who compiled this manuscript; nor is much known about its earlier provenance. A single ownership inscription, 'Thomas Hill 10 June 1759', is written at the head and foot of axioms on astrology on the first parchment leaf.[2] The manuscript later entered the library of the Dukes of Newcastle at Clumber Park, Worksop, Nottinghamshire, and was sold at Sotheby's, London (15 February 1938, lot 1129), to the civil servant and medieval manuscript collector Major Sir Alan Lubbock (1897– 1990) whose bookplate is attached to the inside upper cover.[3] The manuscript was again sold at Christie's, London (29 November 1999, lot 9), and acquired by the Wellcome Library (6 June 2002) from Sam Fogg Rare Books Ltd.

MS 8004 is written in a Middle English dialect, originating (according to the Wellcome Library catalogue) perhaps from 'Nottingham/Lincolnshire/South-East Yorkshire, or possibly Norfolk'. The use of Middle English, rather than Latin, suggests that it was compiled for a practising physician, probably a non-university-trained practitioner, although its lavish illuminations and decorations suggest that its owner had achieved substantial financial success.[4] The Christie's sale catalogue suggests that an area of erasure on the first folio states (under ultraviolet light) that the astrological tables had been 'compiled and drauyne aftyre the consate [conceit or concept] and the devyse [device] of Richard ... of the city of Lincoln'.[5] However, in 2007 Toni Mount confirmed the name 'Richard' but suggested that these erasures read: 'Tabuls compylyd and drauyne aftyre the consate and deuyse of Richard ?etaly limner of the Cite of London'. She proposed its possible author as a noted London surgeon, Richard Esty, who was appointed as Upper Warden of the Surgeon's Guild in 1459 and accompanied Edward IV in 1475 on his French campaigns. His will, drawn up before his departure for France, listed seven books on surgery to be left to the Fellowship of Barbers of London. If Esty was the original compiler of this manuscript, it may have been one of these bequeathed volumes.[6]

---

[1] Freely, *Grand Turk*, pp. 29–43. Barbaro, *Siege of Constantinople*, provides an eyewitness account by a Venetian ship's doctor, Niccolo Barbaro (1420–94).

[2] Amateur sketches on this leaf's verso of a lady in 18th-century dress probably date from Hill's ownership.

[3] The Lubbock MSS collection included an illuminated bible (Paris, *c.*1250–75) (Sotheby's, London, 3 July 2018, lot 10); an illuminated Book of Hours (North Holland, by 'Spierinck' the illuminator, dated 1489) (Koninklijke Bibliotheek, National Library of the Netherlands, MS 79 K 5); and probably the author's presentation copy of 'De precepto prudentia', a treatise on classical poetry (Northern France or Belgium, *c.*1300) (The Morgan Library and Museum, NY, MS M. 1164).

[4] Each text opens with large golden letters with painted grounds and foliage. Some of the calendars, tables and charts contain burnished gold letters and shapes. The two full-page illustrations show the figures of a Phlebotomy or Vein Man (f. 18), with each point for bloodletting pinpointed and a red line leading to the prescriptive text; and a Zodiac Man (f. 40), with signs of the zodiac placed over areas of the body that each reputedly governed.

[5] Christie's, London, Books, Sale 6222, 29 November 1999, lot 9 (sold for £210,500) [online catalogue]. London, Wellcome Library, Western Manuscripts and Archives Catalogue [online catalogue].

[6] Mount, 'Further Adventures', pp. 30–32, also noting that '?etaly' may read '?etasy'. Bale, '"ut legi"', p. 211, describes 'Richard' as a 'London physician'.

This 'Richard' followed a route familiar to earlier generations of English pilgrims and his text is representative of the 'Franciscan pilgrimage industry, which came to dominate the Jerusalem pilgrimage, via Venice, for western European pilgrims from the 1330s until the mid-sixteenth century'.[1] He first obtained a 'wryte of chaunge & a wryte of passage' (costing two shillings) and changed his money in London 'with the lumbardes' – i.e., the Lombards, Italian merchants and bankers trading in Lombard Street and issuing letters of credit to English travellers on the continent. At Dover he was charged four pence for his 'wryte of passage'. The crossing from Dover to Calais cost two shillings for travellers on foot or four shillings and three pence for those with a horse. From Calais 'Richard' passed through Gravelines, Dunkirk, Newport, Ostend, Bruges, Ghent, Mechelen, Aarschot, Maastricht, Aachen, Bergheim and Cologne. From there he followed a familiar route for northern (or 'ultramontane') pilgrims by sailing upstream along the Rhine via Bonn, Andernach, Koblenz, Boppard, Bacharach, Bingen, Mainz, Worms, Speyer, Strasbourg and Basle. Crossing the Alps, he then travelled via Lucerne, Saint Gotthard and into Lombardy, passing through Lugano, Como, Milan and Pavia.[2] Although focused primarily on shrines and relics, the author also occasionally describes other memorable locations such as the Visconti menagerie and castello at Pavia: 'a fayr parke wel wallyd with tyle and therin beyne lyberdes [leopards] & lyons & all maner of odyr der [deer] and mayvelusse maner of fowles and a full stronge castell' (f. 77r).

The text below follows the author's progress from Pavia, down the River Po via Cremona, to Venice. It is not known whether 'Richard' made this part of his journey alone or with a group of other pilgrims. It is likely that he often stayed with fellow Christian travellers at Franciscan, Benedictine and Dominican friaries. At Venice the galley on which he sailed to the Holy Land would have carried about a hundred passengers and drew together a multi-national group of travellers, including secular Christians, priests, members of religious orders and some non-Christians.[3] Each year two galleys usually sailed from Venice, leaving in about the third week of May after the celebration of the Feast of the Ascension during which pilgrims were encouraged to join the traditional procession around the Piazza *San Marco (**Plate 1**). Leaving Venice at this time also enabled the galleys to take advantage of the north-west wind (*Maestro* or *Maestrale*) which assisted vessels sailing southwards down the Dalmatian coast. Passage from Venice to Jaffa was cheaper by sailing ship because they went directly there. But galleys were often preferred because, crewed by rowers, they could make progress when becalmed or escape rapidly from pirates and other hostile vessels.

During the late fourteenth century and the first half of the fifteenth many other English pilgrims had passed through Venice on their way to the Holy Land. Two of the

---

[1] Bale, '"ut legi"', p. 205. The pilgrims sailed in pilgrimage galleys from Venice, calling at Dalmatian ports and Greek islands before landing at Jaffa. They were often guided around the holy sites associated with Christ and the Virgin by Franciscans whose headquarters were on Mount Zion, just outside the Old City of Jerusalem.

[2] Another undated itinerary from this period, starting at Calais, is in Henry Huntington Library, MS EL 26.A.13, f. 115v. The manuscript bears the names of its scribe, John Shirley (d. 1456), his wife Margaret, her sister Beatrice (Lynne) Oxeney (d. 1501) and her husband Avery Cornburgh (d. 1487) who had extensive involvements in maritime affairs, as did his stepson Thomas Oxeney. It is not known, however, if any of these individuals made a pilgrimage via Venice to the Holy Land.

[3] Aboard the galley, the pilgrims lived in dormitory-style arrangements, with each pilgrim allotted about 6 feet by 18 inches for their bedding, a lockable chest for valuables and other portable possessions, including food and drink.

most notable were in 1392–3 Henry Bolingbroke (1367–1413), Earl of Derby (later King Henry IV), and the English mystic Margery Kempe (d. *c*.1438) who was at Venice between January and April 1414 for thirteen weeks, possibly staying at the Benedictine convent of *San Zaccaria.[1] No other first-hand accounts of the experiences of English pilgrims at Venice are known to have survived from the early 1450s.

### Text (Wellcome Library, London, MS 8004, ff. 77r–78r)

[f. 77r] And att *the* end of Pavea is a fayr ryver[2] and a stone brygh ov*er* the ryrd toward*es* Jene.[3] And *the* fery sales[?] unto venysse by wat*er* And iiii myle fro*m* Pavea[4] cometh *the* ryver unto *the* ryver of poo And fro*m* Pavea xl myle downe *the* ryver to Plesaunce[5] is a fayr walled Cytte [f. 77v] And *there* be ii castell*es* in *the* Cytte. And betweene Pavea and Plesaunce is a lytel wallyd towne whych is cald Arena[6] xiiii myle from Pavea. & fro*m* Plesaunce xxx down*e* *the* river to Cremon*a* a fayr wallyd towne And xxxii myle to Bruschell[7] a lytell village And betw*eene* Cremon*a* and Brussell beyn*g* ii lytell wallyd town*es* *that* Rowland was capytayn as men sayn.[8] & *there* be many townyes and castell*es* endlonge *the* Ryver of poo for it is one of *the* iiii Ryver*es* of Crystyndome And fro*m* Brussell xxv myle to Burgoforth[9] a full fayr village & a castell. And from Burgo xii myle to hostilia[10] A fayr lytyll towne & a fayr Castell And xvii myle to Stalat[11] a fayr vyllage And xvii to Corbula[12] a litill village. And xxii to lor[13] a fayr lytyll village And xviii myle to Cloge[14] a fayr lytle Cytte And xxv myle to Venysse all be water a full fayr Cytte & it standyth all in *the* see And *there* is a fayr Pylg*ri*mage to *the* body of seynte Hlyn[15] And to Sancte Zacharis[16] *the* fa*ther* of Saynt John*e* Baptiste And *the* bone of sancte Cristofor And one of *the* arm*es* of Sante George[17] And *there* lyth in *the* towme of Sancte Zacharis the body of Sancte Gregory *the* doctur[18] And *the* body of Sancte Theophile[19] And in *the* mynstyr of *the* Cittye which is of sancte marke[20] *ther*e is a gre*at* stone of red marbule t*he* which *there* at Criste knelyd upon when he pr*ay*d unto *the* fadyr of heuyne. Att Venyse a mane muste tak*e* [f. 78r] hys sale And a mane muste pay for hys passage w*ith*in *the* Gale as *the* patt*ro*ne & he may acorde And *the* moste *that* any mane pay is xvj or lx ducat*es* & to be att *the* patron*es* table bord & *the* bedde will coste *you* An*other* ducett & a haulfe And from*e* Venyse C. myle to Revene a fayr lytell wallyd towne & a mynstyr & *there* lyth *the* body of Sayncte Eufemye.[21]

---

[1] Kempe, *Book*, ed. Bale, pp. 62, 70, 243, 247.   [2] River Ticino.
[3] Genoa lies *c*.130 km due south of Pavia. 'Richard' was travelling east to Venice, via the meandering River Po.   [4] Pavia.   [5] Piacenza.   [6] Arena Po.   [7] Brescello.
[8] The gothic porch of Cremona Cathedral has two columns topped by figures of Roland with his horn and Charlemagne.
[9] Borgoforte.   [10] Ostiglia.   [11] Stellata.   [12] Corbola.   [13] Loreo.   [14] Chioggia.
[15] The body of St Helena, mother of Constantine the Great, was preserved in the church of *Sant'Elena which had been extensively rebuilt by *c*.1435. The saint was popular with English pilgrims because it was erroneously claimed by Geoffrey of Monmouth in *Historia regum Britanniae* (*c*.1136) that she was the daughter of King Coel of Colchester.   [16] St Zacharias's relics were preserved in *San Zaccaria.
[17] Preserved in the church on the island of *San Gorgio Maggiore.
[18] St Gregory the Great (*c*.540–604), Pope from 590, was the fourth and last of the 'Doctors of the Church'.
[19] St Theophilus (d. *c*.183/5), Bishop of Antioch and author of the 'Apology to Autolycus', defending Christianity to a pagan friend.   [20] *San Marco.
[21] St Euphemia, from Chalcedon in Asia Minor, was martyred under Diocletian by being thrown to lions. Her sarcophagus was brought in AD 800 from Constantinople to Rovinj, Croatia.

**[Modernized Text]**

[f. 77r] And at the end of Pavia is a fair river and stone bridge over the road towards Genoa. And the ferry sails[?] unto Venice by water. And 4 miles from Pavia comes the river unto the river Po. And from Pavea 40 miles down the river to Piacenza, [it] is a fair walled city. [f. 77v] And there be 2 castles in the city. And between Pavia and Piacenza is a little walled town which is called Arena Po, 14 miles from Pavia and from Piacenza 30 [miles] down the river to Cremona, a fair walled town. And 32 miles to Brescello, a little village. And between Cremona and Brescello being 2 little walled towns that Rowland was captain [of], as men say; and there be many towns and castles along the River Po, for it is one of the four rivers of Christendom. And from Brescello 25 miles to Borgoforte, a full fair village and a castle. And from Borgoforte 12 miles to Ostiglia, a fair little town & a fair castle. And 27 miles to Stellata, a fair village. And 17 to Corbola, a little village. And 22 to Loreo, a fair little village. And 18 miles to Chioggia, a fair little city. And 25 miles to Venice, all be water and a full fair city and it standeth all in the sea. And there is a fair pilgrimage to the body of Saint Helena; and to Saint Zacharias the father of Saint John Baptist; And the bone of Saint Christopher; And one of the arms of Saint George. And there lieth in the tomb of Saint Zacharias the body of Saint Gregory the doctor; and the body of Saint Theophilus. And in the minster of the city, which is of Saint Mark, there is a great stone of red marble the which thereat Christ kneeled upon when he prayed unto the Father of Heaven. At Venice a man must take [f. 78r] his sail and a man must pay for his passage within the galley as the *patronus* and he may agree. And the most that any man [should] pay is 16 ducats or 40 ducats and to be at the *patronus*'s table board; and the bed will cost you another ducat and a half. And from Venice [it is] 100 miles to Rovinj, a fair little walled town and a minster and there lieth the body of Saint Euphemia.

# 2. 1458/62 – THE 'ITINERARIES'
# OF WILLIAM WEY

**William Wey (1405/7–c.1476)**, an author and pilgrim, was probably from a Devon family.[1] He was elected a fellow of Exeter College, Oxford (1430–42), and bursar at the recently founded Eton College, Windsor (1441–67). His 'Itineraries', also known as 'The Matter of Jerusalem', comprise English and Latin descriptions in fifteen sections of three pilgrimages to Santiago de Compostela (1456), Rome and Jerusalem (1457–58) and Jerusalem (1462).[2] These accounts were probably drawn together after Wey retired in 1467 to the Augustinian Bonhommes priory at Edington, Wiltshire, where he had a replica of the Holy Sepulchre constructed. This model and Wey's manuscript account of his pilgrimages would have offered a rich source of devotional inspiration to his brethren at Edington.[3] It seems possible that Wey himself wrote out much of this manuscript which included blue initials with penwork flourishes in red, rubrics and running headings in red and initials highlighted in red.[4]

Anthony Bale details the diverse range of sources from which Wey drew his material, including acknowledged ones such as St Jerome, Pope Leo the Great, Robert Grosseteste and Bede's commentary on Luke, as well as his major unacknowledged source, Mandeville's *Book of Marvels and Travels*:

> Wey's engagement with Mandeville reveals a medieval editorial process in line with established
> literary habits of *compilatio*, *ordinatio*, and *translatio*: that is, the compilation and reordering

---

[1] Wey, *Itineraries*, ed. Davey, p. 10, states he was born 'probably in 1407, in Devon'.

[2] Mitchell, *Spring Voyage*, provides a detailed account of the 1458 voyage, involving 197 pilgrims in two galleys who sailed from Venice to Jerusalem, including Wey and John Tiptoft, Earl of Worcester (**item 3**). A pilgrim's account of Rome at this period is provided by William Brewyn of Canterbury who spent a considerable amount of time there during the 1460s, although he apparently did not go to Venice (Canterbury Cathedral Archives, dd. MS 68).

[3] Wey donated his manuscript to Edington Priory and it was bound at the priory's expense (note added to back paste-down in the same hand as the contents). It was to be kept in the priory's chapel of the sepulchre (ff. 2r–v, 102r and 105v). Little is known about its post-Reformation provenance. The back paste-down bears the name 'John Edwardes' in a late 16th-century hand; and the front paste-down states: 'Ex dono magistri Tempest 1624', probably the donor to the Bodleian Library.

[4] Boyle, 'William Wey's *Itinerary*', pp. 28–36. Di Stefano, 'How to be a Time Traveller', p. 183. At least two contemporary scribes may have contributed to the compilation of this manuscript with (speculatively) Wey writing out most of it in Anglicana script and another individual completing it from f. 98r in secretary script. The list of contents and bequests may have been compiled during or soon after Wey's final illness. The manuscript was compiled on generally good quality parchment. Its ink foliation is in a much later hand and it has been bound at least twice, once in the 15th century and again in the 19th century (probably after the 1857 Roxburghe Club edition).

of others' texts to produce a new text, repeating and reporting others' material without guaranteeing its accuracy'.[1]

Wey was travelling during the Wars of the Roses (1455–85) between the houses of York and Lancaster but domestic affairs did not seem to impinge significantly on his travel narratives – perhaps because his pilgrimages were undertaken through a desire to escape abroad from these conflicts. Probably a Lancastrian supporter, Wey set off on his third journey on 26 February 1462, eight months after the Yorkist Edward IV had been crowned King of England.[2] The deposed Henry VI was still seeking support in Scotland and his French-born queen, Margaret of Anjou, was intriguing at Amboise with the new King of France Louis XI. As Francis Davey remarks:

> If Henry or Margaret had needed an agent William Wey would have fitted the part ideally. His cover as a pilgrim was impeccable; the records show that many pilgrims acted as spies in the Middle Ages. Wey's powers of observation and attention to detail would have been further recommendations. This additional employment could also explain the apparent ease with which Wey obtained extended leave of absence from his duties at Eton and why he undertook two lengthy Jerusalem pilgrimages.[3]

Wey's account of Venice and its pilgrim galleys is the most detailed by an Englishman at this period. He visited Venice twice, in 1458 and 1462, and his 'Itineraries' contains two sections, one in Middle English and the other in Latin, both of which provide detailed (and sometimes overlapping) information about necessary personal effects, provisions and negotiations with the *patronus* of the pilgrim galley.[4] It seems possible that his 'Itineraries', or selected sections, circulated in manuscript during the late fifteenth century.[5] They were used, for example, by the anonymous compiler of the guide book,

---

[1] Bale, "'ut legi'", pp. 214–21, 220. Wey used a Middle English version of Mandeville, abridged and translated into Latin. Bale notes: 'Wye, in fact, took swathes of his account of the Holy Land from Mandeville, although Mandeville's text is never explicitly acknowledged', ibid., p. 218.

[2] A clue to Wey's political allegiance may lie in his record in July 1462 of visiting a ruined church at Lydda in the Holy Land where he was moved by the hymn 'Miles Christi gloriosa', formerly an antiphon of Thomas of Lancaster, executed in 1322 by Edward II.

[3] Wey, *Itineraries*, ed. Davey, p. 13. Eton College has a document, dated 11 August 1457, recording Henry VI granting to Wey leave of absence with full pay to go on pilgrimage, Wey, *Itineraries*, ed. Williams, pp. iii–iv. See Di Stefano, 'How to be a Time Traveller', p. 183 n. 37, for Wey's travel licences.

[4] Wey's account of preparing for the pilgrim galleys may be compared to advice provided by a German pilgrim, Arnold von Harff (1471–1505), who set out from Cologne and reached Venice in 1497. He details, like Wey, necessary purchases, including a mattress and pillow, wine, water kegs, hen coop, lockable tin box, plague pills, laxatives and a basin for vomiting and washing his feet. He also explains how he changed his money and engaged the services of a multi-lingual Spanish dragoman called Master 'Vyncent'. After boarding a five-decked merchantman (rather than a pilgrim galley) bound for Alexandria, von Harff took careful measurements, noted its ordnance, rigging and huge mainsail (36.5m × 34.7m) painted with an image of St Christopher. He also described Andrea Loredano, its *patronus* from a notable Venetian naval family, his luxurious cabin and the ship's impressive armaments and gunners. See Harff, *Pilgrimage*, ed. Letts, pp. xxi–xxiii and 69–74.

[5] Mary Boyle concludes: 'William Wey was writing for an audience, and perhaps intended that his work be reproduced in multiple copies based upon this manuscript', '*William Wey's Itinerary*', p. 36. Furthermore, given that some of Wey's descriptions of major sites in the Holy Land are comparable to those in Wellcome MS 8004, it is possible that both writers had access to an earlier related source (as well as Mandeville); or Wey knew the text in the Wellcome MS; or even that the author of Wellcome MS 8004 had read Wey's account if his own was compiled later than *c.*1454 (the date usually attributed to Wellcome MS 8004).

*Informacon for Pylgrymes unto the Holy Lande*, London: Wynkyn de Worde, 1498 (**item 6**).[1] Wey's first section offers specific information on currency used in Venice:

> At Venyse be grotys, grossetys, galy halpens, whyche be clepyd ther soldes and bagantynes. For a doket of Venyse xv. grotys, and of grossetys xxx. For a doket of Rome or of Florense a grote lasse; for a grot viii. soldis; for a grosset iiii. soldis; for a solde xii. bagantynes. For a doket of Venyse ye shal have v. li and xiiii. soldis; a punde ys xx. soldis, that be galey halfpennys; and to every solde xij. Bagantynes.[2]

> [*modernized text*] At Venice be groats, grossets, galley halfpennies, which be called there soldi and bagantines. For a ducat of Venice 15 groats and of grossets 30. For a ducat of Rome or of Florence a groat less; for a groat 8 soldi; for a grosset 4 soldi; for a soldi 12 bagantines. For a ducat of Venice you shall have 5 pounds and 14 soldi; a pound is 20 soldi, that be galley halfpennies; and to every soldi 12 bagantines.[3]

Wey's Latin account of Venice, where he arrived on 22 April 1562 after crossing the Alps, is factually informative.[4] Some of his observations, when not drawn from other written sources, were probably compiled as notes in a diary or pocketbook as he moved around the city.[5] He describes a lavish procession in honour of St Mark (**Plate 1**) on the eve of his feast day (25 April) and the entrance of Pasquale Malipiero (Doge, 1457–62) and accompanying Venetian dignitaries into St Mark's on the saint's feast day. He explains the official roles of the doge's councillors, the Procurators of St Mark, the Great Council, and the city's advocates and magistrates. During Wey's visit to Venice Doge Malipiero died on 5 May 1462 and he witnessed the grand ceremonials accompanying the doge's funeral and interment 'high up in the wall in the House of the Dominicans' (*Santi Giovanni e Paolo). His monument by Pietro Lombardo (*c*.1435–1515) can still be viewed today. Malipiero's wife, Giovanna Dandolo, was notable patron of both lacemaking at Burano and the printing presses at Venice, and she received fulsome dedications in some of the earliest books printed in Venice.

Wey also recounts the procedures for the election of the next doge, Cristoforo Moro (Doge, 1462–71). His period of office was dominated by war with the Turks and from 1463 it became more dangerous for western pilgrims to travel to the Holy Land via Venetian galleys. These circumstances underline the importance of Wey's detailed account of his travels to Venice in 1458 and 1462 since documentary evidence from

---

[1] *ODNB*, s.v.

[2] Wey, *Itineraries*, ed. Williams, p. 3.

[3] The Venetian gold or silver ducats, with their numerous subdivisions, were important to pilgrims because they were useable throughout most of the eastern Mediterranean, Ottoman Empire and Holy Land. Pilgrims arriving at Venice would change some of their ducats into smaller value *grotes (grossi), grossets (grosetti), grossines (grossini), tornes (tornesi, torneselli)* and *soldi*, with the money changers charging 5 per cent commission. During the 15th century, the ducat's value remained stable at approximately 124 Venetian *soldi* (or *schillings*). See Lane and Mueller, *Money and Banking*, I.

[4] Wey's section 7, describing his 1458 pilgrimage to Jerusalem, only briefly refers to Venice in relation to distances from other locations on his itinerary. Wey left Venice on 18 May 1458, sailing for Jaffa which he reached on 18 June. He returned to Venice some sixteen weeks after his departure.

[5] Di Stefano, 'How to be a Time Traveller', pp. 182, 185, notes that the 'order in which the churches are listed and their location in the city indicates an actual pilgrimage itinerary'. However, she adds that Wey's listings are sometimes inaccurate or misremembered, 'as if the pilgrim received oral information about the city's sights and then reported this information at a later date when writing up his account'.

pilgrims and travellers in the eastern Mediterranean becomes scarcer during the next two decades.

Wey provides a brief account of the early history of Venice and a selection of information on its major churches and relics, both in the city and on outlying islands such as Murano. One of the most important sections of his 'Itineraries' covers boatbuilding at the Arsenal (**Plate 12**) and a wealth of detailed advice on the practicalities of travelling via Jaffa to the Holy Land aboard Venetian galleys and other merchant vessels.[1] He lists essential provisions, personal effects, medications for the traveller and how to negotiate safely a passage to and from the Holy Land. Wey finally sailed from Venice on 26 May 1562.

In his 'Itineraries', Wey claims to have seen at the Arsenal some eighty galleys, either completed or still under construction. It is unlikely, however, that he or other English visitors to Venice at this period were allowed free access to the Arsenal – the city's major military and naval centre. Nevertheless, during the fifteenth century the Senate did allow pilgrims to inspect prospective pilgrims' galleys and to select the one which appeared the safest or best equipped, along with the most acceptable contracts offered by the *patroni* in terms of routes, meals, cargo and length of time to be spent in ports on the way to and from the Holy Land. Exactly where pilgrims were given access to these galleys remains uncertain. Laura Grazia Di Stefano suggests that they 'were likely authorised to explore only the zone just beyond the Arsenal's monumental "land door" that operated the passage of people and vessels since the mid-fifteenth century'.[2]

Neither Wey nor 'Richard' ('Esty' or 'of Lincoln') offers specific recommendations of where to stay in Venice. However, strict controls were in place to ensure that pilgrims were not exploited or otherwise treated badly. A select committee of the Venetian Senate, the *Cattaveri, watched over their interests by granting licences to innkeepers, inspecting premises and controlling prices. Visitors could also make any complaints directly to the *Cattaveri*; and twelve multilingual *tholomarii* (*tholomagi*) or 'piazza guides', were appointed to assist visiting pilgrims to make necessary purchases, explain currencies accepted in the city and to guide them to their lodgings. German pilgrims often stayed at the inn of *St George*, also known as The Flute, close to their nations' trading centre, the *Fondaco dei Tedeschi. Another cosmopolitan inn was La Storione (The Sturgeon), near the Rialto.[3]

The accounts of Venice by Richard ('Esty' or 'of Lincoln') and William Wey are of considerable historical importance because, after the fall in 1453 of Constantinople to the Ottomans, access to the eastern Mediterranean became more perilous for Western European travellers. During the 1460s and 1470s there was a reduction in the number of English pilgrims undertaking the route via Venice to Jaffa due to the Venetian-Ottoman wars (1463–79). Even by 1480 only one pilgrimage galley, the *Contarina*, was able to leave Venice for the Holy Land in that year. Among its pilgrims were: a French

---

[1] See Mitchell, *Spring Voyage*, pp. 16–20, for these facilities for pilgrims at Venice. They also included the Senate making available lawyers, scribes and witnesses for pilgrims who wished to make their wills before continuing the perilous journey to the Holy Land which became even more dangerous after the capture of Constantinople in 1453 by Sultan Mehmed II.

[2] Di Stefano, 'Pilgrims', 'How to be a Time Traveller', p. 176.

[3] Mitchell, *Spring Voyage*, pp. 47–9.

priest, Pierre Barbatre; Sancto Brascha of Milan, Chancellor to Duke Ludovico Sforza; Félix Faber (Schmidt), a Dominican friar from Ulm; and an anonymous Parisian; all of whom compiled surviving accounts of their voyage.[1]

Nevertheless, although journeys to Rome and Santiago de Compostela were shorter, less fraught with dangers and considered just as beneficial from the spiritual perspective of indulgences, the historical and imaginative importance of Jerusalem remained central to Christian devotions during the last two decades of the fifteenth and early sixteenth centuries. The concept of a 'virtual pilgrimage' – a spiritual experience which did not require the individual to leave their own country or even their cloister, home or private study – became more widespread which, in turn, stimulated the compilation and circulation of manuscript and printed pilgrimage accounts. Nor was it necessarily the case that writers of such guides were expected personally to have visited the locations and routes described and it became common for materials to be copied and adapted from earlier sources. For example, when the pilgrim and visitor to Venice Robert Langton (**item 8** and **Plate 5**), travelling between *c.*1511 and 1514, referred to standard routes to Jerusalem, he directed his readers to Thomas Larke's 1506 account of Sir Richard Guildford's pilgrimage (**item 7**):

> And as for the way with pylgrymage and knowlege of the same to Jerusalem and places of the holy lande I remyt you to mayster Larkes boke made of the same / wherein he comprehendeth all thinges concernynge that holy pylgrymage / insomoche that the redynge the same shall seme rather to se it then rede it. And to me and other englysshe pylgrymes that went this yere it was a grete light guyde and conducte by the whiche we knewe many thinges that by the freres there we sholde not have knowen.[2]

---

[1] Barbatre, *Voyage*, pp. 75–172. Barbatre spent a month at Venice, viewing its festivals and institutions and making practical travel arrangements, before leaving for the Holy Land on 6 June 1480.

[2] Langton, *Pylgrimage*, p. 3.

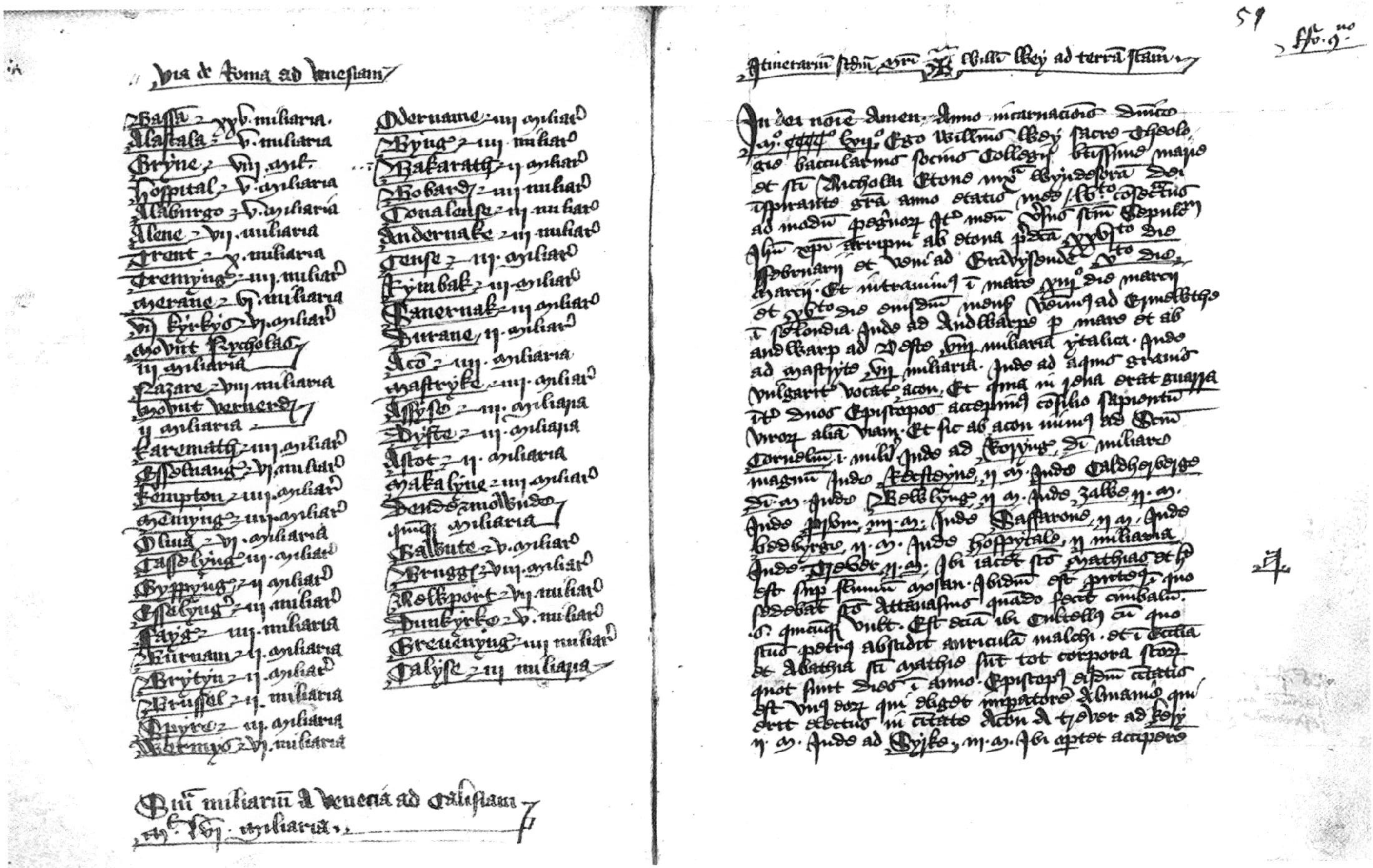

Figure 13.　Sample pages from William Wey's 'Itineraries', listing destinations on his route homeward in 1458 and showing the opening of his account of his 1462 pilgrimage. Oxford, MS Bodl. 565, ff. 50v–51r. By permission of the Bodleian Library.

**Text (*from* Section 2)**[1]

A prevysyoun[2]

A goyd prevysyoun when a man ys at Venyse, and purposyth by the grase of God to passe by the see un to port Jaff in the holy londe, and so to the Sepulkyr of owre Lorde Cryst Jhesu in Jherusalem,[3] he most dyspose hym in thys wyse. Furste, yf ye goo in a galey make yowre covenaunte[4] wyth the patrone by tyme, and chese yow a place in the seyd galey in the overest stage; for in the lawyst under hyt ys ryght smolderyng hote and stynkyng. And ye schal pay for yowre galey and for yowre mete and drynke to port Jaff, and ayen to Venyse, xl. ducatis for to be in a goyd honeste plase, and to have yowre ese in the galey, and also to be cheryschet.[5] Also when ye schal yowre covenant take, take goyd hede that the patron be bounde to yow afore the duke other lordis of Venyse, in an c. dokettis[6] to kepe al maner covenauntis wyth yow; that ys to say, that he schal conduce yow to certeyne havenys by the wey to refresche yow, and to get yow fresche water and fresch bred and flesch. Also that he schal not tary longer at none havyn then thre days at the most wythowte consent of yow all. And that he schal not take yn to the vessel nother goyng nother comyng no maner of marchaundyse wyth owte yowre wylle, to destresse yow in yowre plasys, and also for taryng of passage by the see. And by the havenes he schal led yow yf ye wyl: Furst, to Pole[7] c. myle from Venyse by water; from Pole to Curphw[8] vi. c. myle; from Curphw to Modyn[9] iii. c. myle; from Modyn to Cande[10] iii. c. myle; from Cande to Rodys[11] iii. c. myle; from Rodys to Baffe[12] in Cipres iiii c. myle; from Baffe to Port Jaffe iii. c. myle, withowte more. But make covenaunte that ye com nat at Famagust[13] in Cipres for no thyng, for meny Englysch men and other also have dyde, for that eyre ys so corupte ther abowte, and in the water also.[14] Also that yowre patrone yeff yow every day hot mete twyes, at too melys, in the mornynge at dyner, and after none at soper; and the wyne that ye schal drynke be goyd and yowre water fresch, yf ye may com ther too, and also byscocte. Also ye most ordeyne for yowreselfe and yowre felow, and ye have eny, iii. barellys eche of a quarte, whyche quarte holdyth x. galynnys; too of these barell schal

---

[1] This text is transcribed in old spelling and modernized versions from Wey's Middle English original, Oxford, Bodleian Library, MS 565, with reference to an old-spelling transcription, ed. Williams, *Itineraries,* 1857, pp. 4–7, and a modernized text, ed. Davey, *Itineraries,* 2010, pp. 26–8. I have followed Davey's titles and sub-titles for the various sections of Wey's 'Itineraries'. The list of contents (f. 1r), in two later hands, divides Wey's text into fifteen sections.

[2] Provision, forward planning.

[3] Jaffa and Church of the Holy Sepulchre, Jerusalem; founded in the 4th and reconstructed in the 11th century. It contains the site of the crucifixion of Jesus and his empty tomb.

[4] Covenant, mutual agreement or contract.

[5] Cherished or well cared for.

[6] *Informacon for pylgrymes unto the holy londe* cites this figure as 1,000 ducats.

[7] Pula, on Croatia's Istrian peninsula.

[8] Island of Corfu in the Ionian Sea.

[9] Methoni (Italian, Modone; Venetian, Modon), in Messenia in the Greek Peloponnese; site of an important Venetian fortress.

[10] Venetian name for either Crete or its major city, Heraklion; then a colony of the Republic of Venice.

[11] Rhodes, the largest of the Dodecanese Islands.

[12] Paphos (Baffa; Turkish, Baf) on the western side of Cyprus.

[13] Famagusta (Gazimaðusa) on the east coast of Cyprus.

[14] Wey only visited Famagusta once in 1458 on his return from Jaffa.

**[Modernized Text]**[1]

A provision

A good provision when a man is at Venice and intends by the Grace of God to pass by the sea unto the port of Jaffa in the Holy Land, and so to the Sepulchre of Our Lord Christ Jesus in Jerusalem, is that he must dispose himself in this way. First, if you go in a galley make your covenant with the patron in good time and choose for yourself a place in the said galley in the highest deck, because in the lowest, it is right smouldering hot and stinking.

And you shall pay for your galley and for your meat and drink to the port of Jaffa, and back to Venice, 40 ducats for to be in a good, honest place, and to have your ease in the galley, and also to be cherished. Also, when you shall take your covenant, take good heed that the patron be bound to you before the Doge or other Lords of Venice, for the sum of 100 ducats to keep all aspects of his covenant with you, that is to say, that he will convey you to certain harbours on the way to refresh you, and to get you fresh water and fresh bread and meat.

Also, that he will not tarry at any harbour longer than three days at the most without the consent of you all. And that he will not take into the vessel, either on the outward or return journey, without your agreement any kind of merchandize which might distress you in your berths or delay your sea passage.

And as regards the harbours to which he shall lead you, if you so wish: First to Pula, 100 miles from Venice by water; from Pula to Corfu, 600 miles; from Corfu to Methóni, 300 miles; from Methóni to Candia, 300 miles; from Candia to Rhodes, 300 miles; from Rhodes to Baffa in Cyprus, 400 miles; and from Baffa to the Port of Jaffa, 300 miles, and no further. But make a convenant that you do not visit Famagusta in Cyprus on any account, for many Englishmen and others have died because the air thereabouts is so corrupt, as is the water as well.

Also that your patron shall give you hot meat twice a day, at two meals; at dinner in the morning and at supper in the afternoon; and that the wine you will drink shall be good and your water fresh, if it can be obtained, and also biscuit. Also you must arrange for yourself and your servant, if you have one, three barrels each of a quart, which holds 10 gallons. Two of these barrels will serve for wine and the third for water. In one barrel take red wine and keep it in store and, if possible, do not break into it unto you are homeward bound, unless required by sickness or any other need. For you must especially bear in mind that if you have the flux and if you would give 20 ducats for a barrel, you shall have none after you have gone much past Venice. And that other barrel shall serve when you have drunk all your drinking wine to fill again at the next harbour you come to.

Also, you must buy for yourself a chest to put your things in; and if you have a servant with you, get two or three. I would then buy a chest that is as broad as the barrel is long. In that barrel I would have a lock and key, and a little door, and lay the barrel that you would use first at the same end where the door is. For if the galleymen or other pilgrims come to it, too many will break into it and drink thereof, and steal your water, which you would not often miss for your wine. And in the other part of the chest you may lay your

---

[1] Presented in shorter paragraphs for clarity of reading.

45

serve for wyne, and the therde for water. In that one barel take rede wyne and keep evyr in store, and tame hyt not yf ye may til ye com hamward ayen, withoute syknes cause hyt, other any other nede. For ye schal thys in specyal note, and ye had the flix, yf ye wold yeff xx. doketis for a barel, ye schal none have after ye passe moche Venyse; and that othyr barel schal serve when ye have drunke up yowre drynkyng wyne to fyl ageyne at the havyn where ye next come unto. Also, ye most by yow a chest to put yn yowre thyngys; and yf ye may have a fellow with yow too or thre, y wold then by a chest that were as brode as the barel were long. In that one y wolde have loke and key, and a lytyl dore, and ley that same barell that y wolde spende frust at the same dore ende; for yf the galymen, other pylgremys, may come ther, to meny wyl tame and drynke therof, and stele yowre watyr, whyche ye wold nat mysse oft tyme for yowre wyne. And yn the other part of the cheste ye may ley yowre bred, ches, spyses, and al other thyngis. Also ye most ordeyne yow bysockte to have with yow; for thow ye schal be at the tabyl wyth yowre patrone, notwythstondynge ye schal oft tyme have need to yowre vytelys, bred, chese, eggys, frute, and bakyn, wyne, and other, to make yowre collasyun: for sum tyme ye schal have febyl bred, wyne, and stynkyng water, meny tymes ye schal be ful fayne to ete of yowre owne. Also y consel you to have wyth you owte of Venyse confectynnys, confortatyuys, laxatyuys, restoratyuys, gyngever, ryse, fygys, reysenes gret and smal, whyche schal do yow great ese by the wey, pepyr, saferyn, clowys, masys, a fewe as ye thenge nede, and powder dwke.[1] Also take with yow a lytyl cawdren and fryyng pan, dysches, platerrys, sawserys of tre, cuppys of glas, a grater for brede, and such nessaryes. Also when ye come to Venyse ye schal by a bedde by seynt Markys Cherche; ye schal have a fedyr bedde, a matres, too pylwys, too peyre schetis, and a qwylt, and ye schal pay iii dokettis; and when ye com ayen bring the same bedde to the man that ye bowt hit of and ye schal have a doket and halfe ayen, thow hyt be broke and worne. Also make yowre chaunge at Venyse, and take wyth yow at the leste xxx. doketis of grotys and grossynes. Ye schal have at Venyse xxviii. of new grossetis and dim.;[2] for when ye passe Venyse ye schal have in sum plase xxvi. grossetis or xxiiii. And take also wyth yow iii. other iiii. doketis of soldys that be galy halpanse of Venyse, for every grosset iiii soldys. Take also with you fro Venyse a doket other too of Torneys; hyt ys bras money of Candi, hyt wyl go by all the wey; ye schal have viii. for a sold at Venyse, at Modyn, and Cande oftyn tyme; but iiii. v. other vi. at the most for a solde. Also by yow a cage for half a dosen of hennys or chekyn to have with yow in the galey, for ye schal have nede unto them many tymes; and by yow half a buschel of myle sede of Venyse for hem. Also take a barel wyth you close for a sege for yowre chambur in the galey, hyt is ful nessessary yf ye be syke that [ye] com not in the eyre. Also whan ye com to havyn townys yf ye wyl ye may by eggys, yf ye come by tyme to lond, for then ye may have goyd chep, for they be ful nessessary in the galey, sum time fryed with oyle olyfe, and sumtyme for a caudel.[3] Also when ye come to havyn townys, yf he schal tary there iij. dayes, go by tyme to londe, for then ye may have logyng by fore other, for hyt wyl be take up anone, and yf eny goyd vytel be bee ye sped afore other. Also when ye com to diverse havynnys be wel ware of dyverse frutys, for they be not acordyng to yowre complexioun, and they gender a blody fluxe; and yf an Englyschman have that sykenes hyt ys a marvel

---

[1] *Poudre douce*: a mixture of four spices – ginger, nutmeg, cinnamon and liquorice (or fennel) – used to flavour sweet dishes.

[2] Exchange rate for one ducat.

[3] *caudle*: warm, nourishing drink mixed with wine or spices, often given to the sick.

bread, cheese, spices, and all other things. And you must arrange to have your biscuit with you because, even though you shall be at your patron's table, notwithstanding, you shall often have need of your own victuals, bread, cheese, eggs, fruit, and bacon, wine and other items to make your own meal because sometimes you shall have poor quality bread, wine and stinking water, and many times you will be glad to eat your own provisions..

Also, I counsel you to have with you from Venice confections, confortatives, laxatives, restoratives, ginger, rice, figs and large and small raisins which will give you great ease on the journey, pepper, saffron, cloves, mace, as few as you think necessary, and powder douce. Also, take with you a little cauldron and frying pan, dishes, platters, wooden saucers, glass cups, a grater for bread and such essentials.

Also, when you come to Venice you shall buy a bed near St Mark's Church; you shall get a feather bed, a mattress, two pillows, two pairs of sheets, and a quilt, and you shall pay 3 ducats; and when you come back, bring the same bed to the man from whom you bought it and you shall have a ducat and a half in return, even if it be broken and worn.

Also, change your money at Venice and take with you at least 30 ducats in *grotes* and *grossines* [*grossini*]. You shall have at Venice 28 and a half new *grossets* [*grosetti*]. For when you have passed Venice you shall have in some places 26 or 24 *grossets*. And take also with you 3 or 4 ducats in *soldi* which are galley halfpences of Venice, for every *grosset* equals 4 *soldi*. Also take with you from Venice a ducat or two in *torneys* [*tornesi*], this is brass money from Candia, and it will be useable for the whole journey. You shall often have 8 for a *soldo* at Venice and Candia but 4, 5 or 6 at the most for a *soldo* elsewhere.

Also, buy a cage for yourself for half a dozen hens or chickens to have with you in the galley, for you will need them many times; and buy half a bushel of millet seed of Venice for them.

Also, take a barrel with you to use as a close stool for your chamber in the galley; it is very necessary if you are so sick that you cannot come up into the air.

Also, when you come to harbour towns, if you wish, you may buy eggs; if you are timely in getting ashore, you may have them good and cheap, for they are very necessary in the galley, sometimes fried with olive oil and sometime for a caudle. And when you come to harbour towns, if you shall linger there three days, go ashore quickly, for then you may have lodgings before the others, for they will be taken up quickly. And if any good victuals be there, you must hurry before the others.

Also, when you come to various harbours be very wary of different fruits for they are not suitable for your complexion[1] and they will engender a bloody flux; and if an Englishman have that sickness, it is a marvel if he escapes and does not die from it.

Also, when you shall come to the port of Jaffa, take with you out of the galley onto land two gourds, one with wine and another with water, each of a potel at least, for you shall get no more until you come to Ramys. The wine at Jaffa is very weak and dreadful; and at Jerusalem it is good wine and expensive. Also see that the *patron* of the galley takes charge of your accoutrements within the galley until you come again to the galley. You shall stay in the Holy Land 13 or 14 days.

---

[1] *complexion*: constitution.

and scape hyt but he dye thereof. Also when ye schal come to port Jaff take wyth yow oute of the galey into the londe too gordys, one with wyne another wyth water, eche of a potel[1] at the lest, for ye schal none have tyl ye come to Ramys, and that ys ryght febyl and dyre; and at Jherusalem hyt ys goyd wyne and dere. Also se that the patron of the galey take charge of yowre harnys wythyn the galey tyl ye come ayen to the galey. Ye schal tary yn the holy lond xiii. other xiiii. days.

---

[1] *potel*: pot or tankard, also used as a unit of measurement equating to half a gallon.

## The 1462 Pilgrimage to Jerusalem[1]

This literal translation seeks to convey not only the sense but also the basic style of Wey's original Latin. He does not write in polished or classical Latin, in that he often utilizes vocabulary coined during the late medieval period and his verbs shift erratically within phrases and passages from past to present to future and from active to passive tenses. Hence, this literal translation of Wey's narrative seeks to reflect how an educated Englishman at this period probably thought and spoke in Latin. It represents the linguistic proficiency of an Oxford-educated cleric who wished to record clearly his practical experiences for the benefit of other pilgrims and travellers via Venice to the Holy Land. He writes not to demonstrate his classical erudition and fluency but rather to ensure that those with perhaps only a functional knowledge of reading Latin could still benefit from his advice to ensure that they remained safe during the long and perilous journey to the Holy Land. He wishes to guide his readers how best to prepare themselves for this arduous experience and, no less significantly, to gain the maximum spiritual benefit from undertaking a long-distance pilgrimage while, hopefully, also returning in good health to England.

## [Text translated from Latin, *from* Section 9]

Thence to Venice we came,[2] a large and noble city, on 22 day of April [1462],[3] where on the vigil of the feast of St Mark we saw over St Mark's altar twelve golden crowns full of precious stones and twelve pectoral crosses also full of precious stones and a tall and richly endowed chalice, two great and precious thuribles[4] made of gold or gilded, and four gilded candlesticks; and the high altar was of silver gilt, and the church of St Mark is built in the manner of the temple of the Christians in Jerusalem.[5] And when the most illustrious Doge of that same city entered into this church of St Mark at the first vespers of St Mark, he had in front of him nine very long silver trumpets and three small ones, all bearing his

---

[1] 'Itinerarium secundum Magistri Willelmi Wey ad terram sanctam' (Second itinerary of Master William Wey to the Holy Land), Oxford, Bodleian Library, MS 565. Latin text translated with reference to the Latin text, ed. Williams, *Itinerarie*, pp. 83–93, and the English translation, ed. Davey, *Itineraries*, pp. 117–25. Wey had left England on 13 March 1462.

[2] Wey does not provide specific information about his travelling companions in 1462, although on his 1457/8 pilgrimage he had travelled with John Tiptoft, Earl of Worcester (**item 3**). On entering Italy Wey refers to 'we three pilgrims, each called William'. In a note added to the flyleaf of the 'Itineraries' it was recorded that he had donated to Edington Priory a painting described as 'a cloth stained with three Marys and three pilgrims', probably a memento of this journey and his companions. Wey, *Itineraries*, ed. Davey, pp. 116, 137, 223, suggests that one may have been William Fulford (d. 1475), Canon of Exeter Cathedral. For Wey's will, see Bale and Sobecki, *Medieval English Travel*, pp. 397–400.

[3] Wey also provides detailed information about Venice in his account (section 2) of his 1458 visit. It includes material incorporated into the account of this 1462 visit. The earlier account, written in Middle English, formed the basis of his more detailed Latin account of his 1462 visit. See Wey, *Itineraries*, ed. Davey, pp. 26–32. Both of his journeys were made during the traditional spring (formerly Easter) voyages from Venice to the Holy Land which aimed to benefit from prevailing winds to reach Jaffa by the end of June. In earlier periods there had also been autumn voyages from Venice but these were rare by the mid-15th century. Mitchell, *Spring Voyage*, p. 29.

[4] *thuribles*: metal censers suspended from chains in which incense is burned during services. Swinging the chains disseminates the incense smoke.

[5] Church of the Holy Sepulchre, Jerusalem.

coat of arms.[1] He also had in front of him eight banners with eight gilded crosses in a circle. They also carried before him eight very tall candlesticks with eight white candles. And also on one side one person carried before him a couch with gold cushions and another carried a gilded chair. And after him one carried a canopy of gold cloth and another a sword with a gilded sheath full of precious stones and a long, extinguished candle of white wax. And with the venerable Doge there went the Patriarch of Venice and the Premissory of St Mark in episcopal vestments; the Patriarch with a cross and the Premissory with a crucifer[2] of great worth. And before him were twenty canons clad in amices,[3] also many priests and clerics. And behind him came the lords of the city and a crowd of the people. And on St Mark's Day there came the Fraternities of various saints in a great crowd wearing white habits in the manner of the religious; and in one hand they had candles of wax and in the other scourges; and they had in front of them crosses and processional candles. And there were five hundred members of the Fraternity of St Mark in attendance.

At that time the most illustrious Doge of Venice was called Lord Pascale Malopero.[4] He had with him six Councillors, some of whom are changed each year. There are also under him six Procurators of St Mark who remain in office for life. And they are called the Three Within and the Three Without. There are also in the city ten of the principal citizens who are called the Ten Councillors. And there are also three Advocates who, with the Doge, can conduct all business in the city. And there is also one who is called the Podesta and he is the city's judge. But when all these preceding individuals disagree they summon 150 nobles who are called Precati. These can decide as they wish. Then there is another Great Council to which all the nobles can come and in this said Council they choose officials belonging to the city and to other places outside the city. And they choose each year 800 officers for duties in the city and outside, and some of them hold office for two years and some for one year. Then there are also among the officers, eight who remain in their offices permanently for life; those six Procurators of St Mark, one who oversees the Mint and another the Ropeworks.

And they have in the city a place of great size where they make the galleys for the defence of our Faith;[5] where I saw eighty galleys, either completed or under construction; also below this place they have large armouries of every type, full of all kinds of weapons allocated for the defence of our Faith. On the third day of May, in the year forementioned [1462], Lord Pascuale Malopero, the most illustrious Doge of Venice, departed from this mortal life.[6] He lay dead [i.e., in state] in his palace for three days and on the third day he was taken to his burial. At his funeral all the Schools wearing religious dress processed in front of him, with candles and scourges in their hands. And before them the crosses and processional candles; and behind them the ordinary people of the city, priests, clerics and

---

[1] Gentile Bellini's painting, *Procession in Saint Mark's Square* (Accademia, Venice) (**Plate 1**), although completed in 1496, represents this procession in 1444 and includes many of the officers and ceremonial objects commented upon by Wey.

[2] *crucifer*: usually this term refers to the bearer of a processional cross with a long staff, known as a crucifer, but Wey here elides the two together.

[3] *amice*: in the medieval period, and in some religious orders, this term was applied to a linen cape draped over the head and shoulders.

[4] Pasquale Malipiero, Doge 1457–62.

[5] *Arsenal (**Plate 12**).

[6] Malipiero died 5 not 3 May, as stated by Wey. Chambers, ed., *Venice*, p. 45.

members of the religious orders; and finally there came the Canons of St Mark with a cross and candles; and after them, two men carried his weapons and, after these arms, his body was presented in the following way. On his head he had the biricula,[1] and his face was uncovered; and under his head was a cushion of golden fabric. On his dead body he wore the doge's robe of gold trimmed with fur. And on his feet he wore shoes with gold spurs beside them; and on the other side of his body was a sword with a gilded sheath. And he was buried with all these trappings high up in the wall at the House of the Predicator Brothers [Dominicans][2] in the city of Venice.

After his death and burial, the Venetians convened for the election of a new Doge. They were called together by councillors for this election of the new Doge. And all the nobles of good birth are sworn in to select lords from among the nobles who are faithful to the Catholic faith. They accept, under pain of forfeiting all of their temporal goods, to choose one who was a wiser man, better in status, more faithful to the Catholic faith and more skilful in worldly matters for the city and its dominions. These hundred men with certain notaries will be enclosed in a house from which they cannot leave until they choose forty of the most noble for this office. Afterwards, these forty men will receive the Body of the Lord [Communion] because they will choose such a man whom they believe to be the most Catholic believer in our faith and the most profitable for the city of Venice. And he whom they recognize to have the greatest number of votes, they will accept as their Doge. And the other who has the lesser share, they will not disclose under pain of death. Then he who has the majority of votes and is chosen as Doge will be escorted to his home.

And as he is led there sailors will come to him and say,

'Your goods are our goods'.
He will say,
'I know this well but I ask you to accept among yourselves these hundred ducats and be satisfied'.

And he gives the ducats to them and he scatters coins along the street to his house in order to have the space to return home. And, having made domestic arrangements, he will be led by the lords of the city to the Doge's Palace. And they will make him a knight and then they will dress him with the robes of his office and will put the biricula covered with precious jewels on his head.

The next Sunday he comes to the Church of St Mark and all the Schools will publicly appear before him and one of these will preach a public sermon. Then will come the religious orders in procession with their relics, candles, crosses and canopies. And they will have among them many boys, dressed as angels, and they will be carried by high poles on a litter and they will sing various songs in public to their Lord Doge. And the secular priests sing *Te Deum laudamus* [we praise thee, O God]; *Sermone blando angelus* [with sweet words the angel]; *Ad cenam agni providi* [made ready for the feast of the Lamb].

---

[1] *biricula*: distinctive cap worn by Venetian doges. Wey's terminology may have been derived from the 'biretta', the square cap with three flat projections on top, worn by the Roman Catholic clergy. The Venetian cap was known as the *corno ducale* (ducal horn), adopted instead of a crown because Venice was a republic. These caps were made by the nuns of *San Zaccaria. A new cap was presented to the doge on each Easter Monday, following a procession from St Mark's to the convent.

[2] *Santi Giovanni e Paolo. Doge Malipiero's monument is located in the north aisle.

And thus he will depart from the Church of St Mark with a great procession and a multitude of the people. And he will come to the Palace of the Doge and he will stand in the entrance to his palace, turning his face towards the people, and then all his nobles will walk before him and offer him reverence. These duties completed, he will go to dine in his palace where he will remain for the rest of his life. After his election ambassadors from various provinces will come to visit him, bringing him gifts and offering their congratulations for his elevation to that office.

The name of this doge elected in this year is Christophero Mauro, a truly catholic and faithful man[1] who immediately after his election sent his envoys for the making of peace between Pope Pius and the Austrian Duke.[2] For the glory and honour of God, I shall make clear what I heard, what I saw and what I did on my journey to this holy place with this intention that those things that were well done may become an example for posterity so that those who come after may do the same and better. For the honour of the city, I shall detail later in these writings those things that I saw in the palace of the most illustrious Doge of Venice and the house [room] of his council.

It is read of Pope Alexander III that he was fleeing from Rome in the habit of a Franciscan minor friar[3] because of fear of the Emperor Frederick[4] and he came to the Venetian religious house called Caritas, and it is still so called to this day.[5] And in this house he worked in the kitchen, albeit unknown to everyone. It happened that a certain pilgrim had come to the religious house where he himself was working and here he saw Pope Alexander whom he knew because formerly he had seen him in his church of Saint Peter at Rome. Because of which, he went to one of the lords of the city and intimated to him that Pope Alexander was in that city. This lord took the pilgrim to the Doge called Gayne Zia.[6]

Then the Doge with the lords of the city had come to the house of Charity, asking the prior that he should bring all the monks and servants before him. These all having appeared in his presence, he said to the pilgrim: 'Who is the pope among these?' And he said that he was not there. Then the lord Doge said to the prior: 'Have you any others in this house?' The prior replied: 'There are no others in the house except one who lately came here and serves in the kitchen but let him be called'. When, however, he had come before them, the pilgrim said to the lord Doge: 'This is certainly Pope Alexander'.

Then the Doge and all the others fell at his feet and immediately ordered for him vestments suitable for his office and they led him to the Doge's palace, promising that they would stand surety for his life. And immediately the Doge ordered that many galleys be armed for war against the Emperor. Because this was a matter of faith, the Doge offered

---

[1] Cristoforo Moro (1390–1471), Doge 1462–71.

[2] Enea Piccolomini (1405–64), Pope Pius II (1457–64), and Albert VI (1418–63), Archduke of Lower and Inner Austria (1453–63).

[3] The official Latin name of the order is the Ordo Fratrum Minorum (Order of Little Brothers); informally called friars minor or minorites.

[4] Roland of Siena (c.1100/5–81). Alexander III, Pope, 1159–81, was obliged to spend much of his pontificate outside Rome. In 1153 he led a group of cardinals opposing Frederick I (c.1123–90), known as 'Barbarossa' (Holy Roman Emperor, 1155–90). Wey's reference is mistaken since the Franciscan Order was not founded until 1209 by St Francis of Assisi.

[5] *Santa Maria della Carità.

[6] Sebastiano Ziani, Doge 1172–8.

himself to go to war with the others and he appeared before the Pope in his armour and asked him for his blessing and a plenary indulgence for himself and his men.

And then the Pope first handed to him a sword and said: 'I give you the power to carry out justice.' After this the lord Doge went with his people against the Emperor and he captured the son of the Emperor and took him to the Pope.[1] And on his faith [i.e., parole] he was sent to his father to bring him to the Pope. And when this was done, he [*margin*: Note how it was the Emperor who was taken to the Pope saying][2] fell at the feet of the Pope in the church of St Mark, saying, 'I do this for Peter'. And then the Pope said: 'For Peter and for me.' And then immediately the Pope put his foot on the Emperor's neck, saying, 'You will walk on the asp and the basilisk and you will trample on the lion and the dragon.' And then they were reconciled.[3] Then the Pope said to the Doge, 'Behold, I appoint you Lord of the Salt Sea and as a sign of this I give you a ring with which you will be married to the sea,'[4] which he still does with much ceremony up to this time once a year on the Day of the Ascension of Our Lord. He [the Pope] also gave to him a candle of white wax so that it could be carried before him at great ceremonies. This white candle was given to the Doge of Venice by the Pope because neither in France, England nor in any other kingdoms did he find supporters of our faith but only in Venice. And he wanted a white candle to be carried before the Doge in perpetuity when he crossed to the church of St Mark on feast days for their honour and the continuation of faith. And he also gave him a canopy of golden cloth, eight banners with golden crosses in a circle and eight silver trumpets. And with these items he is led to the church of St Mark's during great ceremonies. He also gave him permission to use a seal with lead.

The city of Venice was built by fishermen in the year AD 200. [*margin*: Note how it was built and the year].[5] But first it was called Realti and afterwards the Province of Venice.[6] St Magnus, the martyr, was the first Bishop of Venice, and his uncorrupted body lies in the Church of St Jeremiah in Venice.[7] This saint had a vision that he should build seven churches in Venice which are these: the first is of St James on the Realto;[8] the second of St John;[9] the third of St Salvator;[10] the fourth is St Mary, the Beautiful;[11] to which come the Doge and Lords of Venice on the Eve of the Purification, and on the

---

[1] The Battle of Legnano (29 May 1176). There seems no conclusive record of the emperor's son, Henry (b. 1165), being captured.

[2] In the manuscript a later hand has added a note in Latin: 'This is the same Alexander 3 who supported St Thomas in exile'. This refers to how Pope Alexander III intervened in the dispute between Henry II and Thomas Becket (c.1119/20–70), St Thomas of Canterbury. King Louis VII of France had offered refuge to Becket at the Cistercian abbey of Pontigny but in 1167 Henry summoned him back to England. Alexander III intervened in 1170 by sending emissaries to England to negotiate a safe passage for Becket if he returned from exile.

[3] On the pavement in front of the great door of St Mark's, a slab of red Verona marble with a white marble lozenge marks the spot where traditionally Barbarossa knelt before Pope Alexander III in 1177.

[4] *Marriage of the Sea.

[5] In the manuscript a later hand has added a note in Latin: 'The city of the Venetians was founded, or rather extended, in AD 450, not by shepherds as in Rome but by more powerful and wealthy strangers of other provinces, fleeing there from the persecution of Attila.'

[6] This paragraph is repeated, with only minor variants, in Wey's section 11, 'A Medley', under 'Concerning the City of Venice'. This section also contains another short section, 'Concerning the Lands and Dominions of the Venetians from Venice to the Holy Land'.

[7] *San Geremia. The relics of St Magnus have been lost.

[8] *San Giacomo di Rialto.          [9] *San Giovanni Evangelista.

[10] *San Salvatore.          [11] *Santa Maria Formosa.

Day itself for Mass, to make offerings to the Most Blessed Virgin for miracles performed there; the fifth church is the Church of St Silvester;[1] the sixth of St Jerome;[2] the seventh, of St Peter, which is the cathedral church and they have there the Patriarch.[3]

Now follows [an account] of relics which are in Venice and its environs[4] In first place in the Church of St Mark the ring and book of St Mark; there is also the stone which was struck by Moses in the desert and which gave water in great abundance,[5] and there is the image of the Most Blessed Virgin on that stone fixed on the wall near the entrance to the palace. And above the door[6] of St Mark is the image of Jesus Christ made in mosaic, and it is very similar to Jesus Christ when he was carrying the cross to Calvary. There is there also in the same church the image on linen cloth of Christ crucified which dripped blood when it was stabbed by a Jew with a dagger; and there is a phial full of this blood in the same place, and those who see the blood on the second hour of night on the Easter vigil will have full remission of their sins and permission to eat meat in the night.

There is also in the same city the body of the martyr Isidore; the bodies of St Sergius and St Bacchus; the body of the almoner St Chrisostom; the body of St Zacharias, the father of St John the Baptist;[7] the body of St Theodore the confessor; the body of St Chorax a hermit; the body of St Lierius the martyr; the body of St Ligorius; the body of St Barbarus the martyr; the bodies of the saints Nichomedes, Gamaliel and Abibon; the body of St Plato the martyr; the uncorrupted body of St Marina the virgin; the body of St Theodore the martyr; the bodies of the martyrs saints Gordian and Epimachus; the body of St Florian; the body of St Paul the first hermit; the uncorrupted body of St Maximus the bishop; the body of St Barbara, the virgin and martyr; the body of St Magnus the martyr; the uncorrupted body of St Lucy the virgin; the body of St Nicetas the martyr; the body of St Crisogonus the martyr; the body of St Constantinus the confessor; the body of St Jonas the prophet; the body of St Hermolaus the martyr; the body of St Nicholas-on-the-Shore; the body of St Theodore, bishop of Giara; the uncorrupted body of St Helena;[8] the bodies of saints Cosmas and Damian; the body of St Cosmas the confessor; the uncorrupted body of St Paul the martyr which has a coronet on his head who was once Duke of Burgundy; the body of St Leo the confessor; the body of St Anianus, bishop of Alexandria; the body of St Donatus, bishop on Murano; the body of St Gerard, bishop and martyr; the body of St Urcus the martyr; the body of St Dominicus the hermit; the body of St Cleodonius, bishop; the body of St Frucia the virgin and martyr; the body of St Antoninus the martyr; the bodies of saints Hermacherus and Fortunatus, martyrs on Marianus; the bodies and bones of many of the Innocents; the body of St John the almoner; the body of St Secundus the martyr; the right hand of St Ciprian the martyr and on his hand there is the blood which fell from his neck when

---

[1] *San Silvestro.

[2] *San Girolamo.

[3] *San Pietro di Castello.

[4] Much of this information is repeated in Wey's section 6, 'Reasons for Pilgrimage to the Holy Land', under 'The Tenth and Final Matter Deals with the Relics of Saints in Various Places along the Road from the Holy Land'.

[5] Cf. Exodus 17:6.

[6] This mosaic is above the door. The Latin 'hostium sancti' is used in the manuscript to mean 'ostium sancti' (holy door).

[7] *San Zaccaria was being rebuilt when Wey was at Venice.

[8] Preserved in *Sant'Elena.

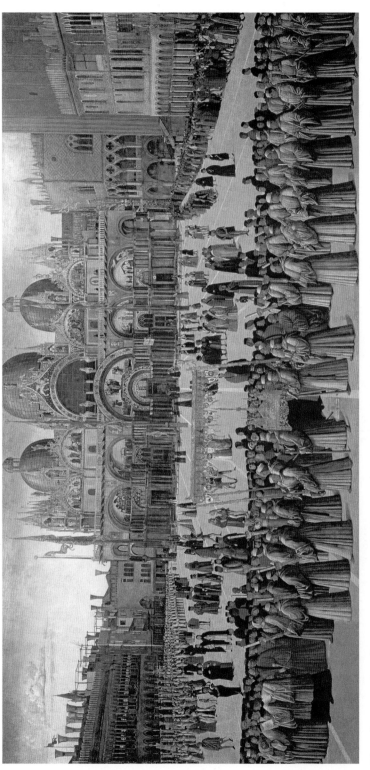

Plate 1.  Gentile Bellini, *Procession in St Mark's Square* (representing the procession in *c*.1444). Oil on canvas, *c*.1496. Gallerie dell'Accademia, Venice. Bridgeman Images.

Map 3.     Untinted frontispiece, 'The Lady of Venice', from Bernard von Breydenbach, *Peregrinatio in Terram Sanctam* (Mainz: Erhard Reuwich, 1486; from the Latin edition, Speyer: Peter Drach, 1502). Special Collections, Brotherton Library, Incunabula, BRE. By permission of Special Collections, Brotherton Library, University of Leeds.

Map 4.  Hand-tinted frontispiece, 'The Lady of Venice', from Bernard von Breydenbach, *Peregrinatio in Terram Sanctam* (Mainz: Erhard Reuwich, 1486). Private Collection, Bridgeman Images.

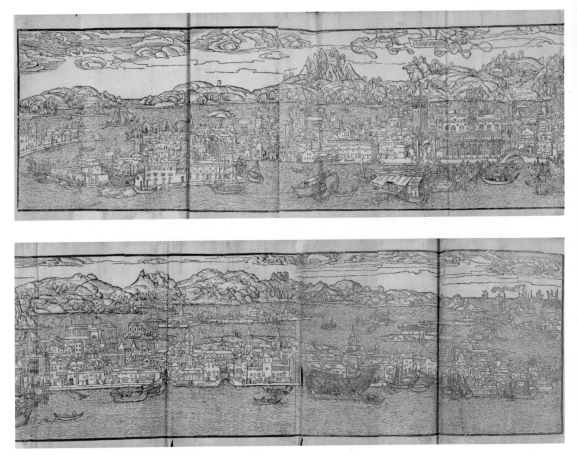

Map 5.    Untinted woodcut map of Venice, from Bernard von Breydenbach, *Peregrinatio in Terram Sanctam* (Mainz: Erhard Reuwich, 1486; from the 1502 Latin edition, Speyer: Peter Drach). Special Collections, Brotherton Library, Incunabula, BRE. By permission of Special Collections, Brotherton Library, University of Leeds.

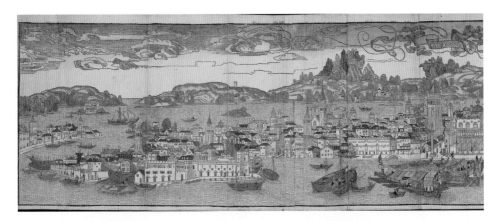

Map 6. Tinted woodcut map of Venice, from Bernard von Breydenbach, *Peregrinatio in Terram Sanctam* (Mainz: Erhard Reuwich, 1486; from the 1502 Latin edition, Speyer: Peter Drach). Bodleian Library, Arch. B c.25. By permission of the Bodleian Library, Oxford.

Map 7.    Tinted detail of woodcut map of Venice, Doge's Palace and Piazzo San Marco, from Bernard von Breydenbach, *Peregrinatio in Terram Sanctam*, British Library, London, Bridgeman Images.

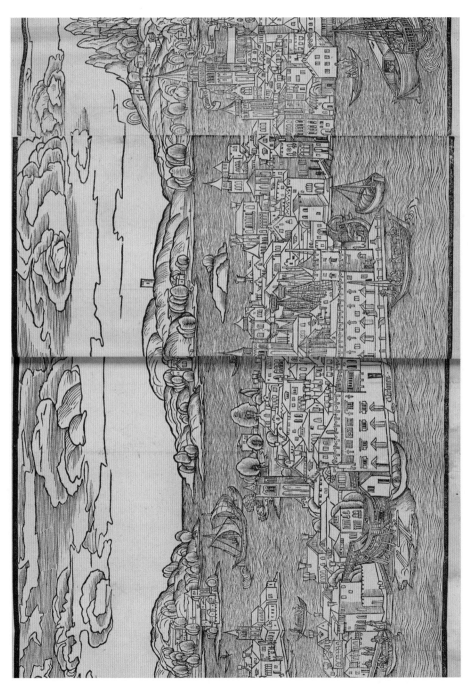

Map 8.   Untinted detail of woodcut map of Venice, customs area and entrance to the Grand Canal, from Bernard von Breydenbach, *Peregrinatio in Terram Sanctam* (Mainz: Erhard Reuwich, 1486; from the Latin edition, Speyer: Peter Drach, 1502). Special Collections, Brotherton Library, Incunabula, BRE. By permission of Special Collections, Brotherton Library, University of Leeds.

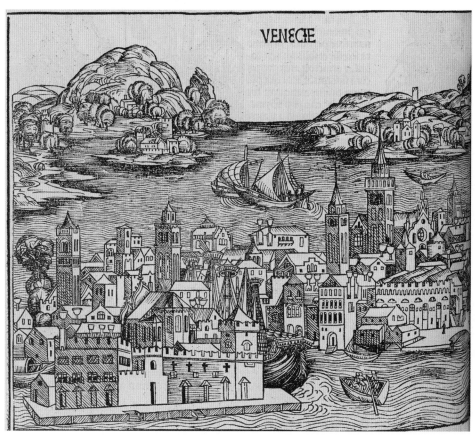

Map 9.  Detail of woodcut map of Venice from Hartmann Schedel, *Liber chronicarum* [Nuremberg Chronicle] (Nuremberg, 1493). Special Collections, Brotherton Library, BRO Coll Safe SCH. By permission of Special Collections, Brotherton Library, University of Leeds.

Map 10.  Detail of woodcut map of Venice from Hartmann Schedel, *Liber chronicarum* [Nuremberg Chronicle] (Nuremberg, 1493). Special Collections, Brotherton Library, BRO Coll Safe SCH.  By permission of Special Collections, Brotherton Library, University of Leeds.

Map 11.  Woodcut from six blocks, Jacopo de' Barbari, aerial view map of Venice (1500). By permission of the Rijksmuseum, Amsterdam.

Map 12.    Detail of wooden Rialto Bridge, from Jacopo de' Barbari, aerial view map of Venice (1500). By permission of the Rijksmuseum, Amsterdam.

Map 13.  Detail of Doge's Palace and Campanile, from Jacopo de' Barbari, aerial view map of Venice (1500). By permission of the Rijksmuseum, Amsterdam.

Map 14. Detail of Arsenal, from Jacopo de' Barbari, aerial view map of Venice (1500). By permission of the Rijksmuseum, Amsterdam.

Map 15.　Plan of Venice, from Georg Braun and Frans Hogenberg, *Civitates orbis terrarum* [from engravings by Bolognino Zaltieri], Part 2, Engraving 4. Cologne, 1572–1617. Private Collection. Bridgeman Images.

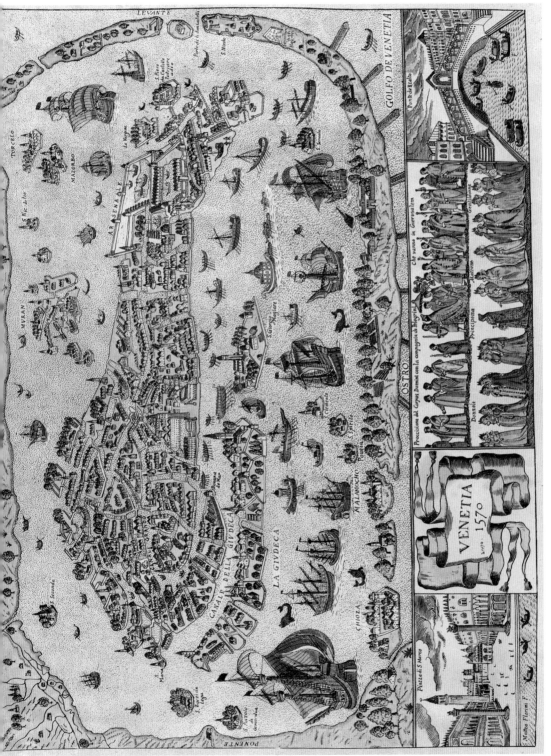

Map 16. Hand-tinted map of Venice by Matteo Florimi, dated 1570 but post 1591. Private Collection. Bridgeman Images.

Plate 2.   Vittore Carpaccio, *Miracle of the Cross at the Ponte di Rialto*. Oil on canvas, *c.*1496. Gallerie dell'Accademia, Venice. Bridgeman Images.

he was beheaded. In St George's Church there is St Christopher's shin bone of great length; also part of Christ's sponge and of His seamless tunic. Also in Venice are the Schools of all languages and the doctors teaching there have for their labours [payment] from the government of the city.

[*margin*: Provisions for pilgrims] Now follows how we put ourselves in order before our departure from Venice. Firstly, it is necessary to agree with some *patronus* or other who is going there how much for a place in the galley and for your food; and choose a place where you will be able to have light and air. In the same way, if you are able to, you will write down the agreements made between you and the *patronus* and put them before the officials of the city because then the *patronus* will keep his pact made with you. And your agreement with the *patronus* should include that your *patronus* will take you to the Holy Land and bring you back to Venice; and that on the way he will take you to certain ports for your benefit and obtain there fresh water, meat and bread; also that he will not delay at a port more than three days without the consent of the pilgrims; also that he will not accept cargo going there and coming back because your room on the galley could be reduced and your sea journey impeded; also that he will take you to these ports: Pole [Pula], of course, about 100 miles from Venice; though the water from Pula to Corphow [Corfu], 600 miles; then to Motyn [Methóni], 300 miles: then to Candea [Heraklion] in Creta [Crete], 300 miles: then to Pafum [Paphos] in Cipria [Cyprus], 400 miles: then to port of Jaff [Jaffa] in the Holy Land, 300 miles. Then make an agreement that the *patronus* will not take you to Famacost [Famagusta] in Cyprus because the air there is very infectious for English people.[1] Also that the *patronus* will give you twice a day hot food and that the wine will be good and the water fresh. And when you come to the port of Jaffa he will guarantee the safe-keeping of your property in his galley.

Secondly, the things that are to be bought by you for your own assistance. Firstly, you must order for yourself and your companions three barrels called 'quarters', each containing gallons, two for wine and the third for water. In one barrel put red wine and serve that wine when you are returning from the Holy Land since it is good for the flux; because even if you were willing to give 20 ducats for one barrel, you would not obtain it once you have left Venice. You can drink from the other barrel and fill it up at port on the way. Thirdly, you must buy a chest for putting your belongings in under wax seal so that you can protect the things which belong to you, be they bread, cheese, spices, fruit and other essentials. Fourthly, you must buy biscuit for a half a year, pork, cheese and eggs and fruit for making meals in the afternoon and evening because what you will get from the *patronus* will be too little and often you will be very hungry. I also advise that you take with you from Venice medical confections, confortatives[2] for example the powder called 'powder duke' [*poudre douce*], laxatives and restrictives, rice, figs, raisins, plums, damsons, pepper, saffron, cloves and other spices. Then you will buy a small frying pan, large and small plates, made both of earthenware and wood, glasses, mixing bowls, baskets for carrying eggs and vegetables and cheese, fish and meats which you will purchase when you come to the different ports where you will need to buy your own victuals. Also you must buy at Venice a small chamber pot because if you are unwell and

[1] Wey's Middle English version (section 2) of his 'Itineraries' provides a more detailed description of this route. This account omits the sections from Candia (Crete) to Rhodes and from Rhodes to Paphos.
[2] *confortatives*: reviving or strengthening medicines.

you cannot climb to the upper parts of the galley, you will be able to do what you need to there. Also you will provide yourself with a lantern and candles. Fifthly, you will buy a bed near St Mark's in Venice. You will have for three ducats a feather bed, a mattress, two pillows, two pairs of small linen sheets and a small quilt; and when you come back to Venice to the vendor he will take them back and give one and a half ducats for the bedding. Sixthly, change 10 or 12 ducats for new Venetian grotes.[1] There you will get 29 for a ducat but in other places you will only get 26 or 24 to the ducat. Take also with you 3 ducats in Venetian soldi [shillings]. Take also 2 ducats in torneys [*tornesi*], you will get 8 for a shilling, but on the way you will not get as many for a shilling and they will be useful on the journey because you will buy victuals with them. You should also buy a mat and a little cord in order to wrap up your bedding. Seventhly, when you come to a port it is good to go ashore among the first people, then you will buy what you need to eat at a better price, for example, vegetables, chicken, meats, fish, fruit and eggs which are very necessary. Then, when you come to different ports, avoid the fruits because many act as a laxative and, in those parts, they cause death for Englishmen … . I will write about our departure from Venice, which cities we went through, what we heard, what we saw and what we did. We left Venice on 26th day of May for the 'Towers of Venice'[2] outside the city and there we remained until 1st day of June; and around midnight we set sail, navigating in the name of God to the Holy Land; and we came to Parense in the land of Istria,[3] about 100 miles from Venice, at about 1.00pm on 3rd of June.

[1] *new Venetian grotes*: rather than referring here to the English or Irish 'groat, Wey means the Venetian silver *grosse*. Its value fluctuated, depending upon the price of silver, approximating to 4 *soldini* or 48 *dinarii*. See also pp. 40 n. 3, 46, 47, 56 n. 1 and 66–7.

[2] Probably the towers of the old *Fortezza di Sant'Andrea.

[3] Poreč (Parenzo), now in western Croatia.

# 3. 1458 AND 1460 – JOHN TIPTOFT, EARL OF WORCESTER

**John Tiptoft (1427–70), Earl of Worcester**, was educated at University College, Oxford, where during the early 1440s he was already planning to make a pilgrimage to the Holy Land. He discussed this ambition with a fellow student, John Rous (*c.*1420/25–91) of Warwick, who advised him to take an artist with him to draw the birds, animals and other memorable sights that he might encounter on his journey.[1] Tiptoft later served as Lord Treasurer of England (1452–4), a Privy Councillor (1453) and Joint Keeper of the Seal (1454–7). These roles placed him in direct contact with the Venetian Senate and its merchants who travelled to London. Each year the Venetian trading galleys brought eight butts of malmsey wine: four for the king, two for the Lord Chancellor and two for the Lord Treasurer. The king also received other luxurious gifts such as those delivered in 1458 which included two painted chests filled with majolica pots containing 'syruped confections, green ginger, melon and quince' and twenty 'gilt glass guard-shaped [gourd-shaped] flasks of rosolio [distilled spirits]'.[2] Tiptoft is also thought to have corresponded with a Venetian sea captain, probably Ser Lorenzo Moro (Mouro), who had commanded a pilgrim galley in 1441 and by the mid-1450s was in overall command of Venetian galleys trading with London and Bruges.[3]

Venetian traders had sailed to England, especially Southampton, in vessels of their renowned 'Flanders Galley' fleet from the early fourteenth to the early sixteenth centuries. Alwyn A. Ruddock describes their vessels:

> The Venetian merchant galley was a long, graceful ship fashioned on the same lines as the light war galley which had been in use in the Mediterranean since the classical age. It was

---

[1] Weiss, *Humanism*, pp. 112–13.

[2] Mitchell, *John Tiptoft*, pp. 14, 24. Rous's conversation with Tiptoft is recorded in Rous's *Historia Regum Angliae*, ed. Thomas Hearne, Oxford, 1716, p. 5. Mitchell, *Spring Voyage*, pp. 42–3. No visual records of Tiptoft's pilgrimage have survived but 147 miniature illustrations are found in Gabriel Muffel of Nuremberg's 'Pilgrim Book' (*c.*1465/7 – translating an account of *c.*1346–50 by the Franciscan friar Niccolo da Poggibonsi and printed at Bologna, 1500), BL Egerton MS 1900.

When Bernardus von Breydenbach (*c.*1440–97), Canon of Mainz Cathedral, undertook a pilgrimage to the Holy Land via Venice in 1482/4 he took with him an artist, Erhard Reuwich of Utrecht. His images included topographical views of Venice, Rhodes, the Holy Land, Egypt and other locations, and animals, local costumes, customs and alphabets were reproduced in woodcuts in *Peregrinatio in Terram Sanctam* (1486). For Reuwich's panorama of Venice, see pp. 26–7 and **Maps 3–8**.

In 1486 Konrad Grünenberg (d. *c.*1494) of Konstanz (Constance) made a pilgrimage to the Holy Land, arriving in Venice in May before boarding one of its pilgrimage galleys. He compiled an illustrated manuscript of his experiences. 'Beschreibung der Reise von Konstanz nach Jerusalem' (*c.*1487) (Description of a journey from Konstanz to Jerusalem). Baden State Library, Cod. St Peter pap. 32, *Grünenbergs Pilgerreise*, ed. Denke, pp. 130–44 (Venice), pp. 222–68 (illustrations) and Plates 1–16.

[3] Mitchell, *John Tiptoft*, pp. 188–9.

wider and deeper than the war galley, however, having an average tonnage below deck of about 250 tons. It carried a mainmast and two smaller ones, the *trinchetto* and the *mezzane*, fore and aft; and depended almost entirely on its sails for speed. The oars were only brought out when nearing port to manoeuvre the galley, or in dead calms at sea. Each ship carried about one hundred and seventy oarsmen, and these, when reinforced by thirty crossbowmen chosen by public contest from among the best shots in Venice, made a fighting force capable of defending the vessel from all but the most formidable of pirate fleets.[1] The entire fleet was in the command of a captain (*Capitaneus*), a nobleman chosen from one of the best Venetian families. He was aided in all nautical affairs by an admiral (*armeraye*), and attended by personal servants, pages, musicians, physicians and notaries as befitted his rank. Each individual galley was commanded by a patron, also of noble birth, who was aided by a navigating officer (*nochero*), a purser and his assistant (*scrivano* and *scrivanello*), a number of pilots picked up *en route*, and many minor officials (*compagno, comito, scalco*, etc.) who were in charge of the rowers, the cargo and feeding the crew. The oarsmen, usually Sclavonians from the Venetian provinces in Dalmatia, were organized into a *scuola*, or society for common worship and mutual aid, having a communal burial place in Southampton. They combined their duties as rowers with other trades, which they plied in the various ports at which the galleys cast anchor. Some were barbers or tailors, others carpenters, oar-makers, caulkers, cooks and shoemakers.[2]

Plans to send Tiptoft to Italy were in hand in the year before his pilgrimage. On 5 August 1457 he was appointed, with Robert Flemmyng and Philip Wentworth, to carry Henry VI's obedience and greetings to Pope Calixtus III.[3] It seems likely that Tiptoft was also keen to use this mission as a means of escaping the simmering tensions between the Yorkists and Lancastrians. Letters of Attorney were issued on 28 January 1458 for Tiptoft to go abroad on a pilgrimage to the Holy Land. No documentary trace can now be found of Tiptoft's route from London to Venice which may have followed one of the traditional pilgrimage and trade routes through Western Europe. Alternatively, it is possible that Tiptoft and his party travelled as passengers aboard one of the Venetian trading ships which came each year to London since his official court roles had familiarized him with these vessels and their merchandise and naval personnel.

Tiptoft arrived at Venice in May 1458 and attended the ceremonial *Marriage of the Sea on Ascension Day (11 May) and then sailed for Jaffa on 17 May with the Milanese soldier Roberto de Sanseverino and the Paduan noble Gabriele Capodilista. In the Holy Land he visited the Church of the Holy Sepulchre with William Wey and they remained travelling companions for a significant part of their respective journeys.[4] Tiptoft returned to Venice on 6 September 1458 and during the autumn stayed on Capodilista's estates in the Euganean hills south of Padua. He then went with Capodilista to the University

---

[1] Pezzolo, 'The Venetian Economy', p. 262, notes: 'The most precious goods were transported on *galee grosse* (great galleys), capable both of defending themselves and protecting each other. A flotilla of three or four such galleys could provide the notable fighting force of 600–800 men, since in addition to crossbowmen and, after 1486, archibusiers, the rowers themselves could also fight …. Galley service as a crossbowman also offered young patricians the chance to get accustomed to life at sea and begin the journey that would eventually lead them to become merchants themselves. Finally, the crews, composed of free men (as opposed to slaves), could provide a well-trained military force in wartime to serve in the fleet.'

[2] Ruddock, 'Merchants of Venice', pp. 274–91, 277. Records survive of the names of captains of Flanders galleys from 1317 to 1533: https://www.british-history.ac.uk/cal-state-papers/venice/vol1/cxxxii-cxxxiv.

[3] Mitchell, *John Tiptoft*, p. 27. This Pope died on 6 August 1458 before Tiptoft could carry out his embassy.

[4] Bale, '"ut legi"', pp. 233–4.

of Padua where he studied from about late 1458 until summer 1461.[1] He formed
friendships there with prominent humanists, such as Ognibene da Lonigo (1412–74)
and Galeotto Marzio (1427–90), and with two English scholars, Peter Courtenay
(c.1432–92), later Bishop of Winchester, and John Free (c.1430–64/5) who assisted
Tiptoft in collecting and annotating manuscripts and books and probably worked as his
secretary.

Tiptoft may have studied during autumn 1459 at the school of Guarino da Verona
(1374–1460) at Ferrara (with whom John Free had also studied) where he probably met
the poet and translator Lodovico Carbone (1430–85), whom he tried to persuade to
accompany him back to England.[2] During summer 1460 Tiptoft visited Florence where
he attended a lecture by the humanist philosopher John Argyropoulos (c.1415–87). He
also commissioned works from the *cartolaio* (manuscript and book merchant) Vespasiano
da Bisticci (1421–98). Tiptoft is now regarded as one of the major figures of the first
phase of English humanist book collectors. For example, Tiptoft owned a copy of a rare
commentary on Juvenal by Ognibene da Lonigo (de' Bonisoli), who divided his time
between Vicenza, Venice, Padua and Mantua.[3] He also commissioned during his stay at
Venice and Padua a richly illustrated manuscript copy of an 'Astronomicon' by Basinio
de' Basini of Parma, now in the Bodleian Library, Oxford.[4]

Henry VI appointed Tiptoft as his envoy to Pope Pius II in 1459. Returning first to
Venice in autumn 1560 and then to Padua, he commissioned from John Free a Latin
translation of Synesius's *Laus calvitii* ('A Praise of Baldness') and from the humanist
translator Francesco Griffolini (1420–90) a Latin text of Lucian's *De calumnia*.[5] As an
able scholar and linguist, Tiptoft compiled English translations of Cicero's *De amicitia*
and Buonaccorso's *De vera nobilitate* (both printed by William Caxton in 1481).
Unfortunately, a collection of his correspondence, *Liber epistolarum Johannis Tiptofti*,
which may have contained information about his time at Venice and Padua, is now lost.[6]

Following Edward IV's accession on 4 March 1561, Tiptoft, a staunch Yorkist and a
cousin of the new monarch, returned to England on 1 September and was appointed in
November to the King's Council. On 2 December 1461 he was named as Constable of
the Tower of London and on 7 February 1462 as Constable of England. This post placed
him in charge of treason trials and he carried out these duties with considerable
ruthlessness and brutality. As Roberto Weiss observes, Tiptoft was the 'English nobleman
of his age who came closest to the Italian prince of the Renaissance', resembling them in
his 'political and intellectual outlook, in his attitude towards humanism, and in his

---

[1] See Tait, 'Letters of John Tiptoft', pp. 570–74, for his letter (c.1460) from Padua to the University of
Oxford, possibly penned by John Free when acting as Tiptoft's secretary. Weiss, *Humanism*, p. 110.

[2] Weiss, *Humanism*, pp. 106–27. Tiptoft and Free were praised in Lodovico Carbone's funeral oration for
Guarino, along with William Gray (d. 1478), Bishop of Ely, John Gunthorpe (d. 1498), Dean of Wells, and
Robert Flemming (1416–83). *ODNB*, s.v.

[3] Bodleian Library, MS Arch. Seld.B.50. Mitchell, 'A Renaissance Library', pp. 73–7.

[4] Bodleian Library, MS Bodley 646. The signature 'Ang. Aquil.' (f. 1v) suggests that one 'Angelo Aquilano'
or 'Angelo da Aquila' may have been its scribe. Mitchell, 'A Renaissance Library', p. 75. Pächt and Alexander,
*Illuminated Manuscripts*, p. 61 (no. 605) and Plate LVIII. Brown, *Venice & Antiquity*, pp. 200, 323. At least
thirty-five manuscripts owned by Tiptoft have been traced by David Rundle, sixteen of which were made in
Italy: https://bonaelitterae.wordpress.com/david-rundles-research-projects/tiptoft/ .

[5] Free was also known as Johannes Phreas, see Weiss, 'Letter-Preface', p. 101.

[6] Mitchell, *John Tiptoft*, pp. 186–7.

generous patronage of scholars which endeared him to the Italians'.[1] Tiptoft became one of Edward IV's most trusted and resolute courtiers but after the king's flight to Flanders in October 1470 Tiptoft escaped from London and hid in the Forest of Weybridge, disguised as a shepherd. Soon after the Lancastrian restoration, he was captured and beheaded on Tower Hill on 18 October 1470. Benjamin G. Kohl concludes of his career:

> Tiptoft may thus be justly called the first Italianate Englishman in two different respects. He brought the texts of the 'new learning' of the University of Padua, Guarino's school in Ferrara, and Medicean Florence back to English libraries, and he applied the harsh lessons of Italian politics to the service of his sovereign, Edward IV, in ways that in the end were to cost him his life.[2]

Tiptoft is of special importance to this study because in 1458 he travelled from Venice to the Holy Land aboard the newly commissioned *Loredana* in the same two-galley expedition as William Wey (**item 2**) who was aboard the *Morosina*.[3] Although he left no personal account of his experiences at Venice – or, if he did, it has been lost – no less than seven accounts of this voyage have survived.[4] Anthony Bale notes:

> The pilgrims thus formed a significant group of literati who probably carried books with them; they may well have exchanged or purchased their books from a common stock and discussed their reading about travel with each other. Certainly, in the 1458 voyage we see the importance of textual consumption and textual production within the experience of pilgrimage ... .[5]

R. J. Mitchell's *The Spring Voyage. The Jerusalem Pilgrimage of 1458* provides a detailed examination of this pilgrimage, involving 197 pilgrims – 100 in the *Loredana* and 97 in the *Morosina* – who sailed from Venice to Jerusalem. In summer 1458 a merchant of Bristol, Robert Sturmy, who had previously shipped pilgrims to Corunna for the Compostela pilgrimage in 1445, 1451 and 1456, was seeking to break into the Mediterranean alum trade then dominated by Genoa. On 9 June his three vessels were attacked and taken by a notorious Genoese-Greek pirate, Giuliano Cataluxus, and Sturmy was killed.[6] It is understandable, therefore, that the Venetian pilgrim galleys also carried about six *balestrieri* (crossbow men) whose primary duty was to protect the galleys and their passengers from hostile marauders. These men did not serve as *galeotti* (rowers) who, at this period, were usually free men of Venice between the ages of twenty-five and

---

[1] Weiss, *Humanism*, p. 112.

[2] *ODNB*, s.v.

[3] The *Loredana* was a Venetian trireme, a vessel with three rowers to each oar (rather than the three banks of oars of classical antiquity). The stern held a large highcastle where the captain had his quarters. Privileged and high-ranking pilgrims, such as Tiptoft, would often dine at the captain's table. A fighting platform was mounted in its bow, manned by *balestrieri*, trained in archery at the *Arsenal (**Plate 12**). The kitchen was on the poop and privies were overhanging one side of the stern.

[4] Mitchell, *Spring Voyage*, pp. 187–90, lists six narratives and their sources by: (1) Roberto da Sanseverino (1418–87), Lord of Caiazzo (near Ancona), a nephew of Francesco Sforza, Duke of Milan; (2) Gabriele Capodilista of Padua travelling with his cousin Antonio; (3) Giovanni Matteo Butigella, a friend of Sanseverino from the Duke of Milan's household; (4) Anton Pelchinger, a professor of Tegernsee; (5) William Wey; and (6) an anonymous Dutch pilgrim. Wey, *Itineraries*, ed. Davey, p. 32, notes a seventh account by William Denys (*c.*1410–79), a Yorkist from Devon and a pilgrim in the *Loredana* who later served as High Sheriff of Devon (1466), Cologne City Archives (deposition from a trial of 1468). See also Bale, '"ut legi"', pp. 232–3.

[5] Bale, '"ut legi"', p. 233.

[6] Wey, *Itineraries*, ed. Davey, p. 33.

forty, signed up at recruiting stations in Piazza San Marco. The rowers, however, could also be armed if the galley experienced a major attack from pirates or Saracens.

Tiptoft was travelling with a large party of twenty-eight retainers, including his cook, barber, chaplain and organist. He arrived in Venice only thirty-six hours before the *Loredana* sailed. He came to an agreement with the Senate's *Cattaveri* that the galley's *patronus*, Antonio Loredano, would act as his personal guide and courier and, instead, Loredano's cousin, Baldessare Diedo, served as its *patronus*.[1] About twenty miles from Rhodes, one of Cataluxus's pirate vessels approached the *Loredana* and ordered it to stop. If they had found Tiptoft – or had known that he was aboard – they would have certainly taken him for ransom. However, Diedo claimed that his galley was a Catalan vessel with cases of the plague aboard. This ruse was successful and the pirates allowed the *Loredana* to continue its voyage towards Jaffa. However, on the return journey from the Holy Land the captain of Tiptoft's galley was advised that Cataluxus had realized that he had been tricked and was determined to ambush the *Loredana*. When they put into Corfu Tiptoft took decisive action and commissioned a Venetian *galea sotil*, a fast-moving and armed patrol boat stationed at Durres (Durazzo), to take him and his party back to Venice, with the other pilgrims arriving later on 6 September.[2]

[1] This contract, Archivio di Stato di Venezia (14 May 1458), is printed in Mitchell, 'Antonio Loredan', p. 85.
[2] Mitchell, *Spring Voyage*, p. 74. Wey, *Itineraries*, ed. Davey, pp. 32–5.

# 4.  *c.* MID-1460s–*c.* EARLY 1470s –
## SIR EDMUND WIGHTON

Before tracing the visit of **Sir Edmund Wighton (d. 1484)** to Venice it is necessary to reiterate the importance for late-medieval travellers to the Mediterranean and the Holy Land of a much earlier and widely read work, already mentioned in the account of William Wey's travels. Over 300 manuscripts, fragments and various early imprints have survived of the *Book of Marvels and Travels* attributed to Sir John Mandeville, although there is no certainty that a single individual of that name ever existed. The *Voyages de Jehan de Mandeville Chevalier*, an account of the known world reputedly based on the travels of its narrator, appeared anonymously in France in about 1357. It proved immensely popular and was translated into English, German, Italian, Dutch, Spanish and other languages. Even though the compiler (or compilers) of the *Voyages* clearly possessed a good knowledge of French and probably had access to a large ecclesiastical library, it was believed in England that the author was a Sir John Mandeville, a knight-adventurer born in St Albans, who had left his homeland in 1322 to travel the known world.[1] The first part of the book focused on routes to the Holy Land and its major sites but it is now accepted that most of its material was drawn from earlier written sources.[2]

Sir Edmund Wighton was a London gentleman and legal attorney who lived in the Aldgate area of London. He came from a family of Norfolk landowning gentry. He was practising law in London by 1447 and his will (made in January 1484 about two months before his death in March) explains that his title of 'Sir' was not due to a royal knighthood but because he was a 'knyght of the sepulchre of Jerusalem'. This confirms that he had made a pilgrimage to Jerusalem and been honoured by this lay confraternity which held chivalric ceremonies in which pilgrim-knights were dubbed with a sword.[3] Wighton travelled at some point during the 1460s or 1470s to the Levant and the Holy Land via Venice. He owned an abridged fifteenth-century Middle English text of Mandeville, now preserved at Manchester, Chetham's Library MS Mun. A.4. 107 (formerly MS 6711). This text contains on its rear flyleaves notes which appear to record information about Wighton's personal experiences in the Mediterranean, suggesting that he took this manuscript with him on his travels.[4] The notes immediately follow the end of

---

[1] Although it has often been assumed that Mandeville's text was originally written in French and in France, recent scholarship suggests an Anglo-French context. See Bennett, 'Mandeville's Travels', pp. 273–92, and Ormrod, 'John Mandeville', pp. 314–39.

[2] *ODNB*, s.v. Mandeville's major source for sites in the Holy Land was William of Boldensele's 'Liber de quibusdam ultramarinis partibus' (*The Book of Certain Regions Overseas*) (*c.*mid-1330s). This author was a German Dominican who had made a pilgrimage to Jerusalem in 1330. See Bale, '"ut legi"', pp. 204–5.

[3] TNA, Prerogative Court of Canterbury, 21 Logge; via A2A. Bale, '"ut legi"', p. 224, n. 77.

[4] For a comparable pilgrim record, see Manchester, John Rylands Library, Latin MS 228, a miscellany with a vellum binding, dating from *c.*1490–1525 when its contents were probably assembled. It contains an

Mandeville's text and begin with a brief record of its number of leaves, perhaps ensuring that later readers would be aware of any losses from this material. The next note (f. 80r) details an itinerary, in Wighton's autograph, 'from venys by the sea callyd mare medeteranneo', describing part of the familiar galley route via Dalmatia to the Holy Land.[1] Most of the places mentioned by Wighton were either towns under Venetian control or long-established locations on the pilgrimage route from Venice to Jaffa. He then diverged from the usual stopping points to visit the Mamluk port of Haifa and then onwards to Constantinople and the Venetian trading post of (La) Tana (the ancient Tanaïs, now Azov) at the mouth of the river Don on the Azov Sea in Russia. It is likely that these notes record Wighton's personal experiences and, if so, it seems probable that he was travelling not in one of the usual Venetian pilgrimage galleys to the Holy Land but instead with Venetian merchants who traded at Haifa, Constantinople and Tana.[2] This supposition seems all the more likely because his account concludes with the word 'trafigo', an anglicized version of the Italian *trafego*, denoting the Venetian commercial galleys utilized in Mediterranean trade between Venice, Alexandria, Beirut and Gaza.[3] As Anthony Bale explains: 'Wighton's route combined a standard, Franciscan pilgrimage route and a late-fifteenth-century voyage of merchantile adventure'. He concludes:

> Wighton's memoranda bear out the hypothesis that, for such an educated gentleman, who had access to the libraries of the London Inns of Court, the pilgrimage to Jerusalem was also an opportunity for an edifying, 'solacious' trip to Venice and its outposts in the eastern Mediterranean.[4]

---

'Itinerarium terre sancta' (ff. 43v–44r), with some brief notes in Latin on distances from Venice to the Holy Land, Rome to Naples and Jaffa to Jerusalem. It also has a short Middle English text giving the 'way from venice unto Jaffe' with distances provided. The two sections are in different hands and its distances differ from those given in the Latin text. Although not necessarily a book owned by a pilgrim, this manuscript again demonstrates English interest in the journey from Venice to the Holy Land: http://www.bbk.ac.uk/pilgrimlibraries/2017/07/26/rylands/.

[1] The final note (f. 80v) details the distance 'from London to venys [by] the sea', suggesting that Wighton did not follow the familiar overland route from England.

[2] Bale, '"ut legi"', pp. 236–7, Appendix, provides a detailed itinerary of Wighton's destinations after leaving Venice, with specific reference to those locations under Venetian control.

[3] The relevant page of notes is reproduced in the University of Manchester Library Image Collections, Mandeville: https://luna.manchester.ac.uk/luna/servlet/detail/Man4MedievalVC~4~4~446609~117667:Memoranda-relating-to-Mandeville-s-?qvq=q:mandeville&mi=168&trs=177.

[4] Bale, '"ut legi"', pp. 223, 226.

# 5.  *c*.1492/3–97 – THOMAS LINACRE

**Thomas Linacre (*c*.1460–1524)** (**Plate 15**), a humanist scholar and physician, was of unknown origins but may have had connections with Kent. In 1484 he was elected to a fellowship at All Souls, University of Oxford, and in 1487 left for Italy, as a member of an embassy sent by Henry VII to Rome, probably accompanied by William Sellyng (1430–94), Prior of Christ Church, Canterbury, and other emissaries. Linacre was studying at Florence by 1489 and was at Rome in November 1490 when he was appointed as a *custos* of the English Hospice. In about 1492/3 he left for Venice and Padua, taking a degree in medicine there in 1496.

At Venice he worked and lived with the printer Aldus Manutius Romanus, a founder of the Aldine Press (1495), and the Neakademia (New Academy), a humanist group founded by Aldus to promote the study of Greek. Linacre's Latin translation of *De sphaera* (Venice, 1499) by the Greek Neoplatonist philosopher, Proclus Lycaeus (AD 412–85), was published by Aldus who lavishly praised 'Thomas Linacrus Britannus' in the dedicatory epistle (dated October 1499) of this volume to his former pupil, Albertus Pius (1475–1531), Prince of Carpi. Aldus also praised Linacre in the dedication of the second volume of the first edition of his Greek text of Aristotle, dated February 1497, in which Aldus refers to 'Thomas Anglicus' as a witness of the care bestowed on the printing of Greek manuscripts at Venice. A friend of Erasmus, William Grocyn (1446–1519), visited Italy (*c*.1488–91) and in a letter to Aldus, printed in *Astronomici veteres*, he paid tribute to the generous civilities received by Linacre at Venice.[1] While at Venice, Linacre also purchased numerous Greek manuscripts and printed texts which he brought back to England.[2]

Linacre became one of the most important figures in the development of English humanism during the first quarter of the sixteenth century. He served from about 1499 as tutor to Henry VII's eldest son, Prince Arthur, and taught Sir Thomas More Greek. He became a close friend of Erasmus, was appointed in 1509 as royal physician to Henry VIII, and tutored his eldest daughter, Princess Mary. Although little is known of his practical medical skills, his renown rests upon his translations from the Greek – probably using his own manuscripts and books acquired during his residence in Italy, especially at Venice and Padua. The first edition of Galen's *Opera omnia* had been published in 1490 at Venice in two folio volumes by the printer Filippo Pinzi and edited by the Brescian physician Diomede Bonardo.[3] The ready availability of new editions of Galen's works at

---

[1] *Catalogus*, ed. Brown, pp. 26–7.

[2] See, for example, Linacre's autographed vellum copy of Aristotle's *Eis Organon Aristotelous. Anônymon: Hçdç biblos Aristotelous logikçs paideiçs*, Venice: Aldus Manutius (1495), Oxford, New College Library, Res. Acc. BT 1.3.4–7, 9, inscribed 'Th. Linacri lib[er]' on title pages of vols 1–3 and 4 (parts 1 and 2).

[3] Fortuna, 'Latin Editions', pp. 394–5.

Venice undoubtedly prompted the compilation of Linacre's own editions of various treatises.[1]

Linacre's pioneering work in medical translations supported his successful royal petition with five other physicians in 1518 to establish a College of Physicians in London. This idea directly imitated the Italian model of teaching medicine under the auspices of local colleges of physicians which controlled all matters of public health. Although this college proved far from successful, due to hostile competition from other medical practitioners and the two universities, Linacre played an important role in bringing to England the higher standards of academic medicine which he had experienced at first hand in Venice and Padua. He also prompted the ambitions of the next generation of English scholars, including John Clement (d. 1572), Edward Wotton (1492–1555) and Thomas Lupset (1495–1530), who continued to study and work with Aldus at Venice.

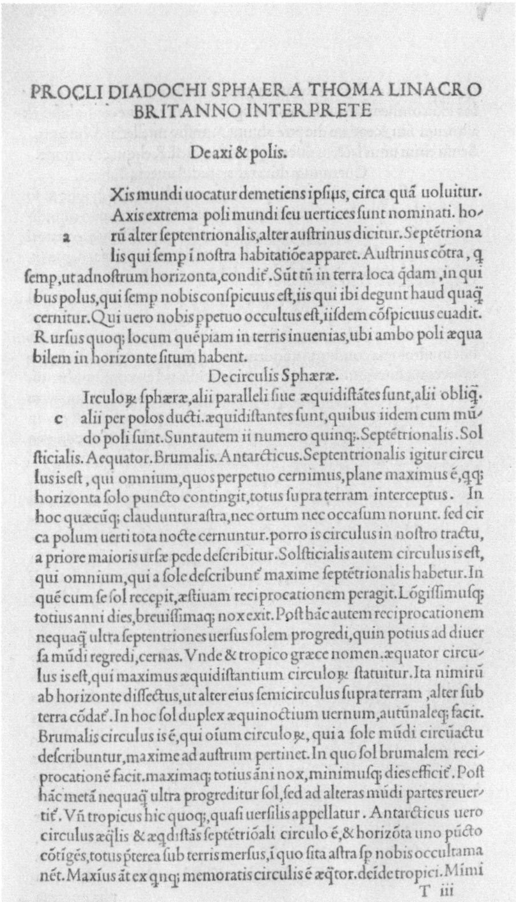

PROCLI DIADOCHI SPHAERA THOMA LINACRO BRITANNO INTERPRETE

De axi & polis.

Xis mundi uocatur demetiens ipſius, circa quã uoluitur. Axis extrema poli mundi ſeu uertices ſunt nominati. horũ alter ſeptentrionalis, alter auſtrinus dicitur. Septẽtrionalis qui ſemp ĩ noſtra habitatiõe apparet. Auſtrinus cõtra, q ſemp, ut ad noſtrum horizonta, condit̃. Sũt tñ in terra loca q̃dam, in quibus polus, qui ſemp nobis conſpicuus eſt, iis qui ibi degunt haud quaq̃ cernitur. Qui uero nobis ꝑpetuo occultus eſt, iiſdem cõſpicuus euadit. Rurſus quoq; locum quẽpiam in terris inuenias, ubi ambo poli æquabilem in horizonte ſitum habent.

De circulis Sphæræ.

Irculoꝝ ſphæræ, alii paralleli ſiue æquidiſtãtes ſunt, alii oblĩq. alii per polos ducti. æquidiſtantes ſunt, quibus iidem cum mũdo poli ſunt. Sunt autem ii numero quinq;. Septẽtrionalis. Solſticialis. Aequator. Brumalis. Antarcticus. Septentrionalis igitur circulus is eſt, qui omnium, quos perpetuo cernimus, plane maximus ẽ, qq; horizonta ſolo puncto contingit, totus ſupra terram interceptus. In hoc quæcũq; clauduntur aſtra, nec ortum nec occaſum norunt. ſed circa polum uerti tota nocte cernuntur. porro is circulus in noſtro tractu, a priore maioris urſæ pede deſcribitur. Solſticialis autem circulus is eſt, qui omnium, qui a ſole deſcribunt̃ maxime ſeptẽtrionalis habetur. In quẽ cum ſe ſol recepit, æſtiuam reciprocationem peragit. Lõgiſſimuſq; totius anni dies, breuiſſimaq; nox exit. Poſt hãc autem reciprocationem nequaq̃ ultra ſeptentriones uerſus ſolem progredi, quin potius ad diuerſa mũdi regredi, cernas. Vnde & tropico græce nomen. æquator circulus is eſt, qui maximus æquidiſtantium circuloꝝ ſtatuitur. Ita nimirũ ab horizonte diſſectus, ut alter eius ſemicirculus ſupra terram, alter ſub terra cõdat̃. In hoc ſol duplex æquinoctium uernum, autũnaleq; facit. Brumalis circulus is ẽ, qui oĩum circuloꝝ, qui a ſole mũdi circũactu deſcribuntur, maxime ad auſtrum pertinet. In quo ſol brumalem reciprocationẽ facit. maximaq; totius ãni nox, minimuſq; dies efficit̃. Poſt hãc metã nequaq̃ ultra progreditur ſol, ſed ad alteras mũdi partes reuertit̃. Vñ tropicus hic quoq;, quaſi uerſilis appellatur. Antarcticus uero circulus æq̃lis & æqdiſtãs ſeptẽtriõali circulo ẽ, & horizõta uno pũcto cõtĩgẽs, totus ꝑterea ſub terris merſus, ĩ quo ſita aſtra ſp nobis occultamanẽt. Maxĩus ãt ex qnq; memoratis circulis ẽ æq̃tor. deĩde tropici. Mĩni

T iii

Figure 14. First Page of Thomas Linacre's Latin translation, published by Aldus Manutius, of *De sphaera* by Proclus, *Iulii Firmici Astronomicorum libri octo ... Procli eiusdem Sphæra, Thoma Linacro Britanno interprete*, Venice: Aldo Manuzio, 1499. Special Collections, Brotherton Library, Incunabula, FIR. By permission of Special Collections, Brotherton Library, University of Leeds.

[1] *De sanitate tuenda* (Paris, 1517); *Methodus medendi* (Paris, 1519); *De temperamentis* and *De inaequali intemperie* (Cambridge, 1521); *De naturalibus facultatibus* (London, 1523); *De usu pulsuum* (London, 1523–4); and *De symptomatum differentiis* and *De symptomatum causis* (London, 1524).

# 6. *c.1498/1500 – INFORMACON FOR PYLGRYMES UNTO THE HOLY LONDE*

This anonymous printed guide nominally recounts the travels of a group of forty-six pilgrims to the Holy Land who sailed from Venice 'in a shippe of a marchaunte of Venyse called John Moreson',[1] captained by 'Luke Mantell'. As regards costs, the author notes that each pilgrim should pay the *patronus* of their galley 'some more some lesse as they myghte accorde', with charges usually ranging between thirty-two and twenty-six ducats. Thirty-four ducats is cited as the typical cost of meat, drink, and a return passage from Venice to Jaffa (f. ciiv). This guide also provides practical information on Venice (routes, currency, provisions, galleys, etc.), much of which was drawn, either directly or via a lost intermediary copy, from William Wey's earlier account.

It is not certain when this pilgrimage was undertaken. However, the text refers at one point to Saturday falling on 14 July which narrows the possible years to 1459, 1464, 1470, 1481, 1487 or 1492. Given that it was published *c.*1498–1500, 1492 has sometimes been suggested as the most likely date but there is no conclusive evidence to support this assumption. Its extensive use of Wey's account may indicate that this pilgrimage took place closer to Wey's two journeys (1458, 1462), perhaps 1470 or one of the two possible years during the 1480s. The original (lost) manuscript may have been written soon afterwards but was only published later through the enterprise of the printer Wynkyn de Worde who in *c.*1500 moved his business to new and expanded premises in Shoe Lane, Fleet Street, at the sign of the Sun. Significantly, at this period he also printed at least three editions of Mandeville's *Marvels and Travels* (1499, 1503 and *c.*1510). Whatever was the exact year of their travels, these pilgrims left Venice on 27 June and arrived at Jaffa on 7 September. They then visited various locations in the Holy Land until they set sail from Jaffa in the following July, arriving back at Venice in mid-October.

This guide begins with a series of itineraries (Calais to Rome via France, Rome to Naples, Rome to Venice, Venice to Milan and Dover to the Holy Sepulchre via the 'Duche waye'). This information is followed by 'Chaunges of money from Englonde to Rome & to Venyse', apparently derived (but not copied exactly) from Wey's account, as this short extract illustrates:

> At Venyse ben grotes & grossettes & *soldes* callid there souldes & bagantynes. For a dukate of Venyse is worth .xxiiii. grossones. and a *solde* and of grossettes xxviij. and .ii. *soldes* for a dukate of Rome or of Florence .iiii. *soldes* lesse for a grote or a grossone, All is one. Viii. *soldes* for a grosset .iii *soldes* for a soulde .xii. bagantynes. For a dukate of Venyse ye shall have . v. li. &

[1] John Moreson: possibly Giovanni Morosini, a member of one of the most distinguished Venetian families which included three doges and the historian Antonio Morosini (d. 1433) who chronicled Venetian life during the early 15th century in the 'Morosini Codex'.

xiiii. *Soldes*. A .li. is worth .xx. *soldes* that ben galy halfpenyes. And to every *solde* xii. bagantynes. (Anon, *Informacon*, sig. biiir)

At Venyse be grotys, grossetys, galy halpens, whyche be clepyd ther soldes and bagantynes. For a doket of Venyse xv. grotys, and of grossetys xxx. For a doket of Rome or of Florense a grote lasse; for a grot viii. soldis; for a grosset iiii. soldis; for a solde xii. bagantynes. For a doket of Venyse ye shal have v. li and xiiii. soldis; a punde ys xx. soldis, that be galey halfpennys; and to every solde xii. Bagantynes. (Wey, *Itineraries*)[1]

The practical details given in *Informacon for pylgrymes unto the holy londe* regarding their arrival at Venice are closely related to that provided in Wey's second section. As with the quotation above, various minor and incidental details are changed but the substance of the advice remains largely the same. This provides an interesting reflection on how information about making a pilgrimage from England to the Holy Land via Venice was shared and disseminated by English travellers during the late fifteenth century. Many such guides must have once existed but, since they were taken abroad on long and arduous journeys as reference books by pilgrims, they were by nature ephemeral. Only one copy of each of the known editions of the *Informacon* now survives (1498/1500, National Library of Scotland, Edinburgh; 1515, Pierpont Morgan Library, New York; and 1524, St John's College, Cambridge). The close textual relationship between the *Informacon* and Wey's account, and the rare survival of these two texts, also raises the possibility that other now lost accounts of the practicalities of pilgrimage to the Holy Land via Venice may have been in circulation during this period.

The following section of text from the *Informacon* not only includes its practical advice relating to a pilgrim's time at Venice and engaging a passage in one of its galleys but also the journey from Venice to Jaffa. In addition it illustrates how English travellers carefully noted which locations on this route were then under Venetian control.


### Text[2]

[sig. b4r] A Good provysyon whan a man is at Venyse & purposeth by goddys grace to passe by the see to porte Jaffe in to the holy londe. and so to the sepulcre of our lorde Jhesu Criste. in Jer*us*alem.[3] he must dispose hym in this wyse.

Fyrste if ye shall goo in a galey, make your covenaunt wyth the patron*us* betyme. And chose you a place in the sayd galey in the overmest[4] stage / For in the lowest under it is ryght evyll & smouldryng [sig b4v] hote and stynkynge. And ye shal paye for youre ship freyghte. and for meete & drynke to port Jaffe and agayn to Venyse. l [50] dukates. for to be in a goode honest place. and to have your ease in the galey and also to be cherysshed.

---

[1] It was once assumed that William Wey was the author of *Informacon for pylgrymes*. See Martin, *Bibliographical Catalogue*, p. 481.

[2] This text is transcribed from the facsimile (included in Duff's edition) of the unique copy of the 1498/1500 edition in the National Library of Scotland, Edinburgh, with the title page copied from the 1515 edition in the Pierpont Morgan Library, New York. An earlier reprint of the Edinburgh copy was edited (but without introduction or annotations) by George Henry Freeling (1789–1841) for the Roxburghe Club, London: 1824.

[3] Church of the Holy Sepulchre, Jerusalem.

[4] *overmest*: overmost or highest.

If a man shall passe in a shyp or a caryk.[1] theñe chose you a chambre as nyghe the myddes[2] of the shippe as ye may / For there is leest rollynge or tomblynge to kepe your brayne & stomache in tempre. And in the same chambre to kepe your thynges in saufgarde. And bye you at Venyse a padlocke to hange on the doore whan ye shall passe in to *the* londe. And ye shall paye for meete & drynke & shyppe freyghte to porte Jaffe & agayn to Venyse .xxx. dukates at the leest.[3]

Also whan ye shall make your covenaunt take good hede that the patron*us* be bounde unto you alle before the duke of Venyse in a .M. [1,000] dukates to kepe all manere covenauntes wyth you. That is to wyte. that he shall condute you to certen havens by *the* way to refresshe you. & to get you fresshe water & fresshe brede & flesshe.

Also that he shall not tary lenger at noo haven than. thre dayes at the moost wythoute consent of you all. And that he shall not take in to the vessel neyther goynge nor comynge noo manere of marchaundyse wythout your licence for to dyseasse you in your places. And also for taryenge of passages by the see. [sig. b5r] And by the havens that here ben folowynge he shall lede you if ye woll.

¶Venyse[4]

| | |
|---|---|
| Fyrste fro Venyse to Pole by water | .C. [100] myles |
| From Pole to Curphu | .vi.C. [600] myles |
| From Curphu to Modone | .iii.C. [300] myles |
| From Modone to Candia | .iii.C.[300] myles |
| From Candia to Rodes | .iii.C.[300] myles |
| From Rodes to Baaffe in Cypres | .iiii.C.[400] myles |
| From Baaffe to porte Jaffe | .iii.C. [300] myles |

wythouten more.[5]

But be well ware ye make covenaunt that ye come not to Famagust[6] in Cypres for no thynge. For many englysshe men & other also have deyed. for that ayre is so corrupt there aboute and the water there also.

Also se that the sayd patron*us* geve you every day hote meete twyes at two meeles. The fore none at dyner. and the after nooñ at supper. And that the wyne that ye shall drynke be good and the water fresshe & not stynkyng. yf ye come to have better. & also the byscute.[7]

Also ye must ordeyne for yourself & your felowe yf ye have ony thre barelles eche of a quart. whiche quart holdyth .x. galons. Two of thyse barrels sholde serve for wyne & the thyrde for water. In the one barell take red*e* wyne. & kepe that ever in store. and tame it not if ye may tyll ye come homeward [sig. b5v] agayn wythout syknesse cause it. or any other specyall need / For ye shall fynde this a specyall note & yf ye had the flyxe[8] / For yf ye wolde geve .xx. dukates for a barell ye shall none have after that ye passe moche Venyse.

---

[1] *caryk*: carrack.

[2] *nyghe the myddes*: near the middle.

[3] This paragraph is not included in Wey's account.

[4] This information is presented in a continuous paragraph in Wey rather than in a table as here.

[5] Pula, Corfu, Methoni, Crete (Candia), Rhodes, Paphos (Baffa) in Cyprus, and Jaffa.

[6] Famagusta.

[7] *byscute*: biscuit.

[8] *flyxe*: flux.

And the other barell shall serve whan ye have spent out your drynkynge wyne to fylle ayen at the haven where ye shall come nexte unto.

Also ye must bye you a cheste to put in your thinges. And yf ye have a felowe with you. two or thre ye nede theñe to bye a cheste that were as broade as the barelles were longe. And in the one ende ye neede locke & key and a lytyll doore. And lay the barel that ye woll came fyrste at the same ende. For if *the* shipmen or other pylgrymes may com*e* therto they wol came & dry*n*ke of it. & also stele your wat*er* whiche ye wolde not mysse ofte tymes for your wyne. And in the other parte of the same cheste ye may laye your brede.chese. spyces / & all other thynges.

Also ye must ordeyne you byscute to have wyth you / For though ye shall be at table wyth the patro*nus*: yet notwythstondyng ye shall full ofte tymes have nede to your owne vytaylles / As brede. chese. egges. wyne & other to make your collac*i*on / For some tyme ye shall have feble brede & feble wyne. & stynkynge water. soo that many tymes ye woll be right fayne to ete of your owne.

[sig. b6r] Also I counsell you to have wyth you out of Venyse Confecc*i*ons Confortatives Laxatives Restrictives Grenegynger Almondes Ryce Fygges Reysons grete & smalle. whyche shall doo you grete case by the waye. And Pepyr Saffron Cloves & Maces a fewe as ye thynke nede and loos sugre also.

Also take wyth you a lytyll caudron. a fryenge panne. Dysshes. platers. sawcers / of tree. cuppes of glasse. a grater for brede. & suche necessaryes.

Also ye shall bye you a bede besides saynt Markys chirche in Venyse / Where ye shal have a fether bede. a matrasse. a pylowe. two payre shetes / and a quylte. & ye shall pay but thre dukates. And whan ye come agayn bring the same bed*e* agayn and ye shall have a dukate & an half for it agayn though it be broke & woren. And marke his hous & his name that ye bought it of ayenst ye come to Venyse.[1]

Also make your change at Venyse. And take wyth you at the least .xxx. dukates in venyse grotes & grossones. Ye shall have at Venyse for a dukate of Venyse .xxviii. grotes & an half. And after ye passe Venyse ye shal have in summe place but .xxvi. &.xxiiii. And take wyth you thre or foure dukates in souldes. that ben galyhalfpenyes of Venyse. For every grote of Venyse .iiii. souldes. And take wyth you from Venyse .i. dukate or .ii. of torneys. it [sig. b6v] is brasse money of Candy. It woll goo all *the* waye by the see. Ye shall have .viii. for a soulde at Venyse. at Modon*e*. & at Candy often but .v. or .vi. at the moost.

Also hyre you a cage for half a dozen of hennes or chekyns to have wyth you in the shyppe or galey For ye shall have need to them many tymes. And bye you half a busshell of myle sede[2] at Venyse for them.

Also take a barell wyth you for a sege for youre chambre in the shyppe. It is full necessary yf ye were syke that ye come not in the ayre.[3]

Also whan ye come to haven townes. yf ye shall tary there thre dayes. go betimes to londe / for theñ ye maye have lodgynge before a nother / for it woll be take up anone. And yf any good vytayle be ye may be spedde before a nother.

Also whan ye come to dyvers havens beware of fruytes that ye ete none for no thynge. As melons & suche colde fruytes / for they be not accordynge to our complexyon & they

---

[1] *And marke his hous … come to Venyse*: not in Wey's account.

[2] *myle sede*: mill-seed, millet seed.

[3] This account omits Wey's advice about buying fresh eggs at port which may then be fried or taken in a caudle on board the galley.

69

gendre a blody flux. And yf any englysshe man catche there that syknesse. it is a grete merveylle but yf he deye therof.

Also when ye shall come to porte Jaffe. take with you oute of the shyppe unto londe. two bottles or two gourdes.[1] one with wyne a nother wyth water eche of a potell at the leest / for ye shall none have tyll ye come to Rames.[2] & that is right feble & dere [sig. c1r] And at Jerusalem there is good wyne & dere.

Also se that the patronus take charge of your harneys[3] within the shyppe tyll ye come agayn to the shyppe. ye shall tary there .xiiii. dayes.

Also take gode hede to your knyves & other smale Japes[4] that ye beere uppon you / for the Sarrasyns wol go talkyng bi you & make gode chere: but thei woll stele from you yf they maye.

Also whan ye shall take your asse at port Jaffe be not to longe behynde your felowes / For & ye come betyme. ye may chese the best mule or asse that ye can / For ye shall paye no more for the beest than for the worste. And ye must geve your asse man there a curteysye a grote of Venyse. And be not to moche before neyther to ferre behynde your felowes for by cause of shrewes.[5]

Also whan ye shall ryde to flume[6] Jordan take wyth you out of Jerusalem brede. wyne. water harde eggys / and chese. and suche vytaylles as ye maye have for two dayes. For by alle that waye. there is none to selle.

Also kepe one of youre botelles with wyne if ye maye whanne ye come from Flume Jordan to Mountquarantyne.[7] And yf ye goo uppe to the place where our lorde Jhesu Cryste fasted .xl. dayes It is passingly hote and right hyghe. And whan ye come downe agayne for any thynge drynke [sig. c1v] noo water. but rest you a lytyll. And thenne ete brede. & drynke clene wyne wythout water / for water after that grete heete gendreth a fluxe or a fevour / or bothe. that many one have deyed therof.[8]

[A short list follows here of 'Tributa in terra sancta'.]

[sig. c2v] IN the seven and twenty daye of the monthe of June there passyd from Venyse vnder saylle out of the haven of Venyse atte the sonne goyng downe. certayn pylgrymes towarde Jerusalem in a shippe of a marchauntes of Venyse callyd John Moreson. The patronus of the same shippe was callyd Luke Mantell. to the nombre of .xlvi. pilgrymes. every man payeng some more some lesse as they myghte accorde wyth the patronus. Some that myghte paye wel payed .xxxii. dukates. and some .xxvi. and .xxiiii. for meete & drynke and passage to porte Jaffe. And from thens to Venyse agayn. ¶ So they passid forth eest southeest by the londe of Slavony.[9] levynge it on the lefte honde / It is two

---

[1] *gourdes*: large, fleshy fruits, when hollowed out and dried used as water vessels.

[2] Ramla, in modern central Israel.

[3] *harneys*: harness, tackle, gear, furniture, armaments or accoutrement.

[4] *Japes*: trinkets or small items.

[5] *shrewes*: scolding or troublesome women.

[6] *flume*: river.

[7] Mount Quarantine (Mount of Temptation) overlooking the Jordan valley supposedly where Christ fasted for forty days in the wilderness (the account in Matthew 4:1–11 and Luke 4:5 mentions a mountain but it is not named).

[8] This account omits the concluding sentence of Wey's account: 'Kep all thes thynges … Jhesus graunt you. Amen'.

[9] Slavonia, Dalmatia, Croatia and Istria form the four historic regions of Croatia.

hundrid myles from Venyse. ¶ And there is a grete cyte callyd Jarre vnder the domynacyon of the Venycians. ¶ And in the same cyte lyeth Simeon Justus.[1] ¶ And they passyd forth by an yle of the ryght honde callyd Lyssa.[2] In whyche ben grete hylles and mountaynes. And in those hylles growyth grete plentee of Rosemary in lengthe as it were fyrses.[3]

After they came to a stronge wallyd towne of the Emperours of Constantinople callyd Aragose.[4] foure hundryd myles from Venyse. ¶ And they saylled soo forth tyll they came to the yle of Corphu on the ryght honde. & Turky on the lyft honde. eyght myle bytwene both londes.

[sig. c3r] ¶ On Frydaye at even they came to the haven of Corphu. There is a good towne & two stronge castelles stondyng on two hyghe rockes. It is a gode yle & a plenteuous. There they speke greke. It is under the Venysyens.

On Sonday next after noon they saylled from thens eest southeest. levynge the londe of Corphu on the ryght honde. & the londe of Turkye on the lyfte honde.

On the Wenesdaye nexte after. to an yle on the lyfte honde callyd the yle of Modon*e*.[5] It is a grete yle & a plenteu*ous*. It is .iii.C. myles from Corphu And there growyth wyne of Romeney.[6] There is a good towne & a stronge castell. It is in Grecc. and under the Venysyens.

On the Thursday nexte after noon they sayled from Modon*e* eest southeest. levynge the londe of Modon*e* on the ryght honde.

On Frydaye nexte after they passyd by a fayre haven towne .xx. myles from Modon*e* callid Corona. It is under the Venysyens.[7] And so they sayled forth tyll they came an hundryd myles from Candy. And there they sayled up & downe thre dayes & two nightes in grete peryl besyde grete rockes. and durste not passe for the wynde was agaynst them. And one of the rockes is callyd in Greke Ouogo.[8] whyche is to say in englisshe. edgyd. An edgydhyll[9] It is shapen lyke an egge. Uppon the lyfte honde. [sig. c3v] vi. myles wythin. there is stondynge yet of t*he* temple wherin Appollo was worshiped. And in the same temple Elena the wif of kyng Menelaus was ravysshed of Parys of Troye & lad in to the cou*n*tree of Asia.[10] And t*he* same yle where the temple was whiche was callyd of the grekes in olde tyme Delphos in latyn Cirigo.[11]

---

[1] *Jarre*: Zadar on the Croatian coast, known in Italian as Zara. Simeon Justus, also known as St Simon the God-Receiver (Luke 2:25–35), met Mary and Joseph at the presentation of Jesus at the Temple on the fortieth day after his birth. His richly decorated casket (1370s), a large, rectangular wooden sarcophagus containing his mummified body, is over the main altar in the Church of Saint Simeon, Zadar.

[2] *Lyssa*: Vis (Italian, Lissa), Croatian island in the Adriatic Sea.

[3] *fyrses*: firs.

[4] *Aragose*: Republic of Dubrovnik was known as Republic of Ragusa (and as Aragose).

[5] Methoni.

[6] *wyne of Romeney*: Rumney (Romney) wine, a popular type of Greek wine exported from Methoni. The name was supposedly derived from *Romania*, then a name for Greece and the southern Balkans.

[7] Koroni (Venetian, Coron), a Venetian possession in the Greek Morea since the early 13th century.

[8] *Ouogo*: perhaps off the coast of Cape Matapan, the southernmost peninsula of Greece, between Koroni and Kythira. On its west side is the Cave of Hades, in Greek legend the home of Hades, the god of the dead. The tip of the peninsula (now with a disused lighthouse) was especially dangerous for shipping.

[9] *edgydhyll*: edged or jagged hill.

[10] According to legend, the Trojans pillaged the Greek island of Kythira (Citera), including its temple, when Paris abducted Helen, wife of King Menelaus.

[11] The island of Kythira (Venetian, Cerigo).

On Wenesday in the mornynge next after they came to Candy .iii. C. myles from Modone. Ther is a stronge castell & a large. & a fayr towne wythout the castell well walled. & a stronge haven wallyd strongly / This yle is a grete yle & a plenteuouse of all manere thynges. Thei be Grekes in that yle And the Venysyens ben lordes there. And every yere or every other yere there is chosen a duke by the same Venysyens. There growyth the wyne callyd malvesey. Somtyme they were callyd Cretes. It is of them wreten in actibus applorum[1] (Cietenses semper mendaces male bestie)[2] ¶ In that londe .xxx. myle from Candy is an olde broken cyte. whyche was callyd Cretina.[3] And a lytyll besyde there stondyth an olde broken chyrche. whyche was buylde in the honour of Jhesu Crist. & halowed in the worshypp of Titus epreus.[4] To whom Poul wrote in actibus aplorum Ad titus)[5] ¶ A lytyll besyde that place there is an hyll callyd Laborintus.[6] and that is a merveylous place wythin forth. wroughte out of harde stone of the rocke. and the grete hylle above. A man [sig. c4r] maye goo wythin that place dyvers wayes. some waye .x. myles. and some waye more / & some waye lesse. And but yf a man be wel ware how he gooth in. he may so goo he shall not come out agayn there be soo many tornynges therin. ¶ In this yle as they saye there were somtyme an hundred cytees & an hundred kynges. In this cyte the sayd pylgrymes taryed a moneth. And there was grete heete / For from May to Halowmasse[7] there groweth noo grasse. it is soo brent wyth the heete of the sonne.

And then aboute Alhalowmesse begynnyth grasse herbes & floures to sprynge. And it is there thenne as Somer in Englonde. so in the wynter it is temperate noo colde but lytyll. There is never snowe nor froste wyth yse. And yf there come ony froste with a lytyl yse. they woll shewe it eche to other for a merveylle.

And from, May tyll the later ende of Octobre there is noo reyne nor clowdes but ryght selde. but ever the sone shyneth ryght clere & hote. And abowte saynt Martyns tyme[8] the sonne is as hote there. as it is in August in Englonde. And so it is in Rodes and Cypres. and alle that countree eestwarde.

From this haven they passyd the Wenesday nexte before the Assumpcion of our lady.[9] and saylled eest southeest. levynge Turky on theyr lyfte honde.

On our lady daye the Assumpcion they came to Rodes before noon .iii. C. myles from Candy on the [sig. c4v] ryght honde. There they taryed .xviii. dayes. There is a fayre castell & a stronge. In whyche castell ben the knyghtes of the Rodes[10] / And there is a goode cyte well wallyd wyth double walles. and a fayr haven closyd with stronge walles & toures. And on the eest party of the haven. there stondeth on a strong walle .xiiii. mylles

---

[1] *in actibus applorum*: Acts of the Apostles, the fifth book of the New Testament.

[2] Citing Acts of the Apostles, Epistle to Titus 1:12–13: 'the Cretans are always liars, evil beasts' (derived from the semi-mythical Greek philosopher Epimenides (7th or 6th century BC).

[3] *Cretina*: an ancient city on Rhodes.

[4] *Titus epreus*: St Titus (1st century AD), a companion and disciple of St Paul the Apostle, traditionally regarded as the Bishop of Crete. The church of St Titus at Heraklion contained the saint's relics which were taken to Venice after the fall of the city to the Turks in 1669. His skull was returned in 1966.

[5] Epistle of St Paul to Titus, a pastoral epistle of the New Testament.

[6] Labyrinth, designed and built by Daedalus for King Minos of Crete at Knossos.

[7] All Hallows' Day or All Saints' Day (1 November).

[8] Feast of St Martin (11 November).

[9] Assumption of the Virgin Mary (15 August).

[10] Knights of Rhodes or Hospitallers.

of stoon,[1] every wyndmyll as it were a strong toure. ¶ Of that place it is wreten that Poul wrote (ad Colosences) to that same place.[2]

The fyrste day of the moneth of Septembre in the even tyde they sayled from Rodes towarde Jerusalem .vii. C. myles eest southeest. levynge Turky on theyr lyfte honde. So they saylled forth fro Rodes & never stryked saylle tyll they came to port Jaffe.

In the vigill of our lady in the feest of the Nativyte they came to port Jaffe. and there they taryied Mondaye & Tewesdaye in the shyppe. tyll they had theyr saufconduyte. And on Wenesdaye in the mornynge they entred in to *the* londe at porte Jaffe. ¶ At porte Jaffe begynnyth the holy londe. There Peter reysed from deth to lyfe Thesbitan[3] the servaunt of the apostles. ¶ There is Indulgence .vii. yeres & .vii. lentes.

And a lytyll besyde southwarde. there is a stoon where Peter stode & fysshed whan our lorde callyd hym. and sayd to hym (sequere me) [follow me] [sig. d1r] ¶ At porte Jaffe they payed as they came oute of the shyppe every pylgryme one dukate of Venyse. for mangery and for saufconduyte[4] to the patron*us*. And at porte Jaffe every pylgryme payed for trybute .vii. dukates & .xvii. grotes.

---

[1] Knights of Rhodes had created (*c*.1402) a fortified rampart (*Petronium*) on the peninsula of Halicarnassus (Bodrum), utilizing stone from the ruined Mausoleum of Halicarnassus, once one of the Seven Wonders of the World.

[2] St Paul's Epistle to the Colossians.

[3] *Thesbitan*: at Jaffa St Peter raised from the dead Tabitha (Dorcas), a disciple of Jesus, Acts 9:36–43, 10:1–4; a location marked by the Church of St Peter (built on the site of a 13th-century citadel).

[4] *mangery and for saufconduyte*: the provision of food or formal dinner and for safe conduct.

# 7.   1506 – SIR RICHARD GUILDFORD'S CHAPLAIN, THOMAS LARKE

**Sir Richard Guildford (Guldeford, Guylforde) (*c.*1450–1506)**, was a prominent Lancastrian courtier and administrator who, like John Tiptoft, may have chosen to undertake a pilgrimage partly as a means of escaping from complex political and personal issues at home. He had been attainted after the abortive rebellion against Richard III in October 1483 and went into exile with Henry Tudor. He returned with him at Milford Haven in August 1485 and was knighted for his loyal service. After Henry's accession as Henry VII, Guildford was named as Master of the Ordnance and Armoury in the Tower of London. By 1487 he was also Master of the Horse and a Privy Councillor and by 1494 he was Controller of the Royal Household. He accompanied Henry VII to Calais for his meeting with Archduke Philip (of Austria, later briefly Philip I of Castile) in June 1500 and was made a Knight of the Garter. In 1501 he assisted in the preparations for Catherine of Aragon's arrival in England.

As Master of the Ordnance, Guildford was heavily involved in national security, the development of the English navy and international intelligence gathering. He organized the building of defences along the Sussex marshes and supplied arms and equipment for various military campaigns, including the Breton expedition (1489–91) and the invasion of France (1492). He was granted £100 in 1486 for shipbuilding, probably including the *Mary Guildford* (which sailed in 1517 with the *Samson* to seek a route to Cathay via a north-west passage) and the 1,000 tonnes carrack *Regent* (which saw action in the Scottish war in 1497 and was destroyed in an engagement with the French ship *Cordelière* in 1513 during the Brest campaign).

As a loyal supporter of Henry VII, Guildford supervised spying missions on the Yorkist claimant to the throne, Edmund de la Pole (*c.*1471–1513), Earl of Suffolk, whose brother John de la Pole (1462/4–87), Earl of Lincoln, had been the designated heir of his maternal uncle Richard III. Edmund and his brother Richard had left England in August 1501 without royal permission and joined the court of Emperor Maximilian I in the Tyrol. Suffolk was resident at Aix between 1502 and 1504 but was imprisoned by Maximilian's son, Archduke Philip, in about April 1504. Philip was unexpectedly forced to land on the English coast during a storm and, as an unwilling guest of Henry VII, was persuaded to hand over Suffolk. The Earl was imprisoned in the Tower of London in March 1506 and Henry VIII ordered his beheading on Tower Hill soon after his accession in 1509, following his father's earlier recommendation.

Despite his long royal service, Guildford was dogged by financial problems and debts. Legal suits for debt had been brought against him as early as 1486 and by 1503 he owed money for wardships, official duties and to private individuals. The situation was serious enough for the management of his debts to be placed in the hands of the Abbot of Battle in November 1503. In June 1505 he was arrested for yet another debt and imprisoned in the Fleet for five months. Although a royal pardon on 4 April 1506 released him from all debts arising from his official duties, his creditors continued to pursue him. Within this context, it seems probable that Sir Richard Guildford's decision to travel via Venice to the Holy Land offered a convenient means of escaping from these unremitting financial problems. As was customary for pilgrims, he made his will on 7 April 1506, the day before his departure from Rye, Sussex. However, the arduous voyage proved too much for him and he was taken ill, possibly with dysentery, on the road between Jaffa and Jerusalem where he died on 6 September 1506.[1]

It should not be discounted that Guildford's motivations for travel abroad also included genuine personal piety since his family took considerable interest in religious matters. His father, Sir John Guildford, was the patron of Tenterden parish church when the noted humanist John Morer (d. 1489) served as its vicar (1479–89). Morer left several books to Sir John, as well as five books and money to Thomas Linacre (**item 5**) who was then based in Florence. Morer may have taught Linacre (**Plate 15**) when he was a schoolboy in Canterbury and it seems likely that Richard Guildford also knew Linacre and shared his interests in Italian scholarship, especially at Florence, Padua and Venice.[2]

**Thomas Larke (d. 1530**), Guildford's chaplain and confessor, was the author of this account of their pilgrimage to the Holy Land. Little was known about him until 2013 when Rob Lutton noted that he was 'almost certainly' the Thomas Larke who was the brother of Thomas Wolsey's mistress Joan Larke (*c*.1490–1532), the mother of his two illegitimate children. Thomas Larke served as Guildford's household chaplain 'from *c*.1495 and by 1511 (and perhaps as early as 1507) was one of Henry VIII's chaplains, and became Wolsey's personal confessor and servant from around 1511'. He was also granted a canonry and prebend of St Stephen's College, Westminster, on 14 November 1511. Larke remained Wolsey's confessor and close friend until his death in July 1530, only four months before the Cardinal's own demise.[3]

Larke's account was published by the stationer Richard Pynson in about 1511 in a text of fifty-nine pages titled *This is the begynnynge, and contynuance of the Pylgrymage of Sir Richarde Guylforde Knight & controuler unto our late soveraygne lorde kynge Henry the .vii. And howe he went with his servaunts and company towardes Jherusalem*, presumably to offer instruction and advice, like the *Informacon for pylgrymes* (*c*.1498–1500) for other prospective travellers.[4] Pynson had been King's Printer since 1506, specializing in legal and constitutional texts. He also published religious and reformist works and an English translation of a French work known as the *Itinerarium* (1496), attributed to Jean

---

[1] *ODNB*. TNA PRO PROB 11/17. Guildford, *Pylgrymage*, ed. Ellis, pp. v–xvi. Lutton, 'Richard Guldeford's Pilgrimage', pp. 41–7.

[2] Lutton, 'Richard Guldeford's Pilgrimage', p. 70; and Lutton's 'Pilgrimage and Travel Writing', pp. 333–4, 340–47.

[3] Lutton, 'Richard Guldeford's Pilgrimage', p. 49, n. 25. Larke later became Master of Trinity Hall, Cambridge (*c*.1517/20–25), and was a friend of Erasmus. He was the Surveyor of the King's Works in the final stages of the building of the chapel of King's College, Cambridge. He also oversaw work at Bridewell Palace in London, Wolsey's first house, and at Cardinal College (now Christ Church), Oxford. His uncle, the Catholic martyr Blessed John Larke (d. 1544), a priest and friend of Sir Thomas More, was executed on the order of Henry VIII. Erasmus wrote in 1519 to Sir Richard Guildford's son, Henry, commending his support for 'sound learning, especially of the sort that makes for true religion'. Henry's father Sir Richard may have met Erasmus during his visits to England in 1499 and 1505/6, Lutton, 'Richard Guldeford's Pilgrimage', pp. 70–71.

[4] Only a single copy of this publication survives, BL, London, G6719.

d'Outremeuse (1338–*c.*1399), and, significantly for English travellers to the Holy Land via Venice, the *Boke of John Mandvyle, Knight of Wayes to Jerusalem* (*c.*1500).[1] Lutton suggests that Pynson may have been commissioned by Henry VIII to print Larke's account because the verso of its title page bears both the arms of the king and the three castles, representing Castile, of Catherine of Aragon. He also notes how both international politics and Guildford family loyalties may have supported its publication:

> In 1511, the year in which the account was published, an English force was dispatched to Spain to assist Ferdinand of Aragon's crusade against the Moors of North Africa. Richard's own son, Sir Henry Guildford, joined the expedition as provost marshal. He may have had a hand in the publication of what was effectively a tribute to his father's own pious exploits. Its promulgation neatly served the dual purposes of emphasizing the continuity between the reign of the young king and that of his father Henry VII, and between the royal service of the young courtier and that of the father Sir Richard.[2]

Guildford was accompanied, according to the title page, by 'his servaunts and company' and by John Whitby, Prior of Gisburn (Gisborough), who had resigned his office only three weeks before joining this pilgrimage party. Little else is known about Guildford's travelling companions, although en route at Alessandria, Piedmont, he was treated hospitably by Sir Christopher (Cristoforo) Pallavicino of Milan (d. 1521) who was related to Guildford's second wife Joan Vaux.[3] Larke was greatly impressed by the treatment his party received from the Pallavicini:

> Saterdaye to Alexandrya and there sonday all daye where Maister Jerom and Augustyn Panyson with the grete Nou*m*bre of their worshypfull parentis & Cosyns whiche two Gentylmen be nyghe Cosyns unto mayster Vaux and to my lady Guylforde made grete honour feestis & chere[4] unto my M. Gulforde *that* myght not be ame*n*dyd & also stuffed us w*ith* vitaylle*s*[5] brede & wyne in our Barge ... (f. iii[r] and Guildford, *The Pilgrimage*, p. 5)[6]

Guildford and Whitby arrived at Venice on 16 May and left on 12 June 1506. It is interesting to trace their experiences in Venetian galleys, both to and from the Holy Land, to illustrate the hardships and dangers faced by English pilgrims at this period. Their galley arrived at Jaffa at night on 18 August, although they were not allowed to disembark until 27 August. This was because the Warden of Mount Syon 'coude no sooner have the

[1] Pynson also published *Here Begynneth a Lytell Treatyse or Booke Named Johan Maundevyll* (1496) which may have been authored by d'Outremeuse.

[2] Lutton, 'Richard Guldeford's Pilgrimage', pp. 50–51.

[3] Joan Vaux was the sister of Sir Nicholas Vaux (1460–1523), a staunch Lancastrian and noted soldier, courtier and member of the House of Commons. Pynson's text prints Pallavicino's name as 'Panyson' (p. 5) and 'Palvasyn' (p. 46). This confusion was probably occasioned by Thomas Larke who clearly knew Guildford's family well. Although Joan Vaux's mother, a lady-in-waiting to Margaret of Anjou (the queen of Henry VI) was known as Katherine Penyson (1440–1509); she was of Italian origin. Her father was Gregorio Panizzone (b. 1415), known in England as Gregory Penistone, from Corticello, Piedmont, which explains their connection with the Pallavicinis. Joan Vaux and her brother Nicholas had been brought up in the household of Lady Margaret Beaufort, the mother of Henry VII. Joan served as governess to the household of Henry VII's daughters, Princesses Margaret and Mary.

[4] *feestis & chere*: feasts and good cheer or hospitality.

[5] *vitaylles*: victuals, provisions or food.

[6] This transcription is from the British Library copy with reference also to Ellis's edition. Ellis, however, modernizes punctuation, capitalization and other incidentals while I have retained most of the original standards of Pynson's printing.

Lordes of Jherusalem and Rama at layser [leisure] to come to us without whose presence and Conducte there can be no Pylgryme passe whiche Lordes be all Mamolukes and under the Soldan' (f. xi<sup>r</sup> and Guildford, *Pilgrimage*, p. 16). Their delight in finally landing in the Holy Land was soon dampened by an outbreak of illness among their party.[1]

Guildford's chaplain recorded:

> Sondeye at nyght we toke oure Journeye towardes Jherusalem / and bycause bothe my mayster and Mayster Pryor of Gysborne were sore seke, therfore with grete dyffyculte and outragyous Coste we purveyed Camellys[2] for them and certayne Mamolukes[3] to conducte theym in safty to Jherusalem / whiche Intreated us very evyll, and toke moche more for theyr payne thenne theyr Covenaunt was. (f. xii<sup>r</sup> and Guildford, *Pilgrimage*, p. 17)

They lodged at the Hospital of St John and began an initial tour of Jerusalem but Larke's account then records the death of Whitby on 5 September and Guildford early on the following morning:

> The saterdaye byfore, mayster Pryor of Gyseborogh disceased, aboute .ii. or .iii. of the Cloke at after noone: & the same nyght late he was had to Mounte Syon and there buryed.
>
> And this same sonday at nyght, aboute .i. or .ii.of the Cloke at after mydnyght, my *Master* syr *Richard* Guylford whom god assoyle[4] disceased & was had *the* same mornynge to mounte Syon afore daye.
>
> And the same monday our Ladyes Evyn *the* Nativite all the Pylgrymes come to mou*n*te Syon, to the buryenge of my sayde Master Guylford*e* where was done by the freres asmoche solempne servyce as myght be done for hym &c. And this was the .vii. daye of Septembre. (ff. xxviii<sup>v</sup>–xxix<sup>r</sup> and Guildford, *Pilgrimage,* p. 40)[5]

Despite these two deaths the rest of the English party continued their pilgrimage to the usual holy places, including Mount Syon, the Holy Sepulchre, Jerusalem, Vale of Josophat, Mount of Olives, Bethlehem, River Jordan and Temple of Solomon.[6] By 14

---

[1] This illness may have been dysentery or 'blood flux', commonly caused by water or food being infected with faecal matter and specifically warned against by William Wey. Just before Guildford and Whitby became sick, Larke recorded that they had drunk from a 'welle of good fresshe watere which was moche to our comforth' and had consumed 'brede, soddyn egges & somtyme other vytaylles' given to them by 'Jacobyns & other feynyed cristen men of sondry sectis'. These refreshments may have caused their fatal illness (f. xi<sup>v</sup> and Ellis, p. 17).

[2] *Camellys*: camels.

[3] *Mamolukes*: mamelukes, members of the regime, originally established by emancipated white military slaves, which ruled Egypt from 1250 until 1517; a military caste in Syria until 1516; or a general term applied to slaves in Moslem countries.

[4] *assoyle*: to assoil; to grant absolution or absolve from sin.

[5] The Scottish cleric and diplomat, Robert Blackadder (*c*.1445–1508), first Archbishop of Glasgow, died on 28 July 1508 while on pilgrimage to the Holy Land. At Venice he had met Doge Leonardo Loredan (**Frontispiece**) and members of the Senate and was invited aboard the Bucentaur for the annual *Marriage with the Sea. On 13 June he made his will at Venice which proved timely because plague broke out on his chartered ship to Jaffa and he was one of 27 casualties out of 36 pilgrims. *CSP Venice, 1508*, items 903, 904, 909. *Informacon for Pylgrimes*, ed. Duff, p. x.

[6] *Informacon for Pylgrimes*, ed. Duff, p. xi, notes that much of Larke's description of Jerusalem was taken from Bernardus von Breydenbach, *Peregrinatio in Terram Sanctam* (1486). See Lutton, 'Richard Guldeford's Pilgrimage', pp. 52, 59–62, and Bale, '"ut legi"', pp. 228–30, for Larke's borrowings from *Mandeville's Marvels and Travels*. Larke's description of Jerusalem may also be compared to an anonymous manuscript account in English, 'Of That Most Blessed Viage to Thee Hooli Citee of Hierusalem', BL Harley MS 2333, which only briefly mentions Venice as a point of departure (f. 1r) and return (f. 37r). See Queen's College, Oxford, MS 357, ff. 7r–41r, for another copy of this pilgrimage account (dated after 1480). Brefeld, 'Pilgrimage', pp. 134–55.

September they were ready to embark for Venice but agreed to a short delay. This was because they had met up again with Sir Christopher Pallavicino and his party who had sailed with Guildford and Whitby from Venice in the same galley but disembarked at Rhodes to take another vessel so that they could travel a different route to Jerusalem via Alexandria, Cairo and St Catherine's Monastery at Mount Sinai. Pallavicino agreed to travel back to Venice with the galley *patronus* who had brought Guildford and Larke to the Holy Land, provided that the English party would delay their departure for a short time so that he could complete his own pilgrimage around various holy sites. The English pilgrims were happy to do so since this enabled them to prolong their own sightseeing and venerations, with the added bonus of travelling back to Venice with the entourage of a wealthy and influential member of the Milanese gentry (f. xxxiii$^v$ and Guildford, *Pilgrimage*, p. 46).

This larger group of pilgrims left Jaffa on 19 September to 'sayle homewarde with ryght grete Joye' (f. xli$^r$ and Guildford, *Pilgrimage*, p. 56) and met up with two other 'galyes of Traffigo' heading towards Venice (f. xlv$^r$ and Guildford, *Pilgrimage*, p. 61).[1] The journey proved extremely unpleasant with challenging weather, frequent risk of shipwreck, supplies of food, wine and clean water running perilously low and a lack of discipline among the galley's crew. By the time they reached Corfu, Pallavicino had decided that these conditions were intolerable. He and his fellow Milanese travellers 'forsoke oure Galye / and gate theym selfe into one of the sayd Galeys of Traffigo / called Conteryn, for theyr better spede and more suerte'[2] (f. lii$^r$ and Guildford, *Pilgrimage*, p. 72). The English travellers were no less frustrated and on 4 January 1507 they secretly hired a smaller vessel (f. lv$^{r-v}$ and Guildford, *Pilgrimage*, p. 76) in the hope that it could return them to Venice more speedily. However, it failed to make any headway against the winds and so they returned despondently to their galley which was still at anchor. Finally, on the night of 25 January 1507 'we come to Venyce late in the nyght, wondre glad & Joyous of our safe Aryvage[3] there'. With obvious relief Guildford's chaplain recalled:

> And there we laye at Venyse unto sonday at nyght that was the laste day of January to per*f*orme
> oure vowes at the Seynt*es* and holy places there whiche occupied us no short tyme / and to
> purvey us at our bankes of money for our retourne.
> The same sondaye at nyght that was the sayde last daye of January we toke our boote to Padua
> / and come thether aboute .viii. or .ix. a Clok the next morne, mondaye, that was the firste
> day of February / and the same day we purveyed[4] us horses to hyre. (f. lvi$^v$ and Guildford,
> *Pilgrimage*, p. 78)

They travelled home along a route familiar to generations of English pilgrims, via Verona, Cremona and Pavia, across the Alps and then through France, arriving back at Dover on 9 March 1507. Immediately following this brief account of the homeward journey, Larke wrote:

> Note that by *th*e afore wryten process*e* of this sayde Journey it apperyth that we dep*ar*ted out
> of Englonde the .viii. day of Apryll, A*nn*o .xxi. and come to venyce the .xvi. daye of May /

---

[1] Venetian *trafigo* vessels were commercial galleys that connected Venice to North Africa and Syria, used from about the mid-15th century.

[2] *suerte*: (Sp.) chance, fate or fortune.

[3] *Aryvage*: arrival.

[4] *purveyed*: arranged (often in advance).

whiche is .v. wekes and .iii. dayes. And there we laye at Venyce unto the .iiii. daye of July, whiche is full .vii. wekes. (f. lviii$^v$ and Guildford, *Pilgrimage*, p. 81).

He also calculated that it had taken six weeks and three days to sail from Venice to Jaffa on the outward journey, a total of some 700 hundred miles. They spent twenty-three days in the Holy Land, before taking an unusually taxing nineteen weeks and one day to travel back from Jaffa to Venice, experiencing 'suche vexacyon and trouble Homewarde by outragyous longe lyenge on the see and were in many daungers & parellys'[1] (f. lix$^r$ and Guildford, *Pilgrimage*, p. 82). The journey from Venice to Calais was completed in five weeks and one day. In total, the entire pilgrimage had taken one year and twenty-nine days.

Thomas Larke also provided an interesting gloss on why their homeward sea journey from Jaffa to Venice had proved so lengthy and problematic. This was primarily because they had left Venice much later than most pilgrimage galleys:

it is no mervayle thoughe that we were so sore troubled for where as Pylgrymes be alwaye accustomed to take theyr Galye immedyatly after Corpus X*hris*ti daye, we dyd not so / but laye styll at Venyce almoste .vi. weke*s* after Corpus X*hris*ti dayc by reason wherof we had no tyme to *per*fourme our Pylgrymage and retourne to Venyce byfore the comyng of *th*e deed wynter season. And so we laye all *th*e stormy wynter wether from Myghelmasse to Candlemasse[2] in the woode wrought see[3] / to our often daunger & grete parell whiche shulde not have ben if we had taken oure Galye at suche tyme as other Pylgrymes have done other yeres passed that come ever ayen to Venyce or than any wynter apperyd; and so is beste and moste surest &c. (f. lix$^v$ and Guildford, *Pilgrimage*, p. 83)

## Text (ff. iiii$^r$–vi$^v$)[4]

[f. iiii$^r$] ¶ The nexte daye Saterdaye byfore the feste of Assencion of oure Lorde that was the .xvi. daye of May we come to Venyse, aboute .ii. of the Cloke at after noone.

The .xii. daye of June that was Fryday we wente by water to Padua by the Ryver of Brente[5] and there we taryed Saterdaye: and Sondaye: Saterdaye was the feeste of Seynt Antony whiche was a grey frere and lyeth ryght fayre at the Grey freres there / there was the same daye a solempne Processyon where at were borne many Relyques / and the noumbre of Doctoures of Cyuyle and physyk[6] was grete excedyngly fin*e* the sayde processyon / we vysyted there many Seyntes and relyques, as seynt Luke and seynt Mathye whiche bothe lye in the Abbey of Saynt Justyne vyrgyn a place of blake Monkes ryght delectable and also Solytarye there be two tables of our blessyd Lady which seynt Luke

---

[1] *parellys*: perils.

[2] *Myghelmasse to Candlemasse*: Michaelmas, feast of St Michael and All Angels (29 September) and Candlemas, feast of the Purification of the Virgin Mary or Presentation of Christ in the Temple (2 February).

[3] *woode wrought see*: extremely perilous sea.

[4] From the British Library copy of Richard Guildford, This is the begynnynge, and contynuance of the Pylgrymage of Sir Richarde Guylforde Knight, *c.*1511, STC 12549, ff. iv$^r$–vi$^v$, and Guildford, The Pilgrimage, pp. 6–9.

[5] River Brenta.

[6] Doctors of Civil Law and Physic.

paynted with his awne handes at Padowa.[1] Also we sawe the Toumbes of Antenore of Troye and of Tytus Lyvyus.[2]

The mondaye folwynge that was the daye of viti & modesti & and the xvi. day of June[3] we retournyd ayen to Venys whiche day was a grete tryumphe [f. iiiiᵛ] and feste there in remembraunce of a Victorye that the Venycyans had the same day in gettynge of Padowa[4] they went over the water to the churche of the sayde Seyntis, whiche is an Arme of the see. upon a brygge layde and made of Galyes and so they do ever whan the Duke & the Senyourye shall passe the same water.

The Relyques of Venyce can not be noumbred there lyeth sanyt Elyn / saynt Barbara / seynt Roke / seynt Zachary / seynt Jervas / and Prothase /[5] and many other Seyntes & grete Relyques / and at the Monastery of seynt Nycholas there lyeth the Holy body of seynt Nycholas, as they seye.[6]

There be also in the Churche of Seynt Marke many grete Relyques and Jewelles. There is a grete Chales of fyne gold of Curious werke set with many precious stones whiche is in heyght .iii. quarters of a yerde / it is to large to use at Masse / But they use it in adhornynge the Aulter at pryncypall tymes / and in theyr processyon on Corpus Xhristi day There be also two grete Candylstykes amonge other of a wonderfull gretenesse that be ryght curyously wrought and are fyne golde garnysshed over all with stones of grete pryce.

There be also .xii. Crownes of fyne Golde and .xii. Pectorals & a Ryche Cappe whiche every Duke is Corowned with at his first Intrononyzacion [f. vʳ] the pryce of all whiche Crownes / Pectorales / and Cappe is inestymable for they be full set with precyous stones of the gretest valoure that may be.

At the Archynale / there be closed within alwaye in a redynesse to set forth whan they woll, an .C. galyes grete bastardes[7] & Sotell besydes all tho that be in voyage and in the haven.

There be workynge dayly at the same Archynale[8] in a place that is in lengthe .M.lxxx. [1,080] fote moo than an .C. men and women that do no thynge but dayly make Ropes and Cables.

Item amonge all wondre and straunge ordynaunce that we sawe there bothe for See & Lande with all maner Artyllary and Ingynes that may be devysyd Pryncypally we noted .ii. peces of Artyllary wherof one was a Pece of ordynaunce of brasse for a Galy bastarde to be devyded in two peces of .xii.M.CCCC. [12,400] and .xix. [19,000?] pounde weyght

[1] *Santa Giustina.

[2] The Trojan hero Antenor was the legendary founder of Padua and his supposed tomb is displayed in the Piazza Antenore in the city centre. An inscribed slab bearing the name Livius was found in Padua, followed by bones in a leaden coffin which were declared to be of the Roman historian Livy and displayed in *Santa Giustina.

[3] Feast (15 June) of the legendary saints Vitus, his tutor Modestus and Modestus's wife Crescentia who were martyred under Diocletian.

[4] Padua was under Venetian rule from 1405.

[5] Saints Helena, Barbara Luke, Roch, Zacharias, Gervase and Protase (Protasius).

[6] *San Nicolò di Lido.

[7] Galley bastards were large galleys. Galley 'subtleties', a general term for other equipment made with ingenuity or subtlety (OED). Cannon sizes (from largest to smallest) used on land and sea included the cannon royal, cannon, cannon serpentine, bastard cannon, demicannon, pedrero, culverin, basilisk, demiculverin, bastard culverin, saker, minion, falcon, falconet, serpentine, and rabinet.

[8] *Archynale*: *Arsenal (**Plate 12**).

with a stopel made by a vyce & and the sayde stopell Joyned by vyce whiche shoteth of yrron .C.l. pounde weight / & the sayde shot of yrron is .xxviii. [18] ynches aboute. This pece is .xxviii. fote of lengthe / and is called a Basylyske / and is for the see.

An other pece there is for the Londe for a Sege devyded in .iii. peces, to be Joyned by vyces weyinge .xxxviii. weyghte / and beryth of lengthe .xxiiii. fote, and [f. v$^v$] shoteth a stone of Iron of .ii. fote depe.

The rychesse the sumptuous buyldynge the Relygous houses and the stablysshynge of their Justyces & councylles with all other thynges that maketh a Cytie glorious Surmounteth in Venyce above all place that ever I sawe. ¶ And specially at .ii. festis wherat we were present. The one was upon the Ascencion daye whiche daye the Duke with a greate tryumphe & solempnyte with all the Seygnyoury went in their Archa triumphali which is in maner of a Galye of a straunge facyon & wonder stately &c. And so rowed out into the see with assystence of their Patriarche / and there spoused the see with a Rynge / The spousal words be / In signum veri perpetuique domini'.[1] And therwith the Duke lete fall the rynge in to the see. The process and cerimonyes wherof were to longe to wryte. &c.

The other feeste was on Corporis Xhristi day where was the most solempne procession that ever I sawe. There went Pagentis[2] of the olde Lawe and the newe Joynynge togyther the fygures of the blessyd Sacrament In Suche noumbre and soo Apte & convenyent for that feeste that it wold make any man Joyous to se it. And over that it was a grete marveyle to se the grete noumbre of Relygyous folkes & and of Scoles that we call bretherhedes or felysshyps / with theyr devyses whiche all bare Lyghtes of wondre goodly facyon / and bytwene every of the Pa [f. vi$^r$] gentis went lytell Children of bothe kyndes gloryously and rychely dressyd berynge in their handes in riche Cuppes or other vessaylles some plesaunt floures or other well smellynge or riche stuffe dressed as Aungelles to adorne the sayde procession / the forme & maner therof excedyd all other that ever I sawe so moche that I can not wryte it.

The Duke sat in Seynt Markes Churche in ryght hyghe estate with all the Seygnyourye and all the Pylgrymes were present / The Duke thus syttynge the sayde procession come by hym and byganne to passe by aboute .vii. of the Cloke / and it was passed .xii. or the sayde procession myght come oones aboute passynge by as faste as they myght goo but one tyme / There was greate honoure done to the Pylgrymes for we all moste and leste wente all there nexte the Duke in the sayd processyon / byfore all the Lordes and other Estates with lyghtes also in our handes of wexe of the fresshet formynge yeven unto us by the mynysters of the sayde procession.

Whyles we were at Venyse we went also to Mestres where the Jewes dwell[3] to Moryan[4] where they make glasse and to many Abbeys and houses of Relygyon that stonde in the see / and grete marveyle it is to se theym stande in suche places and the beauty costely buyldynge and the Relygyous lyfe they kepe in the same &c.

[1] *Marriage of the Sea.

[2] *Pagentis*: pageants.

[3] Mestre, on the mainland, now part of the metropolitan district of Venice. Larke and Guildford visited Venice ten years before the formal establishment of the Jewish Ghetto (29 March 1516) in the Cannaregio *sestiere* of Venice. From the 14th-century Jewish money lenders of German origin had settled in Mestre and it became a centre of mercantile banking. The first Hebrew printing press was also established there during the 1460s by Meshullam Cusi, a rabbi of German origin.

[4] *Murano.

Frydaye the thirde daye of July the Galye departed with all the Pylgrymes oute at the Haven at [f. vi[v]] Venyce & fell to an Ancre in the Rode[1] .iiii. or .v. myle without the Castelles[2] that stande at the mouthe of the sayd Haven / and there we lay all nyght / And saterdaye the .iiii. day of July in the mornynge we made sayle / and with scarce wynde come to Parence in Hystrya.[3]

---

[1] *Rode*: road, sheltered waters near the shore where vessels can safely anchor.

[2] *Castelles*: fortifications on the site of the *Fortezza di Sant'Andrea.

[3] *Parence in Hystrya*: Poreč (Parenzo), in western Croatia on the Istrian Peninsula at the head of the Adriatic Sea below the Gulf of Trieste; then under Venetian control.

# 8.   *c.*1511–14 – *THE PYLGRYMAGE OF MASTER ROBERT LANGTON*

**Robert Langton (1470–1524)** (**Plate 5**), from Appleby, Westmorland, was a well-connected churchman. His uncle, Thomas Langton (*c.*1430–1501), was Archbishop-elect of Canterbury and his cousin Christopher Bainbridge (1461/2–1514) was Archbishop of York (1508) and a cardinal (1511). From 1487 he studied at Queen's College, Oxford, financed by a series of benefices at Lincoln and Salisbury Cathedral and an archdeaconry of Dorset in Salisbury diocese, where Thomas Langton was then bishop. During the 1490s Robert travelled abroad and was recorded in Bologna in 1493, taking his Doctor of Civil Law there in 1498.[1] He continued to gather benefices through the influence of his uncle and, after his death, via the patronage of Christopher Bainbridge, who appointed him as Treasurer of York Minster in April 1509.

Robert Langton's interest in studying in Italy and undertaking an extended pilgrimage would have been fuelled by the diverse international experience of his uncle and cousin. Thomas Langton had been elected by 1462/3 to a fellowship at Pembroke College, Cambridge, but resigned in 1464 to study at Padua, although a shortage of funds curtailed his stay there. He returned to live in Italy between 1468 and 1473 and received at Bologna the degrees of Doctor of Civil Law (1473) and Doctor of Theology (by 1476). In November 1476 Edward IV sent him to Castile to discuss a possible marriage between his son Edward (1470–83), Prince of Wales (later Edward V), and the Infanta Isabella. In November 1477 and March 1478 he was in France seeking to prevent Louis XI from attacking Burgundy; and in the following August he sought to negotiate the betrothal of Edward IV's eldest daughter Elizabeth to the French dauphin, a union which he continued to pursue diplomatically during the next two years. He was also sent in 1480–81 on missions to Maximilian, Duke of Austria. On 29 February 1484 he was appointed by Richard III as his proctor to the Curia in Rome to swear obedience to the new Pope, Innocent VIII, and on his way back to England to negotiate in March a truce with Charles VIII of France. He was elected Provost of Queen's College, Oxford, in 1487 and was translated in 1493 by Henry VII to the see of Winchester, the richest in England.[2]

Christopher Bainbridge probably studied at Oxford before going to Ferrara and Bologna where he was admitted Doctor of Civil Law in October 1492. He was in Rome between 1492 and 1494, becoming in January 1493 a chamberlain of the English Hospice there. He served as a chaplain to Henry VII, witnessed his will and attended the

---

[1] Mitchell, 'Robert Langton's *Pylgrimage*', p. 44.
[2] *ODNB*, s.v.

coronation of Henry VIII.[1] In September 1509 he was appointed as the king's ambassador to Pope Julius II with a brief to strengthen his support for England against France. He arrived in Rome in November 1509 and the Venetian cardinals and ambassadors there sought his support in persuading the Pope to terminate the League of Cambrai against Venice and to lift the interdict against the Senate. By February 1510 the Pope was openly hostile towards the Duke of Ferrara, a key ally of Louis XII, and Bainbridge accompanied him on his military campaign against the duke in Romagna in August 1510. Partly as a reward and partly a diplomatic gesture, Julius II created him curial cardinal at Ravenna, since he now needed Henry VIII's support against France. This led to England joining the Holy League in 1511. Bainbridge served as a papal legate during the campaign against Ferrara and in April 1511 was with the army defending Bologna from the north. He received various benefices in Italy from Julius II and continued vociferously to oppose the French during Leo X's papacy (from March 1513) who granted him additional benefices in Bologna and Vicenza. In 1514 he was appointed as Chamberlain to the College of Cardinals at Rome and died there on 14 July, rumoured poisoned by a servant, Raimondo da Modena (reputedly an agent of the anglicized Bishop of Worcester, Silvester Gigli), who confessed under torture. His lavish funeral was celebrated on 31 July 1514 in the chapel of the English Hospice (now English College) at Rome.[2]

On 11 October 1511 Robert Langton's cousin Cardinal Bainbridge licensed him to go on pilgrimage to Santiago de Compostela, Rome and other places in France and Italy.[3] These travels lasted approximately two and a half years but there is no evidence to suggest that he ever attempted to travel to the Holy Land. Langton was in Rome in March and April 1514 and probably returned, via Venice, to England soon afterwards. He took up residence in the London Charterhouse and maintained another residence in Southampton. In 1516 he financed the building of an antechapel at Queens' College, Cambridge, and work on its provost's lodgings. He died at the Charterhouse in June 1524 and was buried there.

On 18 November 1522 the stationer Robert Copland published *The Pylgrimage of M. Robert Langton Clerke to Saynt James in Compostell and in Other Holy Places of Crystendome*.[4] It is composed in the form of a guidebook in chronological order, beginning at Orleans and providing the names of places and distances on his pilgrimage routes, followed by lengthier glosses on some of the key locations, with specific details of their relics and holy images with, occasionally, other secular details such as the tomb of Dante at Ravenna and the renowned statue of Laocoon (discovered in 1506) at

---

[1] The scholar and diplomat Richard Pace links the circles of Thomas Langton and Christopher Bainbridge. He served from 1493 to 1501 in Langton's household and became his amanuensis and was sent by him to Padua in 1498. In 1509 Pace entered Bainbridge's service whose political sympathies he shared in terms of the Holy League's desire to drive the French out of Italy. Consequently, the 'Venetian republic regarded Pace as a learned and virtuous advocate for its interests, who was to be received as a native Venetian rather than a foreign diplomat'. *ODNB*, s.v.

[2] *ODNB*, s.v.

[3] Langton took an ambitious and circuitous to Oviedo and Compostela, south to Guadalupe and Cadiz, across Andalusia through Seville and Granada, north to Barcelona and on to Italy where he travelled from south to north. From Venice he crossed modern Germany, the Low Countries and on to Calais for the Channel crossing. See Tate, 'Robert Langton, Pilgrim', p. 182.

[4] *STC* 15206, copies at Cambridge University Library and Lincoln Cathedral Library; *The Pylgrimage of M. Robert Langton Clerke*, 1522; rpt and ed. Blackie, 1924.

Rome.[1] Langton's route took him through France to Spain and then back through France to Italy, entering via Mount Cenis so that he could visit Milan and Venice before heading south as far as Naples and returning via Venice to cross by land to Flanders and back home to England. With reference to the routes to Jerusalem, he refers his readers to Thomas Larke's account of Sir Richard Guildford's pilgrimage:

> And as for the way with pylgrymage and knowledge of the same to Jerusalem and place of the holy lande I remyt you to mayster Larkes boke made of the same / wherein he comprehendeth all thinges concernynge that holy pylgrymage / insomoche that the redynge the same shall seme rather to se it then rede it. (p. 3)

A fine portrait of Robert Langton as a pilgrim has survived (**Plate 5**), depicting an elderly man with a long white beard and moustache and an aquiline nose. It was recorded in 1858 at Annesley Hall, Nottinghamshire, the home of the Chaworth family, but later presumed lost.[2] However, it resurfaced in a Christie's sale (9 July 2014) with a provenance related to the 'Congregational Memorial Hall Trust'. Significantly for this study, it was attributed to the Venetian School (*c.*1512–13) and described as follows:

> Portrait of Robert Langton (1470–1524), half-length, in black robes and cap, holding a pilgrim staff in his left hand, from which is suspended a pilgrim hat with badges, and a book in his right, behind a parapet with inscription 'Robertus · Langton · [Lett] doctor: et r:' (upper right) oil on canvas, laid down on panel 34½ × 27¾ in. (87 × 70.5 cm)

The Christie's catalogue continues: 'Executed in Venice in *circa* 1512–13, this portrait of the ecclesiastic and pilgrim Robert Langton constitutes the earliest *ad vivum* portrait of an English sitter painted in Italy by an Italian artist.'[3] Significantly, the catalogue hypothesizes that the portrait may have come from a circle of painters working close to the greatest Venetian artist of the period, Tiziano Vecellio (*c.*1488/90–1576), known as Titian:

> This portrait may have been commissioned on Langton's arrival in Venice and collected on his return visit. Antonio Mazzotta [Università degli Studi di Milano] has observed that the treatment of the gloves and the psychology of the face in this portrait reveal affinities with contemporary portraits by Titian, making it likely that if not actually painted by him, this picture was certainly executed by an artist working in his immediate circle in Venice. The current condition of the picture however precludes any definitive assessment.[4]

Langton's account of Venice (probably compiled from earlier guides and advice from other visitors there), is primarily focused on a selection of its renowned religious relics, although elsewhere in his travel account during his time in Italy he sometimes reveals a keen interest in antiquities. As Brett Foster notes: 'His enthusiasm for antiquities anticipates more secularized, humanist travellers, yet he firmly retains the pilgrim's devotional preoccupations ... his journal subtly reflects the changing conventions of travel

---

[1] De Beer, 'Robert Langton's *Pylgrimage*', p. 58.
[2] Thompson, 'Portrait of Dr Robert Langton', pp. 347–8.
[3] Langton was at Venice in 1514, not 1512–13.
[4] https://www.christies.com/lotfinder/Lot/venetian-school-circa-151213-portrait-5813644-details.aspx. An attribution of this painting to the 'circle' of Titian remains, at best, speculative, although Langton's connections (via his uncle and cousin) with the English royal court would have rendered him a high-status visitor to Venice.

writing, which themselves speak to the evolving values of his milieu.'[1] As the annotations indicate, Langton was largely impervious to the architectural and artistic splendours of Venice – or perhaps simply chose not to write about them because his guide was intended primarily as a devotional support to religious pilgrims in Italy.

**Text**[2]

Venesia.

There is at *th*e trynite chyrche[3] a foote of saynt Demetre.[4] The lyfte hande of saynt Adryan bysshop.[5] A rybbe of saynt Mathew the eveangelyst. The arme of saynt Procupy.[6] A rybbe of saynt Barbara.[7] A piece of the sponge of Cryst / and .ii. thornes of his crowne. The clothe of the Crybbe or Cratche.[8] The ymage of our lady that was sene wepynge thre dayes / whan the plage reygned at Venyce. Also under the hye auter[9] of saynt Markes chyrche lyeth his body. And in the vestiary above is a rybbe of saynt Stephen. Also a piece of the holy crosse. An ymage of our lady paynted by saynt Luke. Also a fynger of saynt Marke. Also a fynger of Mary magdalene. The thigh of saynt George. A thorne of Crystes crowne. A rynge of saynt Markes / and a boke wryten with his handes. And in saynt Antonyes chyrche northwarde fro*m* thens lyeth *th*e body of saynt Saba[10] abbot that had many mo*n*kes under hym / & there are his shoes / and the crosse that he dyde bere. And in *th*e chapell therby northwarde is the whyrlebone[11] of saynt George / and a bone of saynt Blase. Also at saynt zacharies chyrche lyeth his body. id est *pa*tris *san*cti ioannis baptiste[12] / with many other bodyes & relykes. Also in saynt Marynes[13] chyrche lyeth her body. Also there is a nayle of Cryst. At *th*e crucigeris[14] lyeth the body of saynt Barbara. Also a bone and a tothe of saynt Christofre. Also a bone of saynt Laurence. Also saynt Blase cuppe. Also in saynt Lucyes chyrche lyeth her body. Also in saynt Appolynares chyrche

---

[1] Foster, 'Goodliest Place', p. 28.

[2] Text from *The Pylgrimage of M. Robert Langton Clerke*, 1522; rpt and ed. Blackie, 1924.

[3] *Santissima Trinità.

[4] St Demetrios of Thessaloniki (270–304), a Christian soldier and martyr, often paired with St George.

[5] St Adrian of Nicodemia (Nicomedia), a Roman soldier martyred in 290 after converting to Christianity. At his execution his hands were cut off and his legs broken on an anvil.

[6] St Procopius, an ascetic and theologian, martyred in 303.

[7] St Barbara, a 3rd-century saint, executed by her pagan father for converting to Christianity. She was widely venerated at Venice and commemorated by Palma Vecchio (*c.*1480–1528) in his polyptych of six paintings with St Barbara at the centre in the Church of *Santa Maria Formosa.

[8] *Cratche*: crib or manger used to feed animals, specifically applied to the manger at Bethlehem.

[9] *hye auter*: high altar.

[10] St Sabbas, the Sanctified (439–532), a Cappadocian-Syrian monk who lived mainly in the Holy Land. His relics were taken to Venice by Crusaders during the 12th century and preserved in the Church of St Anthony (transferred in 1965 to St Sabbas Monastery in the Kidron Valley, near Jerusalem).

[11] *whyrlebone*: whirlbone, the round head of a bone set in a socket, usually referring to a hip bone, knee bone or patella.

[12] *San Zaccaria was completed in 1515 and Robert Langton was one of its earliest English visitors. He presumably admired its altarpiece, 'Madonna Enthroned with Child and Saints', completed by Giovanni Bernini in 1505.

[13] St Marina. Her relics were reputedly brought to Venice in 1113 and placed in the Church of St Liberalis.

[14] Church of the religious order known as Cruciferes (Fr. *Croisiers*) or the Crusaders' Church. The relics of St Barbara had been brought from Constantinople to Venice in 1003.

is parte of a fynger of saynt Katheryn. And at saynt Symons chyrche is his arme. At saynt Nycolas de Li[d]o there is (as they saye) his body translated from Barry[1] & .ii. of his tethe: his sendalles: & his staffe pastorall. Mary egyptiens fote.[2] The ymage of our lady / ope*re* moseico[3] / made by saynt Luke. One of *the* pottes had in Cana galalee.[4] Also in saynt Elens chriche[5] in an yle on this syde lyeth her body / with a parte of the holy crosse on her breste. ✠[6] Also Constantynes fynger. Two thornes of Cryst. Parte of Mary magdalenes sholder. Also in saynt George chyrche *tha*t is in an yle[7] is a pyece of his heed. Also a hole arme of hym & .ii. thornes of Cryst. The face w*ith*out *the* crowne of saynt James *the* lesse.[8] A pyece of the spo*n*ge of Cryst. Also in a chyrche besyde the gray freres lyeth the body of saynt Roke.[9] And there is a thorne of Cryst that yerely floryssheth. Also in saynt Marcoles chirche is the hande of saynt Johan baptyst / that he baptysed Cryst with.[10] Also in saynt Joh*a*n & Poules chyrche[11] is a bone of saynt Nycolas. A bone of saynt Sebastian, & oyle of saynt Katherin. And in the chyrche of saynt Servace[12] is the ly*ft* hande w*ith*out the thombe of saynt Andrew. Also Mary Cleophe[13] or Jacobyes heed. Also a thorne of Cryst. Saynt Gregoryes eere. Saynt Lukes arme. A piece of *the* holy crosse, & a bone of saint George. In Phylpp & Jacobs chyrche[14] is saynt James heed. A tothe of saynt Appolin, & saynt Phylips arme. Also in Venice is *the* arme of saynt James *the* more & saynt Cecylyes heed. Also in an yle called zoeca lyeth sanc*tus* Athanasi*us*[15] / qui co*m*posuit Quicu*n*que vult.[16]

---

[1] Bari, southern Italy.

[2] St Mary of Egypt (*c.*344–*c.*421), the patron saint of penitents.

[3] *opere moseico*: mosaic work.

[4] *Cana galalee*: the marriage at Cana, when Jesus turned water into wine.

[5] *Sant'Elena.

[6] A cross symbol is inserted in the text here.

[7] *San Giorgio Maggiore.

[8] James 'the Less' (distinguished from James, son of Zebedee) has been identified as either James, son of Alphaeus, or James the brother of Jesus.

[9] *San Rocco (Roch) was completed in 1508, making Langton one of its earliest English visitors.

[10] *San Marcuola.

[11] *Santi Giovanni e Paolo.

[12] *San Servilio (Servolo).

[13] Mary of Cleophas (Clopas), present at the Crucifixion, John 19:25.

[14] *Santi Filippo e Giacomo.

[15] St Athanasius (*c.*296–373), Patriarch of Alexandria.

[16] *qui composuit Quicunque vult*: St Athanasius was at this period thought to have composed the Athanasian Creed, commonly referred to by its opening words *quicunque vult* (whoever will be saved). His authorship, now discredited, was disputed from the mid-17th century.

# 9.   1513 – SIR THOMAS NEWPORT AND SIR THOMAS SHEFFIELD

**Sir Thomas Newport** (*c.* late 1450s–1523) and **Sir Thomas Sheffield** (d. 1524) were only briefly at Venice in September 1513 but their visit provides an informative illustration of Anglo-Venetian diplomatic relations at this period. Newport was a knight of the Hospital of St John of Jerusalem and seems to have entered the order as a hospitaller by 1478 when he was based in Rhodes. He probably took part in the defence of the island against the Turks in 1480 under the command of the order's renowned Grand Master Pierre d'Aubusson (1423–1503). Newport returned to England in 1489 and served as preceptor (officer in charge) of various estates in Yorkshire, Leicestershire and Lincolnshire owned by the order. In 1501 he was elected *Turcopolier* (coastguard commander) in Rhodes and in 1503 was appointed to the lucrative position of bailiff of Eagle in Lincolnshire.

Newport was an experienced and financially shrewd administrator. Between 1489 and 1503 he served as the order's receiver-general for its common treasury in England. He supervised the collection of funds in England and their dispatch, via Venice's banking institutions, to Rhodes. He became one of the wealthiest English hospitallers of his generation with his income estimated at about £800 per year between 1503 and 1523. It seems likely that his earlier travels between England and Rhodes had sometimes been made via Venice and his knowledge of the city, especially its financial facilities, may have dated back to the late 1470s. Newport was summoned back to Rhodes in September 1503 and was able to raise £306 from the order's estates to fund his journey. He set out in late 1505 and spent the winter at Venice before reaching Rhodes in May 1506. While based in London he spent much time at court and by 1513 was recognized as a skilled and knowledgeable ambassador for diplomatic missions to Mediterranean areas, especially Venice. He left England in 1513 and, after travelling through France and Germany, was at Venice by September, accompanied by his fellow hospitaller, Sir Thomas Sheffield.

Newport and Sheffield brought diplomatic letters from Henry VIII to the doge and Senate. They were received with the status of official ambassadors and granted a formal audience on 3 September. The Venetian historian, senator and diarist Marin Sanudo (Sanuto) (1466–1536) made notes of their audience on 3 September with Doge Leonardo Loredan (**Frontispiece**). He observed that the knights were on their way from England to Rhodes, carrying with them credentials and letters of recommendation from Henry VIII. They came first to the *Collegio[1] and were formally presented by the banker

---

[1] *Sala del Collegio.

Antonio Capello and Troian Bollani[1] and privileged to sit beside the doge. Newport had previously lent 400 ducats to Ambassador Andrea Badoer, with a bill of exchange payable at Venice.[2] Sanudo noted that both knights were treated to most cordial reception.[3] The more subtle workings of Venetian diplomacy were also illustrated on 4 September when Sanudo documented Bollani's report on political intelligence gleaned from his informal conversations with Newport and Sheffield. Bollani had received assurances that the King of England was Venice's firm friend and that he disapproved of the King of Spain's truce with France which he had sworn to attack. Among many other narratives, the English knights explained how they had travelled through Germany on their way to Rhodes; and that Sir Thomas Newport was owed 1,700 ducats for money lent to Badoer when Venetian Ambassador in England, for which he had bills of exchange with the Signoria.[4] Four days later, on 8 September Newport and Sheffield were invited to attend Mass at St Mark's with Doge Loredan and the ambassadors of the Pope and Hungary, the secretary of Alfonso d'Este (1476–1534), Duke of Ferrara, and other dignitaries.[5]

The most interesting reflection upon Venetian intelligence gathering is contained in Sanudo's detailed transcript of a report presented to the *Collegio on 5 September by Troian Bollani and read out to the Senate on 10 September. It provides more information about his conversations with Newport and Sheffield, relating to both English and continental affairs:

> The knights said that no king in the world could have endured such a war [League of Cambrai] without yielding. They commended the Signoria, saying that the sovereigns [sic] of Spain were the cause of all mischief, and that King Ferdinand[6] never should have taken Brescia;[7] that King Ferdinand dealt doubly, and had played their King [Henry VIII] several tricks, but two above all. First, when the 10,000 English were sent to Guienne for its seizure, he failed to march his army as promised:[8] but having by means of the English obtained the kingdom of Navarre, the French being unable to succour it, as they were on the other side of the Pyrenees, he then took no further trouble. Secondly, he made truce with France without the knowledge

---

[1] The Capellos were one of Venice's most influential banking families, with long-established commercial and trading links with England. Troian Bollani was a member of a prominent Venetian family, renowned for their financial acumen, scholarship and their Palazzo Bollani, near the Piazza San Marco. Troian had been superintendent of the *Zecca (Mint) in 1498. Domenico Bollani (1514–79), Bishop of Brescia, served as Venetian Ambassador to England (1547–51).

[2] Andrea Badoer was sent to England on official business in 1508–9 and again in 1515.

[3] Sanuto, *Diarii*, XVII, p. 16. *CSP Venice, 1513*, item 285.

[4] Sanuto, *Diarii*, XVII, p. 16. *CSP Venice, 1513*, item 286.

[5] Sanuto, *Diarii*, XVII, p. 22. *CSP Venice, 1513*, item 289. During the Italian wars the Duke of Ferrara had been an ally of Louis XII of France against Venice and the Papacy. He had played a major role in the French victory at the Battle of Ravenna (1512) and so the presence of his secretary at Venice was especially important in terms of Venice's diplomatic relations with Ferrara in 1513.

[6] Ferdinand II (1452–1516), King of Aragon.

[7] Brescia in Lombardy, northern Italy, was sacked in February 1512 during the War of the League of Cambrai. It had previously rebelled against French control and invited a garrison of Venetian troops.

[8] Ferdinand had promised to assist the English in retaking Guyenne (Aquitaine) which had been lost to the French in 1453 by Henry VI. But when the English army landed in 1512 at San Sebastian, his support failed to materialize. Alternatively, Sanudo may be referring (when he writes *Guiena*) to the Battle of Guinegate (Battle of the Spurs) in August 1513 only weeks before Newport's and Sheffield's arrival at Venice. The English military camp had been at Guinegate (now Enguinegatte).

either of the King of England or of the whole island, and sent word to the King of England not to invade France this year. The latter replied that he would cross despite them all, and meant to see who would hinder him.

At the English court the Emperor[1] was considered fickle, and although he was sending 15,000 men towards Lorraine, they met certain persons on the road, who told them they were [already] under command.

Nothwithstanding this, should the King of France come to good terms, the King of England would make peace. On being asked the conditions of such agreement, they said, 'some good tribute;' also that their King derived much profit from peace, whereas war gave him only renown. That in times of tranquillity he levied his duties, the kingdom being frequented by the galleys, which yielded considerable revenue.

Enquired, moreover, on what terms the King of England was with the Duke of Burgundy.[2]

They said the Flemings were averse to war with France, because the Archduke was young; but as the King of England had sent 6,000 men against the Duke of Guelders,[3] without which aid the whole of Flanders and Brabant would have been laid waste and plundered, the lady Margaret had supplied the English with helmets and wagons.

A marriage was being negotiated between the Archduke and a sister of the King of England,[4] and would take place.[5]

In response to Newport's and Sheffield's embassy to Venice, a letter was drafted on 13 September from Doge Leonardo Loredan to Henry VIII. It recorded how he had received Henry's letters, accorded the usual dignities paid to visiting ambassadors and assured them of the Senate's support for their safe passage to Rhodes. The Doge and Signoria expressed their earnest desire for peace between the powers of Christendom and the repression of all those hostile to the Christian faith. The Doge's letter emphasized that the Venetian Republic had earnestly sought peace with the emperor, 'offering the most favourable terms', but its terms had been rejected. This meant that Venetian forces intended to support the emperor were now 'turned against them'. The draft letter concluded by assuring Henry VIII that 'the State will always persevere in its extreme and ancient good will towards him'. The care given to the handling of such diplomatic missives is illustrated by an amendment to this letter, instructing that the 'enclosure for the King of England' should instead be delivered to 'the Cardinal of York' (Wolsey) and that the dispatch of the letter to Henry VIII should be delayed 'until the receipt of surer information from the ambassador Dandolo resident with the King of France'.[6] Newport was back in Rhodes by November 1513 and maintained correspondence with both the King and Cardinal Wolsey before returning to England, probably with Sir Richard Torkington (**item 10**), in time to attend the Field of the Cloth of Gold in 1520. He travelled back to Rhodes in late 1522 but was drowned near Spain on 24 January 1523.[7]

---

[1] Holy Roman Emperor Maximilian I (1459–1519).

[2] Charles II (1500–58), Duke of Burgundy, from 1516 King of Spain (Castile and Aragon) and from 1519 Holy Roman Emperor Charles V.

[3] Charles II (1467–1538), Duke of Guelders and Count of Zutphen.

[4] In 1507 Henry VIII's sister Princess Mary (1496–1533) had been betrothed to Charles, Duke of Burgundy, but the engagement was cancelled in July 1514 and in the following October she married Louis XII of France.

[5] Rawdon Brown's summary translation. Sanuto, *Diarii*, XVII, pp. 42–3. *CSP Venice, 1513*, item 298.

[6] *CSP Venice, 1513*, item 305.

[7] *ODNB*, s.v.

Less information is known about **Sir Thomas Sheffield** who was born in Yorkshire and was the brother of Sir Robert Sheffield (b. by 1462–1518), Recorder of London and Speaker of the House of Commons in 1512. After falling out with Wolsey, Sir Robert was committed to the Tower of London where he died in August 1518. He made his will (proved 28 February 1519) two days before his death, naming his brother Thomas as one of his executors.[1] Thomas was more successful in avoiding Wolsey's lethal hostility and served in England as Preceptor of Beverley and Shingay and as Treasurer of the Order of St John of Jerusalem. He was present at the siege of Rhodes in 1522, commanding the Palace battery, which led to the expulsion of the Knights of St John by the Ottoman forces of Sultan Suleiman I. The remaining knights, including Sir Thomas Sheffield, were given twelve days to leave the island and they defiantly marched out of the town in combat armour with banners and drums. Along with numerous civilians, they boarded fifty ships which took them to the Venetian possession of Crete. Sir Thomas was reported to have died at Viterbo on 10 August 1524.[2]

[1] https://www.historyofparliamentonline.org/volume/1509-1558/member/sheffield-sir-robert-1462-1518 Nicolas, *Testamenta Vetusta*, pp. 555–7.
[2] BHO, 'Houses of Knights Hospitallers: Preceptory of Shingay'.

# 10.  1517 – SIR RICHARD TORKINGTON

**Sir Richard Torkington (fl. 1511–18)** was a Catholic priest and pilgrim but little is known about his personal life or service in the English Church. In 1511 he was presented to the Norfolk rectory of Mulberton by Sir Thomas Boleyn (*c.*1477–1539), later Earl of Wiltshire, whose family residence was Hever Castle, Kent. Sir Thomas was the father of Anne Boleyn (1501–36), whom Henry VIII married as his second wife in a secret wedding on 14 November 1532 and in a public ceremony on 25 January 1533. Torkington was still rector of Mulberton in 1517 when he began a pilgrimage to the Holy Land. He left Rye in Sussex on 20 March for Dieppe and travelled alone through France and northern Italy, visiting Turin, Milan and Pavia before arriving on 29 April at Venice. He stayed there until 14 June when he set out on a galley with other pilgrims to the Holy Land, arriving at Jaffa on 15 July.

Torkington's account of his experiences illustrate how travel memoirs at this period frequently comprised an assembly of personal observations blended – often without acknowledgement – with a range of earlier sources. The intention behind this process was to provide the writer (during the journey and perhaps in recollection afterwards) and other potential readers with material which drew together a wide range of informed and relevant information as a reference compendium rather than a merely subjective account of travels. As Anthony Bale and Sebastian Sobecki explain:

> Much of Torkington's diary appears to be a highly personal eye-witness account, but Torkington's account of the Holy Land is largely indebted to the *Pylgrymage of Sir Richard Guylforde*, probably written by Thomas Larke, concerning a similar journey undertaken in 1506; Larke, in turn, borrowed a significant amount of material from Mandeville. Also, parts of Torkington's descriptions of Crete were taken from the printed guide, *Informacion for Pylgrymes unto the Holy Londe* (which had already been printed in at least two editions, of *c.*1498 and 1515, as well as circulating in manuscript, and which incorporated material from William Wey's *Matter of Jerusalem*). So Torkington's text is a composite of eyewitness testimony and authoritative, widely read accounts.[1]

His return journey proved significantly more problematic. His ship was detained at Cyprus for one month and due to illness he had to disembark at Rhodes for six weeks to convalesce in the care of the Knights of St John. He was grateful for the medical care and kindness shown to him by various members of the community, mentioning, in particular, **Sir Thomas Newport (item 9):**

> ffryday, the xxv day of Septembre, we had sygte of the yle of the rodes Sonnday a for the ffeste of Seynt Michell,[2] we com to the Rodes to dyner And ther my self lay seke by the space of vi wekys.

---

[1] Bale and Sobecki, *Medieval English Travel*, p. 454.
[2] The Feast of St Michael is on 29 September, confirming that Torkington arrived on Sunday 27 September 1517.

Off our chere and well entretyng at the rodys And what comfort was don to us, and Speciall that was seke and disesyd by Syr Thomas Newporte[1] And Mayster William [*deletion*] Weston[2] And Syr John Bowthe[3] and aftyrward by other jentylmen of Englond ther it was to long to wrytte.[4]

His ship was then battered by storms and, rather than returning to Venice, he sailed past Sicily and up the west coast of Italy, visiting Naples and Rome on the way. He finally reached Dover on 17 April 1518, having been out of England for one year, five weeks and three days. He completed his pilgrimage by visiting in May 1518 the shrine of St Thomas Becket at Canterbury. No later details are known of Torkington's life, except that by 1526 he was no longer vicar of Mulberton.[5]

The account of his travels and pilgrimage survives in two manuscript versions: BL Additional MS 28561 (ff. 80r–99v), a sixteenth-century copy (not autograph), beginning: 'Thys ys the begynnyng of the pylgrymage of Syr Rychard Torkyngton Person of Mulberton in Norffolk. And how he went towardys Jherusalem all a lone to the tyme he came to Venesse' (title page f. 2r). Nothing is known about the copyist but several names are associated with the manuscript (probably as owners), including John Potter (alias Warner), Edmund Sellar, Margaret Russell, Edward Russell and Ja:[mes?] Wright. It had originally been paginated (pp. 1–207) but later renumbered as 105 folios (with f. 106 recording: '105 Folios March 1871 J.R.' – probably the date when these folio numbers were added).[6]

The second copy, BL Additional MS 28562, was made probably in the early nineteenth century by the Stratford-upon-Avon based antiquary and collector of Shakespearean memorabilia Robert Bell Wheler (1785–1857), who also published some short extracts from it in an issue of the *Gentleman's Magazine* (October 1812, pp. 316–19). A complete version of Torkington's travels was published in 1884, edited by the London clergyman William John Loftie (1839–1911), under the picturesque but misleading title *Ye Oldest Diarie of Englysshe Travell*.

In his description of Venice Torkington added more details about the specific relics described in Larke's account of Guildford's pilgrimage and provided incidental comments relating to his own experiences, such as his opening remarks about the warm greeting he received at the hostel where he was staying at Venice from its host who spoke good English. Many other English pilgrims travelled via Venice to the Holy Land at this period

---

[1] See **item 9**.

[2] Sir William Weston (b. after 1469–1540), was the last English Prior of the Order of St John before the dissolution of the monasteries. He was the brother of Sir Richard Weston (1465–1541), who served Henry VIII as Governor of Guernsey and Treasurer of Calais. A William Weston, probably his uncle, had defended Rhodes in 1480 against the Turks. He was recorded at Rhodes in 1498 and was resident there until 1510 when he returned to England in 1517, just in time for Torkington's stay on the island. He was one of the few English knights to survive the siege of 1522. With other survivors, he moved to Crete where in 1523 he was appointed *Turcopolier*, commanding the largest ship in the Order of St John's navy, the *Great Carrack* (*Santa Anna*). This vessel, which could carry 500 men, has been described as the first 'iron-clad' because it was sheathed in metal to withstand cannon shots. *ODNB*, s.v.

[3] Probably the *Turcopolier* Sir John Bouch (Buck), who died at the siege of Rhodes (1522).

[4] BL Additional MS 28561, f. 84r; [Torkington], *Ye Oldest Diarie*, ed. Loftie, 57. Page references to Loftie's edition are also supplied, although his transcription is often inaccurate and heavily punctuated.

[5] *ODNB*, s.v.

[6] All references are to these folio numbers.

but records of their experiences are scanty. For example, John Lloyd (or Flude) (*c.*1475–1523), a musician and gentleman of the Chapel Royal at the court of Henry VIII, travelled to Jerusalem in 1519 before returning home in time to join the other members of the Chapel Royal at the Field of the Cloth of Gold (1520). Knowledge of his pilgrimage derives only from his will which he made before his departure. No information survives about Lloyd's experiences in the Venetian pilgrimage galleys or his impressions of the city, especially its renowned excellence in devotional choral works and other church music.[1] Between 1504 and 1508 Lloyd was employed by Edward Stafford (1478–1521), Duke of Buckingham, as director of his musical ensemble of men and boy singers for his private entertainment. Stafford announced in October 1520 his own plans to make a pilgrimage to Jerusalem – perhaps influenced by Lloyd – for which he is likely to have commissioned 'A Lytell Chronicle' about the Middle East, translated from Haytoun of Armenia's 'Fleurs d'histoires' (1307), one of the original sources for Mandeville's *Book of Marvels and Travels*.[2] But again, nothing else is known about Stafford's preparation for pilgrimage which is likely to have included him collecting together earlier written accounts of the experiences and knowledge of other pilgrims.

Torkington's narrative is also of special interest because he provides a detailed account of his personal contact with Federico II Gonzaga (1500–40), whom he describes as 'marchose of Mantua', even though he did not inherit this title until 3 April 1519 after the death of his father Francesco II Gonzaga (1466–1519).[3] When Torkington was visiting Venice, Francesco had been for several years too ill to travel beyond his Mantuan residences due to the ravages of syphilis. However, Federico made an official visit to Venice at this time and his family's personal connections with the Republic were significant.[4] His father Francesco had been a distinguished soldier (*condottiero*) who served as Venice's military land commander (1489–97). However, he later became a leader of the Holy League formed by Pope Julius II against the Venetians, who captured him in autumn 1509 and held him hostage until July 1510. He was only freed by sending his son Federico as a hostage to Rome (1510–13), where he was able to observe the state business of Julius II (d. 1513), his cardinals and visiting dignitaries. It has been assumed that Francesco henceforth harboured an enmity against Venice and he is thought to have refused to serve again as their *condottiero*. Nevertheless, he was still willing to send his son to the city in 1517 as an honoured guest of the doge and Senate during Torkington's visit.

The reasons for this visit were clearly dynastic. Federico had been betrothed in February 1517 to Maria Paleologo (1508–30), the eldest daughter of the Marquess of Monferrato, and was at the French court of François I until April 1517.[5] This betrothal was confirmed

[1] *ODNB*, s.v.

[2] Bale, '"ut legi"', p. 211.

[3] I am grateful to Molly Bourne and Marie-Louise Leonard for their advice on Torkington's meeting with Federico Gonzaga and his family.

[4] Federico was at Casale Monferrato until 27 May and then visited Ferrara and Venice in late May, probably travelling along the River Po. At Venice he attended the Ascension Day festivities with the Venetian Ambassadors Andrea Gritti, Giorgio Coraro and the Doge.

[5] D'Este, *Letters*, pp. 416, 418 n. 313. Federico stopped on his way from France to Italy at Casale Monferrato for his betrothal. This marriage represented a major Gonzaga-French alliance, although it was later dissolved by Pope Clement VII. He eventually married Maria's sister Margherita (1510–66) in 1531. Bourne, *Francesco II Gonzaga*, p. 44.

on 17 April, with plans for Maria to come to Mantua in 1524 to live with her future husband. Then almost seventeen (b. 17 May) Federico was clearly being groomed to be his father's political successor. To this end, there were also plans to send him to the English court to broaden his knowledge of international affairs and this is why Torkington may have been invited to join his entourage at Venice. On 18 April Francesco Chieregato (1479–1539), the Apostolic Nuncio in England, wrote to Francesco Gonzaga to say that Cardinal Wolsey would welcome Federico and personally look after him if he came to London. On Palm Sunday Chieregato was granted an audience with Henry VIII who also welcomed Federico's planned visit to England: 'With regard to the Marquis's son, the King replied that on his coming he would treat him like his own son, that the sooner he came the better, and that he would not let him want for anything.' On 1 May Chieregato was able to add that Henry VIII's close friend, Charles Brandon (1484–1545), Duke of Suffolk, was equally keen for Federico to visit England, 'saying he was very anxious for the coming hither of one of the Marquis's sons, that he might be enabled to show the son how much goodwill he bore the father'.[1] This visit was still being encouraged on 28 May when Chieregato confirmed that Cardinal Wolsey 'had assured him that, should the Marquis send one of his sons to England, he, as well as the King, would act by him as a father, and not allow him to want for anything becoming his noble birth and condition'.[2]

By 1517 there was considerable urgency in completing Federico's political education because his father Francesco was terminally, ill. Although married to the widely admired Isabella d'Este (1474–1539), a noted patroness of the arts in Italy, Francesco was a philanderer and also enjoyed a long association (not necessarily sexual) with his wife's sister-in-law, Lucrezia Borgia (1480–1519).[3] On 29 March 1519 he died of syphilis which he may have first contracted during his military service and perhaps before 1500.[4] His son Federico, was born in 1500 and it has been suggested that he died from congenital syphilis.[5] The disease was medically documented in Italy during summer 1495 and Francesco is one of the earliest high-ranking sufferers on record.[6] He received regular medicinal purges and water-bath treatments but by the time of Federico's visit to Venice his condition was chronic. His spouse, Isabella d'Este, mentioned in a letter to the Duke of Ferrara, dated 13 December 1516, that Francesco had been obliged to cancel his usual Christmas entertainments 'due to his indisposition'.[7] She also resorted to extensive

---

[1] Suffolk was then married to Henry VIII's sister, Princess Mary Tudor, who had previously been the queen of Louis XII of France.

[2] *CSP Venice* (Mantuan Archives), 1517, items 875, 878, 894. This visit to the English court never took place and, instead, Federico returned to the French court in 1518.

[3] Lucrezia was the sister of Cesare Borgia (1475–1507) who was the godfather of Federico II Gonzaga. Cesare, a cardinal and son of Rodrigo de Borja (1431–1503), Pope Alexander VI (from 1492), caught syphilis in the late 1490s and eventually wore a mask to hide his deformities.

[4] Cockram, *Isabella d'Este*, pp. 25–6, 74, 104, 190. D'Este, *Letters*, p. 10. Bourne, *Francesco II Gonzaga*, pp. 39, 43, 45, 62.

[5] Alternatively, Federico may have caught syphilis in later life. Congenital syphilis usually is passed to children via an infected mother. However, there is no evidence that Isabella d'Este suffered from the disease. Nor has syphilis been linked with any of Federico's siblings, many of whom lived long lives: Eleonora (1493–1570), Ippolita (1503–70), Ercole (1506–65), Ferrante (1507–57) and Livia (1508–69).

[6] Tognotti, 'Prevention Strategies', p. 3. The first accurate description of syphilis was provided by the Venetian military surgeon Marcello Cumano.

[7] D'Este, *Letters*, p. 412.

travelling, partly to avoid intimate relations with him. During his visit to Venice in 1517 she was on pilgrimage to the shrine of St Mary Magdalene in Provence. It is likely, therefore that Federico was being accorded by Venice all honours due to a visiting dignitary because it was assumed that he would soon succeed to his father's title and the Gonzaga dominions.

Finally, Torkington's repeated description of Federico Gonzaga (1500–40) as the 'marchose of Mantua' – even though their meeting took place almost two years before Federico inherited this title – has significant implications for the dating of his manuscript. It remains possible that Torkington was simply mistaken in assuming that the youthful Federico was already the marquess when they met at Venice but this seems unlikely, given the strict courtly protocols of the period. Instead, his use of this title suggests that he was drafting his account of his travels at some point after April 1519 when Federico had become Marquess of Mantua, even though nothing is known of Torkington's life after his arrival back in England in April 1518 and his visit to the shrine of St Thomas Becket at Canterbury in the following month. If he was writing sometime after this date, it is easy to imagine that Torkington would have been proud to claim in his travel account that he was personally acquainted with one of Italy's most distinguished noblemen, Federico II Gonzaga, Marquess (and from 1530 Duke) of Mantua.

**Text**[1]

[f. 10r] The same day [Wednesday 29 April 1517) we sayled toward Venys and a bowt iii of the cloke at aftyr none we com to the goodly and ffamose Cite of Venys. Ther I was well at ese ffor ther was no thyng that I desyred to have [f. 10v][2] but I had it shortly.

At Venyse, at the fyrste howse that I cam to except oon the good man of the howse seyd he knew me by my face that I was an englysshman. And he spake to me good englyssh thane I was Jous[3] and glade ffor I saw never englyssh man ffrom the tyme I departed owt of Parys to the tyme I came to Venys which ys vii or viii C myles.

The Reliquies at Venys canne not be nowmbred. Ther lyeth Seynt Elyn Seynt Barbara, Seynt Luke, Seynt Roke, Seynt [f.11r] Zachary Seynt Jervas and Prothase.[4] And many other Seyntis and grett reliques.

May day we went to Seynt Elyn and offerd ther[,] She lith in a ffayer place of religion of whyth[5] monkes ye may se hyr face perfythly hyr body ys coverd with a cloth of whyth Sylke.

---

[1] BL Additional MS 28561, ff. 10r–23v; [Torkington], *Ye Oldest Diarie*, ed. Loftie, pp. 6–16.
[2] 'to have' is repeated in the text.
[3] *Jous*: joyous.
[4] This passage is lifted directly from Thomas Larke's account; see p. 80.
[5] *whyth*: white.

The iii^de Day of May the Invencion of the holy Crosse[1] The patrone of a new goodly sheppe with other Marchauntes Desyred us Pylgrymys that we wold com a bord and see hys shippe withinne which Shippe ley a for Seynt Markys chirche

[f. 11v] And a bowyt viii of the Cloke we went all in to Seynt Markes Churche And aftyr that we went all in to the fforseyd Shippe. Ther they mad us goodly Chere with diverse Sotylties as Comfytes and marche panys,[2] And Swete Wynes.

Also the v^th Day of May the patrone of a nother Shippe whiche lay in the see v myle from Venys he desyered us all [f. 12r] all pylgrymys that we wold come and se hys Shippe And the same Day we went all with hym And ther he provydyd for us a mervelous good Dyner, wher we had all maner of good viteales And wynes And thene we retornyd to Venys a geyne.

At the Archinale[3] ther we saw in making xx/iii[4] new galyes and galye Bastardes [f. 12v] And galye Sotyltes[5] besyd they that be in viage in the haven.

Ther ys Werkying dayly upon thez Galys a m^l men and moo.[6]

Ther be werkying daly at the same Archinale, in a place that ys in lengthe m^l lxxx ffote,[7] mo thanne an C men and women that doo no thyng dayly but make Ropes and Cables.

Ther in that Castyll the Marchauntes shewyd un to us all maner of artyllary [f. 13r] And Ingynes that myght bene devysed ffor warre other be see or ellys be londe.[8]

As grett gunnes that sum of them be dyvided in ii partes and sum in iii partes Joynyd to gedyr be vyres[9] marvell it ys to see.

Also ther ys many howses and Chaumbers full of gunnes, bothe grett and small brygantynes,[10] Crosbowys Swardys byllys halbards Sperys Moryspekys,[11] with all other thynges that ys required necessary for warre.

Wednysday the vi Day of [f. 13v] May, we went by watir to Padua by the Ryver of Brente And there we visite and sawe many Reliquies As Seynt Antonie, whiche was a grey ffryer And lith Rygth ffayer[12] in the body of the Churche In the Vestrye ther ys an herse that

---

[1] Feast of the Invention of the True Cross, celebrating the alleged discovery in 326 of the Cross of Christ by St Helena, the mother of the Emperor Constantine, during her pilgrimage to Jerusalem. The Church of the Holy Sepulchre was then built on this location.

[2] *Sotylties as Comfytes and Marche Panys*: subtleties, table decorations of sugary delicacies; confeits, sweetmeats; and marchpane, marzipan often mounted on wafers.

[3] Most of Torkington's account of the *Arsenal (**Plate 12**) is derived from Thomas Larke's description.

[4] 'xx' written above 'iii', indicating three score.

[5] See n. 2 above.

[6] *m^l men and moo*: 1,000 men and more.

[7] *m^l lxxx ffote*: 1,080 feet.

[8] *other be see or ellys be londe*: otherwise by sea or else by land.

[9] *vyres*: wires.

[10] *brygantynes*: brigandines, body armour made of iron rings or plates, attached to canvas, linen or leather and then covered with similar materials.

[11] *Crosbowys Swardys byllys halbards Sperys Moryspekys*: crossbows, swords, bills, halberds, spears and morris-pikes (supposedly of Moorish origin).

[12] *lith Rygth ffayer*: lies right fair.

stonde full of Chalys to the nowmbyr of xx/iiii or xx/v[1] wher in ys closyd many grett Reliquies, A rybbe of the syd of Seynt Bonaventur whiche translate the holy body of Seynt Antony.

[f. 14r] And also the tong of Seynt Antony, yet ffayer and ffressh whiche tong he covertyd myche peple to the ffeythe of Crist.[2]

Also in the Abbey of Seynt Justine virgyne, a place of blake monkys[3] ryght delectable And also Solytary Ther lithe the holy body of Seynt Justine And Seynt luke, and Seynt Mathew. And ther we see the ffynger of Seynt luke that he wrotte the holy gospell *with*. And also the table of ower blyssyd lady [f. 14v] Whych Seynt Luke poyntyd *with* hys owen hande, berying hyr sone in hyr Army*es*, it ys seyd who so ev*er* be hold thys pitture of *our* blyssyd lady Devowtly onys in hys lyff he shall nev*er* be dep[ri]vyd ffrom [hyr *deleted*] the sight of hyr evlastyng.[4]

Also ther ys ii locures[5] of iii quarter*es* of a yard long, ffull of bonys of Innocentes whyche kyng Herrodye slew ffor malice that he bar to Criste.

Thursday the vii day of May we retornyd by the same Watir [f. 15r] of Brent to Venese ageyne.

Item at Venese ys a place of Nonnys[6] which ys callyd Seynt Johnes Zachari in a Coffer by hynd the hith Auter[7] lies the holy body of Zachari ffather of Seynt John Baptiste And other ii holy body*es* whose namys be wretyng in libro vite.

In the Abbey of Seynt George ther we sey many Reliquies of holy Seynt*es*, bothe martyres and virgines the holy Bodyes and Army*es* of them, the ffaces ther ffyngers the tethe of them it ys grett mervell to see.

[f. 15v] Ther is a parte of the hede of Seynt George hys left Arme w*ith* the holl[8] hande. The arme of Seynt lucie, The Bodys of Seynt Cosme and Damiane.[9]

May day we went to Seynt Elyne to a place of Whith Monkes that stande in the see. There she lyeth in a fayer Chapell Closyd in a Coffer hyr face bare and nakyd that ye may se it perfyghtly. Which Seynt Elyne ffond the Crosse at Jherusalen, Also ther lyes upon hyr brest a lytyll crosse made of the holy Crosse, Also [f. 16r] the Tunge of Constantini magni Sone of Seynt Elyn And a bone of Seynt Mary Mawdleyn.

---

[1] 'xx' written above 'iiii', indicating four score; 'xx' written above 'v', indicating five score.

[2] After his death in 1231 St Anthony, renowned for his preaching, was buried in the Franciscan Church of St Mary, Padua. At the transfer of his body to the new basilica, his coffin was opened and his body found to be reduced to dust except for his miraculously preserved tongue. St Bonaventure was present and gave thanks for the saint's 'blessed tongue'. It was placed in a reliquary and is still displayed in a side chapel in the basilica. St Anthony's other remains and relics were transferred in 1310 and 1350.

[3] Benedictine abbey of Santa Giustina, Padua.

[4] Torkington's description of the abbey is derived mainly from Thomas Larke's account.

[5] *locures*: lockers.

[6] *Nonnys*: nuns.

[7] *by hynd the hith Auter*: Behind the High Altar.

[8] *holl*: whole.

[9] The brothers (reputed twins) Saints Cosmas and Damien, Arab physicians and Christian martyrs.

In the Monastery of blake monkyes callyd Seynt Nicholas De Elio[1] Ther lyes the body of Seynt Nicholas as they sey. Also oon of the pottis[2] that ower lord turnyd water in to wyne, The staff of Seynt Nicholas that he used whanne he was Bushoppe.

In the monastery callyd Accusechirii[3] lyes the body of Seynt Barbare. Also in a nother Auter[4] ys a bone of Seynt Cristofer.

[f. 16v] Also in the Church callyd Sancta Marina lies the holy body of hyr De qua miracula in vitaspatrum leguntur.[5]

Also in a nother Church lies the holy body of Seynt Luce virgyn ye may see perfyghtly hyr body and hyr papys.

In the C[h]urche of Seynt Marke ther ys many grett Reliquies and Jowellys, ther ys a gret Chalis of fine gold of Curius werke, set with many precius stonys whych ys in heyght iii quarters of a yard it ys to[o] large to use at messe. But they use it in ornyng[6] the Auter at principall tymes.

Ther be also iii grett Sensuryes[7] [f. 17r] Of gold as hye as the Chalys ys, and peyer of grett Candylstykes, a mong other a wondeffull gretnesse that be ryght Curiusely wrogth and are[8] fine gold garnyshed over all with stones of great Pryse.

Ther be also xii Crownes of fine gold. And a Riche Cappe which every duk ys Crowned with at hys ffirst Intrononyzacions.[9] The price of all with Crownes Pectorales. And a Coppe[10] ys inestymable. ffor they be full sett with precious stonys[11] of grett value that may be.

Also ther be viii grett Copyes of fyne gold garnyshed over with precius stonys.

[f. 17v] All these thynges I sawe whanne they war shewyd to the marchose of mantua.[12] Which browght with hym many Knyghtes and Gentylmen in Riche aperell.

Thys don we passed owt of the Vestre. And so to the hye Auter. And a non it was sett opyn.[13] And ther was ii torches brynyng. The Marchose had a Candyll govyn to him in hys hande bornyng. The gold the precius stonys in the Auter wh[en?] they Glysteryd And shone it was grett mervell to See.

[1] *San Nicolò di Lido.
[2] *oon of the Pottis*: one of the pots.
[3] *Accusechirii*: Probably the Church of *Santa Maria de Crociferi, described by Fynes Moryson as 'Saint Mary de Crostechieri', *Itinerary*, I.179. Hammerton, pp. 155–6.
[4] *a nother Auter*: another altar.
[5] *De qua miracula vitaspatrum leguntur*: of which miracles may be read in the lives of the (three desert) fathers (then attributed to St Jerome).
[6] *ornyng*: adorning.
[7] *Sensurys*: censers.
[8] *are*: Loftie reads this word as 'urn'.
[9] *Intrononyzacions*: enthronization, formal installation to an office.
[10] *Coppe*: cope, ecclesiastical vestment.
[11] *stonys*: stones.
[12] Torkington joined the party of Federico Gonzaga, the eldest son and heir of Francesco II Gonzaga, Marquess of Mantua (d. 1519).
[13] *a non it was sett opyn*: promptly it was set open.

[f. 18r] The Richesse, the sumptuous buyldyng, The religious howses and the stablyssyng[1] of ther Justyces and Councellyes with all other thynges that makyth a Cite glorius Surmownteth in Venys a bove all places that ever I Sawe.

And specially at ii festis wher at we war present the on[e] was upon the Assencion day The Duke with grett Triumphe and solemnyte with all the Senyorye went in ther Archa triumphali which ys in maner of a sayle of a straange facion and wonder stately, etc.

And the marchose of Mantua was with them in the forseyd Galye.

[f. 18v] And so they rowed in to the see with the assistens of ther Patriarche and ther Spoused the See with a ryng. The spousall wordes be In signum veri perpetuique Domini And therwith the Duke lete fall the ryng in to the see, the processe and the cerymonyes wherof war to long to wryte.[2]

Thanne thaye Rode to the Abbey of Seynt Nicholas of blake monkys that stond by juste be them And all thaye brake ther fastes And so retornyd a a[3] geyne to Venys To the Dukys palace. Wher they had provyd for them a mervelows Dyner. wher at we pilgrymes war present and see them servyd. at which dyner ther was viii [f. 19r] Corse of soundery metys. and att every Corse the Trumpettes and the mynystrellys com inne a for them.

Ther was excedying myche plate. As basons Ewers wonders grett and of a straunge facion every iiii persons had a bason and an Ewer to washen ther hands Also ther was a grett Vesell of Sylver. And it had at every ende rounde rymys gylte and it was iiii cornarde And it had at every ende iiii rynges that ii men myght bere it betwyne them ffor to Cast owt the watyr of ther basons whanne they had washed ther handys

[f. 19v] Ther Dysshys ther platers ther Sawcers all was of Sylver and gylte.

And while they satt at dyner ther was parte of the Dukys Chapell singing dyverse balyttys.[4] and sumtyme they song with Orgones. And aftyr that ther cam on[e] of the Trompetores and he pleyd with the Organs all maner of messur the excellent conyng man that ever I hard with diverse Instrumentes I hard nor never see a ffor.

And whanne dyner was don the Duke sent to the pilgrymes gret basons full of marchepanyes And also commfytes and maluysey [f. 20r] And other Swete Wynyes as myche as ony man wold ete and drynke.

Thys don ther cam on that was disgysyd and he gestyd a for the Duke and the Marchose and the company and made them very mery.

And aftyr that ther came dauncers and some of them disgysyd in womenes clothes that daunsyd a gret while.

And after them come Tombelers both men And Children the marvelows ffelaws that ever I saw so myche that I canne nott writt it.

---

[1] stablyssyng: establishing.
[2] *Marriage of the Sea.
[3] 'a' repeated.
[4] balyttys: balletts, a form of part-song in dance rhythm.

[f. 20v] The other ffest was oon Corpis *X*ris*t*i day wher was the most Solemne procession that ever I saw. Ther went Pargent*es* of the old law and the new law Joynyng to gedyr The ffygmyes[1] of the blyssyd sacrament in such nowmb*er* and so apte and convenient for that ffest that it wold made any man Joyus to se it. And over that it was a grett merveyle to se the grett nowmbre of Religius ffolkes and of Scolys that we call Bachelors or ffelachippy*es*[2] Clothid all in *white* gramens *with* diverse bag*es*[3] on their [f. 21r] brestis which bar all light*es* of wondyr goodly facion. And be twyne every of the pagent*es* went lityll childern of both kynd*es* gloriously and rechely dressed beryng in ther handys ryche Cuppes or other vessales of gold and silver Rychely inamelyd and gylt ffull of plesaunt fflowers and well Smellyng which chyldern [r?]est the flowers upon the lord*es* and pylgrymes. They war dressed as Aungellis *with* clothe of gold and crymsyn velvet to order the seyd procession. The forme and manner therof excedyd all other that [f. 21v] ever I Saw. so myche that I canne nott wryte it.

The Duke Satt in Seynt Markes Churche in ryght hye astate in the Qwer[4] on *the* ryght syd *with* senyoryte which they call lord*es* in riche apparel as purpyll velvet cremsyn velvet ffyne Scarlett.

Also all the pylgrymes war commandyd to com in to the ffor seyd Qwer and ther we Satt all of the left syd on the quere. The Duke thus Syttyng *with* hys lord*es*, the seyd procession be ganne to com by hym a bowte viii of the clok and it was xii or the seyd procession myght [f. 22r] Com oonys a bowt passyng by as faste as they myght goo but on tyme.

Thanne the Duke rose up *with* hys lord*es* and company to folow the fforsayd procession He commaundyd hys lordys that they shuld in the procession every oon of them take a Pylgryme on hys Right-hande hys servaunt*es* gevyng to us grett Candyls of wax whych Candelys eve*ry* pylgrim bar a-way the procession doon at hys owen plesur. We procedyd owt of [the dukes palace *deleted*] Seynt Markes Churche in to the Dukys pales, and so went procession *with* inne the seyd place be cause it was [f. 22v] Reyne wedyr and so retornyd in to the Churche a geyne of Seynt Marke and ther made ende of the seyd Procession.

Sonday aftyr Corpus *X*ris*t*i Day, the xiiii day of June we dep*a*rtyd from Venys in a lytyll bott whyche bott browght us to the Shippe that lay iiii myle *with*owt the Castellys a good new shippe whiche mad nev*er* Jorney a fore of viii C tunne, The name of the patrone was callyd Thomas Dodo.[5]

Tuesday, the xvi day of [f. 23r] June, whiche was the translac*io*n of Seynt Richard,[6] a bowt v of the Clok in the mornyng we mad sayle with scace Wynde.

[1] *ffygmyes*: sacred elements, from the Latin *figmenta*.
[2] *ffelachippys*: fellowships.
[3] *bags*: badges.
[4] *Qwer*: Choir.
[5] *Thomas Dodo*: a member of the patrician Duodo family of Venice, who may be the same Tommaso Duodo who served as 'Lord of the Arsenal' in 1501. Lane, *Venetian Ships*, pp. 192–3. De Bainville was shown at the Arsenal the arms of one 'Francisco Dodo' who had 'fought his ship against 25 *Turkish* Galleys, run several of them a-ground, and forced the rest to retire very much shattered', *Travels*, I, p. 528. The Villa Duodo was built during the 1590s at Monselice, near Padua, by Vincenzo Scamozzi (1548–1616), a pupil of Palladio.
[6] *Seynt Richard*: probably St Richard of Chichester (1197–1253), Bishop of Chichester and patron saint of Sussex.

Thursday, the xviii of June, we cam to Ruyne[1] in histria x. myle from Parens,[2] C myle and x. from Venys. Ther we went a lond and lay ther all nyght. ffryday in the morning we hard messe.

ffriday, the xix day of June a lityll a for nyght we com all to the Shippe a geyn.

Ther we lay Satyrday all Daye at a naker[3] in the havyn ventus erat *contrarius*.[4]

Sonnday a for Midsom day [f. 23v] a bowyt vii of the cloke in the mornyng we made Sayle And passyd by the Costes of Slavone and histria and also pole[5] which ys xxx myle from parence a good havyn ffor many Shippy*es* and galyes towche ther rather thane at Parence / We passyd also by Gulfe of [Zara?][6] that ys the entre in to hungeri.

---

[1] Rovigno.

[2] Poreč (Parenzo).

[3] *at a naker*: at anchor.

[4] *ventus erat contrarius*: the wind was contrary.

[5] Pola.

[6] Probably Gulf of Zara (Zadar) but the word is not written clearly and is smudged or overwritten.

# 11.  *c.*1521–*c.*1526 AND 1532–6 – REGINALD POLE

**Reginald Pole (1500–58)** (**Plate 6**), was a cardinal and Archbishop of Canterbury.[1] His father was a cousin of Henry VII and his mother, Margaret (Plantaganet) Pole (1473–1541), Countess of Salisbury, was the daughter of George, Duke of Clarence (1449–78), the brother of Edward IV.[2] At Oxford University (*c.*1512–*c.*1519) he was tutored by William Latimer (*c.*1457–1545), a friend of Erasmus and Thomas More (1478–1535), and, possibly, the scholar and physician Thomas Linacre (**item 5** and **Plate 15**). Pole travelled in *c.*1521 to Padua, a city under Venetian control since 1405, and the Signoria honoured him as a visiting dignitary with close royal connections, lodging him in the Palazzo Roccabonella (formerly the home of Pietro Roccabonella, a Venetian-born professor of medicine at Padua), thereby following the distinguished tradition of William Grocyn, Thomas Linacre, William Latimer, Cuthbert Tunstall (1474–1559) and Richard Pace (*c.*1483–1536), who had also studied at Padua.[3]

Although Pole's time is often assumed to have focused primarily on Padua, Robert Barrington has recently demonstrated that the 'description of Pole's circle as Paduan is a misnomer, as it was as much centred on Venice as Padua … he probably maintained a house in Padua, but was often staying in Venice even during the course of his studies'. A letter from Pole's domestic chaplain George Lily (Lilly) (d. 1559) to the humanist reformer Thomas Starkey (*c.*1495–1538) remarked that Pole 'prefers this air [at Venice] to that of Padua' and Barrington has traced Pole's residential itinerary at Venice and Padua during the mid-1530s.

In 1535, for example, Pole lived in the Santa Croce *sestiere* of Venice until 2 July; he then went to stay with his close friend Alvise Priuli in Padua, while his servants remained in Venice. They then moved to 'my lord's villa at Murano, and at Venice in the house of Messer Edmondo [Harvell]' (**item 12**). However, Pole found Harvell's residence to be 'small and cold and foul' and by 21 October he had moved to 'a fine house on the Grand

---

[1] Pole was not a priest for most of his life but was created cardinal in December 1536 by Pope Paul III and then priest-cardinal by Pope Paul IV in December 1555. He was finally ordained as a priest in March 1556.

[2] *ODNB*, s.v. Pole's father, Sir Richard Pole (1462–1505), was the son of Edith St John, the half-sister of Lady Margaret Beaufort, the mother of Henry VII. Pole's mother was executed in May 1541 at the order of Henry VIII after Pole refused to attend the king's summons to return to England. Other executed members of Pole's Plantagenet family included his mother's father, George, Duke of Clarence; her brother, Edward Plantagenet (1475–99), Earl of Warwick; his eldest brother, Henry (1492–1538), 1st Baron Montague; and his sister Jane's brother-in-law, Edward Neville (*c.*1481–1538). His youngest sister Ursula married Henry Stafford (b. 1501), 1st Baron Stafford, whose father Edward Stafford (1478–1521), 3rd Duke of Buckingham, and grandfather, Henry Stafford (1455–89), 2nd Duke of Buckingham, had also been executed as Plantagenet heirs. The Poles, Nevilles, Staffords and the Tudors all claimed descent from Edward III.

[3] Pole had also briefly visited the University of Padua in 1519. In 1521 his studies were supported by a £100 annual grant from Henry VIII. Barrington, 'Two Houses', p. 897.

Canal, between the house of Foscari and the ferry of St. Barnabas'. Still not content, on 14 November Bernardino Sandro reported to Thomas Starkey that 'Il Signore and all are well, at the house of M. Donato'. Barrington concludes that 'Pole's household was therefore not Paduan at all. If anything, it was Venetian, but a more accurate description would be peripatetic.'[1]

It should also be noted that Thomas Starkey's renowned polemical 'A Dialogue Between Pole and Lupset' (mainly written *c.* 1529–32 with a dedicatory letter to the king and some later revisions) was originally intended for Pole but then redirected towards Henry VIII. It offered the first major attempt to analyse comparatively the political state of monarchic England and the Venetian Republic, especially in terms of how Venetian models of mixed government (the rule of the doge, Senate and councils) and its civic humanism might be productively incorporated into English society.[2] Starkey was familiar with Venice and Padua, having first visited them in about 1522 with Reginald Pole and again later in the early 1530s, witnessing the MD there in 1533 of the physician Thomas Bill.[3] In his 'Dialogue' Starkey sought 'to correcte the fautys [faults] in our pollycy' under the English constitution by pointing to the example of Venice:

> the most nobul cyte of venyce, wych by the reson of the gud ordur & policy that therinys usyd, hath contynuyd above a thousand yerys in one ordur & state, where as the pepul also by the reson of theyr sobur & temperat dyat be as helthy & welthy as any pepul now I thynke lyvyng upon the erth, therfor mastur lup[set]. By statute made & commynly receyvyd concerning our dyat we must be compellyd at the first to follow thes men in soburnes [soberness] & temperance & then you schold never have any occasion to dowte therof, nor feare the stabylyte of our prosperouse state, & gud pollycy specially as I sayd yf we may so tempur our polytyk ordur & rule that theyr schal rest no faute theryn, for that ys the sure ground of the conservation of the commyn wele in the polytyke body ... (f. 109r)

More controversially, Starkey also praised Venice's republican election of its doges, pointedly comparing it to the monarchic and aristocratic rule of England which could be prone to 'daunger of tyranny' (f. 111r):

> I can not wel tel you that yf hyt were restraynyd as I have sayd befor ther wold not be so grete ambycyon therof as ther ys now, for in venyce ys no grete ambycyouse desire to be ther duke, bycause hye ys restreyned to gud ordur & polytyke , so wyth us also schold be of our kyng yf hys powar were temperyd aftur the maner before descrybyd whereas now every man desyryth hyt bycause he may make hymselfe & al hys frendys for ever rych, he may subdue hys ennemys at hys pleasure, al ys at hys cummandement, & wyl & thys hathe movyd cyvyle war in tyme past notwythstondyng thys ordynance of succession, but we wyl not entur no ferther in dysputacyon now ... (f. 111v)[4]

---

[1] *LP*, IX, items 512, 659, 673, 819. Barrington, 'Two Houses', p. 899. Sandro served as Pole's butler, household manager and transcriber of manuscripts.

[2] *ODNB*, s.v. The only extant manuscript (TNA SP, Henry VIII, 1/90) seems a working draft (with the dedicatory letter in another hand) and may have come into the hands of Thomas Cromwell after Starkey's death in 1538. If a final presentation copy was sent to Henry VIII, it is now lost. Mayer, *Thomas Starkey*, pp. 89–105. Hadfield, *Literature*, pp. 21–4.

[3] Woolfson, *Padua*, pp. 213, 274. Bill's MD was also witnessed by Starkey's friend John Friar (MD Padua, 1536; d. 1561), Pole's servant Michael Throckmorton and Bartholomew Bainham. He later became physician to Henry VIII, Edward VI and Princess Elizabeth in 1549.

[4] TNA SP 1/90. Starkey, *Dialogue*, ed. Meyer, pp. 119, 122–3.

Heavily influenced by his reading of Gasparo Contarini's *De magistratibus et republica Venetorum* (Paris, 1543) Starkey promulgated, as demonstrated by these short quotations, an idealized perspective on Venetian/Paduan humanism and its aristocratic republicanism. As Cameron Wood observes, Starkey adopted:

> the Venetian propagandist view that the perfect commonwealth could only be constructed and maintained through civic education of the natural rules, the nobility, who needed to study classical, political, medical and philosophical texts, which argued that rule by a mixed government was superior to the other political constitutions that Plato and Aristotle examined in *The Republic* and *Politics*.[1]

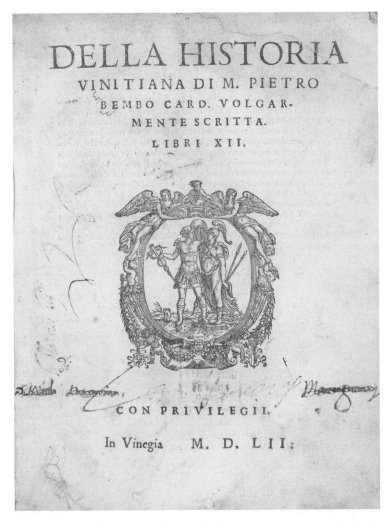

Figure 15.    Title page of Pietro Bembo, *Della historia vinitiana di m. Pietro Bembo card. volgarmente scritta. Libri XII*, Venice: Gualtero Scotto, 1552 edition. Special Collections, Brotherton Library, Strong Room for. 4vo 1552 BEM. By permission of Special Collections, Brotherton Library, University of Leeds.

[1] Wood, "'A commyn wele of true nobylyte'", p. 29.

Given the proximity of Venice and Padua, it is understandable that many of Pole's contacts at Padua possessed strong Venetian links. He was befriended by the leading Paduan humanist Pietro Bembo (1470–1547), the author of a major history of Venice, *Della historia vinitiana* (Venice: 1551) from the 1480s to 1513, who had been born at Venice and whose father Bernardo had served as an ambassador for the Venetian Republic to Austria, France, Florence and Rome. Pole was tutored by another distinguished Venetian-born scholar of Epirote Greek origins, Niccolò Leonico Tomeo (1456–1531), who had been professor of Greek at Venice (1504–12) with most of his writings published at Venice.[1] He was also taught by Lazzaro Bonamico (1477/8–1552), who was born in the Venetian town of Bassano del Grappa and had recently moved to Venice in 1527. Pole fostered wide-ranging contacts with numerous other notable Italian scholars and churchmen, including Pope Leo X's chief minister, Gianmatteo Giberti (1495–1543) who had been appointed as Bishop of Verona at the request of the Doge of Venice and later served as Apostolic Nuncio to Venice (1534–37); and Marcantonio Flaminio (1498–1550), a humanist poet born in Serravalle, a small village in the Veneto.

At Venice and Padua Pole also knew Jacopo Sadoleto (1477–1547), a noted opponent of John Calvin; Gianpietro Carafa (1476–1559), the future Pope Paul IV; Rodolfo Pio (1500–64), later a diplomat and cardinal; Otto Truchsess (1514–73), a German prince-bishop; the Pole Stanislaus Hosius (1504–79), later a cardinal; and two other churchmen who became cardinals, Cristoforo Madruzzo (1512–78) and Giovanni Morone (1509–80). He also befriended three notable scholars later condemned as heretics: Pier Paolo Vergerio the Younger (*c.*1498–1565), who was born in Istria then part of the Venetian Republic; the reformist theologian Pietro Martire Vermigli (Peter Martyr) (1499–1562); and the Venetian Bishop of Bergamo, Vittore Soranzo (1500–58). The young Belgian polemicist against Martin Luther, Christophe Longueil (1488–1522), died in Pole's household. He bequeathed to Pole his extensive library, resulting in Pole's first publication, a biography (1525) of Longueil. During his time at Padua Pole also became known to Erasmus through the English humanist Thomas Lupset (1495–1530). Pole's closest friend and lifelong companion was Alvise Priuli (d. 1560), a member of a wealthy Venetian banking family and brother of two Venetian doges, Lorenzo (1556–9) and Girolamo (1559–67).

A wide range of Englishmen were also associated with Pole at Padua and Venice during the 1520s and 1530s, although they were not necessarily members of his household. These included: Richard Morison (1513–56); John Friar (d. 1561), an illegitimate son of Cardinal Wolsey; Thomas Winter (d. after 1537); Thomas Lupset; Thomas Starkey; George Lily; and Pole's trusted agent and messenger Michael Throckmorton (Throgmorton) (*c.*1503–58).[2] Although Pole was not always resident at Padua, after his return there in 1532 it was regarded as the focal point for young English scholars abroad, not least because of Pole's distinguished academic reputation. The university was also of importance to visiting Englishmen because it was one of only two Italian universities

---

[1] Tomeo These included *Aristotelis Parva quae vocant Naturalia*, Bernardino Vitali, Venice 1523; *Opuscula*, Bernardino Vitali, Venice 1525; and *Conversio in latinum atque explanatio primi libri Aristotelis de partibus animalium*, G. Farri, Venice 1540.

[2] See **item 27** for his relative Arthur Throckmorton.

(Bologna was the other) 'to have reached a favourable opinion on the two questions related to the king's divorces'.[1]

Pole left Padua in about July 1526 and travelled through France back to England. He was sent on a diplomatic mission to Paris from October 1529 until summer 1530 to seek approval for Henry VIII's divorce from Catherine of Aragon. Clearly finding his position at court problematic (compounded by his lack of religious preferment), he left England again in early 1532, staying at Avignon and Carpentras before travelling via Verona to Padua where he took up residence again in October. At this time he befriended Cosmo Gheri (1513–37), the youthful Bishop of Fano, and the Venetian Gasparo Contarini (1483–1542), Ambassador to the Papacy and Emperor Charles V who was later appointed as cardinal and became a leading figure in the reform movement at Rome. Contarini is of special importance to this study because his *De magistratibus et republica Venetorum* (Paris, 1543) was translated into English by the soldier and courtier Lewis Lewkenor and published in 1599 as *The Common-Wealth and Government of Venice* (**item 35**).

Pole was called to Rome in July 1536 and strongly opposed the new religious order in England, as was made clear in his lengthy treatise, *Pro ecclesiasticae unitatis defensione* ('In Defence of Ecclesiastical Unity'), published at Rome in 1536 and presented to Henry VIII possibly by Michael Throckmorton.[2] It attacked the king's claim of royal supremacy over the English Church and vigorously defended the spiritual authority of the Pope. Pole was made a cardinal in December 1536 and appointed by Pope Paul III as head of the English Hospice at Rome in March 1538. He attended a conference at Nice in April–June 1538 when the English Ambassador, Sir Thomas Wyatt (**item 13** and **Plate 16**), tried but failed to establish meaningful negotiations with him. Henry VIII continued to view Pole as a constant threat to both his secular and religious authority. He was attainted in May 1539 and outlawed from England, prompting him to head back to Italy in September.

During summer 1541 Pole, while residing at Viterbo, developed a close relationship with the aristocratic poet Vittoria Colonna (1490/92–1547), Marchioness of Pescara. After the execution of Pole's mother in May of that year the marchioness treated him as a son (although she was only ten years older than him). She was also a friend of Contarini and a spiritual mentor to the artist Michelangelo Buonarroti (1475–1564) who dedicated fulsome sonnets to her and sketched her portrait when she was about fifty (British Museum, London). She also had her portrait painted in oils, probably in the 1520s (Museu nacional d'art de Catalunya), by the Venetian artist Sebastiano del Piombo (*c*.1485–1547) who had trained at Venice with Titian and Jacopo Palma il Vecchio (*c*.1480–1528). With other humanist scholars, notably Marcantonio Flaminio (fl. 1540s) and Pietro Carnesecchi (1508–67), Pole was involved in the production of the popular devotional tract *Beneficio di Cristo* ('The Benefit of Christ's Death') published in 1543 with reputedly over 40,000 copies sold at Venice alone. In October 1542 Pole served as one of the three papal legates to the Council of Trent and attended the reconvened Council in December 1545, returning to Rome in November 1546. Throughout this period, he was under constant threat of assassination from Henry VIII's agents, especially the notorious mercenary Ludovico dall'Armi (da l'Armi) (**item 12**).

---

[1] Barrington, 'Two Houses', p. 902.
[2] Overell, *Italian Reform*, p. 265.

At some point, probably during the 1540s, Pole also had his portrait (Hermitage Museum, St Petersburg) painted by Sebastiano del Piombo (**Plate 6**). He worked for much of his career at Rome which is where it is likely that he painted Pole. Sebastiano was supported by Michelangelo and they worked closely together to challenge the dominance of Raphael's workshop over papal commissions and young artists coming to Rome to study. By the 1520s Sebastiano had established himself as Rome's most renowned portrait painter, leading to his portrait of Vittoria Colonna and a series of acclaimed images of Clement VII (Pope, 1523–34) which earned him the office of keeper of the papal seal (made of lead, hence 'del Piombo'). His striking portrait of Cardinal Pole echoes a formula based on Raphael's painting of Pope Julius II which provided a template for the iconography of high-ranking ecclesiastical portraits. Sebastiano's image captures what is known from contemporary descriptions of Pole's facial features: thin-faced and ascetic with an aquiline nose and a large, often unkempt bushy beard. It has been proposed that Vittoria Colonna may have commissioned this portrait after promising in 1546 to obtain one for Cardinal Cristoforo Madruzzo (1512–78), who was himself painted by Titian (São Paulo Museum of Art, Brazil).

Pole's attempts at conciliation after the death of Henry VIII and accession of Edward VI, via Protector Somerset, were unsuccessful, not least because a western rebellion in 1549 called for Pole's restoration and his membership of the royal council. He was a strong candidate for the papacy after the death of Pope Paul III in October 1549 but, instead, Giovanni Maria Ciocchi (1487–1555) was elected as Pope Julius III and worked amicably with Pole. The accession of Queen Mary in July 1553 opened the possibility of his return to England, although the imperial ambassador at Venice strongly opposed his membership of a papal legation to England formed in early August. By late summer 1554 it seemed more likely that Pole would return to England, following his expression of approval of Mary's marriage to Philip of Spain. On 20 November he crossed from Calais to Dover, his attainder was reversed two days later and on 30 November he led the formal reconciliation of the English realm to the papacy.

Succeeding Thomas Cranmer, who was burnt at the stake on 21 March 1556, Pole became Archbishop of Canterbury on the following day until the accession of Queen Elizabeth in November 1558. The papacy of his long-time opponent, Gianpietro Carafa, elected as Pope Paul IV in May 1555, led to the withdrawal of Pole's legatine power in April 1557. The difficulty of his position had been exacerbated by the arrival in England in March 1557 of King Philip II of Spain, who was viewed as a political opponent of the Papal States. Although Pole was summoned to Rome by the Pope in June 1557, he declined to go since he knew that he would face the Inquisition there. Instead, he sent to Rome in August Nicolò Ormanetto, his datary (an office of the Roman Curia), to deliver personally to the Pope an *apologia* and to express his willingness to return to Rome, even if it meant his imprisonment. However, by September 1558 Pole was seriously ill and he died on 11 November, during an influenza epidemic, some twelve hours after Queen Mary's demise.

# 12.  *c.*1520s–1550 – EDMUND (SIGISMUND) HARVELL[1]

The community of scholars and churchmen associated with Reginald Pole (**Plate 6**) has usually been taken to suggest that the major point of intellectual community for Englishmen visiting the Veneto was Padua rather than Venice itself. However, as already explained, the work of Robert Barrington has demonstrated that while Pole's academic and religious associates in Padua were certainly a dominant cultural and theological force during Henry VIII's reign, the residence of the merchant and English representative at Venice, **Edmund Harvell (d. 1550)** provided a major secular focus for Englishmen in this part of Italy. He was exceptionally well connected within the political, commercial and religious circles of the city, having been resident there since at least the 1520s when he acted as 'banker and aide both to the English community and the English ambassador'.[2] He was also used to receiving and sending diplomatic mail and, in effect, occupied the role of an unofficial secretary to the English embassy. During 1529–30 he received financial payments from Henry VIII, apparently with the expectation that he would pass them on to Richard Croke (*c.*1489–1558) who had been delegated by the king to elicit a favourable opinion on the royal divorce from the University of Padua. He also housed the possessions of John Stokesley (1475–1539), Bishop of London, who was Croke's assistant on this mission.[3] As already noted, this endeavour proved successful with the University of Padua, along with that of Bologna, publicly supporting Henry's marital position.

Harvell was from 1535 English Agent at Venice and in January 1539 Thomas Cromwell (1485–1540) appointed him as English Ambassador to the Republic.[4] Furthermore, with his extensive commercial and personal links with other nations, most notably the Germans and their trading house the *Fondaco dei Tedeschi, Harvell could provide his English visitors with valuable contacts, not only with Venetian and other Italian Catholics but also with northern European Protestants, leading Barrington to conclude, that 'the house of Edmund Harvell in Venice was the true centre of the English community'.[5] His residence acted as a kind of refuge and meeting point for English visitors to the city:

---

[1] Edmund Harvell is named as 'Sigismund' and 'Arruel' in a posthumous inventory of his goods, compiled 3 February 1550 at Venice. Archivio di Stato, Proprio Mobili, R 16.C.152. Brown, 'Inventory', p. 72. 'Sigismund' was an alternative to Edmund, sometimes with distinct Protestant connotations. Harvell's Protestant brother Richard went into exile at Padua and Venice during Mary's reign. Garrett, *Marian Exiles,* pp. 180–81, 346–7.

[2] *LP*, IV.iii, items 6491, 6540, 6595, 6607.

[3] *LP*, IV.iii, items 6192, 6235, 6595, 6607, 6620, 6670, 6694–6, 6786. In Sept. 1533 Stokesley christened Princess Elizabeth, the future queen.

[4] *CSP Venice*, 1545, item 354, 1550, p. 616.

[5] In 1537 Harvell married Apollonis Uttinger, the daughter of a Protestant German merchant. Venice, Archivio di Stato, Proprio Vadimoni R.33.51ᵛ. Brown, 'Inventory', pp. 70–71. Barrington, 'Two Houses', p. 905.

For those Englishmen in Venice who knew Pole but also acted independently of his household – which is in fact most of those usually mentioned as his household – the focal point was undoubtedly Edmund Harvell. Indeed, it may be that as a clearing house for English travellers and scholars, Edmund Harvell was at least as important as Pole. He was often visited by many of the English Paduans, including Pole himself. [1]

Despite living away from England from the 1520s until his death in 1550, Harvell always seemed well connected at the English court. His business interests were probably looked after by his brother John who was a London merchant. He was able to maintain amicable relations with Thomas Cromwell right up to his execution in July 1540 and also fostered contacts with Sir Anthony Denny (1501–49), Sir John Russell, Sir Francis Weston and Thomas Wriothesley. He made productive use of numerous English visitors to Venice – now often known only through their fleeting connection with Harvell – by asking them to carry messages and correspondence back to England. [2] Another important messenger for Harvell was the Venetian merchant Hieronimo Molins who travelled between Venice and England on several occasions and carried his messages for various members of the English court. [3]

Records from 1541 indicate that a significant number of Englishmen were living with Harvell during that year, including John Hoby, Richard Shelley (c.1513–87), and Raphael White. Another young man, John Denny, the nephew of the courtier Sir Anthony Denny, stayed with Harvell for several years, learning 'luting, vauting and th'Italian tongue'. When he was required to return to England by Christmas 1543 Denny begged his uncle to allow him to stay longer, claiming that 'having made a good beginning in learning, [he] begs leave to stay a year or two longer, so that it may be known he has been in Italy'. [4] The Hobys, in particular, provided a useful and lasting court connection for Harvell. When the young Thomas Hoby (1530–66) was passing through Venice in 1547 he wrote in his diary:

> Here I lay in Mr. Edmund Harvells house, Ambassador resident for the King's Majesty, where I found also Mr. Jhon Yong, with whom I laye, Mr. George Speake, Mr. Thomas Fitzwilliam, Mr Thomas Straung, and diverse other Englishmen.

Returning to the city three years later, he found that Harvell had died but noted:

> In Venice I rested a daie with Mr. Jhon Arundell, where I visited Mr. Edmund Harvelle's wyff, whom she had buried that summer, complaining greatlie of the loss of so worthie a husbande (as he was indeed), as gentle a gentleman as ever served king, of whom all Englishmen found great lacke. [5]

Harvell was also an able scholar and linguist who involved himself in Venetian literary circles. From the 1540s, following Henry VIII's break with the Catholic Church, he seems to have been especially sympathetic towards Protestant writers. In 1544 he sought to assist Francesco Strozzi who was being questioned by the Inquisition, following his

[1] Barrington, 'Two Houses', pp. 896, 902, 904.

[2] Barrington, 'Two Houses', pp. 910–11, recording various English messengers for Harvell called Mr Farmer, Mr Perkins, John Walker, Cokerel, John Hutton, Henry Farthing, Mr Rowse, Thomas Theobald, Anthony Budgegood, Ralph Sadler, Mr Bucler and John Leigh.

[3] *LP*, IV.iii, items 6491, 6540, 7686.

[4] *CSP Venice*, V, 1542, item 282. *LP*, XVIII, items 576, 725, 714. Barrington, 'Two Houses', pp. 903–4.

[5] Hoby, 'Booke of the Travaile' (BL Egerton MS 2148), p. 8, **item 17**.

translation of Coelius Secundus Curione's *Pasquini in estasi*; and in the same year Curione dedicated to him his *Arameus, seu de Providentia Dei.* In 1548 Ortensio Lando in his *Lettere di molte valorose donne*, described Harvell as the 'protector of great authority and blessed with great judgement'.[1] His most significant literary connection was with the poet and satirist Pietro Aretino (1492–1556) who had settled in Venice in 1527 and was a close friend of Titian. While it is well known that Aretino dedicated a collection of his letters to Henry VIII, it is rarely mentioned that it was Harvell who arranged for the presentation copy of the volume to be sent to the king.[2] Aretino also remained on friendly terms with Harvell's widow Apollonis after Harvell's death in January 1550.[3]

The mercenary Ludovico dall'Armi (*c.*1515–47) has already been mentioned in the context of a possible assassination attempt on Cardinal Reginald Pole (**item 11**). Harvell came across this troublesome individual, and their contacts provide a telling example of the personal challenges facing an English representative at Venice within the complex political and diplomatic interactions of England, Rome and Venice during the 1540s. Ludovico was the nephew of Cardinal Campeggio (1474–1539) who had been sent to England in 1528/29 by Pope Clement VII during Henry VIII's attempts to annul his marriage with Catherine of Aragon (finally achieved in May 1533). In 1544 Henry was in France with the English forces against François I under the command of Sir John Russell (**item 13**). Dall'Armi managed to inveigle his way into the English camp, despite Russell's suspicions over his character and motives, and persuaded Henry to appoint him as an official agent for hiring Italian mercenaries to fight with the English forces against the French.[4]

Dall'Armi was sent to Venice to seek recruits but Harvell distrusted him on sight, not least because of his known connections with Rome and his intimacy with the papal legate at Venice and other French residents in the city. He felt strongly enough to write personally to Henry VIII on 25 January, noting:

> S[or] Ludovico de Larmy, your Majesty's servant, has since appeared with letters from your Council to me, to help him in your service. Before his coming was a rumour that you designed to make men in Italy, but it is now more confirmed. He pretends great devotion to you, but here I have observed him to have great familiarity with the Bishop's legate and others of the French faction. I esteem this as done for some policy, but must report it. He warned me of his visiting the Legate, his old friend, to see if he could learn anything.

He added that afterwards the French legate had advised him that he held dall'Armi in 'great suspicion'.[5] However, within two weeks news came from Brussels to the English court that the Ambassador of Ferrara there had reported that 'Ludovico de Liarmi, a gentleman Boloignese, the King's servant, is much spoken of in Italy and may have 6,000

---

[1] Barrington, 'Two Houses', p. 908.

[2] Harvell's successor at English Ambassador to Venice, Peter Vannes (Pietro Vanni) (**item 18**) also seems to have been involved at the English court in the delivery of Aretino's letters to Henry VIII.

[3] *LP*, XVII, item 841. They later fell out when Aretino claimed that Harvell had not passed money on to him which Henry VIII had sent in reward for his dedication. Barrington, 'Two Houses', p. 909.

[4] Harrison, 'Henry the Eighth's Gangster', pp. 265–74. Russell noted in a letter, 20 Aug. 1544, to Secretary of State William Paget that 'he nor yet any other Italian should have tarried and seen our doings here, for I know their natures and treasons'.

[5] *LP*, XX.i, item 87.

Italians to serve the King if he will'.[1] By 1 March Harvell felt obliged to revise his opinion (at least publicly) of dall'Armi and he wrote to Henry VIII that 'Ludovico de Larme entertains many captains at great charge, looking for Henry's commission, and evidently loves and esteems his Majesty'.[2] On 29 March Harvell advised Henry that dall'Armi was so successful in his recruiting campaign that he was under threat of assassination from the French:

> Ludovico de Larmye entertains a great band and is here in peril of life from the Bishop and the French part, for 12 men were lately sent by Piero Maria de San Secondo, the French king's captain, to slay him. He is apt and willing as any young man in Italy.[3]

Officials at both Venice and Rome remained much more sceptical and regarded dall'Armi as a highly untrustworthy individual who was now problematically ensconced as a servant of the heretical King of England and arch-enemy of the Apostolic See. Cardinal Ardinghelli (1503–47), who directed secret affairs on behalf of Pope Paul III, remained determined to remove dall'Armi from Venice and impressed upon Francesco Venier (1489–1556), the Venetian Ambassador at Rome (and later Doge, 1554–6), that dall'Armi posed a genuine threat to the internal security of both Venice and Rome.[4] Venier was instructed by Ardinghelli, and even the Pope in person, to ensure that dall'Armi was removed from Venice but Venier reasonably stated that the importance of maintaining good Anglo-Venetian relations made it difficult to expel any official agent of Henry VIII.[5]

Following yet more pressure from the papal nuncio at Venice, the Council decreed that all foreign enlistment was to be banned throughout Venetian territories. But when dall'Armi was summoned to appear before them, Harvell's secretary, Baldassare Alcherio (Balthasar Alterius?), came instead, claiming that dall'Armi was away from the city on official business for Henry VIII.[6] Eventually, he was allowed to continue his residence in Venice but, given his volatile temperament, he was identified in early August as one of several young thugs who had attacked a Venetian security patrol led by the city's Captain of Boats. Yet again, however, his association with the English king made it impossible for the authorities to prosecute him, even though other members of his unruly entourage were arrested, interrogated and possibly tortured for drawing weapons against Venetian officials. However, it was then claimed on 11 August that dall'Armi had hired three assassins to murder an individual named Curio Bura at Treviso. He and his associates were promptly declared outlaws with arrest warrants issued.[7] Harvell was obliged to register a half-hearted protest and, despite his clear reservations over dall'Armi, he wrote personally to Henry VIII on 3 August, claiming that he had been framed by agents of the

[1] *LP*, XX.i, item 192.
[2] *LP*, XX.i, item 292.
[3] *LP*, XX.i, item 447.
[4] Alessandro Farnese (1468–1549), Pope Paul III (1534–49), had decreed the second and final excommunication of Henry VIII (1538) and opened the Council of Trent (1545). He was the father of Pier Luigi Farnese (1503–47), 1st Duke of Parma, and commissioned Michelangelo to direct the construction of St Peter's Basilica, Rome.
[5] *CSP Venice*, V, 1545, items 334–5.
[6] Ibid., V, 1545, items 337–8.
[7] Ibid., V, 1545, items 344–8.

Pope, while also pointedly noting that he was renowned for his 'proud, vindictive and seditious nature'.[1]

Dall'Armi fled from Venice to the English court and once again managed to ingratiate himself there, eliciting an English diplomatic request that he should be granted by the Venetian Council a safe-conduct for no less than five years. After much debate and controversy, further diplomatic pressure from England resulted in dall'Armi being readmitted to Venice and the new Doge, Francesco Donato, even wrote to Henry VIII, claiming that the delay in their decision had been caused by the death of his predecessor, Doge Pietro Lando.[2] In New Year 1546 dall'Armi headed southwards across the Alps, bearing a letter of protection from Henry stating that he was his Majesty's 'noble and beloved familiar'. Once again, he was supposedly seeking to recruit mercenaries to serve with the English army against the French but he continued to attract controversy wherever he went. He was accused of complicity in the murder of an Italian banker, Ser Mafio Bernardo, but his former reliance upon his association with Henry VIII vanished with the king's death on 28 January 1547.[3]

Dall'Armi fled from Venice to Milan but was soon identified there and arrested. Once the Signoria had received from Harvell on 2 March official confirmation of the English king's death, renewed demands were made for dall'Armi's return to Venice.[4] Official notes of communications between Harvell and the Venetian authorities were recorded and preserved in the Venetian Archives:

> In the matter of Lodovico da l'Armi the ambassador of the King of England, Harvel, stated that this affair caused him such great pain that he knew not what to say. He had at all times known the courtesy of this State towards his King, and the respect had for him, both heretofore when Da l'Armi perpetrated those outrages here and at Treviso, after which he was granted the safe-conduct at the request of his Majesty, to whom it gave extreme satisfaction, as also on this last occasion, on which Harvel acknowledged that not only had this man offended the majesty of the Republic, but also the majesty of his [Harvel's] King, who has been greatly deceived in him, as frequently happens to Princes with regard to their servants. That he wrote about this at the time of the affair at Treviso, and therefore Da l'Armi always bore him ill will, and laid many plots against him, and lately when Da l'Armi was summoned by the Chiefs, Harvel came to the Signoria to know what he was to write to the King.[5]

This time, dall'Armi could no longer hide behind the personal favour of Henry VIII. He arrived back at Venice on 29 April under armed guard and was interrogated that evening in handcuffs. On 11 May he was sentenced to death and on 14 May, by a motion of the *Council of Ten and Junta, he was taken to St Mark's Square where, according to his official sentence, he was to be placed 'between the Two Columns, where on a lofty scaffold his head shall be severed from his shoulders so that he die'.[6] While Harvell seems to have

[1] *LP*, XX.ii, item 124, 287.

[2] *CSP Venice*, V, 1545, items 363, 365–7.

[3] Ibid., V, 1545, item 367, 1546, items 420–24, 432–3; 439–40, 1547, items 452, 455. *LP*, XXI.i, items 466, 655, 667.

[4] *CSP Venice*, V, 1547, items 449, 456–9, 474, 476, 480.

[5] Ibid., V, 1547, item 466.

[6] Ibid., V, 1547, items 487, 495, 497, 500, 502, 508. The Junta (Zonta) refers to additional members of the *Senate.

left no written response to this execution, he would have been much relieved to know that his dealings with such a problematic and disreputable individual as dall'Armi were at an end.

Harvell continued to serve English interests at Venice for three more years before his death in January 1550. His duties and business dealings had made him rich enough to be buried in the basilica of *Santi Giovanni e Paolo, a traditional mausoleum for doges where only the wealthiest foreigners were usually interred.[1] His household at Venice, therefore, should be held alongside Pole's at Padua when considering the significant presence of Englishmen in the two cities during the reign of Henry VIII. Although they may have harboured differences of religious belief and monarchic loyalty, Harvell always seemed happy to liaise with both Catholics and Protestants at Venice and Padua. There were also regular interchanges between Pole's and Harvell's respective circles and Harvell maintained friendly relations with Pole himself until at least the late 1530s. Robert Barrington concludes that although there must have been some key differences of opinion between Pole and Harvell, 'there is very definitely an air of intellectual unity about these Englishmen abroad'. Through their respective contacts with numerous Englishmen, Italians and commercial gentlemen of other nations, 'the intellectual "spirituali"' and the protestant merchants at Venice 'were able to come together to influence the English community'. No less importantly, the 'strong intellectual contacts between Englishmen and Venice clearly placed the Republic in a unique position to influence English political philosophy in the 1530s and beyond'.[2]

---

[1] His family paid 50 ducats and 5 grossi to purchase a tomb there from the Dominicans. Brown, 'Inventory', p. 71.

[2] Barrington, 'Two Houses', pp. 212-13.

# 13. 1527 – THOMAS WYATT AND SIR JOHN RUSSELL

The brief embassy to Venice in 1527 of **Thomas Wyatt (*c*.1503–42) (Plate 16)** and **Sir John Russell (*c*.1485–1555)** illustrates the complex political challenges and extreme personal dangers faced by English diplomats in Italy at this period. Wyatt is now chiefly remembered as one of the most talented lyric poets of the Henrician court. He was the son of Henry VIII's Treasurer of the Chamber, Sir Henry Wyatt (*c*.1460–1536), a distinguished soldier and long-serving courtier to Henry VII and Henry VIII. For those with the requisite language and negotiating skills, international diplomacy often became a key part of a prominent English courtier's public duties. Sir Henry Wyatt had accompanied Henry VIII to Calais (1513 and 1519) and to the Field of the Cloth of Gold (1520). The family's residence at Allington Castle, Kent, brought them into close contact with the Boleyns who lived at nearby Hever Castle. The eldest son, Thomas studied at St John's College, Cambridge, a centre of humanist learning. His first experience of international diplomacy came in April 1526 when he travelled with Sir Thomas Chenye (*c*.1485–1558) to Bordeaux to congratulate François I on his release from imprisonment by the Emperor Charles V and 'to urge him to enter a league with the Italian powers against imperial aggrandizement'.[1] At the Battle of Pavia (24 February 1525) the French army led by François I had been defeated by the combined Habsburg Imperial-Spanish forces, leading to the imprisonment of the French King by Charles V and, for the French, the humiliating Treaty of Madrid (January 1526).

**John Russell, first Earl of Bedford**, was fluent in both French and Italian, and possibly Spanish, and may have lived abroad during his youth. He became intimate with Henry VIII through their shared interest in jousting and court tournaments. In 1514 he was sent to Paris as one of the English observers of the marriage of Henry's sister, Princess Mary Tudor (1496–1533), to Louis XII of France. Working closely with Wolsey, he conspired against another Plantagenet claimant to the throne and relative of Reginald Pole (**item 11** and **Plate 6**), Richard de la Pole (1480–1525).[2] In 1520 Russell accompanied Henry VIII and Sir Henry Wyatt to the Field of the Cloth of Gold. He served as a special ambassador to France from July to September 1523 and was often during abroad the next two years as a royal envoy in France and Italy. He sometimes travelled in disguise as a merchant when carrying funds for military operations and participated in the Battle of Pavia.

---

[1] *ODNB*, s.v. Brigden and Woolfson, 'Wyatt in Italy', pp. 464–6, 471–3. This account of Wyatt's embassy draws extensively on their informative article.

[2] Richard was the son of John de la Pole (1442–92), 2nd Duke of Suffolk, and Elizabeth of York (1444–*c*.1503), the younger sister of Edward IV.

On 22 May 1526 a league for the defence of Italy was agreed, known as the League of Cognac, with François I, Pope Clement VII, Venice and Francesco Maria Sforza (the recently deposed Duke of Milan) as its signatories and with Henry VIII as a guarantor. However, as defence turned to aggression two of its military leaders – Francesco Maria della Rovere (1490–1538), Duke of Urbino and Captain-General of the Venetian army, and Francesco Guicciardini (1483–1540), Lieutenant-General of the Papal army – sought to liberate Milan and other cities in Lombardy from the imperial army. But neither François I nor Henry VIII were inclined to offer significant practical or financial support to the League's cause and relations between the Pope and the emperor rapidly deteriorated to the point that Charles V was even threatening to disavow his obedience to the papacy. Imperial forces threatened Mantua and the Papal States, the League's military forces were outmanoeuvred, and the Venetian Senate desperately called on Henry VIII to act in their support.[1]

On 7 January 1527 Thomas Wyatt was sent with Sir John Russell to Italy to attend the court of Pope Clement VII at Rome. Wyatt was probably glad of an opportunity to leave England because he had recently separated from his wife and was regarded by some as too intimate with Anne Boleyn whom Henry VIII had begun to pursue in spring 1526. Clement VII, as Giulio de'Medici (1478–1534), had been Cardinal Proctor of England (1514) and continued to hope for friendly relations with Henry VIII in order to bind the English King to the defence of Italy against imperial incursions. Wyatt and Russell first met with François I at Poissy and then travelled via Paris, Lyons and Chambéry towards Piedmont under the protection of Charles, Duke of Savoy. They were advised that they must cross the mountains quickly otherwise imperial troops might cut them off. Leaving most of their party to follow, Russell and Wyatt pressed on by riding day and night, until they reached Savona on 28 January from where they took a boat for Civitavecchia. Arriving on 4 February they were welcomed by the renowned Admiral Andrea Doria (1466–1560) who escorted them with an armed guard to Rome where they arrived two days later. They stayed with Gregorio (Sir Gregory) Casale, English Envoy at Rome and had a papal audience on either 7 or 8 February, handing over 25,000 ducats to assure Pope Clement of Henry VIII's amity. However, on 28 January the Pope agreed a three-year truce with the imperial forces which created fears in Venice that 'this truce would kindle a greater war and bring the ruin, not only of Italy, but of all Christendom'.[2]

Russell offered to go to Venice to consult the Signoria and was perhaps intending some duplicity. The Milanese ambassador suspected that he was promising the Pope that he would persuade the Venetians to support the armistice while tacitly intending to advise against it. He set out on 24 February with Wyatt from Rome for Venice, almost certainly intending to play the situation there either to firm up the peace or intensify the war. The journey through Lombardy was perilous because of the threat of capture by imperial troops or brigands but, instead, another crisis ensued. Somewhere in the region of Terni, Narni or Rieti (contemporary reports differ) Russell broke his leg when his horse stumbled, necessitating his return to Rome carried in a litter. Clement VII refused Casale's offer to go to Venice instead of Russell and so the youthful Wyatt (then only twenty-three or twenty-four) was thrust into the diplomatic limelight:

---

[1] Brigden and Woolfson, 'Wyatt in Italy', pp. 474–5.
[2] Ibid., p. 478.

Casale instructed Russell to send his commission to Prothonotary Giambattista Casale, English ambassador in Venice. Thus Wyatt went on alone, beyond advice or instruction from Rome or England, to the Signoria of Venice and to the Duke of Ferrara, who were poised to take decisions of the greatest consequence.[1]

Wyatt arrived at Venice on about 1 March 1527 and probably stayed at Casale's usual lodgings there at *San Giorgio Maggiore. It seems likely that Wyatt also met with Edmund Harvell (**item 12**), as is suggested by a letter sent by Harvell to Russell on 12 June 1526, just before he and Wyatt embarked from England for their Italian embassy. Addressing Russell as 'Mag. viro Joanni Russello equiti aurato, unico patrono suo optimo, Londini' (To the great man John Russell, distinguished knight, his best and only patron, of London), Harvell recorded various items of Italian news and offered his personal services to Russell. Given that Harvell was probably expecting Russell and Wyatt to arrive together at Venice, he could have been of considerable assistance to Wyatt who was now without his far more experienced diplomatic colleague.[2] On 2 March Wyatt and Casale formally attended at the Ducal Palace and went before the College (*Collegio), the Republic's executive committee responsible for issues of peace or war. Venice was of crucial importance in these negotiations between England, France and the Papacy because it was the most powerful of all the Italian states in terms of its territories and wealth. At the same time, the English delegation would have realized that Venice always put its own political security and commercial interests above other (even Italian) considerations. Furthermore, the 1520s were proving problematic times for Venice, as Bridgen and Woolfson explain:

> Its losses in the War of the League of Cambrai (1509–17) haunted the military and political thinking of the Most Serene Republic, which feared that France and the empire aspired to partition Venice and its terraferma as they had Milan. Having allied with both Francis and the emperor, the republic was now accused by both monarchs of having betrayed them.[3]

Wyatt and Casale explained to the College the details of the Pope's proposed truce with the imperial forces and invited the Venetians to support it or at least not to make immediate preparations for war. They tried to keep their instructions from the eyes of the French ambassador, but the Venetians would not act without his consent and he was advised of the Pope's proposed truce on the same day. On 3 March the papal Ambassador to Venice, Altobello Averoldi (1468–1531), the Florentine Ambassador, Casale and Wyatt had an audience with Doge Andrea Gritti (**Plate 4**) who advised them that he was awaiting a personal communication from the Pope before taking any further action. On 6 March Casale and Wyatt left for Ferrara, travelling by barge because the roads were too dangerous. They went, with the approval of the League's ambassadors, to deliver to Alfonso d'Este (1476–1534), Duke of Ferrara, letters from Henry VIII and Wolsey. However, they were just too late. On 5 March the Duke had left to meet near Modena with the imperial generals and had agreed that the imperial army should march on Florence. Pope Clement VII, considering himself abandoned by England and France, agreed an eight-month armistice on 15 March, much to the dismay of the Venetians. While Casale returned to Venice to communicate the Duke of Ferrara's rejection of the

---

[1] Ibid., 'Wyatt in Italy', p. 481.
[2] *LP*, IV.i, item 2244. Barrington, 'Two Houses', p. 904.
[3] Brigden and Woolfson, 'Wyatt in Italy', p. 468.

League's proposals, Wyatt rode on alone to Ferrara, carrying letters from the Florentine Ambassador in Venice and from Giambattista Casale to his brother Gregorio.

Although Wyatt left Ferrara under the duke's safe-conduct and with one of his couriers, he was captured outside the walls of Bologna by a company of Spanish light horse. His letters were seized and those sections not in cipher were copied and sent to Charles V. The soldiers of the imperial forces were suffering from dire conditions, battered for months by heavy rain and then freezing snow, severely undernourished and close to mutiny. Wyatt's position was perilous in the extreme with only limited verbal communication with his Spanish (and perhaps German) captors. His ransom was set at 3,000 ducats which equated to approximately one-eighth of the entire sum sent by Henry VIII to relieve the League. Raising such a ransom was unlikely and, given the chaos among the discontented imperial forces, it was improbable that the beleaguered commanders of these troops could exercise much power over them. Instead, direct approaches were made to the Duke of Ferrara, with the implicit threat that the continuing captivity of Wyatt, the son of the king's highly respected treasurer, could well alienate Henry VIII from the emperor.[1] This tactic proved successful and by 24 March Wyatt had been freed and he was safely at Bologna by 1 April. He then travelled on to Rome to meet up again with Russell who was working closely with Gregorio Casale in attempting to persuade the Pope against agreeing a truce with the imperial forces. Both Wyatt and Russell left Rome, just before the sacking of the city by imperial troops on 6 May and were back in England by late May 1527.

Both men continued to perform important diplomatic duties for Henry VIII. Wyatt served as High Marshall of Calais (1529–30) and in October 1532 he accompanied Henry VIII, his mistress Anne Boleyn and Sir John Russell to Calais to meet François I. Wyatt was knighted on Easter Day 1535 but his later court career became dangerously problematic. He was imprisoned in the Tower of London on 5 May 1536, due to his close relationship with the Boleyns and intimacy with Anne, although he escaped the fates of the queen's brother George Boleyn, and Mark Smeaton, Henry Norris, Francis Weston and William Brereton, who were all executed for treason and alleged adultery with Anne. After his release Wyatt was sent abroad in April 1537 as ambassador to the court of Charles V in an attempt to improve diplomatic relations with the emperor who was the nephew of Catherine of Aragon.

Although Wyatt never again visited Venice, he did have dealings with the now most notorious (from a Protestant point of view) English resident of Venice and Padua – Cardinal Reginald Pole (**item 11**). Wyatt remained abroad for most of the next two and a half years, travelling to Paris, Lyons, Avignon, Barcelona, Saragossa and Nice. He was briefed to seek a marriage between Princess Mary and the Portuguese *infante*, as well as attempting to prevent the emperor forming a league with François I which would exclude England. Seeking to foster discord between the emperor, the French king and the Pope,

---

[1] Close relations between the English court and the dukes of Ferrara had been fostered since the latter half of the 15th century. Alfonso's father, Duke Ercole I (1431–1505), had been buried wearing his Order of the Garter bestowed on him by Edward IV and Alfonso had visited England in 1504 with English emissaries visiting Ferrara in subsequent years. Two members of the Gonzaga family of Mantua, Ercole (1506–65) and Ferrante (1507–57) – nephews of Duke Alfonso of Mantua and younger brothers of Federico who met Sir Richard Torkington at Venice in 1517 (see **item 10**) – acted as intermediaries in the negotiations to free Wyatt. Brigden and Woolfson, 'Wyatt in Italy', p. 489.

Wyatt proposed that his secretary, the experienced diplomat John Mason (1503–66), should be sent to the papal legate Cardinal Pole to seek advice and information but nothing came of this suggestion. Charles V and François I concluded a treaty while Wyatt was back in England reporting to Henry VIII. He returned to Barcelona in July 1538 to attend the imperial court and then moved on to Toledo but, while still abroad, he was accused of treacherous dealings with Pole and it was rumoured by his enemies that he had even expressed a desire for the king's death. Pole attended the imperial court in February 1539 and, probably in a futile attempt to damage the impending alliance between the Pope, the emperor and the French king, Wyatt became embroiled in a vague plot to assassinate Pole.

Wyatt returned to England during the second half of 1539 but was sent in November to the emperor in France, again in the hope of formulating a breach between him and François. He was recalled from Spain in April 1540 without having achieved any significant diplomatic objectives. His chief patron, Thomas Cromwell, was arrested in June 1540 and executed on 28 July. Wyatt was himself imprisoned in the Tower in January 1541, largely through the accusations of Edmund Bonner (c. 1500–69), Bishop of London, over his contacts with Cardinal Pole. After his release he was sent in April 1541 to command a force of 300 horse at Calais; and in August 1542 unfounded rumours suggested that he would be appointed as admiral of the English fleet against France. However, he died, probably of a fever, in early October 1542.

As a final point of interest relating to Wyatt's 1527 brief mission to Venice, one of his most famous lyric poems, known as 'They Flee From Me', often thought to be associated with his rumoured intimacy with Anne Boleyn, may have been prompted by the availability of printed texts of Petrarch at Venice. Wyatt's poem casts the mistress as a 'hind' or female deer who, once loving, now seeks to escape from him (supposedly as her relationship with Henry VIII was developing):

> Whoso list to hunt, I know where is an hind,
> But as for me, hélas, I may no more.
> The vain travail hath wearied me so sore,
> I am of them that farthest cometh behind.
> Yet may I by no means my wearied mind
> Draw from the deer, but as she fleeth afore
> Fainting I follow. I leave off therefore,
> Sithens in a net I seek to hold the wind.
> Who list her hunt, I put him out of doubt,
> As well as I may spend his time in vain.
> And graven with diamonds in letters plain
> There is written, her fair neck round about:
> Noli me tangere, for Caesar's I am,
> And wild for to hold, though I seem tame.

This poem was an English versification of Petrarch's sonnet 190 in his *Canzoniere*, beginning:

> Una candida cerva sopra l'erba
> verde m'apparve, con duo corna d'oro,
> fra due riviere, all'ombra di un alloro,
> levando 'l sole a la stagione acerba.

119

(A white hind on the green grass
appeared to me, with two horns of gold,
between two streams, in the shade of a laurel,
the sun rising in the unripe season.)

Wyatt possessed an extensive familiarity with Petrarch's poetry, printed texts of whose verse were readily available at Venice. In 1501 the Venetian printer Aldus Manutius published a major edition of Petrarch's poetry, edited by the humanist scholar Pietro Bembo who also wrote a detailed defence of Petrarch's use of the Tuscan language, *Prose ... della volgar lingua* ('Writing in the Vernacular', Venice: 1525) and a major history of Venice, *Della historia vinitiana* (Venice: 1551). Wyatt may have seen both works at Venice and he definitely had access to Alessandro Vellutello's edition (Venice: 1525), which rearranged the poems into a coherent narrative tracing Petrarch's love for Laura and provided textual annotations. It is possible that he acquired a copy of this edition during his 1527 embassy to Venice and, if this was the case, such a purchase may be regarded as a landmark moment in Italian influences on the development of English lyric poetry.[1]

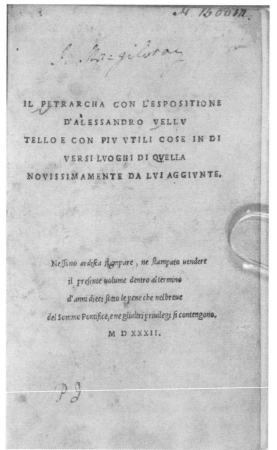

Figure 16.    Title page of *Il Petrarcha con l'espositione d'Alessandro Vellutelloe con piu utili cose in diversi luoghi di quella novissimamente da lui aggiunte*, Venice: Maestro Bernadino de Vidali Venetiano, 1532 edition. Special Collections, Brotherton Library, Strong Room for. 8vo 1532 PET. By permission of Special Collections, Brotherton Library, University of Leeds.

[1] Thomson, 'Wyatt and the Petrarchan Commentators', pp. 225–33.

# 14. *c.*1538–42 – ANDREW BO(O)RDE

**Andrew Bo(o)rde (*c.*1490–1549)** was a Carthusian monk, physician and author who was born in Sussex and brought up in Oxfordshire.[1] In 1517 he was nominated while still a young man as Suffragan Bishop of Chichester but was dismissed by papal bull in 1521, allegedly, for having been 'conversant with women'. He was released from his vows in 1528 or 1529 and went abroad to study medicine. He returned to England in 1530 and resided with Sir Robert Drewry (Drury).[2] He also provided medical care to Thomas Howard (1473–1554), Duke of Norfolk, and claimed to have attended Henry VIII. By 1532 he was again abroad, meeting medical practitioners in Orleans, Poitiers, Toulouse, Wittenberg and Rome. He undertook a pilgrimage to Santiago de Compostela where he also consulted with surgeons at the city's university. When he returned to England he took the Oath of Conformity in 1534 but was briefly imprisoned for unspecified reasons. He then became associated with Thomas Cromwell who had him freed from prison and sent him abroad in 1535 to assess continental views of Henry VIII's divorce from Catherine of Aragon. He travelled widely through France, Spain and Portugal, describing his experiences in a manuscript diary, 'The Itinerary of Europe', which he lent to Cromwell and who, he claimed, lost it 'bycause he had many matters of [state] to dyspache for al England'.[3]

By April 1536 Boorde was based in Glasgow (under the alias of 'Karre'), passing on intelligence to Cromwell, and in 1537 in Yorkshire, Cambridge and London where his *Almanake and Pronostication for 1537* was published. In either late 1537 or 1538 he left on pilgrimage to the Holy Land and Jerusalem, travelling there via Venice and on his return journey via Naples and Rome. He stayed for a while at Montpellier where in 1542 he wrote his *Pryncyples of Astronamye* and finished *The Compendious Regiment, or, Dyetary of Helth*, which he dedicated to the Duke of Norfolk. In the same year he wrote *The Fyrst Boke of the Introduction of Knowledge* which included his description of Venice. Dedicated on 3 May 1542 to Henry VIII's daughter Princess Mary (1516–58), this volume was ostensibly intended as a medical treatise but it became something of a hybrid volume. It is written in prose, verse and dialect and each chapter, focusing on one country, is headed by a crude woodcut illustrating its inhabitants. A supposed representative of each nation recounts in doggerel his compatriot's characteristics, followed by a prose account of details of local customs, currencies, fashion, food, commerce and useful phrases. This aspect of Boorde's *Introduction* echoes other practical handbooks, such as William Caxton's *Instructions for Travellers* (*c.*1483), which provided basic language guides for English travellers. At the same time, his volume promotes the idea of the cultural stereotypes of

---

[1] *ODNB*, s.v. Bo(o)rde, *Introduction*, ed. Furnivall, pp. 36–74.

[2] Probably the lawyer Sir Robert Drury (d. 1535), of Hawstead, Suffolk; Speaker of the House of Commons and Privy Councillor.

[3] Bo(o)rde, *Introduction*, ed. Furnivall, pp. 24, 145.

other nations to enhance an awareness of the qualities and distinctiveness of the English. He proudly claims that the great and 'noble citie of London precelleth all other', including 'Constantynople, Venis, Rome, Florence, Paris [and] Colyn' (sig. B1r).[1]

Boorde returned to England in 1547 and lived in the house of the Master of the Hospital of St Giles-in-the-Fields and then at Winchester. However, he was charged by John Ponet (1514–56), the married chaplain of Thomas Cranmer (1489–1556) and later Bishop of Winchester (from 1551), with keeping three prostitutes in his chamber at Winchester. Boorde was committed to the Fleet prison where he was still incarcerated when he drew up his will on 9 April 1549. He died later that month and his will was proved on 25 April.[2]

The publication history of *The Fyrstt Boke of the Introduction of Knowledge* is far from clear. While its dedication to Princess Mary is dated 3 May 1542, the first surviving edition was published by William Copland in about 1555 (*STC*, 3383), when he was trading from 'the sign of the Rose Garland' in Fleet Street. Two other lost editions are mentioned in Boorde's other works. His *Hereafter Foloweth a Compendyous Regiment or a Dietary of Helth, Made in Montpyllier* (1542), refers to one printed by W. Middleton (*STC* 3378.5); and *The Breviary of Helthe* (1547), refers to another by Copland (*STC* 3373.5). Yet another edition was published in about 1562 by Copland (*STC* 3385) and it is likely that other now lost editions were produced of this wry and idiosyncratic text.

## Text[3]

The .xxiiii. chapter treateth of Venys, and of the
naturall dysposicyon of the people of the
country of ther mony and of theyr spech.

> [f. 3r] I am a venesien both sober and sage
> In all myne actes and doynges I do not outrage
> Gravite shalbe founde ever in me
> Specially yf I be out of my countrey
> My apparell is ryche, very good and fine
> All my possession is not fully myne
> For part of my possession, I am come tributor to the Turke
> To lyve in rest and peace in my cytye I do lourke
> Some men do saye I do smell of the smoke
> I passe not for that, I have money in my pooke[4]
> To pacyfe the pope, the turke, and the Jue[5]
> I say no more good felow now adew.

Yf I should not bring in & speke of Venes here, I sholde not kepe the circuit of Europe. whosoever that hath not seene the noble citie of Venis, he hath not sene the bewtye and

[1] Shrank, *Writing the Nation*, pp. 27–49.
[2] TNA PRO PROB 11/32, ff. 217–218. *ODNB*, s.v.
[3] Text from 1555 edition.
[4] *pooke*: a small bag or sack.
[5] *Jue*: Jew.

ryches of thys worlde. Therbe ryche marchauence and marchauntes,[1] for to venys is a great confluence of marchauntes as well christians as all sortes of infydels. The citie of Venis doth stande .vii. myle wythin the sea, *the* sea is called the gulf it doth not eb nor flow. Thorow the stretes of venys ronnyth the water, and every marchaunt hath a fayre lytle barge standynge at his stayers[2] to rowe thorow and aboute the citie and at bothe sydes of the water in every street a man maye go whyther he wyll in Venys; but he must passe over many bredges. The marchauntes of Venys goeth in longe gownes lyke preestes, with close sleves. The venyacyo*n*s wyll not have no lordes nor knyghtes a monges theym, but only the Duke. The duke of Venys is chosen for terme of hys lyfe, he shall not mary by cause hys sonne shall not clayme no inheritaunce of the dukedomshyp [f. 3v] the duke may have lemons[3] & concubyns as manye as he wyl, the duke shall never ryd nor go nor sayle out the cyte as longe as he dothe lyve. The duke shall rule the senyorite,[4] and the seniorite shall governe and rule the comynalte[5] and depose and put to deth the duke if they do fynd a lawful cause. The duke weryth a coronet over a cap of sylke the which stondeth up lyke a podynge or a cokes come bekyng forward[6] of .iii. handfoll longe. The duke do not come to the butyful church of saint Marke but certen hygh feastes in the yere & the first eyght daies after that he is made duke to shew hym selfe. I dyd neer se within the cyte of Venis no poverte. But al riches. ther be non inhabitours in the cite that is nede & pour vitelles[7] there is dere. venys is one of the chefest portes of all the world the venyscions hath great provision of warre for they have ever in a redynes tymber readye made to make a hundred gales or more at tyme they have all maner of artillery in a redynes. They have greate possessions and Candy, and sco[8] with other Iles and portes cites and landes be under ther dominion Whan they do heare masse & se the sacrament they do inclyne, & doth clap theyr hand on theyr mouth and do not knock them self on the brest, at high masse they do use prycksong[9] & playnsonge the orgins and the trumpates if ther be any gospel red or song of saynt Marke, they wyl say seqencia santy evangely secundum istium[10] poyntyng theyr finger to *st* Mark the whych do ly in the church[.] the people do pol their heades,[11] and do let ther berdes grow. Theyr speche is Italion ther money is gold that is to say duccates and bagantins is brasse, .xii. bagantyns is worth a galy halpeny & there is galy halpens.

---

[1] *marchauence and marchauntes*: trading and merchants.

[2] *stayers*: poles or anchorage to which gondolas and boats were moored.

[3] *lemons*: lemmons, lemans: unlawful lovers or mistresses (*OED*).

[4] *senyorite*: \*Signoria.

[5] *comynalte*: commonalty, the people of a nation, state or city.

[6] *a podynge or a cokes come bekyng forward*: a pudding or cock's comb beaking forward.

[7] *vitelles*: victuals or provisions.

[8] *Candy, and sco*: Candia (Crete) and Scio.

[9] *prycksong*: music sung from notes written or pricked, as opposed to music sung from memory or by ear; written or printed vocal music.

[10] *seqencia santy evangely secundum*: 'sequentia sancti evangelii secundum', the Latin formula used in the liturgy to announce the Gospel reading.

[11] *pol their heads*: to shear or cut off hair.

# 15.   1545 – THE SINKING OF THE *MARY ROSE* AND VENETIAN SALVAGE ATTEMPTS

While the sinking of the English flagship the *Mary Rose* (**Plate 7**) in July 1545, and its raising in 1982 from the Solent, are events now renowned in British maritime history, it is much less well known that initial attempts to raise her between 1545 and 1549 were entrusted by the English authorities entirely to teams of Venetian salvage experts based in England. The following brief account illustrates how close links had developed between England and Venice over maritime and naval affairs during Henry VIII's reign. It also provides an example of one of the various small communities of Venetians who had taken up residence in London and on the south coast of England during the mid-sixteenth century.

The 500-ton displacement, 60-gun carrack *Mary Rose* had been launched in 1511 and saw action during the Brest (1512–13) and Scottish (1513–14) campaigns and the Second French War (1522). She was substantially rebuilt in 1536, raising her to 700 tons and adding an extra tier of broadside guns to her already formidable armaments.[1] During the Third French War (1544–5), King François I sent a large fleet under the command of Admiral Claude d'Annebault (1495–1552) to land troops on English soil. By 19 July French galleys were threatening the becalmed English fleet and Portsmouth harbour, under the command of the Lord Admiral, John Dudley (1504–53), Viscount Lisle. As the wind picked up, the *Mary Rose* and the *Henry Grace à Dieu* advanced across the Solent against the French galleys and main fleet but the *Mary Rose* heeled over to starboard. Heavy armaments and other equipment shifted, allowing water to flood rapidly through the lower-deck open gunports. She sank about one mile offshore in six fathoms (about 36 feet). The majority of her 400 or more crew were drowned with many trapped either inside the vessel or by the anti-boarding netting on her sides. Their cries as they drowned were audible onshore from where Henry VIII was watching the unfolding action. Her commander, Vice Admiral Sir George Carew (*c.*1504–45) (**Plate 8**), and her captain, Roger Grenville (1518–45), the father of the renowned Sir Richard (1542–91) of the *Revenge*, also drowned.

The rediscovery in 1971 of the wreck of the *Mary Rose* led to her raising by the Mary Rose Trust in October 1982. However, the first attempt to raise the vessel, resting on her side 60 degrees to starboard in the thick mud of the Solent, was begun only days after the sinking. Henry VIII's Secretary of State, William Paget (1506–63), ordered a salvage attempt, supervised by one of the king's most trusted courtiers, Charles Brandon, Duke of Suffolk, who was then in charge of the land fortifications at Portsmouth. Rather than

---

[1] The *Mary Rose* had not experienced problems of stability during her first twenty-seven years of service. These modifications substantially increased her draught and may have rendered her unseaworthy in strong winds, with her lowest gunports only a few feet from the waterline.

utilizing English expertise, the vessel's recovery was entrusted to Venetian salvage operators based at Southampton. They were led by Piero de Andreasi (Petre de Andreas) and Simone de Marini (Symond de Maryne) who formed a team comprising a Venetian master-carpenter and thirty Venetian and sixty English mariners. They planned to run cables under the ship's hull at low tide, attaching them to large vessels of approximately equal tonnage to the *Mary Rose* positioned on either side. Two ships from the English fleet, the *Jesus of Lübeck* and *Sampson of Lübeck*, were emptied of as much of their ballast, cargo and fitments as possible to increase their buoyancy.[1] As the tide rose, the cables were tightened with capstans so that they might pull the *Mary Rose* up from the deep silt and clay of the Solent seabed and then drag her to shallower water to be emptied and pumped out.

The sails and yardarms of the *Mary Rose* were brought ashore on 5 August by the Venetian salvage team and Suffolk informed Paget that she should be raised 'tomorrow'. Although this proved impossible, on 7 August the Lord Admiral told Suffolk that 'he had good hope of the weighing up of the *Mary Rose* this afternoon or tomorrow'. However, by 9 August her main mast, the primary point of connection for the cables, had snapped and all subsequent attempts to raise her failed. On 8 December the Venetian salvage team was paid off, with Andreasi and de Marini receiving forty marks.[2] Further salvage work was undertaken from July 1546 until about August 1549 to remove accessible weapons and anchors from the wreck by a team formed by another Venetian expert, Piero Paolo Corsi, whose team was led by his Guinean lead diver, Jacques Francis (Jaques Frauncys).[3] It is significant that from 1545 until 1549 Lord Admiral John Dudley, Secretary of State William Paget, the Duke of Suffolk and, presumably, the king himself, all chose to entrust attempts to raise and gather salvage from the wreck of the *Mary Rose* entirely to Venetian salvage experts rather than English naval engineers.

[1] The 700-ton carrack *Jesus of Lübeck* had been purchased at Hamburg. Records of this attempt to raise the *Mary Rose* refer only to the *Sampson* but this vessel was the *Sampson of Lübeck*, as recorded in the Lord Admiral's 'Order of Battle' (compiled August 1545). This list refers to the *Jesus* as the *Johannes Lubeck* and includes the *Venetian*, also known as the *Great Venetian*, a commandeered Venetian merchant vessel commanded by Sir Peter Carew, the younger brother of the English Vice-Admiral, George Carew. Corbett, *Fighting Instructions*, pp. 15–18.

[2] *LP*, XX.ii, items 2, 14, 16, 38–9, 61, 81, 951.

[3] When Corsi was accused of theft from another wreck in the Solent, the *Sancta Maria and Sanctus Edwardus* (owned by the Venetian merchant Francesco Bernardi and leased by a partnership of England-based Italian merchants), he was imprisoned in the Tower of London. Jacques Francis was called as a witness in his trial, thereby becoming the first black man to give evidence to an English court (High Court of Admiralty). See Ungerer, 'Recovering a Black African's Voice', pp. 255–71.

PART II

ENGLISH TRAVELLERS TO VENICE
1548–1600

# 16.   1545/8 – *THE HISTORIE OF ITALIE* BY WILLIAM THOMAS

**William Thomas (*c.*1507–54)** was of unconfirmed parentage but probably of Welsh descent. He possessed a good knowledge of Latin and may have been educated at Oxford or Cambridge. When in the service of Sir Anthony Browne (1500–48), Henry VIII's Master of the Horse, he was accused of embezzling some of his employer's money to pay off gambling debts. To escape incarceration, he fled abroad in late 1544 or early 1545 and deposited funds at London with an Italian banker, Acelyne Salvago (Anselm Salvage), receiving in return bills of exchange which he cashed with the factor of the 'House of Vivaldes' at Venice.[1] A servant of Edward Seymour, Earl of Hertford, was sent in pursuit of Thomas and the Privy Council issued instructions to Edmund Harvell, the English Ambassador at Venice (**item 12**), to return Salvago's bill of exchange, making it payable to Sir Anthony Browne.[2] After his arrival at Venice on 10 April 1545 Thomas immediately presented himself to Harvell, through either contrition, cunning or desperation. He was briefly imprisoned until the bill of exchange was repaid to Browne.[3] He travelled to Bologna and Florence (winter 1546–7) before returning to Venice where he wrote a eulogy for the recently deceased Henry VIII (d. 28 January 1547), titled 'Peregryne' in the form of a dialogue between the narrator and gentlemen of Bologna.[4]

By Christmas 1547 Thomas was in Rome and was commissioned by an English friend at Venice, John Tamworth (*c.*1524–*c.*1569), to compile an Italian grammar and dictionary which was printed in 1550 as *Principall Rules of the Italian Grammer, with a Dictionarie for the Better Understandying of Boccace, Petrache and Dante*.[5] Thomas probably arrived back in England soon after the death of his former patron, Sir Anthony Browne (d. 28 April 1548), and completed *The Historie of Italie, a Boke Excedying Profitable to be Reade: Because it Intreateth of the Astate of Many and Divers Common*

---

[1] Adair, 'William Thomas', 2012, chapter 21. Thomas, *History of Italy*, ed. Parks, pp. ix–xviii. Partridge, 'Thomas Hoby's English Translation', pp. 776–8. Hadfield, *Literature*, pp. 24–32. Thomas also spent time at Rome, Naples, Genoa, Mantua, Ferrara and Urbino.

[2] *LP*, XX.i, item 836.

[3] Harvell noted on 13 April 1545 (*LP*, XX.i, p. 514) that Thomas was carrying '16 ducats and crowns and one angel broken, with 4s in white [silver] money', and that he was making 'incessable wepinges for his trespasses which semith to greve him no lesse than deth'.

[4] BL Cotton MS Vespasian D.xviii, pr. *Il pellegrino inglese*, 1552.

[5] London, 1550, based on Alberto Accarigi (Accarisio), *Vocabulario* (1543; rpt Venice, 1550) and Francesco Alunno, *Le richezze della lingua volgare* (1543). The author's preface was addressed to 'Maister Tamwoorth. At Venice' and dated 'Padoa the thirde of Februarie, 1548'. John Tamworth (*c.*1524–69) was a relative of Thomas Cranmer and the brother-in-law of Sir Francis Walsingham. Either he or his cousin Christopher was with Sir Thomas Hoby at Padua in August 1554. Garrett, *Exiles*, pp. 302–3. Woolfson, *Padua*, p. 275. Bartlett, *English in Italy*, p. 220.

*Weales, How Thei Have Ben & Now be Governed* (1549).[1] He dedicated it to John Dudley (1504–53), Earl of Warwick (from 11 October 1551, Duke of Northumberland). Although Dudley was executed for instigating the Lady Jane Grey usurpation of the English throne, his remaining family – most notably his son Robert Dudley (1532–88), Earl of Leicester (**Plate 23**) – sustained extensive interests in Italian politics, literature, and the visual arts.

Thomas was elected in January 1552 as MP for Old Sarum, Wiltshire, through the influence of Dudley's ally, William Herbert (*c.*1501–70), first Earl of Pembroke; and he was returned as the member for Downton, Wiltshire, in March 1553.[2] He also served from 29 April 1550 as Clerk of the Privy Council and in 1551 as secretary to the embassy to France of William Parr (1513–71), Marquess of Northampton. This work and his powerful patrons drew Thomas into the personal circle of King Edward VI. In *c.*1552/53 he presented the King with a manuscript translation: 'The narration of Josaphat Barbaro, citezein of Venice, in twoo voyages, made th'one into Tana and th'other into Persia'.[3] Thomas clearly retained his interests in Venice because on 14 August 1552 he wrote to Sir William Cecil (1520–98), asking to be sent there for a year or two in some official capacity:

> And Sr whereas at my departure we talked of Venice considering the stirre of the worlde is noe like to be very great these waies I coulde finde in myne heart to spende a yere or two there if I were sent I have not disclosed thus much to any man but to you nor entende not to do. Wherefore it may please you to use it as you shall thinke good.[4]

Thomas sent this letter from Wilton House, the residence of the Earl of Pembroke, whose wife, Anne Parr, was the sister of Henry VIII's sixth wife, Queen Catherine Parr. It is not known exactly how Thomas became associated with Pembroke but since both were firm Protestants, it is likely that they were fearful of the already frail health of Edward VI (who died on 6 July 1553). Thomas was probably seeking to absent himself abroad if the ardently Catholic Princess Mary acceded to the throne. Pembroke had allied himself with John Dudley, Duke of Northumberland, and his plot to place his daughter-in-law, Lady Jane Grey, on the throne. After Edward's death Pembroke initially supported her claim and had married his eldest son and heir, Henry, to Jane's sister, Lady Catherine Grey on 25 May 1553 – the same day as Jane married Northumberland's son, Guildford Dudley. As soon as Pembroke realized that Mary would become queen, he had his son's marriage to Catherine Grey annulled and managed to distance himself from the Grey and Dudley conspiracy. The Duke of Northumberland was executed on 22 August 1553 and Lady Jane Grey and her husband Guildford Dudley, on 12 February 1554. Her father, Henry Grey, Duke of Suffolk, was executed on 23 February.

The Wyatt Rebellion (late January to early February 1554), against Queen Mary's proposed marriage to Philip of Spain, proved a pivotal event for both Pembroke and

---

[1] Hoby, 'Book of the Travaile', 4, records Thomas Hoby at Strasbourg in January 1548 and the preface to Thomas's *Italian Grammer* is dated 3 February 1548. Hoby was at Strasbourg until July 1548 and so Thomas probably arrived there during this period. Thomas, *History of Italy*, ed. Parks, p. x.

[2] Thomas also compiled a devotional tract, *The Vanitee of this World* (1549), dedicated to Pembroke's wife, Anne (Parr) Herbert (1515–52), Queen Catherine Parr's younger sister.

[3] BL Royal MS 17 C x, pr. in Italian, 1543–5, recounting a Venetian embassy to the Persian ruler, Uzun Hasan (1423–78).

[4] Quoted in Barbaro, *Travels to Tana and Persia*, p. ix.

Thomas. While Pembroke regained the Queen's favour by playing a prominent role in its suppression, Thomas was arrested as one of the leading conspirators. He was convicted of treason and on 18 May was drawn on a hurdle from the Tower of London to Tyburn where he was hanged, drawn and quartered. Thomas's head was displayed on London Bridge and his other body parts over Cripplegate.[1] Although specific details of Thomas's role in the conspiracy are uncertain, it may be that his Italian expertise ultimately proved his downfall.

The leader of the rebellion, Sir Thomas Wyatt the Younger (1521–54), was the son of the poet Sir Thomas Wyatt who in 1527 had undertaken with Sir John Russell an embassy to northern Italy, including Venice (**item 13**). Before his execution on 11 April 1554 Wyatt claimed that the plot had originally been conceived by Edward Courtenay (1526–56), first Earl of Devon, who had been regarded as a possible spouse for Queen Mary.[2] Courtenay had been imprisoned in the Tower of London from 1538 after charges were brought against his father, Henry Courtenay, who was executed in 1539, supposedly for his treasonable contacts with the self-exiled Cardinal Reginald Pole (**item 11**).

While imprisoned Edward Courtenay had translated from the Italian a popular devotional tract, *Beneficio di Cristo* ('Benefit of Christ's Death'), published at Venice in 1543.[3] He dedicated it in 1548 to Anne Stanhope, the wife of the Lord Protector, Edward Seymour (c.1500–52), first Duke of Somerset, who was the uncle of Edward VI.[4] It is possible that Thomas had supplied Courtenay with a copy of this Venetian imprint since his mother employed tutors for him during his incarceration in the Tower of London.[5] Courtenay was released on Mary's accession but again imprisoned in the Tower in February 1554 and exiled in April 1555 for his alleged involvement in Wyatt's Rebellion. If successful, it was rumoured that Mary would have been deposed in favour of Elizabeth, with Courtenay as her consort. He was granted a licence to travel in October 1555 and resided in Venice, establishing a house in the city by mid-January 1556. He also studied at the University of Padua, dying there of a tertian fever, although it was widely rumoured that he had been poisoned by English or Imperial agents.[6] Thomas's involvement in the Wyatt Rebellion, leading to his gruesome execution, may have developed from an association with Courtenay and his letter to Cecil in August 1552, requesting to be sent to Venice, could have been an implicit attempt to extricate himself from an increasingly perilous political position..

Thomas's *The Historie of Italie* is the first printed English book on Italy. His lengthy account of Venice systematically details from close personal observation the city's geography, republican constitution, pageantry, buildings and administration.[7] It forms a key section of an overtly didactic work, aimed not only at the educated courtier and wealthy private citizens but also at prospective ambassadors, diplomats and merchants

[1] *ODNB*, s.v. The indictment against Thomas is printed in Barbaro, *Travels to Tana and Persia*, pp. x–xi.

[2] Courtenay was the great-grandson of Edward IV and cousin of Cardinal Reginald Pole (**item 11**).

[3] Overell, *Nicodemites*, p. 97.

[4] Cambridge University Library, MS Nn.4.43. This manuscript has two autograph annotations by Edward VI. Overell, *Nicodemites*, pp. 97–8.

[5] Overell, *Italian Reform*, pp. 61–80.

[6] *ODNB*, s.v. Woolfson, *Padua*, pp. 227–8.

[7] Thomas may also have had access to printed works on Venetian history, perhaps the recently published *Historia ... dell'origine di Vinegia*, 1545, translated into Italian by Lodovico Domenichi from Bernardo Giustiniani, *De origine Urbis Venetianum rebusque ab ipsa gestis historia*, 1492.

interested in the Venetian model of republicanism and the city's reputation as an international trading centre. Given its lavish dedicatory preface, it was probably also intended as a means of enhancing Thomas's own ambitions at the English court and to indicate his potential as a foreign agent or even ambassador. His visit to Venice between 1545 and 1548 occurred during an important period of the city's architectural developments. For example, his descriptions of the *Fortezza Sant'Andrea and the *Palazzo Ducale (Doge's Palace) indicate that they were still under construction.

## Text[1]

### [p. 73r] ¶ The Venetian astate.[2]

Because the mervailouse Situacion of the citee of Venice, amongest other thynges seemeth unto me moste notable, I therefore have thought good fyrst to treate therof: and than consequently to procede vnto the declaracion of the Venetians astate, theyr customes and procedynges.

### ¶Of the mervailouse Site.

Whan I consider what thinges necessitee causeth (havyng an earnest proufe for my parte therof) I nothyng mervaile, to see the wonders that it worketh. For he that beholdeth the place, where Venice standeth, and would imagine it to be without any buildyng or habitacion, shoulde saie it were the rudest, unmeerest,[3] and unholsomest place to builde upon or to enhabite, that w[e]re againe to be founde thoroughout an whole worlde: It standeth open upon the maine sea, foure miles from the neerest maine lande, in suche a marishe, as at every low water leaveth the muddy ground uncovered, and at every full sea drowneth it cleane.

And yet men (constreigned of necessitee) have brought this marishe to suche a passe, that it is now not onely excedyng full of people, and riche of treasure and buildynges: but so holesome withall (throughe the muche haunte of people and the great noumbre of continuall fyres) that I thynke none other citee hable to shewe so [p. 73v] many olde men. But were it not, that as it seemeth nature hath of purpose made a banke two or thre miles of[f], betwene it and the sea, it were impossible to be enhabited: Because the citee standyng equall with the water, the floudde by reason should passe through the houses at every full sea. But this banke, that beginneth at *Chiozza*,[4] and stretcheth towardes the citee of *Concordia*,[5] 60. myles of length, dooeth so defende the water floudde, that within those marishes it hath nothyng the lyke force as on the other sea costes. For it is a great mattier whan the sea swelleth in Venice .iiii. or v. foote above the lowe water marke: Notwithstandyng that the citee seemeth to be rather in a part of the sea, than in a marisshe. For everie chanell[6] (as who woulde saie every streete) is full of

---

[1] Transcribed from *The Historie of Italie*, 1549, *STC* 24018, 73r–112v.

[2] *astate*: estate.

[3] *unmeerest*: of no great importance or significance.

[4] Chioggia.

[5] Concordia Sagittaria.

[6] *chanell*: the standard English translation of '*canale*' was 'channel' from the French '*chenal*'. This word was still being used by John Evelyn in his description of Venice during the mid-17th century.

water, and the chanels are so many, that you maie row through all partes of the citee: though there be waies also, to goe on land if you list. Whiche streetes for the most parte are verie narow, and the houses nothyng so faire as on the water side. And in the marisshe, betwene the citee and the maine lande, whan the water is low, the most parte of the chanels are so shalow, that the botes have muche a dooe to passe to and fro. For the mudde encreaseth daiely, by reason of the lande flouddes, that a noumbre of rivers fallyng into the same, dooe carie with theim. And a wonderfull treasure the Venetians spend in continuall diggyng and cariyng awaie of that mudde, to preserve theyr foresaied chanelles, and to defende, that theyr citee joygne not to the maine lande.

The banke before rehersed, is broken in .vii. places, through the whiche botes maie come in: but no shippe [p. 74r] can passe to Venice, savyng at the porte of Malamoco,[1] or at the two Castelles of Li[d]o. The entrie wherof is so daungerous (by reason the sand*es* are movable here & there) that whan any shippe cometh in, she taketh fyrst pilottes to sounde the waie: whiche in effect is reputed to be one of the greatest sureties, that the Venetians have for defence of theyr citee, against all ennemies by sea: and than by lande it is impossible to hurt or besiege it, unlesse the enemie were hable to occupie .150. myle compasse with his armie.

## Of buildynges.

nexte unto the situacion, the maner of theyr buildyng is most to be mervailed at. For almost every man that buildeth an house, maketh his foundacion lower than the water: and er ever he set in hand withall, is constreigned to make suche a stronge pale of pyles and mudde betwene his buildyng and the water, as shall be hable to defende his woorke, whan (after he hath closed it well) the water and mudde that resteth within, is clensed and emptied out. Than causeth he stronge pyles of timber of a great length, to be driven in, and therupon with stone and gravell beginneth his foundacion. So that whan he hath brought it to the full sea marke, he rekenneth[2] to have furnished one halfe of his buildyng: notwithstandyng that above water I thynke no place of all Europe, hable at this daie to compare with that citee for numbre of sumptuouse houses, specially for theyr frontes. For he that woull rowe throughe the Canale grande,[3] and marke well the [p. 74v] frontes of the houses on bothe sydes, shall see theim, more lyke the doynges of princes than private men.

And I have been with good reason persuaded, that in Venice be above .200. palaices able to lodge any kyng.

But now to the particuler of theyr notable buildynges: The new Castell[4] at the mouthe of the haven Li[d]o for strengthe and beautie is one of the rarest thynges dooen in these daies.

The churche of S. Marke is a verie antike thyng,[5] furnisshed with goodly pillers of fine marble to the noumbre of .900. (as they saie, besides the floore under foote of small

---

[1] Malamocco.

[2] *rekenneth*: reckons.

[3] *Grand Canal.

[4] *Fortezza di Sant'Andrea. Thomas witnessed the final stages of its construction (completed 1549). His brief description is the first published reference to it by an Englishman.

[5] *San Marco.

marble stones, wrought in knottes of divers colours, and foure faire brasen horses over the fronte.[1]

The Dukes palaice is a verie sumptuouse buildyng and not yet finished.[2]

The streete called, La Piazza di San Marco, is verie fayre and large, and the one syde is built of harde stone, all uniformely with faire glasen wyndowes, and the streete by low,[3] paved over with bricke.[4]

Saincte Markes steeple is a veraie hyghe and fayre toure of bricke, so well built, that within foorth an horse maie be ledde up into the bellfroy.[5]

The Rialto is a goodly place in the hert of the citee, where the merchauntes twyse a daie assemble.[6]

The schooles of S. Rocke and S. Marke are two notable thynges: the frontes wherof are fayrest and costliest that ever I have seen.[7]

Finally, the Arsenale in myne eie excedeth all the rest.[8] For there they have well neere two hundred galleys in suche an ordre, that upon a verie small warnyng [p. 75r] they maie be furnisshed out unto the sea. Besydes, that for everie daie in the yere (whan they woulde goe to the cost) they shoulde be hable to make a new galey: havyng suche a staple of tymber (whiche in the water within Th'arsenale hath lien aseasonyng, some .20. yere, some .40. some an .100. and some I wote not[9] how longe) that it is a wonder to see it. And every of these galeys hath his coveryng or house by hym selfe on the drie lande: so that the longe liyng unoccupied can not hurt theim. Their mastes, cables, sailes, ankers, rooders, ores,[10] and every other thyng are redy in houses of offices by theim selfes, that unseen, it is almost incredible: with suche a quantitee of artillerie, bothe for sea and lande, as made me to wonder, besides the harneyse and weapons, that suffise (as they saie) to arme an 100000. men. Finally, the noumbre of woorkemen waged for terme of life about those exercises, is wonderfull. For by all that I could learne, theyr ordinarie is never lesse than .600. woorkyng in the Arsenale, be it peece or warre. And because thei have such a numbre of botemen, that continually live by gaine upon the water within the cite: they neede not to seeke further for mariners to furnishe their galeys withall. For it was crediblie tolde me that there are no lesse than 12000. botes daiely servyng in those theyr chanelles:[11] and almost no bote rowed, but of a sufficient mariner. So that if the Venetians had ben men, as the Romans were, geven as well unto chivalrie by lande, as unto the exercise on the water: no doubt thei might many yeres agoen have subdued the worlde. But sure theyr

[1] *San Marco, Bronze Horses.

[2] *not yet finished*: after a fire in 1547, rebuilding at the *Palazzo Ducale was not completed until c.1559.

[3] *by low*: below.

[4] * San Marco, Piazza, now much altered from the 1540s. The Library of St Mark (Libreria Sansoviniana) on the west side was still under construction during the 1540s.

[5] *San Marco, Campanile. Its Loggetta, at the base of the campanile, was still being completed during Thomas's visit.

[6] *Rialto. Thomas does not refer to a bridge at the Rialto, even though this was the city's only bridged crossing point at this period.

[7] *Scuola Grande di San Rocco. Thomas probably witnessed the building of its main facade, completed 1549; and *Scuola Grande di San Marco.

[8] *Arsenal (**Plate 12**).

[9] *wote not*: know not.

[10] *rooders, ores*: rudders, oars.

[11] *chanelles*: canals.

power hath been more warely governed than valiantly enlarged. [p. 75v] For sens[1] Constantinople was gotten by the Turkes,[2] theyr dominion hath decreased, bothe by reason (as the fame gothe) they rather practise with money, to bie[3] and sell countreys, peace and warre: than to exercise deedes of armes: and for that moste Venetians are at these daies become better merchauntes than men of warre.

And now methynketh it convenient to speake in this place, of the armorie that is in an hall of the Dukes palaice, called *La Sala del Consiglio d'i dieci*, whiche surely is a verie notable thyng.[4]

There be (as thei recken) a thousande cotes of plate, parte covered with clothe of golde and velvette, with gilte nayles so fayre, that their princes myght weare theim: besides divers other fayre harneyses made of late, whiche are bestowed in so fayre an ordre with theyr dyvers kyndes of weapons, furnisshed of the beste sorte, that a great while lookyng on, could not satisfie me. This hall is divided into divers severall porcions, as the hous dooeth geve it, and every porcion hath his soret by him selfe verie handsomely.

Finally for provision of fresshe water it is a wonder to see theyr noumbre of costly welles, made onely to receive the raine that falleth from the houses. I call theim costly, because fyrst every well hath his bottome as low as the salt water, and must therfore be so surely walled and stopped with sande on the utter[5] syde, that it defende the salte water from sokyng in. And on the inner side it must have his vent to receive the water, that falleth from the houses, gravell within to passe thorough, and last of all a fayre pavyng of bricke or stone [p. 76r] in the bottome closed about lyke a cesterne, to preserve the purged water.

And though they have a great noumbre of those welles, and plentie of raine, yet the poore men, that dwell in the countrey, doe gaine yerely aboue .20000. crownes, by bringyng theyr botes laden with fresshe water from the rivers to Venice. Yet all this notwithstandyng, you shall many tymes heare muche lamentacion amonge the poore folke for lacke of water.

### Of the dominion.

Besides all those townes and habitacions that are in theyr marishes, and on that longe banke betwene theim and the sea, as Murano, Mazzorbo, Torcello, Malamoco, Chiozza,[6] and others, they have on the maine lande the countrey of Friuli,[7] anciently called Forum Julii, the citees of Treviso, Padoa, Vicenza, Verona, Bressa, Bergamo, and Crema,[8] with theyr appurtenaunces.

The most part of the countrey of Istria, and upon the costes of Dalmatia (now called Schlavonia) they have Zara and Zebenico:[9] In the mouthe of the Adriatike sea the ile of Corfu: and in the Levant seas, otherwise called Mare Mediterraneum, the notable ilandes

---

[1] *sens*: since.

[2] Constantinople had been captured after a 53-day siege by the Ottoman army, commanded by Sultan Mehmed II, on 29 May 1453. This conquest effectively marked the end of the Byzantine Empire.

[3] *bie*: buy.

[4] *Sala d'Armi del Consiglio dei Dieci.

[5] *utter*: the outer or exterior part.

[6] Murano, Mazzorbo, Torcello, Malamocco and Chioggia.

[7] Friuli Venezia Giulia, in northern Italy bordering Austria, Slovenia and Adriatic Sea.

[8] Brescia, Bergamo and Cremona.

[9] Zadar (Zara) on the Croatian coast; and Šibenik (Sebenico), in central Dalmatia.

of Candia and Cyprus. So that if the grounde that thei be lordes of, were in one mans handes, he should be no lesse woorthie to be called a kyng, than most kynges that are knowen at these daies. For not longe agoen Cyprus (a parte of this) hath had a kynge alone. And how and whan they gotte these thynges, this briefe historie, hereafter folowyng particulerly declareth.

[f. 76v] **Of revenue.**

As I have been crediblie enformed by some gentilmen Venetians, that have had to dooe therin, they leavey of theyr subiectes little lesse than .4. millions of golde by the yeere, whiche (after our olde reckenyng) amounteth to the summe of tenne hundred thousande poundes sterlyng. A thyng rather to be wondred at than beleeved, consideryng they reyse it not upon landes, but upon customes after so extreme a sorte, that it would make any honest herte sorowfull to heare it. For there is not a graine of corne, a spoonefull of wine, a corne[1] of salte, egge, byrde, beast, foule, or fisshe bought or solde, that paieth not a certaine custome. And in Venice specially the customers[2] part in many thyng*es*, is more than the owners. And if any thyng be taken by the waie uncustomed, be it merchaundise or other, never so great or small, it is forfeited. For those customers kepe suche a sorte of prollers[3] to serche all thyng*es* as they come to and fro, that I thynke Cerberus was never so greedie at the gates of hell as they be in the chanelles about Venice. And though thei in serchyng a bote, finde no forfeiture, yet woull they not departe without drinkyng money. And many times the meanest labourer or craftesman throughout all theyr dominion, paieth a rate for the Poll by the moneth. Insomuche that a Candiote[4] my friende (one that had dwelled in Constantinople) sware to me by his faieth, the Christians lived a great deale better under the Turke, than under the Venetians. It is almost incredible, what gaine the Venetians receive by the usurie of the Jewes, bothe privately and in common. For in every [f. 77r] citee the Jewes kepe open shops of usurie, takyng gaiges of ordinarie[5] for .xv. in the hundred by the yeere: and if at the yeres ende, the gaige be not redemed, it is forfeite, or at the least dooen awaie to a great disadvantage: by reason wherof the Jewes are out of measure wealthie in those parties.

**Of dignitees and offices.**

Thei have a Duke called after theyr maner, Doge, who onely (amongest all the rest of the nobilitee) hath his office immutable for terme of life: with a certaine yerely provision of .4000. duckates or theraboutes. But that is so appoincted unto him for certaine ordinarie feastes, and other lyke charges, that his owne advauntage therof can be but small. And though in apparaunce he seemeth of great astate, yet in veraie deede his power is but small. He kepeth no house, liveth privately, and is in so muche servitude, that I have hearde some of the Venetians theim selfes call hym an honourable slave: For he can not goe a mile out of the towne without the counsailes licence, nor in the towne departe extraordinarily out of the palaice, but privately and secretely: And in his apparaile he is

[1] *corne*: grain.
[2] *customers*: tax collector.
[3] *prollers*: prowlers, searchers.
[4] *Candiote*: resident of Crete.
[5] *gaiges of ordinarie*: items of value pledged or pawned as a regular custom or practice.

prescribed an ordre: so that in effect, he hath no maner of preeminence but the bare honour, the gifte of a few small offices, and the libertee, Di mettere una parte,[1] whiche is no more, but to propounde unto any of the counsailes his opinion, touchyng the ordre, reformacion, or correction of any thyng: and that opinion every counsaile is bounde taccepte into a triall of theyr sentences by Ballot: (the maner [f. 77v] of whiche ballottyng shall hereafter appeare) and this privilege, to have his onely opinion ballotted, no man hath but he. And wheras many have reported, that the Duke in ballottyng shoulde have two voices, it is nothyng so: for in gevyng his voice he hath but one ballot, as all others have.

Next unto the Duke are three called the Signori Capi, or Cai,[2] whiche outwardly seeme inferiour to the Duke, and yet are of more auctoritee than he. For theyr power is so absolute, that if there happen cause why, they maie arrest the Duke. And all suche proclamacions as concerne the maiestee of theyr common welth, goe foorth alwaies under theyr name: Lyke as we use to saie in the kynges name, so saie they, Da parte dei Signori Cai.[3] Two of whiche Cai, or one of theim, with one of the Avogadori,[4] have power, Di metter una parte,[5] suche as is before rehersed of the Duke.

Than have they .vi. counsaillours of the most woorthy amonge theim, who are joygned with the Duke to sitte in the college for audience of ambassadours, and other mattiers of importaunce: and these specially are called *La Signoria*.[6] For notwithstandyng there be divers joygned in the same college with them, as, Gli savij della terra ferma,[7] and other moe: yet those .vi. counsaillours are of most reputacion in that place: and accordyngly go alwaies apparailled in skarlet or crimsen silkes.

In deede, *La Signoria*, is commonly used as the name of theyr whole maiestee, and principally it doeth include the Duke, with the reste of the chiefe officers or senatours (to the numbre of three score) that accompanieth him, [f. 78r] whan in his solemnitee he cometh to churche, or goeth unto any of the ordinarie ceremonies abroade in the citee.

Now of suche as have auctoritee to consulte upon mattiers of importaunce (as we shoulde saie, the kynges maiestees privie counsaile) they have .xvii. persons appoincted, called Il Consiglio di dieci:[8] Of whiche the Duke, the three Cai, and the .vi. counsailours are part.

For mattiers of conclusion of peace, of warre, of astate, or of other lyke greatest importaunce, they have a counsaile called, Pregadi,[9] into the whiche entreth the Duke, with the Consiglio de dieci, and of the other principall officers, to the numbre of .200. or theraboutes.

[1] *Di mettere una parte*: present a motion.

[2] *Signori Capi, or Cai*: chief lords; three presidents of the criminal court of appeals (*quarantia criminale*) who sat in the *Signoria and served in rotation for two months.

[3] *Da parte dei Signori Cai*: on behalf of the chief lords of the Capi.

[4] *Avogadori*: *Avogadori de Comùn*: investigating magistrates or public prosecutors and defenders, responsible for overseeing the interests of the *Commune Veneciarum* and handling cases of corruption or breaches of constitutional legality.

[5] *Di metter una parte: di mettere una parte*, to present a motion.

[6] *Signoria.

[7] *Gli savij della terra ferma*: council for the mainland, comprising five members which combined with two other groups of ministers to make up the *Collegio of twenty-six members.

[8] *Council of Ten.

[9] *Pregadi*: literally, the invited or elected; the Senate, the usual legislative assembly of 120 members. Only members of the *Collegio could initiate motions in the Senate.

For mattiers of justice, there be dyvers other offices, as Il Consiglio di Quaranta,[1] Il Consiglio di trenta,[2] gli avogadori, gli Signori di notte,[3] gli Auditori vecchie nuovi,[4] and many mo[r]e: whiche have theyr degrees and orders so appoincted, that not one of theim woulle meddle with an others office: beyng a thyng no lesse fearefull unto theim than poyson. For theyr principall profession is libertee: and he that shoulde usurpe upon an other, shuld incontinently be reputed a tyranne: whiche name of all thynges they can not abyde. For whan a subiect of theyrs saieth: sir, you are my lorde, you are my maister, he taketh it for the greatest villanie of the worlde.

The Signor della Sanita[5] hath the charge to see the citee kept cleane, and the sicke provided for. And as for other particuler officers, that have the oversight of all maner provisions and assise of vittailes, it shall suffise to saie, that there cometh nothyng unto theyr citee, [f. 78v] but it is viewed, and an ordinarie price appoincted unto the seller, to the entent the byer be not deceived.

## Of the great counsaile.

Nowe it behoveth me to saie somewhat of theyr great counsaile, whiche seemeth to be the whole staie of theyr common wealth.

There be about .200. families of name, as Contarini, Morosini, Donati, Badoeri, Foscari, and suche others: of whiche families be welneere the noumbre of 2500. gentilmen. And all they that are of the age of 25. and upwardes, dooe entre into the great counsaile: the ordre of whose admission into the same is: Whan a gentilman is growen unto .20. yeere olde, his father or friendes dooe present him unto the Avogadori, who taketh his name, and with other names of the same sort, putteth it into a boxe, untill the .iiii. of Decembre: beyng the daie appoincted, that all they of that age resorte unto the Duke, unto whom (besides this boxe) there is brought an other boxe, with so many balles, as the names amount unto: of whiche every fifte ball is golde, and all the rest silver. Than taketh the Duke a bill out of one boxe, and a ball out of an other, and if the bill meete with a golden ball, than is that gentilman allowed: and if he meete not, than must he abide a better chaunce the next yere, or els the age of .25.

This foresaied great counsaile[6] maie be lykened to our parliament: For unto it manie mattiers of importaunce are appealed, and that that it dooeth, is unreformable. By it all offices are geven. And into it [f. 79r] entreth the Duke, and all the other officers. And finally there passe so many thynges through that great counsaile (specially offices) that ordinarily everie holidaie, and many times the workendaies,[7] the same sitteth from diner till nyght. The ordre beyng this.

---

[1] *Il Consiglio di Quaranta*: Council of Forty; the three courts of Venice, two *civile* and one *criminale*.

[2] *Il Consiglio di trenta*: Council of Thirty.

[3] *gli Signori di notte*: night commissioners, six district police magistrates.

[4] *gli Auditori vecchie nuovi*: investigating magistrates.

[5] *Signor della Sanita*: health commissioner.

[6] The electorate which chose most officials from the doge down; it was not, however, a legislative body.

[7] *workendaies*: weekend or days at the end of the week. This word is not recorded in the *OED* and 'weekend' is rare before the 19th century. It probably represents Thomas's adaptation of the Italian, *giorni del fine settimana* (weekend days).

They have an hall verie fayre and large, in the principall parte wherof, at the one[1] ende, sitteth the Duke with certaine counsailours. And over against hym at the other ende the Cai: and on the sides the Avogadori, with the other magistrates. Than in the body of the hall there be tenne longe benches from the one ende therof unto the other, and so made, that the gentilmen maie sitte by two rewes on a benche backe to backe. And so every man beyng set, in what place it shal please him to take at his comyng in, the doores are shutte: and the chauncellour standeth up, and readeth the office that is voide, with the names of theim that desyre it: and he that in the election hath most ballottes (so that they passe the halfe noumbre) is admitted officer. If there be none that hath more than halfe the voices as of a 1000. to have .501: than is the election put over till an other daie. This maner of gevyng theyr voices by ballotte, is one of the laudablest thynges used amongest theim. For there is no man can knowe what an other dooeth.

The boxes are made with an holow place at the top, that a man maie put in his hand, and at the ende of that place hange .ii. or .iii. boxes, into whiche he will, he maie let fall his ballot, that no man can perceive hym. If there be but two boxes (as commonly it is in election) the one saieth yea, and the other saieth naie: And [f. 79v] if there be .iii. boxes (whiche for the most part hapneth in cases of judgement) the one saieth yea, thother saith naie, and the thyrde saieth nothyng: and they are all well enough knowen by theyr dyvers colours. By this ordre of ballottyng they procede in judgement thorough all offices, upon all maner of causes: beyng reputed a soveraigne preservacion of justice. For oftentymes the judges maie graunt theyr voyces, and neverthelesse (whan they come to the hearyng of the mattier) dooe as theyr consciences shall leade theim: aunswearyng afterwardes, that they did theyr best, but they could not prevaile.

Finally in the disposyng of theyr offices they use this ordre: that all offices of preeminence, as of the Signoria, that are before rehersed, or the beeyng Potestate,[2] Capitaine, or Governour of any citee, castell, towne, or countrey, maie be geven to none other, but unto gentilmen Venetians. All offices, that be under commandement, as chauncellour, secretaries, and suche others, are bestowed amongest theyr best knowen citesins. For though there be many of those offices of commaundement verie profitable, yet can no gentilman have the benefite therof. Either because they woull mainteyne in theyr personages a certeine maiestee, with theyr lybertee, or els because they woull advoide the inconveniences that maie growe of perpetuitee. For all maner of gentilmens offices, from the highest to the lowest (the Dukes dignitee onely excepted) ar removable, some from yere to yere, some every .ix. monethes, some more, some lesse (for no gentilman maie longe enjoie one office): So all offices, that appertaine unto theyr citesins, are durable [f. 80r] for terme of live without any chaunge.

Amongest all other, this notable ordre they have, that two gentilmen of one familie can not be in one magistrate or hygh office together at ones. By reason wherof those gentilmen, that of one name are fewest in numbre, grow a great deale sooner and oftner to authoritee, than they that be of the most: whiche is thought a wonderfull helpe of their unitee and concorde. For if many of one name shoulde rule at ones, they might happen so to agree, that it should be an undoyng of their common wealthe.

---

[1] *the one*: printed as 'the tone', probably an uncorrected alteration at press of type-setting from 't[']one' to 'the one'.

[2] *Potestate*: Podestà, chief magistrate or senior official.

**¶Of the proctours and treasure.**

There be certeine principall officers, whiche shulde seeme exempted from theyr common wealth, and be neverthelesse head*es* of the same, that is to were xii. of the principallest called *Procuratori di San Marco*,[1] out of whiche numbre the Duke is alwaie chosen: and those have theyr offices for terme of life, with a certeine stipende of an hundreth dukates a yere, or there about. Theyr charge is, some to governe the revenewes and treasure of the common wealth, and some the rentes and treasure of saincte Markes churche.

As for the treasure of theyr common wealth I could never fynde the meane to see it: but I have been crediblie enformed, that it is a great summe of readie money locked up in chestes, (that no man maie come at) whiche is sometyme more and sometyme lesse, as theyr wealth or charges encrease. And thoughe theyr revenewe be [f. 80v] verie great, yet consideryng the often warres that they have, the great wages that the senatours and officers receive, the noumbre of straunge capitaines that they wage for terme of life, the noumbre of castels and fortresses that they maintaine, fortified with watche and warde, theyr continuall costly buildynges, and finally the unreasonable charge of theyr Arsenale, and of their galeys abrode, I thynke they can not laie up any great some at the yeres ende.

The other treasure of sainct Markes churche, I have seen: the principall thing wherof is a table on the high aulter, plated over with silver, graven and enameled, and set full of preciouse stones of all sortes. And than in a little stronge corner on the southsyde of the churche are certeine plates of golde muche lyke womens partelettes[2] set full of riche stones, a goodly imperiall crowne for theyr Duke, two fayre unicornes hornes, and divers other thynges, the value wherof consisteth onely in the preciouse stones: For the golde that is about theim is but small in quantitee, but the stones are many in numbre, excellent great and fayre, and almost inestimable of price.

Finally to retourne unto the Proctours, theyr reputacion is the greatest next the Dukes, and there is none can clymbe unto that dignitee, but either he must be so woorthy, auncient and notable a man, as fewe lyke are to be founde amongest theim: or els so riche, that in time of neede he hath before his election releaved the common wealth with the lone of a notable summe of money. Whiche seconde sort of election is also commen uppe of late, sens[3] money (as some saie) hath entred in more reputacion than vertue.

[f. 81r] **Of lawes.**

Theyr advocates (as we shoulde saie our men of law) studie principally the civile lawes,[4] and besydes that the statutes and customes of the citee: whiche are so many, that in maner they suffise of theim selfes. But he that substancially considereth the maner of theyr procedynges, shall plainly see, that all mattiers are determined by the judges consciences, and not by the civile, nor yet by theyr owne lawes. For in every office there be dyvers judges, and that parte that hath most ballottes, prevaileth ever: be it in mattier of debt, of title of lande, upon life and death, or otherwise. And in every triall of thefte, murder, or suche other, the partie hym selfe is never suffred to speake. But there be certeine advocates waged of the common revenewe, whiche with no lesse studie pleade in their defence, than the Avogadori, in the contrarie. One daie the Avogador cometh into the

---

[1] *Procuratori di San Marco*: Procurators of St Mark (**Plate 21**).

[2] *partelettes*: ornamental neckbands.

[3] *sens*: since.

[4] *civile lawes*: based upon Roman law.

courte, and laieth against the felon that, that either by examinacion, by torture, or by witnesse hath been proved: And an other daie cometh in th'advocate, and defendeth the felon with the best aunsweare he can devise: so that many tymes the prisoner tarieth .ii.iii. and sometyme .iiii. yeres, er ever he come unto his triall of life and death.

This ordre they observe in Venice onely. For out of Venice the gentilman Venetian, that is Potestate of the citee, towne, or place, hath absolute power to judge upon all mattiers hym selfe alone: how be it every of theim, hath a counsaile of learned men, to advise hym what the law commaundeth. Besides that, every .v. [f. 81v] yeres there be certaine inquisitours, called Sindici,[1] sent foorth to refourme extorcions, and all other thynges that they finde amisse, throughout theyr whole dominion.

Finally there is a law in Venice, that no gentilman Venetian maie speake with any ambassadour, without licence of the Signoria, for feare of intelligence, or of daungerouse practise. And because they feare, least civile sedicion might be the destruction of their common wealth, as of dyvers other it hath been, therefore they have provided an ordre, that whan any two gentilmen happen to fall out, either they dooe so dissemble it, that theyr malice never appeareth to the worlde, or els they agree within theim selfes. For if it come to the Signorias knowlage, it can not be chosen, but he that is most faultie receiveth a great rebuke, and many tymes in those cases divers are banished, or sharpely punished. As for theyr other lawes, though I were sufficiently expert in theim, yet partly for briefenesse, and partly because they are not so muche necessarie to my purpose, I passe theim over. But this is cleere, there can be no better ordre of Justice in a common wealth than theirs, if it were duely observed. How be it corrupcion (by the advocates meanes) is so crept in amongest the judges, that poore men many times can want[2] no delaies in the processe of theyr mattiers.

## Of warre.
I Finde two sortes of warre, one by sea, an other by lande.

By sea[3] the Venetians theim selfes governe the [f. 82r] whole, and by lande they are served of straungers, both for generall, for capitaines, and for all other men of warre, because theyr lawe permitteth not any Venetian to be captaine over an armie by lande. (Fearyng, I thynke, Caesars example).[4] Neverthelesse with theyr armie by lande, they sende foorthe dyvers of theyr gentilmen, some as legates, some as paiemaisters. So that theyr general, (what noble men so ever he be) hath alwaies a counsaile of the Venetians about him, by whom in maner all thynges are dooen.

And by sea every Galey hath one gentilman Venetian for capitaine, by the name of Sopracomito,[5] and over a noumbre of galeys one Legate (as it were, an admyrall) that maie hange and punisshe at his pleasure. This is ordinarie both in peace and warre. For though the peace be never so sure and quiet, yet faile thei not to send forth yerely certaine

---

[1] *Sindici*: controllers or inspectors.

[2] *want*: lack or avoid.

[3] The senior Venetian naval commander was the Captain General of the Sea (*Capitano Generale da Mar*).

[4] To avoid the risk of a military coup Venetians were not appointed as commanders of land armies. Instead, foreigners, known as *condottieri* (contracted), were chosen with their leadership monitored by two senior patricians. They were often granted residences on the Grand Canal and estates on the mainland. This custom explains why Shakespeare made Othello commander of the Venetian forces on Cyprus in *The Tragedy of Othello the Moor of Venice* (*c*.1603/4).

[5] *Sopracomito*: chief captain.

armed galeis to kepe the seas against Corsales,[1] and Pyrates: not onely because their merchaundise maie passe saufely to and fro, but also for the honour that they claime in the dominion therof. For yerely on the ascension daie, the Duke, with the senate in theyr best araie use to goe into the haven at Li[d]o, and there by throwyng a rynge into the water, to take the sea as theyr espouse.[2]

Finally whan they happe to have any daungerouse warre by sea or lande, they create a Proveditore,[3] who (out of Venice) is of no lesse authoritee, than the Dictatour was wont to be in Rome, specially by sea. And lightly they never make a Proveditore, but either they be in great feare, or perill. And throughout all theyr dominion, within any citee or walled towne, no man maie carie weapon without a speciall licence.[4]

## [f. 82v] Of common provision, and charitable deedes.

Theyr diligente use in provision for graine is notable. For be it deare or good cheape theyr common graner (whiche is a myghtie great house) is in maner alwaies furnisshed. So that lyghtly in the citee can be no great dearth, because many tymes of their owne common purse, they are contented to lose for the poore peoples reliefe (though an other tyme they paie theim selfes the double).

They have also certaine schooles or felowships gathered together for devocion, as one of sainct Marke, an other of sainct Rooke, one of this sainct, an other of that: which (beyng for the most part substanciall men) dooe releeue a noumbre of the poore after this sorte.

[margin: Poore people.] They geve theim ones a yere a course liverey, with a certaine small stipende, for the whiche the poore man is bounde to carie a taper at one of the bretherne or sisters buriall, and besides that to attende certeine holidaies at the schoole, where the principall bretherne assemble, to dispose unto the mariage of poore younge women and in other good woorkes, that part of money that theyr rate for the time dooeth allow: and afterwardes (with theyr priestes and clerkes) goe a procession a certaine circuite, in the whiche the poore men lykewyse carie their tapers before theim.

[margin: Hospitals.] Furthermore there are certaine hospitalles, some for the sicke and diseased, and some for poore orphanes, in [sig. 83r] whiche they are nourished up till they come unto yeres of service: and than is the man childe put unto a craft, and the maidens kept till they be maried. If she be fayre, she is soone had, and little money geven with hir: if she be foule, they avaunce hir with a better porcion of money.

For the plague, there is an house of many lodgeynges, two miles from Venice, called the Lazaretto,[5] unto the whiche all they of that house, wherin one hath been infected of the plague, are incontinently sent, and a lodgeyng sufficiente appoincted for theim till the infection ceasse, that they maie retourne.

[margin: Prisoners] Finally for prisoners they have this ordre: Twyse a yere, at Christmas, and Easter, the Auditori[6] dooe visite all the prisones in Venice, and there geve

---

[1] *Corsales*: variant of *corsaro*, corsair.

[2] *Marriage of the Sea. The Bucentaur in service at the time of Thomas's visit to Venice was used from 1526 until 1606.

[3] *Proveditore*: literally a purveyor, high commissioner or chief commissar.

[4] See pp. 203–4 for Philip Sidney's application to bear arms during his residence at Venice.

[5] *Lazzaretto Vecchio.

[6] *Auditori*: examining magistrates of the civil courts.

audience unto all creaditours that have any debtour in prison for the summe of .50. duckates and under. If the partie be hable to paie, daies are geven,[1] and sureties founde: and if the debt be desperate, than dooe they theim selfes agree with the partie for more or lesse, as the likelyhode is, and paie hym of the common purse. So that ere ever they depart, they emptie the prisones of all theim that lie for that summe.

**Of customes in their lyvyng.**

To speake of the gentilman Venetians private life and customes, I wote not whether it be best to folow the common reporte: or to dissemble the mattier. And yet me seemeth I can not dooe more indifferently [f. 83v] than recite what is used to be said on both sides.

If any man woulde saie, there were no woorthy men amongest the Venetians, he shoulde greatly erre. For (as I beleve) there be some, and specially of those olde fatherly men, as wyse, as honest, as faiethfull, as honorable, and as vertuous, as in any place can be found. Lykewise some of the younge men, as gentill, as liberall, as valiaunt, as well learned, as full of good qualitees, as maie be. But to speake of the greatter numbre, straungers use to reporte, that the gentilman Venetian is proude, disdeinfull, covetouse, a great nygarde, a more leachour, spare of livyng, tyranne to his tenant, finally never satisfied with hourdyng up of money. For though (saie they) he have .viii. ix. or .x. thousand duckates of yeerely revenew, yet woull he kepe no moe persones in his house, but his wife and children, with ii. or .iii. women servauntes, and one man, or two at the most, to row his Gondola. He woull goe to the market hym selfe, and spende so miserablie, that many a meane man shall fare better than he. Of his .10000. duckates a yere, if he spend three or .iiii.C. in his house, he estemeth it a wonderfull charge.[2] Besides all this, he hath .ii. or .iii. Jewes, that choppe and chaunge[3] with him daiely: by whose usurie he gaineth out of measure. And yet woull be rather see a poore man starve, than relieve hym with a penie. It is true, he woul have his wife goe gaie and sumptuously apparailed, and on his woman besides, if he be a lover (as in maner they be all) he woull sticke for no coste. To the mariage of his daughter .30 . 40 . or . 50. thousande duckates is no mervaile. Finally his greatest triumphe is, whan [f. 84r] saincte Marke hath neede (for under that name is comprehended theyr common welth) to be hable to disburse an huge summe of money in lone, to receive yerely till he be repaied .10. 12 . or . 15. of the . hundreth.

This kynde of prest[4] the Signoria useth to take (borowyng of all them that are hable to lende) whan they happen to have warres. And they that maie, doe the more willyngly lende: because they are not onely well paied againe with the usurie, but also the more honoured and favoured as long as theyr money is out of their handes.

This is theyr trade,[5] saieth the straunger. But the Venetian to the contrary defendeth hym selfe on this wyse.

Admitte (saieth he) that this report were true, If I be proude, I have good cause, for I am a prince and no subjecte. If I be spare of livyng, it is because my common wealth alloweth no pompe, and measure is holesome. If I kepe few servantes, it is because I nede

---

[1] *daies are geven*: due dates given (for release).

[2] *charge*: expense. During Thomas's time at Venice the ducat was equal to about 5 shillings and 4 pence; this equates to 4 ducats (21 shillings and 4 pence), close to an English guinea (21 shillings).

[3] *choppe and change*: buy and sell; trade and negotiate.

[4] *prest*: loan.

[5] *trade*: common practice (of moneylending and usury).

no moe. If I bye my meate my selfe, it is because, I woul eate that, that I love, & that (having little a do) I woul exercise my selfe withall. As for my tenaunt, he liveth by me, and I am no tyranne for husbandyng myne owne. If I gaine, I gaine upon my money, and hide not my talent in the grounde. If I love, I hate not: if she be fayre, I am the more woorthie. If I spende little, I have the more in my purse. If I spend largely with my daughter, it is because I woull bestow hir on a gentilman Venetian, to encrease the nobilitee of myne owne bloudde, and by meane of suche aliaunce to atteine more habilitee to rule and reigne in my [f. 84v] common wealth: Besydes that, my money: if hir housbande die, is hirs and no mans els. If my wyfe goe gaie, it is to please myne eie, and to satisfie hir. In kepyng my money to lende unto sainct Marke, it is both an helpe to my common wealth, and a profite unto my selfe.

And thus defendeth the Venetian it, that in maner all the worlde layeth unto his charge.

But surely many of theim trade and bringe up theyr children in so muche libertee, that one is no sooner out of the shell, but he is hayle felow with father and friend, and by that time he cometh to .xx. yeres of age, he knoweth as muche lewdnesse as is possible to be imagined. For his greatest exercise is to goe amongest his companions, to this good womans[1] house and that. Of whiche in Venice are many thousandes of ordinarie, lesse than honest. And no mervaile of the multitude of theyr common women, for among the gentilmen is a certeine use, that if there be divers brethern, lightly but one of theim dooeth marie: because the numbre of gentilmen shoulde not so encrease, that at length their common wealth myght waxe vile:[2] wherfore the rest of the brethern dooe kepe Courtisanes, to the entent they maie have no laufull children. And the bastardes that they begette become most commonly monkes, friers, or nunnes: who by theyr friendes meanes are preferred to the offices of most profite, as abbottes, priours, and so foorth. But specially those Courtisanes are so riche, that in a maske, or at the feast of a mariage, or in the shrovyng tyme: you shall see theim decked with jewelles, as they were Queenes. So that it is thought no one citee [f. 85r] againe hable to compare with Venice, for the numbre of gorgeouse dames. As for theyr beaultie of face, though they be fayre in deede, I woull not highly commende theim, because there is in maner none, olde or yonge unpeincted. In deede of theyr stature they are for the most parte veraie goodly and bygge women, well made and stronge.

### ¶ The libertee of straungers.

Al men, specially strangers, have so muche libertee there, that though they speake verie ill by the Venetians, so they attempt nothyng in effecte against theyr astate, no man shall controll theim for it. And in theyr Carnovale time (whiche we call shroftide) you shall see maskers disguise theim selfes in the Venetians habite, and come unto theyr owne noses in derision of theyr customes, theyr habite, and miserie.

Further, he that dwelleth in Venice, maie recken him selfe exempt from subiection. For no man there marketh an others dooynges, or that meddleth with an other mans livyng. If thou be a papist, there shalt there want no kinde of supersticion to feede upon. If thou be a gospeller,[3] no man shall aske why thou comest not to churche. If thou be a Jewe, a Turke, or beleevest in the divell (so thou spreade not thyne opinions abroade) thou arte free from

---

[1] *good womans*: mistress or prostitute.
[2] *vile*: poor.
[3] *gospeller*: protestant or evangelical.

all controllement. To lyve maried or unmaried, no man shall aske the why. For eating of flesshe in thyne owne house, what daie so ever it be, it maketh no mattier.[1] And generally of all other thinges, so thou offende no man privately, no man shall [f. 85v] offende the[e]: whiche undoubtedly is one principall cause, that draweth so many straungers thither.

## An abbridgement of the Venetian histories from the edificacion of the citee vnto this daie.

[Thomas provides a chronicle history of Venice from its earliest foundations. Only the section referring to the period from the 1450s until the 1540s is reproduced here.]

[f. 107v] ¶About this tyme the Turke wonne Constantinople,[2] in the takyng wherof the emperour of Grece,[3] with divers gentilmen Venetians, valiauntelie resistyng their ennemies, both by sea and lande, were slaine, besides a numbre of others taken prisoners, with the losse of theyr navie and substaunce. Wherfore the bishop of Rome[4] toke upon him the appeasyng of the Italian warres: agreyng the parties on this wise: that *Sforza*[5] shoulde restore unto the Venetians all that that he had taken [f. 108r] from them in those warres (the castelles of *Gieradadda*[6] onely excepted) that the kynge of Naples shoulde do the like to the Florentines (*Castiglione*[7] excepted) and the Florentines to doe the lyke to the *Senese*.[8] And that whan anie controversy shoulde happen of newe betwene them, the bishop of Rome should order the mattier without any businesse of warre.

The Genowaies[9] were left out of this peace, by meane of the kyng of Naples.[10]

Federike emperour of Almaine[11] requyred ambassadours from all the princes of Europe, to make a newe league against the Turke.

But this meane whyle *Bartholomeo Marcello*[12] retourned from Constantinople with an ambassadour of the Turkes, that brought certeine articles of agreement to the senate,

---

[1] This level of religious tolerance was not always shown to Venice's own citizens, as illustrated by the Venetian Inquisition's rigorous questioning of Orazio Cuoco, a choirboy who was taken back to England by Edward de Vere, Earl of Oxford, see pp. 220–21.

[2] 29 May 1453.

[3] Constantine XI Dragases Palaiologos (Palaeologus) (1405–53), the last reigning Roman and Byzantine Emperor.

[4] The Italian Dominican Pope Nicholas V (1397–55; Pope, 1447–55). His attempt to rally Christian military forces to defend Constantinople was unsuccessful but he commanded ten papal ships, with others from Venice, Genoa and Naples, to sail to the city which fell before they arrived. He then preached the need for a Crusade against the Ottomans but without success.

[5] Francesco I Sforza (1401–66), founder of the dynasty and 4th Duke of Milan (from 1450); praised by Niccolò Machiavelli in *The Prince*.

[6] *Gieradadda*: relating to the Battle of Gieradadda (Gieredada) in 1509.

[7] Castiglione della Pescaia, central Tuscany, renowned for its medieval fortress.

[8] *Senese: Sienese*.

[9] *Genowaies*: Genoese.

[10] Alfonso the Magnanimous (1396–1458), King of Aragon, Valencia, Majorca, Sardinia, Corsica and Sicily. He was also King of Naples from 1442 to 1458.

[11] Frederick III (1415–93), Holy Roman Emperor 1452–93.

[12] On 17 July 1453 the Venetian envoy Bartolomeo Marcello was sent by the Senate to Constantinople to negotiate with Mehmed II a renewal of a peace treaty (confirmed 18 April 1454) which Venice has signed with his predecessor Murad II on 10 September 1451. This treaty granted the Venetians protection for their trade and properties within the Ottoman Empire and free access to Constantinople and other Turkish ports. Marcello was also appointed as *bailo* (bailiff or head) of a Venetian trading colony at Constantinople. Freely, *Grand Turk*, pp. 58–9.

whiche the Venetians accepted: and therupon was confyrmed amitee betweene the Turke and theim.

[*margin*: Pasquale Malipiero 1457.] After the death of *Foscaro*[1] succeded *Pasquale Malipiero,* of whom I fynde nothyng of importaunce, savyng that in his time hapned the terrible earthquake in Italie, that specially in the realme of Naples did so muche hurte:[2] and that emprintyng was than fyrste invented.[3]

[*margin*: Christofero Moro. 1462] After him succeded *Christofero Moro,*[4] in whose time the Turkes wanne by force, and rased to the earth the Venetian walle, made upon *Istmus* of *Morea,* and after didde in maner what they woulde thoroughout all that region.[5]

This *Morea,* aunciently called *Peloponnessus,* is the chiefe parte of Greece, a verie riche countrey, [f. 109v] compassed about with the sea, except in one narow place, that it seemeth tacked unto the maine lande: in whiche place beyng about six myle over, was suche a walle made, as with reasonable furniture had been sufficient to resiste a wonderfull power. But the Venetians (because they fyrste of Christian princes, entred in amitee with those infidelles) trustyng to muche in theyr newe friendship, attended more to the undoyng of theyr neighbours at home, than to the earnest provision that so worthie a countrey, agaynst so puissaunte an ennemie, the Turke, requyred. So that shortly after the losse of that wall,[6] they were shamefully discoumfited at *Patrasso:*[7] *James Barbarico*[8] beyng theyr *Proveditore.* And than also they loste *Negroponte,*[9] where was suche a slaughter of Christians, as woulde make any Christian herte wepe to heare it. Besides a huge summe of money, that they were constreigned to geve to the kyng of Hungarie,[10] to resist the Turkes passage, that with an other armie by lande was than comyng towardes *Dalmatia.*

[*margin*: Nicolo Trono. 1471] Than succeded *Nicolo Trono,*[11] who was cause of the establishement of *Ercole da Este* in the duchie of *Ferrara.*[12]

---

[1] Francesco Foscari (1373–1457), Doge 1423–57.

[2] A major earthquake, centred on Benevento, north of Naples, occurred on 30 Dec. 1456.

[3] Moveable type printing, traditionally developed by Johannes Gutenberg (c.1400–68) at Mainz, reached Venice with a press established there by Johannes of Speyer (de Spira) (d. 1469) who was granted a five-year monopoly.

[4] Cristoforo Moro (1390–1471), Doge 1462–71.

[5] First Ottoman-Venetian War (1463–79).

[6] Probably a reference to the Hexamilion Wall, a defensive structure constructed across the Isthmus of Corinth, protecting the major land route into the Pelo peninsula from mainland Greece; abandoned c.1460.

[7] Patras.

[8] Giosafat (Giosaphat, Josaphat) Barbaro (1413–94), a member of the notable patrician Barbarigo family of Venice; Marco (1413–86) was Doge from 1485–6 and was succeeded by his brother Agostino (1419–1501), Doge from 1486–1501. An account of Barbaro's travels, *Viaggi fatti da Vinetia, alla Tana, in Persia* (1543–5), was published by the sons of Aldus Manutius and Thomas seems to have used a copy when compiling his history of Venice. He also later presented King Edward VI with a manuscript translation of this work, BL Royal MS 17 C x.

[9] Negroponte, the Venetian name for the city of Chalcis on the Greek island of Euboea; also used as a name for the island itself. After its fall to the Turks in 1470, the Venetians signed a collaborative pact with Naples, the Papal States, Cyprus and the Knights of Rhodes against the Turks.

[10] Matthias Corvinus (1443–90), King Matthias I of Hungary and Croatia from 1458–90.

[11] Nicolò Tron (1399–1473), Doge 1471–3.

[12] Ercole I d'Este (1431–1505), became Duke of Ferrara in 1471 with assistance from the Republic of Venice, enabling him to succeed his half-brother Borso while the latter's son, Niccolò, was in Mantua. Niccolò later led a coup when Ercole was away from Ferrara but was captured and beheaded on 4 September 1476.

He entred in league with *Usnucassan* kyng of *Persia* (whose successour is nowe called *Sophie*) against the Turke.[1]

In his tyme the Venetians gatte the realme of *Cyprus* by this meane. James, last kyng of the same, for the great amitee betweene his forefathers and the Venetians, came unto Venice, and requyred the *Signoria* to adopt one of theyr daughters, as daughter of theyr common wealth: and than woulde he be contented [f. 109r] to accepte hir unto his wyfe.[2]

This large offer was soone accepted, and *Katheryn Cornaro*, a goodly yonge gentilwoman espowsed to the kynge, who therupon retourned into his realme continuyng in peace the tyme of his life. At his deathe, (leavyng his wife great with childe) he ordeined, that she and hir childe not yet borne, shoulde enjoy the realme· But the childe after the birth lived not longe.

[*margin*: Cyprus wonne.] Assoone as the Venetians hearde of the kynges death, they armed certaine galleys, and sent them with *Georgio Cornaro*, brother to the Quene into Cyprus,[3] to comforte hir on the *Signorias* behalfe: with this wile, that whan *Cornaro* shoulde arrive before *Famagosta* (the principall citee of Cyprus) he should feigne him selfe so sicke, that he might not go out of the shippe, and whan his sister the Quene, with hir barons shoulde come to visite hym, than shoulde he kepe theim sure from retournyng, and sodeinelye entre the citee, subduyng it with the whole realme, unto the Venetian obedience. As it was devised, so it happened from poinct to poinct, albeit that the Quene was counsailed not to go abourde the galey, and that some businesse was made after for it, yet in effect the Venetians prevailed, & the Quene was brought to Venice, where she passed the rest of hir yeres.

Some esteme this doing treason, but many men allow it for a good policie.

[*margin*: Nicolas Marcello 1473.] After *Trono* folowed *Nicolas Marcello*,[4] in whose tyme happened no notable thyng, other than the victoriouse defence of the towne of *Scodra* in *Albania*[5] against an infinite numbre of Turkes.

[*margin*: Peter Mocenigo. 1474.] Next hym succeded *Peter Mocenigo*, whiche at the [f.109v] tyme of his election, was capitaine of an armie by sea, wherwith he had in Cyprus quieted a great rebellyon, preserved *Scodra* from the Turkes furie, and restored the kynge of *Carramania* to his astate.[6]

---

[1] Uzun Hasan (Uzun Hassan) (1423–78), 9th Shahanshah of the ghuz Turkic Aq Qoyunlu dynasty, ruled 1453–78. The Sofi (Sophy, Sophie, Soffi) refers to the rulers of the Safavid dynasty in Persia from the time of its founder Ismail I (Sofi, 1501–24).

[2] Cyprus formally became a Venetian possession in 1489 (until 1571 when it was conquered by Ottomans). Thomas refers to the marriage by proxy in 1468 of King James II of Cyprus (*c.*1438/39–73) with Catherine Cornaro (1454–1510) from a patrician Venetian family. The marriage was celebrated in person in November 1472. After James II's death – rumoured to have been caused by Venetian agents – Catherine acted as regent and then queen when their infant son James III died in 1474. During her reign the island was effectively controlled by Venetian merchants but she was forced to abdicate on 14 March 1489 so that Cyprus's administration could be taken over by the Republic. Thomas's reference to a daughter may be to one of James II's two illegitimate daughters, Charlotte (d. *c.*1469) or Charla (d. 1480).

[3] Giorgio Cornaro (1452–1527), known as 'Padre della Patria', Knight of the Holy Roman Empire and Procurator of St Mark's.

[4] Nicolò Marcello (1399–1474) was Doge for only a short period (13 Aug. 1473–1 Dec.1474).

[5] Shkodër (Shkodra, Scutari), Albania.

[6] Pietro Mocenigo (1406–76), Doge 1474–6, distinguished admiral who placed Queen Catherine Cornaro under Venetian protection and defeated the Turks who were then besieging Shkodër. King Ibrahim ruled Carramania (Cicilia), a south coastal region of Asia Minor, when it was captured by the Ottomans.

For these woorthie deedes, and for his other vertues was in his absence first made Proctour of. S. Marke, and than (as I saied) created Duke. And beyng called home from the armie, to governe the dominion, *Antonio Loredano*[1] was sent foorth in his stede: who delivered *Lepanto* from the Turkes siege, and used great diligence in the conservacion of the countrey of *Morea*.

[*margin*: Andrea Vendramino. 1476.] After *Mocenigo, Andrea Vendramino*[2] was elected Duke. In whose tyme the Turkes retournyng into *Albania*, came fyrste before *Croia*,[3] and after overran all the countreis betwene that and the river of *Tagliamento* in *Friuli*:[4] so that the Venetians were faine to call backe the capitaine *Carlo Montone*,[5] who not long before put out of wages was than gone into *Tuscane*.

This Duke attempted a peace with the Turkes, but his purpose was interrupted by meanes of the kynge of Hungarie and of Naples.

[*margin*: John Mocenigo 1478.] After *Vendramino* folowed *John Mocenigo*, brother to Peter beforenamed.[6]

This man agreed with the Turke, after they had warred with him .17. yeres. The articles of accorde were, that the Venetians shoulde yelde into the Turkes handes *Scodra*, the principall citee of *Albania*, with the ilandes of *Corfu, Tenaro*, and *Lemno*,[7] and besides that shoulde paye him .8000. duckates a yere. In consideracion wherof the Turke for his parte graunted theim safe passage for trafficque of merchaundise into the sea [f. 110r] nowe called *Mare Maggiore*, and auncientlie named *Pontus Euxinus*:[8] and that the Venetians shoulde have power to sende an officer of theirs under the name of *Bailo* to Constantinople, to judge and order all their merchauntes businesse.

Not longe after this agreement, the Ile of *Corritta* in *Dalmatia*,[9] was broughte under the Venetian dominion.

And in the .iiii. yere of this mans rule, warre was moved against *Ercole* Duke of *Ferrara*, for the breache of certeine articles betwene hym and the Venetians.[10]

After that Robert of. S. *Severino*[11] was sente with an armie against *Ferrando* kyng of Naples,[12] in whiche enterprise the Venetians discomfited *Alfonse* Duke of

---

[1] Antonio Loredan (1420–82), Captain of Shkodër (Scutari) and Governor in the Morea (1466), Split (1467–9) and Albania (1473); Venetian commander during the successful defence of Scutari (1474) and during the seizing of Cyprus; Procurator of St Mark (1578).

[2] Andrea Vendramin (1393–1478), Doge 1476–8; his brief reign was largely preoccupied with the final stages of the Second Venetian-Ottoman War.

[3] Croia (Krujë), in north central Albania. The Ottomans finally took control of it in 1478 after a fourth siege.

[4] River Tagliamento, north-east Italy, flowing from the Alps to the Adriatic Sea between Trieste and Venice; its source lies on the border between the Veneto and Friuli-Venezia Giulia.

[5] Carlo di Montone (1421–79), a noted condottiero, served the Venetians in Friuli against the Turks in 1575 but then accepted alternative paid military service in Tuscany; recalled to Friuli by the Venetians in 1476/7 to strengthen their fortifications.

[6] Giovanni Mocenigo (1409–85), the brother of Pietro Mocenigo, was Doge 1478–85.

[7] Corfu, Cape Tenaro (Matapan) and Lemnos.

[8] The Black Sea, known as Mare Maggiore, *c.* AD 500–1500, and Pontus Euxinus, *c.* 700 BC – AD 500.

[9] Corrita (Gorrita, Corita, Korita), now in Croatia.

[10] In 1482–84 Giovanni Mocenigo, allied with Pope Sixtus IV, fought the War of Ferrara against Ercole I d'Este, Duke of Ferraro, over a salt monopoly. Ercole I ceded Polesine under the Peace of Bagnolo and the Venetians regained Rovigo.

[11] Roberto Sanseverino d'Aragona (1418–87), *condottiero*, Count of Colomo (1458–77) and Caiazzo (1460–87).

[12] Ferdinand I (1423–94), also known as Ferrante, King of Naples (1458–94).

*Calabria*,[1] sonne of the foresaied kynge. But those warres, by meane of the other Princes of Italie, were soone appeased, whan the Duke of *Ferrara* (besides the losse of *Comacchio*)[2] had susteined verie great damage, for his parte takyng.

[*margin*: Marco Barbarico 1485.] Nexte to *Vendramino* succeded, *Marco Barbarico*,[3] who never seking to be avenged on his enemie, woulde saie, *It suffised a discreate prince, to have power to revenge, wherby his ennemie shoulde have cause to feare him.* Therfore he used severitee against the transgressours of the common wealth, and not against theim that privately offended hym. In his daies hapned littell adoe.

[*margin*: Agostino Barbarico 1486.] The contrarie wherof folowed in the tyme of his successour *Agostino Barbarico*.[4]

Firste by reason of the warres with Edmonde Duke of Austriche, for the interest of certain mynes of yron: in whiche enterprise the Venetian capitaine Robert of. S. [f. 110v] *Severino* died:[5] than thoroughe the comyng of *Charles* the .viii. Frenche kynge into Italie, who at lengthe, partly through the Venetian force was constreigned to retyre into Fraunce:[6] but most of all they were troubled with the Turkes, who fell out with theim, overanne all their countreis as farre as *Tagliomento*,[7] slew above. 7000. persons of the Venetian parte, and toke from theim *Lepanto, Modone, Corone,* and *Durazo*.[8] Nevertchelesse this meane whyle the Venetians gatte *Cremona*, and divers other townes in Italie, whiche is rather a reproche to the*m*, than an honor that wolde lieffer[9] warre upon their christen neighbours, than bende their power to resist the Turkes.

[*margin*: Leonardo Loredano. 1501.] After *Barbarico, Leonardo Loredano*[10] was elected to the astate: in whose tyme all Christian princes about the Venetians, conspyred by one accorde utterly to destroie theim. And the league was suche, that in one selfe tyme the emperour *Maximilian*, Lewys the .xii. Frenche kynge,[11] *Ferrando* kyng of Spaine and of Naples,[12] *Julius* bishop of Rome, with the Dukes of Mantua and *Ferrara*,[13] should warre upon theim, beginnyng about the yere of grace .1509. So partly by force, after many

---

[1] Alfonso II (1448–95), also known as Alfonso of Aragon, Duke of Calabria and King of Naples (1494–5); fought as a *condottiero* in the War of Ferrara.

[2] Commachio, situated in the lagoon at the mouth of the River Reno in the province of Ferrara.

[3] Marco Barbarigo (*c*.1413–86), Doge 1485–6.

[4] Agostino Barbarigo (1419–1501), Doge 1486–1501.

[5] Sigismund (1427–96), Duke (1439–77) and Archduke (1477–96) of Austria, seized iron and silver mines from the Venetians at Primiero and Val Sugana. Sanseverino died at the Battle of Calliano.

[6] Charles VIII (1470–98), King of France 1483–98. René of Anjou (1409–80) had left the Neapolitan throne to his father, King Louis XI (1423–83), which led to his invasion of Italy in 1494–8.

[7] River Tagliamento.

[8] Agostino Barbarigo's contacts with the Ottoman Sultan Bayezid II (1447–1512) became strained from 1492, leading to a Venetian-Ottoman War (1499–1503). Venetian merchants at Constantinople were arrested and Venetian territories in Dalmatia as far as Zara (Zadar) were occupied, The Battle of Zonchio (1499), also known as Battle of Sapienza, saw the defeat of the Venetian fleet and the loss of Lepanto, followed by Modone, Corone and Durazzo (Durrës). These losses deprived Venetian merchants of most of their usual stopping points for the Levant trade.

[9] *lieffer*: gladly or willingly.

[10] Leonardo Loredan (Loredano) (1436–1521), Doge 1501–21 (**Frontispiece**).

[11] Maximilian I (1459–1519), Holy Roman Emperor; and King Louis XII (1462–1515).

[12] Ferdinand II (1452–1516), King of Aragon (1479–1519); King of Castile as Ferdinand V (1474–1504); King of Naples as Ferdinand III (1504–19); and King of Navarre (1512–19).

[13] Pope Julius II (1443–1513); Francesco II Gonzaga (1466–1519), Marquess of Mantua; and Alfonso d'Este (1476–1534), Duke of Mantua.

discoumfitures of the Venetians power, partly by accorde: in maner all the Venetian dominion with in the maine lande was divided amongest these princes. The frenche kyng had *Bressa, Bergamo, Cremona,* and *Crema*: the emperour *Maximilian, Verona, Vicenza, Padoa,* and parte of *Friuli*: The kyng of Spaine, the citees and portes in *Puglia,* that the Venetians before had gotten: *The bishop* of Rome, *Arimino, Faenza, Ravenna,* and *Cervia,* with the rest of *Romagnia*: and the [f. 111r] Duke of *Ferrara* the *Pollisene di Rovigo*. So that the Venetians had so little dominion lefte on the maine lande· that the emperour *Maximilian* came to *Maestie*:[1] v. little myles from Venice, as neere as the sea would suffre hym to approche: and there for a triumphe or despite, shotte of his artillerie to Venicewardes: though he coulde dooe it no hurt. Wherfore the Venetians, provoked in maner by despayre, and through an oracion made by theyr Duke, that encouraged theim rather to die lyke men, than to suffre theim selfes thus vilie to be eaten up and despysed, renued an armie by lande, recovered *Padoa,* than negligently kept, fortified it and *Treviso,* fought dyvers tymes with variable fortune against theyr enemies, fought to be revenged on the Duke of *Ferrara,* against whom they sent .xvii. galleys and 400. botes to assaile the Ferrarese dominion by the river of *Pò*: and finally behaved theim selfes so manfully, that the kyng of Spaine, and the bishop of Rome, made a new league with them against the frenche kyng: who at that tyme, besydes the state of Myllaine, had gotten Bononia,[2] and was become so great in Italy, that they were all afearde of hym.[3] Upon conclusion of whiche league the citesins of *Bressa* retourned to the Venetian obedience, so that for defence of that citee against the Frenchemen, *Andrea Gr[i]tti*, with certeine other noble Venetians and capitaines, and a convenient noumbre of souldiours, were sent thither: where after a sore conflict with the Frenchemen, they were all discoumfited, slaine or taken, and the principall prisoners sent to Myllaine to *Mounser du Foys*, than governour there, who s[e]nt *Andrea Gritti*, as a singuler presente, [f. 111v] prisoner to the Frenche kyng.[4]

The Venetians not a little troubled for this losse, caused the campe of the league, that than laie before Bononia to draw towardes Ferrara: and in succour of that campe, made a new armie by water, wherwith they sacked *Argenta,* toke *Mirandula,* and did muche hurte to the Ferrarese dominion, till at laste the *Vice Roy,* of Spaine generall of the saied campe, came before Bononia, and from thense to *Ravenna* for feare of the Frenche host, that from Myllaine pursued him. Unto whiche Frenche armie the Duke of Ferrara united his power, and so together folowed the armie of the league to Ravenna: where on Easterdaie[5] in the mornyng was fought the blouddiest battaile betwene theim, that hath ben heard of in our daies: and so many thousand*es* slaine on bothe sydes, that it coulde scarcely be judged who had the better: Savyng that the Frenchemen obteined the victorie, toke *Ravenna,* put it to sacke, and after gatte divers other townes in *Romagnia*.

[1] Mestre.

[2] Bologna.

[3] The Holy League, organized in 1511 by Pope Julius II against King Louis XII of France, by 1512 was supported by Venice, Spain, the Holy Roman Empire, England and Switzerland. The French were driven out of Milan in May 1512 and defeated at the Battle of Novara (June 1513).

[4] Andrea Gritti (1455–1538), a distinguished military commander and later Doge (1523–38) (**Plate 4**). After the Venetian defeat at the Battle of Agnadello (1509) Gritti was appointed proveditor of their army at Treviso and facilitated the return of Padua to Venetian control. During the war of the Holy League he held negotiations with France which led to Venice leaving the league and allying with France. The French Governor of Milan was Gaston de Foix (1489–1512), Duke of Nemours.

[5] The Battle of Ravenna was fought on Easter Day, 11 April 1512.

[*margin*: Douchemens hall in Venice]Whilest these thynges were doyng, the Douchemens hall in Venice, called *il fondago di Tedeschi*,[1] was reedified: a very faire and great house: and of a mervailouse rent. For they affyrme, that it yeldeth to the Venetians above .100. duckates a daye: whiche after our old reckenyng amounteth above .7000. pounde sterlyng by the yere.

[*margin*: Antonio Grimani.] After *Loredano* succeded *Antonio Grimani*,[2] who beyng in exile, was called home, made proctour of sainct Marke, and finally Duke.

[*marginal note*: Andrea Gritti] Than *Andrea Gritti*, before named, newly retourned out of Fraunce, was elected Duke: by whose meanes [f. 112r] the Venetians entred in league with the frenche kyng: and so recovered *Bressa*, redeemed *Verona* for a great summe of money, and ayded the Frenchemen to recover Myllaine, and to doe many feates in the realme of Naples: how be it, the frenchemen not longe after, lost all againe through theyr ill governaunce and tyrannie.

Finally practisyng[3] now with Fraunce, now with the emperour, now with the bishop of Rome, as best served for the common wealth: this Duke left it in good ordre, tranquillitee and peace, and so died, greatly bewailed of his citesins.

Than folowed *Peter Lando*,[4] in whose daies the Turke made warre to the Venetians, because they joigned with the emperour against him: so that they to obteine peace, were faine to geve hym the stronge and notable citees in *Napoli*, and *Maluagia*[5] in Greece: and beside that the summe of .300000. duckates.

It was thought, that the Turke woulde have been appeased with a muche lesse gifte, but beyng secretely advertised by the Frenche ambassadour, how the Venetians had geven theyr *Bailo* or ambassadour commission, that rather than the warre should continue to make this offer: he woulde none other wise agree with them.

This knowlage came through intelligence, that the frenche ambassadour had with one of the Venetian Secretaries, who through corrupcion of money, disclosed all the procedynges of the privie counsaile: whiche at length beyng discovered, the same Secretarie fledde into Fraunce, and .ii. other Venetians of his confederacie were taken and hanged.

By this mans time *Andrea Doria*,[6] with a great navie [f. 112v] of the emperours, of the bishop of Romes, and of the Venetians together, enterprised a journey against Barbarossa, admirall of the Turkish navie:[7] and yet metyng with him at great advauntage, both of

---

[1] House of the German merchants (*Fondaco dei Tedeschi).

[2] Antonio Grimani (1434–1523), Doge 1521–3. He had been appointed in 1594 as *Capitano Generale da Mar* but in 1499 he presided over two major defeats by the Ottoman forces, Spaienza and Zonchio. He was threatened with the death penalty but this was reduced to exile, first on the island of Cherso and then in 1509 at Rome. He was able to return to Venice in the same year, thanks to the intercession of his sons. As Doge, he was involved in the Italian War of 1521 when Venice was the only remaining ally of France.

[3] *practising*: in alliance with.

[4] Pietro Lando (1462–1545), Doge 1538–45. In 1540 he signed a peace treaty with Suleiman I (1494–1566), ceding Venice's few remaining possessions in the Peloponnese to the Ottomans.

[5] Monemvasia, Aegean port in the Morea or Peloponnesus.

[6] Andrea Doria (1466–1560), Italian condottiero and Admiral of Genoa. This conflict took place in 1538.

[7] Hayreddin Barbarossa (Barbaros Kheireddin Pasha) (*c.*1478–1546), Admiral of the Ottoman fleet. Barbarossa's forces had defeated Andrea Doria's fleet at the Battle of Preveza (September 1538) which facilitated Ottoman dominance over the Mediterranean until the Battle of Lepanto (1571) (**Plate 13**). Venice signed a peace treaty with Suleiman I in October 1540, recognizing his territorial gains. In September 1540 Emperor Charles V attempted to persuade Barbarossa to change sides and become his Admiral-in-Chief and ruler of

power, and place, Doria retyred: for what cause no man can tell. He lefte the Venetian Galeon, the notablesse vessell of the worlde, in the middest of the Turkes navie. And yet after she had been assayled .v. houers on all sydes, she came hir waies safe, in despite of theim all, leavyng an infinite numbre of hir shotte in the Turkish beten shippes and galleys.

[*marginal note*: Francesco Donato] After *Lando Francesco Donato*[1] was elected unto the astate, about two yeres and an halfe before the writyng hereof. And because in his tyme hitherto hath not hapned anie woorthie thyng to the Venetians, I woull referre the reste to theim that hereafter shall finde occasion to write.

---

Spanish territories in North Africa. But when Barbarossa refused, Charles laid siege to Algiers, attempting to curtail piracy against Spain and Christian shipping. Doria opposed this campaign and withdrew his fleet to open waters to avoid it being wrecked on the shore, although many ships from the Spanish fleet were lost. Soon afterwards Charles was obliged to withdraw his forces and admit defeat.

[1] Francesco Donato (1468–1553), Doge 1545–53. He was elected on 24 Nov. 1545, suggesting that Thomas was compiling this history of Venice in about May 1548.

# 17.   1548/50 AND 1554/5 – SIR THOMAS HOBY AND THE PROTESTANT ENGLISH COMMUNITY AT VENICE AND PADUA

**Sir Thomas Hoby (1530–66)** was born in Leominster, Herefordshire. His elder half-brother, Sir Philip Hoby (1504/5–58), was a prominent diplomat, courtier and administrator and, when at Venice in the mid-1550s, befriended Titian and Pietro Aretino.[1] Thomas matriculated from St John's College, Cambridge, on 20 May 1545 and was taught by the classical scholar and statesman, John Cheke,[2] tutor to both Prince Edward and Princess Elizabeth. Leaving England in late 1547, he spent about one year in Strasbourg studying classics and theology with the Protestant reformer Martin Bucer (1491–1551). During autumn 1548 his brother, then serving as English Ambassador at Augsburg, arranged for him to visit Italy and he spent time at Venice, staying with Edmund Harvell (**item 12**), and at Padua.

Thomas Hoby also travelled south to Rome, Naples and as far as Sicily before returning to Naples by sea. He headed northwards in spring 1550 to rejoin his brother at Augsburg and they arrived back in England together in December, enabling Thomas's introduction to the court of Edward VI during the Christmas season. In May 1551 he travelled to France with the embassy of William Parr (1513–71), Marquess of Northampton, to invest King Henri II with the Order of the Garter.[3]

As a firm Protestant Thomas spent much of Queen Mary's reign (1553–8) abroad and her regime remained suspicious of the loyalty of both Hoby brothers.[4] In 1552–3 Thomas was based at Paris where he translated Castiglione's *Il cortegiano*, first published at Venice in 1528 and in England in 1561 as *The Book of the Courtier*. This translation

---

[1] Sir Philip served (1532–4, 1538, 1548–50) at the English embassy to the court of Charles V and in April 1538 he accompanied Hans Holbein the Younger abroad, on a mission to obtain portraits of potential marriage partners for Henry VIII. He also travelled (November 1539) to the court of Anne of Cleves to negotiate her marriage with Henry VIII. During Edward VI's reign he was abroad for extensive periods, at the emperor's court and in France and the Low Countries. During Mary's reign he went into exile on the continent and when in Italy, especially at Venice and Padua, he was suspected of consorting with Protestant plotters against her regime. Philip and Thomas Hoby returned to England in January 1556 and Philip died at his London house in Blackfriars on 9 May 1558. Garrett, *Exiles*, p. 185. *ODNB*, s.v.

[2] Sir John Cheke (1514–57) had studied abroad during the 1530s and served as tutor (1544) to Edward VI and as Regius Professor of Greek (1540–51) at the University of Cambridge. He was the brother-in-law of Sir William Cecil. Due to his intimacy with the Duke of Northumberland, he was committed to the Tower of London on Queen Mary's accession but discharged in spring 1554 and granted a royal licence to travel abroad with Richard Morison and Anthony Cooke. Ludovico Leoni designed a medal commemorating his time in Italy. He was kidnapped in May 1556 en route to Brussels and committed to the Tower of London. Garrett, *Exiles*, pp. 114–17. Woolfson, *Padua*, pp. 221–2.

[3] 'Sir Thomas Hoby', *ODNB*, s.v.

[4] Partridge, 'Thomas Hoby's English Translation', p. 779.

also linked Thomas Hoby with the circle of Cardinal Reginald Pole (**item 11** and **Plate 6**) at Venice and Padua. He dedicated the published translation to Henry Hastings (*c.*1536–95), the son and heir of Francis Hastings, second Earl of Huntingdon. As a youth Henry had been educated by John Cheke, Anthony Cooke and Roger Ascham. He was also the nephew and protégé of Pole, who had been consecrated as the last Catholic Archbishop of Canterbury on 22 March 1556. While resident in Italy Pole had formed friendships with several of Castiglione's close acquaintances, including Vittoria Colonna, to whom Castiglione refers in his preface to *Il cortegiano*, and Pietro Bembo, who delivers crucial speeches within the dialogues.[1]

In 1553 Thomas Hoby met up again with his brother Philip at Brussels and returned to England in the following September. In 1554 he accompanied Philip to Brussels and Padua where they shared a house with Thomas Wroth,[2] John Cheke and Anthony Cooke.[3] In 1555 the Hoby brothers visited the baths at Caldiero, near Verona, and Venice before returning home later that year.[4] It is probable that Thomas Hoby, like numerous other English students, took the opportunity during his various visits to Venice and Padua to expand his personal library with works from the Venetian presses. His Cambridge college, St John's, has a copy of a Venetian edition of Dante's *Divina commedia* (1544), stamped with Hoby's initials on its covers and his inscription on a preliminary leaf.[5] Louisiana State University has a copy of Benedetto Bordone's *Isolario* (Venice, 1528; 1547 edition) about ancient and modern islands, with its title page bearing Hoby's signature and his personal Latin motto, 'Tendit in ardua virtus' (Virtue strives for what is difficult). Originally published in 1528 as an illustrated guide for sailors, it went through several editions and became popular with both real and armchair travellers. The *Isolario* contained illustrations of the known world, new discoveries in the Americas and aerial views of cities, and a renowned view of the Venetian lagoon.[6]

Following Philip Hoby's death on 9 May 1558 Thomas inherited Bisham Abbey, Berkshire, which his brother had purchased in 1552. On 27 June Thomas married Elizabeth Cooke (1528–1609), the daughter of the humanist scholar Sir Anthony Cooke who had also tutored Prince Edward. He was knighted at Greenwich on 9 March 1566 and appointed Ambassador to France in the same month. He died at Paris on 13 July

[1] Partridge, 'Thomas Hoby's English Translation', pp. 775–80, supports the hypothesis (first made by P. J. Laven in 1954) that William Thomas had also been translating *Il cortegiano* – a scheme truncated by his execution in May 1554 (**item 16**).

[2] Thomas Wroth (1518–73) of Enfield, Middlesex, had been Chief Gentleman of the Bedchamber to Edward VI. He had supported John Dudley, Duke of Northumberland, and Lady Jane Grey but, after a brief imprisonment, was released, only to become implicated in the Duke of Suffolk's second rising. He escaped to the continent with Sir John Cheke and they shared a house at Padua in July 1554 and at Venice in 1555. He returned to England in 1558. Garrett, *Exiles*, pp. 344–6. Woolfson, *Padua*, p. 288.

[3] Sir Anthony Cooke (1504–76), of Gidea Hall, Essex; Knight of the Bath. He was committed with Sir John Cheke to the Tower of London on 27 July 1553 on suspicion of complicity in the Lady Jane Grey usurpation but was pardoned and headed abroad with Cheke. He was resident at Padua in 1554. He married Anne, daughter of Sir William Fitzwilliam, and was father-in-law to Thomas Hoby, and also to Sir William Cecil and Sir Henry Killigrew. Garrett, *Exiles*, pp. 124–6. Woolfson, *Padua*, pp. 226–7.

[4] Woolfson, *Padua*, pp. 245–6.

[5] https://www.joh.cam.ac.uk/library/special_collections/early_books/hoby.htm.

[6] https://news.blogs.lib.lsu.edu/2013/10/09/sir-thomas-hobys-book-of-islands-1547/.

1566 and was buried on 2 September in Bisham parish church where a lavish monument to him and his half-brother Philip remains.[1]

Sir Thomas Hoby was a member of the exiled Protestant English community in Italy, centred around Venice and Padua. Kenneth R. Bartlett explains the political importance to the post-1558 Elizabethan regime of this loose grouping of individuals:

> Significantly, the Marian exile community which enjoyed the largest and most consistent representation in Elizabeth's Parliaments was the Venetian, a group of essentially political rather than religious refugees. It is of course manifest from their choosing a Catholic country that the Venetian émigré community had motives which were fundamentally different from those of the exiles in Germany and Switzerland whose concern was to find a climate congenial to their religious beliefs. This difference is emphasized by the social status of the group in Italy, which tended to attract only protestant laymen of good birth and education who had fled abroad without their families after the failure of Northumberland's coup d'état or Wyatt's rebellion. A great many of these men had been holders of high office under Edward VI, and most of the remainder were university men, especially from Cambridge, who were attracted to the Venetian Republic by the growing interest in Italian culture in England and by the reputation of the University of Padua.[2]

These individuals took up residence at Venice and Padua for two purposes: to further their own immersion in Italian humanism and to oppose the government of Queen Mary and, from July 1554, her Spanish spouse Philip. Since before the death in July 1553 of Edward VI, the Venetians had been intriguing to limit the potency of Imperial influence in England and they even lent a cannon from a Venetian vessel moored in the Thames in support of the Wyatt rebellion in January 1554.[3] It has been calculated that of the forty-two Marian refugees returned to Parliament between 1559 and 1593, twenty-four had been resident in Italy, mostly at Padua and Venice. An important centre for their clandestine activities was the residence of Edward Courtenay, Earl of Devon, who was himself a claimant to the English throne.[4] Other Protestant members of the Venetian-Paduan community included Henry Killigrew,[5] William Morley,[6] John Pelham,[7] Thomas Dannett,[8] John

---

[1] Hoby, *Travels*, 1902, pp. viii–xvi. *ODNB*, s.v. Woolfson, *Padua*, pp. 245–6.

[2] https://www.historyofparliamentonline.org/volume/1558-1603/survey/appendix-xi-role-marian-exiles.

[3] *CSP Spanish*, XII, items 88, 113, 122–3.

[4] Edward Courtenay (1526–56), 1st Earl of Devon, great-grandson of Edward IV, was a former suitor to Queen Mary and a cousin of Cardinal Pole. He resided in Venice, with a house there from mid-January 1556, and studied at the University of Padua. He was often under the threat of assassination and was allowed by the Signoria in February 1556 to retain a bodyguard of 25 armed men. Garrett, *Exiles*, pp. 130–31. Woolfson, *Padua*, pp. 227–8. *ODNB*, s.v.

[5] Henry Killigrew (*c.*1528–1603), a former member of the household of John Dudley, Duke of Northumberland; served as his agent in Italy in 1546. He met Thomas Hoby at Padua in 1549 and travelled with him in Italy. He attempted to persuade Edward Courtenay, Earl of Devon, to come from Ferrara to France to support a rebellion against Queen Mary. He married Catherine, the daughter of Anthony Cooke. Woolfson, *Padua*, pp. 248–9.

[6] William Morley (*c.*1531–97), a member of Francis Russell's household in Italy and a cousin of John Pelham. He served as Consiliarius of the English nation at Padua (1556), taking over this post from Francis Walsingham. Garrett, *Exiles*, p. 231. Woolfson, *Padua*, p. 258.

[7] John Pelham (Paleus, Puleus) (1537–80), was granted with his brother Anthony a licence to travel abroad (1552); Consiliarius of the English nation at Padua (1556–7) and remained there until after Queen Elizabeth's accession. Woolfson, *Padua*, p. 263.

[8] Thomas Dannett (fl. 1550s), probably the uncle of Leonard Dannett (1530–91). Thomas and Leonard were implicated in the Wyatt Rebellion (1554) and were committed to the Tower of London but soon released and

Tamworth,[1] Edmund Tremayne,[2] Hugh Fitzwilliam,[3] Thomas Randolph,[4] Sir Nicholas Throckmorton,[5] John Astley,[6] Humphrey Michell,[7] Sir Peter Carew[8] and – perhaps the two

---

pardoned (Leonard in May and Thomas in October 1554). Thomas then went to France with his family and returned after Queen Elizabeth's accession. His son, Thomas (1543–c.1601) travelled widely in France and Spain and wrote *The Description of the Low Countries* (1593), an 'Epitome' of Guiccardini (dedicated to William Cecil, Lord Burghley) and translated Philippe de Commines's *History of France* (1596 and 1600). Garrett, *Exiles*, pp. 139–40.

[1] John Tamworth, see p. 125 n. 5.

[2] Edmund Tremayne (c.1525–82), of Collacombe, Devon; a first cousin of Sir Francis Drake; from 1553 servant of Edward Courtenay, Earl of Devon. He was tortured in the Tower of London after the failure of the Wyatt Rebellion in an attempt to make him testify against his master. He was released on 18 Jan. 1555 and accompanied Devon to the continent but left his household in 1556. His brother Nicholas carried messages from Sir Henry Dudley in France to the Earls of Devon and Bedford at Venice. Garrett, *Exiles*, pp. 309–10. *ODNB*, s.v.

[3] Hugh Fitzwilliam (fl. 1550s), from Yorkshire; as a youth he had joined the household of William Fitzwilliam (c.1490–1542), Earl of Southampton (from 1537). He was possibly the 'Mr. Phitzwilliam' recorded at Paris in 1559 who was returning to England from Italy where he had been a student during Queen Mary's reign. Garrett, *Exiles*, p. 154.

[4] Thomas Randolph (1523/6–90), of Haslemere, Kent; the brother of Edward Randolph (d. 1566) who was implicated in the Wyatt Rebellion. Both brothers are known to have taken refuge at Paris and Dr Nicholas Wotton, English Ambassador in France, procured a pardon for Edward and employed Thomas. Little is known about Thomas's time at Venice, although he remained on friendly terms with Sir Thomas Wroth and Sir Anthony Cooke. Garrett, *Exiles*, pp. 266–7. *ODNB*, s.v.

[5] Sir Nicholas Throckmorton (1515/16–71), of Coughton, Warwickshire; diplomat and MP; father of Arthur Throckmorton (**item 27**). He had lived in France for almost a year as a page to Henry Fitzroy (1519–36), Duke of Richmond (Henry VIII's illegitimate son). As a gentleman of Edward VI's Privy Chamber, he is said to have suggested that William Thomas (**item 16**) should prepare political documents for the king's consideration. He was imprisoned in the Tower of London in February 1554 for supporting the Wyatt Rebellion. After his release in January 1555 and the failure of the Dudley Plot in 1556, he fled to France and Italy, returning to England in May 1557. Garrett, *Exiles*, pp. 306–7. *ODNB*, s.v.

[6] John Astley (Ashley) (c.1507–95/6), of Hill Morton and Melton Constable, Norfolk; Marian exile and author of *The Art of Riding* (1584), based on Xenophon. His mother's sister, Elizabeth, was Anne Boleyn's aunt and he served in the households of Prince Edward and Princess Elizabeth. He travelled in Italy (1553–4) and was commended by Roger Ascham for his ability to speak Italian. He married Katherine Champernowne, who was an aunt of the three Denny brothers and had been governess to Princess Elizabeth from 1547. He returned to England in 1555 and during Elizabeth's reign was appointed a Gentleman of the Privy Chamber, Master of the Jewel House, Keeper of St James's Palace and an MP. His portrait, dated 1555, is in the National Portrait Gallery, London, attributed to an 'unknown Netherlandish artist'. *ODNB*, s.v.

[7] Humphrey Michell (1526–98), a servant of the Earl of Devon and then the Earl of Bedford at Padua and Venice (1555–6); expert in hydraulic engineering. Woolfson, *Padua*, p. 257.

[8] Sir Peter Carew (c.1514–75), of Mohun's Ottery, Devon; soldier and Wyatt Rebellion conspirator. He was sent to the French court aged twelve, and spoke fluent French. In 1528 he saw military action with the French army outside Naples. He was not at the Battle of Pavia (1525) or the sack of Rome (1527), as claimed by his earliest biographer, John Hooker, but did serve in Italy until 1530 with the army of Philibert, Prince of Orange. He returned to England c.1531/2 but went abroad again in the 1530s, travelling via Venice to Constantinople (1541) before returning to Venice and England.

Carew had been renowned at the Henrician court as a soldier and jouster. In 1545 he was given command of the 700-ton *Great Venetian*, a commandeered Venetian merchant vessel, and was present when his elder brother George (c.1504–45), the Vice-Admiral of the English fleet, drowned aboard the *Mary Rose* (**item 15**). He was drawn into the Wyatt Rebellion as one of its principal conspirators in Devon and Cornwall but then, sensing its likely failure, fled abroad into exile. By December 1555 he was soliciting a pardon from Philip and, following what seems to have been a staged kidnapping in Flanders, returned to England with John Cheke in May 1556. Garrett, *Exiles*, pp. 104–8. *ODNB*, s.v.

most influential émigrés during Elizabeth's reign – Thomas Wilson[1] and Francis Walsingham.[2]

After Courtenay's death in September 1556, the highest ranking and most influential Protestant exile was Francis Russell, second Earl of Bedford,[3] who attracted several of Courtenay's former followers. Fourteen members of his household were granted permission by the Signoria in July 1555 to bear arms, including Thomas Wyndham,[4] Sir John Chichester,[5] John Brooke (alias Cobham, a younger son of the ninth Lord Cobham),[6] Thomas Fitzwilliams,[7] Henry Kingsmill,[8] Humphrey Michell and William

[1] Thomas Wilson (1523/4–81), of Strubby, Lincolnshire; humanist scholar; friend of Roger Ascham (**item 19**) and John Cheke; tutored the sons of John Dudley, Duke of Northumberland, and fled abroad after his fall; delivered the funeral oration at Padua for Edward Courtenay, Earl of Devon; accused of heresy by the Roman Inquisition; imprisoned and tortured for anti-Catholic comments in his *Arte of Rhetorique* (1553). He owned a portrait of 'a widow of Venice'. Woolfson, *Padua*, p. 285. *ODNB*, s.v.

[2] Francis Walsingham (*c*.1532–90), later Principal Secretary to Queen Elizabeth; matriculated from King's College, Cambridge, in spring 1548, when Sir John Cheke was its Provost. According to the inscription on his tomb, he travelled abroad after leaving the college on 29 September 1550 and had returned to England by 1552. He escorted his cousins, the three Denny brothers, to Basle in autumn 1555 and was at Padua by the end of that year, serving as Consiliarius of the English nation (29 December 1555–6). Garrett, *Exiles*, pp. 319–20. Woolfson, *Padua*, pp. 280–81. *ODNB*, s.v.

[3] Francis Russell (1526/7–85), 2nd Earl of Bedford, declared his support for Lady Jane Grey in 1553; briefly detained by the Sheriff of London but pardoned and placed under house arrest; granted a licence to travel abroad (20 April 1555) he was resident at Padua (from June) and arrived at Venice (31 July) where he was permitted to carry arms, together with fourteen other Englishmen (*CSP Venice*, 1555, items 169, 171). He spoke fluent Italian and also visited Rome, Naples and Ferrara. He may have been at Venice again in spring 1557. He led the English forces supporting Philip II of Spain at the Battle of St Quentin (August 1557) and returned to England in the same year. A catalogue of his personal library compiled in 1584 included 12 books in Italian and histories of Italy. *ODNB*, s.v. Garrett, *Exiles*, pp. 275–7. Woolfson, *Padua*, p. 267.

[4] Thomas Wyndham (d. 1599), met by Thomas Hoby at Padua in 1554 and licensed to carry arms at Venice in July 1555 (Venice, Archivio di Stato, Consiglio di X, Parti Communi, Reg. 22). He should be distinguished from the naval officer, navigator and trader with the Barbary coast, Thomas Wyndham (d. 1554), of Felbrigg, Norfolk. Thomas's half-brother Edmund (Sigismund) Wyndham was Consiliarius of the English nation at Padua in 1556. Woolfson, *Padua*, pp. 288–9. Bartlett, *English in Italy*, pp. 225–6.

[5] Sir John Chichester (d. 1569), of Yolston, Devon, son of Edward Chichester (d. 1522) and Elizabeth, daughter of John Bourchier (1470–1539), 1st Earl of Bath. In 1554 he joined the entourage of the Earl of Bedford travelling to Italy and he was a member of the Earl's household at Venice in 1555 where he was licensed to bear arms. After returning to England he was briefly imprisoned for his involvement in the Dudley conspiracy (1556). Garrett, *Exiles*, p. 118.

[6] John Brooke (1535–94) (alias 'Sigismund'), probably the son of George Brooke (d. 1558), Lord Cobham; if so, John was the first cousin of Sir Thomas Wyatt the Younger. He was captain of the galleon *Foresight* (built 1570) which served during the Spanish Armada crisis (1588), at Lisbon (1589) and at the Azores (1591). Childs, *Tudor Sea Power*, p. 291. John's elder brother William Brooke (1527–97) studied at Padua and Venice (1543) where he was licensed with his tutor John Schiere to carry arms and to view the city's munitions (Venice, Archivio di Stato, Consiglio di X, Lettere ai Capi, filza note 45, 11 Oct.1543, ff. 204, 214, 217, and Parti Communi, Reg. 17, f. 37). John resided at Padua (1554) and Venice (1555) but was in Frankfort by 1557. Garrett, *Exiles*, pp. 97–8. Woolfson, *Padua*, p. 214.

[7] Thomas Fitzwilliam(s) (fl. 1550s), was probably not the illegitimate son (d. 1562) of William Fitzwilliam, Earl of Southampton, as has been suggested. Bartlett, *English in Italy*, p. 205. He encountered Thomas Hoby in Edmund Harvell's house at Venice (1548) and visited Padua in the same year and in 1554. He was permitted to carry arms in Venice in 1555 while in the train of the Earl of Bedford. Garrett, *Marian Exiles*, p. 155. Woolfson, *Padua*, p. 235.

[8] Henry Kingsmill (*c*.1534–*c*.1577), shared a house with Thomas Hoby at Paris (1552) and met him again at Padua (1554); joined the household of Francis Russell, Earl of Bedford, at Venice (1555); member of Queen Elizabeth's household by 1560. Garrett, *Exiles*, p. 208. Woolfson, *Padua*, p. 249.

Page.[1] While all of these individuals were able to return to England after the accession of Queen Elizabeth, their collaborative influence exerted a significant influence over English politics and court life for much of her reign.

## Text

Sir Thomas Hoby's 'A Booke of the Travaile and lief of me Thomas Hoby *with* diverse thing*es* woorth the noting*e*' (BL Egerton MS 2148, ff. 5–182), covers the period 1547 to 1564 and was presumably compiled during the last two years of his life.[2] He left Augsburg on 5 August 1548, travelling via Brixen, Kollman, Trent, Castelnuovo, Bassano, Treviso and Marghera and arriving at Venice 'by water'. Much of his account of Italy is first-hand but it also draws upon Leandro Alberti's *Descrittione di tutta d'Italia*.

[f. 10v; p. 8] here I laye in Mr. Edmund Harvell*es* house,[3] Ambassaodo[r] resident for the King*es* ma*jes*tye, where I found also M[r] Jhon Yong[4] with whom I laye, [f. 11r] m[r] George Speake,[5] m[r] Thomas Fitzwilliams, m[r] Thomas Straung,[6] and dyverse other Englishemen. From hense I went to padoa and m[r] Fitzwilliams with me, which was the xv[th] of August. In this towne laye manye Englishmen as S*ir* Thomas Wyatt,[7] m[r] Jhon Cotton,[8] m[r] Henry williams,[9] m[r] Fraunc*es* williams his brother which died both in England the yere, 51,[10] m[r]

---

[1] William Page (fl. 1550s), a servant of the Italian Catholic, Peter Vannes (d. 1563), English Agent at Venice (1550–56), and then a member of Sir Philip Hoby's household. *CSP Venice*, 1555, item 145. Venice, Archivio di Stato, Consiglio di X, Parti Communi, Reg. 22, July 1555. Vannes was suspected of hiring assassins to kill Sir Peter Carew (see p. 156 n. 8) and of being involved in a plot to poison Edward Courtenay, Earl of Devon. *ODNB*, s.v.

[2] The title page also bears a note in a later hand: 'The yeers in this booke begyne upon Newyers day, accordynge to the Romysh Computatione' (f. 5r; 1902, p. 1). Marginal notes are not included in this transcript because they were added by Hoby's son Edward at a later date. The manuscript's contemporary pagination (probably by both Sir Thomas and his son Edward) is erratic and incomplete with many pages numbered two or three times. A more consistent folio numbering has been added in a later hand. This transcript provides page references to both this later manuscript foliation and Edgar Powell's 1902 edition.

[3] See **item 12**.

[4] John Young; Garrett, *Exiles*, pp. 347–8, suggests that this is perhaps a 'misappropriated Englishman', citing a source to suggest that this name may refer to Johannes Jung from Bischofszell, Switzerland. However, Hoby's reference may be to another, otherwise unidentified, Englishman then at Venice and Padua.

[5] George Speake, an individual of this name, from White Lackington, Somerset, was recorded at Paris in 1577. Poulet, *Copy-Book*, pp. 16–17.

[6] Unidentified.

[7] Sir Thomas Wyatt the Younger (1521–54), son of Sir Thomas Wyatt (**item 13** and **Plate 16**), travelled abroad (1544–50), partly on military service. Leader of the Wyatt Rebellion (1554); found guilty of treason and beheaded 11 April 1554, with his quartered limbs publicly displayed. Woolfson, *Padua*, p. 288. *ODNB*, s.v.

[8] John Cotton (fl. 1550s). Perhaps related to Thomas Cotton who was an intelligencer at Antwerp (1566) and at Padua (1567). He advised William Cecil that the tomb of Edward Courtenay, Earl of Devon, had been removed and the coffin thrown into a cloister. He made the arrangements with the Venetian government for the tomb to be reinstated. Woolfson, *Padua*, p. 227.

[9] Unidentified.

[10] Francis Williams (d.1551)

Jhon Arundle,[1] m[r] Jhon Hasting*es*,[2] m[r] Christopher Alen,[3] m[r] Jhon Sheres,[4] m[r] Jhon Handford,[5] and dyverse other. Here I applied my self as well to obtain the Italian tung as to have a farther entrance in the Latin.

[Hoby then provides a detailed description of Padua, noting:]

[f. 12v; p. 10] the govenar's house of the [f. 13r] towne, whiche is continuallie a gentleman of venice and changed every yere. At the other end are prisonnes & dongeons. The towne is ruled by two principall heades, the on[e] is governor, called in Italian Podesta, and his authoritie is in the day time. The other is the Captain over the sowldiers and the garison, and his authoritie is in the night. They have two severall faire howses belonging to their offices. At everie yeres end of there abode here they are chaunged, but not bothe at on*e* time. They count the governance of this towne on*e* of the cheeffest offices belonging to the Syniorye of venice, and not much inferior to Candia and Cyprus. No man wearethe his weapon within the towne, but such as are licenced by the Podesta, which is the maner both of venice and all the townes under the dominion of it. And by everie newe Podesta this license is confirmed, yf he thinke it so expedient.

[On 7 January 1549 Hoby left Padua with [f. 14r; p. 11] 'm[r] Edward murphin'[6] and 'm[r] Henry Killigrewe'[7] to visit Mantua and to witness the arrival there of Prince Felipe (1527–98), later Philip II of Spain.]

[f. 17v; p. 13] We came back again into padoa the xix[th] of January: And shortlie after I went to venice where as after the entrie of the prince into Trent, Duke Maurice th'elector[8] with the Cardinall of Auspurghe[9] cam from his Cowrt to see the Citie of Venice, and were then newlie arrived there. They were honorablye receaved and greatly banqueted on the Syniories charge.[10] When Supper was doone they cam*e* bothe with other companye in a maskerye and daunsed with [p. 14] the gentlwomen a good space. There was at that Supper don Juan di mendozza,[11] the emperores Ambassado[r] there resident, who satt uppermost and took the upper hand of them all.

---

[1] Unidentified.

[2] Unidentified.

[3] Unidentified.

[4] John Schiere (Schieres, Sheres, Shire) (fl. 1550s–1560s), tutor who travelled with William Brooke in 1541; possibly at Padua and Venice (1543–45); offered to collect antique busts for William Cecil; still in the Veneto during the 1560s. Woolfson, *Padua*, p. 270.

[5] Unidentified.

[6] Edward Murphin (fl. late 1540s), left Padua in 1549 with Hoby and Henry Killigrew and visited Rome with Hoby, Francis Peto (Freitto) and other Englishmen in the same year. Woolfson, *Padua*, p. 259.

[7] See pp. 154 n. 3 and 155 n. 5.

[8] Maurice (1521–53), Duke (1541–7) and Elector (1547–53) of Saxony.

[9] Otto Truchsess von Waldburg (1514–73), Prince-Bishop of Augsburg (from 1543) and Cardinal (from 1544).

[10] Francesco Donato was then Doge (1545–53).

[11] Diego Hurtado de Mendoza y Pacheco (1503–75), diplomat and writer. He had been sent in 1537 to England to arrange marriages between Henry VIII and Christina of Denmark (the widowed Duchess of Milan) and between Mary Tudor and Prince Louis of Portugal. In 1539 Emperor Charles V (1500–58) appointed him as Ambassador to Venice where he was a prolific collector of books and manuscripts. He also served as a Plenipotentiary at Rome (1547–54).

At Shroftide after there came to venice to see the Citie the lustie yong Duke of Ferrandin,[1] well accompanied with noble menn and gentlemen, where he with his companions in Campo di San Stefano shewed great sport and muche pastime to the Gentlmen & Gentlwomen of Venice, [f. 18r] bothe on horsback in running at the ring with faire Turkes and Cowrsares, being in a maskerie after the Turkishe maner, and on foote casting of egges into the wyndowes among the Ladies full of sweete waters and damaske poulders. At night after all this triumphe in a bankett[2] made purposlie at mowrano,[3] a litle owt of venice, by the Siniorye, to honor him withall he was slaine by a varlett belonging to a gentlman of the Citie. The occasion was this: the Duke cuming in a brave maskerye with his companions went (as the maner is) to a gentlewoman whom he most fancied among all the rest (being assembled there together a .l. or lx).[4] This gentlwoman was wyff to one Mr Michael Venier.[5] There came in another companye of Gentlmen Venetiens in an other maskerye: and one of them went in like maner to the same gentlwoman that the Duke was entreating to daunse with him, and somwhat shuldredd[6] the Duke, which was [f.18v] a great injurie. Upon that, the Duke thrust him from him. The gentlman owt with his dagger and gave him a strooke abowt the short ribbes with the point, but it did him no hurt, because he had on a jacke of maile. The Duke ymmediatlie feeling the point of his dagger, drue his rapire, whereupon the gentlman fledd into a chambre there at hand and shutt the dore to him. And as the duke was shovinge to gete the dore open, a varlett of the gentlmannes cam behind him and with a pistolese[7] gave him his deathe's wounde, and clove his head in such sort as the one side honge over his shulder by a little skynn. He lyved abowt two dayes after this stroke. There was no justice had against this gentlman, but after he had a while absented him self from the Citie the matter was forgotten. The varlett fledd, and was no more hard of. This Gentlman was of the house of Giustiniani in venice.[8]

[f. 19r] Abowt this time there fell an other straung chaunce in venice. In the Countrey of Friuli are two great families, whiche of long time have bine deadlie enemies thone to thother, Della Turre [p. 15] and Soveragnani.[9] Of th'origion of this hatred betwixt them, I could never gather other reason than this: at such times as the venetiens sawght first to

[1] The identity of Hoby's 'Duke of Ferrandin' is uncertain. However, contemporary references to 'Ferrandine' or Neapolitan galleys of Naples may link him to the descendants of either Ferdinand I (*Aragonese*: Ferrando; also known as Ferrante) (1423–94), King of Naples. Or Ferdinand II (Ferrando) (1452–1516), King of Aragon.

[2] banquet.

[3] *Murano.

[4] 50 or 60.

[5] Unidentified.

[6] shouldered?

[7] *pistolese*: defined in the margin: 'A Pystolese is a shorte broadsword.'

[8] The Giustiniani were one of Venice's most distinguished families with branches in Genoa, Naples and the Greek islands of the Archipelago. The Palazzo Giustinian, next to Ca' Foscari, overlooks the Grand Canal. Thomas Hoby, William Thomas and other English travellers to Venice may have known the history of Venice by Bernardo Giustiniani (1408–89), *De origine urbis Venetiarum rebusque ab ipsa gestis historia* (1492), which had recently (1545) been translated into Italian by Ludovico Domenichi (1515–64), *Historia di B. Justiniano, dell'origine di Venetia*.

[9] The Della Torre (Torriani) family were prominent in Lombardy and in the 13th century preceded the Visconti as lords of Milan. Francesco Torriani served as councillor to Emperor Ferdinand I and was his ambassador to Venice (1558). Hoby's 'Soveragnini' probably refers to the Severgnini family.

be Lordes over that Countrey of Friuli, they had the house Della Torre whiche was somewhat the mightier on their side, But the Soveragnani could never be browght to yelde to yt. Upon this they fell at debate and contention, thone for their libertie, and thother to bring in a straunge nation. So that muche slawghter ensued of that sundrie times. At last the venetiens obtained their purpose and could never sett these two howses at one. About this Shroftide there were certaine Justes[1] proclaymed in padoa to all commers at the tilt. [f. 19v] The best price[2] was a great cheine of Golde, the second a rapire dagger and gyrdle faire wrowght and gylt. The third was a Coronett of gold sett with pearle and stone, which was the ladies' and gentlwomennes cost: and whosoever came into the feelde with this traine best besene and galantest to the eye, withe slyghtest cost, his shuld this coronett bee. To these Justes dailie repayred sundrie gentlmen owt of all the Countreys abowt, som to be doers, and a number to be lookers on. Emong other these two howses chaunced to runn bothe with their fawtors[3] on their parties well apointed. There were great gentlmen that were put in suritie for them and bound them selves to the Syniorye that repayring to thes Justes there shuld no hurt be done. Notwithstanding as they mett at a chaunce together by the Santo there was a great fraye and one [f. 20r] of the howse Della Torre slaine and certain on bothe parties sore hurt. Thus they left for that time hooping for a reveng at more leyser.[4] This matter was taken upp by the Siniorye of venice, and their sureties that were thus bound for them were handled to the most extremitie. They thowght it behouffull to banishe the Count Jhon Delli Soverignani,[5] who was judged to bee the beginner of this Fraye. When sentence of banishment was geven, he prepared him selfe therto, and taking wyff, children bagg and baggage with him cam to venice, entending to saile from thence to Candia and there to remaine in exile. As he thus taried in venice a season attending for passag, being lodged upon the Canal grand over against San Geremia,[6] he tooke bote manie times to goo upp and downe abowt sundrie his affaires. At his return upon a [f. 20v] time he was watched, and by the walles side over against the house of Quirini[7] there lingred a bote, suche a one as communlie carie frutes uppe and downe venice, upon their [p. 16] frutes they use to laye mattes to keepe them freshe and to defend them from the heate of the Sunn. There were no mo[re] in syght but two within the bote. Under the mattes there laye vii or viii parsons withe eche of them a hackbutt[8] in his hand. When the Gondalo that Count Jhon Soveragnani was in came directlie against them they shott all together levelling all at one marke. Count Jhon was shott throwghe in manie places of his bodye. This enterprise thus acheved, as manie as were in the bote fell to rowing and made so sweftlie awaye that none were able to folowe them, nor decern who they were nor yet whither they went. The deade bodye was browght into the house of Quirini where it laye to be seene of all menn. [f. 21r] When the Siniorye understoode of this murther, they cawsed ymmediatly Francesco Della Turre to bee taken who was then in venice. But for all they putt him to the torment

---

[1] *justes*: jousts.

[2] *price*: prize.

[3] *fawtors*: fautor, a supporter, adherent or patron.

[4] *leyser*: leisure.

[5] *Count Jhon Delli Soverignani*: probably one Count Giovanni Severgnini; unidentified.

[6] *San Geremia.

[7] *Palazzo Querini (Stampalia).

[8] *hackbutt*: hackbut, an early portable form of fire-arm.

of the cord,[1] they coulde never make him confesse that he was condescending or of counsel[2] to this kind of murther. And the lawe is except a man confesse his trespasse when he is putt to this torment, he shall never suffer deathe for yt. This chaunce happened in lent. Abowt the Ascension daye the Duke and Dutchesse of Urbin[3] came to Venice, where the Dutchesse, Cardinall Farnese syster, for that she was never there before, was mett a mile or two withowt the citie upon the Seea, and receaved into the venetiens' vessell of Triumphe called Bucentoro, wherin were diverse of the Syniorye and nyghe two hundrithe gentlwomen to accompanie herr to the Duke herr husbandes palaice within the Citie. There a man might have seen the Seea almost [f. 21v] covered with sundrie kinde of botes, Sume made like Shippes, other like Galies, Some other like pinaces richlie dect within and withowt, besides manie other pretie vesselles full of minstrelsye, daunsing and maskaries. After herr arrival she was greatlye feasted. And before herr departure thense she sawe the Arsena[4] of venice where all their Galies, Shippes, artillarye, munition and such other matters were. After she had bine leade abowt yt, which lackethe little of a mile in compasse, she was browghte into a larg room where she had a costlie bankett prepared for herr and all her companie richlie served of all kinde of dilicaties. Yt was in the after noone abowt fowre of the clock. Herr cuming to venice was to see the Sensa,[5] which is a great feast there. And upon the place of Saint Markes is a great faire for certain dayes. The daye of the Ascension the Duke of venice with all the Siniorye goethe [f. 22r] into [p. 17] this vessell the Bucentoro and after they are a litle from the Land, they have a wonderous great Ceremonie abowt the marying of the See. For the Duke takethe a ring off his finger and castethe yt into the Seea, thinking by this meane to knitt yt so sure that yt shall never depart and leave the Citie upon the Drie land: As it is like to do in processe of time yf it contineue to diminishe still as yt hathe begone sith the memorye of man. Yet have they dailie provisions and officers appointed to the same to see the sandes and whatsoever is in the bottome in the shalowe places voided.

My jorney into Tuscane.

I departed owt of padoa towardes venice the vii[th] of June, where m[r] Jhon Hastinges[6] and I were onse purposed to goo with the great Gallies into Sorria.[7] From whense m[r] Edward murphin[8] was abowt that time returned. [f. 22v] After I had taried a yere somtime in Padoa and somtime in venice and obtayned some understanding in the tung, I thowght yt behouffull to travaile into the middes of Italye, as well as to have a better knowleg in

---

[1] Hoby probably refers here to the strappado (il tormento della corda) when the victim's hands were tied behind the back and then suspended by a rope attached to the wrists, usually resulting in dislocated shoulders and ligament damage. Another form of torture by the cord (mancuerda) involved winding cord around the arms of the victim and then pulling it so tight that it cut through the flesh to the bone.

[2] condescending or of counsel: agreeing to or aware of.

[3] Guidobaldo II della Rovere (1514–74), Duke of Urbino. After the death of his first wife, Giulia da Varano (d. 1547), he married in 1548 Vittoria Farnese, the daughter of Pier Luigi Farnese (1503–47), Duke of Parma, and sister of Cardinal Alessandro Farnese (1520–89).

[4] *Arsenal (Plate 12).

[5] *Marriage of the Sea.

[6] See p. 159 n. 2.

[7] Syria.

[8] See p. 159 n. 6.

the tung, as to see the Countrey of Tuscane so much renowned in all places. I departed from venice the xxiiii^th daye of August, and went to Ferrara by water, which is abowt fowre score and tenn miles.

[While at Siena Hoby learned of the political turmoil back home in England:] [f. 27v; p. 21] 'This yere was the rebellion in England in Norfolk and Devonshire, and the Duke of Sommersett¹ deposed from his protectorshippe by the onlie malice of the Erle of Warwicke, afterwards created Duke of Northumberland.² And before that the Duke of Sommersett had cawsed Sir Thomas Seymer, lord admerall his owne brother to be beheaded at the towre hill.³

[At Rome Pope Paul III had died on 11 November 1549 and Hoby, with a small group of Englishmen including [f. 38v; p. 25] 'm^r Barker,⁴ m^r Parker'⁵ and 'Whitehorn'⁶ delayed their departure from the city in the hope that they could be present for the election of Cardinal Reginald Pole (**item 11** and **Plate 6**) as the new pope:]

[f. 38r; p. 26] It was thowght Cardinall poole shulde have bine pope. Yf he had receaved the Cardinalles offer overnight as he entended in the morning folowing, he had surelie bine so. And in the morning when all the souldiers of Roome, and a great multitude of people besides were assembled in the markett place of Saint peters to have seene Cardinall poole proclaimed pope, he had lost by the Cardinall of Ferrara⁷ his meanes the voice of manie cardinall*es* of the Frenche partie, persuading them that Cardinall poole was both Imperiall and [f. 38v] also a verie Lutheran. So that morning passed withowt anie thing done, contrarie to the expectation of all menn. After the election of Cardinall poole was thus passed the commune opinion was, that by the reason of the factions Emperiall and Frenche that were among them, they would not so soone agree afterward, for there was no on*e* in the [w]hole Consistorie that was generallie so well beloved as he was of them all, and never declared him self neyther Emperiall nor Frenche.

[Hoby left Rome in early May to visit Siena and left there on 19 July to meet his half-brother Philip at Augsburg. Travelling via Bologna and Ferrara he came to:] [f. 92v; p. 61] Chioggia, which is an yland within the Seea built as Venice is. From hense com all the abundance of mellones that in the sommer time are in venice. Afterward we sailed to

---

¹ Edward Seymour (1500–52), 1st Duke of Somerset, Lord Protector of England (1547–9). His sister Jane (*c*.1508–37) was Henry VIII's third wife and the mother of Edward VI. He was executed in January 1552.

² John Dudley (1504–53), Earl of Warwick and Duke of Northumberland.

³ Thomas Seymour (*c*.1508–49), Lord High Admiral, was executed on 20 March 1549.

⁴ William Barker (*c*.1522–*c*.1576), Cambridge graduate and translator; at Rome with Hoby and Peter Whytehorne and Henry Parker; later an MP and secretary to the Duke of Norfolk; implicated in his plot and imprisoned in 1571. Woolfson, *Padua*, p. 211.

⁵ *Mr. Parker*: Garrett, *Exiles*, pp. 243–4, notes a Roger Parker of Essex who was then abroad but it is not known whether this individual ever visited Rome or knew Hoby.

⁶ *Whitehorn*: Either Thomas Whytehorne, a musician who was travelling in Italy in 1554 or Peter Whytethorne, the translator of Machiavelli's *Arte della guerra*. Woolfson, *Padua*, p. 283.

⁷ Ippolito (II) d'Este (1509–72), Cardinal of Ferrara. Giovanni Maria Ciocchi del Monte (1487–1555), was elected as Pope Julius II on 7 February 1550.

venice, which is xx miles. In venice I rested a daie with m$^r$ Jhon Arundell,[1] where I visited m$^r$ Edmund Harvelles wyff,[2] whom she had buried that sommer, complayning greatlie of the loss of so [p. 62] worthie a husband (as he was indeede) and gentle a gentleman as ever served king, of whom all Englishemen found great lacke.

[Hoby continued his journey northwards via Marghera and Treviso which was [f. 93r] 'now so fortified by the venetians, that it is reckoned on*e* of the strongest holds in all Italye'. He then reached Bassano, 'a prettie Towne under the venetiens, situated upon the Brenta that goeth to Padoa'.

His narratives also include an account of his brother Philip's [f. 144r; p. 104] 'journey Into Italy' in 1554 from England which he also joined. His account of their stay at Padua is especially interesting because of the number of English residents there which he names.]

[f. 157r; p. 116] We arrived in Padoua the xxiii$^{th}$ of the moneth of August, where as we mett with S*i*r Thomas Wroth, S*i*r Jhon Cheeke, S*i*r Henry Nevell,[3] S*i*r Jhon Cutt*es*,[4] m$^r$ Bartye,[5] m$^r$ Taumworth, with iii of S*i*r Anthonie Denies sonnes,[6] m$^r$ Henry Cornwallis,[7] m$^r$ Jhon Ashley, m$^r$ Drurye,[8] m$^r$ Henry Kingsmell, m$^r$ Windam, [p. 117] m$^r$ Roger Carewe, and mathew, his brother,[9] m$^r$ Brooke, m$^r$ Orphinstrange[10] with dyverse other. And shortlie after here arrived S*i*r Anthonye Cooke. Besides all these here I found m$^r$ Thomas Fitzwilliams whom in fore time I had left in Fraunce, whose studie and industrie

[1] Unidentified.

[2] See **item 12**.

[3] Sir Henry Neville (*c*.1520–*c*.1593), of Billingham, Berkshire; godson of Henry VIII and Gentleman of the Privy Chamber to Edward VI; knighted 1551; at Padua (1554); member of Earl of Devon's household at Venice (1556). Woolfson, *Padua*, p. 260.

[4] John Cutts (d. 1555), Sheriff and Cambridgeshire and Huntingdonshire (1551); member of Marquis of Northampton's embassy to Paris (1551); probably at Padua (1554) due to his opposition to Queen Mary; died at Venice of pleurisy (by 9 May 1555). Garrett, *Exiles*, p. 139. Woolfson, *Padua*, p. 229.

[5] Probably Richard Bertie (1517–82), who married in *c*.1553, Katherine, widow of Charles Brandon, Duke of Suffolk; he was formerly her steward. He was licensed to go abroad in June 1554 to collect debts owing to his wife. He was at Venice in the same year where he was permitted to view the Treasury of *San Marco (*CSP Venice*, 1554, item 122). After returning to England, probably in January 1555, he and his wife fled abroad in disguise; various attempts to arrest them failed. They had returned to England by 1559. Garrett, *Exiles*, pp. 87–9. Woolfson, *Padua*, p. 212.

[6] Charles (b. 1536? but sometimes wrongly referred to as the third son, Garrett, *Exiles*, p. 143), Henry (1540–74) and Anthony Denny (1542–72), sons of Sir Anthony Denny (1501–49), Henry VIII's Groom of the Stool. He had sent in 1543 his nephew John Denny to study at Venice under the care of Edmund Harvell (**item 12**). The three brothers were supervised by John Tamworth. Woolfson, *Padua*, p. 231.

[7] Henry Cornwallis (b. after 1519, d. before 1599), his elder brother, Sir Thomas Cornwallis (1518/19–1604), had been sent by Queen Mary to confer with Sir Thomas Wyatt and he later sat on the commission for his trial. Henry may have been either a Protestant exile or merely a Catholic traveller when he met Hoby at Padua; returned to England in 1555. Garrett, *Exiles*, pp. 128–9. Woolfson, *Padua*, p. 227.

[8] William Drury (d. by 1590), Regius Professor of Civil Law, Cambridge University (1559–61); converted to Catholicism on his deathbed. Woolfson, *Padua*, pp. 231–2.

[9] Roger Carew (*c*.1528–90), brother of the Marian exile Matthew Carew (1531–1618), who was with him at Padua. They were uncles of the three Denny brothers. Roger had returned to England by 1559. Woolfson, *Padua*, p. 218.

[10] John Orphinstrange (d. 1589), Consiliarius of the English nation at Padua (1552–3); awarded DCL at Padua (1555). Woolfson, *Padua*, p. 261.

in obtayning of vertuous knowlege hathe spred abrode a worthie fame of it self. And indede it was no small contentation of mind unto me to find him here whose unfayned frendshipp I had always tasted of in sundrie places, and now receaved of the frutes of the same.

[On 21 October 1555 Thomas Hoby left Padua with his brother, Mr Wroth, Mr. Cooke and Mr. Cheeke to travel to Mantua. His entries for 1555 contain some interesting miscellaneous records for events at Venice and Padua.]

[f. 161v; p. 120] The ix^th of maye Sir Jhon Cuttes departed owt of this woorlde at venice of a pleurisie as it is judged.

...

The xii^th of June my Lord of Bedfort[1] arrived in padoa and Sir Anthonye Cooke departed towards Germanie.

In the monethe of July Sir Anthonye Browne, Viscount Montague,[2] returned by padoa from Roome, and the bisshopp of Ely[3] arrived at Venice in his jorney towardes England again, where my brother went to see him.

[f. 162r] The xv^th of July my brother departed owt of padoa towards the baynes of Caldero, besides Verona.[4]

...

[f. 170r; p. 120] After xxii dayes abodd[5] at Caldero to take the water, we departed thense in cumpanie with mr Wrothe and m^r Cheeke who were then cumm from padoa for that the plague that was ceased before ow^r cumming from thense, begann again to encrease.

---

[1] Francis Russell, 2nd Earl of Bedford, see pp. 11, 155 n. 6 and 157 n. 3.

[2] Appointed Ambassador Extraordinary to Venice in 1555.

[3] Thomas Goodrich, Bishop of Ely, died 10 May 1554; and Thomas Thirlby (1506–70), formerly chaplain to Henry VIII and Bishop of Norwick, was nominated on 10 July 1554. Thirlby was heading back to England after serving as ambassador to the court of Emperor Charles V (Apr. 1553–Apr. 1554).

[4] The thermal baths of Caldiero (Caldero), situated in the Veneto, c.90 km west of Venice and 15 km east of Verona.

[5] *abodd*: abode.

# 18.  1550–56 – PETER VANNES (PIETRO VANNI OF LUCCA), ENGLISH AMBASSADOR TO VENICE

**Peter Vannes** (*c.* 1488–1563) provides an example of a native-born Italian who was one of many living in Tudor England but, exceptionally, was sent to Venice to serve as King Edward VI's and Queen Mary's official ambassador there. He was born in Lucca, Tuscany, the son of Stefano Vanni, a relative of the humanist scholar Andreas Ammonius (Cosma della Rena) (1476–1517), who had travelled to England in about 1506 to seek court patronage. Ammonius became the friend of Erasmus, Sir Thomas More, Thomas Linacre (**Plate 15**) and Richard Pace, and also served Henry VIII as his Latin Secretary (1511). In 1513 he encouraged Vannes to come to England as his assistant. Silvestro Gigli (1463–1521), absentee Bishop of Worcester and a native of Lucca, introduced Vannes to Cardinal Thomas Wolsey.[1] Vannes was appointed as Wolsey's Latin Secretary (1514) and he acquired several ecclesiastical livings in England.

Vannes's training as a diplomat and personal contacts with Venice began in 1527 when he accompanied Wolsey and More to France to negotiate a league between England and the Holy Roman Empire, France and Venice. He was then sent in late 1528 as a special ambassador to Pope Clement VII at Rome to seek his confirmation of Henry VIII's marriage to Catherine of Aragon as void *ab initio* and, on the same mission, met with the French king, François I, in December 1528. While at Rome he also met the Venetian cardinal Gasparo Contarini (1483–1542), who described him as 'really a most amiable person and partial to the Signoria, being a Lucchese'.[2] Vannes stayed at Rome until October 1529 and this absence probably contributed to his survival of Wolsey's fall. Soon afterwards he became Latin Secretary to Henry VIII while continuing to accumulate lucrative English benefices and being granted the desirable post of collector of papal taxes (*colletaria*) – usually held by an Italian – until its suspension soon afterwards, following Henry's break with Rome. He was sent in 1533 to meet with the Pope at Marseilles and was Dean of Salisbury by 1536. He also successfully cultivated the favour of Thomas Cromwell (executed 1540) and Edward Seymour (executed 1552), Duke of Somerset.

Edward VI retained him as Latin Secretary and in May 1550 he was appointed as English Ambassador to Venice with a salary of 40s per day.[3] He arrived there in August

---

[1] At Wolsey's instigation, from 1512 Gigli had consistently undermined the authority of Bishop Christopher Bainbridge, the cousin of Robert Langton (**item 8**), then serving at Rome effectively as the Cardinal Protector of England. When Bainbridge died on 14 July 1514, possibly poisoned, one of his household claimed under torture to have administered poison at Gigli's direction. Although the Pope eventually absolved him of responsibility for the murder, it terminated his ambitions to become a cardinal. 'Peter Vannes', *ODNB*, s.v.

[2] *CSP Venice*, 1529, item 398.

[3] Ibid., 9 Aug. 1550, item 679.

and his duties included monitoring closely Protestant Englishman in Italy and those with reputed Catholic sympathies who frequented the circle of Cardinal Reginal Pole (**item 11**).[1] He was commended by the English Council for the quality of his regular reports from Venice and sought permission to attend Venetian religious services in order to integrate himself into the community but certainly not 'for the worshipping of idols and images'.[2] As part of this process, as a noted Italian scholar, Vannes soon became the focus of attention at Venice from other Italian writers. The humanist Ortensio Lando (*c.*1510–*c.*1558) dedicated to him his *Miscellaneae questiones,* printed at Venice in 1550. Lando worked at Venice as a printer's scribe, translator, editor and compiler of collections and was best known in England for his translation into Italian of Sir Thomas More's *Utopia* (Venice, 1548). Vannes also sent a spy to Rome to check on the activities of two friends of Cardinal Pole, William Peto and Richard Pate, who still held titles to English bishoprics.[3]

Soon after his arrival, Vannes experienced some personal difficulties with another Englishman then at Venice, named Robert Stafford, 'who behaved in an unbecoming and discourteous manner' in the ambassador's residence. The *Council of Ten immediately summoned Stafford and 'reproved him as his temerity deserved, admonishing him to abstain for the future, lest they have cause to proceed further against him, as they would have done at present, had not the ambassador interposed, requesting them to do nothing more'.[4] This problematic individual, Sir Robert Stafford, was, as Christina Garrett notes, a well-known 'turbulent adventurer' and troublemaker while travelling around the continent between 1549 and 1559. A son of Sir Humphrey Stafford of Blatherwick (and not, as sometimes claimed, a nephew of Cardinal Pole), he met Sir Thomas Hoby in Siena during autumn 1549 and later at Rome. He fled to France in 1554 with Thomas Stafford (who was a nephew of Cardinal Pole) but when in Paris in 1556, his 'melodramatic and incessant quarrels with Thomas Stafford elicited from [Henry] Wotton the sarcasm, "If ever there were a tragico-comedia played, surely these men played it".' He even quarrelled aggressively with John Calvin over the custody of the son of his elder brother, Sir William Stafford, who had died at Geneva in May 1556.[5]

Between 1550 and the death of Edward VI on 3 July 1553, as Ann Overell explains, Vannes loyally represented in Venice the English Protestant regime's 'radical evangelical government', but then managed with considerable skill the 'vertiginous transition' to Queen Mary's ardently Catholic rule, with confirmation of his reappointment finally reaching Venice on 3 November 1553.[6] In late February 1554 the doge and *Collegio

---

[1] The doge and *Collegio* informed Daniel Barbaro, Venetian Ambassador in England, that the 'Rev. D. Peter [Vannes] arrived lately at Venice, having been appointed by the King of England to reside with them as his ambassador'. On 8 Aug. he had attended an audience with the Collegio, accompanied by numerous senators. 'After presenting his credentials, he stated his commission with great gravity and prudence, bearing ample testimony to the King's goodwill towards them.' The Collegio commended Vannes for his 'learning and eminent qualities and parts'. *CSP Venice*, 1550, item 679.

[2] *CSP Foreign, 1547–53*, pp. 361, 378.

[3] Ibid., p. 313. Overell, *Nicodemites*, pp. 82–3.

[4] *CSP Venice*, 1550, item 687.

[5] *CSP Foreign, 1553–58*, pp. 264, 282, 299. Garrett, *Exiles*, 293–4. This Sir William Stafford was the father of Sir Edward Stafford, English Ambassador to France during the Spanish Armada crisis.

[6] Overell, *Nicodemites*, p. 76, in her chapter, 'The Volte-Faces of Pietro Vanni'.

wrote to Giovanni Michiel, the Venetian Ambassador at London, to record how Vannes and the Imperial Ambassador had come together to inform them about the successful suppression of the Wyatt Rebellion ('the battle between the insurgents and the Queen's troops, her Majesty remaining victorious').[1] Sometimes, however, there were questions over Vannes's personality and suitability for such a diplomatically demanding role. In August 1554 Marc'Antonio Damula, Venetian Ambassador at the Imperial court, wrote to the doge and Senate explaining that Sir John Mason (1503–66), his English ambassadorial counterpart at the court, had recounted how Vannes had written to Queen Mary, reporting 'certain words uttered in Venice' by one of his own servants, called William (sometimes referred to as George) Page, claiming that he wished to kill the queen. Vannes had gone to the Senate to demand the arrest of his servant but had been told that he was over-reacting:

> you told him it was of no importance (*che non importava*), nor should the words of similar persons be heeded (*nè era da metter a mente le parole di tali*), and that at Venice there was liberty for good men and for rogues (*era libertà alii buoni et alii tristi*), and that he himself was to make him hold his tongue. So as Vannes did not think fit to allow this outrage against the Queen to remain unpunished he went to Mantua, where the Cardinal [Ercole Gonzaga] and the Duchess [the Regents of Mantua] conceded him the apprehension of the servant, who, on being examined, confessed to having said the words, and thereupon many witnesses were examined.

Sir John Mason had advised Marc'Antonio Damula that he considered Vannes 'very timid' and had even advised him against contacting the queen, in case she might 'subject him to reproof as well as detriment' (*egli ne ricevesse biasimo et danno anchora*). Damula replied:

> I said to Sir John Mason that fear was by certain persons appropriately styled a tie and ligature (*vincido et legame*), and that some had too much of it, as seemed to have been the case with Mr. Vannes, who was as it were bound (*legato*), and knew not what to do, and that occasionally, under other circumstances, I had seen him in greater fear about ridiculous matters; nor was it becoming to imprison men for light causes, such as the words of a base menial (*un vil servitor*), who was either mad or drunk, and that I believed when the Queen heard them they would move her to laughter; nor are trifles of this sort held in account at Venice.

Mason confirmed this assessment and told Damula that he recalled letters from Venice sent to King Edward VI about Vannes's timidity and that he had even in the past seen him 'cry from fear'. They agreed that Mason should write to Queen Mary, apologizing for Vannes's panic in taking Page's idle words so seriously, remarking that 'since the last Parliament, this liberty of speech is greater in England than in any place in the world, whereas previously, one word of the sort constituted *crimen laesae Majestatis*, which, seeming too harsh and unjust, they therefore repealed the statute'.[2]

Only one week later, more tribulations came the way of Peter Vannes. This time Marc'Antonio Damula reported to the doge and Senate how Vannes had reported the presence at Venice of Peter Carew, 'the leader of the Cornish insurrection', and how he

---

[1] *CSP Venice*, 1554, item 860.

[2] *CSP Venice*, 1554, item 936. Page was eventually imprisoned for three months but on his release entered the service of Francis Russell, 2nd Earl of Bedford. Overell, *Nicodemites*, pp. 87–8.

had often tried to speak to Vannes who refused to see him.[1] Once again, Vannes was beginning to panic but Sir John Mason remarked:

> in no place could Peter Carew do less mischief than in that noble city (*quella inclyta città*), where he might learn obedience and quiet, and repent himself, which Masone admitted, and seemed glad of it, as I added, that the least harm Peter Carew might have done would have been to turn corsair, like the others, and plunder English subjects.

Damula also noted how he had communicated this view to Michiel, the Venetian Ambassador in England, and that Mason had attempted to reassure Vannes that he should feel free to talk to Carew because Mason had written to Queen Mary to reassure her that Carew could not be 'in a better place than Venice, and that he should be entertained, because he is not naturally bad'.[2] In his later manuscript biography, 'The Life and Times of Sir Peter Carew' (*c*. late 1570s), John Hooker (*c*.1526–1601) claimed that Vannes had hired Venetian ruffians to assassinate Carew.[3]

In early 1555 Vannes requested permission to hire two Venetian ships to transport grain from the Levant to Lucca but the *Council of Ten turned him down, explaining that shortages across the Mediterranean meant that all Venetian ships were required to keep its own citizens supplied with grain.[4] In July 1555 Vannes experienced more success in applying on behalf of Francis Russell, second Earl of Bedford, for permission for the Earl and fourteen of his men to bear arms for their own protection both within the city of Venice and in all of its possessions.[5] However, in early October 1555 he entered into an acrimonious correspondence with Cardinal Pole (who was then at Greenwich) about the collection of 'Peter's Pence'. One of Pole's letters, dated 4 October and written in Italian, attempted to smooth over this issue and reaffirmed his unwavering 'goodwill towards Vannes'. Nevertheless, this dispute remained indicative of Vannes's ability to take personal offence and constantly question the motives of others towards him – neither of which qualities is helpful for an ambassadorial diplomat.[6] By the end of 1555 it would probably have been a relief to Vannes if he had known of a confidential report to the doge and Senate of Giovanni Michiel, the Venetian Ambassador in England, which noted: 'The Queen is about to recall all her ambassadors save the one in France, to save their cost; such business as necessary to be transacted by those remaining in the King's [i.e., the Emperor's] name, for her likewise; and Mr. Vannes, the resident at Venice, will soon have orders to return.'[7]

In spring 1556 Vannes travelled to Padua to meet with Bona Sforza (1494–1557), Dowager Queen of Poland. He found himself having to justify to her the burning at the stake of Thomas Cranmer on 21 March, despite his recantations in which he had recognized papal authority and that of the queen and king of England (even though he then withdrew them as he stood at the stake). In his report to Queen Mary Vannes

---

[1] For Carew, see pp. 11 and 156 n. 8.

[2] *CSP Venice*, 1554, items 941, 944.

[3] Lambeth Palace Library, London, MS 605. Overell, *Nicodemites*, p. 89.

[4] *CSP Venice*, 1555, items 19–20.

[5] Ibid., 31 July 1555, item 169. The Earl's supporters were listed as Sir John Chichester, Thomas and Clement (servants), Mr William Godolphin, John Broke, Thomas Rayme, John Eustace, Anthony Trulo (or Trewlock or Trewlove), Thomas Fitzwilliam, John Morley, Thomas Toylson, Henry Kingsmel and John Rug.

[6] *CSP Venice*, 1555, item 233.

[7] Ibid., 3 Dec. 1555, item 297.

explained how he had emphasized how Cranmer's 'iniquity and obstinacy was so great against God and your Grace that your clemency and mercy could have no place with him but you were constrained to minister justice'.[1] He then had to deal with the controversial arrival at Venice in April 1556 of Edward Courtenay, Earl of Devon, whom he invited to stay at the ambassador's residence, although (probably much to Vannes's relief) Courtenay opted to reside at Ferrara instead and then moved to Padua. Rumours circulated that he might be married to Princess Elizabeth and then usurp the English throne from Mary and Philip. However, within two months he was dead (on 18 September) and yet another set of rumours circulated, implying that Vannes had somehow been complicit in Courtenay's demise.[2]

The English Council had decided upon Vannes's recall two days before Courtenay's death and Vannes may also have requested soon afterwards that his embassy should be terminated. He was back in England soon after October 1556. Queen Elizabeth allowed him to retain his church livings and he died between 28 March and 1 May 1563. His will (two versions were compiled on 1 July 1562) revealed considerable wealth. He provided generously for his sister Margaret and his brother's illegitimate daughter, also named Margaret. His principal heir was one 'Benedict Hudson, alias Vannes', probably his illegitimate son, who received his family lands in Lucca and bequests to his mother Alice. To Sir William Petre (1505–72), Royal Secretary (1554–7), he bequeathed a 'new black satin robe adorned with black velvet newly acquired from Venice'.[3]

[1] BL Harleian MS 5009, ff. 94r–95r; quoted in Overell, *Nicodemites*, p. 90.

[2] Overell, *Nicodemites*, pp. 107–12. Vannes sent an account of Courtenay's death to Queen Mary, but the exact circumstances remain murky. According to Vannes, he had been flying a falcon on the Lido when he was caught in a violent storm from which he developed a fever which left him too weak even to take Communion in the hours before his death. He was buried with a grand monument in the Basilica of St Anthony of Padua. Other accounts suspected death from syphilis or malaria or a fall down the stairs.

[3] TNA: PRO, PROB 11/46, f. 173v. *ODNB*, s.v.

# 19.  1552 – ROGER ASCHAM

**Roger Ascham (1514/15–68)**, of Kirby Wiske, Northallerton, North Yorkshire, was an author and royal tutor. As a youth he joined the household of Humphrey Wingfield, a Suffolk lawyer, royal commissioner and MP who modelled his household on Sir Thomas More's. Ascham matriculated from St John's College, Cambridge, in 1530 where he developed his knowledge of Greek under the guidance of John Cheke. Ascham did not come from a wealthy family and much of the later 1530s and 1540s was spent in seeking patronage and modestly paid academic employment, coupled with recurrent bouts of bad health (possibly malaria). He compiled a manual on archery, *Toxophilus* (1545), cast as a dialogue between Philologus (devoted to academic study) and Toxophilus (devoted to archery). Ambitious in his pursuit of court patronage, Ascham dedicated the work to Henry VIII and sent personal presentation copies to Prince Edward, Sir Anthony Denny (whose three sons were sent to study at Padua and Venice) and William Parr, the brother of Queen Katherine Parr. Ascham's bid for patronage was successful and he was granted a royal pension of £10 and appointed Public Orator (1546–54) at the University of Cambridge.

In January 1548 Princess Elizabeth's tutor, William Grindall, died and Ascham was appointed, at Elizabeth's request, as his replacement. He taught her languages through the technique of 'double translation', utilized later by Philip Sidney (**item 22**, **Plate 17** and **Figure 17**) and other Englishmen preparing for a diplomatic career or travelling abroad.[1] He also taught calligraphy to Elizabeth and her brother Prince Edward and perhaps also Lady Jane Grey. He was friendly with Elizabeth's governess Katherine (Campernowne) Astley and her husband John who later took up residence at Venice as a Marian exile. In 1548 Princess Elizabeth moved to the household of Sir Anthony Denny whose three sons were also exiles with John Astley during Mary's reign at Padua and Venice.

In September 1550 he joined the embassy of Sir Richard Morison to the Emperor Charles V and wrote six letters describing his journey from England to Germany. He served as Morison's secretary who, in turn, began to teach him Italian. By late 1552 he was resident at Augsburg and compiling an account of the emperor's court, probably for the benefit of friends back in England such as John Astley, using Machiavelli's *History of Florence* and *Discourses* as models. He returned to England in August 1553 and, heavily in debt, returned to Cambridge, In May 1554 he was appointed as Queen Mary's Latin Secretary and received a royal pension of £20 a year for life. He also became friendly with Cardinal Reginald Pole (**item 11** and **Plate 6**). Wisely, however, he retained amicable

---

[1] Gallagher, *Learning Languages*, p. 92. In a letter to Sidney, dated 1 Jan. 1574, Hubert Languet explained this method, using Cicero's letters: 'Many believe that it is extremely useful to choose some passage from the letters, and to translate it into another language, then, having put the book away, to translate it back into Latin, and finally to look at the book again and see how close you have come to Cicero's style.' Sidney, *Correspondence*, I, p. 77.

relations with Princess Elizabeth and continued to study with her, deeply impressed by her linguistic skills, classical erudition and political understanding. After her accession, Elizabeth continued to read with him after dinner, a custom which prompted him to write his educational manual, *The Scholemaster*. During the last years of his life, Ascham was troubled by illness and financial problems, at least in part occasioned by his large family and other dependants. Nevertheless, he maintained a wide circle of academic contacts with the likes of George Buchanan and the Regius Professor of Greek at Cambridge University, Bartholomew Dodington, to whom he gave a copy of Carlo Sigone, *De republica Atheniensium libri III*, published at Venice in 1565.

His educational manual, *The Scholemaster*, contained two books and was published posthumously in 1570 by the stationer John Daye. The first, heavily dependent upon Plato, outlines the ideal tutor and pupil; and the second, drawing upon Cicero, demonstrates the proper imitation of classical models and the pedagogic value of 'double translation'. A manuscript version of the first book survives (BL Royal MS 18 B. xxiv, ff. 47r–78r), completed *c.*1563, and the second book and preface were completed shortly before his death on 30 December 1568 (probably from malaria). The completed work considered the educational and moral development of young men intended for public service and he wrote in English to attract as wide an audience as possible. *The Scholemaster* remained a popular text throughout the rest of Elizabeth's reign, going through five editions by 1590. On the basis of a visit to Venice of only nine days in duration, the first book of *The Scholemaster* closes with a sustained diatribe against young Englishmen travelling to Italy, prompted by his discussion with Sir Richard Sackville about his son's academic and moral education, with a particular emphasis upon ensuring that he did not fall into loose or lascivious ways.

## Text[1]

[p. 23r] Syr *Richard Sackvile*,[2] that worthy Jentleman of worthy memorie, as I sayd in the begynnynge, in the Queenes privie Chamber of Windesore, after he had talked with me, for the right choice of a good witte in a child for learnyng, and of the trewe difference betwixt quicke and hard wittes, of alluring yong children by jentlenes to love learnyng, and of the speciall care that was to be had, to kéepe yong men from licencious livyng, he was most earnest with me, to have me say my mynde also, what I thought, concernyng the fansie that many yong Jentlemen of England have to travell abroad, and namely to leadde a long lyfe in Italie.[3] His request, both for his authoritie, and good will toward me,

---

[1] Text from *The Scholemaster* (1570), *STC* 832. See also Ascham, *The Schoolmaster* (1570), ed. Ryan, pp. 60–75; and Wyatt, *Italian Encounter*, pp. 159–63.

[2] Sir Richard Sackville (*c.*1507–66), a cousin through his mother's line of Anne Boleyn, was a financial administrator, MP and Queen Elizabeth's Under-Treasurer of the Exchequer (from 1559). He claimed to have been mistreated and beaten by his own childhood tutor and was interested in finding a more suitable way of educating his son Thomas. *ODNB*, s.v.

[3] Sir Richard's son, Thomas (1536–1608), later 1st Earl of Dorset (from 1604), was an MP and held various financial positions. He travelled to Rome in 1563 where he was briefly imprisoned, perhaps for spying, although it has been suggested that he was seeking to negotiate some form of reconciliation between Protestant England and the Papacy. It may be significant in the context of this trip to Italy that his mother, Winifred Brydges (d. 1586), was reputed to have been a devout Catholic. Thomas Sackville was also co-author of the first English

was a sufficient commaundement unto me, to satisfie his pleasure, with utteryng plainlie my opinion in that matter. Syr quoth I, I take goyng thither, and living there, for a yonge jentleman, that doth not goe under the kepe and garde of such a man, as both, by wisedome can, and authoritie dare rewle him, to be mervelous dangerous. And whie I said so than, I will declare at large now: which I said than privatelie, and write now openlie, not bicause I do contemne, either the knowledge of strange and diverse tonges, and namelie the Italian tonge, which next the Greeke and Latin tonge, I like and love above all other: or else bicause I do despise, the learning that is gotten, or the experience that is gathered in strange contries: or for any private malice that I beare to Italie: which contrie, and in it, namelie Rome, I have alwayes speciallie honored: bicause, tyme was, whan Italie and Rome, have bene, to the greate good of us that now live, the best breeders and bringers up, of the worthiest men, not onelie for wise speakinge, but also for well doing, in all Civill affaires, that ever was in the worlde. But now, that tyme is gone, and though the place remayne, yet the olde and present maners, do differ as farre, as blacke [p. 23v] and white, as vertue and vice. Vertue once made that contrie Mistres over all the worlde. Vice now maketh that contrie slave to them, that before, were glad to serve it. All men seeth it: They themselves confesse it, namelie soch, as be best and wisest amongest them. For sinne, by lust and vanitie, hath and doth breed up euery where, common contempt of Gods word, private contention in many families, open factions in every Citie: and so, makyng them selves bonde, to vanitie and vice at home, they are content to beare the yoke of servyng straungers abroad, *Italie* now, is not that *Italie,* that it was wont to be: and therfore now, not so fitte a place, as some do counte it, for yong men to fetch either wisedome or honestie from thence. For surelie, they will make other but bad Scholers, that be so ill Masters to them selves.

...

[p. 24v] I know diverse noble personages, and many worthie Jentlemen of England, whom all the *Siren* songes of *Italie,*[1] could never untwyne from the maste of Gods word: nor no inchantment of vanitie, overturne them, from the feare of God, and love of honestie.

But I know as many, or mo, and some, sometyme my deare frendes, for whose sake I hate going into that countrey the more, who, partyng out of England fervent in the love of Christes doctrine, and well furnished with the feare of God, returned out of *Italie* worse transformed, than ever was any in *Circes* Court. I know diverse, that went out of England, men of innocent life, men of excellent learnyng, who returned out of *Italie,* not onely with worse maners, but also with lesse learnyng: neither so willing to live orderly, nor yet so hable to speake learnedlie, as they were at [p. 25r] home, before they went abroad.

...

[p. 26r] But I am affraide, that over many of our travelers into *Italie,* do not exchewe the way to *Circes* Court: but go, and ryde, and runne, and flie thether, they make great hast to cum to her: they make great sute to serve her: yea, I could point out some with

---

play in blank verse, the political drama *Gorboduc* (1561), and contributed a prefatory sonnet to the first English translation of Castiglione's *Book of the Courtier* (1561) by Sir Thomas Hoby (**item 17**) and verses to the poetic miscellany, *The Mirror for Magistrates* (1563 edition). 'Thomas Sackville', *ODNB*, s.v.

[1] Sirens, creatures in Greek mythology, part woman and part bird, which lured sailors to destruction on rocks through their enchanting singing and music.

my finger, that never had gone out of England, but onelie to serve *Circes*, in *Italie*. Vanitie and vice, and any licence to ill livyng in England was counted stale and rude unto them. And so, beyng Mules and Horses before they went, returned verie Swyne and Asses home agayne: yet everie where verie Foxes with sutlie and busie heades: and where they may, verie wolves, with cruell malicious hartes. A mervelous monster, which, for filthines of livyng, for dulnes to learning him selfe, for wilinesse in dealing with others, for malice in hurting without cause, should carie at once in one bodie, the belie of a Swyne, the head of an Asse, the brayne of a Foxe, the wombe of a wolfe. If you thinke, we judge amisse, and write to sore against you, heare, what the *Italian* sayth of the English man, what the master reporteth of the scholer: who uttereth playnlie, what is taught by him, and what is learned by you, saying, *Englese Italianato, e vn diabolo incarnato*, that is to say, you remaine men in shape and facion, but becum devils in life and condition.

...

[p. 29r] I was once in Italie my selfe: but I thanke God, my abode there, was but ix. dayes: And yet I sawe in that litle tyme, in one Citie, more libertie to sinne, than ever I hard tell of in our noble Citie of London in ix. yeare. I sawe, it was there, as free to sinne, not onelie without all punishment, but also without any mans marking, as it is free in the Citie of London, to chose, without all blame, whether a man lust to weare Shoe or pantofle.[1] And good cause why: For being unlike in troth of Religion, they must nedes be unlike in honestie of living. For blessed be Christ, in our Citie of London, commonlie the commandementes of God, be more diligentlie taught, and the service of God more reverentlie used, and that daylie in many private mens houses, than they be in Italie once a wéeke in their common Chirches: where, masking Ceremonies, to delite the eye, and vaine soundes, to please the eare, do quite thrust out of the Chirches, all service of God in spirit and troth. Yea, the Lord Maior of London, being but a Civill officer, is commonlie for his tyme, more diligent, in punishing sinne, the bent enemie against God and good order, than all [p. 29v] the bloodie Inquisitors in Italie be in seaven yeare. For, their care and charge is, not to punish sinne, not to amend manners, not to purge doctrine, but onelie to watch and oversee that Christes trewe Religion set no sure footing, where the Pope hath any Jurisdiction. I learned, when I was at *Venice*, that there it is counted good pollicie, when there be foure or five brethren of one familie, one, onelie to marie: & all the rest, to waulter,[2] with as litle shame, in open lecherie, as Swyne do here in the common myre. Yea, there be as fayre houses of Religion, as great provision, as diligent officers, to kepe up this misorder, as Bridewell is, and all the Masters there, to kepe downe misorder. And therefore, if the Pope himselfe, do not onelie graunt pardons to furder thies wicked purposes abrode in Italie, but also (although this present Pope, in the beginning, made som shewe of misliking thereof) assigne both meede and merite to the maintenance of stewes and brothelhouses at home in Rome, than let wise men thinke Italie a safe place for holsom doctrine, and godlie manners, and a fitte schole for yong jentlemen of England to be brought vp in.

Our Italians bring home with them other faultes from Italie, though not so great as this of Religion, yet a great deale greater, tha*n* many good men can well beare. For commonlie they cum home, common contemners of mariage and readie persuaders of

[1] *pantofle*: slipper or loose shoe; also applied to high, cork-soled Venetian chopins.
[2] *waulter*: welter.

Plate 3.    Gentile Bellini, *The Miracle of the Cross on San Lorenzo Bridge*. Oil on canvas, *c*.1500. Gallerie dell'Accademia, Venice, Bridgeman Images.

Plate 4.    Titian (Tiziano Vecellio), posthumous portrait of Doge Andrea Gritti (1455–1538). Oil on canvas, *c.*1546–8. National Gallery of Art, Washington DC, USA. Bridgeman Images.

Plate 5.    Unknown artist, Venetian school, portrait of Robert Langton. Oil on canvas laid on panel, *c.*1514. Private Collection. Bridgeman Images.

Plate 6.   Sebastiano del Piombo, portrait of Cardinal Reginald Pole. Oil on canvas, *c*.1540s. State
Hermitage Museum, St Petersburg, Russia. Bridgeman Images.

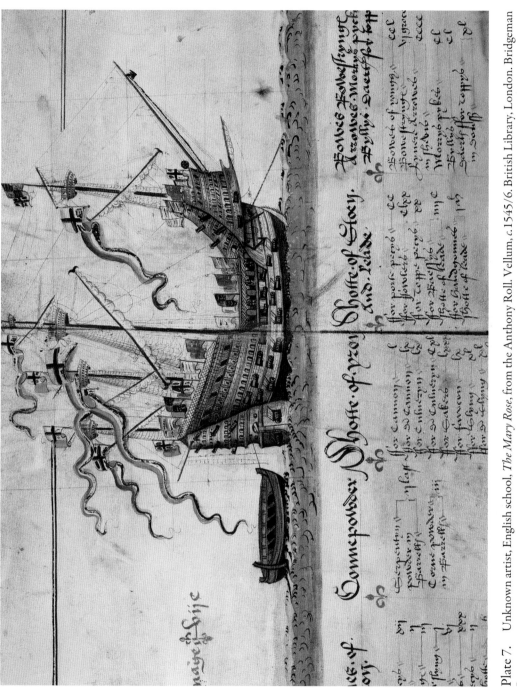

Plate 7.　Unknown artist, English school, *The Mary Rose*, from the Anthony Roll. Vellum, *c.*1545/6. British Library, London. Bridgeman Images.

Plate 8.    Hans Holbein the Younger, portrait of Sir George Carew, commander of the *Mary Rose*. Oil on panel, *c.* early 1540s. The Trustees of the Weston Park Foundation, UK. Bridgeman Images.

Plate 9.   Andrea Vincentio, *Doge Mocenigo and Patriarch Trevisan Welcoming Henri III, King of France, to the Lido in 1574*, detail. Oil on canvas, *c*.1593. Palazzo Ducale, Venice. Bridgeman Images.

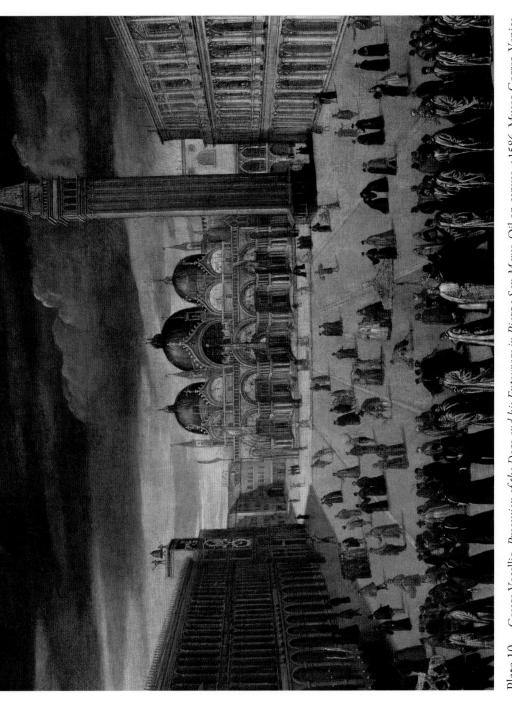

Plate 10.   Cesare Vecellio, *Procession of the Doge and his Entourage in Piazza San Marco*. Oil on canvas, c.1586. Museo Correr, Venice. Bridgeman Images.

all other to the same: not because they love virginitie, nor yet because they hate prettie yong virgines, but, being free in Italie, to go whither so ever lust will cary them, they do not like, that lawe and honestie should be soch a barre to their like libertie at home in England. And yet they be, the greatest makers of love, the daylie daliers, with such pleasant wordes, with such smilyng and secret countenances, with such signes, tokens, wagers, purposed to be lost, before they were purposed to be made, with bargaines of wearing colours, floures, and herbes, to bréede occasion of ofter meeting of him and her, and bolder talking of this and that &c. And although I have seene some, [p. 30r] innocent of all ill, and stayde in all honestie, that have used these thinges without all harme, without all suspicion of harme, yet these knackes were brought first into England by them, that learned the*m* before in *Italie* in *Circes* Court: and how Courtlie curtesses[1] so ever they be counted now, yet, if the meaning and maners of some that do use them, were somewhat amended, it were no great hurt, neither to them selves, nor to others.

An other propertie of this our English *Italians* is, to be mervelous singular in all their matters: Singular in knowledge, ignorant of nothyng: So singular in wisedome (in their owne opinion) as scarse they counte the best Counsellor the Prince hath, comparable with them: Common discoursers of all matters: busie searchers of most secret affaires: open flatterers of great men: privie mislikers of good men: Faire speakers, with smiling countena*n*ces, and much curtessie openlie to all men. Ready bakbiters, sore nippers,[2] and spitefull reporters privilie of good men. And beyng brought up in *Italie*, in some free Citie, as all Cities be there: where a man may freelie discourse against what he will, against whom he lust: against any Prince, agaynst any governement, yea against God him selfe, and his whole Religion: where he must be, either *Guelphe* or *Gibiline*,[3] either *French* or *Spanish:* and always compelled to be of some partie, of some faction, he shall never be compelled to be of any Religion: And if he medle not over much with Christes true Religion, he shall haue free libertie to embrace all Religions, and becum, if he lust at once, without any let or punishment, Jewish, Turkish, Papish, and Devillish.

A yong Jentleman, thus bred up in this goodly schole, to learne the next and readie way to sinne, to have a busie head a factious hart, a talkative tonge: fed with discoursing of factions: led so contemne God and his Religion, shall cum home into England, but verie ill taught, either to be an honest man him selfe, a quiet subject to his Prince, or willyng to serve God, under the obedience of trewe doctrine, or with [p. 30v] in the order of honest living.

I know, none will be offended with this my generall writing, but onelie such, as finde them selves giltie privatelie therin: who shall have good leave to be offended with me, untill they begin to amende them selves. I touch not them that be good: and I say to litle of them that be nought. And so, though not enough for their deserving, yet sufficientlie for this time, and more els when, if occasion so require.

And thus farre have I wandred from my first purpose of teaching a child, yet not altogether out of the way, bicause this whole taulke hath tended to the onelie

---

[1] *curtesses*: courtesies.

[2] *nippers*: someone who verbally nips or snipes.

[3] Members of the two great parties of medieval Italian politics, the Guelphs and Ghibellines, who supported, respectively, the Papacy and Holy Roman Emperors. Ascham's usage predates the first citation in the *OED*: Edmund Spenser, 'All Italy was distraict into the Factions of the Guelfes and Gibelins', *The Shepheardes Calendar* (1579), gloss to 25 June.

advauncement of trothe in Religion, an honestie of living: and hath bene wholie within the compasse of learning and good maners, the speciall pointes belonging in the right bringyng up of youth.

But to my matter, as I began, plainlie and simplie with my yong Scholer, so will I not leave him, God willing, untill I have brought him a perfite Scholer out of the Schole, and placed him in the Universitie, to becum a fitte student, for Logicke and Rhetoricke: and so after to Phisicke, Law, or Divinitie, as aptnes of nature, advise of frendes, and Gods disposition shall lead him.

The ende of the first booke.

# 20.   1564 – RICHARD SMITH'S ACCOUNT OF SIR EDWARD UNTON'S VISIT TO VENICE

**Sir Edward Unton (Umpton) (1534–82)**, of Wadley, Berkshire, and Langley, Oxfordshire, married on 29 April 1555 Anne Seymour (1538–87), daughter of Edward Seymour, Duke of Somerset, and widow of John Dudley (*c.*1527–54), Earl of Warwick, son of John Dudley (1504–53), Duke of Northumberland. The Dudleys had sought to place Lady Jane Grey on the throne of England and Unton was arrested in November 1555 by order of the Privy Council and incarcerated in the Fleet Prison for over a month. His marriage was eventually approved and, probably through the influence of his brother-in-law, Robert Dudley (**Plate 23**), he was appointed as a Knight of the Bath at Queen Elizabeth's coronation in January 1559. He was a Member of Parliament for Malmesbury (1554), Oxfordshire (1563) and Berkshire (1572) and entertained the queen in 1572 and 1574 at his manor house at Langley, Oxfordshire. He was granted a licence to travel abroad in 1563 and an incomplete account of his continental travels, written by his servant Richard Smith, is preserved in BL Sloane MS 1813. This travel narrative was compiled in a small pocketbook of fifty-seven folios titled: 'The jorney of Sr. Edward Unton and his company into Italy wherein is contiened the names of the townes where he bayted and laye, and the distaunce of myles betwene them wherein is to be noted that one Dutche myle conteyneth iii Englishe myles.' It is also stated that 'This jornall was written by Richard Smith gentleman, some time servaunt to Sʳ. Edward Unton of Wadley in the countye of Bercks knight.'[1] Unton, Smith and their party boarded ship at Dover on 12 March 1564.

Nothing else is known of Richard Smith's life or career but he was an engaged and perceptive observer of rural and urban landscapes on their route and the fashions and interests of their inhabitants. A. H. S. Yeames observes:

> Mr Richard Smith had many merits as a traveller .... He was quick to note the manners of the people as they appeared to him in the inn or the market-place, and to describe with curious detail the fashions of their dress. He was interested in agriculture, and observed the crops and fruits which were cultivated by the road ... . He remarks singular ways of building and is warm in his praise of Antwerp, of Augsburg, of the Cathedral at Florence, and, with some hesitation, of that of Siena. Rome depressed him. Like his contemporary Du Bellay, he found but little trace of its ancient splendour, but he admired the Vatican, to which Pius IV was then adding, and foresaw the magnificence of St Peter's. His description of Rome, however, is so brief that

---

[1] BL Sloane MS 1813, f. 4r. The second statement about Richard Smith's authorship has been added in a different and probably later hand. The ink in parts of the manuscript is faded, especially in the section dealing with Venice. Smith's manuscript is not foliated or paginated and so I have confirmed and followed the foliation of Yeames, 'Grand Tour of an Elizabethan', pp. 92–113. MS 1813 was acquired by the British Museum, following the death of Sir Hans Sloane (1660–1753); it is not known from where Sloane acquired it. It bears earlier manuscript references, 'MS 1681' and '682' (deleted), followed by '1813'.

he is clearly more at home in the fields and the inns by the roads than in a city which bewildered him. We may conjecture that it was the contrast with the life of Berkshire which chiefly roused his interest in his journey through foreign lands.[1]

While Smith was happy to praise the Pope's building projects in Rome, he was more sceptical of the attractions of Venice. His diary is incomplete (whether through being unfinished or later loss of the concluding part of a completed account) and continues only as far as the journey from Strasbourg to Mainz during the return trip on 27 October 1564. It is clear from this section of his narrative that Smith was familiar with William Thomas's *History of Italy* (**item 16**) and among several books once belonging to the Untons are two which act as memorials of their Italian travels. The first is the *History of Nicolo Machiavelli*, a copy of the 1541 edition printed at Venice of the *Istorie fiorentine*, bound with the *Arte della Guerra* (1537) and bearing a short inscription by Unton.[2] The second is a copy of the popular guidebook, *Le antichità della Città di Roma*, printed at Venice in 1562. This volume has on its title page the initials 'H. V.' of Sir Edward Unton's second son, Sir Henry (*c.*1558–96), and its first flyleaf bears the inscription: '*Questo è il libro di Thomaso Vntono è costaua – 16ᵈ. ob*'.[3]

Sir Edward died on 16 September 1582 and was buried in Faringdon church. His will (made on 14 September 1581 and proved 19 September 1582) granted to his eldest son, Edward, the custody of his widow Anne, Countess of Warwick, since from May 1566 she had been a 'lunatic enjoying lucid intervals'. He also advised his second son, Henry, 'to govern himself', by the advice and guidance of his trusted friend, Sir Francis Walsingham (**Plate 24**). This Henry became a noted diplomat and soldier, establishing during the 1590s a close working relationship with King Henri IV of France. He also undertook a continental tour during the 1570s, through France to Padua and Venice, probably with his father who accompanied him for at least part of his travels (**item 25**).

### Text[4]

[f. 32v] from trent[5] my master rode the 21 of Aprill toward venyce leavynge me there to sell his horse trent is an old cytye situated in a very barron contry among the hills as is aforesayd a very swyfte river runynge by the towne which ysuethe[6] oute of the hills in dyvers places between trente and bowlsane[7] / ffrom trent I roode the 25 of Aprill to an old towne called burgo[8] / the way muche worse amonge the mountains then in any place

[1] Yeames, 'Grand Tour of an Elizabethan', p. 94. *ODNB*, s.v. Sir Henry Unton [Umpton]: https://www.historyofparliamentonline.org/volume/1558-1603/member/unton-sir-edward-1534-82.

[2] Chaney, *Evolution of the Grand Tour*, pp. 78, 98, notes that that he inspected this copy when in the possession of 'the late Professor J. H. Whitfield'. On the final endpaper, a previous owner or reader had written: 'Machiavelli Maxima / Qui nescit dissimulare / nescit vivere' and Unton had added the comment: 'Vive et vivas / Edw. Unton'.

[3] http://www.berkshirehistory.com/bios/euntonsr.html. These two books were first recorded in Nichols, 1841, pp. xxxviii–xxxix. The identity of this Thomas Unton remains uncertain.

[4] From BL Sloane MS 1813; and Yeames, 'Grand Tour of an Elizabethan', pp. 105–7.

[5] Trento.

[6] *ysuethe*: issueth, flows from.

[7] Bolzano, due north of Trento.

[8] Borgo Valsugana.

before this is called the welshe contrye[1] [f. 33r] the people speak the ytalian tong they ar very craftye beggars and sluttyshe in all thear doings from trent to burgo ar iiii leages ffrom alborgo I rood the 27 of Aprill to a towne called bassane[2] 6 leages from alborgo the way very ill and strayte baytinge[3] by the way att an ostary[4] called prymolane[5] in the myd waye aboute 2 Italyan myles beyond prymolane / ther is a strayt passage which is kept wheras we entered the land of venyce / this passage devydeth the land of tyrole from venyce land / bassane is vii leages the next waye from venyce wherof one leage is by water / bassane standethe at the farthest parte of the mo[n]strous hills / even at the fote of the mountains [f. 33v] ffrom bassane I roode the 29 of Aprill to a cytye called treviso[6] 5 leages ffrom bassane the contry between very fayre and plesaunte wher as they have as it apperth very good rye / wheet / benes / otes / and fatches / but no barly / between every land of corne as it wer in the forows tres planted of dyvers ffruites as plums cherys walnuts fyggs / and many other kynds settynge vynes between the said trees / which spred from tre to tre very plesaunte to be hold / also many playne commons where theyr cattell feed / the grasse semeth not to be very good beinge very full of horrible wormes lyke [f. 34r] unto serpents grene of coloure ffrom Treviso I went by a cotche the 2 of maye to a towne called mestre[7] ii leages from trevyso / wheras I was stayed all nyghte / this towne standeth nere unto the place wher as the passage botes ar taken to go unto venyce and is one leage by water from thence / from thence to venyce the 3 of maye whence I went to paduaye to my master the 4 of may / paduay is from venyce xx myles Italian / ther are ordynar[y] botes masse between bothe evening and morning . [f. 34v] padyuay is a cytie under the venecians estaste and is very lardge and mervelous stronge / wherin is a unyversitie / ther is also the tombe of Antheno[r][8] and the house of tytus Lyvius / it standeth in a pleasaunte contrye; build[ed] at the first by anthenor ffrom thence we departed 21 of maye to venyce wher we contynewed 2 monthes / venyce one of the ffayrest syties of sumptuous byldinges in chrystendon cytuated in the [f. 35r] salt water in the mouthe of the sea Adryatyke thear maners lawes and customs you shall in the [erasure] boke of William Thomas[9] although as it semeth unto me as well as to others that hath ben there that he speketh more in the prayse of itt than it dothe deserve I sawe in venyce a certain horrible beast which was taken in Ethiopia ix monthe before we sawe hym / this best was supposed to be a cocodrill[10] / he was by estim[e] [f. 35v] a bowte 14 fote long his scales so harde and thike that no pyke was able to perce hym to do hym harme / his hinder legs wer longer then his for legs / his nayles grete and longe / his tayle cuttynge lyke a saw / his hed longe his mouthe very wyde his tethe very grete / he was taken wythe gret iron hookes and a

---

[1] *welshe contrye*: Smith's grammar and meaning here are unclear but may mean 'welsh' in old sense of foreign.

[2] Bassano.

[3] *baytinge*: providing food and water for horses or taking refreshment on a route.

[4] *ostary*: hosteria, an inn, hostelry or eating house.

[5] Primolano. Smith's account is confused here. The route he followed was a standard one from Borgo Valsugana, via Primolano to Bassano del Grappa. It seems that he was writing the diary retrospectively.

[6] Treviso.

[7] Mestre.

[8] Antenor and Livy, see p. 80 n. 2.

[9] See **item 16**. Smith's reference to William Thomas's *History of Italy* demonstrates how it had become a standard guidebook to Italy by the 1560s.

[10] *cocodrill*: crocodile.

shepes hed[1] and a gret chayne of iron / [f. 36r] from venyce we went the 19 Julye and toke horse at mestre aforesayd and roode to paduaye which is 18 myle of / from paduay the next mornynge toward fferrara[2] / and lay at Rovigo[3] a towne of the venecyans 30 myle from paduaye ffrom thence the 21 of Julie to fferrare 25 myle ffrom thence note that in paduay is one of the chefeste universities in all Italei; and better [f. 36v] served of good vitailles and better chepe the[n] in venyce.

[1] *shepes hed*: sheep's head.
[2] Ferrara.
[3] Rovigo.

# 21.   1570 AND 1589 – HENRY CAVENDISH

**Henry Cavendish (1550–1616)** provides an example of an Englishman who made two separate trips to Venice, almost twenty years apart, during the latter half of the sixteenth century. He was the eldest son of Sir William Cavendish (1508–57), of Chatsworth, Derbyshire, and his third wife, Elizabeth Hardwick (1527–1608), renowned as 'Bess of Hardwick', the daughter of John and Elizabeth Hardwick of Hardwick, Derbyshire, and widow of Robert Barley (d. 1544), whom she had married in 1543 when he was thirteen and she was fifteen or sixteen.

Born on 17 December 1550 the young Henry Cavendish belonged to a world of influential family court connections. At his christening his godparents were Princess Elizabeth, Henry Grey, Marquis of Dorset (the father of Lady Jane Grey), and John Dudley, Earl of Warwick (from October 1551 Duke of Northumberland). He briefly attended Eton College in 1560 but was then tutored at home and admitted to Gray's Inn in 1567. As a child he became a tool of his mother's dynastic ambitions. His mother had married Sir William Loe (1518–65) as her third husband and, following his death, she married in 1568 George Talbot (1528–90), sixth Earl of Shrewsbury. In a double ceremony held on 9 February 1568 her son Henry, aged seventeen, was married to his stepsister, Shrewsbury's eight-year-old daughter Grace; and Bess's daughter Mary (1556–1632), aged twelve, was married to Shrewsbury's heir, Gilbert (1552–1616), then aged fifteen.[1]

Soon after these two weddings, Henry Cavendish and Gilbert Talbot were sent to the continent to broaden their education. They met in Germany and travelled to northern Italy, visiting Padua and Venice, before returning to England in early 1572. Henry's younger brother, Charles Cavendish (1553–1617), was also with them in Italy. On 4 November 1570 Henry wrote to his parents from Padua, providing details of their travels together and asking for advice on whether they should remain abroad or begin to come home to England:

> To my Lorde and my Lady geve thes,
> Pleaseth yt your honores tunderstand that synce our last lettars to you, whych we sent from Spyres[2] we have traveled thorough the cuntry of Swycerland into Italy whear for the shorte tyme of our travel we have seen many goodly Cittyes, as Myllan, from whence we traveled to Pavia, and so to Genua: and from that Cytty dyrected our journey to Venyce, betwyxt with [*sic*] tow townes lyeth the greatest bredthe of al Italy, and tooke thes famous Cyttyes in our waye Fortona, Placentia, Parma, Mantua, Verona, Vicenza, Padua, to whych towne we came the ix of October, whear after we had rested tyl the xxviiith of the same moneth we went to see Venyce, whych doonne we returned agayne to Padua whear we remayne tyl we knowe your honoures pleasures, eyther for our farther travel, aboode hear, or returne: whych your

---

[1] *ODNB*, s.v. 'Henry Cavendish'. Cavendish, *His Journey*, ed. Wood, pp. iii–x.
[2] Speyer, in the Rhineland-Palatinate.

Honours' myndes to us once knowne we shal accordynge to our dewtyes very wyllyngly dooe any of thes. what we have seen in thys journey and the decryption of the townes to the best of our poure, with eych dayes travel (accordynge to your honors commaundements) would we have now sent wrytten in bookes, but that at thys present we had not fully fynyshed them and so ar constrayned to let them staye tyl the next post. Thus most humbly cravynge your Honours' daly blessynges I end beshechynge god longe to to contynew your honors in perfect health and great prosperytye. From Padua the iiiith of November.
Your honors obedient sonne
Henry. Cavendishe.[1]

It is interesting to note that Cavendish states that he and Talbot were compiling detailed accounts of 'eych dayes travel (accordynge to your honors commaundements)' and intended to send them back to their respective parents 'wrytten in bookes' as soon as they were finished. These travel diaries are now lost (assuming that they were ever completed and transported safely back to England) but such a process was expected by parents and guardians from most young travellers on the continent at this period.

Gilbert Talbot also wrote to his parents on the same day (4 November) and it is clear from the contents of the two letters that the two young men probably wrote them together:

To my Lord & lady geve thes
My moste humble deuty remembred unto your honors, pleaseth it you tunderstand that (thankes be to god) in moste perfite helthe we came hither to Padoa the 9 of october wher we are now well sattelled in suche a convenient place for our study or any other good exercise *th*at we doute not but to imploye the tyme yat we tary here according to your honours' expectation of us.
We fulfill your honours' commaundement in wrytynge the discource of our travayle which we would have sent with thes lettres but *th*at it could not be caryed so conveniently with them as it may be with the next lettres we wryte./ thus moste humbly cravynge your honours' daly blessinge I ende, beseching the living god to preserve your honours together in good helthe with muche increace of honor. Amen. Wrytten at Padoa the 4 of November. Anno Salutis. 1570
Your honors moste humble and obedient sonne
Gilbert Talbott[2]

While Cavendish admitted that their detailed travel diaries were not yet completed, Talbot merely claimed that they 'could not be caryed so conveniently' with their letters but would be dispatched with 'the next lettres we wryte'. In August 1571 Henry and Charles Cavendish and Gilbert Talbot witnessed the DCnCL (Doctorate in Canon and Civil Law) at the University of Padua of the recusant John Le Rous (d. 1590), a ceremony which also included his profession of Catholic orthodoxy.[3]

On Henry Cavendish's return to England in 1572 he served as MP for Derbyshire in the same year (and in 1584, 1586, 1589 and 1593) and Sheriff of Derbyshire (1582–3 and 1608–9). However, he was of a restless temperament, 'fiery, turbulent and

---

[1] Arundel Castle, West Sussex Archive, Autograph Letters, no. 83. https://www.bessofhardwick.org/letter.jsp?letter=226&view=normal&menu=date.

[2] Lambeth Palace Library, Talbot Papers, MS 3206, pp. 571–4: https://www.bessofhardwick.org/letter.jsp?letter=171.

[3] Woolfson, *Padua*, pp. 218, 251. Charles Cavendish was also suspected of harbouring Catholic sympathies.

adventuous' according to Anthony C. Wood, and during an affray in 1574, in which he was prominently involved, a man was killed.[1] In 1578 he raised a regiment from his own estates of 500–600 men to fight with the army of William of Orange. It played a prominent role in the victory over the Spanish at Rijmenam in August 1578 but, in reality, it was under the direct command of Cavendish's experienced lieutenant-colonel, Richard Bingham (1527/8–99) – a veteran of St Quentin (1557) and the Battle of Lepanto (1571) (**Plate 13**) – rather than of Cavendish who appears to have absented himself from this engagement. In March 1579 he returned home, abandoning the regiment with major debts which amounted to £3,000 by 1584. After his return from the continent Cavendish became alienated from his wife, Grace, whom in 1605 he openly called a 'harlot' and he produced no legitimate heir, although he is known to have had at least four illegitimate sons and four illegitimate daughters.

Cavendish had made a brief trip to Portugal in 1579 and in March 1589, when aged thirty-nine, he left England to make an expedition to Constantinople. This trip may have been motivated by a desire for adventure or, alternatively, there could have been a more commercial purpose behind it. Cavendish was travelling with the merchant Richard Mallory who had trading interests in the Levant and acted as an overseas agent for Sir Francis Walsingham (**Plate 24**). Mallory replaced at short notice Cavendish's intended travel companion, the scholar Anthony Wingfield (b. *c.*1552, d. in or after 1611), whose mother Mary was the younger sister of Bess of Hardwick.[2] It is possible that Cavendish and Mallory were exploring various trading options because the Earl and Countess of Shrewsbury had significant import-export interests, including shipping lead and minerals and luxury goods, with the Earl possessing his own international trading vessel, the *Talbott*. His countess, Bess of Hardwick, acquired for her residences European and Chinese silks, Persian and Anatolian carpets and a Gujarati embroidered bed-cover; and, after her husband's death, she maintained her family's involvements with lead, coal and glass manufacturing.[3]

Cavendish's wife, writing on 27 June 1589 to her mother-in-law, the Countess of Shrewsbury, hoped that he had reached Constantinople by that date: 'For by a nott he left wyth me at hys goinge of hys days jurneys (wherin he hath altered but one day as appeareth by hys letters) he was at Constantinople the XX of thys month'.[4] One of Cavendish's entourage, known only as 'Fox, his servant', kept a simple diary record of their travels.[5] Although Fox was clearly a man of limited education and cultural curiosity, his record remains an interesting perspective on the experiences of travellers to and through Venice at this period. The diary begins by noting that Cavendish took with him three servants and was travelling with 'Mr Rychard Mallory of London'. Their party left England on 28 March 1589, crossing by sea from Leigh in Essex to Stade in Germany where they arrived on 2 April. They travelled via Hamburg, Nuremburg and Augsburg

---

[1] Cavendish, *His Journey*, ed. Wood, p. iv.

[2] During the late 1570s Wingfield was Reader in Greek to Queen Elizabeth and on 21 March 1589 he was granted leave of absence by Cambridge University, where he was public orator, to go abroad in the queen's service which may also imply that Cavendish's journey to Turkey was more than merely a cultural or personal trip. *ODNB*, s.v.

[3] https://www.bessofhardwick.org/background.jsp?id=152.

[4] Cavendish, *His Journey*, ed. Wood, p. v.

[5] Chatsworth House, Derbyshire, Devonshire MSS, HM/45a; rpt Cavendish, *His Journey*, ed. Wood.

which they reached on 22 April: 'a fre stat of yt self and a plac of great beawty, the most beawtyfullest that we yet cam thorow'. After exploring the town and the various residences and business premises of the Fuggers, renowned as bankers and merchants, they began to make preparations for their journey to Venice:

> At thys toune we hyred horses to Venys for xvii crounes a horse and the postmaster or curayer to fynd and bear all chargys bothe for horse and men to Vennys whyche ys 240 myles.
>
> At this plac ther was a good fellowly man that had the Italyan tong that kept my master company all the tyme of our being ther. Hys name ys Moor.

Their party set out for Venice on 24 April, passing through Lansberg, Ammergau, and 'veary hylly contry under the Alpes' in the company of a German gentleman who was heading to Padua with two young charges. This German and Cavendish 'began to speak Lattyn' as they continued their journey together, stopping for food and rest at an unnamed village 'wher we found the lord Mountygue's armes sett up in the in', located before their stop for the night at Seefeld. These arms were probably those of Anthony Browne (c. 1528–92), Viscount Montagu, who had served as English Ambassador to the Papacy and Venice in 1555.

Reaching Innsbruck, they were offered accommodation by a Mr Lea, an Englishman in the service of Duke Ferdinand, the brother of Emperor Maximilian II and uncle of Rudolf II. They were shown around the duke's palace and he graciously provided 'hys passport under hys hand and seale for our better safty in our travel in hys contry'. They then followed the usual route south to Venice, via Steinach, Brixen and Bozen, reaching Primolano on 2 May. Fox's account of Venice matches Ascham's in terms of his personal disgust at the reputed immorality of its wealthy citizens:

> So leaving Jarmany we cam to Bassano in Italy to our lodging. My master and some others, being weary of ther horses, hyred a coche to Castell Franco[1] wher we bayted, and from thenc to Venys by water.
>
> Uppon Satterday the third of May we cam to thys great cytty wher we stayed for the receipt of mony and convenient shyping for Ragusa[2] untill Satterday the xth of May at nyght. I will leave the report of thys cytty to others that doe understand the estat of yt better, but in my simple opynyon yt ys a pryson of so much liberty and a plac of all maner of abomynacyon. The gentellmen be marchantes and veary ryche and therfor proud. They have wyves but for facyon sake, for they prefer a common cutyzan befor ther maryed wyves, for they constrayn ther wyves to honesty by locking of them. If he fynd hys wife to be so lyberall of her honesty her punnyshment ys deathe, but not by the lawe, but by the blody hand of her husband. If the frends of any gentellwoman so kylled would have satysfaccyon they must have yt by the sword. These men love thys swet synn so well that they tearm them most vertues that I think to be most vyccyous, but why should not the cyttyzyns be lyk the cytty, whyche ys a foule stinking synk, as evell kept as the kepers be evell condycyoned. They honor Saynt Mark by whyche they hould ther tytles of honor. Therbe many places of good note as the Ryalita, the Cannell Grand, Saynt Marke's church, the Duke's pallase and the Arceanall whyche ys the storehouse for ther navgacyon wythe dyvers other good places. Yt was creadyably reported unto us that ther wear viii thowsand curtyzans in thys cytty aloud by the senat, whyche yelded muche profytt to ther treasury.

---

[1] Castelfranco.

[2] Ragusa, in southern Sicily.

At thys plac we hyred a frygat of Cattara[1] for iii chekenes[2] a man to cary us to Ragusa, and upon Satterday the xth of May in the nyght [sic]; and we aryved at Ragusa upon Satterday the xviiith, whyche was Whyttsonne even; but we aryved at many places first, at Rovygo,[3] in the iles of Sayt Jeronymy[4] for freshe water, then at Sara,[5] wher we lay ashor all nyght. Thys Sara ys a toune of the Venecyans in the whyche they kepe a garrison bothe of footmen and horsemen and have ther gallyes for war in readiness. (ff. 17v–19r)

Henry Cavendish and his servant Fox left Constantinople on 29 June with a janissary and a dragoman but avoided another Mediterranean voyage and passage via Venice by travelling back across Europe, through Bulgaria, Romania, Moldavia, Poland and Germany. Cavendish had returned to England by late 1591 when he engaged in a violent feud with his neighbour William Agard of Foston during which both sides had armed men clashing with one another. Cavendish's travelling companion from the early 1570s, Gilbert Talbot, now seventh Earl of Shrewsbury, had to intervene and on 30 May 1592 requested that the Privy Council should instruct both men to agree that 'all matters of quarrel and pyke betwixt them and theyrs' should be adjudicated by him (Shrewsbury) and Robert Devereux (1565–1601), Earl of Essex.[6] In 1602 Cavendish became embroiled in a plot to liberate his Catholic niece, Arabella Stuart (1575–1615) – a potential heir to the throne – from the custody of his mother (and Arabella's grandmother), Bess of Harwick.[7] She condemned her son's behaviour to the Privy Council and disinherited him from her will. They still remained unreconciled when she died in 1608 and he did not attend her funeral. Cavendish moved into Chatsworth but his ever-mounting debts required him in 1609 to sell the reversion and most of his lands to his younger brother William Cavendish, later first Earl of Devonshire. He was able, however, to remain at Chatsworth until his death in 1616.

---

[1] Cattaro (Kotor, in Montenegro), under the rule of the Venetian Republic from 1420 until 1797.

[2] Venetian zecchino (chequing), equivalent to $c$.7s to 9s in English currency.

[3] Rovigo, 80 km south-west of Venice.

[4] The cult of St Jerome, patron saint of Croatia, was strong in Dalmatia (under Venetian rule from 1409) during the 15th and 16th centuries.

[5] Zara (Zadar).

[6] Talbot MSS, Volume 2, f.102.

[7] Arabella's mother, Elizabeth, was Henry Cavendish's younger sister.

# 22. 1573–74 – PHILIP SIDNEY, WITH GRIFFIN MADOX, HARRY WHYTE, JOHN FISHER, THOMAS CONINGSBY, LODOWICK BRYSKETT AND EDWARD, LORD WINDSOR

**Philip Sidney (1554–86)** (**Plate 17** and **Figure 17**) was born at Penshurst, Kent. His father, Sir Henry Sidney (1529–86), served Queen Elizabeth as her Lord Deputy in Ireland and President of the Council of the Marches in Wales and his mother, Mary Dudley Sidney (*c.*1530–86), was the daughter of John Dudley (1504–53), Earl of Warwick and Duke of Northumberland.[1] On 25 May 1572 Queen Elizabeth granted Philip Sidney a licence to travel for two years on the continent to study languages which specified that he should not visit 'territories or countries of any prince or potentate not being with us in amity or league', implying Italy or Spain.[2] He was also instructed to avoid 'any person being our subject born, that is departed out of our realm without our licence or that contrary to our licence doth remain in the parts of beyond the seas, and doth not return into our realm as he ought to do' – usually English recusants or Catholic sympathizers living abroad. Sidney took with him four companions – a Welshman, Griffin Madox, who was a trusted Sidney family servant; Harry Whyte (d. 1589), probably an uncle of Rowland Whyte (d. 1640), who became the long-time servant and advisor of Philip's younger brother Robert Sidney; and John Fisher, probably another Sidney family servant perhaps related to the Robert Fisher who was bailiff in 1572 of lands owned by Sir Henry Sidney at Tattershall, Lincolnshire.[3]

Sidney also travelled with a gentleman companion, Lodowick Bryskett (*c.*1546–1609/12), who had served Sir Henry Sidney in Ireland from 1565 and was paid a generous stipend of £20 in 1573, presumably towards his own costs during Sidney's time on the continent. Bryskett was the son of Antonio Bruschcetto (d. 1574), a naturalized Genoese merchant who by 1523 had settled in London.[4] Lodowick read and spoke Italian fluently, translating, probably during the 1580s, a philosophical treatise by Giambattista Giraldi Cinthio, *Tre dialoghi della vita civile* (the second part of *De gli hecatommithi*, 1565), which was published in 1606 as *A Discourse of Civill Life, containing the Ethike Part of Morall Philosophie*. His sister Lucrece (1539/40–1608) had married Vincenzo Guicciardini (d. 1581), a member of a wealthy Florentine mercantile family with extensive trading and intelligence links across Europe. Vincenzo was probably the nephew of Francesco Guicciardini (1483–1540), the author of *Historia d'Italia* (published

[1] See pp. 135, 154 n. 2 and 163 n. 2.
[2] Oxford, New College MS 328/2/40. Buxton and Juel-Jensen, 'Sidney's First Passport', pp. 42–6. Osborn, *Young Philip Sidney*, p. 3.
[3] *HMC De L'Isle & Dudley*, I, p. 251.
[4] TNA, PROB 11/56/381 (Antonio Bruschetto's will).

Figure 17.   Renold Elstrack, portrait engraving, c. 1616–18, of Sir Philip Sidney. Private Collection.

1561).[1] Lodowick had previously travelled in Italy during 1569, presumably on business for the Sidneys, since they paid him £3 for the period he was abroad.[2] His eldest brother Sebastian (1536–92), a Catholic recusant, was then living in Venice and Lodowick either stayed on in the city (or returned there) long after Sidney's departure, for example, meeting Wolfgang Zünderlin in St Mark's Piazza on 19 June 1575 and again meeting with him in late October before returning to England.[3]

For much of his journey through northern Europe Sidney was accompanied and guided by an older academic and personal mentor, the distinguished French scholar and diplomat Hubert Languet (1518–81). As will be illustrated below from their extensive

[1] Jones, 'Lodowick Bryskett', pp. 243–362. *HMC De L'Isle & Dudley*, I, p. 249, 'Lodowike Briskett's stipend, £20'. TNA, PROB 11/80/195 (Sebastian Bryskett's will). Guicciardini's *Historia*, containing information about Venitian affairs from 1490s to 1530s, was translated into English by Geoffrey Fenton (1579; rpt 1599).

[2] *HMC De L'Isle & Dudley*, I, pp. 413–14: 'To Lodwick Briskett, in full payment of annuity at £5 *per annum*, during the time he remained in Italy, 22nd Nov., 1569, £3'.

[3] Sidney, *Correspondence*, I, pp. 365, 464, 545.

correspondence, Languet strongly opposed Sidney's excursions into Italy, especially the length of time he chose to spend in Venice and Padua. Languet shared Roger Ascham's negative views of the temptations offered to inexperienced young Englishmen by licentious Venetian society and was also anxious over its notoriously unhealthy environment with the ever-present threat of contagion. Such fears were well grounded since one of the major outbreaks of bubonic plague at Venice during the sixteenth century killed about 50,000 people (almost one-third of the city's population) between 1575 and 1577, beginning less than a year after Sidney's departure.[1]

Sidney's access to regular funds while he was abroad was arranged via letters of credit drawn up by the Florentine merchant and banker Acerbo Vitello (Vetturelli/Vellutelli) who resided in England.[2] These two carefully planned connections with Bryskett and Vitello suggest that Sidney – probably with the support (or even at the instigation) of his uncle Robert Dudley, Earl of Leicester (**Plate 23**) – was determined from the outset of his travels to visit Italy and spend significant time at Venice and Padua. The Sidneys are known to have had strong personal interest in the Italian language and Philip's uncle, the Earl of Leicester, read and spoke Italian. The Sidney's family accounts include details of 'Mistress Maria, the Italian' who in 1572 and 1573 probably taught the children (and likely their mother Mary Dudley Sidney) Italian and one 'Mr Lodwicke' (almost certainly Lodowick Bryskett) who was 'skolemaster' to Philip's younger sister Ambrosia.

With experience of Italy clearly intended from the outset of Sidney's travels, in late October 1573 his party headed southwards to cover the c.600 km from Vienna to Venice. At this point in his continental explorations it becomes apparent that Sidney was not always keeping Languet fully briefed on his intentions. This was probably because while at Vienna Languet had openly disapproved of the Italian aspects of his plans. This would have placed Sidney in an awkward position, given it seems likely that an opportunity to familiarize himself with northern Italy had been encouraged by both his uncle Leicester and his parents who educated their children in the Italian language. Furthermore, the exotic attractions of Venice, ranging from its renowned architecture and artworks to its republican political structures and cosmopolitan mercantilism (not to mention its carnival, festivals and courtesans), would surely have been far more alluring to Sidney than meeting yet more middle-aged scholars, politicians and diplomats whom Languet had been keen for him to encounter at Heidelberg, Frankfurt, Strasbourg and Vienna.

On 22 September a testy Languet wrote from Vienna, querying why Sidney 'did not dare entrust me with your plans. Perhaps you were afraid that I would set snares upon your path.' In this case, Sidney had only gone to Pressburg (Bratislava), about 60 km from Vienna, a trip that should have taken about three days although he stayed away from Vienna rather longer. Languet also speculated that 'Your friend Coningsby has [doubtless] already flown across the Alps' a week earlier. This individual, Thomas Coningsby (1550–1625), was the son of Humphrey Coningsby (1516–59) of Hampton Court, Herefordshire. Like Sidney, he had been licensed to travel abroad from 1572 for three years and, after they met in Vienna, he became one of Sidney's companions during

---

[1] See **item 24** for Hugh Lochard's description of Venice during the plague of 1575–7.

[2] *HMC De L'Isle and Dudley*, I, p. 247, recording the £20 stipend for Bryskett and noting payment of £161 15s 0d to Acerbo Vitello. Brennan and Kinnamon, *Sidney Chronology*, pp. 32–44. In 1575, at the request of Robert Dudley, Earl of Leicester, Queen Elizabeth granted Vitello a monopoly over the importation of currants into England.

In questa guisa si ueggono le maschere in Vinegia nel Carnouale, d'ogni qualita di persone le quali sogliono quasi tutte alle hore . 23. ridursi su la piazza di san stefano, é quiui passeggiando tratenersi fino a quasi due hore di notte
Giacomo Franco Forma con Priuilegio

Figure 18.    Giacomo Franco, *La Città di Venetia* (1614). A scene from the carnival in Piazza San Stefano, illustrating carnival disguises and masked revellers. By permission of Special Collections, Brotherton Library, University of Leeds.

his north Italian explorations.[1] When he returned to England Coningsby married Sidney's cousin Philippa Fitzwilliam (d. *c.*1617) – the daughter of Anne Sidney, sister of Philip's father Sir Henry – and became a friend of Philip's younger brother Robert. While at Vienna Sidney and Coningsby had taken shared accommodation with one 'Raichel' and so, by going on ahead to Venice, Coningsby may have agreed with Philip to find suitable accommodation there either for their entire party or for Bryskett, Madox, Whyte and Fisher. On 19 December 1573 Philip mentioned in the conclusion of one of his letters to Languet that 'Coingsby and Bryskett greet you as their greatest patron and friend', implying that they were all still resident together in Venice.[2]

Coningsby is of more importance to Sidney's Venetian experiences than has previously been realized. He had his portrait painted in 1572, probably just before he set out for the continent (**Plate 18**). This portrait by an unknown artist, representing Coningsby with a falcon, bears mixed Latin and Italian inscriptions (probably added after his continental travels): 'IVVENTVS' (*Lat.* young man), 'INDISIP[L]INABILE' (*It. indisciplinabile*, rebellious or undisciplinable), '1572 Æ[t] SUÆ 21 THO: CONYNGESBY NEL LA IVVENTVTE' (*Lat.* and *It.* 1572 aged 21 Tho: Conynsby in his youth), and some damaged or incomplete wording: 'SED NUNC C' and on the line below 'AB'.[3] The painting's allegorical intent may suggest that Coningsby's falconry symbolizes youth and indiscipline versus a hoped-for maturity and control developed through his experiences abroad. Such a mixed Latin/Italian inscription fits well with both Coningsby's and Sidney's bold impetuosity (at least from Languet's perspective) in unexpectedly leaving the relative safety of Protestant Europe to explore the dangers of Catholic Italy and Venice.

The distinctly peeved tone of Languet's next surviving letter to Sidney, dated 19 November, makes clear that he had not known in advance of these Venetian plans. It also conveys some of the anxieties which those close to young travellers were likely to feel when the transmission of letters and news between continental cities (and England) was so slow and unpredictable:

> From what care and worry, from what fear indeed, you would have freed me if once in a while you had written to me on your journey. I did not need an effortful missive, but just one that would say 'Today we have arrived here safely,' or something like that. You remember how strongly I asked you this when you left. But you will say, '[Surely] it is unimportant for you to know that. When I get to Padua or Venice, then I will write to you.' You could have done both: and had you done so, I would have considered myself to have received a great favour from you. Still, I would rather believe that you met no one to whom you could give letters for us, than either that you cared too little what you had promised, or that you are already weakening in your affection for me, to the vehemence of which those tears of yours witnessed at your leave-taking, which scarcely let you say goodbye to me. [In any case,] I will easily forgive

[1] TNA E 157/1/1.

[2] Osborn, *Young Philip Sidney*, p. 75, is incorrect in stating that Coningsby was a first cousin of Sidney since he was not the son of 'Philippa, Sir Henry Sidney's sister' (i.e., Sir Henry did not have a sister Philippa). Sidney, *Correspondence*, I, pp. 22–3, 42–3, 64.

[3] National Portrait Gallery (N4348), lent to Montacute House, Somerset. This portrait has been attributed to George Gower (*c.*1540–96), predating his earliest documented works, companion portraits of Sir Thomas Kytson and his wife Lady Kytson, Tate Gallery, London. Strong, *Tudor & Jacobean Portraits*, I, pp. 49–50, II, Plate 89. See also Strong, 'Sidney's Appearance Reconsidered', II, pp. 171–87, for two portraits (1578, 1612) of Thomas's wife, Lady Philippa Coningsby, and other portraits at the Coningsby's Hampton Court home. Strong incorrectly states (ibid., II, p. 174) that she was the daughter of 'Agnes' Sidney (i.e., Ann Sidney).

this, and whatever future offences you commit against me, if only you will take care not to let your desire to learn and explore many things plunge you into any kind of danger.

Languet's letter specifically warns Sidney of the potential political and military dangers which he might face in northern Italy since the strategic positions of the Pope and the King of Spain (referred to in his letter as a composite Catholic 'Satan') were proving increasingly perilous:

> Satan murmurs already, because he sees his kingdom shaken: nor can he honestly swear that his affairs are prospering in France and the Netherlands: so there is no doubt that he will stir up his ministers to savagery against many, for so far he has [always] thought that the only way he could safeguard and defend his realm: which is why I am sure that if you were to entrust youself to them [now] you would be in more danger than you might have been in previous years Forgive my love for you which impels me to remind you of this too often.[1]

Sidney's party had travelled via the Semmerling Pass, through Klagenfurt and Bad Villach, before descending through the Carnio Alps to Udine. They had reached Venice by Friday 6 November when Sidney raised the enormous sum of £400 from Acerbo Vitello's Venetian correspondent. Sidney was never noted for his personal frugality and having so much money available may have been significant to his lack of hesitation in commissioning a portrait from a Venetian painter of the social pre-eminence (and prices) of Paolo Caliari, known as Veronese (**Plate 20**).

There was no accredited English ambassador resident at Venice after Queen Mary's appointment in 1555 of Sir Anthony Browne until the accession of King James I in 1603. Protestant English travellers who did venture into its territory were largely left to their own devices since they were not meant to be there under the terms of their licences to travel. But Sidney and perhaps Coningsby, as two high-ranking young visitors, may have been able to stay instead at the French Embassy in the Palazzo Michiel on Fondamenta Rio della Sensa (Cannaregio 3218), near the Jewish ghetto.[2]

If so, they probably met there the resident French Ambassador, Arnaud (Arnaul) du Ferrier (1508–85) – who twice served in this diplomatic post (1563–7 and 1572–82), and, significantly for Sidney and his English party, was rumoured to be sympathetic to Protestantism. Through this embassy Sidney also encountered the German political intelligencer Wolfgang Zünderlin, the French writer François Perrot de Mézières and Cesare Pavese, a friend of Bernardo Tasso (the father of Torquato) who forwarded Sidney's letters and belongings after he had left Venice in August 1574.[3] Sidney also seems to have spent some time during summer 1574 at the household of Edward, Lord Windsor (c.1532–75), third Baron Windsor of Stanwell, a prominent English recusant who had taken up residence at Venice sometime after June 1573.[4] Lord Windsor, the

---

[1] Sidney, *Correspondence*, I, pp. 33–4, 72, 84. Osborn, *Young Philip Sidney*, p. 104.

[2] Roger Kuin describes Sidney as 'staying at the French embassy near the Jewish ghetto', 'The Sidneys and the Continent: The Tudor Period', p. 207.

[3] Sidney, *Correspondence*, I, pp. 82, 465. On 24 June 1574 Zünderlin noted in a letter to Sidney (then at Padua) that Sidney had 'come to look for me several times at my house', ibid., I, p. 266.

[4] In a letter to Sidney of 20 June 1575 Zünderlin mentioned that 'you were staying with that friend of yours the Baron', probably Lord Windsor although, as Roger Kuin notes, this individual could perhaps have been Fabian, Baron and Burggrave of Dohna, Sidney, *Correspondence*, I, p. 266. Stewart, *Philip Sidney*, p. 121, casts this passing reference more definitely, stating: 'Philip forsook his customary lodgings and moved into the Windsor house, a no-go area for many of his other acquaintances.'

brother-in-law of Edward de Vere, seventeenth Earl of Oxford (**item 23**), had made his will on 20 December 1572, probably just before leaving his estate at Bradenham, Buckingham, for the continent because of his Catholic faith. He left his wife and children behind in England and the numerous clauses in his lengthy will were aimed primarily at securing their financial future. He also added a codicil on 18 June 1573 while at Spa and at some point after this date he travelled south into Italy to take up residence at Venice.[1] Lord Windsor may have already been known to the Sidneys since he appointed as the first overseer of his will Thomas Radcliffe (1526/7–83), Earl of Sussex, who had married Sir Henry Sidney's sister Frances and preceded Sir Henry as Lord Deputy of Ireland.[2] Lord Windsor corresponded from Venice with William Cecil, Lord Burghley, and gathered intelligence for the Earl of Sussex in the hope of being appointed as Queen Elizabeth's official agent at Venice.[3]

Sidney, Bryskett, Coningsby and their party would have soon met up with other members of the English community at Venice and Padua. These included Richard Shelley (d. 1574) and Robert Corbet (1542–83). Shelley was a distant relative of Sidney's and has been mistakenly identified with the much older Sir Richard Shelley (*c.*1513–87), a diplomat, Prior of the Hospital of St John of Jerusalem and from 1561 Grand Prior of the Knights of Malta.[4] Although he was resident at Venice in 1574 it is unlikely that this sixty-year-old man was the individual with whom Sidney regularly consorted, even though it is probable that Sidney did meet him. Instead, Roger Kuin suggests that this Richard Shelley was Sir Richard's nephew who was serving as his personal assistant on the continent at this time. This identification is correct since it was a young man called Richard Shelley who accompanied Corbet to Vienna to deliver to Languet Sidney's portrait by Veronese. This individual was taken seriously ill on the journey and then died in July 1574, with his uncle the Prior later confirming in a letter to Burghley in May 1575 that his nephew was 'dead by the way'.[5] Robert Corbet was the eldest son of Sir Andrew Corbet of Moreton Corbet in Shropshire and was training to become a diplomat. His younger brother Vincent had been at Shrewsbury School with Sidney.[6]

Following his letter of 19 November Languet wrote again on 27 November, complaining about Sidney's 'stubborn silence' because it was now one month since he had left Vienna. Sidney would have received this letter sometime after his nineteenth birthday on 30 November but it seems that he had neither let Languet know that he had arrived safely at Venice nor where he was staying. Languet was also concerned to ensure

---

[1] TNA PROB 11/57/216–19. In 1563 Edward, Lord Windsor, and his wife Katherine de Vere, unsuccessfully challenged the legitimacy of Edward de Vere, Earl of Oxford (Katherine's half-brother by her father's second wife). TNA SP 12/29/8, ff. 11–12. Nelson, *Monstrous Adversary*, pp. 40–41.

[2] Lord Windsor was married to Katherine de Vere (1538–1600). Their eldest son Frederick (1559–85) was named as his will's first executor, although he was only 15 or 16 when his father died in 1575. The other executors were Sir John Throckmorton, John Talbot and Peter Vavasour, the son of Lord Windsor's sister, Elizabeth. TNA, PROB 11/57/332.

[3] *Calendar of the Cecil Papers*, II, pp. 67–9 (10 Jan. 1573/4).

[4] *ODNB* identifies him as the older man. This Sir Richard offered the Earl of Oxford lodgings at Venice in 1575 (**item 23**).

[5] Sidney, *Correspondence*, I, p. 295.

[6] *ODNB*, s.v. Sidney, *Correspondence*, I, pp. xxxix, lviii, lxiii, 191. Philip Sidney's aunt Anne's half-sister-in-law, Mary Fitzwilliam, had married the Prior's brother, John Shelley, the probable father of the Richard Shelley who befriended Sidney at Venice. Stewart, pp. 120–21.

that Sidney safeguarded both his own and Languet's reputations when consorting with the residents (English, Italian and other nationalities) of Venice:

> But take care to safeguard your own and my reputation with those who knew you here and are fond of you: for as, trusting in your promises, I told them that you would write to us about what happened to you on your journey, and about what you would decide about your affairs when you got to Italy; and as they see you doing none of those things, they are laughing at my naivety for having believed that you valued me enough to take such trouble on my account... But away with suspicions: you can annihilate them all with one little line from the letter I go on hoping you will send us. Meanwhile I prefer to believe you still remember us and bear in mind that here I was devoted to you and wanted to please you and be of service to you.
>
> When I am sure where you have arrived, and where you have decided to stay, I will sometimes sprinkle my letters with some comments on public affairs, although dwelling as you will be in the light of the city of Venice you will not be ignorant of anything that is done anywhere in the world.[1]

It has usually been assumed that the youthful Sidney was merely a negligent correspondent, but it is just as likely that he was keen to avoid having to discuss with Languet his firm intention to stay at Venice for some considerable time. He was certainly corresponding with others as he neared Venice. In a letter of 3 December, addressed to Sidney 'a Venise ou a Padoue', the priest and diplomat Jean de Vulcob (c.1535–1607), French Ambassador at Vienna, acknowledged receipt of a letter from Sidney dated 21 November about Henri of Valois's reluctant progress towards Cracow to take up the crown of Poland. It is likely that Vulcob and Languet may have collaborated over enabling Sidney to stay at the French Embassy at Venice.[2]

Languet wrote again on 4 December (received by Sidney on 19 December), noting that he had sent three previous letters without any reply before he finally received with great relief 'the one you wrote me at your arrival in Venice', presumably in late November. He sensed that Sidney was being secretive in his plans and pleaded: 'I [want to] ask you not to hide anything from me, and if you decide about your affairs otherwise than you had decided here, to let me know.' He also asked Sidney to thank 'Master Coningsby' for speaking well of him to 'your men' and to pass on his thanks to 'Master Bryskett' for ensuring that Sidney's party arrived safely at Venice. In this letter Languet was also concerned by the risk of Sidney falling into temptations at Venice – whether political, religious or moral – about which he had previously warned him. He pleaded with him to promise:

> to take scrupulous care for your health and safety, and not to follow your overeagerness, or the idle talk of those who will make light of the dangers you would plunge into should you come to those places we have often spoken of.[3]

Sidney's first surviving letter to Languet from Venice, dated 5 December 1573 (but not received by Languet until 24 December), states that he had written two previous ones. He proposed that they should 'talk once a week by letter' and mentioned that on his arrival at Venice the 'French Ambassador [du Ferrier] received me with great kindness'.

---

[1] Sidney, *Correspondence*, I, pp. 35–6.

[2] Ibid., I, pp. lxi, 38–9, II, p. 1331. One of Sidney's now lost letters was sent to Vulcob from Padua on 9 Apr. 1574.

[3] Ibid., I, pp. 40–43, 63.

Perhaps more duplicitously, he added that he would soon be back with Languet at Vienna once 'that Polish King has freed France from his presence'.[1]

In a letter written on 12 December Languet notes from one of Sidney's lost letters that some aspects of Venetian life had disappointed him, enabling him to give full vent to his innate hostility towards Italian lifestyles:

> I divine from your letter that the ornaments of the city of Venice have not come up to your expectations. Yet Italy has nothing that can compare to them: so if you dislike them, you will hate the rest. But you will admire the intelligence and the wisdom of the people. Mind you, while there are clever and intelligent men, there are also many among them who are more show than substance, and most of them spoil their wisdom with too much ostentation and become revoltingly affected. Even if our German friends are less supple in spirit, they are perhaps not far behind in gravity of judgement. Of course, I have been away from Italy for so many years that I am not the one to judge all this, but I will hear what you think when you come back to us.[2]

Sidney continued to correspond from Venice (although some of his letters have been lost) and Languet was unremitting in expressing his reservations of any lengthy sojourn in Italy. On 18 December he explained that his most pressing desire was for Sidney to attend the imminent coronation at Cracow of Henri of Valois as King of Poland. He also admitted with some regret:

> I wrote that I was afraid that you might be overwhelmed by the magnificence and elegance of things Italian, and by the charms of those regions, and view Germany and Poland with contempt ... I did advise you against an Italian journey, as I saw winter approaching ... . So you see that it was not for my own sake that I advised you against a journey through Italy ... . I have asked you not to go incautiously to those places in Italy where you would not be safe and I have asked that again, often, and greatly exaggerated the danger of everything.[3]

It is important to remember when reading Sidney's Venice- and Padua-based correspondence with Languet that it usually took at least two weeks for letters to be delivered to either party. Writing on 19 December, for example, Sidney explained that he had only received on the previous day Languet's letter of 4 December. Similarly, this letter from Sidney of 19 December was received by Languet on about 1 January 1574. In a luxuriant phrase deftly attuned to Languet's cynicism over Italy, Sidney proposed in this 19 December letter that he would only be staying at Venice among 'these magnificent magnificoes' magnificences' for 'another fortnight' before moving on to Padua. His movements were limited by the fact that after arriving at Venice he had sold all of his horses since they were useless amid the canals of the city. He also thanked Languet for sending to him twenty crowns and promised that when Languet advised him that 'the time is right' he would 'prepare the gift for Master Abondio', adding: 'I should like to know what he has done'. This passing reference is to Antonio Abondio (1538–91), an Italian sculptor and

---

[1] Ibid., I, pp. 44–6, 68. There were other activities which Sidney probably wished to keep from Languet. A light-hearted letter from a young Frenchman whom he knew at Vienna, Jacques Bochetel (*c.*1554–77), sent 'A Venize' on 10 Dec. 1573, refers to Sidney's apparent liaison at Vienna with 'madame your hostess' (perhaps a Viennese *cortegiana honesta*) and expects that 'those beautiful courtesans' will keep Sidney at Venice, ibid., I, pp. 47–8.

[2] Ibid., I, p. 55.

[3] Ibid., I, pp. 59–60.

medalist working at Vienna who was a pioneer of the techniques for creating coloured wax bas-relief portrait miniatures. Sidney's letter concludes with warm compliments to Languet from Coningsby and Bryskett who 'greet you as their greatest patron and friend', indicating that these three young men were still exploring Venice together.[1]

Sidney's connections with the French community at Venice remained of importance to both his safety and introduction to the political and cultural elite of the city. On 24 December Languet reported that when he told Vulcob, the French Ambassador at Vienna, that Sidney would not be staying for much longer at Venice the ambassador seemed 'to be afraid of something or other'. More positively, Vulcob had told him that Du Ferrier, the French Ambassador at Venice, greatly admired Sidney's 'spirit' and through Vulcob's letter had the 'occasion of striking up a friendship with you' – thereby confirming that Vulcob had written a letter of introduction for Sidney to present to Du Ferrier on his arrival at Venice.[2] On Christmas Day 1573 Sidney informed Languet that he planned to go within the week to Padua where he had already taken lodgings at the Pozzo della Vacca (the Cow's Well), owned by one Hercole Bolognese.[3]

While at Venice and Padua Sidney was regularly socializing with the international community there. In a letter of 7 January Languet commended his friendship at Padua with another of his young protégés, 'His Excellency Count Hanau' and his trusted steward 'the excellent Master Welsperg'.[4] He also noted that he was 'glad you have finally decided to move to Padua; the city is quieter than Venice and better for study'. He advised Sidney before leaving Venice to ensure that the merchant Camillus Crucius continued to handle their letters because he did not want them to fall into the hands of the French Ambassador du Ferrier.[5] The Ambassador had apparently invited Languet to write to him regularly with political and court intelligence but, since his close friend Vulcob, the French Ambassador at Vienna, already served in this capacity as an intelligencer for du Ferrier, Languet feared that Vulcob 'might suspect me of either wanting to appear more knowledgeable than he, or of writing something I was not telling him'.[6] These concerns hint at just how circumspect Sidney had to be in his own correspondence with Languet when based at Venice and Padua.

At this point in the narrative of Sidney's time at Venice the loss of yet another of his letters to Languet proves crucial. In a letter of 15 January Languet refers to this missing letter which had advised him that Sidney's health was not good and he was feeling 'even

[1] Ibid., I, pp. 63–5.

[2] Ibid., I, p. 71.

[3] Ibid., I, pp. 74, 188. Sidney probably planned to make this trip in one day by boat, usually a *burchiello tirato* (towed barge), ibid., I, figure 6.

[4] The German aristocrat Philip Ludwig I von Hanau-Müzenberg (1553–80) had been raised by his guardians Philipp of Hanau-Lichtenberg, Johann of Nassau (William of Orange's elder brother) and Elector Palatine Frederick III. He was educated at Strasbourg, Paris (where he met Languet and, like Sidney, had a narrow escape from the St Bartholomew Day Massacre), Basle and Padua. The Austrian Paul von Welsperg (Welsberg), served as Hanau's Hofmeister (steward or chamberlain) and accompanied him on all of his travels. He was a close friend of Languet. Sidney, *Correspondence*, I, pp. xliv, lxii.

[5] The delivery of Languet's and Sidney's letters to one another between Vienna and Venice was handled by one 'Camillus Crucius' who has previously been assumed to be an Italian, Camillo Cruci. Kuin, however, has pointed out that the name Crucius was also familiar in Germany and the Netherlands. He was probably a merchant whose communication channels for trade correspondence were being utilized by Languet and Sidney. Sidney, *Correspondence*, I, p. 72, n. 26.

[6] Ibid., I, pp. 77–85.

more melancholy than usual'. Languet's keenness to get him away from Venice is obvious:

> Flee those lagoons, than which nothing is more unhealthy as soon as one has seen whatever is worth seeing in the city. I have been surprised that you have stayed so long in that perpetual din and stink, especially since you write that you have not yet made the acquaintance of anyone whose company you greatly enjoy. So hurry to Padua, to your friend Count Hanau and to the other good men who are remarkably fond of you and long enormously for your company.

Languet made this recommendation for Sidney to meet up at Padua with Hanau and Welsperg because they were planning a trip to:

> those parts of Italy than can be visited without danger. Make sure you do not neglect the opportunity to join them as a companion on that trip, for you could not choose a more delightful and suitable company. But you will have to make sure early enough that you have all the information you need for the journey, so that some difficulty does not come up when it is time to carry out your plan.[1]

On the same day (15 January) Sidney wrote to Languet from Padua where he had just arrived and had already paid his respects to Count Hanau and the wealthy Bohemian Baron Michael Slavata (c.1554–post 1577) who was then a student at Padua University. He also mentioned his regret over his tardiness in writing to the artist Abondio: 'I am very concerned not to be writing to Abondio, because of his great kindness, but I will take care of that shortly; meanwhile please greet him cordially from me.'[2]

In a letter of 22 January Languet mentioned his sadness over how long it might be before they could next meet in person and suggested that 'a picture of you might bring me some relief'. He continued:

> Even though your image is so engraved on my mind that it hovers always before my eyes, I would ask you, if it is not a burden to you, to indulge my longing so far as to send it [a portrait] to me (in some form), or to bring it when you come back to us. Another reason I so long to have it is to show it to those to whom I mention my feelings for your noble nature, and what hopes I have conceived of your virtue. For, as they think that nobody could combine so many gifts without signs of them shining in his body, and especially in his face, they are all dying to see what you look like. But I am asking you this in perfect freedom for you to refuse without offending me: I would not want to ask you something I thought would be a bother to you.

He also mentioned, after viewing Sidney's 'likeness at our friend Abondio's recently', that he had been moved to pen some panegyric 'little verses', probably a Latin distich or quatrain (now lost), which he enclosed with this letter. He asked Sidney, if he did have his portrait taken, that he should have these verses 'copied on to the picture you order painted'.[3]

In another letter of 28 January Languet expressed his relief that Sidney had extricated himself from 'those irksome affairs that kept you in Venice' – possibly genuine financial or personal concerns or perhaps simply because Sidney wished to spend more time in Venice and claimed to Languet that he had unfinished business there. Whatever the reason for his delay in moving to Padua, Languet was confident that Sidney's health would improve and

---

[1] Ibid., I, pp. 87–8.
[2] Ibid., I, pp. 87–93.
[3] Ibid., I, pp. 97–8.

he would meet more like-minded young friends there.[1] In response to Languet's request for a portrait Sidney wrote on 4 February 1574: 'I am delighted that you ask me so insistently for my portrait' and promised that 'As soon as I go back to Venice I will have it done either by Paolo Veronese or by Tintoretto, who at the moment are easily the first in that art' (**Plates 19** and **20**). However, he hesitated over having Languet's fulsome Latin poem attached to this picture but concluded by offering Languet 'that portrait Abondio made, and will either send or bring to him the price for it'.[2] Languet was clearly keen to ensure that Sidney had his portrait taken and even seemed happy for him to return to Venice to have it painted. To this effect, he concluded his next letter, dated 5 February 1574, with the reminder: 'remember what I wrote you about your picture.'[3]

Sidney was still in Padua on 11 February and expressed his hope of soon seeing Languet again at Vienna (even though he did not finally leave there until the following August). On 19 February Languet concluded another of his letters by thanking Sidney 'for what you so generously promise about your portrait' in agreeing to have it painted by either Tintoretto or Veronese.[4] Although Sidney had mentioned both Paulo Caliari (1528–88), a native of Verona (known as Veronese), and Jacopo Robusti (1519–94), a native of Venice (known as Tintoretto), in his letter of 4 February 1574 to Languet, sitting for Veronese was always a more likely choice. While the older Tintoretto tended to specialize in official portraits of influential Venetians, lavishly adorned with the regalia of their public status, Veronese's portraits – especially his private commissions of which about thirty-eight survive (27 male, 11 female) – specialized in conveying 'courtly elegance' and 'knowing nonchalance', a style which would have appealed far more readily to a nineteen-year-old of Sidney's tastes. Veronese was a brilliant colourist and his mastery of flesh tones and facial expressions was unrivalled in Venice of the 1570s. Many distinguished Venetians sat for him, including individuals from the Barbaro, Contarini, Soranzo and Venier families.[5] One of Veronese's biographers, Antoine Orliac, notes that he 'excelled at interpreting the distinction of high breeding' and communicating the 'charm and attraction of his models', hinting at 'subtle psychological values' – qualties which would certainly have appealed to Sidney.[6] One of his most renowned paintings, of an unknown Venetian woman sometimes called 'La Bella Nani', is now displayed in the same room as Leonardo da Vinci's Mona Lisa in the Louvre, Paris (**Plate 14**). It exemplifies Veronese's consummate skills a as portrait painter, as well as providing an interesting insight into the contemporary dress of wealthy Venetian women during the mid-sixteenth century.[7]

---

[1] Ibid., I, pp. 97–8, 101.

[2] Ibid., I, pp. 105, 107. In the only surviving version of this letter in Latin (Stadtbibliothek, Hamburg) 'Tintoretto' is written 'Tintorello', probably an error by the copyist since Sidney, whose handwriting was notoriously scrappy, apologizes at the end of this letter for his 'mess of mistakes and corrections'.

[3] Ibid., I, p. 112.

[4] Ibid., I, pp. 106–7, 123.

[5] Rosand, 'Dialogues and Apologies', p. 238. Garton, *Grace and Grandeur*, pp. 9–10, 61. In contrast, c.154 portraits attributed to Tintoretto have survived. Strong, *Tudor and Jacobean Portraits*, I, p. 290, states that Sidney 'visited Venice (meeting Tintoretto and Paolo Veronese)'. There is no evidence that Sidney ever met Tintoretto in person.

[6] Orliac, *Veronese*, pp. 13, 25; quoting Osborn, *Young Philip Sidney*, p. 152.

[7] While this portrait is no longer thought to be associated with the Venetian Nani family, it has been suggested that the sitter may be a member of the Giustiniani family of Venice, perhaps Giustiniana Giustiniani, due to the sitter's possible resemblance in both facial features and clothing to Veronese's portrait of Giustiniana at Villa Barbaro at Maser, Treviso, built by Andrea Palladio for the brothers Daniele and Marcantonio Barbaro.

Figure 19.   Giacomo Franco, *Habiti d'huomeni et donne venetiane* (1610), A Venetian woman taking fruit from a tray held by a page. By permission of Special Collections, Brotherton Library, University of Leeds.

Sometime between 11 and 26 February Sidney travelled back to Venice since on the 26 he wrote to Languet, noting that 'Today one Paul of Verona [*Paulus quidam Veronensis*] has begun my portrait', presumably at his workshop in the Calle di Ca' Mocenigo, Salizada San Samuele. He explained that he would need to 'stay here two or three more days' for further sittings before returning to Padua.[1] Languet's next letter, dated 5 March, teasingly refers to Sidney being yet again 'Back in your Venice, as if looking down from an exalted place', despite the primary purpose of this return being for him to sit for the portrait which Languet so earnestly desired. Languet also added: 'If you do not have good lodgings in Padua, you can have some in the citadel of Milan, if you feel like going that far.'[2] On 12 March the emotionally unpredictable Languet wrote that he wished he had 'not mentioned your portrait to you, as I see that business is a bother to you'. Perhaps also intending to remind Sidney of his irregularity as a correspondent, he concluded by asking him to thank Bryskett 'for his extraordinarily elegant letter'.[3] Sidney seems to have suggested that his sittings for Veronese could be fitted into three or four days, unless later ones went unmentioned in his surviving (or lost) letters. It is unlikely that he attended these sittings entirely alone and, although he could probably speak Italian with reasonable proficiency, he may have been accompanied by one or more experienced Italian speakers, such as Lodowick Bryskett, Robert Corbet, Richard Shelley or Edward, Lord Windsor.

At this point it is useful to consider what is known about the reputation and working habits of Veronese's workshop. Paolo Caliari (Cagliari) had been born in Verona, then Venice's largest possession on the mainland (since 1405), the son of a skilled stonecutter and sculptor, Gabriele Bazaro. He had reputedly adopted the name Caliari from his mother Catherine who claimed to be the illegitimate daughter of a nobleman, Antonio Caliari. He moved to Venice in *c.*1553 and by early 1574 he was at the height of his artistic powers, internationally renowned alongside Tintoretto and the aged Titian (d. 1576). At Venice he established a lucrative family workshop which included his younger brother, Benedetto (1538–98), who specialized in completing the architectural backgrounds to their paintings, his nephew Luigi Benfatto (*c.*1551–1611) – also known as Luigi Alvise dal Friso – and from the 1580s his sons Gabriele (1568–1631) and Carlo (1570–96).[4] Other Venetian artists, such as Giovanni Antonio Fasolo (1530–72), trained at his workshop and he collaborated extensively with several other distinguished artists based at Venice such as Giovanni Battista Zelotti (1526–78).

By February 1574 Veronese's reputation as a portrait painter was rivalled by only by Tintoretto since Titian, then in his eighties, devoted himself mainly to religious subjects during the last two years of his life. Veronese's public and ecclesiastical commissions during the early 1570s, such as the *Madonna of the Rosary* (painted for San Pietro Martire,

---

[1] Sidney, *Correspondence*, I, pp. 130–32. The location of Veronese's house, where he lived from about 1567 and died in 1588, '*in Calle di Ca' Mocenigo*' (San Samuele 3338), is given by Kuin, 'New Light', p. 33. Salomon, *Veronese*, pp. 15, 28. Veronese was also working in Padua in 1574/5, completing *The Martyrdom of St Justina* at the Church of St Justina. Fenlon, pp. 278–9.

[2] Sidney, *Correspondence*, I, pp. 134–5.

[3] Ibid., I, p. 139.

[4] Garton, 'Veronese's Art of Business', p. 765, notes that at this period portraits from the Veronese workshop may sometimes have been collaborations between Paolo and his brother Benedetto Caliari. See also, Garton, *Grace and Grandeur*, pp. 201–14.

Murano; Accademia, Venice) and *The Adoration of the Magi* (painted in 1573 for *San Silvestro, Venice; National Gallery, London) brought him great public acclaim. A major fire at the Doge's Palace broke out on 11/12 May 1574, gutting the administrative offices in the top floor of the east wing. Various reorganizations of rooms had to be made and Veronese was entrusted with the redecoration of the ceiling of the Sala del Collegio. He also produced for the same room a huge mural, *Allegory of the Battle of Lepanto*, celebrating the victory of the Venetian fleet over the Turks on 7 October 1571, which was displayed above the doge's throne (**Plate 13**). As an interesting insight into the workings of Veronese's workshop, it is known that Paolo's brother Benedetto played a major role in the execution of both the *Madonna of the Rosary* and the *Allegory of the Battle of Lepanto*.[1] The young Sidney, therefore, was commissioning his own portrait, no doubt at considerable expense, from one of the major Venetian workshops (although it is not known how much of his portrait was from the hand of Veronese himself).

The price paid for this Veronese portrait is not recorded in Sidney family accounts, although, given Philip's temperament and the fact that he had recently received a large sum from Acerbo Vitello, it seems that expense was not a primary consideration. Roger Kuin explains:

> for a quarter of a century Venice had only one choice of painters: Veronese or Tintoretto. He was the more expensive of the two: Tintoretto boasted of being able to paint like Veronese but for a much lower price. By the 1570s he was receiving an increasing number of private commissions, several of which were from foreigners; to the point where his brother Benedetto, who had been helping him since 1555, no longer sufficed, and he took on a new assistant, Alvise Benfatto, a.k.a. Dal Friso, who worked for him until 1584.[2]

Sidney's friend at Venice, Edward, Lord Windsor, died on 25 January 1575 about five months after his departure from the city in early August 1574. The Neapolitan nobleman Don Cesare Carrafa, who had been close to Windsor, wrote to Sidney, detailing his death and grandiose funeral. In his letter, dated 3 February 1575, Carrafa described how after 'twelve days of a wicked fever' (perhaps typhus) he had died a 'saintly death'. Carrafa had personally managed his funeral arrangements and burial in *Santi Giovanni e Paolo where the Doge at this period, Alvise Mocenigo (d. 1577) was also later buried.[3] During the late sixteenth century this basilica was generally regarded as the most prestigious place to be buried in the city and it was unusual for a non-Venetian to be interred there, unless he had made a major contribution to the wealth or security of the Venetian empire.[4] Lord Windsor's monumental classical tomb, attributed to Alessandro Vittoria (*c.*1525–1608), can still be seen today at Santi Giovanni e Paolo. This connection affords another

---

[1] Rearick, *Art of Paolo Veronese*, p. 102.

[2] Kuin, 'New Light', p. 34.

[3] Sidney *Correspondence*, I, pp. 386–7. See ibid., I, p. 586, for another letter from Carrafa to Sidney (2 Dec. 1575), mentioning his contact with Ludowick Bryskett and the departure of Lord Windsor's nephew, Thomas Sandys, from Venice. Carrafa also described Lord Windsor's death and funeral in a letter to Marco Antonio Colonna (22 Jan. 1575), *CSP Vatican* [Rome], *1572–78*, item 376.

[4] The codicil added to Lord Windsor's will at Spa on 18 June 1573 had specified that his body should be buried in the cathedral church of Liège and his 'heart to be enclosed in lead and sent into England to be buried in the chapel of Bradenham'. The latter (but not the former) wish was followed and the leaden casket was preserved in the family vault at Bradenham, although it bore an incorrect inscription, claiming that Lord Windsor had been buried at Spa. TNA, PROB 11/57/332. Anon., 'Antiquarius', p. 328.

interesting link since Vittoria worked closely with Titian, Tintoretto and Veronese and his reputed portrait (New York, Metropolitan Museum of Art) was painted by Veronese sometime in the mid-1570s – close to when Sidney was sitting for his own portrait.[1]

The reason for Lord Windsor being granted this great privilege is uncertain. It may have been due to him having fought with the Anglo-Spanish forces at the Battle of St Quentin (1557) against the French during the Italian (or Habsburg-Valois) War (1551–9) which, through the Treaty of Cateau-Cambrésis (1559), led to the independence from France of the Duchy of Savoy. Robert Dudley, Earl of Leicester (**Plate 23**), had also fought at St Quentin, along with his brothers Ambrose and Henry (who was killed in a subsequent siege), and Henry Herbert, later second Earl of Pembroke (husband of Philip Sidney's sister Mary). The Dudley and Windsor families had been close during the reigns of Henry VII and Henry VIII when Edward, Lord Windsor's grandfather Andrew – a cousin of Edmund Dudley (the Earl of Leicester's grandfather) – was Keeper of the Wardrobe from 1504 until 1543. It is, therefore, possible that it was Robert Dudley, Earl of Leicester, who had arranged for his nephew Philip to make contact at Venice with Edward, Lord Windsor.

In his letter of 12 March 1574 Languet also commended Sidney for cultivating a friendship with Wolfgang Zünderlin (1539–1600) who was then resident at Venice as a political reporter and observer for Elector Frederick III and other German princes. He concluded by giving vent to his hostility towards Italy because of its papistry and acquisitive materialism, as evidenced by the ostentatious wealth of Venice:

> I do not admire the splendour of the Italian cities, since for so many years it has absorbed the spoils of so many peoples whom the impostures of the Italians, or rather their own stupidity, have forced to undergo the yoke of the Roman Court.[2]

On 18 March Languet scolded Sidney for only letting him know that he was going to visit Genoa on the north-western Italian coast just before leaving Padua since he had sent a packet of confidential letters to Sidney to be distributed to Count Hanau and other friends.[3]

Languet's numerous letters continued to oscillate between extremes of affection, scholarly solicitude and accusations of inconstancy and lack of communication. Sidney was clearly finding Languet's personal interventions in his plans increasingly irksome and this well-intentioned hectoring may have served only to enhance his growing interest in Venice. Given his hatred of the Papacy, Languet was also genuinely disturbed by Sidney's continuing presence in a Catholic country. On 26 March he gave full vent to his Protestant suspicions of an international Catholic conspiracy:

> The Roman Pontiff is twisting himself into every shape to prop up his crumbling tyranny, but God is turning his criminal plans to his ruin. It is from him and nowhere else that the plans came for the nobleman's execution in the Netherlands, for that monstrous slaughter of so many innocent people in France, and for the Polish election.[4]

---

[1] Garton, *Grace and Grandeur*, p. 206.

[2] Sidney, *Correspondence*, I, pp. 338–9.

[3] Ibid., I, p. 141. Stewart, *Philip Sidney*, p. 124. Genoa then had strong links with Spain since the Genoese were the Spanish state's principal bankers.

[4] Sidney, *Correspondence*, I, pp. 146–7. Languet refers to the beheading of the Counts of Egmont and Hornes in Brussels in 1568; the St Bartholomew's Day Massacre in August 1572; and the 1573 Polish election, which, influenced by Catherine de' Medici, elected the Catholic Henri of Valois to the Polish throne.

Similarly, Languet's letter of 9 April reiterated his unwavering suspicions of Italian religion and culture:

> I was afraid, when you were going to go off into Italy, that something of the customs of that people would slowly steal into your soul, which even if it did not quite stain its radiant purity would nevertheless make it slightly dingy. But as you promised not to cross the Apennines and to come back to us quickly, I thought that you could bring back your spirit to us pure and untainted; especially as you had decided to live among the Venetians and the Paduans, who seem still to maintain something of the simplicity of those nations from whom they took their origin.[1]

On a more positive note, on 15 April Sidney wrote from Venice (but mentioning that he was about to return to Padua) to say that two 'English noblemen' would soon be visiting Languet at Vienna. These were his Venetian friends Robert Corbet who spoke good Italian and, he assured Languet, was a firm Puritan; and the young Richard Shelley, who also spoke Italian but was 'most devoted to Papist superstition'.[2] Before receiving this letter, Languet warned Sidney on 16 April not to 'set foot in those places that are under Spanish government' (Naples, Sicily and the Duchy of Milan). He also counselled against staying for long at Genoa because the Genoese were the Spanish state's principal bankers and he even mocked how Sidney might be seeking to enhance his naval knowledge there, noting:

> I am not sure how safe it is for you to stay there longer. But perhaps you are taking pleasure in watching the shipbuilding that usually goes on there; or the sound of the chains used to bind the wretched rowers.[3]

By 23 April Languet was relieved to know that Sidney had returned 'safely from Liguria [i.e., Genoa] to Padua or Venice' and mentioned that he had sent various letters to him for distribution to other individuals at Venice such as Welsperg. Sidney had made a four-week excursion to Genoa and Florence with Ludowick Bryskett perhaps on the advice of Arnaud du Ferrier, the French Ambassador or simply because Bryskett's father was Genoese.[4] Sidney had also mentioned Veronese's portrait in a now lost letter, apparently suggesting that the painting could be sent to him at Vienna and, in reply, Languet remarked in his letter of 23 April: 'About your picture you can decide as you like. If you hoped soon to come to us, there would be no need to send it before; but in that business you make haste extremely slowly.'[5]

Sometime before 29 April Sidney had petitioned the *Council of Ten for his retinue to bear arms and his application is still preserved in the Archivio di Stato at Venice:

> 29 aprile 1574
> L'Illustre Signor Filippo Sidnei figliolo dell'Illustrissimo Signor Henrico Governatore della Provincia di Gales si ritrova qui in Venetia, et vol partir per Padoa, dove dissegna fermarsi

---

[1] Ibid., I, p. 155.

[2] Ibid., I, pp. 163–4.

[3] Ibid., I, p. 167.

[4] Osborn, *Young Philip Sidney*, p. 158, suggests that Sidney may have been tempted into this arduous excursion by the possibility of accompanying one of the couriers from the French embassy who made regular trips between Venice and Genoa.

[5] Sidney, *Correspondence*, I, pp. 174–7.

qualche tempo allo studio. Desidera non esser molestato Lui, né un suo gentil-huomo con tre servitori per il portar dell'armi, et però si supplicano le eccellentissime etc.

Il nome del gentil-huomo e il Signor Lodovico Bruschetto

li servitori sono

> Harrigo Vita
> Grifone Appiano
> Gio. Fisher[1]

[Translation]

29 April 1574

The Illustrious Sir Philip Sidney, son of the most Illustrious Sir Henry, Governor of the Province of Wales, finds himself here in Venice, and wishes to leave for Padua, where he plans to stay some time for study. He desires neither himself, nor his gentleman, nor his three servants to be molested for carrying arms, and, therefore, they petition the most excellent [members of the Council], etc.

The name of the gentleman is Sir Ludovick Bryskett

The servants are

> Harry White
> Griffen Madox
> John Fisher

The patent was promptly approved and issued by the *Council of Ten on the next day:

30 Aprile 1574                    Patentes

Universis et singulis, Rectoribus quarúcunq; civitatum, praesertim Padua[r], terrarum et locarum nostrorum, Magistratibus huius urbis nostra[r] Venetiarum, officialibus, et ministris nostris quibuscunq; tam praesentibus quam futuris significamus, heri in cons°. nostro Decem captam fuisse partem tenoris infrascripti vz. che al Signor Filippo Sidnei Inglese figliolo dell' Ill. S[or.] Henrico Sidnei governator della provincia di Gales, che si ritruova qui per andar a Padoa, ove disegna fermarsi per studiar, sia concessa licentia di portar le armi si in questa Città di Venetia come in ogni altra città, terra, et luogo del Dnio nostro, con un suo gentil'huomo appresso di lui nominato Ludovico Bruscheltto, et con tre servitori, li nome d'i quali siano notati in quest città nell'officio d'i capi disquesto cons°. et di fuori, nelle cancellarie delli luoghi, ovi si ritroverà, giurando, che stiano in casa sua, et a sui spese. Quare auctoritate sopradicti consilii mandamus vobis, ut supradictam concessionem observetis, et ab omnibus observari faciatis. Dat, Die 30, Aprilis 1574.

> Vigore partio captae in cons°. X
> Die 29. Aprilis 1574.[2]

[Translation] 30 April 1574          Licences

To one and all, rulers everywhere, of states, especially Padua, of all our lands and territories, to the magistrates of this our city of the Venetians, to our officials and ministers whoever they may be; we signify both for the present and future, that yesterday in our Council of Ten, as described below

viz. that to the Englishman Sir Philip Sidney, son of the most illustrious Sir Henry Sidney, governor of the province of Wales, who finds himself here in order to go to Padua, where he plans to stay to study, be given licence to carry arms in this city of Venice, as also in every other city, land and place of our dominion, with his intimate gentleman by the name of Ludovic Bryskett, and with three servants, the names of whom are noted in this city in the office of

[1] Consiglio dei Dieci, Parti Comuni, R. 31, c. 127r; pr. Osborn, *Young Philip Sidney*, p. 523.
[2] Capi del Consiglio dei Dieci, Lettere. Fil. 75, pr. Osborn, *Young Philip Sidney*, p. 523.

the heads of this council and beyond in the chancelleries of other places where he [Sidney] will find himself, on oath that they are in his house and at his expense. Wherefore by the authority of the abovenamed Council we send to you that observed the abovementioned permission, and that you ensure that it is observed by all. Given the 30th Day of April 1574.

Formally recorded in the Council of Ten<br>29th day of April 1574

On 29 April Sidney was back in Padua and wrote to Languet to say that the French Ambassador to the Sublime Porte of the Ottoman Empire, François de Noailles (1519–85), Bishop of Dax, had just returned to Venice and he hoped to be able to make his acquaintance. He also mentioned that 'Master Du Ferrier and Zünderlin continue to treat me with the greatest kindness'.[1] By 3 May Zünderlin was expecting Sidney back in Venice and was grateful for news of him from Ludowick and Sebastian Bryskett (1536–91) and Edward, Lord Windsor. However, Sidney was still at Padua on 7 May, although he mentioned that he had recently received intelligence about the Battle of Mook Heath (April 1574) in which William of Orange's two brothers, Louis and Henry of Nassau, were killed and their armies routed, 'not from obscure men but from the Council of Ten itself', implying that he had recently been back to Venice. He may have gleaned this information when submitting his application to bear arms.

Sidney also mentioned in his letter of 7 May that he had written to his uncle, Robert Dudley, Earl of Leicester (although this letter has not survived).[2] It is likely that Sidney remained in regular touch with Leicester throughout his continental travels and it is to be regretted that this part of his correspondence is now lost, not least because Leicester was then building up a major art collection for his main residences at London and Kenilworth and would have been interested in Sidney's contacts with Veronese and the art world at Venice. It is also clear that he was keeping Leicester fully briefed about political intelligence acquired at Venice and Padua because Wolfgang Zünderlin had also been informed of the contents of Sidney's latest letter to Leicester, as is made clear by Zünderlin's comments in his own letter to Sidney written on 10 May:

> To return to your letter: I was especially pleased by what you tell me you have written to your most illustrious uncle [Leicester]. Truly, you could not have chosen a subject more worthy both of him and of yourself. For born as you are to the highest office in the state, you write of the state's affairs to a man who most loves, as I hear, your country: you write of what touches the motherland you share, such things as he could not receive more accurately from anyone else than you, who equally love your England, nor more happily than as an uncle from his beloved sister's son.[3]

On 28 May Sidney was back in Venice and he wrote a letter to Languet mentioning that he was 'expecting a letter from my father' (Sir Henry Sidney), suggesting that he was also writing regularly to his family back home in England. As with his correspondence with Leicester, these letters are also lost. Nevertheless, Sidney's letter to Languet of 28 May provides an interesting example of the kind of detailed intelligence he was able to glean from Venetian sources about international affairs:

---

[1] Sidney, *Correspondence*, I, p. 182. On 13 May Languet doubted whether this report of the French Ambassador to the Ottoman court was correct, ibid., I, p. 217.

[2] Ibid., I, pp. 191, 201–3.

[3] Ibid., I, p. 210.

I think it is the Spaniards who hold La Goletta and Tunis. In fact they say they are quite roasting in that heat. The Sultan, though, is said not to be able to mount any large attack this year for lack of oarsmen.[1] Which likewise is widely said about our Queen.[2] I have mentioned that all the English have for some time now been shut up on board the ships of Orange.[3] Much is reported about John of Austria. Some are agreed that he will leave for Flanders with a large force of Italians; others say that he will be recalled to Spain, some that he will stay in Italy. My own opinion is that Philip is using John like a Delphic sword, so that he can be seen to have such a commander both against the Turk and the King of France, if they try anything; and also against the rebelliousness of the Italians, which rebellion they [the Italians] are beginning to fear his [Don John's] presence would subdue; and that he might keep the Dutch in order by the expectation of his coming. My own wish is that while meddling in so many things he ends up getting nothing done.[4] The Ragusans have furnished Philip with 40 ships to prepare that Biscayan fleet of his.[5] De Foix, the French ambassador, is 'held in the highest honour' in Rome: not an unusual expression, but in this case apt and proper, for he is clearly (as an honest and trustworthy man told me) being held in such a way that he cannot escape [even] if he wants to.[6] But enough of that.

At the end of this letter Sidney also mentioned that Robert Corbet, whom he had met at Venice, was preparing to set out for Vienna to bring Veronese's portrait of Sidney to

---

[1] A combination of Spanish and Italian forces held La Goleta and Tunis which were recaptured by the Turks in a fierce conflict lasting from 15 July to 3 September 1574. Rumours at Venice in late May about the Turks' lack of oarsmen were clearly incorrect because the triumphant Turkish fleet comprised c. 250–300 vessels. This was a decisive campaign which ensured that North Africa fell under Muslim rather than Christian rule. It also had a broader European significance because early in 1574 William of Orange and Charles IX of France (who died in May 1574), via his pro-Huguenot Ambassador to the Ottomans, François de Noailles, Bishop of Dax, had sought to obtain the support of Sultan Selim II against Philip II of Spain. The Spanish writer Miguel de Cervantes (c.1547–1616) served as a soldier at the siege of Tunis. Many of the captured Christian soldiers were enslaved on the Ottoman galleys.

[2] This negative Venetian view of the English fleet is intriguing because galleys and their oarsmen played only a minor role in the Tudor navy during the early 1570s. It also seems that Sidney's sources at Venice were unaware of the steady expansion of the English fleet during the early 1560s and 1570s. During the 1560s seventeen vessels were added to the English navy but these included only three galleys: two (*Speedwell* and *Trywright*) taken as prizes from the French and the other (*Ellynore*) gifted by them. Between 1570 and 1574 the galleons *Foresight* (1570) and *Dreadnought* (1573), the pinnaces *Swiftsure* (1573) and *Swallow* (1573) and the smaller ship *Achates* (1573) were all built and later saw action during the Spanish Armada crisis (1588). Childs, *Tudor Sea Power*, pp. 292–3.

[3] During the Dutch revolt English merchants attempted to sustain free trade but in late 1573 an English vessel was captured by Flushingers, or possibly pirates, and its crew was imprisoned. This incident led to a formal protest by Queen Elizabeth to the Prince of Orange and an increase in the political tensions between England and the Low Countries.

[4] Don John of Austria (1547–78) was an illegitimate son of the Holy Roman Emperor Charles V and the half-brother of Philip II of Spain. Although he had distinguished himself at the Battle of Lepanto (October 1571) (**Plate 13**) – in which Miguel de Cervantes also served and was wounded – Sidney was essentially correct in his Machiavellian assessment of Don John's later ineffectiveness, as a 'Delphic sword', which, like the ambiguous Delphic Oracles, inconclusively cuts both ways.

[5] The Republic of Ragusa (Dubrovnik) claimed neutrality within the Adriatic and Venetian affairs but supported Philip II against the Dutch and English.

[6] Paul de Foix (1528–84) had served as French Ambassador to Scotland (1561) England (1562–6) and Venice (1567–70). He had also attempted to negotiate a marriage in 1570 between Queen Elizabeth and the Duke of Anjou (1551–89), later King Henri III of France. Arnaud du Ferrier was probably Sidney's source of this information about Foix.

Languet, although he would probably not be able to bring his servant 'as he is much too ill to make such an effort'.[1]

Sidney's letter to Languet of 4 June illustrates how English visitors to Venice and Padua were also able to socialize freely with the German community there. He explained that Languet's German protégé Count Hanau, with whom he planned to travel back to Vienna, wished to stay in Italy for at least three more weeks and so his own departure would be delayed. He was, however, able to include with his own letter, ones to Languet from Hanau and two of his entourage, Paul von Welsperg and Jacques Le Goulx. He also mentioned a new German acquaintance:

> There is in this city [Padua] a certain exceedingly noble German called the Baron and Burggrave of Dohna in Prussia. Stirred by your reputation, he already loves you greatly and hopes to become your friend. For that reason he has persistently asked me to commend him to you: in accepting this (although I know that it will be as much of a pleasure to you as to him since, to put it in a nutshell, he far excels all the Germans who live in this city, in every virtue) you [will] let me satisfy him all the better.

This individual was Fabian Dohna (1550–1621) who became a distinguished military commander and Prussian statesman. During a serious illness at Padua, contracted about the time of Sidney's acquaintance with him, he converted to Protestantism and continued his studies at Geneva. He was able to meet Languet at the Diet of Ratisbon (1576) and after the death of the Emperor Maximilian (October 1576) Languet found him employment with Johann Casimir (1543–92) of the Palatinate. As he was drafting this letter Sidney was also interrupted at his lodgings by a social visit from Jacob Monau (1545–1603) from Breslau, 'a good man who sends you cordial greetings'. He concluded his letter with the cynical but largely accurate comment: 'In Padua there is no news, except (and that is not new) that our Doctors are completely out of date.'[2]

Along with dutifully socializing with sound German Protestants, Sidney was clearly not averse at Padua and Venice to mingling with English recusants and Catholic exiles. Perhaps introduced to members of this community by Sebastian Bryskett and Edward, Lord Windsor, on 7 June Sidney and Griffin Madox witnessed the examination of the doctoral dissertation in law of John Hart, then a student at the University of Padua.[3] Hart and another witness, the civil lawyer Nicholas Wendon, were listed in an English official document in 1575 as fugitives living abroad.[4] Hart was later imprisoned in England in 1581–5 and supplied evidence on Catholic recusants to Francis Walsingham (**Plate 24**). He eventually became a Jesuit, dying in Poland in 1586. Wendon was ordained in 1578 as a priest at Rome.[5]

On 11 June Languet confirmed that he had received a letter from Sidney, personally delivered by Corbet although he had not as yet met Richard Shelley who was then in poor health. He also recounted how Corbet had delivered to him Sidney's Veronese portrait:

---

[1] Sidney, *Correspondence*, I, pp. 232–3.
[2] Ibid., II, pp. 248–9.
[3] Padua, Archivio di Stato, Notarile, 5007, ff. 26r–27v. Stewart, *Philip Sidney*, pp. 120, 338.
[4] TNA SP 12/105/105.
[5] Woolfson, *Padua*, pp. 243, 271, 282,

Master Corbet set your picture before me which, to fill my eyes, I kept by me for several hours, but by my gazing upon it my longing was increased rather than diminished. It seems to me rather to represent someone who looks like you than you yourself, and at first I thought it was of your brother. Most of your features are beautifully expressed, but it is far more youthful than it should be. I think you must have looked not unlike this when you were twelve or thirteen years old.

Languet went on to wonder why Sidney had still not clarified when he was intending to return to Vienna, suspecting that 'you have some plan you do not want me to know about'. Corbet had explained that Sidney was waiting for a letter from his father, Sir Henry, before making any decisions on the next stage of his travels, although Languet remained keen to ensure that Sidney did not move on to Rome or Constantinople.[1]

In another letter from Languet, written on 18 June, Sidney was sternly warned against adopting Italian political science (references to Machiavelli often crop up in their correspondence), social culture or personal morality. Languet's anxious words encapsulate the fear of all things Italian inculcated into young English travellers after 1570, following the publication of Roger Ascham's concerns (**item 19**) in that year:

To be honest with you, I do not admire the wisdom of the Italians so much that I take each of their sayings for an oracle, nor do I much approve the thinking of those who believe that they have brilliantly ordered their lives if they come as close as possible to those people's manners. At least, all the nations I can remember who followed their ideas for running their commonwealth have involved countries in the greatest calamities.

I will not even speak of their crimes. Are not the people most praised in Italy those who know how to dissemble? Who know how to flatter, and by various means to creep into the favour of the powerful, and so to attune themselves to those men's moods that whatever is proposed by the grandiose folly of one they have once decided to serve, would be sacred to them, and they would feel they should fight for it as for their homes and hearths? No: ever since their spirits were broken by long servitude, they willingly endure any indignities and insults if only they are not separated from their money and their shameful pleasures.[2]

By 20 June Sidney and Lodwick Bryskett were still residing at Hercole Bolognese's Pozzo della Vacca (the Cow's Well) at Padua, to where Wolfgang Zünderlin sent a brief letter from Venice. It is clear, however, that Sidney had recently been back to Venice because Zünderlin apologized for not being at home when Sidney had 'come to look for me several times at my house' and also noted that Sidney had been staying at Venice with Edward, Lord Windsor.[3] Sidney purchased on 20 June at Padua a copy of Francesco Guiccardini's *History of Italy* (Widener Library, Harvard). This text would have been of considerable interest to both Sidney and Bryskett because Lodovick Bryskett's sister Lucretia (1539/40–1608) had married in 1558 Vincent Guiccardini, who was probably the nephew of this historian Francesco.

Whilst hoping for so long that Sidney would soon return to Vienna, from late June Languet experienced a dramatic change of heart. This was occasioned by the death of Charles IX on 30 May 1574 and the visit to Venice of his successor Henri of Valois, Duke of Anjou, now King Henri III (**Plate 9**). He was lavishly entertained at Venice (18–25 July 1574) as he headed back from Poland to claim the crown of France. Languet saw

[1] Sidney, *Correspondence*, I, p. 254.
[2] Ibid., I, pp. 260–61.
[3] Ibid., I, pp. 266–7.

Figure 20.    Giacomo Franco, *La Città di Venetia* (1614). A Venetian ball in honour of visiting princes. By permission of Special Collections, Brotherton Library, University of Leeds.

this royal visit as an ideal diplomatic opportunity for Sidney, and by 25 June had already written to one of his numerous French contacts, Gaspard de Montmorin de Saint-Hérem (*c.*1535–77), a trusted member of Henri III's entourage, to recommend Sidney to him and the new French king. Languet reported that Henri III and his huge entourage had arrived at Vienna on 24 June and reported that 'Some people think that the King will come to where you are [Venice], and go back to France via southern Switzerland', although at this point Languet doubted that this would happen. Nevertheless, he recognized that the French king's itinerary offered a valuable opportunity for Sidney who was a fluent French speaker and the son and nephew of two of the most influential men in England, Sir Henry Sidney and Robert Dudley, Earl of Leicester. Languet insisted: 'If you should happen to have the opportunity to greet the King on his journey, I should like you to take it with both hands. You can use the good offices of Montmorin, and if he is not there, of Bellièvre, to whom I will entrust you.'[1]

By 28 June Languet was able to advise Sidney that Henri III was indeed going to travel across the Alps via northern Italy, 'so as to be able to see the city of Venice, and to form a closer friendship with that commonwealth and its neighbour princes'. He insisted that Sidney should be a 'spectator at the ceremonies with which he will be welcomed by the Venetians: I do not doubt that they will be splendid and absolutely worth seeing'; and he supplied him with a lengthy list of French contacts to exploit, headed by Du Ferrier and Montmorin.[2] On 10 July Languet imagined that Sidney would soon be filling his 'soul with the Venetian spectacles and pomp with which they will be receiving the King of France'. On 17 July he expressed his relief that Sidney had 'completely abandoned' the idea of making a short trip to inspect the antiquities of Rome, even though he was probably by then 'sated with Venetian spectacles'. It may also have been the case that Sidney was not up to such a journey because Languet noted from a now lost letter from him that he had been 'suffering from dreadful headaches, and drinking immoderate amounts of water'.[3] Henri III arrived in Venice on 18 July and, although no account of these celebrations has survived from Sidney's own hand, it is clear that he was specially honoured by the French king, no doubt through the good offices of Du Ferrier and Languet's other French associates in the royal party. Sidney had previously been honoured as a *gentilhomme de la chambre* by Charles IX and Henri III graciously retained him in that rank while at Venice. On 4 August Sidney withdrew the remaining money in his account with Acerbo Vitello via his Venetian agent, perhaps as an indication that he was finally intending to leave Venice.[4] Certainly, by 27 August the Huguenot François Perrot de Mésières (1537–after 1612), a close friend of Du Ferrier and long-time resident of Venice, was writing from there to Sidney who was then back at Vienna, to provide him with more news about Henri III's progress back to France. He referred to two printed accounts of the recent Venetian and other Italian entertainments for the king, copies of which he assumed would be sent directly to Sidney.[5]

---

[1] Ibid., I, pp. 270–72. Pomponne de Bellièvre (1529–1607), a jurist and diplomat, was Henri III's Superintendent of Finance and one of the new king's most influential courtiers.

[2] Ibid., I, pp. 275–6.

[3] Ibid., I, pp. 291, 296.

[4] Stewart, *Philip Sidney*, pp. 129–30.

[5] Sidney, *Correspondence*, I, pp. 305–8. Porcacchi, *Le attioni d'Arrigo terzo re di Francia*, 1574, and Anon., *Entrata ... Henrico III di Francia*, 1574.

Sidney's connections with Venice and Padua, however, were not entirely severed by his departure from northern Italy and he sustained for the rest of 1574 a detailed correspondence with several residents there. On 6 September Zünderlin wrote to Sidney from Venice to thank him for a letter, delivered by Ludowick Bryskett, which he had written when leaving Padua. On 27 September a German resident at Padua, Matthaüs Wacker (1550–1619), updated him on news from there and expressed his personal sadness at the loss of his company. François Perrot wrote to Sidney from Venice on 9 October, thanking him for his letter dated 24 September and promising to keep him updated on 'news from hence, as I know this pleases you' and about the activities of Henri III in France. Zünderlin wrote again from Venice on 5 November, replying to a lost letter from Sidney, supplying him with information about the aftermath of the Ottomans taking La Goleta and Tunis. He described the arrival at Corfu of a Turkish fleet of trireme galleys with 1,200 Spanish and Italian prisoners and 10,000 Africans in fetters and, most notably, Gabrio de Serbelloni (1508–80), the former commander of the fort at La Goleta, in foot-shackles. Perrot wrote again from Venice on 26 November, in response to a letter from Sidney dated 12 November, enclosing a copy of some Italian verses (perhaps some of his own, later published as *Perle elette di Francesco Perotto ... di CL. [p]salmi di David*, Geneva, 1576) and reporting that he had passed on Sidney's compliments to Du Ferrier. Zünderlin again wrote from Venice on 27 November, with news about the Turks and the forthcoming Jubilee Year at Rome.[1]

Similar correspondences continued into 1575. A German acquaintance from Padua, Otto I (1550–1612), Count of Solms-Sonnewalde, wrote to Sidney from there on 6 January, recalling their friendship and his own visit to England as a guest in 1573 of Edward Manners (1549–87), third Earl of Rutland, at his Belvoir estates. Perrot wrote again from Venice on 8 January in reply to a letter from Sidney dated 4 December 1574, in which he had apparently enquired as to the current whereabouts of Ludowick Bryskett. Zünderlin had informed Perrot that his brother Sebastian had advised him that Ludowick would not be in Venice for another two weeks, mysteriously adding that 'he did not want to say where he was' but Perrot promised to write again once he had any more news about Bryskett.[2] Zünderlin himself wrote to Sidney from Venice on 9 January, advising him not to overtax himself through excessive study. He also added his own sparse information about the secretive activities of Ludowick Bryskett:

> I return your letter. I have given the one which accompanied it to your servant [perhaps Harry Whyte], to whom it was addressed: he said he would reply to you by this same messenger. Your man Bryskett I have not seen for several months: what has become of him I have often asked his brother, who replied that he knew nothing, and was surprised that he had had no letter from him. But just recently he told me when I asked him again that he would soon be here, though where he would be coming from he did not add, even though I asked him.

Zünderlin wrote again on 30 January with news about the death of Sultan Selim II (on 13 December 1574) and the Kings of Spain and France but nothing else about Bryskett's activities. Sent in the same packet of letters was the one to Sidney from Cesare Carrafa describing the death and funeral of Edward, Lord Windsor. Perrot wrote again from Venice on 20 February, replying to a letter from Sidney dated 9 February with news about

---

[1] Sidney, *Correspondence*, I, pp. 311, 315–17, 322, 336–8, 341–3, 350–53.
[2] Ibid., I, pp. 362–3, 365–6.

the new Sultan at Constantinople, Murad III (1546–95), Rome and France and mentioning that he had 'communicated your letter to the English gentleman you wrote to me about' – perhaps Ludowick or Sebastian Bryskett. Wacker wrote from Padua on 24 February and Perrot from Venice on 27 February, whose letter was carried to Sidney at Frankfurt by the Venetian publisher and bookseller Pietro Longo (who was later accused in 1587 of Protestant sympathies by the Inquisition).[1]

Such a sustained correspondence, coupled with Sidney's lengthy stay at Venice and Padua, caused Languet considerable anxiety. On 10 March 1575 he wrote from Prague to Sidney who had begun his homeward journey to England to say that his friend Edward Wotton (1548–1628) had brought him a letter from Francis Walsingham, indicating that 'your people have begun to have some suspicions about your religion, since you are on more comfortable terms with the Venetians than is usual with those who profess a religion different from yours'. Languet promised to write to Francis Walsingham to reassure him that such suspicions were entirely unfounded but also instructed Sidney to 'take the trouble to convince others of it also'. He also counselled Sidney 'to cultivate a friendship with Master Walsingham' – advice which proved both politically and personally shrewd since Sidney married Walsingham's daughter Frances in 1583.[2]

Sidney sailed for England from Antwerp on 4 May 1575 but continued his correspondence with Languet and other contacts made during his almost three years of continental travel. On 6 June Languet wrote from Prague, offering Sidney his more considered thoughts on the Veronese portrait after having the canvas stretched and mounted:

> While I had the good fortune to enjoy your company, I did not fully appreciate your portrait which you gave me, and hardly thanked you for that splendid gift. Missing you made me, when I had come back from Frankfurt, have it fixed to a board and put in a place where it would be easily seen. Since that has been done, I find it so elegant, and such a true portrayal of you, that now I have nothing among my possessions that is dearer to me. Master Vulcob so admires its elegance that he is looking for a painter to copy it. The painter has portrayed you a little melancholy and pensive. I should have preferred you to have been wearing a merrier face when you went to be painted.[3]

This portrait is known to have still been in Languet's possession when he died at Antwerp on 30 September 1581 and may have been brought back to England by the Earl of Leicester and Sidney who were at Antwerp in February 1582 for the installation of the Duke of Anjou as titular ruler of the Netherlands. Its present whereabouts – if it has survived – is unknown.[4] Philip Sidney's last known comments on Italy and Venice were made in a letter of advice about continental travel to his younger brother Robert, dating from about 1579:

---

[1] Ibid., I, pp. 372–4, 383–4, 386–7, 390–91, 393–4, 397–400.

[2] Ibid., I, pp. 404–6.

[3] Ibid., I, pp. 449–50.

[4] Goldring, 'A Portrait of Sir Philip Sidney', pp. 548–54. Kuin, 'New Light', pp. 19–47, and 'Languet and the Veronese Portrait of Sidney', pp. 42–4, suggests that this Veronese portrait may have been taken to the château at Saumur of Languet's close friend and protégé Philippe de Mornay whose wife, Charlotte Arbaleste, had nursed Languet during his final illness.

As for Italie, I knowe not what wee have, or can have to do with them but to buye their silkes and wynes And as for the other pointes except Venice (whose good Lawes & Customes we can hardly proportion to our selfes, because they are quite of a contrary government) there is litle their but Tyrannyous oppressyon and servile yeeldinge to them that have litle or no right over them. And for the men you shall have ther (although indeed some be excellentye learned) yet are they all given soe to counterfeit learninge as a man shall learne emonge them more false groundes of thinges then in any place else that I knowe: for from a Tapster upward they are all disoursers in fine certaine qualityes; as Horshemanshypp, weapons, vawtinge, and suche are better there, then in the other Countryes. But for other matters, aswell (if not better) you shall have them in these neerer places.[1]

[1] Sidney, *Correspondence*, I, pp. 881–2.

# 23.   1575–6 – EDWARD DE VERE, EARL OF OXFORD

**Edward de Vere (1550–1604)**, seventeenth Earl of Oxford, was probably born at Castle Hedingham, Essex, and was known as Viscount Bulbeck until the death in 1562 of his father John de Vere, the sixteenth earl. He spent about one year at the University of Cambridge (1558–59) and it has been assumed that he was then tutored at home by the Protestant Thomas Fowle (*c.*1530–post 1597) within the family of Sir Thomas Smith (1513–77).[1] This household was a cultured and intellectual one and Smith himself had made a continental tour, including stays at Paris, Orleans and Padua between May 1540 and January 1542.[2] He was a member of the Marquess of Northampton's embassy to France in May 1551, seeking to agree a marriage between Edward VI and Princess Elisabeth of France. He served as English Ambassador to France (1562–6) and made another brief trip to France in March 1567 in a fruitless pursuit of the return of Calais. His library contained works by Castiglione and Machiavelli but as a staunch Protestant he remained deeply suspicious of Italy, once notoriously commenting at court that the 'hardest punishment for all papists by mine advice should be to confine them into Italy and let them live by sucking the pope's teats'.[3] After his father's death, Edward de Vere became a royal ward under the charge of Sir William Cecil, Master of the Court of Wards.[4] Cecil arranged for him to be tutored by Laurence Nowell (*c.*1516–76) who, with his brother Alexander (*c.*1516/17–1602), had fled in 1555 to the continent during Queen Mary's reign.[5]

   Despite the best efforts of his tutors and guardian, Oxford proved an undisciplined youth. On 23 July 1567 he killed an undercook, Thomas Brincknell, during fencing practice with Edmund Baynham but, through Cecil's influence, the coroner's jury found that the unarmed but drunken Brincknell had supposedly committed suicide by running

---

[1] Fowle had been ejected from his fellowship at St John's College, Cambridge, during Queen Mary's reign. Although he remained in London, secretly ministering to a congregation of Protestants, his greatest sympathies would have been with the Marian exiles at Venice and Padua. During the early 1570s he was active on commissions in Norfolk prosecuting Catholic recusants.

[2] Smith's visit to Padua is recorded in *ODNB* but not listed in Woolfson, *Padua*.

[3] *ODNB*, s.v. TNA, SP 70/52/411. Recently, doubt has been cast on whether Oxford did live in Smith's household at Ankerwyke, Berkshire. The reference in Smith's household inventory (1569) to 'my Lorde's chamber' may refer to the chamber of an earlier owner of the house, Edward, 1st Lord Windsor (1467–1543), the grandfather of Edward, 3rd Lord Windsor, who befriended Philip Sidney (**item 22**, **Plate 17** and **Figure 17**) at Venice: http://www.oxford-shakespeare.com/Oxmyths/Oxmyths Oxford.pdf (p. 3).

[4] TNA WARD 8/13.

[5] The Nowell brothers are known to have stayed at Strasbourg and Frankfurt but their complete itinerary abroad is unknown.

onto Oxford's sword.[1] From late 1569, following the outbreak of the Northern Rebellion, Oxford expressed a desire to gain military experience on the continent but, instead, was sent to Scotland under the command of Thomas Radcliffe (1525–83), third Earl of Sussex. In December 1571 he married Anne Cecil (1556–88), the daughter of William Cecil, now Lord Burghley, a union which proved disastrous. In 1569 she had been contracted to marry Philip Sidney (**item 22, Plate 17** and **Figure 17**), creating a lasting personal enmity between these two young men. Oxford was also suspected of Catholic sympathies when in 1572 he remonstrated with Cecil over the imprisonment of Thomas Howard (1536–72) who had been imprisoned in the Tower of London in 1569 for scheming to marry Mary Queen of Scots.[2] After his release Howard became embroiled in the Ridolfi Plot with Philip II of Spain to put Mary on the English throne and restore Catholicism to England. Oxford was suspected of being involved in an attempt to rescue Norfolk from the Tower, prior to his execution for treason on 2 June 1572. By summer 1573 Oxford was already making plans to travel on the continent although this trip, perhaps due to his already huge debts (estimated at £6,000), never came to pass.[3] In July 1574 Oxford travelled without permission to Flanders where several members of the northern English Catholic nobility were based.

Oxford was forcibly brought back to England but then granted a licence to travel abroad for one year in January 1575.[4] Queen Elizabeth also provided him with two letters of introduction to foreign monarchs and dignitaries, one cast in general terms and the other to the Emperor Maximilian, describing him as 'an illustrious youth much adorned with many virtues, the offspring of a most ancient family of England'.[5] Evidence has survived to show how Oxford financed the expensive process of travelling abroad, especially for someone of his excessive tastes who also needed to pay off substantial debts before his departure. Nina Green explains:

> Prior to his departure Oxford entered into two indentures. By the first indenture, dated 20 January 1575, he sold his manors in Cornwall, Staffordshire and Wiltshire to three trustees for £6000. By the second indenture, dated 30 January, he entailed the lands of his earldom on his first cousin, Hugh Vere, giving as his reason that 'he hath not any issue of his body as yet born', and if he should die abroad without heirs the lands of the earldom would therefore descend to his sister, Mary [d. 1624, his younger sister], 'being next of his kind of the whole blood'. The indenture also provided for payment of debts in an attached schedule amounting to £9,096 10s 8½d, of which sum £3,457 was owed to the Queen in the Court of Wards.[6]

It is clear that Oxford had developed interests in Italian literature and culture well before his travels. Records of books bought for him in 1569 include two in Italian and early in 1572 he wrote a Latin epistle for Bartholomew Clerke's *De curiali*, a translation

---

[1] TNA KB 9/619, m.13. Nelson, *Monstrous Adversary*, p. 47. It has been proposed that Brincknell thought that Oxford and Baynham were fighting in earnest and had sought to separate them, just as Romeo's intervention in *Romeo and Juliet* (III.i) leads to Tybalt accidentally killing Mercutio with his sword.

[2] Nelson, *Monstrous Adversary*, pp. 53–4, 80–82, 84.

[3] Ibid., pp. 99–104.

[4] Ibid., pp. 108–14. TNA E157/1/1. For Oxford's licences to travel, see TNA E 157/1, Jan. 1574 and 2 Mar. 1575.

[5] Nelson, *Monstrous Adversary*, p. 119. CUL MS Dd.3.20, ff. 98v, 99r–v.

[6] Essex Record Office, D/DRG2/25: http://www.oxford-shakespeare.com/OxfordsBiography/Oxford's Biography.pdf.

into Latin of Baldassare Castiglione's *Il cortegiano*. In the following year he provided a commendatory letter and verses for Thomas Bedingfield's *Cardanus' Comfort*, a translation from the Latin of *De consolatione libri tres* by the Italian mathematician and physician, Girolamo Cardano.[1]

Oxford left England during the first week of February 1575 with two gentlemen, two grooms and a housekeeper. With the assistance of the English Ambassador, Valentine Dale (*c.*1520–89), he was presented at Paris on 6 March to Henri III and his queen, Louise of Lorraine. He also met Jacques Amyot (1513–93), the translator of Plutarch, and probably Catherine de' Medici and Henri of Navarre.[2] The Venetian Ambassador at Paris, Giovanni Francesco Morosini, provided him letters of introduction to the Doge and his own friends and reported to the Signoria on 12 March 1575:

> An English gentleman, whose name is the Earl of Oxford, has arrived in this city: he is a young man of about twenty or twenty-two years of age. It is said that he fled England on account of his inclination to the Catholic religion; but having returned he received great favour from the Queen, who gave him full licence to travel and see the world, when she ascertained that he had resolved to depart under any circumstances.[3]

On 17 March Oxford wrote to Burghley from Paris, expressing his pleasure at news of his wife's pregnancy and his keenness to see Venice. On that day or soon afterwards he travelled to Strasbourg and visited the Protestant reformer Johan Sturmius (1507–89).[4] With the arrival of spring, it became safer to cross the Alps and he left Strasbourg on 26 April and entered Italy via the Brenner Pass. He travelled by canals and rivers to Verona and arrived at Padua in late April and Venice by mid-May.[5]

A significant number of other English visitors – some now largely unknown unless briefly recorded in State Papers or the records of the University of Padua – visited the Veneto during the mid-1570s.[6] On 16 April 1575 Cesare Carrafa (who had written on the previous 3 February to inform Philip Sidney of the death of Edward, Lord Windsor) (**item 22**) wrote from Venice to Marco Antonio Colonna at Rome to note the arrival there of Sir William Russell (*c.*1553–1613), later first Baron Russell of Thornhaugh. He was the grandson of Sir John Russell who had travelled to Venice with Thomas Wyatt in 1527 (**item 13** and **Plate 16**), and the fourth son of Francis Russell (1526/7–85), second Earl of Bedford. Sir William Russell's father John had also visited Venice when, after his father's death in 1555 and escaping from the Catholic regime of Queen Mary, he received

---

[1] Ward, *Earl of Oxford*, pp. 31–3. Nelson, *Monstrous Adversary*, pp. 67, 237.

[2] TNA SP 70/133/178–80. Ward, *Earl of Oxford*, p. 101. Anderson, *'Shakespeare' by Another Name*, pp. 75–6. The clergyman poet Nathaniel Baxter (fl. 1570s–1610s), who claimed to have tutored Philip Sidney in Greek, also seems to have been a member of Oxford's continental entourage. William Lewin travelled with him probably from England and certainly from Paris to Strasbourg. Ralph Hopton (d. 1580), whom Lewin claimed had previously been a servant to Philip Sidney, joined Oxford's entourage at Venice. http://www.oxford-shakespeare.com/StatePapersOther/SP_70-133_ff_178-80.pdf.

[3] *CSP Venice*, 1575, item 619.

[4] TNA SP 70/133/186.

[5] Ward, *Earl of Oxford*, p. 102. Anderson, *'Shakespeare' by Another Name*, pp. 78–81.

[6] Oxford apparently knew Luke Astlow (d. 1575) at Padua. He had travelled with Robert Persons (1546–1610) and the physician George Lewkenor via Antwerp and Frankfurt to Padua in 1574 to study law where they shared 'a very commodious house' with John Lane (1542–78). Oxford reported his conversion to Catholicism and Astlow intended to follow the renowned Jesuit priest Robert Persons (Parsons) to Rome but died before leaving Padua. Woolfson, *Padua*, pp. 209, 250, 263.

a licence to travel abroad. He visited Brussels and then set out for Venice, where he learned Italian, and also visited Rome, Naples and Ferrara before taking up residence at Zurich to study under the guidance of the Protestant reformer Henry Bullinger and returning to England in 1557.[1] Carrafa observed:

> Three days ago [13 April] there arrived here Sir William Russell, son of the Earl of Ubelfort [Bedford], a great lord of England, and one of the Queen's Council of State. He is going to Rome or Naples. Our ambassador makes much of him, as do also the Signoria. He dined with me the day before yesterday. His Serenity is a great friend of his father. The Arsenal has been shown him, and other things worth a visit, and it has fallen to my lot to be ever with him.[2]

Sir William Russell continued his travels on the continent until 1579 and in late March 1576 accompanied the Earl of Oxford back to Paris.[3] After his arrival back in England Russell served in a military capacity in Ireland and in 1585 joined the Earl of Leicester's campaign in the Low Countries where he was appointed Lieutenant-General of Horse. He was renowned for his valour on the battlefield and led the English attack at Zutphen on 22 September 1586 when the English forces were outnumbered by Spanish *tercios* (infantry). Sir Philip Sidney (**item 22**, **Plate 17** and **Figure 17**), who received a mortal wound at this engagement, acknowledged Russell's comradeship by bequeathing to him his best gilt suit of armour. Russell also succeeded on 1 February 1587 to Sidney's post of Governor of Flushing.

In late June Oxford applied for access to the chambers of the Doge's palace where the *Council of Ten met, perhaps to view the spectacular art works there. On 12 July William Lewin (d. 1598) wrote from Strasbourg with retrospective news of Oxford's activities. Lewin had possibly served William Cecil as tutor to his daughter Anne during the mid-1560s and after her marriage he was appointed as Oxford's Receiver of Revenues. Burghley had presumably wished Lewin to travel with Oxford on at least part of his continental tour and they had left Paris together on about 17 March with Lewin staying with Sturmius when Oxford decided to head off into Italy. His comments provide a useful insight into how correspondence from England was distributed in Italy and to Venice by means of resident merchants:

> On 4 June I wrote from Strasbourg to a certain merchant of Venice that your letter had been sent, asking that he convey it to my lord and write to me about what he was doing concerning it. Now a few days after June 5, it has been reported to Sulcher by that same merchant that he has sent your letter to my lord at Padua. I desired a fuller reply. But from this report I think it can be gathered that my lord was at Padua at the time and that your letter has been given to him. For thus Sulcher has instructed: if my lord was at Venice, to give him the letter personally, or, were he elsewhere in Italy, to attend to its transmission with diligence. This is why he wrote that it had been sent to my lord at Padua: he did this on his own initiative, because he understood he was at Padua at the time, and I hope he was diligent in doing this, since it was requested that he act with all diligence.

[1] 'Francis Russell', *ODNB*, s.v.
[2] *CSP Vatican, 1572–78* [Rome], item 395. http://www.oxford-shakespeare.com/DocumentsOther/CSPR_1575_395.pdf.
[3] TNA SP 70/137/322–3. 'My Lord of Oxford hath passed through all the camp very well, and is arrived here in very good health, and Mr William Russell with him.'

Lewin then provided more news which referred to Philip Sidney and expressed his own uncertainty over Oxford's destinations and activities in Italy, comparable in his anxiety to Languet's concerns over Sidney's movements between Venice and Padua:

A few days ago I received a not dissimilar report from an Italian: he understood that at the beginning of this month of June a certain English nobleman was at Venice, and that he had taken into his company some young man who had been at Venice with that right decorous youth Philip Sidney. Although he called him by a different name. I imagine that this nobleman was my lord and that the young man whom he took into his company was Ralph Hopton, a former servant of my lord. Yet I would prefer not to have believed this without further details, as long as I could hope to discover more. But I perceived that this city is distant from the commerce of the Venetians, so that everything comes to us rather slowly, and also that my lord had either altered or abandoned his plan in such a way that he wrote nothing about it to myself. Indeed I should be satisfied with whatever is granted me, but I desire to have reported to me all the things that are being done as accurately as possible, rather than merely what is being done. Although I earnestly exerted myself that your lordship learn from me, as if from an intermediary, those things which would be pleasant for you to hear and could be written by me with honesty, nothing can be offered, since this depends on the will of other men. I dare not write to Venice more frequently, and I am afraid that I be held suspect for my diligence rather than being accused of negligence. And yet what I have written you has been rhetorical and literary. I should give it substance and content, if what he said pleased him at the time he was leaving here had pleased him in his absence, for he said that he would write to me for the sake of practicing his style. This was my sole intention, to inspire his mind with a desire for literary studies, to steer his thoughts away from other subjects and towards that one. I was of the opinion that, when he had been a few months at Venice, he could be brought back to Germany out of longing for Dominus Sturm, by whom he originally seemed to be wonderfully delighted. But if what I hear mentioned in certain men's conversation is true, that my lord's delay has been extended, even if I should imagine that he will not linger long at Venice, since he will tire even of Italian things, I think he will choose to continue in his journey rather than turning back, since for those wearied of things, nothing seems preferable to seeing that which they have not yet seen.

Lewin advised Burghley that he had decided to wait a few more days to see if Oxford contacted him and then, if not, he would 'return to my own nation' from Strasbourg. He concluded by assuring Burghley that his greatest hope was that 'our ever-living God' would 'gladdend all your hoped-for wishes and joys concerning' Oxford and that the earl should 'realise how blessed he is in his affairs, and that he might gloriously increase the joy both of yourselves and of your ladies with the joy of new offspring, and grant him all else happily and prosperously'.[1] Clearly, both Lewin and Burghley were soon to be seriously disappointed in this respect.

At this point it is important to clarify a longstanding myth about Oxford's time at Venice. His only surviving legitimate son, Henry de Vere (1593–1625), also visited Venice in 1617 and was presented to Doge Giovanni Bembo (1543–1618) and the *Collegio by the resident English Ambassador, Sir Henry Wotton (1568–1639) (**Plate 26**). Henry was offering to raise a body of military volunteers to serve the Republic in its conflict with Austria over control of the Adriatic and Wotton was seeking to assert his family's longstanding loyalty to the city of Venice. This audience, conducted in

[1] TNA SP 70/134/238–9. http://www.oxford-shakespeare.com/StatePapersOther/SP_70-134_ff_238-9.pdf.

Italian with Henry de Vere waiting outside the audience room in the Palazzo Ducale, was recorded in the Cancelleria secreta (secretarial office and archives relating to foreign affairs) and translated by Logan Pearsall Smith in *The Life and Letters of Sir Henry Wotton* as: 'when he arrived in Venice, [Edward de Vere] took no trouble to see the rest of the country, but stopped here, and even built himself a house'.[1] However, Noemi Magri has demonstrated that the original Italian has been misunderstood ('il quale […] non si curò di veder altra parte della ditta Provincia: et vi si fermò et vi fabric anch'una casa').[2]

Wotton would certainly have known that Henry's father, Edward de Vere, had travelled widely in Italy and not restricted himself to the city of Venice alone. Wotton, then, was concerned to emphasize in his first phrase ('il quale […] non si curò di veder altra parte della ditta Provincia') that Edward de Vere had been especially attached to Venice itself and that his son shared the same passion. Smith's translation of the second phrase ('et vi si fermò et vi fabric anch'una casa') misunderstands the diversity of meaning of the Italian word *fabbricò*. Rather than literally meaning that Oxford built himself a house – clearly an impossibility during the relatively short time he spent at Venice – Wotton was suggesting that, instead of staying at an inn, he had provided himself with a desirable home (the Italian *casa* meaning both 'house' and 'home'). Almost certainly, Oxford had rented a comfortable (or, knowing his lavish tastes, luxurious) house or *palazzo* which probably included the furnishings (implied by *fabricò*).

Oxford also visited Genoa but was back in Venice by 23 September, according to his servant Clement Parrett who wrote to Lord Burghley on that date, clearly wishing not only to provide him with information about Oxford's activities and health but also to quash any unfavourable rumours which might be reaching England:

> Right Honourable,
> My most humble duty remembered, I am sorrow [*sic*] that afore this time I could not, according to duty, write to your Honour of my Lord's success and good disposition in this his travel, but my daily and continual service about my Lord hath rather hindered than furthered my good intention and service, which always hath been and is employed to obey your Honour's commandment.
> At this present your Honour shall understand my Lord's better disposition, God be thanketh, for now last coming from Genoa his Lordship found himself somewhat altered by reason of the extreme heats, and before his Lordship hurt his knee in one of the Venetian galleys, but all is past without further harm.
> Of any other reports that your Honour hath understood of my Lord, no credit is to be given unto. It is true that a while ago at Padua were killed unawares, in a quarrel that was amongst a certain congregation of Saffi[3] and students, two noble gentlemen of Polonia, and the bruit ran *Gentilhomini Inglesi*.
> This I can assure your Honour of, that other thing there is not chanced in my Lord's journey that might proceed to my Lord's or your Honour's displeasure, nor hope will not until his Lordship return into England, where with all my desire and careful duty I wish his Honour to return in health., which I hope will be shortly, for many strangers will be soon weary in

[1] Wotton, *Letters*, II, p. 113, n. 3.
[2] Magri, 'Edward de Vere Did Not Build Himself a House in Venice', pp. 11–16. She also notes (p. 14) that the registers of taxpayers for 1575–6 in the Venetian State Archives, which recorded both Venetian and foreign owners of properties in the city, contain no reference to Oxford.
[3] *congregation of Saffi*: unidentified.

218

these parts considering their estate, life and government, as your Honour doth know, besides the danger of sickness and other inconveniences.

Of any other certain news I cannot advertise your Honour but that I hope in doing my duty and faithful service in this journey towards my Lord and master your Honour shall find satisfaction, and in all the dealing it hath pleased his Lordship to employ me.

Thus craving pardon if duty and affection doth presume to trouble your Honour, that nevertheless the fault may be accepted in good part of him that prayeth daily to Almighty God for the preservation of your noble person.

From Venice in haste the 23 September 1575.

Yours Honour's most humble servant,

Clement Parrett.[1]

At about this time Oxford received news that his wife had given birth on 2 July but, rather than coming home, he wished to see more of Italy and Germany. He also mentioned that he had been sick with a fever which had limited his travelling, although he escaped the bubonic plague which began to hit Venice, at first slowly and unreported, from about July 1575.[2] Writing from Venice on 6 October Pasquale Spinola, the brother of the London-based Genoese banker Benedetto (Benedict) Spinola (1519/20–80), congratulated Lord Burghley on Oxford's safe return to Venice from Milan. By 27 November he was back in Padua, from where he wrote to Burghley about the sale of more of his lands to ease his debts. These land transactions may have facilitated his receipt of money on 11 December from Pasquale Spinola at Venice which enabled him to leave for Florence on the next day.[3] On 2 December 1575 Cesare Carrafa wrote from Venice to Philip Sidney:

A servant of the Earl of Oxford has arrived here, who I had thought would bring a letter from Your Lordship;. he gave me to understand that you are well and in favour with her Majesty our Queen and beloved by all the court, which has pleased me enormously .... My greetings to His Excellency, your father [Sir Henry Sidney], and my Lord Oxford [*sic*]; and commend me to the excellent Master Bryskett. And may Our Lord grant all your Lordship's desires.[4]

Close to Christmas, Oxford left Florence to explore more southerly regions of Italy.[5] On 3 January 1576 Oxford wrote to from Siena in response to complaints about his still-unpaid debts to the queen, his sister and other creditors and instructed that yet more of his lands should be sold off to pay them. His whereabouts after this date remain uncertain, although he may have visited Rome and even further south (perhaps Sicily).[6]

On 2 March 1576 Oxford's licence to travel was renewed for another year but for reasons which are unclear he elected to leave Venice on 6 March only days before one of

---

[1] Hatfield House, Cecil Papers, 7/106. Perrett was one of Oxford's servants from England and he was neither Italian nor a Venetian banker, even though he has sometimes been referred to as 'Clemente Peretti'. http://www.oxford-shakespeare.com/CecilPapers/CP_7-106.pdf.

[2] Ward, *Earl of Oxford*, p. 106. Anderson, *'Shakespeare' by Another Name*, pp. 93–6. Michael Delahoyde: https://public.wsu.edu/~delahoyd/shakespeare/continent.html.

[3] TNA SP 70/136/113–14.

[4] Sidney, *Correspondence*, I, pp. 585–7. Carrafa must have known that Oxford was still in Italy and so his possible reference to 'Lord Oxford' ('Milorth Auberth in the original letter, BL MS Add. 15914, ff. 25–6) may be to another individual, perhaps to one of the Lords Howard at the English court. http://www.oxford-shakespeare.com/BritishLibrary/BL_Add_15914_ff_25–6.pdf.

[5] Ward, *Earl of Oxford*, p. 109. Anderson, *'Shakespeare' by Another Name*, p. 97.

[6] Edward Webbe (**item 31**) claimed to have encountered Oxford in southern Italy.

the most virulent outbreaks of the plague to hit Venice during the sixteenth century.[1] Perhaps prompted by this news to head north and curtail his itinerary, he travelled homewards via Milan, Lyons and Paris where he had arrived by 21 March.[2] The huge expense of Oxford's lifestyle while abroad may be gauged by a reference made to a London-based Italian merchant, Benedetto (Benedict) Spinola, having arranged for a total of £3,761 4s 5d to be paid to Oxford when he was in France and Italy.[3] On 3 April 1576 the Venetian Ambassador at Paris noted:

> The Earl of Oxford, an English gentleman has arrived here. He has come from Venice, and, according to what has been said to me by the English ambassador here resident [Dale], speaks in great praise of the numerous courtesies which he has received in that city; and he reported that on his departure from Venice your Serenity had already elected an Ambassador to be sent to the Queen, and the English Ambassador expressed the greatest satisfaction at the intelligence. I myself, not having received any information from your Serenity or from any of my correspondents, did not know what answer to give concerning this matter.[4]

After his extended travels abroad, gossip proliferated about Oxford's suspect personal morality. He was rumoured by Stephen Powle (**item 29**) to have associated at Venice with a renowned courtesan, Virginia Padoana, and when he returned to Paris with various fashionable Italian items of dress he also had with him a sixteen-year-old Venetian choirboy, Orazio Cuoco (sometimes mistakenly called Cogno), whom he employed as a page at his London residence for eleven months. While crossing the Channel, his ship was waylaid by Flushing pirates and he lost many of his clothes and other souvenirs.[5] Landing at Dover on 20 April he returned to London by river wherry to avoid his wife Anne, who had given birth to a daughter Elizabeth on 2 July 1575 (whose paternity Oxford denied).[6]

Oxford's Venetian choirboy returned to Venice in 1577 and was questioned on 27 August on behalf of the Venetian Inquisition (Santo Ufficio) by Pasquale Ciconia (Cicogna), Doge of Venice from 1585 until 1595 (**Plate 22**). A complete transcript of the

---

[1] Nathaniel Baxter, who seems to have been travelling with Oxford, claimed in his poem *Ourania* (1606) that he had been summoned home by the queen: 'Vigilant then th'eternal Majesty ... / Induces us to make speedy repair.'

[2] Woolfson, *Padua*, p. 280. TNA E157/1/2–3. Benedetto (Benedict) Spinola advised Burghley on 23 March that he had received a letter, dated 26 Feb., from his brother Pasquale at Venice, stating that Oxford would leave Venice after its Carnival had finished. Francis Peyto wrote to Burghley on 31 March, stating that Oxford had already passed through Milan. Ward, *Earl of Oxford*, pp. 110–12. Anderson, *'Shakespeare' by Another Name*, pp. 101–7.

[3] Spinola was born at Genoa. He was associated in London with Acelyne Salvago who took cash deposits from travellers, including William Thomas (**item 16**), in return for bills of exchange which could be cashed with merchants, factors and bankers in Italy. On 15 June 1580 Oxford purchased property and land near Aldgate, London, from Spinola for £2,500. TNA C54/1080 and REQ 2/178/60.

[4] *CSP Venice*, 1576, item 653. Valentine Dale also wrote to Burghley on 31 March, noting Oxford's arrival at Paris with William Russell. TNA SP 70/137/332–3.

[5] Michel de Castelnau (*c*.1520–92) described to Henri III Oxford's losses as 'une infinite de belles hardes d'Italie', a phrase which includes not only clothes but other personal goods, including furniture and art. Robert Beale was sent by the Privy Council to the Low Countries to seek recovery of the goods and noted that the pirates had bribed officials with 'golden stuff' stolen from Oxford. TNA 31/3/27/75–8. BL Cotton MS Galba C V, ff. 252–3.

[6] Nelson, *Monstrous Adversary*, pp. 141–54.

questions and responses has survived.[1] Its purpose was to establish whether Cuoco had lived as a dutiful Catholic while in England, as well as seeking information about Venetians who had associated with Oxford during his time at Venice and Venetians resident in England.[2] These enquiries established that Oxford, whom Cuoco confirms was fluent in Latin and Italian, followed Catholic requirements at Venice by eating fish on Fridays and fast days and attending Mass at San Giorgio dei Greci, the Greek Orthodox Church situated east of St Mark's where Mass was always said in Greek.[3] But, back in England, although he allowed religious freedom to two male servants who were Catholics, he was happy to eat meat on Fridays and fast days. He also permitted Cuoco to attend Catholic Mass in the households of the ambassadors of France and Portugal. Cuoco explained that his singing in the choir of Santa Maria Formosa had prompted Oxford to invite him to accompany him back to England where he sang before Queen Elizabeth.[4] Cuoco had then returned to Venice because some merchants feared that he would be *pervertido* (corrupted in a spiritual sense) by being converted to Protestantism and one of them, a Milanese merchant, Christopholo da Monte, paid 25 ducats for his secret embarkation on a ship to Flanders with a group of Italian merchants. After Oxford invited him to come to England he had sought advice from his parents who approved of this plan but soon afterwards they died of the plague which had begun to ravage Venice.[5] Hence, Oxford had effectively saved young Cuoco's life by taking him into his household at Venice on the Thursday (1 March) before Lent and then leaving Venice with him on the following Monday of Carnival (5 March).

Cuoco's information about Venetian residents in London is especially interesting. The Inquisition was concerned to establish whether anyone in England had encouraged him to read prohibited (i.e., Protestant) books or to teach him 'the doctrine of heretics'. In response, Cuoco stated that there had been and listed the following Venetians:

A man called Master Alexandro,[6] I think he has been banned from Venice on account of religion. Another one, Ambroso da Venezia who is a music-player of the Queen of England: he has two children and has got married there, even though, as I have heard, his wife lives here in Venice and, so they say, he used to send money to her.[7] And there are also five Venetian brothers who are musicians of the Queen and play the flute and the viola;[8] and there is a

---

[1] Archivio di Stato di Venezia, Savi all'Eresai, Santo Uffizio, b. 41. Magri, 'Orazio v Nelson', pp. 6–11, provides the most accurate transcription of this document, written in Latin (the questions) and Venetian dialect (Cuoco's responses). She confirms that the boy's name was Cuoco (not Cogno, Coquo or Cocco). http://www.oxford-shakespeare.com/DocumentsOther/Archivio_di_Stato_1577.pdf.

[2] Information about Venetians living in England is repeated in the margins of the document.

[3] Magri, 'Oxford and the Greek Church in Venice', p. 1.

[4] *Santa Maria Formosa.

[5] His father was Francesco Cuoco, an 'altarist' (probably a sacristan) at *Santa Marina. Early cases of the plague between July 1575 and February 1576 were kept secret and the Carnival was allowed to take place during February–March 1576. In summer 1576 the plague rapidly spread and lasted until early 1577, killing c.50,000 citizens, about one-third of Venice's inhabitants.

[6] Identified as 'Alexander Forlan' in the margin of the document.

[7] Identified in the margin as 'Ambrosio da Venezia, a musician of the Queen of England; he has two children and has got married'.

[8] Identified in the margin as 'Five Venetian brothers who are musicians of the Queen: they play the flute and viola'. These were the Bassano brothers (Alvise, Anthony, Jasper, John and Baptista), the sons of Jeronimo Bassano, whose family was originally from Bassano del Grappa. Another brother, Jacomo, remained based in Venice. For Antony Bassano's will (1574), see TNA PROB 11/56/512. See also Lasocki and Prior, *The Bassanos*, pp. 17–31, 143–238; and Ongaro, 'New Documents', pp. 409–16.

Venetian gentlewoman from Ca' Malipiero who has a school and teaches reading and the Italian language.[1]

Oxford delighted in perfumed jerkins and embroidered gloves and was widely mocked as the embodiment of the dandified and effeminate Italianate gentlemen. Gabriel Harvey (1545–1630), a noted scholar of Italian literature and close associate of Philip Sidney (**item 22**, **Plate 17** and **Figure 17**), paid Oxford conventional compliments in dedicating to him the fourth volume of his panegyrical collection, *Gratulationes Valdenses* (1578), but also circulated a vicious satire, 'Speculum Tuscanismi', deriding him as an Italianate Englishmen, clad in a 'little apish hatte, cowched fast to the pate, like an oyster' and as 'delicate in speech, queynte in araye: conceited in all poyntes ... a passing singular odde man'.[2] In August 1579 Oxford insulted Sidney in a dispute over the use of a tennis court at Greenwich, calling him a 'puppy'. Queen Elizabeth insisted upon the protocol of Oxford's superior rank, forbidding them a duel and ordering Sidney to defer, leading to rumours that the increasingly erratic Oxford was planning to have Sidney murdered.[3]

After his return from Italy, it was rumoured that Oxford remained sympathetic towards Catholicism, but in December 1580 he denounced his formerly close friends Henry Howard (1540–1614), Charles Arundel (d. 1587) and Francis Southwell (d. 1581) as Catholic sympathizers. However, Oxford was himself imprisoned in the Tower of London for a few days.[4] On 23 March 1581 one of Queen Elizabeth's maids of honour, Anne Vavasour (fl. 1580–1621), gave birth to a son, Edward Vere (d. 1629), and Oxford found himself in the Tower once more because she had been his mistress since about 1579. Oxford was released to house arrest on June 1581 and reconciled with his wife Anne (Cecil) but in March 1582 he fought in the street with Anne Vavasour's uncle, Sir Thomas Knyvet (1545–1622), with both men being wounded. The enmity continued for over a year, resulting in the deaths of retainers on both sides. Oxford's first wife died of a fever of 5 June 1588 and he was married again in about January 1592 to Elizabeth Trentham, who gave birth to his only legitimate son and heir, Henry de Vere (1593–1635), who succeeded him as eighteenth Earl of Oxford.

Unpredictable and financially profligate, but also intelligent and cultured, Edward de Vere's reputation seemed to embody the weaknesses represented in *The Scholemaster* by Roger Ascham in the character of the Italianate Englishman and youthful frequenter of Venice. More positively, he is now recognized as a skilled lyric poet and literary patron, attracting twenty-eight literary dedications between 1564 and 1599. Since the 1920s he has also become the focus of claims to have been the author of poems and plays written by William Shakespeare.

---

[1] Ca' Malipiero is situated in Campo Santa Maria Formosa. The Malipieros were one of the most distinguished families in Venice.

[2] Spenser, *Three ... letters*, sig. E2.

[3] Nelson, *Monstrous Adversary*, pp. 195–200, 230. Sidney, *Correspondence*, I, pp. 914, 921–5. On 27 January 1580 Arthur Throckmorton (**item 27**) noted in his diary that Oxford had challenged Sidney to a duel, leading to his confinement in his chambers at Greenwich until 11 February. Rowse, *Ralegh and the Throckmortons*, pp. 77–8.

[4] Nelson, *Monstrous Adversary*, p. 249.

# 24.   1575/7 – SIR JOHN NORTH AND HIS SERVANT HUGH LOCHARD

**Sir John North** (*c.*1550/51–97), was born at Kirtling, Cambridgeshire, the second son of Roger North, second Baron North (1531–1600). His mother Winifred (d. 1578) was the widow of Sir Henry Dudley (d. 1544), the son of John Dudley, Duke of Northumberland. His father was a close ally of Northumberland's son, Robert Dudley, Earl of Leicester (**Plate 23**). John North matriculated at Peterhouse, Cambridge (Fynes Moryson's college, **item 33**) but then migrated to Trinity College in 1567 when his tutor, John Whitgift, later Archbishop of Canterbury, became its master. He was awarded an MA in 1572 and was admitted in the same year to Gray's Inn.

In May 1575 North was granted a licence to travel on the continent for two years and he left England in the second week of September, arriving in Italy in October.[1] On 5 September 1575, as he was about to leave England, he began to keep a personal journal (Oxford, Bodleian Library, MS Add. C.193), first noting the expenses 'for my voyage and in the same' (f. 2r).[2] With a small entourage he travelled through Bruges and Antwerp and then down the Rhine through Germany and Swiss territories. He encountered a suspected outbreak of the plague at Mantua and arrived at Padua on 7 November where he lodged at the 'I[n]n of the Son, wher the lodginge was good and the fare lykewise' (f. 16r) before renting a room in the town.

At this point the diary breaks off and does not begin again, near the back of the volume, until two years later when he was leaving Venice. Significantly, this entry in his diary was made in Italian, in North's italic hand (commonly adopted at Padua by English students) rather than the traditional English secretary form used in the earlier part of his diary:

> Settembrio, alli 24. del'qual'mese, a 6 hore della mattina, io mi partiva da Venetia con due gentilhuomini Venetiani fratelli chi s'hanno il nome Octtaviano Buon, & Philippo Buon, & con un altro Grego mercatante di Zante, Levantino. P[er] la gondola – 3£ (f. 88v)

> [Translation] September, on the 24 of this month, at six o'clock in the morning, I left Venice with two Venetian gentlemen, brothers with the names Ottaviano Buon & Philippo Buon, and with another Grego, a merchant of Zante, a Levantine, for the gondola – 3£[3]

North had clearly put considerable efforts into his acquisition of both spoken and written Italian and he was proud, for example, that on the road to Calais a group of

[1] TNA E 157/1.

[2] This analysis draws extensively from John Gallagher's article, 'The Italian London of John North', pp. 88–131. See also his *Learning Languages*, pp. 75, 177–8.

[3] This habit of writing in Italian was also adopted in 1580–81 when the French essayist Michel de Montaigne was travelling in Italy. Montaigne saw it as a means of practising his linguistic skills in the language rather than producing a fluently polished account of his observations. Gallagher, 'The Italian London of John North', p. 91.

soldiers mistook him for an Italian national (f. 75v). After arriving back in England he continued the diary, keeping records, still in sometimes idiosyncratic Italian, of his daily activities at London, the royal court and his Cambridgeshire home.

No information has been located to explain why North did not continue his diary once he arrived in the Veneto. It is possible that he simply gave up keeping it once he became immersed in the academic and social life of Padua and Venice. Alternatively, he may have chosen to keep another record of his time in Italy in a different (now lost) manuscript. More dramatically, the disastrous outbreak of the plague at Venice in 1575–7 may have disrupted or even curtailed many of his planned educational activities during his continental itinerary, including his language learning and diary keeping.

Fortunately, several other records survive which testify to North's experiences in the Veneto and his later involvements with Italians living in England. His diary refers to 'S[ignor] Jacomo', namely, Giacomo Castelvetro (1546–1616), a well-travelled humanist writer and educator from whom North hired a horse for his journey from Brescia to Mantua (f. 11r). Castelvetro accompanied North on some of his continental travels but returned to Italy in 1578 after the death of his father. However, his Protestantism made it dangerous for him to remain there and in 1580 he took up residence in England where he sought patronage from Philip Sidney (**item 22**, **Plate 17** and **Figure 17**) and Sir Francis Walsingham (**Plate 24**).

Castelvetro maintained personal contact with the North family. He sent, with a handwritten dedication, a copy of Juan Gonzáles de Mendoza's *L'historia del gran regno della China* (1587) to North's father, stating that he was writing 'in casa del Signor suo figliuolo mio padrone' (in the house of the Signor your son my patron').[1] In 1592 Castelvetro was appointed as Italian tutor to King James VI of Scotland and his queen, Anne of Denmark. He also continued his peripatetic lifestyle in search of employment and patronage, travelling extensively in Denmark, Sweden, France, Switzerland and Germany. In 1598 he returned to Italy and took up residence at Venice where he edited manuscripts on contemporary Italian poetry and fiction for the printer G. B. Ciotto.[2]

Following his return to England in November 1577 North volunteered to fight with the Dutch but had returned to England by 1580. Probably in the same year, he married Dorothy (d. 1618), the daughter of Sir Valentine Dale, then Master of Requests and formerly the English Ambassador to France, who had assisted Edward de Vere, Earl of Oxford (**item 23**), when he was passing through Paris on his way to Strasbourg and Italy.

North assiduously maintained his Venetian contacts during the 1570s and 1580s and had books shipped from Venice as well as buying Italian works in England, including in 1578 (f. 41r) John Florio's English-Italian language guide, *First Fruites*.[3] He also exchanged letters with Jerome Sapcot(e) ('S[ignor] Gieron: Sapcote', f. 11r), the son of John Sapcot, an MP (1559) and recusant, who was first recorded at Padua in 1565 and lived in the Veneto during the 1570s and 1580s. He wrote a legal textbook, *Ad primus leges Digestorum de verborum et rerum significatione* (Venice, 1579), dedicated to Giovanni Grimani, Patriarch of Aquileia. Jerome Sapcot appears to have married and

---

[1] Copy in Columbia University, Butler Library (B899.63 G581).

[2] In 1609 Giacomo Castelvetro's brother Lelio was burnt at the stake as a heretic at Venice and he was himself imprisoned by the Inquisition in 1611. He was only freed at the intervention of the English Ambassador, Sir Dudley Carleton.

[3] Gallagher, 'The Italian London of John North', pp. 94–5.

settled permanently at Venice and an Anthony Sapcot, very likely Jerome's son, supplied Dudley Carleton with *objets d'art* from Venice between 1618 and 1620.[1] North's sustained interest in Italian was presumably also supported by his father's brother, Thomas North, best known as the translator (from the French) of Plutarch's *Lives* but also in 1570 of an Italian tract, *La moral filosophia del Doni*, dedicated to Robert Dudley, Earl of Leicester (**Plate 23**), whom he described as one who 'understandeth the Italian tongue very well, and can perfitely speake it' (sig. A3v). He was also willing to assist members of the Italian community in London, as illustrated by a series of letters (10 October 1585 to 27 January 1586) in which he requested that the MP Sir William More (d. 1600) should extend a lease in Blackfriars for the Italian fencing master Rocco Bonetti (d. 1587) which Bonetti had purchased from the poet and dramatist John Lyly (1553–1606), the private secretary of Edward de Vere, Earl of Oxford (**item 23**).[2]

His nephew, John North, was also closely associated with Leicester, after whom he named his eldest son Dudley (1582–1667) since Leicester was his godfather. Leicester was one of the major patrons of Italian émigrés and refugees in England and his household became a popular centre for academics and courtiers interested in Anglo-Italian affairs. Along with Sir Francis Walsingham and Philip Sidney (**item 22**, **Plate 17** and **Figure 17**), Leicester was widely praised for his interests in Italian scholarship, culture and politics. Elizabeth Goldring explains:

> he took under his wing expatriate Italians, many of whom were Protestants seeking refuge from the terrors of the Inquisition and the Counter-Reformation. As a result Leicester's household became a focal point for Italians living in Elizabethan England. Pietro Bizzarri, the Cambridge-educated historian, and Alberico Gentili, the Oxford-educated jurist, were perhaps the most intellectually distinguished members of this group. But others who benefited from the earl's patronage include the calligrapher Petruccio Ubaldini; the writers Giacomo Concio and John Florio; Queen Elizabeth's Italian tutor Giambattista Castiglione; and the riding master Claudio Corte, who helped Leicester – appointed master of the horse at Elizabeth's accession – to introduce French and Italian Renaissance equestrian practices at the English court.[3]

The philosopher Giordano Bruno (1548–1600) commended Walsingham, Sidney, and especially Leicester, as 'so praised from the hearts of generous Italian souls, who were received especially by him with particular favour (accompanying that of his Lady), and were always befriended [by him]'.[4] The London-based Genoese banker, Benedetto (Benedict) Spinola, worked closely with Leicester and his circle of Italian and English associates. In 1577 North borrowed money from him and relied on Spinola's international network to bring home his books and possessions from Venice via Antwerp. He also probably utilized his connections to import the wines and luxury fabrics recorded in his diary.[5] Benedetto's brother, Pasquale, moved between London and Venice as their commercial transactions required and provided finance to both the Earl of Oxford and John North while they were at Venice. North's diary refers to him, in a casual attempt to disguise his identity, as 'S[ignor] P*sq*l Sp*n*l*' (f. 84v).

[1] Woolfson, *Padua*, pp. 268–9.
[2] Surrey History Centre, LM/COR/3/382–3, ff. 387–8.
[3] Goldring, *Robert Dudley, Earl of Leicester*, p. 17.
[4] Gallagher, 'The Italian London of John North', p. 97.
[5] TNA, C 2/Eliz/N3/59.

North was with Leicester's entourage when he accompanied the Duke of Anjou to the Netherlands for his installation as Governor-General and he served in the Low Countries until 1584, amassing large debts with Dutch merchants. He was elected MP for Cambridgeshire in 1584 and served in the Parliaments of 1586 and 1588. He was in Ireland in 1595–97, involved in suppressing the Earl of Tyrone's uprising, and was knighted there in April 1596. He returned to the Low Countries in 1597 where he died on 5 June.[1] Possessing a combative nature, North was never entirely successful as a soldier or military leader and was prone to alienating more experienced officers.[2]

It is frustrating that the missing section of North's diary would have covered his time at Padua and Venice, not least because it coincides with one of the most serious outbreaks of plague at Venice during the sixteenth century, during which approximately one-third of the city's population died. However, North's quarrelsome nature inadvertently provides some interesting information about this period, due to an acrimonious lawsuit from the mid-1590s between North and his former servant, Hugh Lochard, who had accompanied him on his continental itinerary.[3] Lochard attested that North had been resident outside Venice when the plague was most virulent but on three separate occasions he had sent Lochard into the city to obtain money from a Venetian merchant. The first time was reputedly when 500 people per day were dying, the second when this figure had escalated to 700 and the third when the morality rates had reached 900 per day. The relevant section of Lochard's account is reproduced below, providing a rare (and possibly unique) account of an English traveller to Venice during the terrifying days of the 1575–77 outbreak of the plague when Lochard personally witnessed the multitude of 'dead bodyes carried uppon heapes in barges'.[4]

## Hugh Lochard's Description of Venice During the Plague of 1575–7[5]

Theruppon the [plaintiff, i.e., North] undertakinge a course to traveyle beyonde the seas *the* defend*ant* [Lochard] was willingly content to [*page damaged*] to doe *the* [plaintiff] the best service he colde, where the defend*ant* served *the* [plaintiff] about twoe yeares, enduring some harde wronge*s* & abuses at his hands & und*er* goeinge verye extreme p*er*ils

---

[1] For Sir John North's will, see TNA PROB 11/90/25 (8 June 1597). A possible portrait is at The Vyne, Basingstoke, Hampshire: http://www.nationaltrustcollections.org.uk/object/719398; https://artuk.org/discover/artworks/sir-john-north-15511683-mp-220149.

[2] *ODNB*, s.v.

[3] Although Hugh Lochard is described here as 'English', the Lochard family was probably of Scottish ancestry. A Hugh Lochard was born at Hereford in 1562 and may have been a relative rather than this Hugh (since he would only have been about 13 or 14 during the events at Venice described in this litigation). This Hugh had previously been an usher at his brother Richard's fencing school, attended by John North.

[4] For a detailed eyewitness account of the 1575–7 outbreak of the plague at Venice by the notary Rocco Benedetti, see Chambers and Pullan, *Venice, A Documentary History*, pp. 117–19. I am grateful to Alex Bamji for this reference.

[5] TNA, C 2/Eliz/N3/59, 'Hugh Lochard's First Rejoinder, 5 June 1595'. Parts of this document are badly damaged and creased. It comprises North's original statement (in January 1595), Lochard's rejoinder (5 June 1595), followed by shorter responses by North and Lochard (neither dated). Paragraphing has been added to assist the reader. I am grateful to John Gallagher for allowing me to consult his transcript of this document. http://discovery.nationalarchives.gov.uk/details/r/C5704912.

for *the* [plaintiff] good & avayle ffor duringe *the* [plaintiff] beinge in *the* [*page damaged*] venetians and his monye faylinge & not knowinge otherwyse to be furnyshed, then from one Seign*or* Pasquell Spindelo[1] a venetian march*a*unte whoe then was dwellinge & abydinge in *the* City of Venyse where was soe [ex? *page damaged*] and plauge [*sic*], *that* the fame & reporte was co*m*men, *that* ther died every daye fyve hundred p*er*sons, Soe as without inevytable occasions few or none durst nor wolde travayle thither, yet *the* defend*ant* uppon *the* [plaintiff] heavy [cheare?] for want of [*page damaged*] willingly contente to goe to venyce for a Supply of his wante w*hich* accordingly he did & havinge receaved monye from *the* said march*a*nte Seign*or* Spindelo after some staye & enforcement to lodge in *the* said city of Venyse [*page damaged*] to the [plaintiff] lyeinge at Peove Saccoe[2] beinge (as *the* defend*ant* reme*m*breth) aboute sixtene myles from venyce and deliv*er*ed *the* [plaintiff] the monye.

And shortly after *the* [plaintiff] beinge agayne in distres throughe lacke of monye & [knowe not? *page damaged*] without supply from the said Seign*or* Spyndelo whoe still remaynde in Venyce wher *the* plauge was increased Soe *that* there died by reporte about Seaven hundred p*er*sons in a daye, The defend*ant* *the* seconde tyme [*page damaged*] notwithstandinge *that* greate & extreame daunger where *the* defend*ant* was forced to staye twoe or three dayes or he colde receave monye wher he founde lodginge hearde to get & verye daungerous & much to his [*page damaged*] receaved monye the defend*ant* retorned & deliv*er*ed it to *the* [plaintiff] lyeinge then at Castell ffranco[3] within *the* territoryes of *the* venetians. And *the* [plaintiff] shortlie after beinge *the* thirde tyme in want of monye & makinge [gr? *page damaged*] he knewe not what to doe unlesse he were releaved, w*hich* he knew not how to pro*c*ure but only from Venyce, & from *the* foresaid March*a*nte Seign*or* Spyndelo, where he was usually remayninge & the plauge & infection [*page damaged*] soe as *the* fame was *that* there died daylie about nyne hundreth yet *the* defend*ant* tenderinge much *the* state of *the* [plaintiff] (notwithstandinge *that* the defend*ant* himself lacked noe monye, as was well knowen to *the* [plaintiff] [*page damaged*] some monye of the defend*ant* for *that* the [plaintiff] had by some meanes (unknowen to the defend*ant*) discovered & founde out *that* the defend*ant* had forty crownes in his portmantowe)

The defend*ant* adventured *the* thirde tyme [*page damaged*] season to goe to Venyce to *the* said Seign*or* Spyndelo for monye to supply *the* [plaintiff] wante, where the defend*ant* founde the saide Seign*or* Spyndelo shutt upp in his howse, & not p*er*mittinge the purveyor of his owne [victualls? *page damaged*] & soe by his owne reporte he had remayned by *the* space of six weecks, where alsoe the defend*ant* sawe the deade bodyes carried uppon heapes in barges, & *the* men appoynted to carry out *the* deade bodyes did were [*page damaged*] *that* they might be knowen & avoyded where alsoe *the* defend*ant* colde get noe lodginge, but was forced to hier a howse for to staye in untill he might receave the monye he was sente for & forced to lye uppon the flore & to goe into *the* markett [*page damaged*] buye his owen victuals & dresse it himselfe during *the* tyme of

[1] Pasquale Spinola, the brother of the London-based Genoese banker Benedetto Spinola. See pp. 219, 220 n. 2, 225 and 227 n. 1.
[2] Piove di Sacco, about 25 km south-west of Venice.
[3] Castelfranco Veneto, about 40 km north-west of Venice.

his abodde there, which was by the space of ten or twelve dayes, aboute which tyme the defendant havinge receaved such monye as the [plaintiff] sente for the said Seignor Spyndelo knowinge that noe man mighte passe from any place infected with the plauge, unto any other cytie or towne that was cleare uppon payne of death wept & said he sholde never see the defendant agayne & that he wolde not undertake the carriage [page damaged] to the [plaintiff] for a grete some of monye, notwithstandinge the defendant confidently undertooke to carry the monye to the [plaintiff] which accordingly he did perform.

And havinge receaved his lettres of [? illegible] to passe, the defendant came to Mastryck,[1] the only waye to [page damaged] venyce unto Castell ffranco, where the [plaintiff] wherfore the necessitie of passage & for that the saide towne of Mastrick helde of the state of venyce the defendant mighte passe throughe there but none wolde gyve the defendant lodginge & if [page damaged] wandring person not knowinge whether to goe they used to execute them wherby he was forced to goe into a dutchmans howse whose famely was newly come from the spittle howse,[2] for that that not longe before his [fa– page damaged] with the plauge & for the same cause [? illegible] his goodes [? illegible], where the defendant caused his supper to be prepared & pretended he must lye els where. But after supper he was forced to tell the hoaste that he muste lye, & that he wolde [page damaged] was as good for him to die in his howse if he wolde [stayve?] with him as to be hanged if he were takin in the towne, wheruppon at length the hoast consented to lodge him which he did, but in a place under a payre of [stayres?] defendant thinketh never any man had lien before, but it was lykelie that many a dogge had been lodged there, which the defendant afterwards did shewe the [plaintiff] in their travaile

And the defendant pleased the hoast by spendinge much money there [page damaged] the valew of x[s] or xv[s] for his dyet and lodginge that nighte, althought the [plaintiff] never allowed the defendant above xii[d] a daye, And by that means the hoaste the next daye made the defendant to be acquaynted with the [Sou? page damaged] men at the gates on whom the defendant was forced to bestowe much coste at Breakfast & dynner and often drinckinge and all at his owne coste without anye allowance had at anye time of the Playntiffe [page damaged] the defendant at lenght havinge Libertie to walke out of the Towne to take the ayre and [vewe?] of the feilds the defendant departed quiet from the towne But if he had otherwise attempted to have done And that it had ben knowen [page damaged] the towne comming so latelie from Venice, he should have byn executed, for the defendant had see[n] such executions done before his face, But the defendant thus passed into the wild feilds & knewe not whether to goe, for the escape of [this? page damaged] an other And firste the defendant buried his Lettres of passe which he had of his beinge & departure from Venyce leste they beinge founde about him he should streight waies be executed then beinge in the feilds he there [wandred? page damaged] [faded word] two or three dayes without cominge to anye towne or village without eatinge or drinckinge or by havinge any other lodginge then was to be had in the fields.

[1] *Mastryck*: perhaps Mestre.
[2] *spittle house*: institution for the indigent or diseased; a lazar house.

And at lenght the defendant seeinge two poore men [dytching?] [page damaged] Castylle ffranco where the [plaintiff] was and he made his [mone?] to them pretendinge he had loste his Pursse & that he came newlie into that countrye, & was a meare stranger and had never byn at Venice (for he was [drin? page damaged] they refreshed the defendant with their victualls & on of the Laborers for a good peece of Monye (how much certeynlie the defendant now remembreth not went to the next towne or village procured a passe in his owne name which [page damaged] that he [illegible] the same as if he had byn the self same partie, might goe to anye towne, which havinge gotten, the defendant came to Treviso & there staied certayne daies & after came with a passe from there to the gates of the towne of Castill franco, where beinge knowen by on of the [Soldiers? page damaged] he would not suffer the defendant to come into the towne, sayinge your master (meaninge the [plaintiff] had sayde how he had sent him to Venice and that if he should be taken there were no [waye?] but death.

And [therupon the? page damaged] advised the defendant to take him the passe and that the defendant should goe through the towne and he would followe And yf anie man stayed the defendant he should saye the Souldier had his passe which was done And the defendant [page damaged] the defendant of [pinge?] the towne caused that the Plaintiff should have notis of the defendant beinge abrode, wherof advertysed he came and received the monye & left the defendant to shifte for his lyffe And the defendant [page damaged] the foresaide passe went to an other towne about tenne or twelfe myles distante and there stayed untill the tyme was expired that the defendant might lawfullie goe to anye towne by the passe of the [towne? page damaged] the defendant did lye. And yet besides, the defendants passe was examined by a Justice of that countrye And the defendant was forced to lye there at his owne chardge except after the rate of xij$^d$ by the daye [page damaged] [these?] damages the [plaintiff] sent the defendant to Padova in the territory of the venetians for certeyn things there lefte where the plauge was so violent at that time that the defendant passinge from the gate of the towne called [cada longu?] [page damaged] called Plazza della [? illegible] beinge about one mile in leght and mett not anie person but onlie three persons being such as guided twoo Carts loden with dead Carcasses of the people of the Cytie and notwithstanding [as? page damaged] [ad?]ventures the [plaintiff] delt so unkindlie with the defendant as he put him out of his service and turned him to shift for himself at twelve a clock of the night beinge in a strange countrye as afore is declared, for no other cause [page damaged] than for that the defendant had advysed him not to use a Basse & beggery dutch man soe famyliarly as he did but rather to make choyse of assocyates worthy of him selfe & the defendant.

Thus travayling out of service in Italy, did at vicenza[1] in the territory of the venetians [by the? page damaged] [Englysh?] gent & others namly m$^r$ Edward Umpton & Sir Henrye Umpton[2] that now is, & one Doctor [delabere?][3] unto whom beinge well knowen, the said mr Umpton wolde uppon the defendant comminge backe unto him gyve the defendant enterteynment [page damaged] as the [plaintiff] was a noble mans sonne he

[1] Vicenza, about 60 km west of Venice.
[1] See **items 20** and **25** for Edward and Sir Henry Umpton (Unton). Lochard's reference confirms that the brothers were then travelling together in Italy.
[1] Unidentified.

wolde use him well & loath such a matter sholde fall out, for *that* it was saied in these countryes, *that* amongste all countrymen Inglyshe men colde not agree amongst themselves And uppon m^r [Umpton[s]? *page damaged*] and his le*tt*re to the [plaintiff] there was an agreement made betwixte the [plaintiff] & the defend*ant* and the defend*ant* served him in those p*a*rtes beyonde the seas untill his returne into Ingland w*hich* was aboute twoe yeares[.]

# 25.   *c.*1575 – SIR HENRY UNTON

**Sir Henry Unton (Umpton)** (*c.***1558–1596**) (**Plate 25**), was born at either Ascott-under-Wychwood or at another of his family's houses at Wadley, near Faringdon, Berkshire, the second son of Sir Edward Unton (*d.* 1582) (**item 25**) and his wife Anne Dudley (1538–88), eldest daughter of Edward Seymour, Duke of Somerset, and the widow of John Dudley, Earl of Warwick. His elder brother Edward accompanied Robert Devereux, Earl of Essex, on his Portugal Voyage (1589) but died at Plymouth on his return. He studied at Oriel College, Oxford (BA 1573), and enrolled as a law student of the Middle Temple in 1575. Soon afterwards, he undertook a continental tour, although no written records of his experiences have survived, other than brief incidental details.[1] It is known that he travelled through the French Midi and met Henri de Montmorency-Damville (1534–1614), the governor of Languedoc, later Duke of Montmorency (1579) and Constable of France (1593). As detailed below, he visited Venice and Padua and matriculated at Basle University in 1577. Hugh Lochard's complaint against Sir John North (**item 24**) also makes clear that Henry Unton was then travelling in Italy with his elder brother Edward.

The exact date when Henry returned home is unknown, although in 1580 he was in England and married the wealthy Wiltshire heiress, Dorothy Wroughton (d. 1634). When his father Sir Edward died on 16 September 1582 his feckless elder brother Edward (d. 1589) was in Italy and the funeral may have been delayed for two months in the hope that he could return home. If so, this plan was foiled when Edward was seized by the Inquisition as he was travelling from Padua and was imprisoned at Milan. He was only freed through the efforts of his brother Henry who travelled via Paris to Lyons, then the axis of Franco-Italian relations, with letters of recommendation from Sir Francis Walsingham and Sir Henry Cobham (1537–92), the English Ambassador to France. Henry spent three months abroad negotiating for his brother's release. An agent called Pyne promised to extricate Edward but after the expenditure of over 300 crowns he was still imprisoned in late April 1583. Solomon Aldred, the Catholic papal agent who had been sent to Lyons to negotiate with Henry, either grew more sympathetic – or accepted bribes – and Edward was eventually released in a sickly state and under suspicion of having converted to Catholicism.[2]

Philip Sidney's uncle, Robert Dudley, Earl of Leicester (**Plate 23**) – the brother-in-law of Unton's father – supported Henry's early parliamentary career as MP for New Woodstock (1584–5) and Henry also served as Oxfordshire's Deputy-Lieutenant (1587–93). In June 1586 he crossed to the Low Countries and was at Zutphen where on 22 September 1586 Sidney received his fatal wound. Unton was knighted by Leicester on 29 September and was one of the twelve knights who escorted Sidney's coffin at his

---

[1] A travel licence was issued to Sir Henry and his father Sir Edward in September 1574. TNA E 157/1.
[2] Strong, *Cult of Elizabeth*, pp. 91–2.

funeral at St Paul's, London, in February 1587. He was appointed as Ambassador to France in July 1591 and formed a productive working relationship with King Henri IV during the French civil wars. He returned to the English court in June 1592 but was reappointed as Ambassador to France in December 1595 with the virtually impossible mission of preventing a peace treaty between France and Spain. However, he died of a fever during the siege of Spanish forces at La Fère in north-west France on 23 March 1596. His body was transported back to England aboard a mourning ship with black sails for burial at Faringdon church on 8 July. His widow erected a lavish monument there (completed 1606) which was severely vandalized in 1646 during the English Civil War. Some surviving fragments, including the kneeling figure of Lady Unton, were later installed in the west transept of the church.[1]

Sir Henry Unton was an accomplished linguist, probably speaking proficient Italian and French.[2] His library at Wadley House was inventoried (11 May 1596) after his death and contained 220 volumes: 'many books of diverse sortes, to the number of ccxx', although no more specific details are supplied. It is likely that he purchased some volumes during his visit during the mid-1570s to Venice and Padua.[3] His time there is primarily known from a large (74 cm × 163.2 cm, oil on panel) 'narrative' painting (**Plate 25**), now in the National Portrait Gallery, London, commissioned from an unknown artist by Sir Henry's widow, Lady Dorothy.[4] At the centre of this memorial portrait, Sir Henry is shown half-length seated and writing at a table with a cameo of Henri IV (not as previously thought Queen Elizabeth) visible on it. This image is surrounded by a sequential narrative of his private life and public career, flanked by the figures of Fame with a trumpet and bearing a coronet and Death as a *memento mori* with an hourglass in, respectively, the top right-hand and left-hand corners of the picture. The scenes comprise (anticlockwise from the bottom right):

1. Henry as an infant (*c.*1558), held by his mother, Anne Seymour, formerly Countess of Warwick, in their family house at Ascott-under-Wychwood.
2. At Oriel College, Oxford (BA, 1573).
3. Travelling via the Alps to Venice and Padua (*c.*1575).
4. Serving with the Earl of Leicester (**Plate 23**) and Sir Philip Sidney (**Plate 17** and **Figure 17**) in the Low Countries (1586), with Nijmegen in the background.
5. His embassy to Henri IV at Coucy Le Fère (1595–96).
6. Sir Henry on his deathbed, tended by probably the royal physician, Andreas Laurentius (1558–1609), sent by Henri IV.
7. His body being brought back to England aboard a black pinnace.
8. His hearse on the way to Wadley House, Faringdon, Oxfordshire.
9. (*centre right*) Sir Henry's life at Wadley House: scenes depicted him sitting in his

---

[1] *ODNB*, s.v. Woolfson, *Padua*, p. 279.

[2] His ambassadorial duties during the 1580s and 1590s confirm his fluency in French. One of his travelling companions when abroad, Charles Merbury, commended Unton's knowledge of languages and thanked him for help in compiling a collection of Italian proverbs in his *Discourse of Royal Monarchy* (1581).

[3] Nichols, *Unton Inventories*, p. 3, Leicestershire Record Office, 26D53/2583.

[4] In her will (1634) Lady Unton left 'the Picture of Sir Henry Unton' to her niece, Lady Unton Dering. This individual was Unton Gibbes, the third wife (from 1629) of Sir Edward Dering (1598–1644). Nichols, *Unton Inventories*, p. 34. Strong, 'Sir Henry Unton and his Portrait', pp. 53–76.

study (*top*); talking with learned divines (*bottom left*), a quartet of viols accompanying a boy singer (*above left*); presiding at a banquet with musicians and a masque of Mercury and Diana, accompanied by a train of maiden huntresses. His funeral procession from Wadley passes a group of the poor and lame lamenting his death.

10. Faringdon Church with his funeral (8 July 1596) in progress and showing (*foreground*) an early design for his monument with Unton recumbent and the figure of his widow kneeling.[1]

Recent research, using X-radiography and infrared reflectography of the painting and its wooden panels, has suggested that it may have been first intended as a temporary memorial to Sir Henry Unton and placed on display in Faringdon Church until the stone monument commissioned by his widow was completed in 1606.[2]

Finally, Sir Henry Unton may have also travelled as far as Hungary, probably during the late 1570s, because in 1582 a young Hungarian poet, Stephanus Parmenius (1555–83) of Buda, dedicated a Latin poem to him on Psalm 104 which implied that he had first met Unton in Hungary.[3] Parmenius was well known to Richard Hakluyt who provided him with accommodation at Christ Church when he came to Oxford in 1581. Hakluyt introduced him to Sir Humphrey Gilbert when he was organizing his expedition to colonize Newfoundland. Parmenius accompanied him on this voyage and Unton may have been an investor in this venture. Parmenius, sailing aboard the *Swallow*, served as the chronicler of this expedition and wrote a lengthy letter to Richard Hakluyt offering his observations on the landscapes and weather of Newfoundland, in which he also requested news of 'how my patron and master, Henry Unton, doth take my absence'. On 3 August 1583 Gilbert's small fleet of five ships reached St John's Harbour which was already utilized as a seasonal camp for fishermen from England, Portugal, France and Spain. On 2 August they set sail again to explore further south, with Parmenius onboard the *Delight*. However, on 29 August his ship encountered shallow waters, ran aground and broke up with Parmenius among those who drowned. Hakluyt included his single letter from Newfoundland in the 1600 edition of his Principal Navigations.

[1] Strong, 'Sir Henry Unton and his Portrait', pp. 53–76; *Tudor and Jacobean Portraits*, I, pp. 315–19; *The Cult of Elizabeth*, pp. 84–110. Foister, *National Portrait Gallery Collection*, p. 39. Two versions of another portrait of Unton, on which this central portrait is modelled, are at Arundel Castle (Duke of Norfolk) and the Tate Gallery, London. Both were probably painted abroad to commemorate his involvement in the Low Countries campaign.

[2] https://www.npg.org.uk/research/programmes/making-art-in-tudor-britain/case-studies/the-portrait-of-sir-henry-unton-c.-1558-1596.

[3] *Paean ad psalmum Davidis CIV conformatus*, London: 1582.

# 26.  1580 – JAMES CRICHTON

**James ('the Admirable') Crichton (1560–82)** was born in Dumfriesshire, the eldest son of a lawyer Robert Crichton (d. 1582) by his first wife Elizabeth Stewart of Beath, Fife. Robert served Mary Stuart as Lord Advocate and acted for the crown in the prosecution in 1566 of the murderers of David Riccio and in 1567 of James Hepburn, fourth Earl of Bothwell, for the murder of Henry Stuart, Lord Darnley. James was taught as a child by Alexander Hepburn, author of *Grammaticae artis rudimenta* (1568) and perhaps in Edinburgh by the Catholic schoolmaster William Robertson. He matriculated in 1570, aged ten, at the University of St Andrews and graduated BA (1573) and MA (1575). Returning to Edinburgh, he met the scholar George Buchanan, the sternly authoritarian tutor to the boy-king James VI.

For reasons which remain unclear (but seem to have involved disputes with his father) James left Scotland in autumn 1577 and may have travelled to Paris. He later claimed to have served as a soldier in France. By spring 1579 he was at Genoa where he delivered an oration (later printed) on the biennial election of magistrates. By summer 1580 he had moved on to Venice and was taken up by the printer and publisher Aldus Manutius the Younger (1547–97) who vigorously promoted his young protégé's reputation.[1] It was claimed in an anonymous handbill, *Lo scozzese, detto Giacomo Crionio* (Venice, 1580), that Crichton was fluent in ten languages, learned in philosophy, theology, mathematics and astrology, skilled in public debate and adept at the courtly skills of horsemanship, jousting and swordsmanship.

On his twentieth birthday, Crichton was invited (probably through Manutius's influence) to address the Council of Ten which reputedly rewarded him with 100 gold crowns. At the residence of the Patriarch of Aquileia he debated the orthodoxy of the doctrine of the Procession of the Holy Spirit from the Father to the Son. However, he fell ill during the winter of 1580–81 and withdrew to a villa on the River Brenta where he prepared for a display of his disputation skills to be held at Santi Giovanni e Paolo. He was active in debating at Padua in March 1581 where he met Giacomo Luigi Corner (Jacobus Cornelius) and Sperone Speroni, although later in that year he was defeated in a debate by the noted philosopher Jacopo Mazzonin (1548–98). Nevertheless, his erudition and personal accomplishments were greatly admired by Cardinal Guglielmo Sirleto and by summer 1581 he had been invited to Rome by Alfonso Chacón, the historian of the Papacy.

Crichton was invited to debate before Cardinal Luigi d'Este and his secretary, Annibale Capello, commended his skills to the Duke of Mantua's secretary, Aurelio Zibramonti. He was invited to the court at Mantua and was established there by early 1582. He was commissioned to design fortifications for the city and was also sent

---

[1] Manutius the Younger, *Jacomo di Crettone*, 1581; and his 'Dedication', in *Ciceronis de officiis*, 1581.

back to Venice on diplomatic business relating to the proposed marriage of the Duke of Mantua's daughter to Archduke Ferdinand of Austria. He took this opportunity to return to Padua where he renewed his friendship with Giacomo Luigi Corner. He was back in Mantua by May 1582 but then seems to have incurred the enmity of the duke's son and heir, Vincenzo Gonzaga (1562–1612). During the early morning of 3 July Crichton became involved in a brawl with other youths. He killed Vicenzio's companion, Hippolito Lanzone, but Vicenzio then wounded Crichton fatally. He was buried in an unmarked grave in the Church of Santi Simone e Guida, Mantua.[1]

During his time at Venice, Crichton wrote a Latin poem, 'In suum ad urbem Venetam appulsum' (On his Arrival at the City of Venice), published over fifty years later in *Delitiæ poetarum scotorum huius illustrium* (Amsterdam, 1637, pp. 268–72).[2] Like most of Crichton's literary output at Venice, these verses sought to promulgate his scholarly virtuosity and flatter the patronage of Aldus Manutius the Younger. Displaying his knowledge of classical and Mediterranean mythology, the poem begins with his imaginary encounter with a mythical Naiad:[3]

> Whilst far from my fatherland, near the shores of the Adriatic Sea,
> I was overcome with admiration for the city
> Standing high in the midst of the waves,
> To which befall the laws of the savage trident,[4]
> The constant power and the eternal dominion of the open sea.
> I often reflected in my mind on my misfortunes,
> I often moistened my face with dripping tears
> While the divine and worthily venerated shape of a Naiad,
> Once recognised near the banks of the River Eridanos,[5]
> Placed herself before me; a Naiad indeed beloved by the learned Muses.[6]

Addressing Crichton's negative state of mind, triggered by personal problems and fears of *pestis* which had spread across Europe and decimated the population of Venice between 1575 and 1577, the Naiad advises him to take solace by regarding the pestilence as a punishment from the gods for the Promethean hubris of mankind. In particular, the Naiad explains that Crichton should find consolation simply from being at Venice which has now succeeded Athens as the true home of the Muses and from his friendship with Aldus Manutius, whose fame and scholarship has spread throughout the world. Aldus, the nymph promises, will formally present Crichton to the Doge and his Senate so that he can truly appreciate the grandeur and

---

[1] *ODNB*, s.v. Irving, *Scottish Writers*, pp. 258–68. Douglas, *Life*, pp. 3–18.

[2] This volume also contained Crichton's short Latin ode, 'Ad Aldum Manutium', in praise of Aldus Manutius (pp. 272–3).

[3] In Greek mythology the Naiads presided over fresh water and were often associated with the Mediterranaean.

[4] Neptune.

[5] Virgil named the Eridanos as one of the rivers of Hades. It was also associated with the River Po.

[6] See *Venice*, tr. Robert Crawford for a full text of the poem. I am grateful to Robert Crawford for sending me a copy of his translation.

magnificence of the Republic. The poem concludes by lavishly praising the aged Doge Nicolò da Ponte's virtue and affirming that, whilst Diana continues to draw the sun through the sky, the illustrious state of Venice will stand firm forever to the glory of her people.[1]

[1] Nicolò da Ponte (1491–1585) was elected, aged 87, as Doge in 1578. In his youth he had studied philosophy and medicine at Padua and later became a wealthy merchant. Despite his great age, he proved a wise and adept politician, presiding over an extended period of peace, limiting the powers of the clergy and reforming (1581–2) the Council of Ten during Crichton's visit to Venice. Tintoretto's *Triumph of Doge Niccolo da Ponte* adorns the ceiling of the Sala del Maggior Consiglio in the *Palazzo Ducale.

# 27. 1581 – ARTHUR THROCKMORTON

**Arthur Throckmorton (c.1557–1626)** was the second son of Sir Nicholas Throckmorton (1515/16–71) and his wife Anne, daughter of Sir Nicholas Carew (1496–1539). Sir Nicholas had been a childhood companion of Henry VIII and a distinguished diplomat and courtier but in 1538 he fell foul of Thomas Cromwell who staged-managed his trial for his supposed treasonable contacts with Cardinal Pole (**item 11**), leading to his beheading on Tower Hill in March 1539. Negotiating dangerous familial relationships and the vicissitudes of Protestant and Catholic enmities became a key element in Arthur Throckmorton's life. Aged fourteen, he inherited in 1571 extensive estates in Northamptonshire, Buckinghamshire, Oxfordshire, Warwickshire and Worcestershire.[1] In the same year he matriculated from Magdalen College, Oxford, where he was in his own words a 'careless and negligent student', and then proceeded to the Inns of Court. In 1576–7 he joined the embassy to France of Sir Amyas Paulet and in 1578 served briefly in the militia of John Norris in the Netherlands. From 26 July 1580 he undertook two years of travel on the continent, returning home in early 1582. He met up during his itinerary with various other young Englishmen, including at Nuremberg Robert Sidney (the younger brother of Philip Sidney, **item 22**, **Plate 17** and **Figure 17**), Henry Neville and others from the Pelham, Carew, Harmer, Smyth and Savile families.[2] In about 1586 he married Ann Lucas (d. 1629), the daughter of Sir Thomas Lucas of Colchester and one of Queen Elizabeth's ladies-in-waiting. Arthur was returned to Parliament MP for Colchester in November 1588 through the influence of his father-in-law and Sir Francis Walsingham (**Plate 24**).[3] Arthur was also friendly with another visitor to Venice, Edward de Vere, Earl of Oxford (**item 23**).

In autumn 1591 Arthur's sister Elizabeth or 'Bess' (1565–c.1647), a lady-in-waiting to Queen Elizabeth, secretly married Sir Walter Ralegh (c.1552/4–1618) and their son Damerei was born in March 1592 but died as an infant. This relationship prompted a prolonged period of royal disfavour for the couple, resulting in their house arrest and incarceration in the Tower of London. Nevertheless, a close intimacy developed at this period between the Throckmorton and Ralegh families. Arthur and Robert Devereux, Earl of Essex, were party to the Raleghs' secret marriage and both stood as godparents to Damerei.

In 1596, through the influence of Ralegh and Essex, Arthur joined as a gentleman volunteer the controversial Cadiz Expedition, led by Essex and Charles Howard (1536–

---

[1] Arthur became at his majority his father's primary heir because his elder brother William (b. 1553) was mentally and/or physically incapacitated. See The National Archives, PROB 11/54/109, will of Sir Nicholas Throckmorton: http://www.oxford-shakespeare.com/Probate/PROB_11-54_ff_64-5.pdf.

[2] Rowse, *Ralegh and the Throckmortons*, p. 84.

[3] http://www.historyofparliamentonline.org/volume/1558-1603/member/throckmorton-arthur-1557-1626. Rowse, *Ralegh and the Throckmortons*, chapters I–XI.

1624), Earl of Nottingham, and he was knighted by Essex during the voyage. On his return home he resided at his estate at Paulerspury, Northamptonshire. Unlike his Catholic Throckmorton cousins who led the 'Throckmorton Plot' (1583) to assassinate Queen Elizabeth, Arthur remained a loyal Protestant. This plot was led by Sir Francis Throckmorton (1554–84), whose father Sir John (1524–80) was the Catholic brother of Arthur's father, Sir Nicholas. Sir John had served as Master of Requests during Queen Mary's reign and was a witness of her will. Francis and his brother Thomas were travelling on the continent (1580–83) at the same time as Arthur where they had become involved with exiled Catholics and agents of Mary Queen of Scots. After a confession extracted under torture, Francis was tried for high treason and executed in July 1584. Another of Arthur Throckmorton's cousins, Job Throckmorton (1545–61), the son of his father's brother Clement (c.1515–73), became embroiled in 1588/89 in the publication of the Marprelate Tracts which viciously lampooned the Anglican hierarchy of the English Church, especially the Episcopacy.[1] With such dangerous family affiliations, Arthur Throckmorton continued to make determined efforts to present himself as a loyal Protestant. In 1605 he took part in searching the Northamptonshire houses of Catholic suspects in the Gunpowder Plot, including Robert Catesby's.[2] He was seriously ill in 1606 and suffered from poor health during the rest of his life, dying at Paulerspury on 21 July 1626.

During his time in Italy in 1581 Arthur Throckmorton enjoyed extended stays at Padua, Venice and Florence. He recorded his experiences and purchases in the form of a personal diary with an entry for each day (although some days were left blank). Arthur left Vienna on 20 April 1581, having arranged for a trunk of possessions to be carried to Venice separately.[3] Crossing the Alps, his diary records his arduous journey on horseback via Friesach, Villach, Vinzon, Spilenberg and Conegliano. From this town he travelled by coach to Treviso and then on to Padua where he arrived on 4 June and hired a 'chamber with a stable and a garderobe in Borgo Socco [Borgo Zucho] in John Bassan's house'. He spent his time there purchasing books, learning how to play the lute and enhancing his knowledge of the Italian language. He also purchased black silk grogram, white and black taffeta and velvet for his own clothing.[4] While resident at Padua he boarded with one Antonio Milanese and met the Florentine Giacomo[?] Guicciardini and two Jesuit priests, Fathers Fant and Brookes on their way from Rome to Poland.

Arthur Throckmorton arrived at Venice on 29 July and stayed at 'the George' inn (probably The George, often favoured by German travellers).[5] He listed various English visitors to the city, took music and calligraphy lessons and left for Florence on 16 September. Venice was then a likely meeting point, for either temporary transit or

---

[1] Although the authorship of these tracts has never been conclusively determined, Job Throckmorton has been proposed as one of their major authors, along with John Penry (b. 1559, executed 29 May 1593) and John Udall (Uvedale) (c.1560–92).

[2] Arthur's prominent role in hunting down the Gunpowder conspirators was motived not only by loyalty to the Crown but also self-preservation since he was cousin to four of the conspirators and a cousin of the wife of a fifth.

[3] This is probably the trunk he had bought in England for 8s 10d. Rowse, *Ralegh and the Throckmortons*, p. 81.

[4] Rowse, *Ralegh and the Throckmortons*, pp. 89–91. Woolfson, *Padua*, p. 130.

[5] See pp. 241 n. 3 and 249.

prolonged visits, for young Englishmen in northern Italy and those studying at Padua. The city also possessed earlier family associations for the Throckmortons. John Throckmorton (*c.*1529–56) – the great-nephew of Arthur's father Sir Nicholas – was recorded by the Venetian Ambassador as being at Venice in 1551/2. John was perhaps in the company of his kinsman George Throckmorton (*c.*1523–*c.*1573) – the brother of Arthur's father – who was also then at Venice to learn the Italian language and observe its political structures and lucrative trading ventures.[1] On 17 August 1552 the *Council of Ten decreed that 'the armoury halls of this Council and the jewels of the Sanctuary [in St. Mark's church] could be shown to Mr. George Trock-morton, an Englishman'.[2]

In his will, made 26 January 1625, Arthur Throckmorton left to his son-in-law, Sir Thomas Wotton (*c.*1583/87–1630), who in 1608 had married his daughter Mary (*c.*1585–1660) and was an overseer of his will, a great gilt cup engraved with the Carew and Throckmorton arms, presented to his father by Mary Queen of Scots in France. Significantly, another overseer of the will, Sir Thomas Wotton's uncle, Sir Henry Wotton (1568–1639) (**Plate 26**), was left the papers of Arthur's father, Sir Nicholas, concerning his missions to France and Scotland.[3] Sir Henry (**item 32**) had first visited Venice in the early 1590s and again in 1602. He was appointed by King James I as English Ambassador to Venice in 1604 where he remained for the next twenty years (except for 1612–16 and 1619–21). He returned to London early in 1624 and in July was installed as Provost of Eton College. It may be that during the last two years of his life Arthur Throckmorton was able to reminisce about his visit to Venice in 1581 with Sir Henry Wotton who knew the city so well.

Also of special interest is Throckmorton's generous bequest from his personal library of 230 (or more) Latin, Italian, French and Spanish printed books to Magdalen College, Oxford, many of which were probably purchased during his continental itinerary.[4] Thirty of these volumes were printed at Venice and included such titles as Boccaccio, *Decameron* (1538 edition); Castiglione, *The Courtier* (1541); Dante, *Divine Comedy* (1578); Gasparo Contarini, *La republica, e i magistrati di Vinegia* (1551); Giovanni Batista Ramusio, *Terza editione delle nauigationi et viaggi* (1563) and Leandro Alberti, *Descrittione di tutta l'Italia & isole pertinenti ad essa* (1577).[5]

---

[1] http://www.historyofparliamentonline.org/volume/1509-1558/member/throckmorton-george-1523-73-or-later;
http://www.historyofparliamentonline.org/volume/1509-1558/member/throckmorton-john-ii-1529-56.

[2] *CSP Venice, 1534–1554* http://www.british-history.ac.uk/cal-state-papers/venice/vol5/pp370-371# highlight-first. Another member of the family, the staunchly Catholic Michael Throckmorton, was in the service of the exiled Cardinal Pole at Venice and Padua (**item 11**).

[3] http://www.historyofparliamentonline.org/volume/1558-1603/member/throckmorton-arthur-1557-1626. Wotton handed these papers over to King Charles I for the national collection of State Papers. Rowse, *Ralegh and the Throckmortons*, p. 58.

[4] Throckmorton's original bequest could have been larger because the college may have disposed of duplicate copies. His English books were retained by his wife Anne, including some Shakespeare quartos. http://www.magd.ox.ac.uk/libraries-and-archives/treasure-of-the-month/news/throckmorton/.

[5] Some of these volumes may have been acquired at Italian locations other than Venice since Throckmorton was a keen book buyer at both Padua and Ferrara. Also, some of his Venetian imprints were clearly obtained after his continental travels, such as his edition of Ariosto, *Orlando Furioso* (1585) and Paolo Sarpi, *History of the Council of Trent* (1619).

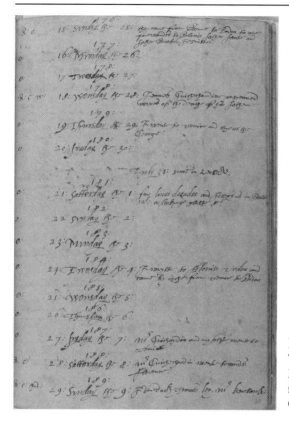

Figure 21.   Page from Arthur Throckmorton, Diary, Hales Papers, MS U. 85, Box 38, 3 vols, I (1578–83), f. 67r. By permission of Canterbury Cathedral Archives.

**Text**[1]

Arthur Throckmorton's record of his time at Venice and Padua offers a rare survival of a visitor's private manuscript diary. It comprises three columns for each day. The first column usually contains letters or symbols, probably indicating either the weather (presumably 'R:' = rain; '☉:' = sun; 'C:' = cold; 'H:' hail; 'W:' = wind; 'thund' = thunder) or astrological notations (e.g. '☉' = sun). The second column contains (above the entry) the number of days since his departure from England (beginning, '176:'); number of days in sets of thirty, i.e. the number of degrees in each sign of the zodiac (beginning on f. 64r, '15:') and the day of the week and date (beginning, '15: Sunday the 25:'). The third column contains specific information about his activities, individuals, purchases, etc. Although these entries are often mundane, hastily scribbled and faded (rendering many illegible), Throckmorton's private manuscript diary remains the only such document roughly recording the first-hand experiences and impressions at Venice by an Englishman of this period. It illustrates not only his daily activities but also his personal contacts with Italian intelligence gatherers such as James (Giacomo) Guicciardini and his own (now lost) reports to Sir Francis Walsingham.

[1] Canterbury Cathedral Archives, Hales Papers, MS U. 85, Box 38, 3 vols, I (1578–83), II (1583–96) and III (1609–13), I, ff. 64r–67r.

| [f. 64r1] | 176: | |
|---|---|---|
| R: ☉: | 15: Sunday the 25: [July] | ther came from Rome to Padoa to goe fourwardes to Polonia father Fante and father Brookes Jesuites:[1] |
| | 177: | |
| ☉: | 16: Monday the 26: | |
| | 178: | |
| ☉: | 17: Twesday the 27: | |
| | 178: | |
| R: C: W: | 18: Wensday the 28: | Jeames Guichechardine[2] resceaved newes of the dathe of his father |
| | 179: | |
| ☉: | 19: Thursday the 29: | I wente to venice and laye at the George[3] |
| | 180: | |
| ☉: | 20: fryday the 30: | |
| | | July 31: sune in Leo ☉: ♌:[4] |
| | 181: | |
| ☉: | 21: Satterday the 1: [August] | For lives[5] decades and Josephus in Italian 12ˡ: a lookynge glasse 8ˡ:[6] |
| | 182 | |
| ☉: | 22: Sunday the 2: | |
| | 183: | |
| ☉: | 23: Munday the 3: | |

[1] Laurence Fant (c.1553–91), was educated at Merton College, Oxford (c.1568), Louvain and Munich (1572). He lectured in divinity at the English hospice at Rome (1575) and was sent by Pope Gregory XIV to be rector of the Jesuit College at Poznań, Poland (1581). Woolfson, *Padua*, p. 233. Throckmorton's reference seems to be the only information known about this Father 'Brookes', ibid., p. 215.

[2] Giacomo (or James) Guicciardini was born in London and was the nephew of the Anglo-Italian Lodowick Bryskett (Ludovico Bruschetto), a friend of Philip Sidney (**item 22**, **Plate 17** and **Figure 17**) and Edmund Spenser. Bryskett had travelled with Sidney through France, Germany and Italy and was with him during his extended stay at Venice in late 1573 and 1574. Following disputes over his father's will, Giacomo travelled to Florence and during the early 1590s acted there as the agent of Robert Devereux, Earl of Essex. He also corresponded, on behalf of his uncle Lorenzo, an influential official at the court of the Grand Duke, with William Cecil, Lord Burghley. Hammer, *Polarisation of Elizabethan Politics*, p. 179. See also TNA, SP 98/1/3, the intelligence gatherer Lorenzo Guicciardini (d. 1593) to Arthur Throckmorton, 12 July 1582.

[3] George Inn, Venice.

[4] This and later similar entries contain astrological symbols (e.g. the Sun ☉ and Leo ♌) indicating the planetary positions at the time of observation.

[5] *lives*: Livy's.

[6] These two books are probably the copies listed among Throckmorton's books in the library of Magdalen College, Oxford: Livy, *Deche di Tito Liuio Padouano delle historie romane*, Venice, 1575; and Josephus, *Giosefo Della guerra et ultima destruttione di Gierusalem & del suo regno, sotto Vespasiano Imperadore*, Venice, 1570; or his *Delle antichità giudaiche*, Venice, 1560.

| | 184: | |
|---|---|---|
| ⊙: | 24: Twesday the 4: | I wrytte to Aloniso Vedoa[1] and came by coche from venice to Padoa |
| | 185: | |
| ⊙: | 25: Wensday the 5: | |
| | 186: | |
| ⊙: | 26: Thursday the 6: | |
| | 187: | |
| ⊙: | 27: fryday the 7: | M^r Guichardin and my selffe wente to venice |
| | 188: | |
| R: C: | 28: Satterday the 8: | Mr Guichechardin wente towardes Florence: |
| | 189: | |
| R: C: thnd:[2] | 29: Sunday the 9: | I dined with Thomas ley, m^r Kerton[3] &c: |
| [f. 64v] | 190: | |
| R: C: thund ⊙: | 30: Monday the 10: 191 | I came to Padua from venice |
| the ⊙: in the first point of leo: ⊙ in ♌: ⊙: | 1:[4] Twesday the 11 | geaven to the taillor for makynge 2 doublettes and one payre of hosse 29^l: |
| | 192: | |
| R: C: thund:[?] | 2: Wensday the 12: | |
| | 193: | |
| ⊙: | 3: Thursday the 13: | I write to my mother,[5] my L: chamberlyn,[6] my couson Midellmore,[7] M^r Secretary |

[1] Unidentified.

[2] *thnd*: thunder?

[3] Unidentified.

[4] This '1:' is placed in the first column due to lack of space in the second.

[5] Anne (Carew) Throckmorton. After Sir Nicholas's death (1571) she married in 1572 Adrian Stokes (1519–86), the second husband and former Master of Horse of Frances (Brandon) Grey, Duchess of Suffolk.

[6] Thomas Radcliffe, 3rd Earl of Sussex, was Queen Elizabeth's Lord Chamberlain in 1581. Alternatively, Arthur's father, Sir Nicolas Throckmorton, had served as Lord Chamberlain of the Exchequer from 1564 until his death in 1571 and so Arthur may be referring here to his successor, Thomas Randolph (d. 1590).

[7] In his will, TNA PROB 11/54/109, Arthur's father, Sir Nicholas Throckmorton, left various bequests to his 'cousin' Henry Middlemore (1535–c.97). When Sir Nicholas was sent in 1567 on a mission to Mary Queen of Scots, Middlemore served as his secretary. Bell, *Handlist*, p. 242.

| | | Walzyngeyam,[1] A Agard:[2] Jhon White and dated my lettres the the 15th: payed for byndynge Josephus and Livy 3:ͥ: |
|---|---|---|
| | 194: | |
| | 4: fryday the 14: | |
| | 195: | |
| R: C: thund: | 5: Saterday the 15: | I sente a letter to Mr Asheby to venice ~~and from~~ by Thomas [Rowlley?] lles and from there to Praga: Thomas ley a traguetto di [camon?] Sto apresso St Apostolo: |
| | 196: | |
| | 6: sunday the 16: | |
| | 197: | |
| R: C: | 7: Munday the 17: | |
| | 198: | |
| ☉: | 8: Twesday the 18: | I entered to learne of Romano[3] on the Lutte: payed to Romano 7:ͥ: |
| | 199: | |
| ☉: | 9: Wensday the 19: | Mr de Saint vallier duke d'Aumale['s] brother[4] came hether to Padoa: payed for my lute 9ͥ: payed to Mr Antonio Millaneso[5] for a mounthes boarde 4ˢͥ: and 4ͥ: extraordinary |
| ☉: | 200: | |
| | 10 Thursday the 20: | |
| | 201: | |
| | 11: fryday the 21: Magdalena[6] | I resceaved a letter from Jhon Whytte and ane other from Aloniso vedoa and from Thomas ley: |

[1] Sir Francis Walsingham (c.1532–90) maintained a wide network of continental correspondents who supplied him with intelligence about foreign states and discussions of English affairs abroad. Arthur had met personally with Walsingham, recording in his diary for 14 August 1579: 'Mr. Secretary Walsingham spake with me about her Majesty's letters for myself', Rowse, *Ralegh and the Throckmortons*, p. 75.

[2] Arthur Agard (1540–1615), an antiquary who had been appointed in 1570 as Deputy-Chamberlain to Arthur's father, Sir Nicholas. He was one of the witnesses to Sir Nicholas' will and 'the writer of three of these last sheets of this present testament'. TNA PROB 11/54/109.

[3] 'Romano' was Arthur's lute tutor at Venice. At Padua he had employed 'Bergamasco' for 8ˡⁱ per month and he had written to Thomas Ley (Leigh) for his 'luting book' which cost 6s. Rowse, *Ralegh and the Throckmortons*, pp. 89–90.

[4] Unidentified.

[5] Antonio Milanese, with whom Throckmorton boarded at Padua.

[6] This name seems to have been added in a different ink.

| | | |
|---|---|---|
| | 202: | |
| | 12: Satterdaye the 22: | I writte to Aloniso vedoa: |
| [f. 65r] | | |
| | 203: | |
| ☉: | 13: Sunday the 23: | |
| ☮: | | |
| | 204: | |
| R: C: ☉: | 14: Munday the 24: | |
| | 205: | |
| R: C: ☉: | 15: Twesday the 25: | |
| | 206: | |
| ☉: W: | 16: Wensday the 26: | Draco Volans[1] flied in the nether Region of the ayr from the north to the southe betwyn 7: and 8: at nyght leaving his coursse to be soon halffe a quarter of an [hower?] after hym:[2] M^r Ratcliffe brought me from Millan 2: payre of sylke stokynges 5: crownes a payre. |
| | 207: | |
| ☉: | 17: Thursday the 27: | I writte to my mother my cousen H. Midellemour, A: Agard: Jhon Dawson[?] Jhon Whitte, H. Parvis, Thomas Ley and dated my letters the 5^th of August, and to my father in lawe And: Stokes: |
| | 208: | |
| ☉: | 18: fryday the 28: | |
| | 209: | |
| ☉: | 19: Saterday the 29: | |
| | 210: | |
| | 20: Sunday the 30: | |
| | 211: | |
| ☉: | 21: Monday the 31: | I wrytte to M^r W Asheby: |
| | | August: 31: ☉: in ♍: virgo |
| | 212: | |
| R: | 22: Twesday the 1: [September] | The rector[?] was chosen by the 23: nations counsellors: |
| | 213: | |
| ☉: | 23: wensday the 2: | |

[1] 'Draco volans' (flying dragon) was a late Latin term occasionally used to describe a fiery meteor (*OED*, s.v.)
[2] An example of Throckmorton's celestial observations. See Rowse, *Ralegh and the Throckmortons*, p. 90.

| | 214: | |
|---|---|---|
| ☉: | 24: Thursday the 3: | |
| | 215: | |
| ☉: | 25: Fryday the 4: | |
| | 216: | |
| ☉: | 26: Saterday the 5: | |
| | 217: | |
| ☉: | 27: Sunday the 6: | Mr [S?]entry and Mr James Critton dined with us Scottishemen:[1] |
| [f. 65v] | | |
| | 218: | |
| ☉: | 28: Munday the 7: | Mr Nowelle[2] Mr Savelle[3] and Mr George Carew,[4] came to Padoa, my truncke came to venice: |
| | 219: | |
| ☉: | 29: Twesday the 8: | I wryte to W Ashby and sent a [illegible] to hym: |
| | 220: | |
| ☉: | 30: wensday the 9: | |
| | 221: | |
| | St: Laurance: | |
| ☉: in the firste pointe of virgo: ☉: in ♍ | 1 Thursday the 10: | |
| | 222: | |
| | 2: fryday the 11: | |
| | 223: | |
| W: ☉: C: | 3: Saterday the 12: | |

[1] Unidentified.

[2] Probably Laurence Nowell, perhaps a cousin of the Marian exiles, Alexander (1507–1602) and Laurence Noel (d. 1576). A 'Mr Noel' had tutored the Harington brothers at Padua in 1558. This Laurence Nowell travelled widely in 1568–70, visiting Venice and Padua, and was again recorded at Padua in 1583. Woolfson, *Padua*, pp. 260–61.

[3] Henry Savile (1549–1622), later a distinguished mathematician, astronomer and Greek scholar who was involved in the foundation of the Bodleian Library, Oxford. He travelled on the continent during 1578–81 with Arthur Throckmorton, Robert Sidney, Henry Neville and George Carew. At Venice he knew Wolfgang Zünderlin, one of the friends and correspondents of Philip Sidney. Woolfson, *Padua*, p. 269.

[4] George Carew (d. 1612), later a lawyer and diplomat who travelled in 1580–81 with Henry Savile and Henry Neville. He met with his cousin, Arthur Throckmorton, in Nuremburg (1580) and Prague and Padua (1581). While at Padua he wrote to Hugo Blotius, the imperial librarian at Vienna. Woolfson, *Padua*, p. 217.

| | 224: | |
|---|---|---|
| | 4: Sunday the 13: | I writte to Mr Robert Sidney[1] and to Thomas Leye |
| | 225: | |
| R: C: | 5: Munday the 14: | I resceaved a letter from Thomas Ley |
| | assension of our lady: | |
| | 226: | |
| | 6: Twesday the 15: | |
| | 227: | |
| R: H: C: | 7: wensday the 16: | |
| | 228: | |
| R: ☉: | 8: Thursday the 17: | |
| | 229: | |
| ☉: | 9: fryday the 18: | |
| ☉: | 230: | |
| | Satterday the 19: | payed to Mr Antonio for a monnthes bourd 8: crownes: resceaved of Mr Spensser[2] 10: crownes: I enteredto learne to wryghte to whom I gave a doucate[?] by the monethe. |
| | 231: | |
| ☉: | 10: Sunday the 20: | I write to Mr Agard: |
| | 232: | |
| ☉: | 11: Monday the 21: | I resceaved a letter from my mother dated the 8th of Jully I sent Edward to venice for my truncke geave him 4l: |
| [f. 66r] | | |
| | 233: | |
| R: | 12: Twesday the 22: | I resceaved my trunke here at Padoa |
| | 234: | |
| ☉: | 13: wensday the 23: | |
| | 235: | |
| ☉: | St Bartelomew | |
| | 14: Thursday the 24: | |
| | 236: | |
| ☉: | 15: fryday the 25: | |

[1] Robert Sidney was the younger brother of Philip Sidney and had travelled with Throckmorton from Nuremberg.
[2] Richard Spenser (c.1553–1624), later an ambassador and MP. He was Consiliarius of the English nation at Padua in 1581–2 and delivered a letter from Arthur Throckmorton to Hugo Blotius at Vienna in 1581. Woolfson, *Padua*, p. 273.

| | | |
|---|---|---|
| | 237: | |
| ☉: | 16: Satterday the 26: | |
| | 238: | |
| ☉: | 17: Sunday the 27: | payed for the byndynge of my tulles offices and de amicitia[1] &c in 2 volumes in quarto 35ˢ |
| | S Augustins daye | |
| | 239: | |
| ☉: W: | 18: Munday the 28: | |
| | S. Jhon | |
| | 240: | |
| ☉: | 19: Twesday the 29: | |
| | 241: | |
| ☉: | 20: wensday the 30: | I write to Mʳ Aga[rd ]: and dated my lettere the 4ᵗʰ of September: |
| | 242: | |
| ☉: | 21: Thursday the 31: | |
| | | September 30: |
| | 243: | ☉: in Libra: 1581: |
| ☉: | 22: fryday the 1: | I resceaved a letter from my mother and 2 letters from my couson Agard wᵗʰ 2: billes of exchange of 120: doucates to Sgʳ: Agres: silao marro:[2] and a letter from my coson Joh Throkmorton: |
| | 244: | |
| ☉: | 23: Satterday the 2: | resceaved 2: letters from A [illegible]: 1: from Mʳ Henry Midellemore and 1: from Mʳ W. Ashby: a freyer[?] [illegible] 4: frensche gentellmen [?] Mʳ [four illegible French names], and sent a letter to Thomas Ley: |
| [f. 66v] | | |
| | 245: | |
| ☉: | 24: Sunnday the 3: | I resceaved a letter from Thomas ley |
| | 246: | |
| ☉: thund: W: R: at nyght: | 25: Munday the 4: | monsieur Pinson, Mr Bonaronissy[?], Mʳ Sᵗ: Katerinie[?]: mʳ R[illegible] to the governour of [illegible]: of the housse of bourbon: |

[1] Cicero's *De officiis* and *De amicitia*. Cicero was often called Tully (Tullius) in this period.

[2] Unidentified.

[3] Apart from difficulties in deciphering Throckmorton's idiosyncratic French and erratic script, the ink is badly faded in this section of his diary.

| | | |
|---|---|---|
| lightenynge [?] at nyght: | | Bell[*illegible*] of [*illegible*] messieur [*illegible*] Ronn[?] 2 brothers: 2 brothers Antragnes[?] m[r] N[*illegible*][3] |
| | 247: | |
| [*symbol*]:[1] R: W: ⊙: m[2] thunder lightenynge [?] | 26: Twesday the 5: | |
| | 248: | |
| ⊙: W: | 27: wensday the 6: | I wryte to my mother, M[r] H. M. my L: L[*illegible*] m[r] G. Scote, mr Jhon Whyte, my couson Joh Throkemorton, m[r] A Agard, m[r] W. Ashby, Thomas Ley, |
| | 249: | |
| | 28: Thursday the 7: | |
| | 250: | |
| ⊙: R: n:[4] [*illegible*]: | 29: fryday: the 8: | I wente ~~w[th]~~ to Pro obecies house[3] and from there to mons [*illegible*] and so homewardes to the bathes of S[ta]: hellena by la Battaiglle and spent 5[l]: |
| | 211:[5] | |
| ⊙: | 30: Satterday: the 9: | |
| | 212: | |
| ⊙: in the firste pointe of Libra: ⊙: R: C: W: Light | 1: Sunday: the 10: | M[r] Nowel and m[r] [*illegible*] wente towards vicensza:[?] |
| | 213: | |
| ⊙: R: | 2: Monday the 11: | I wrytte a letter to W Ash: by m[r] [*illegible*] and dated my letters the 16th of Sept[ember] and sente one other to hym of the 18th by Thomas Ley I wrytte a letter to Doctor Blotius[6] in frenche by mr Spenser |

[1] Added above the line.
[2] Added above the symbol ⊙.
[3] Added above the line.
[4] Unidentified.
[5] The original number here was '221', revised to '251'. Subsequent numbers have been similarly revised.
[6] Hugo Blotius (1533–1608), a Dutch scholar appointed in 1575 by Emperor Maximilian II to direct his imperial library.

| [f. 67r] | | |
|---|---|---|
| | 214: | |
| R: W: | 3: Twesday the 12: | I resceaved a letter from m$^r$ W: Ash: dated the 22 of Auguste 1581: w$^{th}$ a pakett to m$^r$ Agarde: |
| | 215: | |
| | 4: wenesday: the 13: | I came to venice from Padoa |
| | 216: | |
| | 5: Thursday the 14: | |
| | 217: | |
| | 6: fryday the 15: | I resceaved of Agisilao [?] 120: doucates: |
| | 218: | |
| | 7: satterday the 16: | I wente from venice w$^{th}$ the poste Baldo of Florence to whom I gave 6: crownes for my selffe and 4: crownes for the carriage of my trunke and other thinges w$^{ch}$ wayed [*deletion*] 158$^l$. and for every $^l$: I muste paye 4. soldes. I sette out from the George in venice and came in to the boate at 12: at nyght and saylled all the reste of the nyght: we came by porto de mallamocco, and by porto de chodsi,[1] 45: milles: |
| | 219: | |
| | 8: sunday: the 17: | [arrived at Loreto] |

---

[1] Chioggia.

# 28.   1581 – LAURENCE ALDERSEY

**Laurence Aldersey (1546–97/8)** was born at Aldersey Hall, Spurstow, Cheshire as the sixth child of Thomas (d. 1557) and Cecilia (Garnet) Aldersey (fl. 1513–94). His father was sheriff (1538–9) and mayor (1549–50) of Chester. Laurence went to London in the mid-1560s and, under the guidance of his relative and experienced international trader Thomas Aldersey (1521/22–98), became a merchant, sea captain and traveller.[1] Sailing from London on 1 April 1581, on a trip lasting just over nine months, he crossed through Holland and Germany to Venice, from where he embarked for Cyprus. He then sailed in a smaller barque to Jaffa and travelled overland to Jerusalem, where he visited various sites between 12 and 22 August 1581.

Laurence Aldersey undertook a second voyage, commanding the *Hercules of London*,[2] between February 1587 and February/March 1588 to transport Turks who had been brought by Sir Francis Drake from the West Indies to William Harborne, English Ambassador at Constantinople.[3] This trip took him to Malta, Zante, Chios, Cyprus, Tripoli, and Cairo before returning via Alexandria, Tunis and Algiers. Aldersey died, heavily indebted, during a diplomatic mission begun in May 1597 to carry letters from Queen Elizabeth to the Emperor of Ethiopia.

Aldersey's description of Venice provides an important account of the city's Jewish community which has been compared to William Shakespeare's depiction of Shylock's society in *The Merchant of Venice* (c. 1595–8, pr. 1600). He reveals his curiosity over their living arrangements 'in a certaine place of the Citie' (the *Ghetto). He was allowed to visit a synagogue to observe their forms of worship and was impressed by how their singing of the Psalms of David was comparable to Protestant English usage.

Aldersey's account also conveys a vivid impression of the challenges facing an English visitor to Venice, involving a six-day crossing of the Alpine pass and, when leaving the

---

[1] Laurence Aldersey's relationship with Thomas Aldersey (1521–98) is unclear. This Thomas was born at another Aldersey estate, Lower Spurstow, Cheshire. Laurence's father Thomas may have been a son of Hugh or Robert or Richard Aldersey, the brother of John (c.1494–1554), who was the father of Thomas (1521–98). In this Thomas's will (written 1595) Laurence received only £5 and, pointedly, forgiveness for large debts and behaviour 'dyvers waies offensive to me' (TNA: PRO, PROB 11/93/10). See [Lancashire and Cheshire], 'Pedigrees ... 1613', pp. 5–9 (Laurence, p. 7); Cheshire Archives and Local Studies, CR 69, 469; Earwaker and Bridgeman, *Family of Aldersey*. I am grateful to Mark Bland for his advice on the Alderseys. http://www.cheshire-heraldry.org.uk/visitations1613/1613.pdf.

[2] For another account of this ship's return voyage, see Federici, *Voyage and Travaile*, 1588. The Levantine merchant and traveller John Eldred (1552–1632) was also a member of this return voyage to England, see Hakluyt, *Principal Navigations*, 1599, II.i, pp. 268–71.

[3] *ODNB* states that the *Hercules of London*, commanded by Aldersey, left Bristol on 21 February 1587 and returned to Dartmouth on 1 February and London on 7 February 1588. However, Eldred's account of this voyage in *Principal Navigations* states that he arrived back in the Thames on 26 March 1588 and Hickock's translation of Federici's account is dated 25 March 1588.

city by sea, the vicissitudes of waiting for favourable winds (or until the captain had enough passengers or cargo to make the trip worthwhile). Fortunately, Aldersey decided against boarding an earlier vessel which was lost with many passengers drowning when it sank close to Venice. His own vessel came close to being captured by a Turkish galley with only a sudden gale of favourable winds resolving his predicament.

## Text[1]

[*margin*: Venice][2] The fift of May, I departed from Augusta towards Venice, and came thither upon Whitsunday, the thirteenth of the same moneth. It is needlesse to speake of the height of the mountaines that I passed over, and of the danger thereof, it is so wel knowen already to the world: the heigth of them is marveilous, and I was the space of six dayes in passing them.[3]

I came to Venice at the time of a Faire, which lasted fourteene dayes, wherein I sawe very many, and faire shewes of wares. I came thither too short for the first passage, which went away from Venice about the seventh or eight of May, and with them about three score pilgrims, which shippe was cast away at a towne called Estria, two miles from Venice,[4] and all the men in her, saving thirtie, or thereabout, lost.

Within eight dayes after fell Corpus Christi day, which was a day amongst them of procession, in which was shewed the plate and treasure of Venice, which is esteemed to be worth two millions of pounds, but I do not accompt it worth halfe a quarter of that money, except there be more then I sawe.[5] To speake of the sumptuousnesse of the Copes, and Vestments of the Church, I leave, but the trueth is, they be very sumptuous, many of them set all over with pearle, and made of cloth of golde. And for the Jesuits, I thinke there be as many at Venice, as there be in Colen.[6]

[*margin*: The number of Jewes in Venice] The number of Jewes is there thought to be 1000, who dwell in a certaine place of the Citie,[7] and have also a place, to which they resort to pray, which is called the Jewes Sinagogue. They all, and their offspring use to

---

[1] (from) 'The first voyage or journey, made by Master *Laurence Aldersey*, Marchant of London, to the Cities of Jerusalem, and Tripolis, &c. In the yeere 1581. Penned and set downe by himselfe', in Hakluyt, *Principal Navigations*, 1599, II, pp. 150–54. This text has also been reprinted in MacLehose and Sons, 1903–5, V, pp. 202–14.

[2] Aldersey arrived at Augsburg (Augusta) on 3 May 1581, toured the city's sights and purchased a horse for Venice before beginning the usual Alpine crossing.

[3] Although Aldersey does not give any details of his Alpine journey from Augsburg to Venice, a common route for travellers was via Innsbruck, the Brenner Pass, Bolzano, Trento, Verona and Padua.

[4] *a towne called Estria*: The peninsula of Istria, is approximately 80 km to the east of Venice, now lying in Italian, Croatian and Slovenian territories. It is usually visible on the first day of a voyage from Venice. But if this location is a 'towne' and only 'two miles from Venice', then it presumably lay somewhere close to the Lido di Venezia or southwards in the direction of the town of Choggia.

[5] Corpus Christi feast day and procession (**Plate 1**).

[6] *Colen*: Cologne. Saint Ignatius of Loyola (1491–1556), the founder of the Society of Jesus (Jesuits), first came to Venice in 1523 while undertaking a pilgrimage to the Holy Land. In 1535 he returned to the church of *Santa Maria Assunta with a group of followers who were ordained as priests. The Jesuits thrived in the Venetian lagoon area until 1606 when they were exiled from the city until 1657, due to an interdict prompted by hostilities between Pope Paul V and the Venetian authorities.

[7] *Ghetto.

weare red caps,[1] (for so they are commaunded) because they may thereby be knowen from other men. For my further knowledge of these people, I went into their Sinagogue upon a Saturday, which is their Sabbath day: and I found them in their service or prayers, very devoute: they receive the five bookes of Moses, and honour them by carying them about their Church, as the Papists doe their crosse.[2]

Their Synagogue is in forme round, and the people sit round about it, and in the midst, there is a place for him that readeth to the rest: as for their apparell, all of them weare a large white lawne[3] over their garments, which reacheth from their head, downe to the ground.

The Psalmes they sing as wee doe, having no image, nor using any maner of idolatrie:[4] their error is, that they believe not in Christ, nor yet receive the New Testament. This Citie of Venice is very faire, and greatly to bee commended, wherein is good order for all things: and also it is very strong and populous: it standeth upon the maine Sea, and hath many Islands about it, that belong to it.

To tell you of the duke of Venice,[5] and of the Seigniory:[6] there is one chosen that ever beareth the name of a duke, but in trueth hee is but servant to the Seigniorie, for of himselfe hee can doe little: it is no otherwise with him, then with a Priest that is at Masse upon a festival day, which putting on his golden garment, seemeth to be a great man, but if any man come unto him, and crave some friendship at his handes, hee will say, you must goe to the Masters of the Parish, for I can not pleasure you, otherwise then by preferring of your suite: and so it is with the duke of Venice, if any man having a suite, come to him, and make his complaint, and deliver his supplication, it is not in him to helpe him, but hee will tell him, You must come this day, or that day, and then I will preferre your suite to the Seigniorie, and doe you the best friendship that I may. Furthermore, if any man bring a letter unto him, hee may not open it, but in the presence of the Seigniorie, and they are to see it first, which being read, perhaps they will deliver it to him, perhaps not. Of the Seigniory there be about three hundreth, and about fourtie of the privie Counsell of Venice, who usually are arayed in gownes of crimsen Satten,[7] or crimsen Damaske, when they sit in Counsell.

In the Citie of Venice, no man may weare a weapon, except he be a souldier for the Seigniorie, or a scholler of Padua, or a gentleman of great countenance, and yet he may not do that without licence.[8]

[1] *red caps*: In 1394 Jews had been required to wear a yellow badge which was changed to a yellow hat in 1496 and then a red hat in 1500.

[2] Aldersey does not give any specific details of this synagogue (or schola). By the late-16th century Venice housed communities of German Jews (schola founded 1528), Ashkenazi Jews (1531/32), Sephardic Levantine Jews (1541), Italian Jews (1575), and Spanish and Portuguese Jews (c.1580).

[3] *lawne*: lawn, fine white linen resembling cambric, originally made at Cambrai, France.

[4] Metrical versifications of the Psalms of David, mostly in ballad metre, by Thomas Sternhold and John Hopkins were popular with Protestant exiles on the continent during the reign of Queen Mary (1553–8). This collection was expanded by various editors at Geneva until the London stationer John Day published *The Whole Booke of Psalmes* (1562), with metrical versions of 150 psalms. This collection was often reprinted and bound with the Geneva Bible.

[5] Nicolò da Ponte (1578–85), although he was 87 when elected Doge, his reign lasted for seven years and proved productive; he died aged 94 in July 1585.

[6] *Seigniory*: Councillors of the Seignory governed Venice from 1404–1797.

[7] *gownes of crimsen Satten*: Venetian procurators traditionally wore a gown of crimson velvet (**Plate 21**).

[8] See pp. 202–4 for Philip Sidney's and pp. 11, 157–8, 169, for the Earl of Bedford's petitions to the *Council of Ten for them and their gentlemen to bear arms.

[*margin*: The excesse of the women of Venice] As for the women of Venice, they be rather monsters,[1] then women. Every Shoomakers or Taylors wife will have a gowne of silke, and one to carie up her traine, wearing their shooes very neere halfe a yard high[2] from the ground: if a stranger meete one of them, he will surely thinke by the state that she goeth with, that he meeteth, a Lady.

[*margin*: His embarking at Venice for Jerusalem] I departed from this Citie of Venice, upon Midsommer day, being the foure and twentieth of June, and thinking that the ship would the next day depart, I stayed, and lay a shippeboord all night, and we were made beleeve from time to time, that we should this day, and that day depart, but we taried still, till the fourteenth of July, and then with scant winde wee set sayle, and sayled that day and that night, not above fiftie Italian miles: and upon the sixteene day at night, the winde turned flat contrary, so that the Master knewe not what to doe:[3] and about the fift houre of the night, which we reckon to be about one of the clocke after midnight, the Pilot descried a saile, and at last perceived it to be a Gallie of the Turkes, whereupon we were in great feare.[4]

The Master being a wise fellowe, and a good sayler, beganne to devise howe to escape the danger, and to loose little of our way: and while both he, and all of us were in our dumps,[5] God sent us a merry gale of winde, that we ranne threescore and tenne leagues before it was twelve a clocke the next day, and in six dayes after we were seven leagues past Zante.[6] And upon Munday morning, being the three and twentie of the same moneth, we came in the sight of Candia[7] which day the winde came contrary, with great blasts, and stormes, untill the eight and twentie of the same moneth: in which time, the Mariners cried out upon me, because I was an English man, & sayd, I was no good Christian, and wished that I were in the middest of the Sea, saying, that they, and the shippe, were the worse for me.[8]

---

[1] *monsters*: extraordinary, marvellous or unnatural. Aldersey refers to the elevation of these ladies because of their high shoes or *chop(p)ines*. He was perhaps also recalling the title of *The First Blast of the Trumpet Against the Monstrous Regiment of Women* (1558), by the religious reformer John Knox (*c*.1514–72), denouncing the unnatural (or monstrous) rule (or regiment) of women (i.e., the Catholic reign of Queen Mary). Knox was of particular interest to mariners because, after the capture of St Andrew's Castle in 1547 by the French fleet, noble prisoners were taken hostage to castles in France while Knox and other commoners were committed to the French galleys. He spent 19 months in this naval captivity, sometimes rowing in chains.

[2] *shooes very neere halfe a yard high*: shoes elevated to extreme heights by cork soles, worn by Venetian women to enhance their attractiveness and to avoid the mud and dirt of the Venetian *calle* (street). Their height was also often thought to reflect the woman's social status. They were usually referred to as *chop(p)ines*, with the earliest citation in English dating from 1577. *OED*, 'What, my young lady and mistress! By'r lady, your ladyship is nearer to heaven than when I saw you last, by the altitude of a chopine' (*Hamlet*, II.ii.418–19).

[3] Aldersey was probably travelling in some kind of merchant ship rather than a traditional pilgrim galley. The latter utilized both sail and oars which were deployed when winds failed.

[4] Venetian shipping was under threat in the Mediterranean from not only Turkish but also Spanish, Portuguese and English piracy, see Tenenti, *Piracy*.

[5] *in our dumps*: depressed, discouraged or melancholy.

[6] *Zante*: Greek island of Zákynthos in the Morea was Venetian from 1484 until 1797.

[7] *Candia*: Iráklion (Heraklion) on the island of Crete. The city had been bought by Venice in 1204. It was besieged by the Ottoman army from 1645 until 1669 when it finally fell to Turkish rule. The Venetian administrative district of Crete was known as Regno di Candia (Kingdom of Crete); 'Candia' was often used to refer to the whole island.

[8] Aldersey arrived at Cyprus on 2 August 1581.

# 29.   1587/8 – STEPHEN POWLE

**Stephen Powle** (*c.*1553–1630), was born at Cranbook, Essex, and studied at Broadgates Hall (later Pembroke College), Oxford, from about 1564 (BA 1569; MA 1572 from Corpus Christi College). He entered the Middle Temple in November 1574 and roomed with the young Walter Ralegh. He left England in November 1579 and stayed at Paris as the guest of the English Ambassador Sir Henry Cobham where he practised the French language and perhaps also began to learn Italian. Intending to move on to Protestant Geneva, he found it expedient among French Catholics to claim that his intended destination was the University of Padua. He made his way, via Dijon and Lyons, with a group of dyers who were experienced travellers and arrived at Geneva in early 1580. He attended sermons delivered by the Calvinist preachers Theodore Beza and Lambert Daneau (who dedicated his *Geographiae poeticae* to Philip Sidney (**item 22**, **Plate 17** and **Figure 17**) in the same year).[1] Prompted by an outbreak of the plague, Powle then moved on to Basle before enrolling on 6 April 1581 at Strasbourg University. In a long letter to his father (completed on 20 June), he summarized the knowledge he had so far attained of European countries.[2] He was already interesting himself in the potency of the Venetian Republic, noting that while it was only one city it had extended its territories into various islands of the Mediterranean.[3] Leaving Strasbourg on 12 August he also visited Speyer, Heidelberg and Frankfurt before returning to Strasbourg to meet up with Robert Sidney, Philip's younger brother, who had been at Christ Church, Oxford, when Powle was at Corpus Christi College. They left together for France on 26 September 1581 and stayed at Paris before returning to England by probably mid-March 1582.

Soon afterwards, as a key moment in Powle's career in public affairs, he entered the service of William Cecil, Lord Burghley, and in April 1585 he moved to Heidelberg where he became Burghley's agent at the court of Duke John Casimir and also studied at the city's university. He returned to England in March 1586 with letters from the duke and in March 1587 Sir Francis Walsingham (**Plate 24**) dispatched Powle as one of his intelligence agents to Venice, from where he sent regular newsletters and information about rumoured papal plots against Queen Elizabeth. This posting lasted just under one year before he returned to London in late 1588.[4]

Early in 1589 Powle sought permission from Burghley to travel to Switzerland and Walsingham considered him for service at the court of the Duke of Brandenburg. However, further international employment was not forthcoming and he remained in London, marrying Elizabeth Hobart (1556–90) in March 1590, who died in childbirth

---

[1] Stewart, *Philip Sidney*, pp. 188, 247.

[2] Oxford, Bodleian Library (letter book) MS Tanner 169, ff. 149r–173r.

[3] Ibid., f. 159r.

[4] Stern, *Sir Stephen Powle*, pp. 19–57. This account of Powle's continental travels draws extensively on Virginia Stern's biography.

on Christmas Eve of the same year. In late 1593 he married a wealthy widow, Margaret Smyth (née Turner) and resided with her at Smyth Hall, Blackmore, Essex. His father Thomas (1514–1601) was high steward to Queen Elizabeth and a chancery clerk but, as he became frail with age, Stephen was appointed deputy clerk of the Crown in chancery and in 1601 took over his father's public offices. He resided at his London houses in Chancery Lane and Mile End and his wife's country estate at Blackmore. He was knighted by King James I on 8 July 1604 and became one of the thirteen original council members of the Virginia Company, enrolling as an adventurer in March 1609, as well investing in Ralegh's second expedition to Guiana (1617). When his wife died in April 1621 her house passed to her heirs and Stephen married Ann (d. 1631), the widow of Sir Richard Wigmore, and took up residence at her London home in King Street, Westminster.

## Stephen Powle at Venice and His Intelligence Reports

On 12 December 1586 Powle wrote to Lord Burghley, telling him of his father's failing health and seeking some sort of employment for himself either in England or abroad. He requested a licence to travel so that he could go either to the forthcoming fair at Frankfurt or some other part of Europe. In a postscript, he suggested that it might be useful for English intelligence to order copies of the monthly Venetian newsletters produced at Padua, Venice and Augsburg since they drew together valuable information from weekly intelligence letters circulated within various parts of Europe. This was a useful suggestion since England had not maintained an official embassy at Venice since 1555. Burghley passed on Powle's letter to the queen's principal secretary, Sir Francis Walsingham, who also directed her international intelligence gathering. Soon afterwards an order was issued for Powle to travel to Venice and reside there, supported by 'a yearly pencion out of hir maiesties purse of 50[li] and 30[li] in my purse to convey me to venyce'.[1] In late March 1587 he left England in the party of a former ward of Lord Burghley, Edward, Lord Zouche, which also included Powle's servant, Daniel Simpson; Henry Hawkins, a former proctor of Cambridge University;[2] a French schoolmaster called Holliband;[3] and one of Zouche's personal servants called Warde. They travelled together via Hamburg to Frankfurt where

---

[1] MS Tanner 309, ff. 65v–66r. Many of Powle's papers are preserved in MS Tanner 309 (letter book) and MSS Tanner 168 and 169 (commonplace book). Other material relating to Powle is in MSS Tanner 76, 78, 130, 231, 283, 284 and 314. Manuscript documents relating to Powle's time at Venice are also in BL Harleian MS 296, ff. 48r–49v; *CSP Domestic*, 1586–88, SP 99/1/28 and SP 101/81; and Bodleian Tanner MS 130, ff. 132r–134r.

[2] Henry Hawkins had matriculated in 1568 from Peterhouse, Cambridge (BA, 1571/2; MA, 1575; LL.D. 1591), and was elected to a fellowship there in 1575. He served as a university proctor (1583–4) and was admitted to Gray's Inn in the same year. On 2 July 1586 he was granted a royal licence to travel 'beyond seas' with Lord Zouch to Prague. University of Cambridge, Alumni Database: http://venn.lib.cam.ac.uk/Documents/acad/2018/search-2018.html.

[3] Claudius Hollyband (Claude de Sainliens) (1534–94), was a Huguenot refugee from Moulins who came to London in about 1564. He published several books on learning French, including *The French School-master* (1573); *De pronuntiatione linguae gallicae* (1580); and *Treasurie to the French Tongue* (1580). He also knew Italian and published *Campo di Fior, or the Flowery Field of Four Languages* (1583) and translated *The Pretie and Wittie Historie of Arnalt & Lucenda, from B. Maraffi's Italian version* and *Certain Rules and Dialogues set foorth for the learner of th' Italian tong* (1575).

Powle delivered letters from Walsingham to Horatio Palavicino (d. 1600), Elizabeth's financial agent. He then wrote on 8 April to Burghley from Frankfurt, detailing some of the challenges and dangers which awaited him at Venice:

> Touchinge my goeinge to venyce which is the other parte of M[r] Secretarys Comandement, although I heare that the Inquisition is more streightly observed there than eaver heretofore: for of late one Donzellino a learned Phisitian[1] was drowned there only for that he had a booke of the Religion sent him enclosed in a lettre: yet I meane by the favoure of God to remayne there, till sum extraordinary occasion drive me from thence, be it neaver so dangerous: and am to depart hence wednesday in Easter weeke (which is the ende of the Mart) with the merchants of this Towne. I would it stood with your Lordships pleasure to commaunde me any particular service by message of worde of mouth, or by other mens lettres; and not by your owne writing: for the tymes beinge so dangerous your Honors lettres woold be construed in the worst sence, if they shoold be intercepted. Without any commission from your Lordship I will presume to send your Honor suche thinges as I shall valew at any worth for rareness beinge harde to be recovered, or newnes beinge of any singular invention.[2]

Zouche and Powle then moved on to Heidelberg, arriving there on 13 April. While Zouche's party remained there, Powle pressed on for Italy.[3] They passed through Augsburg, where Powle had arranged to meet merchants from Frankfurt with whom he was to travel to Venice. This group left Augsburg on 15 April and in a letter to Walsingham he expressed the anxieties which young Protestant Englishmen must have often felt as they approached Venice:

> Hoapinge that your Honor will leave this free to my sealf, that if I finde it dangerous in respect either of Inquisition, passage, or other troubles, to lye elcewhere thereabouts ... I presume to intreate this at your Honours hands because of late one Donzelliny was drowned att venyce for having a booke only sent unto him that was of the religion enclosed in a letter: for that it dooth appeare heerby that the force of the Inquisition dooth creepe in there also. But wheresoever I remayne your Honour shalbe enformed eavery three weekes of the occurrents by me: and though I adventure never so many dangers, I will by the favor of God goe to venyce to take order that the weekly advices be sent me: And if any other Intelligences may be procured by my industrie, I will acquaint your Honour therewith likewise: But heerin if I doe not performe so muche as your Honour looketh for, then if it please you to commande M[r] D[r]. Whyte of St. Dunstane in London to put downe my errour heerin by letter, he will convey the same to me by the waye of Nuremberge and Augsburg. And if there be any impossibillity for any englysh man to enter venyce, then if it shall please your Honour to apply me to some Dutche [i.e., German] service, I will discharge that parte of my duty with all faythfulnes and seacrisie [secrecy].[4]

Powle arrived at Venice on 27 April 1587, after delays caused by his need to obtain safe conduct passes through each province of Germany. As the focus of multiple trade routes from both the west and east, Venice acted as a hub for international news about

---

[1] Girolamo Donzellini (Donzellino) (*c*.1513–87), a Protestant physician who had graduated from the University of Padua in 1541. He was tried five times by the Venetian Inquisition and in March 1587 was condemned to death by drowning in the Lagoon.

[2] MS Tanner 309, f. 66v.

[3] Oxford, Bodleian Library, MS Tanner 309, ff. 65v–67v. *CSP Foreign, 1586–88*, p. 263. Stern, *Sir Stephen Powle*, pp. 65–6.

[4] MS Tanner 309, f. 68r–v. Stern, *Sir Stephen Powle*, pp. 67–8.

politics, commerce, war, religion and the activities of individual potentates and their advisors. Powle's first bi-weekly newsletter from Venice was sent to Walsingham on 16 May.[1] He sometimes wrote in English and Italian, reporting uncontroversial information in Italian and more politically sensitive intelligence in English (assuming that Italians intercepting his post would not bother to have the English sections translated).[2] Powle's newsletters regularly incorporated factual reports, rumours and casual gossip about events in Germany, France, Spain, Persia and the Ottoman Empire. Predictably, his news about Venice and activities in northern Italy was usually the most accurate. On 16 May 1587 he informed Walsingham about Italian (especially Venetian) attitudes towards England. This was crucial information during the escalating tensions between England and Spain, culminating in the Armada attack of July and August 1588:

> The Cheef Princes that wishe good successe to her ma*jesty*s proceedings, be the Dukes of Mantoa, Ferrara, Florence, and the Signorye of venyce: All mooved therunto by the generall dislike of the Spanyard*es* tyranizinge greatnes, hir M*ajesty*s knowne enemye ... The Duke of Florence also hath at this tyme a private different wi*th* the Pope (whome I account a principal member of Spayne) about a claime the Pope maketh to Borgo Sa*nt*o Sepolchro,[3] that many yeares since did belonge to the Sea of Rome but became the Dukes because it was not redeemed after it had been pawned for money: the money this Pope Sixtus Quintus offereth to paye, *th*e Duke refuseth it: moreover, he would have him at the leaste pluck downe the Castle thereof, because it standeth too nigh Forli,[4] a frontier forte of Romagna: And sundrie banditi from Rome be harbored in Tuscan to encrease the heartburninge betwixt them.
>
> The venetian in particular honoreth hir ma*jesty* in regard of hir gracious, calme, & peacable government in these stormy tymes: and that nowe all hir neighboures Cuntryes be afyer, hir Highnes only keepeth hir Realme in a moderate temper. He is also well affected to our Cuntrie in respect of his sale of his cheefest com*m*odities in those parts to his exceedinge gaine: moreover, sundrie principall men of this State have remained longe in England and doe dayly encrease their wealth by tradinge thither, as Giacomo Foscarini, Ragazzoni, and sundrie others of lesse account.[5]

The concluding section of this letter sent on 16 May was concerned with the aftermath of the execution of Mary Queen of Scots on the preceding 8 February at Fotheringay Castle. It seemed to Powle that most of the Italian princes and the Venetian Senate approved of Queen Elizabeth's actions in so ruthlessly removing this threat to her sovereign power. But concerns had been expressed over the open treatment and execution of a figure of royal status – the implication being that the ruthless Venetian state would probably have disposed of Mary more covertly. His letter closed with an informative insight into the complex and often dangerous world of intelligence gathering at Venice:

---

[1] MS Tanner 309, ff. 63r–65r.

[2] The simplicity of Powle's techniques for trying to hide sensitive material was in sharp contrast to the sophisticated cryptographic methods adopted by Venetian intelligence gatherers, including ciphers in several languages, musical cryptograms and recipes for invisible ink. A state-controlled and regulated department of cryptology was housed in the Ducal Palace and from 1543 'oversaw several cryptology functions, including the creation of ciphers, deciphering encrypted messages, training chancery staff in the use of cipher keys, breaking enemy ciphers, and even the development of a distinct training and development regime for Venetian state cryptologists'. Iordanou, *Venice's Secret Service*, pp. 129–57, 132.

[3] Sansepolcro (formerly Borgo Santo Sepolcro).

[4] Forli, situated in Emilia-Romagna region, south of Venice.

[5] MS Tanner 309, ff. 63v–64r.

I deliver unto your Honour at this preasent diffusedly suche occurrants as my small continuance & acquaintance have afforded me meanes to attaine. If I had a direction from your Honour by writinge to sende them: I might bothe adventure to deale with the Secretaries heere of Ferrara, Mantua, & Florence, as beinge warranted therby: and also it would be a good shielde of defence against any of my promotinge Cuntrimen: which lurke heere to put suche into the Inquisition as they finde to hinder your endeavors by any labour or letter. I write thus muche because sundrie have been drowned heere for religion since Donsellinus execution, boath of frenche & dutche by means of the Inquisition; and Wolfgangus[1] a secrett Intelligencer here for the Duke of Saxony (and not an Agent for his [?] to the State of venyce) had a Commission from his Prince to the same ende, which hee was constrayned to shewe to the Signoria of late beinge accused by the frenche kinges Ambassadour to lye here as a spie.

Thus with the humble remembrance of my duty I beseeche Almighty God to blesse you in this worlde with encrease of honor, and after this life, to bestowe on you everlastinge happines. From Venyce 16 May 1587.

> Your Honours for ever moste bounden.[2]
> S.P.

In his second letter to Walsingham, dated 30 May, Powle mentioned that his first letter had been carried by one Jieronimo di Bonna (probably a regular courier), enclosed in a letter addressed to the London-based merchant Niccolo di Gozzi.[3] He supplied some local Italian news, but the end of this letter and the opening of his next letter, dated 18 June, are now missing.[4] In a letter dated 20 June 1587 to his elder brother Thomas, Powle apparently did not wish to admit to him that he was in Italy and, instead, described through hearsay ('*audita*' not '*visae*') various aspects of the current state of Italy, its people and its rich agriculture, adding that he hoped to return to England during the spring of 1588. He especially praised the Signoria of Venice for the extent of its empire and its all-powerful navy. Keeping up the pretence over his current location, Powle told his brother that he was still based at Strasbourg and hoped to be in Frankfurt by September. He even suggested that Thomas could send letters to him via English merchants in Germany who would forward the letters to him (i.e., to Venice but giving Thomas the impression that they would be sent on to Frankfurt).[5]

Powle's next letter to Walsingham, dated 12 July 1587, was written in English and Italian, confirming a facility in the language of both the author and its recipient (since Walsingham had lived at Padua during Queen Mary's reign). After requesting assurance that his letters were being received in England, he explained to Walsingham how difficult they were to compile in that the reports to which he subscribed at Venice, including those from Naples, Rome and Milan, frequently offered conflicting and contrasting views of

---

[1] Unidentified.

[2] MS Tanner 309, f. 65r. Stern, *Sir Stephen Powle*, pp. 71–4.

[3] See *Calendar of The Cecil Papers ... Addenda*, p. 516, for the petition (in Italian) of Niccola di Menze, executor of the will of Niccolo de Gozzi (d. *c.* Nov. 1594), a 'gentleman, and a merchant of Raugia' [Ragusa?]. Gozzi had left various generous bequests to charities in Italy and elsewhere but his estate had been claimed for the queen because of its beneficiaries' 'superstitious observances [i.e., Catholicism] contrary to the laws of this kingdom'. Niccola di Menze was disputing this claim, stating that the will had previously been read and approved by the Archbishop of Canterbury.

[4] MS Tanner 309, f. 69v. Stern, *Sir Stephen Powle*, p. 74. Parts of two different letters have been bound together at this point in Tanner 309.

[5] MS Tanner 309, ff. 17r–21v. Stern, *Sir Stephen Powle*, pp. 74–5.

the same subject. Nevertheless, he promised to synthesize as best he could these various sources of information so that the news sent to Walsingham might be as reliable as possible but not necessarily taken as definitive. He reported in Italian how Algerian galliots[1] were conducting raids around Sicily and Otranto and the threats posed by Turkish pirates. More significantly for Walsingham, who with Burghley was responsible for the personal security of Queen Elizabeth, Powle noted that letters received from Rome suggested that some members of the English College, along with other Englishmen and Scotsmen in Italy, thought that after the recent execution of his mother, King James VI might no longer be concerned to cultivate Elizabeth's friendship. Instead, it was rumoured that he was now set upon reintroducing Catholicism in Scotland and had recalled from abroad three bishops who had previously wished to re-establish the Catholic Church in Scotland.

Turning back to writing in English, Powle then considered current speculation among Venetian merchants about who might be created cardinals by Pope Sixtus V.[2] He described how those in the running included 'Dr. Allen,[3] Dr. Lewes,[4] m[r]. Hayes an Irishman,[5] and my lord Prior'.[6] However, he noted:

> My lord Prior beinge sick of the Stone and in great want requested me to remember his duty to mhy Lord Treasorer and your Honor, as his moste honourable Patrons, with this request that his annuities and rents for his houses, one in Trinity lane, and 2. in westminster might be sent him for relief. Considering he sayth your Honors knowe that though in religion he be a Catholick, yet in hart he is a moste dutifull subiect, preferringe the good of his Cuntrie before his private advancement: in regarde whereof he has refused a pension from the Kinge of Spayne.

Reverting to Italian, Powle then summarized reports recently received from Venice, Milan, Rome and Genoa before commenting in English on a report about Sir Francis Drake's recent activities near Cape Saint Vincent in southern Portugal. He also noted that a group of Englishmen, who had recently made a brief trip to Naples, had returned to Venice on 4 July. He recommended, if they returned to England, that they should be questioned about what naval preparations they had seen there since they could be valuable eyewitnesses (*occulati testes*). Powle was clearly referring here to preparations for an 'Impresse' of importance (elsewhere referred to as the 'Enterprise of England') which became in the summer of 1588 the launching of the Spanish Armada fleet and the Duke of Parma's preparations in the Low Countries for a military invasion force for England. This letter of 12 July concluded with more information about how Powle and Walsingham communicated with one another. Powle recommended that outgoing letters to him from England could be dispatched either via 'Master Loe', a merchant based in Milk Street, London, or via other London-based Venetian merchants who had their own

---

[1] *galliots*: small ships with oars and sails (*OED*).

[2] Felice Piergentile (1521–90), elected as Pope Sixtus V in April 1585.

[3] William Allen (1532–94) was created on 7 August 1587 cardinal-priest of SS Silvestro e Martino. He established colleges for the training of English missionary priests and was an ardent supporter of the Spanish Armada (1588). If this invasion had been successful, he would have become Archbishop of Canterbury. He also ordered the Douai-Rheims translation of the Bible.

[4] Unidentified.

[5] Unidentified.

[6] Richard Shelley (*c*.1513–87), see pp. 110, 192 and 260.

established communication networks. Apparently, Loe regularly sent post to Nuremberg which was then forwarded to Venice on a weekly basis.[1]

Powle's next letter from Venice was dated 24 July 1587 and over half was written in Italian.[2] It contained more valuable information about Philip II's 'Enterprise of England'. He provided in English details of the Altanni brothers whom the Spanish King had appointed to take from Venice to the Spanish Ambassador at Constantinople important documents relating to his planned invasion of England. However, the brothers had mysteriously disappeared for five months and it seemed that the letters had never been delivered. In response, Philip II had requested that the Venetian Signoria should apprehend the Altannis because he suspected that they had passed on these letters to English agents who would have sent them to England so that Sir Francis Drake could prepare to foil his 'enterprise'. Following the death of the Spanish secretary who had attempted to prosecute them, the brothers had been freed without any punishment or penalty.

This letter also contained news of the death of the Grand Prior Richard Shelley on about 15 July who had argued with some Jesuits who were sympathetic to English traitors executed in the previous summer.[3] He had left to his trusted servant 'John' the arrearages of his various properties in London and John planned to travel to England to persuade Walsingham to assist him in obtaining this money. Shelley had died with considerable debts outstanding to merchants at Rome. The Knights of Malta had arranged his funeral but also seized all of his goods in Italy as their rightful property. Powle also noted that the 'Enterprise of England' had now been delayed, enabling men levied in Italy for this venture to be utilized in Algiers, although he noted that men were still being levied in every Italian state to support the King of Spain. He concluded this letter by again requesting confirmation of its receipt, although he did not know that Walsingham was currently unwell with kidney problems and was temporarily unable to continue with his official duties.[4]

Powle's next letter to Walsingham, dated 10 August 1587, began by noting that his previous letter of 24 July had been sent, to ensure its security, by one 'Bonna' to the merchant Niccolo di Gozzi in London.[5] Still uncertain as to whether Walsingham was receiving his letters, Powle repeated much of the information contained in his missive of 24 July about military levies in various Italian states in support of Philip II and the names of captains employed in Italy and how the Spanish King was financing these levies via his credit with the Fuggers bankers. Powle also confirmed receipt at Venice on 30 July of the

---

[1] MS Tanner 309, ff. 70r–75v. Stern, *Sir Stephen Powle*, pp. 75–7.

[2] MS Tanner 309, ff. 73v–76v.

[3] Ibid., f. 75r–v. They had probably been discussing the aftermath of the Babington Plot (1586) to assassinate Queen Elizabeth and put Mary Queen of Scots on the English throne. The first group of conspirators to be hanged, drawn and quartered included Anthony Babington (1561–86), the Jesuit priest John Ballard, Chidiock Tichborne (*c.*1562–86), Thomas Salisbury (1564–86), Henry Donn(e), Robert Barnewell and John Savage. A second group, including Edward Habington, Charles Tilney, Edward Jones, John Charnock, John Travers, Jerome Bellamy and Robert Gage, were executed soon afterwards but, as an act of royal mercy, they were allowed to hang until dead before disembowelling and quartering.

[4] MS Tanner 309, f. 76r. Stern, *Sir Stephen Powle*, pp. 77–9.

[5] MS Tanner 309, ff. 76r–78r. This 'Bonna' was probably Jieronimo di Bonna referred to in Powle's letter to Walsingham of 30 May 1587.

news that Robert Dudley, Earl of Leicester (**Plate 23**), was back in the Low Countries near Sluys.

Not all of Powle's letters to Walsingham have survived, as evidenced by a letter, dated 12 September, which Walsingham sent to Burghley, recommending that it should be read to the queen.[1] Although Powle's letter is now lost, Walsingham's comments suggest that Powle thought that the young Huguenot leader, Henri of Navarre, was the French leader whom the queen should be supporting since, following the death of the Duke of Anjou, he was heir-presumptive to the French throne. In August 1587 Henri had sought financial support from England to levy German troops to suppress Guise aggression and the Catholic League. However, despite Walsingham's personal support for Powle's recommendation, Queen Elizabeth was unwilling to commit funds to this venture, although she later relented.

In a light-hearted letter, dated 27 September 1587 and sent by Powle to John Chamberlain (1553–1628) whom he had first met at the Middle Temple, he mentioned that he had instructed his servant Daniel Simpson (who had already returned to England) to brief Chamberlain on his activities abroad.[2] He noted how he had travelled from Augsburg, via Innsbruck and Trent, to Venice under the guidance of 'Moyses the proccaccio' (postal carrier).[3] He then went on to describe his first impressions of Venice in his letter which was to be delivered to Chamberlain by 'Master Egerton':

> By m[r] Luthers direction I was provided of a very good lodginge where I grewe acquainted with the Gentleman the bearer hereof m[r] Egerton a knights sonne and heyre[4] my especial frende with whome I desire you to be acquainted for my sake. The seate of venyce when I behold it in my Gondolo as I came from Margera, me thought resembled some flemish painted table of Landskipt, or some mathematicall demonstration in perspective: the towers and monasteries in the Sea and especially of Muran devided from venyce resembled it so well. But howe this place contented me when I came in, I must tell you my opinion. At the first I was rather amazed then delighted therewith because beinge the day of the Dukes marriage in the Bucentaure to the Sea[5] at Lio,[6] the streets weare stuffed up with a worlde of people. But since that by continuance I have been acquainted with the infinite number of delightes heere, I thinck it be the Paradise of all pleasures that may be possibly devised or Imagined: the patterne of all well governed common wealths for policy: and for territory & jurisdiction the greatest state in all Italy.

---

[1] BL Harleian MS 6994, f. 96r.

[2] MS Tanner 309, ff. 53v–57r. Chamberlain's father Richard (d. 1566) was an alderman and sheriff of London and twice Master of the Worshipful Company of Ironmongers. He left a considerable bequest to his sickly son which meant that he never had to work for a living. He matriculated in 1570 from Trinity College, Cambridge, but left without taking a degree and was almost certainly the John Chamberlain who enrolled in 1575 at Gray's Inn. During the 1570s he may have travelled to Venice since Powle in his letter offers his initial description of Venice to him as 'a later edition than that which you do daily behold within your own memory'.

[3] Ibid., f. 54r.

[4] Powle had earlier met 'Master Luther' at Nuremberg and delivered a 'token' to him from John Chamberlain. Luther recommended comfortable lodgings to Powle. Stern, *Sir Stephen Powle*, p. 82. The identity of this Mr Egerton is uncertain but it is possible that he was the Edward Egerton to whom Powle sent a letter on 26 December 1587; see p. 267.

[5] *Marriage of the Sea (**Plate 11**).

[6] *at Lio*: at the Lido.

Since my com*m*inge hither, I have seen the Arcinall,[1] the Sala di dieci:[2] the Patriarke of Aquileyas antiquities,[3] S[t]. markes treasure: and all other places worth the beholdinge. I have been at Troviso, Padoa, vinconza, verone, Bressia & Bergamo: I have seene Mantoa, & was at the coronation of the younge Duke the 22nd of September.[4] I have seene Ferrara, Ravenna, Rimini, urbin, Pesaro, Ancona, Loretto, Augubio, Perugia, Borgo S*an*to Sepolchro, Concordia, Imola, Faenza, Furli, Siena, Florence, Bologna, Goro, and chiozza.[5] If I go any farther I am a fearde I shall make you a map of Italye in this letter. Though it be of a latter edition then that w*h*ich you doe dayly behoulde w*i*thin your owne memory, yet it can not be so perfecte because I did see these places, tanquam Canis Nilum: bibit et abit.[6] And nowe that I am returned hither, I am but where I was at the first, w*h*ich I make the Centre where I doe quiescere [i.e., rest] this winter. This rest have been but my circumpherences.

Our Comediantis many yeares since banished venice,[7] be renewed at Muran: wheare I wish you to hear madona Francischina,[8] Horatio, and old Pantalon w*i*th his Zane.[9]

In describing his lodgings at Venice, Powle informs Chamberlain how he has found himself living amidst the world of Venice's renowned courtesans. He also refers to rumours that Edward de Vere, seventeenth Earl of Oxford (**item 23**), had consorted with one such notorious figure,[10] Virginia Padoana:

If to be well neighboured be no smalle parte of happines I may repute my self highly fortunate: for I am lodged emongst a great nomber of Signoraes. Isabella Bellochia in the next howse on my right hand: And Virginia Padoana, that honoreth all our nation for my Lord of Oxfords sake, is my neighbour on the lefte side: Over my head hath Lodovica Gonzaga the French kinges m*i*stris her howse: you thinck it peradventure preposterous in Architecture to have hir lye over me. I am sorry for it, but I can not remedye it nowe: Pesarina w*i*th hir sweet entertainment & brave discourse is not 2 Canalls of[f]. Ancilla (m[r] Hattons[11] handmayde) is

[1] *Arsenal (**Plate 12**).

[2] *Sala dei Dieci.

[3] Daniele Barbaro (1513–70), Patriarch of Aquileia, had served as Venetian Ambassador to England (1548–50). He was also an architect, renowned for his commentaries on Vitruvius (Venice, 1556) which is displayed in his portrait by Veronese (Amsterdam, Rijksmuseum). His portrait was also painted by Titian (Museo del Prado).

[4] Vincenzo I Gonzaga (1562–1612), Duke of Mantua and Montferrat (from 22 September 1587). His father, Guglielmo Gonzaga (1538–87) had died on 14 August.

[5] While some of these locations are clear, others cannot be definitively identified. Powle perhaps means Borgo Santo Spirito (Vatican), Sansepolcro (formerly Borgo Santo Sepolcro), Concordia Sagittaria (Veneto), Goro (Ferrara Province) and either Chioggia (Veneto) or Chiozza (Lucca Province).

[6] 'just as the dog at the Nile: he drinks and he departs', a proverbial saying originating in Aesop's fable 'The Dog and the Crocodile'.

[7] In 1530 Andrea Gritti (Doge, 1523–38) (**Plate 4**) had banished some types of comedy from the city of Venice due to their licentious nature.

[8] The name 'madona Francischina' probably indicates a comic, bawdy performer or singer. The title 'madon[n]a' also suggests a member of a religious order. It may recall old sexual scandals relating to canonesses such as Madonna Franceschina di Alvise Boldù or Madonna Franceschina Giustiniani. Lowe, *Nuns' Chronicles*, pp. 83, 171.

[9] In the Commedia Dell'Arte the aged, wealthy and greedy Pantalone often characterized the Venetian mercantile classes. Zanni (Zane, Zani) was a devious servant or trickster. Powle's 'Horatio' refers to 'Il Signor Horacio', a lyrical gentleman lover.

[10] Powle was the son-in-law of John Turner (d. 1579), who had been a servant of John de Vere (1516–62), 16th Earl of Oxford, and was an executor of this earl's will. John Turner leased his residence, Crepping Hall Manor, from Edward de Vere, the 17th Earl (**item 23**). In 1593 Powle married Turner's widowed daughter Margaret (Turner) Smyth.

[11] Unidentified.

in the next Campo: Paulina Gonzaga is not farre of[f]. Prudencia Romana with hir courtly trayne of frenche gentilmen every nighte goeth a spasso [walking] by my Pergalo. As for Imperia Romana hir date is out which flourished in your tyme. I must of force be well hallowed emongst so many Saintes. But in troath I am a frayde they doe condemne me of heresye, for settinge up so fewe tapers on their high Altars ... [1]

This letter, however, does not necessarily prove that this 'Virginia Padoana' (presumably a native of Padua) was Oxford's mistress during his time at Venice. Nina Green explains:

It was the custom at that time for the wives of prominent Venetians to remain secluded at home, and it was these accomplished and polished courtesans who were the female companions of wealthy and titled Venetians at public events and entertainments. It would have been difficult for Oxford, as a nobleman visiting Venice, to have avoided meeting these courtesans in the company of the men whose mistresses they were. Powle's remark about Virginia Padoana is evidence of nothing more than the fact that Virginia Padoana still remembered and admired Oxford eleven years after his visit to Venice.[2]

Returning to Powle's letter to John Chamberlain, he continues by describing some of the city's most famous entertainers and then his own state of mind in view of having to compile more serious missives for Burghley (and probably Walsingham, although he does not mention these intelligence-gathering duties to Chamberlain) and the worrying state of his father's finances:

I doe observe Guicciardins method, *tha*t in every Citties description, forgetteth not the persons *tha*t flourished therein: and you havinge hearde the names of the cheef Ladyes of account, I must put downe likewise the names of *th*e famous Mountebankes: Antonio milanese[3] for a cunninge Ciarlatano:[4] Lucasino[5] for a good voice: but of all Tabarino[6] passeth for a Zane, and Frittado[7] for a maske balle, and shorte Comedyes in the Piazza of S[t] marke.

Doe you not merveill S*i*r to see me write in this kynde[?] I am boulde to make my self merry in your companye hoaping no man shall see these follies of myne but your owne self in your private Chamber. And I doe use this kynde of musick as an Antidotum against melancholy, wherew*it*h I am som times overcharged, when I tourne my thoughts to beholde *tha*t dayly decayinge house,[8] and almoste ruinated to the foundation: for I heare the lande is morgaged. Moreover I have been writing these twoe dayes to my L*or*d Treasoror of matters of more gravity, and therfore I delight in this vayne for change. This humor of voluntary is almoste spent, now to set songes. The occurrants, followed of that weeke as in *Signo*r Georgios[9] hand*es* appeareth: and I writte unto him besides many other particularities of Persia, Polonia, Turkye: and of sundry discontentments betweene the Princes in Italye, and of a proffered marriage to Parmaes sonne Prince Ranuccio by the Pope for Madona Flavia his Niece: by Florence of his

---

[1] MS Tanner 309, ff. 54v–55v. Stern, *Sir Stephen Powle*, pp. 81–4. In 1565 a guide was published detailing noted Venetian courtesans, *Catalogo de tutte le principal et più honorate cortigiane di Venetia*, Venezia: Centro internazionale della grafica, 1984.

[2] http://www.oxford-shakespeare.com/Oxmyths/OxmythsOxford.pdf.

[3] Powle boarded with Antonio Milanese at Padua.

[4] *ciarlatano*, a charlatan or trickster.

[5] Unidentified.

[6] Giovanni Taborino was a famous Venetian actor who also worked at the Imperial Hapsburg court.

[7] Unidentified.

[8] Powle's family residence at Aldersbrook.

[9] Unidentified.

Figure 22.    Giacomo Franco, *Habiti d'huomeni et donne venetiane* (1610). A courtesan with mirror with her hair being dressed. By permission of Special Collections, Brotherton Library, University of Leeds.

Daughter:[1] of Lorraine of his daughter: of the death of Admirall Occialli[2] in Turkye: and of his successor, Ebriam Basha,[3] the Turkes sonne in lawe.

I meane to putt you m$^r$ Chamberlaine to your cipheringe because I scribble this *lettre* in haste.

I performe in measure that w*hich* I want in weight, and I make you a misers feaste, because havinge longe tyme starved you, I glutte you w*ith* a volume of lines.

If you write to me every 14. dayes, I will requite it after the manner of the olde worlde: ware for ware, when com*m*utatio mercium[4] was used.

Sende by Farrington, not by Parvis brother,[5] to me because I like him not: not for injurynge me, but because I heare many complaine that he hath a Com*m*ission to open mens *lettre*s.

Of m$r$ Gents not writinge to me from Nuremberge,[6] being in my debt for a token and a letter from Bremen: I take Parvis to have been the cause of all this unkyndness, whom etc. *sed motos praestat componere fluctus*[7] Com*m*endacions to m$^r$ Cope,[8] m$^r$ Bodleigh,[9] m$^r$ Litton,[10] m$^r$ Evers,[11] m$^r$ D$^r$ Gilbert.[12]

On a far more serious note, Powle wrote to Walsingham on 7 November 1587, to warn him of a potential assassination plot against Queen Elizabeth, with an increased tone of urgency since he thought that an earlier letter about the matter had not been

[1] Alessandro Farnese (1545–92), Duke of Parma, and his son Ranuccio (1569–1622) who married in May 1600 Margherita Aldobrandini (1588–1646), niece of Ippolito Aldobrandini, Pope Clement VIII. However, Ippolito did not become Pope until 1592 and the pope to which Powle refers here is Felice Piergentile (1521–90), who was elected Pope Sixtus V in April 1585. This 'Madonna Flavia' is likely to have been Sixtus V's niece, Flavia Peretti, who married Virginio Orsini (1572–1615), 2nd Duke of Bracciano.

[2] Unidentified.

[3] Unidentified.

[4] 'exchange of commodities'.

[5] Farrington and Parvis's brother were either personal servants or regular mail couriers. Arthur Throckmorton wrote to a 'H. Parvis' when he was at Venice and Padua in 1581; see p. 244.

[6] Powle seems to have first met this William Gent at Paris in November 1581 when Gent taught him the dubious skill of how to swallow a knife without discomfort and, more usefully, how to divide any circumference with a compass. He may also have borrowed money from Gent, possibly without paying it back. Stern, *Sir Stephen Powle*, pp. 49, 124.

[7] 'but it is better to calm the aroused waves': Virgil, *Aeneid*, I, 135.

[8] Walter Cope (*c.*1553–1614), Gentleman Usher to William Cecil, Lord Burghley. Stern, *Sir Stephen Powle*, p. 65. *ODNB*, s.v.

[9] Before leaving England in November 1579, Powle deposited his yearly allowance from his father and some other small sums with a London merchant, 'Master Bodley', to create a bill of exchange from which he could draw money when abroad. This is likely to have been John Bodley (*c.*1520–91), a merchant from Exeter who had been a Marian exile on the continent. He returned to England in September 1559 and settled in London, becoming a freeman of the Drapers' Company. His son, Thomas Bodley (1545–1613), later a diplomat and founder benefactor of the Bodleian Library, Oxford, left England in 1576 for four years to undertake travels and study in France, Italy and the Holy Roman Empire. See TNA E 157/1 for his travel licence. The elder Bodley sent a letter of credit to his son at Lyons on behalf of Powle. Stern, *Sir Stephen Powle*, pp. 33, 223 n. 1. *ODNB*, s.v.

[10] Unidentified.

[11] Powle had earlier met 'Master Evars' at Frankfurt in the company of Horatio Palavicino. 'Evars' had spent a year studying at Heidelberg. Stern, *Sir Stephen Powle*, p. 82.

[12] Unidentified. Two copies of Chamberlain's reply, dated 25 December 1587, were preserved by Powle: one is Chamberlain's autograph copy (MS Tanner 309, ff. 300r–301v) and a scribal copy of its latter section (f. 56r). Stern, *Sir Stephen Powle*, p. 84.

Greco  Francese  Capelleto  Spagnolo  Turchi  Inglese

*Intartenimento che dano ogni giorno li Ciarlatani in Piazza di S. Marco al Populo*
*d'ogni natione che matina e sera ordinariamente ui concore*
*Giacomo Franco Forma con Priuilegio*

Figure 23.    Giacomo Franco, *La Città di Venetia* (1614). Performances in the Piazza San Marco by jesters, watched by foreign visitors. By permission of Special Collections, Brotherton Library, University of Leeds.

delivered.[1] Three years previously Powle had met Stephen Rodway[2] in Bohemia and had sent him to Rome to gather information there. On his return to Venice, Rodway fell into conversation in a coach near Verona with four men. One, an Italian merchant from Bergamo called Giuseppe Giraldo told Rodway about his cousin Michael Giraldo who had recently returned from a trading visit to Constantinople. As soon as he had arrived back at Venice Michael made a secret trip to Rome and then briefly came back to Venice before leaving for England, supposedly for trade purposes. However, Giraldo told Rodway that his cousin was carrying '*una pasta nella scatula per la regina d'Inghilterra*'[3] which may have contained poison and that Michael was undertaking this mission at the orders of Pope Sixtus V. He had asked his cousin Giuseppe to pray for the success of his mission and Powle was convinced that the plot was a real one. He was able to establish that only two vessels had left Venice during the summer: *La Stella Evidale* (in July or August) and the *Gallion Tizzon* (in August). Further research suggested that Michael Giraldo had been travelling on *La Stella Evidale*, as Powle was able to confirm in a later letter to Walsingham. Fortunately for the queen, the ship had been shipwrecked off the Isle of Wight in late September and this assassination attempt thwarted.[4]

On 26 December 1587 Powle wrote from Venice to his friend Edward Egerton who had recently departed for London.[5] Egerton had already sent him three letters and Powle hoped that he would soon be safely back home and married to an honourable gentlewoman. He also described a perilous mission which he had recently undertaken, apparently at Walsingham's request, which he noted:

> was boath lesse dangerous, and more comfortable to me by the good companie of m[r] Geratt.[6] For whose courtezie I thanke you as the author: and I repute my self greatly bounde unto him, for beinge an actor with me in so dangerous a Tragedie as this voyage might have brought us unto. What was the cause wee performed not every point of our former determinacion I suppose m[r] Geratt hath himselfe acquainted you by Letter. Nevertheles I account that travaill boath to have been pleasant & profitable, and so muche to have satisfied me, as no other like unto it that ever I made: Not that I gained any thinge more therby then varietie of solaces, which was the only fruite I gathered. And in truth, s[r] I have learned this one thinge since I came into Italie that Chi va et ritorna fa bon viaggio.[7]

Such thoughts enhanced Powle's homesickness, prompting his longing for the sight of English chimneys and oak trees. He confessed: 'I looke for sume restraint of this unpleasant libertie I enjoye by sume good meanes shortly of calling me home by commandment from hir Majesty'.

On 2 January 1588 Powle replied to three questions which Walsingham had sent to him in a letter of 15 October about the preparations for a Spanish invasion of

[1] BL Harleian MS 296, f. 48. Stern, *Sir Stephen Powle*, pp. 85–6.

[2] Three years after their initial meeting, Powle had travelled with Stephen Rodway (Rodwey) from Frankfurt to Nuremberg. Rodway spoke French and Dutch so fluently that he could pass as a native and he continued to supply Powle with intelligence reports. He also corresponded with John Chamberlain (BL Lansdowne MS 88, f. 41r) and hoped to marry Powle's niece Jane. However, Powle and Rodway later fell out, with Rodway claiming in October 1601 that Powle owed his brother £200. Stern, *Sir Stephen Powle*, pp. 82, 85, 94, 123–5.

[3] 'a pastry in a box for the queen of England'.

[4] Stern, *Sir Stephen Powle*, 88. TNA SP 101/81, 7 November.

[5] MS Tanner 309, f. 57r–v. Stern, *Sir Stephen Powle*, pp. 86–7.

[6] Unidentified.

[7] 'He who goes and returns makes a good journey'. Italian proverb.

England.[1] First Walsingham asked if a potential peace offered by the Duke of Parma was genuine or a trick. Powle was sure that it was no more than a snare to lure the English into complacency. Secondly, Walsingham wondered why the invasion now seemed a realistic possibility when it had been previously deferred on a number of occasions. Powle felt that Philip II was being egged on by the support of the Pope and, since he was now sixty, also wished to ensure that his son Philip (1578–1621) should eventually inherit Portugal, the Low Countries and the Indies. However, these territories were considered by the Spanish to be at considerable risk due to Queen Elizabeth's military presence in the Low Countries, the predatory raids of her navy and privateers, and the presence of Don Antonio in England.[2] Thirdly, Walsingham requested intelligence on what knowledge France and Scotland might have of these affairs. Powle could only answer to this question that their positions were uncertain but he doubted that the Scottish king would seek actively to plot against Queen Elizabeth. In each case, Powle emphasized that his responses should be regarded as no more than his personal opinions, and those of his friends at Venice, and should not be weighed 'in comparison with your Honour's experienced judgement'.[3]

On 16 January 1588 Powle expressed to Walsingham his concerns over the problematic conditions for foreigners in Venice.[4] New regulations had been passed to limit the circulation of intelligence information about the political situation and visitors with no specific reason to be in Venice were being encouraged to leave the city. Powle had been unable to renew his permit (*bolletino*) for more than fifteen days and he claimed to be the only one of 'our English gentlemen' still resident at Venice. He hoped that Walsingham would either procure him a warrant to extend his stay or find somewhere else for him to be based because Venetian officials regularly sought to inspect his credentials. In the meantime, he continued to send home his intelligence reports, most significantly about preparations for the invasion of England. Although there were rumours at Venice that the fleet would soon be ready, he had heard of letters from Lisbon received in late December which suggested that these preparations would take at least another six months because of the poor condition of the fleet and the exhaustion of its sailors. It was reported that the fleet had tried to put to sea at the beginning of December but, due to unusually stormy weather, it had been driven back to the coast of Portugal, thereby placing impossible demands on the food and accommodation resources of Lisbon.

In response to these personal concerns and the useful intelligence supplied in his earlier letters to Walsingham, Lord Burghley wrote to Powle on 15 February 1588, thanking him for the length and quality of his newsletters. He expressed his special gratitude for Powle's letter sent in late November which had systematically assessed the political sympathies of all the Italian states. Burghley's letter, which reveals the care with

---

[1] TNA SP 101/81. Stern, *Sir Stephen Powle*, pp. 88–9.

[2] António (1531–95), Prior of Crato, was a grandson of King Manuel I and a claimant to the throne during the early 1580s.

[3] Walsingham clearly trusted Powle's judgement and ordered the compilation of an 'Abstract of the principal pointes of the letters from M[r] Powle', covering his reports from late December and early January 1587/8. TNA SP 101/81. Stern. *Sir Stephen Powle*, p. 89.

[4] TNA SP 101/81. Stern, *Sir Stephen Powle*, pp. 87–8. See also ibid., pp. 205–13, for Powle's detailed intelligence report, dated 13 February 1588, to Walsingham.

which he treated his most trusted intelligence field agents, is worth quoting here in full:

> Master Powle, I shoold condemne my self deeply, if I thought that you did looke for my letters of thanks or commendacions either so often or in so large a measure[1] as you have deserved the same, by your contynuall writinge to m<sup>r</sup> Secretary [Walsingham], wherof beinge made a participant, I have receaved towards my self a consolation to see the various proceedings of the world; and conceaved in you a great liking, to see your capacitie and judgement, in your advertisements & reportes, wherto for your commendacion I must needs adde, a greate labor and industrie, in writinge at suche length, (as I have observed) in your monthly letters. But settinge that a part which concerneth your publick letters to m<sup>r</sup> Secretary, for the which I am sure he giveth you greate thanks, I can not but particularly acknowledge my self very hartely gladded with a long lettre written by you to me in the latter ende of November; wherin you did at greate length and in a good method anatomize the whole bodie of Italie, describing the Condicions, the sympathyes, and Jointures of all the States and Potentates in suche plaine and probable manner, as anie discourser or inwarde Counsellor of their Cuntries were hable to doe. And truly for my satisfaction therin, I could not finde any thinge lackinge therin to be required. And though I doe frequently reade the advices which commonly come from Italye: and doe take pleasure to see the motion of the worlde that can not rest; yet the substance of your lettre containinge the aspects (as the Astronomers saye) of every particular state one to the other either by Conjunction or opposition; I doe the easiler judge of the probability of all other Common advices, which doe manie times so varie, as without a common rule, (for which your longe discourse dooth serve me) it weare harde to determyn amongst the advertizements what is true, and not true. Thus you see what proffitt I have taken of your writing: and at this tyme perceavinge your servants purpose to come to you, I could not without some note of unkyndnes, but write to you heerofe as I doe. and though you may pretend that I may challendge thus muche of you, because you have knowledged me as your master yet suerly [surely] I esteeme your labour bestowed in your lardge discourse to be of more value then any service at anie time, since I have had servants hath been. And now to ende. I wishe you health to continue as you doe: and therewith I wishe you to be circumspect in the place where you are, to avoide the craftines of false brethren, and the mallice of suche as may be your enemies for your Cuntries sake.
>
> ...
>
> And so I ende with my moste heartie thancks, and therto I must adde a Confession of my debt, for the delicat and costly token that you sent me which was certaine faire spoones of mother of pearle.
>
> From the Court at Greenwyche     .15. Febr. 1587
>      Your assured loving
>        rende
>        W. Burghley[2]

On 28 February (10 March) Powle noted in this newsletter that it was the thirty-first he had sent to Walsingham.[3] He took the opportunity to convey just how demanding –

---

[1] Burghley first wrote 'manner' but then drew a line above this word – his mode of deletion – before adding 'measure'.

[2] MS Tanner 309, ff. 46v–47r. Stern, *Sir Stephen Powle*, pp. 80–81, 213–15. In Tanner MS 78, f. 101r, Powle states that Burghley's letter was written in his own hand.

[3] TNA SP 101/81. Stern, *Sir Stephen Powle*, p. 88.

and expensive – the role of an intelligence gatherer at Venice had become during his year in the city. He noted how he had personally had to pay for intelligence reports and the significant fees required to have his weekly letters transported back to England. Also noting that his father could no longer afford to subsidize his residence at Venice, he respectfully asked if his official allowance could be set at one French crown per day, otherwise he would be forced to give up his role as an intelligence gatherer. Concluding this letter in Italian, Powle expressed the general view that war was imminent in Italy and noted that various tracts were then circulating at Venice, denouncing the execution of Mary Queen of Scots and calling for vengeance. He had bought up as many copies as he could (again at his own expense) and had tried to limit their further circulation, although he could not suppress them entirely. He confirmed that in the previous week he had sent to Walsingham the name of the recently-created cardinals and information about the Spanish king's treasure brought from the Indies by his latest fleet. It is interesting to note that this letter, although in Powle's hand and bearing his seal, is signed 'N. N.' – standing for 'Nomen Nescio' [I do not know the name] – as were some of his other more secret communications back to England.[1]

Powle's Commonplace Book contains a fragment from his thirty-second letter to Walsingham, dated (Saturday) 19 March 1588. It provided details of Spanish preparations for the invasion of England and specific particulars of ships, men, money, and victuals. Powle was astonished that such a large number of men were being mobilized, observing that at Venice it was hoped that Sir Francis Drake would sail down to the coast of Portugal to threaten the Spanish fleet.[2] On the same day he also wrote to a Master Kyrton at Ferrara, apparently a wealthy young Englishman but one who had failed to supply Powle with his full address.[3] The few Englishmen remaining in northern Italy tended to keep in touch with one another, both for security and general information, but Powle's letter could only be addressed to Kyrton at 'Ferrara'. He mentioned that he had not recently heard from Master Rodway and also wished Kyrton success in his suit to become a gentleman to the Duke of Ferrara.[4] On the following Wednesday, 23 March, he received from Kyrton his full address and Powle wrote to him again, gently suggesting that he should be more economical with his paper because Powle had been obliged to pay a large sum for the carriage of his previous letter to him. He also mentioned that he was planning to leave on the following Monday 28 March for Verona on foot (about sixty-five miles) because he was almost choked for his lack of exercise at Venice. If his legs did not hold out he would resort to being a 'Centaure' (i.e., hiring a horse). He was planning to be away from Venice for about eight days and hoped that at Easter they could travel to Ferrara together. Perhaps most significantly, Powle mentioned to Kyrton that he had received a note from Milan which provided details about plans for the King of Spain's 'Emprese of England', including information about provisions for the armada and details of some 400 fighting men.

[1] Ibid., pp. 89–90.
[2] MS Tanner 169, f. 40r. Stern, *Sir Stephen Powle*, p. 90.
[3] MS Tanner 309, ff. 58r–59v. Stern, *Sir Stephen Powle*, pp. 90–94. This 'Kyrton' may have been related to the Thomas Kirton recorded at the English Hospice at Rome (*c.*1563–70) and at Padua (1581).
[4] Alfonso II d'Este (1533–1597), Duke of Ferrara (from 1559).

Walsingham had requested Powle to give his opinion on the prospect of a peace to be concluded between England and Spain. In his Commonplace book Powle listed arguments for and against such an agreement, with the latter far outweighing the former.[1] He then included this judicious assessment in his thirty-third letter to Walsingham, dated 26 March 1588. Powle felt that such a peace would be tactically problematic because it would certainly require relinquishing Holland and Zeeland to Spain and he also estimated that the strength of Philip II's navy and militia was much overrated. Although all the signs suggested that an invasion was imminent, Powle thought that the Spanish king might well prefer a peace because his age might leave him more disposed toward quietness. After such lengthy and expensive preparations, Powle felt that Philip would certainly feel dishonoured if his Armada did not sail. However, he also noted that the Spanish king had numerous other problems to deal with which could well limit his potential aggression towards England. For example, it was rumoured that the Turks might send their galleys to threaten Malta, Naples or Sicily; Emperor Maximilian[2] was then imprisoned in Poland and the cost of his release would have to be borne by Philip. Equally, the Low Countries campaign was proving immensely expensive and English privateers under Sir Francis Drake were threatening Philip's treasure fleets from the Indies and, if this source of finance were removed by English privateering, he would be obliged to levy money from the likes of the Fuggers. On balance, therefore, Powle considered that the Armada might well never be launched. Although his speculation was proved incorrect when the fleet finally set sail from Lisbon in May 1588, Powle was accurate at this time in realizing that Philip was so financially overstretched that his navy was inadequately equipped. No less significantly, continuing military actions in the Low Countries limited the Duke of Parma's ability to become involved in the planned invasion; or perhaps more likely, Parma had already shrewdly realized the impossibility of Philip's invasion plans and so was not intending to commit his troops to such a foolhardy mission.[3]

On 6 April Powle wrote again to Kyrton, expressing his puzzlement over the dating of his letters because, while his from Venice arrived within one day, Kyrton's seemed to be taking at least four days to be delivered to Powle. He also sternly advised him to be circumspect about what he wrote since letters could readily be opened and read by hostile eyes. He passed on news of the Prince of Condé's poisoning, the arrival of Queen Elizabeth's commissioner at Ostend and the imminent signing of a peace treaty at Antwerp. He was also expecting the arrival of letters from Rodway at Frankfurt and promised to pass on any interesting news to Kyrton.[4]

A section of Powle's thirty-fourth letter from Venice to Walsingham has survived, dated 20 April 1588, providing the following intelligence:

> Not foure dayes since as I came from Verona in the companye of a younge gentleman of
> Naples, that was going into Flaunders as he tould me, supposinge me (whom he thought to

[1] MS Tanner 237, ff. 26r–31r.

[2] Maximilian III (1558–1618) of Austria was briefly known as Maximilian of Poland during his claim in 1587 to the Polish throne. Some of the Polish nobility duly elected him but others chose Sigismund III Vasa (1566–1632), Prince of Sweden. Maximilian initiated the War of the Polish Succession but was defeated in January 1588 and taken captive at the Battle of Byczyna. He was only released after some eighteen months, following the intervention of Pope Sixtus V.

[3] MS Tanner 169, ff. 40v–41v. Stern, *Sir Stephen Powle*, pp. 92–3.

[4] Ibid., pp. 93–4.

be French) to have a place in the spoile of Eng*la*nd. I heard this discoursed on, that the Armata [*sic*] beinge nowe in a readines to goe forthe, and the D*uke* of Parma beinge furnished with all thing*es* necessarie for the Impresa, there wanted nothinge but to reducesse certi piccioli impedimenti[1] that the K*ing* of Scots had in his owne countrye, by reason of his preachers, wh*i*ch he forthwithe would take order in to perfect the whole enterprise. The resolution betwene whom and the K*ing* of Spain was to settle him in her M*a*jesties seate, And after to give him his daughter, the Infanta, in marriage. And for a dowrye to give her the Kingdome of Portugall. These greate matters of momente the Neapolitan had begune and ended, with one mile ridinge. Many other suche fabulous report*es* and dream*es*, I dayly heare, whych I do not acquainte yo*u*r Hono*u*r with because as there is a brainsicke follye of suche as conceave them in their idle thought*es*, so there is a kinde of offence in writinge them and the harmonye in reading thereof is very harshe and unpleasant.[2]

It is not clear whether this letter was ever sent because in another hastily written letter to Walsingham, dated 29 April 1588, Powle noted that his last letter had been sent on 14 April. Since then his servant, presumably Daniel Simpson, had arrived at Venice from England with Walsingham's orders for him to return to England, along with £50 to cover his travelling expenses. Powle promised to leave Venice as soon as possible, perhaps even that same day, and stated that he would travel back to England via Hamburg, aiming to arrive home by the end of May. This letter was signed with a primitive form of invisible ink, leaving Powle's signature visible only when viewed with a light behind the paper.[3] When he arrived home in late May or early June he found that he had been honoured by a grant of arms designed by William Dethick (*c.*1542–1612), Garter King of Arms, presumably at the instruction of Burghley or Walsingham. He based himself at his father's house in Maiden Lane and wrote a letter to Burghley, bringing him up to date with Italian news from just before his departure from Venice, adding further information about activities in Western Europe gleaned during his travels home. He also noted to Burghley that he had been ordered home by Walsingham because of the escalating dangers to his welfare at Venice.[4]

[1] 'reduce certain small hindrances'.
[2] MS Tanner 169, f. 35r–v. Stern, *Sir Stephen Powle*, p. 94.
[3] Stern, *Sir Stephen Powle*, p. 94.
[4] Ibid., pp. 95–7.

# 30. VENETIAN INTELLIGENCE ABOUT THE SPANISH ARMADA IN 1588

'Venice', as Logan Pearsall Smith notes, 'was the first State in Europe to form a regular diplomatic service' and it was 'regarded as the best place for the training of an ambassador'.[1] Hence, the lack of formal diplomatic contacts between England and Venice for the entirety of Queen Elizabeth's reign proved in 1587 and 1588 a self-inflicted disadvantage for her regime. While Sir Francis Walsingham (**Plate 24**) was obliged to gather crucial continental information from a network of informal intelligence gatherers and amateur spies like Stephen Powle, England and Queen Elizabeth were placed at a distinct disadvantage during the build-up to the Armada crisis by its lack of direct diplomatic channels with the Venetian Republic. As Garrett Mattingly explains:

> Though in the years of her [Queen Elizabeth's] greatest danger her Secretary Sir Francis Walsingham build up for her protection what some historian has described with awe as 'an omnipresent network of spies', this impressive system of counter-espionage in England dwindles on inspection to a few underpaid agents of varying ability whose efforts were supplemented by casual informers and correlated by a single clerk who also handled much of Walsingham's ordinary correspondence – a system hardly larger or more efficient, except for the intelligence of its direction and the zeal of its volunteer aids, than that which every first-rate ambassador was expected to maintain for his own information, one which the governments of Florence or Venice would have smiled at as inadequate for the police of a single city.[2]

In sharp contrast, Venice's Council of Ten systematically organized the collection, communication and evaluation of formal reports from state officials, along with other miscellaneous pieces of intelligence gleaned from disparate sources. As Ioanna Iordanou notes:

> As Venice's spy chiefs, in an exemplary display of political and organizational maturity, the Council of Ten developed and administered an elaborate system of information flow with and between their informants and other underlings. To achieve this, they oversaw and managed a far-flung, yet interconnected network of private informants and public servants whose role was to supply them with vital intelligence for the political and, by extension, economic conduct of the Venetian Republic.[3]

Spain's imperial ambitions were viewed at Venice with grave suspicion and throughout the latter half of 1587 and 1588 the doge and Senate received detailed and well-informed

[1] Wotton, *Life and Letters*, I, p. 51.

[2] Mattingly, *Spanish Armada*, pp. 23–4.

[3] Iordanou, *Venice's Secret Service*, pp. 2–3. See ibid., pp. 42–7, for Spanish intelligence networks and Venice's contacts with them. The Spanish embassy at Venice during Philip II's reign became a key geopolitical focus of military and commercial espionage.

intelligence reports from its various European ambassadors concerning the preparations, sailing and ultimate defeat of the Spanish Armada. The Venetian authorities regarded Protestant England as a staunch opponent of Spanish military ambitions in Western Europe and especially of Philip II's fanatically Catholic crusade which bonded him so closely with the other major threat to Venice's republican independence and commercial prosperity – the Papacy. Hence, it seems likely that, if Anglo-Venetian diplomatic relations had been productively maintained in London and Venice during Queen Elizabeth's reign, the surreptitious exchange of military intelligence about the Spanish Armada preparations would have been both possible and probable.

Numerous substantial reports, detailing both verified facts and rumours about Spanish naval and military preparations, were submitted to the doge and Senate by Hieronimo Lippomano (Venetian Ambassador to Spain), Giovanni Gritti (Rome), Giovanni Dolfin and Giovanni Mocenigo (France), Vincenzo Gradenigo (Germany) and Giovanni Moro (Constantinople). Their reports provide a vivid and often exceptionally well-informed commentary on the intended Spanish invasion of England and reveal just how momentous a political event it was considered throughout both Western Europe and as far as Constantinople. They also demonstrate how knowledgeable the Venetian Senate was about Spanish naval preparations. This level of intelligence would have been invaluable to Sir Francis Walsingham, William Cecil, Lord Burghley, and Charles Howard, Lord Howard of Effingham – if only they had been able to access it. However, due to the lack of reciprocal ambassadors between England and Venice, Queen Elizabeth and her Privy Council were deprived of potential access to one of the most efficient and wide-reaching intelligence services in Europe.

Little was known about these diplomatic reports until after their publication as the *Calendar of State Papers ... Venice* (1894–1905). This pioneering work of research and translation was first undertaken by Rawdon Lubbock Brown (1806–83) who, as an employee of the British Public Records Office, worked for twenty years in the Venetian archives. After his death this project was taken over in 1889 and completed by the Scottish historian Horatio Robert Forbes Brown (1854–1926).[1]

As early as 2 January 1588 Gritti had reported from Rome that 'his Holiness will assist the King of Spain with money for the attack on England' (615); and on the same day Lippomano sent from Madrid news of the activities of English corsairs around Cape St Vincent and a detailed breakdown of troops mustering at Lisbon (616, 617).[2] Lippomano also noted on 8 January: 'His Majesty [King Philip II] shows that he will not submit to the Queen of England any longer' (619). From France came reports from Dolfin and Mocenigo that the English fleet was sailing towards Flanders 'to oppose any force which the Duke of Parma may set in motion' and Sir Francis Drake was sailing towards Spain to monitor Spanish navel movements (620). On 20 January Lippomano wrote again from Madrid, noting that the Spanish fleet was to be 'victualled for eight months with provisions for sixteen thousand troops and six thousand sailors'. He also noted that reports had been received in Spain of Queen Elizabeth's mustering of her troops at the southern ports and the size and power of her fleet which, he rightly thought, 'will be able to inflict some further damage on Spain and Portugal'. Lippomano was equally prescient

---

[1] Rawdon Brown and Horatio Brown were unrelated.
[2] These references cite item numbers in *CSP Venice ... 1581–1591.*

in observing that the Spanish fleet could well find it problematic to join 'their forces with those of the Duke of Parma' in Flanders (621). He also reported on 13 February the death of the intended admiral of the Armada fleet, the Marquis of Santa Cruz (1526–88), and the king's appointment in his place of the unwilling Alonso Pérez de Guzmán y de Zúñiga-Sotomayor (1550–1615), Duke of Medina Sidonia, 'in spite of his want of experience at sea' (627, 628).

On 11 March Mocenigo reported from France that the 'house of Guise is pledged to the King of Spain' (637) and that Queen Elizabeth was sending five commissioners, including Ferdinando Stanley (1559–94), Earl of Derby, and William Brooke (1527–97), Lord Cobham, the Governor of the Cinque Ports, to negotiate with the Duke of Parma (639). On 12 March Gritti recounted his conversation with Sixtus V (Pope 1585–90), during which the Pope revealed his warm personal regard for Queen Elizabeth, especially her diplomatic statecraft in her dealings with the Ottoman Empire:

> His Holiness then said, 'We hear that the Turk is preparing a great fleet, and that the Queen of England is urging him to send it out; for this she promises him three hundred thousand ducats'. He added, 'She is a great woman: and were she only Catholic she would be without her match, and we would esteem her highly. She omits nothing in the government of her kingdom; and is now endeavouring by way of Constantinople, to divert the King of Spain from his enterprise'. (640).

Throughout spring and summer 1588 Lippomano continued to supply the doge and Senate with detailed information about Spanish military and naval numbers and preparations while Mocenigo in Paris always seemed very well informed about English naval manoeuvres and land preparations against invasion, noting on 8 April that the English fleet would render it very difficult for the Spaniards even 'to approach the English coast' (648). On 18 May Moro advised the Senate from Constantinople that Murad III (Sultan 1574–95) had told him: 'The Venetians are not behaving as well as they used to. I am informed that they are helping the King of Spain, who is my enemy, against the Queen of England, who is my ally' – a worrying statement in view of Ambassador Lippomano's personal intimacy with Philip II of Spain. Moro was so concerned that he immediately sent his secretary to 'inform the English Ambassador of the questions I had been asked'. The Ambassador, William Harborne (c. 1542–1617), advised Moro that this was probably no more than a malicious rumour spread by someone who wished to foster discord between the Republic of Venice and the English queen (665). Moro even sought to persuade the Sultana to assure Sultan Murad that Venice was not supplying galleys to Spain to assist with their planned invasion of England, noting that 'light galleys like ours are not built for ocean navigation' (668). In fact, three Venetian merchantmen did sail with the Spanish Armada with dire consequences for their owners, crews and soldiers. *La Regazzona* returned to Spain seriously damaged and sank off La Coruña; *La Lavia* ran aground north of Sligo on the west coast of Ireland; and *La Trinidad Valencera* was wrecked on 16 September 1588 at Kinnagoe Bay, County Donegal.

Once the Spanish fleet had set sail from Lisbon on 29 May, Lippomano kept the doge and Senate regularly informed of its movements since he was clearly receiving from someone within Philip II's close circle of advisors detailed intelligence about the fleet's ships, numbers of soldiers and intended route. His report to the Senate written on 2 July also made it clear that he had direct access to the despatches sent to the Spanish court by

Medina Sidonia from the fleet and that Philip II was in poor health, suffering from gout in his hand and doing little more than passing 'day and night in prayer'. Lippomano was clearly growing more and more sceptical of the wisdom of Philip II's plans to invade England and sensed that they were based more on religious fanaticism rather than pragmatic naval and military strategy. His despatch concluded cynically: 'Spain is full of processions, austerities, fasting and devotion' in the hope that such devotions would enhance the Armada's chance of a successful outcome.

This same report also disclosed that Lippomano had an informant aboard one of the Spanish ships who wrote to him in Italian. This individual, perhaps an Italian volunteer or mercenary, had sent him a detailed account from La Coruña of the Armada's progress (680). However, such intelligence leaks were highly dangerous for not only the Spanish fleet and the on-board informant but also for Lippomano himself if he was caught receiving such documents and on 12 July he reported:

> The Duke of Medina Sidonia has issued orders forbidding, upon pain of death, any information about the Armada to be sent to anyone. This causes great difficulty in procuring news; all the same I am informed that the departure of the Armada cannot take place for many days, and that many ships are lying in the ports of Galicia too badly damaged to be able to join the rest of the fleet. (687)

Clearly, the latter part of this statement indicates that Lippomano was still hopeful of obtaining such useful and detailed intelligence. Furthermore, the level of his infiltration of Philip II's personal circle is evidenced by his next statement, describing how the king insisted on 'studying and directing every detail' and how he had even 'sent to the commander-in-chief [Medina Sidonia] the order and plan of an engagement with Drake, a copy of which I enclose'. He must have been confident in the security of his dispatches to Venice because he casually remarked that he had been 'able to have it copied from the original which lay on his Majesty's desk' (687).

Similarly, Mocenigo was able to send back from France on 18 July detailed information about the location and tactics of the English fleet and how it was 'always to the windward of the Spanish fleet, and to fight it at a vantage should it enter the channel and attempt to effect a junction with the forces of the Duke of Parma' (691). Once the two fleets had engaged in battle, Meconigo sent virtually daily briefings throughout August back to Venice on the ensuing disaster for Spain, including a vivid account of the English fire ships and 'continual losses for the Spanish' (713). Gritti at Rome was also able to send secretly back to Venice on 3 September a copy of a letter written by the Duke of Parma on 12 August, claiming that he had 'all of his men embarked and ready' (728); and Gradenigo sent from Prague on 6 September the dispiriting news for the Spanish that the 'Armada itself has been borne northward' (731).

Lippomano had also gained access to some of the Duke of Parma's dispatches to Philip II, copies of which he sent back to Venice, 'detailing the misfortune which befell the Armada' (732). From early October onwards Lippomano's reports from Spain were uniformly grim, describing on 1 October the returning remnants of the Armada as 'in a very bad plight' but noting (inaccurately) that the 'three Venetians are all safe'. He concluded that 'there are serious differences between the Duke of Medina Sidonia and the Duke of Parma, each one trying to throw the blame on the other' (747). On 7 October he was still hoping for news of the 'three Venetian ships which formed part of the Armada', although he heard that Medina Sidonia had told the king that the *Regazzona* had done very well in that brush with the enemy' (750). As soon as it became clear that the Spanish fleet had been scattered and many vessels lost, Mocenigo regularly met with the English Ambassador at Paris, Sir Edward Stafford (1552–1605), to exchange news about the aftermath of the Armada and how both sides would be well served if England and Venice could strengthen their political contacts through diplomatic means.[1] Mocenigo reported on 24 October that they had met, ostensibly to discuss customs dues, but really to discuss Anglo-Venetian diplomatic relations:

> He [Stafford] then went on to say that he knew how acutely her Majesty felt it that your Serenity had never sent an Ambassador to her Court as to that of her predecessors, and more especially to that of her brother, who was of the same religion as herself. I endeavoured to assure his Lordship that the esteem of the Republic for his mistress was in no way diminished by this fact. The Ambassador replied, 'I do not desire to go into the motives which govern Venice, but I would only point out that at the present juncture of affairs it would be as well to foster friendly relations by all possible means.' (767)

As both Mocenigo and Stafford clearly realized, England and Venice could have done much to assist one another during the Armada crisis, if it had been possible to sustain collaborative diplomatic relations during the reigns of Edward VI and Queen Elizabeth.

It is difficult to assess whether Stafford was involving himself in this kind of discussion with Mocenigo with the approval of the English Council or if he was taking the initiative in seeking to foster productive Anglo-Venetian collaborations. This situation is rendered even more complex by well-founded suspicions that Stafford (who had run up substantial gambling debts while in Paris) was also meeting informally from early 1587 with Bernardino de Mendoza (*c*.1540–1604), the Spanish Ambassador at Paris, during the Armada crisis. Mendoza had previously served from 1578 as Spanish Ambassador to London until his expulsion in 1584 due to his involvement in the Catholic Throckmorton Plot against Queen Elizabeth. He was especially close to Philip II and they used to correspond in a code (supposedly) known only to both of them. He then served from 1584 until 1590 as Spanish Ambassador to France and, as an ardent supporter of Philip's interventionist foreign policies and desire to restore Catholicism to England, acted as a paymaster for the extremist Catholic League aimed at eradicating the Huguenots in France and, ultimately, Protestantism in England. Given Mendoza's ready access to Habsburg funds to support this league, it is likely that Stafford was tacitly receiving payments from him for passing on intelligence about the English fleet and even deliberately feeding misinformation back to England. For example, on 24 January 1588 Stafford sent the startling (and dangerously inaccurate) intelligence that the Armada fleet had been disbanded. Howard of Effingham (whose sister Douglas had married Sheffield in 1579) incredulously commented in a letter to Walsingham:

> I cannot tell what to think of my brother Stafford's advertisement; for if it be true the King of Spain's forces be dissolved, I would not wish the Queen's Majesty to be at this charge that

---

[1] Sir Edward Stafford was the son of the Marian exile, Sir William Stafford (b. by 1512, d. 1556), who was the elder brother of Sir Robert Stafford. See p. 167 n. 5. Through his mother, Dorothy, Sir Edward was descended from Edward IV's brother, George (1449–78), Duke of Clarence. His father's first wife, Mary Boleyn (1499–1543), was Queen Elizabeth's aunt and his mother Dorothy served Elizabeth for many years as her Mistress of the Robes.

she is at; but if it be a device, know that a little thing makes us too careless, then I know not what may come of it.

It also seems likely that Stafford disclosed to Mendoza advance warning of Sir Francis Drake's raid on Cadiz (April–May 1587) and information relating to the gathering of the English fleet.[1]

Mendoza was a master of misinformation and Stafford's attempt in January 1588 to hoodwink English intelligence into thinking that the Armada fleet had been disbanded may well have been initiated by Mendoza. Similarly, by 12 August the Spanish fleet had been defeated at the Battle of Gravelines and its remnants were fleeing northwards. On the same day Mendoza was granted an audience with the French king, Henri III, whom he hoped to assure of the triumphal success of the Spanish forces until he was handed a letter, dated 8 August, from M. Gourdan, the Governor of Calais, which offered a very different picture. It detailed how the Armada had been dislodged by the English fire ships and fled into the North Sea, except for one galleass which had run aground below Calais Castle. Mendoza continued to receive conflicting and often false news, including claims that fifteen English galleons had been sunk off Scotland and that Sir Francis Drake had been captured when attempting to board the *San Martin* and was being held as a prisoner of Medina Sidonia. Despite growing doubts over the veracity of these reports, Mendoza still tried to assure Philip II of the success of the Armada expedition. The Spanish Ambassador at Prague, Don Guillén de San Clemente (1550–1608), remained no less confident of an ultimate Spanish victory. Similarly, at the Vatican the Spanish Ambassador, Enrique de Guzmán (1540–1607), Count Olivares, advised Pope Sixtus V that a *Te Deum* should be celebrated in all Roman churches to mark the triumph of Spanish Catholicism over Protestant England.

In contrast, the first definite news on the continent of the English victory came via Giovan Francesco Morosini (1537–96), Papal Nuncio at Paris, who sent to Rome on 17 August a manuscript 'Journal of all that Passed between the Armies of Spain and England from July 28th to August 11th, 1588, According to News from Divers Places'. Although this document was written in French and bore New Style dates, its content was based upon English Privy Council reports, closely resembling the 'Abstract of Accidents Between the Two fleets', which Howard of Effingham had submitted to the Council. Morosini confirmed that his original source was English and it seems virtually certain that Stafford had personally supplied him with this information.[2] After the Armada campaign Stafford seems to have gradually ceased passing on information to Mendoza while Giovanni Mocenigo, the Venetian Ambassador, was still meeting with him. On 23 September Mocenigo noted that Stafford had told him of Queen Elizabeth's personal displeasure with Henri III who seemed to have done 'all he can to assist her enemies' [i.e., Philip II]. He concluded with a report which seems to have been based upon his conversations with Stafford:

> We have no news here of the Armada. The English fleet is out again. A detachment of the fleet has passed over to Havre de Grace to capture a Spanish galleon which has been driven in there by storm. The galleon lies outside the harbour, and has put on shore forty thousand crowns and other provision of war. The Ambassador found some difficulty in recovering this property, which was claimed by the Admiralty; but the King has sent orders to surrender it

---

[1] It is known that Stafford accepted 3,000 crowns from the Duke of Guise for allowing him to read English diplomatic correspondence. *ODNB*, s.v.

[2] Mattingly, *Spanish Armada*, pp. 319–25.

all. The Queen of England has returned to London to comfort her people. There is a scheme for fortifying all the coast on both sides of Margate, which is the place where a landing might most easily be effected, and where it was discovered that the Spaniards actually intended to land. This can be done at very small cost, and in a very short time. (742)

Almost one month later on 20 October Mocenigo informed the doge and Senate that Stafford had told him that nineteen Spanish ships had been lost around the coast of Ireland, with some four thousand men dying. Stafford had also reported how:

> The Queen received this news from Ireland with tears of joy in her eyes, as it were the final liberation from this attack, the power of which has been estimated rather from the length of preparation and Spanish confidence in its success than from any secure foundation in the enterprise itself. (762)

This news prompted Mocenigo's and Stafford's friendly discussions on 24 October (767, quoted earlier) over the possibility of closer diplomatic relations between Venice and England, although Mocenigo did not report any further contacts with Stafford between November 1588 and the end of January 1589. However, on 2 February Mocenigo confirmed to the doge and Senate that he had passed on to Stafford their demand 'for the liberation of the crew of the "Balanzara," detained in Ireland', noting that 'His Lordship promised so to act that the Queen will give every satisfaction' (810).

This vessel was one of three Venetian traders requisitioned in Sicily, against the wishes of its captain Horatio Donai, by the Spanish for the Armada campaign. Renamed the *Trinidad Valencera* (a Spanish corruption of her original Venetian name) and fitted with twenty-eight bronze guns, she was the most heavily armed ship in the Levant Squadron of the Armada which included ten other converted Mediterranean merchant ships. She carried 281 Neapolitan soldiers, a cadre of officers and 79 crew – most of whom, presumably, were the sailors whose safe return the Venetian Senate had requested. The *Trinidad Valencera* saw action during the Battle of Gravelines before fleeing northwards. On 12 September she was caught in a storm of the north coast of Ireland and anchored two days later in Kinnagoe Bay. On 16 September she split in two and sank, although most of those still aboard seemed to have safely reached the shore. After being tricked into laying down their arms 300 were slaughtered by Anglo-Irish soldiers. All but two of the ship's officers were murdered at Dublin on the personal orders of the Lord Deputy, Sir William Fitzwilliam (c. 1526–99), who regarded his forces in Ireland as too small and lightly armed to sustain a large prison garrison. Only thirty-two crew members managed to escape to Scotland and were granted safe passage by James VI to France.[1] After these unfortunate circumstances, the Venetian State Papers do not record any further intimate discussions between Mocenigo and Stafford, who vacated his embassy for England in 1590.[2]

---

[1] Paine, *Warships*, p. 175.

[1] On 12 May Mocenigo advised the doge and Senate that there was now 'no English Ambassador in this country' because Stafford had returned to England due to his perilous financial position. However, Queen Elizabeth instructed him to return to France and he spent much of the autumn at Henry of Navarre's camp outside Paris. He then finally returned to England in November 1590. Mocenigo had been instructed to seek assistance in either tracing or freeing a 'son of the Admiral' and noted: 'If I am summoned to the King it is possible that I may find a way to help him by sending letters to Mons. de Stafford, who was Ambassador at this Court, and who courteously undertook to protect other Venetian subjects who had suffered in the operations against England [i.e. the Armada]' (932). https://www.historyofparliamentonline.org/volume/1558-1603/member/stafford-edward-ii-1552-1605.

# 31.   1588 – EDWARD WEBBE

Although **Edward Webbe (1553/4–after 1592)** was only briefly at Venice in 1588, his account of his experiences is included here because it provides a rare insight into the brutal life of a sailor and military man who not only travelled widely but also experienced several years as a galley slave in the Turkish navy.[1] He was eventually freed through the intervention of the English Ambassador at Constantinople but on his way back to England he fell under suspicion of being an English spy and was subject to interrogation and torture at Naples. While most of his sensational narrative cannot be verified from other contemporary sources, Webbe insisted in his 'The Epistle to the Reader' upon the veracity of his accounts:

> And this I protest, that in this booke there is nothing mentioned or expressed but that which is of truth, and what mine owne eyes have perfectly séene. Some foolish persons perhaps wil cavil & say, that these are lies and fained fables, and that it conteineth nothing else: but to those I answere, that what soever is herein mentioned, he whosoever he be, that shall so finde fault and doubt of the trueth hereof, let him but come and conferre with me or make enquiry of the best and greatest Travellers and Marchantes about all this land: and they doubtles shall be resolved that this is true which is here expressed: with a great deale more, which now I cannot call to remembrance, for that my memorie faileth me, by meanes of my great and gréeuous troubles. (sig. A3r)

The printed account of his experiences, *The Rare and Most Wonderfull Things Which Edw. Webbe an Englishman borne, Hath Seene and Passed in his Troublesome Travailes* (1590), dedicated to Queen Elizabeth, offers a sensational account of daily life on Mediterranean battle galleys from a slave's point of view, as well as a record of the dangers for an ordinary Protestant Englishman travelling through Catholic Italy during this period.[2]

Edward Webbe was born at St Katherine's by the Tower of London, the son of Richard Webbe, a 'master gunner of England' (sig. A4r), but nothing else is known about his family background. In his narrative he states that at the age of twelve his father placed him in the service of Captain Anthony Jenkinson (1529–1611), English representative to Russia, who sailed on his third voyage from England to Muscovy on 4 May 1566 with the unenviable brief of discussing trade deals with Ivan IV Vasil'evich ('Ivan the Terrible') (1530–84). Webbe was Jenkinson's personal servant and remained in Russia with him until 1568.[3] He then sailed in 1570 in the *Hart* with Captain William Borough for Narva

---

[1] Webbe's description of being an English galley slave may be compared to a later account, Davies, *True Relation*, p. 1614.

[2] Webbe's account proved so popular that it went through five printings in 1590 (*STC* 25151.5, 25151.7, 25152. 25153, 25154), and was sold by three stationers (William Wright, William Barley and Thomas Pavier). Quotations here are taken from *STC* 25152.

[3] A brief account of Jenkinson's mission is included in Hakluyt, *Principal Navigations*, I, pp. 372–4.

in the Gulf of Finland and was in Moscow on 24 May 1571 when it was burnt by Crimean Tartars. Although he escaped from the ruined city he was captured by the Tartars, taken with seven other Englishmen to Kaffa in the Crimea and enslaved for five years, required to carry out menial tasks:

> we were set to wipe the féete of the kings horses, and to become ordinary slaves in the sayd Court, to fetch water, cleave wood, and to doe such other drudgerié. There were we beaten thrée times a wéeke with a Bulls pissell,[1] or a horse tayle. (sig. a4v)

He was eventually ransomed for 'thrée hundred crownes which is seven shillings sixe pence a péecé, of currant English money' (sig. A4v). This section of his narrative, however, remains suspect because elsewhere in *The Rare and Most Wonderfull Thinges* Webbe states that he was serving in the *Royal* as a master gunner with the Christian forces under Don Juan of Austria when Tunis was captured from the Turks in October 1572.[2]

After returning to England Webbe sailed again aboard the *Hart* and with thirty other ships to Russia but on the return journey was shipwrecked and lost all of his possessions. Setting sail once again in another ship called the *Henry*, he was bound for the Levant via Leghorn. Unbeknown to Webbe and most of the crew, this ship had already been sold to one 'Doctor Hector and other Italian Marchants'. Once they had arrived at Leghorn they were required by the 'factors of those that were the owners thereof' (sig. B1r) to carry merchandise to Alexandria with Webbe promoted to the rank of master gunner. But on the voyage back to Leghorn (Livorno) they encountered:

> fiftie saile of the Turkes Gallies: with which Gallies we fought two daies and two nightes, and made great slaughter amongst their men, we being in all but thréescore men, verie weake for such a multitude, and having lost fiftie of our 60. men: faintnes constrained us to yéeld unto them, by reason wée wanted winde to helpe our selves, and the calme was so great a helpe unto them, as there was no way for us to escape. Thus did the Turkes take the Ship & goods, and in the same found ten of us living whom they tooke prisoners, and presently stripped us naked, and give us 100. blowes a péece with an Oxe Pissell, for presuming to fight against them. (sigs. B1r–v)

The survivors were transported to Constantinople and 'committed unto the Gallies' (sig. B1v) for the next six years. Webbe's account of his experiences in the Turkish galleys may be taken as typical of the brutal treatment meted out by both Turks and Christians to slaves in their navies.

> First, we were shaven head and face, and then a shert of Cotten and bréeches of the same put upon us: our legges and féete left naked: and by one of the feete is each slave chained with a great chaine to the Gallie, and our handes fastned with a paire of Mannacles. The foode which I and others did eat, was verie black, far worse then Horse bread:[3] and our drinke was stinking water, unlesse it be when wée come to the places where we tooke in fresh swéet water, at which time we supposed our diet to be verie daintie.
>
> Thus as I said before, I remained six yeares in this miserable estate, wonderfully beaten & misused every day: there have I séene of my fellowes when they have béene so weake as they

---

[1] *Pissell*: pizzle, penis.

[2] *ODNB*, s.v.

[3] *Horse bread*: bread made of beans, bran, etc. for the food of horses (*OED*).

could not rowe by reason of sickenes and faintnes: where the Turkes would laie upon them as upon Horses, and beate them in such sort, as oft times they died, and then threw them into the Sea. (sigs. B1v–B2r)

To avoid starvation, Webbe revealed to his captors his 'good skill in Gunners Art' (sig. B2r) and he served as a gunner with the Turkish army during their campaign to Persia. These travels, he claimed, took him to Calabria, Damascus, Cairo, Goa, Bethlehem, Jerusalem, Syria and 'the land of prester John, who is by profession a Christian' (sig. B3r).[1] However, even when serving as the 'maister Gunner of the Admirals Gally' Webbe was 'yet chained gréevously, and beaten naked with a Turkish sword flatling, for not shooting where they would have me, and where I could not shoote' (sig. B3v). Back at Constantinople, he was imprisoned with two thousand other Christians, 'pinde up in stone walles lockt fast in yron chaynes' (sig. C2v). Five hundred, including Webbe, broke out of the prison but all were recaptured and savagely beaten: 'seven hundreth blowes a péece with a bulls pissell upon the naked skinne, viz. thrée hundred on the belly, and foure hundred on the backe' (sig. C3r). In 1589 Webbe and 'sundry other English captives' (sig. C3r) were ransomed (through a subscription by London citizens) with the assistance of the English Ambassador William Harborne (1542–1617), who had successfully persuaded Sultan Murad III not to support Spain in its struggle with Protestant England:

> At the same time that I was released, there were set at libertie about twentie English men, whereof I was one of the last: some of them are at this present in England. My selfe and others were released by meanes of her Majesties favourable letters sent to the great Turke, brought by the aforesaide maister Harborne, some by the ransome money gathered at sundrie times by the Marchants in the Citie of London, for that godly purpose: of which, some of their names that were released were these. Hamond Pan, Iohn Béere, Iohn Band, Andrew Pullins, Edward Buggins and others. (sig. C3v)

Webbe explained that after being freed in Turkey he travelled overland towards Venice:

> I intending my journey towards England, cam by land to Venicie, where I met at Padua thirtie Englishmen students, I met also with an Englishman, who lived in the state of a Fryer, he brought me before the high Bishop, where I was accused for an heretike, and he brought in two false witnesses to be sworne against me (having before knowne me in Turkey) nevertheless I disproved his witnesses, and they were found forsworne men, then was I set at libertie, and constrained to give fiftéene Crownes towards the finishing of our Ladies shrine at Padua, and my accuser and his witnesses were punished. (sig. C4r)

At Ferrara he was 'well entertained and liberally rewarded with a horse and five and twentie Crownes for the sake of the Quéenes Maiestie of England'. Bearing a passport for safe travel, Webbe reached Bologna where an English bishop, 'Doctor Poole', treated him kindly. At Florence Webbe met 'John Stanley'[2] (sig. C4r) but at Rome he was suspected of heresy by Cardinal William Allen (1532–94). Allen had been made a cardinal by Pope Sixtus V on 7 August 1587 in advance of the Armada Expedition. He

---

[1] Webbe states that this location was within 18° of the equator ('within eightéene degrées of the Sunne, everie degrée being in distance thrée score miles', sig. C1v). Prester John is usually associated with Ethiopia (approximately 5°–15° north of the equator). Webbe could perhaps have visited it after his visit to Goa but he may have meant a location on the North African coastline, given that he precedes this reference with sites in the Holy Land.

[2] *Doctor Poole* and *John Stanley*: unidentified.

was an active supporter of Philip II's planned invasion of England after which, if successful, he would have been made Archbishop of Canterbury and Lord Chancellor. Webbe's account continues:

> And from thence I went to Rome, there I was nyntéene daies in trouble with the Pope, and the English Cardinal Doctor Allen, a notable Arch papist, where I was often examined, but finding nothing by me, they let me passe, and understanding that I had béene a Captive a long time in Turkey, the Pope gave me his blessing, and twentie and five crownes. And before I went out of Roome, I was againe taken by the English Colledge, and put there into the holy house thrée dayes, with a fooles coate on my backe halfe blew, halfe yeallowe, and a cockescombe with thrée belles on my head, from whence I was holpen by meanes of an Englishman whom I found there, and presented my petition and cause to the Pope: who againe set me at libertie. (sigs. C4r–v)

Continuing on to Naples, he was denounced as an English spy by an unnamed Genoese, leading to his imprisonment and severe torture. He was 'committed to a darke dungeon fiftéene dayes, which time they secretly made enquiry where I had lyen before, what my wordes and behaviour had béene while I was there, but they could finde nothing by me' (sig. D1r). The tortures applied to Webbe in the hope of extracting a confession were typical of the period:

> Thrice had I the strappado, hoysted up backward with my handes bound behind me, which stroke all the jointes in my armes out of joint, where a Phisition was readie to set my armes in joynt againe presently, I was also constrained to drinke salt water and quicklyme, and then a fine lawne or callico thrust down my throat and pluckt up againe, readie to pluck my hart out of my belly, all to make me to confesse that I was an English spye. After this there were foure barde horses[1] prepared to quarter me, and I was still threatned to dye, except I would confesse some thing to my harme. (sig. D1r)

Webbe remained incarcerated for another seven months until the viceroy, supposedly on the recommendation of Philip II himself, was ordered to appoint him as a gunner with pay of 35 crowns per month. He eventually escaped on board the ship *Grace*, commanded by Nicholas Nottingham,[2] noting how dangerous it would have been if his ship had been taken by the Spanish:

> At my comming over into England from Rome, I was faine to steale away, being then reteined in yéerly fée to the King of Spaine, to be one of his chéefest Gunners. And if the Ship wherein I came over, had béen taken, both they and I my selfe had died for that offence. (sig. D2v)

Webbe arrived back in England 'on the first of May. 1589', he claimed, for the first time in thirteen years.[3]

After recounting these experiences, Webbe also notes that he met at Palermo in Sicily (perhaps in about 1575/76 when he was a slave in Turkish galleys) Edward de Vere, Earl of Oxford (**item 23**):

---

[1] *barde horses*: clad in bards, a protective covering for the breast and flanks of war-horses.

[2] Unidentified.

[3] Despite this claim, there is a record of the Attorney General, John Popham (1531–1607), consulting a Mr Webbe on 8 April 1587 about expanding the trade in English cloth to Muscovy. *CSP Domestic, 1581–90*, p. 403.

One thing did greatly comfort me which I saw long since in Sicilia, in the citie of Palerms, a thing worthie of memorie, where the right honourable the Earle of Oxenford a famous man for Chivalrie, at what time he travailed into forraine countries, being then personally present, made there a challeng against all manner of persons whatsoever, and at all manner of weapons, as Turniments, Barriors with horse and armour, to fight and combat with any whatsoever, in the defence of his Prince and countrie: for which he was very highly commended, and yet no man durst be so hardie to encounter with him, so that all Italy over, he is acknowledged ever since for the same, the onely Chivallier and Noble man of England. This title they give unto him as worthely deserved. (sig. D1v)

Little else is known about Webbe's life. In November 1589 he travelled to France and was appointed chief master gunner by Henri IV at the Battle of Ivry (14 March 1590), prompting the jealousy of other French gunners who tried to poison him. The king's physician treated him and saved his life with a potion supposedly made from unicorn's horn. He then returned to England and at his lodgings at Blackwall, completed his account of his travels on 19 May 1590. He was appointed as a cannonier for life on 14 January 1592, with a fee of 10 shillings per day, but then disappears from all records.[1]

---

[1] *CSP Domestic, 1591–94*, p. 172.

# 32. 1591 – SIR HENRY WOTTON

**Sir Henry Wotton (1568–1639)** (**Plate 26**), served on three occasions as English Ambassador to Venice (1604–10, 1616, 1621), official residences which fall outside the chronological span of this study. However, Wotton also made a short visit to Venice in 1591 as a young man which merits recording here, along with some of his impressions of Venice compiled in *c.*1593/4.

Wotton was born at Boughton (Bocton) Hall, Kent, the son of an estate manager, Thomas Wotton (*c.*1521–87), and his second wife Eleanor (née Finch) Morton. His half-brother was the diplomatic and administrator Edward Wotton (1548–1628), a friend of Sir Philip Sidney (**item 22**, **Plate 17** and **Figure 17**) and later Baron Wotton of Marley. After studying at Winchester College he matriculated from New College, Oxford, on 5 June 1584 but then migrated to Hart Hall in the following October, where he was taught civil law by the Italian jurist Alberico Gentili (1552–1608), the university's Regius Professor of Civil Law (through the patronage of Robert Dudley, Earl of Leicester, **Plate 23**) and a pioneer in the study of international law. At Hart Hall, Wotton met the poet and later clergyman John Donne (1572–1631) and graduated BA in June 1588. He then migrated to Queen's College where he wrote and staged a lost play, 'Tancredo', based on Tasso's *Gerusalemme Liberata* which suggests an early interest in the Italian language.[1]

After his father's death in January 1587, he received a legacy which enabled him to undertake travel on the continent to gain experience of diplomacy and languages. He left England in October 1589 and travelled through north Germany before studying law for six months at Heidelberg University. He became a fluent German speaker and during 1590 travelled through Bavaria and Austria until he took lodgings with Hugo Blotius (1533–1608), the Dutch librarian of Emperor Rudolf II. In late August 1591 he resumed his travels, disguised as a Catholic German scholar, and headed south to Italy to visit Venice, Rome and Florence. He arrived at Venice at 8 am on 4 November 1591 but stayed only for four days before leaving for Padua, fearing, in a letter to Blotius, the climate of the city as 'unwholesome'. Furthermore, 'not being made of stone', he felt that he could not trust himself among the beautiful Venetian courtesans.[2] At Padua he became friendly with Edward Zouche (*c.*1556–1625), eleventh Baron Zouche of Harringworth, whom he had first met at Altdorf near Nuremberg. Zouche had been abroad since 1587 and had travelled in Germany with Stephen Powle (**item 29**). He was also befriended by Italian scholars, one of whom, Orazio Lombardelli, dedicated to him a small volume, *I fonti toscani d'Orazio Lombardelli, senese, accademico umoroso* (Florence, February 1593), designed to assist young Englishmen with the acquisition of the Italian language.[3] In

---

[1] Wotton, *Life and Letters*, I, p. 5.

[2] Vienna, Hofbibliothek, MS 9737.Z.17, Letter from Padua to Hugo Blotius, 30 Nov. 1591. Wotton, *Life and Letters*, I, p. 18.

[3] Wotton, *Life and Letters*, I, p. 22.

June 1593 Wotton made his way to Geneva where he lodged for over a year with the classical scholar Isaac Casaubon (1559–1614) before returning to England in August 1594.[1]

While still at Geneva, Wotton drafted an essay, 'The State of Christendom' (first printed 1657), recording his views on international affairs, with particular reference to England's dealings with Spain, Don Antonio of Portugal, Henri IV of France, Pope Clement VIII and the various states of Germany and Italy. It was drafted to demonstrate his youthful mastery of international politics and statecraft. One of his comments on Venice, for example, noted how power could shift between traditional enemies and even close neighbours:

> And such as all and every one of these Nations have been, such they will be as long as they do and shall inhabit the same Climate, and receive breath from the same Air. And as these Nations naturally hate one another, so by nature they desire not to be subject one unto another; and therefore, if against their nature, one of them chance to have never so little authority over the other, the one commandeth imperiously, and the other obeyeth most unwillingly: and yet it so hapneth oftentimes, that the Commander is commanded; and they that once obeyed, many times command. So did *Padua* command *Venice*, and now *Venice* commandeth *Padua*: So did *Rome* rule *Spain*, and now *Spain* ruleth *Rome*: So did *France* sway the Empire of *Germany*, and now *Germany* precedeth *France*.(1667 edition, p. 9)

Wotton was impressed by the toleration of Jews at Venice, noting: 'Besides the Pope himself, the Dukes of *Mantua*, *Ferrara*, *Florence*, and *Baviera*, together with the Seigniory of *Venice* suffer *Jewes* to live in their Country' (p. 134). He also recalled watching an execution at Venice, probably staged according to tradition between the two columns in front of the Doge's Palace; and he noted how England, unlike Venice, did not assume jurisdiction over crimes committed outside the realm:

> And I remember that I saw a man executed at *Venice* because he killed his own Wife in *Turky*; and the reason why they proceeded against him, was the heinousness of the Fact, and for that his Wife (although she were not so) was their natural Subject. And yet I confesse that our Common Laws regard not offences committed without our Realm; wherein me thinketh they have small reason. (p. 199)

He also illustrated how ruthlessly the Venetian authorities pursued their own internal security, even if it meant breaching the traditions of ambassadorial immunity:

> The Seigniory of *Venice* understanding that certain Traitors who had revealed their secrets to the Turk, were fled to hide themselves to the French Ambassadors house at *Venice*, sent certain Offices to search the Ambassadors house for them, and when the Ambassador forbad and refused to suffer those Officers to enter into his house, the Senate made no more ado, but sent for certain peeces of great Ordnance out of their Arsenal, whereby they would have beaten down the house, had not the said Ambassador as soon as he saw the same Ordnance, yielded the Traytors to their mercy and discretion. (p. 210)

By late 1594 Wotton was back in England and employed in the service of Robert Devereux, Earl of Essex. He began to set up a network of informants and intelligence gatherers who kept him briefed on continental politics and current affairs from numerous locations, including Siena, Florence, Geneva, Heidelberg, Basle, Vienna, Prague, Utrecht

---

[1] *ODNB*, s.v.

and The Hague. In 1596 he and the poet John Donne joined the naval expedition to raid Cadiz, led jointly by Charles Howard, Lord Howard of Effingham (the commander of the English fleet during the repulse of the Spanish Armada), and the Earl of Essex. They also sailed together in the following year on Essex's inconclusive Azores expedition; and Wotton followed Essex to Ireland in April 1599 for his problematic military campaigns there against the Earl of Tyrone. As Essex's personal difficulties with the queen escalated, Wotton wisely left his service and undertook another short continental tour, this time with his nephew Pickering Wotton, the eldest son of his half-brother Edward, including visits to Paris and Florence where he met Ferdinand I (1549–1609), Grand Duke of Tuscany. This encounter led to one of the more bizarre manifestations of the 'Italianate Englishman'. Ferdinand had heard rumours of a plot to poison King James VI of Scotland and he requested that Wotton should take a box of antidotes prepared by his own physician to the Scottish king. Leaving Florence in May 1601 Wotton chose to travel in disguise as an Italian merchant, 'Ottavio Baldi'. He was warmly welcomed at Dunfermline (since the king was still recovering from the stresses of the Gowrie conspiracy in 1600) and, having disclosed his true identity to James and his advisors, maintained his Italianate disguise throughout his time in Scotland.

Wotton returned to Florence in May 1602 and, following the death of Queen Elizabeth on 24 March 1603, he wrote from Venice in May to Robert Cecil, pledging his loyalty and support, despite his previous allegiance to the Earl of Essex who had been executed for treason on 25 February 1601. Given his previous loyal service to King James VI who was now James I of England, Wotton was rapidly drawn into the new regime's ambassadorial ranks by being appointed on 26 December 1603 as English Ambassador to Venice, the country's first resident ambassador since the 1550s. Wotton returned to London in April 1604 and, as befitted his new international status, was knighted on 8 July. He arrived back in Venice on 24 September and took up residence in a small palazzo in Cannaregio, near the Grand Canal.

As the diplomatic representative of the King of England and Scotland, Wotton was keen to clarify the specific courtly etiquette of his formal reception by the doge. Secretary Giovanni Carlo Scaramelli was instructed to call upon him to finalize the arrangements. Scaramelli had been sent to England in late January 1603 to facilitate the renegotiation of Anglo-Venetian diplomatic relations and, presumably, was already known to Wotton.[1] Scaramelli's report to the Venetian *Collegio provides an interesting insight into the formalities and nuances of Anglo-Venetian diplomacy when it was in the process of being re-established after a gap of almost fifty years. He first noted that Wotton, as a weary traveller just arrived at Venice, had reasonably requested to remain incognito for a few days to settle himself into his new abode and also to 'take a purge'. Scaramelli continued:

> Although the Ambassador has been in Venice before he knows no official persons except myself; he accordingly begged me to wait upon him, in order to arrange the details of his public entry and first public audience.

[1] Scaramelli had arrived in England on 28 January, just in time to have an audience on 9 February at Richmond with the aged Queen Elizabeth. A key aspect of his mission was to seek to limit the damage to Venetian shipping caused by English pirates and they discussed this issue in Italian. Rutter, "'Hear the Ambassadors!'", pp. 272–86. *Elizabeth I's Foreign Correspondence*, p. 99. Levin and Watkins, *Shakespeare's Foreign Worlds*, pp. 111–13.

I informed the Savii,[1] who told me to obtain the permission of the Chiefs of the Council of Ten and to wait on the Ambassador at the hour indicated. I did so, and after some formal remarks the Ambassador said he desired to know when and in what state he would be received, for his master was inferior to no reigning Sovereign, and as King of Scotland was the oldest and the first Sovereign to receive baptism, and by the Union of the kingdoms of England and Ireland he acquired that power which all the world recognises now, and his Ambassador expected to be no less honourably treated than other Ambassadors.

I satisfied him on that score, and explained the usual ceremony observed in the case of Ambassadors of Crowned heads. We settled his entry for Friday afternoon. He will withdraw for this purpose to a convent on one of the little islands near by. His first audience will be on Saturday. In conversation he said he had two qualifications, the good will and the confidence of his Majesty, which would assure him attention for all that he might put forward in the course of his negotiations here. He said that he was well aware of the regard your Serenity had for religion, and so he desired before being introduced to say that he, too, was obliged to place his religious convictions before all other considerations, that he could not live without his religious rites, but these will be carefully limited to the service of himself and his staff; and he promises not to admit Flemish or Germans and barely the English, who are not in his suite, for to tell the truth most of the English resident in Venice are Catholics. This undertaking will secure that no scandal, public or private, shall take place in this City. The service will always be conducted in English. The King had given him special instructions on the subject.

He enquired how the Ambassadors of France and Spain conducted themselves on entering the Chamber, for he had heard that Spain only uncovered on reaching the steps that lead up to the throne. I replied that both these Ambassadors and the Imperial Ambassador and the Papal Nuncio uncovered at the door. He argued over this for some time, till I told him that the Doge rose from his seat on the entry of the Ambassador, whereupon he was pacified, remarking, 'Oh! if the Doge rises the Ambassador certainly must uncover.' He added, 'I was anxious on this point, for I could not accept a difference of treatment, which might serve as a pretext for arguing that my Sovereign was in any way inferior to the others. Of course we Ambassadors will visit and dine with each other, and will have company each in his own house, but on the score of religion I shall not be able to attend his Serenity at public functions, and thus any question of precedence will be avoided. Should his Serenity ever invite me to table I hope it will be when I am to be alone; and that I suppose will be rarely.' He spoke with great prudence and eloquence, and begging me to kiss your Serenity's and your Excellencies' hands he gave me my leave.[2]

For Wotton's formal reception, which took two full days, his gondola, followed by his personal entourage and English residents at Venice and students at Padua, was taken on the first day, (*giorno d'entrata*) across the lagoon to the island of S. Spirito and its monastery. They were joined there by sixty Venetian senators who exchanged formal greetings and then, in pairs with the Venetians on the left of the Englishmen, they returned to the gondolas and were taken back to Venice and the ambassador's residence. Once the Venetians had left, gifts of malmsey wine, loaves of sugar, sweetmeats and other confections were delivered on silver plates. On the next day of the audience (*giorno*

---

[1] The *Savii* (Savi del Consiglio or Savi[i] Grandi) ('Wise Men of the Council'), were senior magistrates, responsible for preparing and executing office business. The six members of the Savii were chosen from the Consiglio dei Pregadi (Senate) and appointed on a staggered basis: three on 1 October, 1 January, 1 April and 1 July, serving for a period of six months. They attended meetings of the Cabinet (*Collegio) and when the *Council of Ten (*Dieci*) discussed foreign affairs.

[2] *CSP Venice*, 1604, item 282 (Collegio, Secreta Esposizioni Principi).

*d'audienza*) the Venetian senators led the English Ambassador and his entourage to the *piazzetta* before the Doge's palace. They then went up the staircase to the *Collegio to be presented to Doge Marino Grimani (1532–1605) and his Collegio. The new ambassador made a triple bow, at which the Doge stood up as Wotton advanced to kiss his hand and then they embraced. After presenting his credentials, Wotton made a speech in fluent Italian, expressing King James I's high regard for the Venetian Republic and praising its distinguished history, beneath the Collegio's magnificent ceiling depicting 'Venice Enthroned' and Veronese's expansive representation of 'Thanksgiving for the Battle of Lepanto' (**Plate 13**).[1]

---

[1] *CSP Venice, 1603–07*, items 190, 275, 279–80, 282. Wotton, *Life and Letters*, I, pp. 49–55. When Provost of Eton over twenty years later, Wotton had in his lodgings a painting recording the splendours of the *Collegio. All of Wotton's audiences were recorded verbatim and Scaramelli was the scribe appointed to this duty, Rutter, "Hear the Ambassadors!", pp. 284–6.

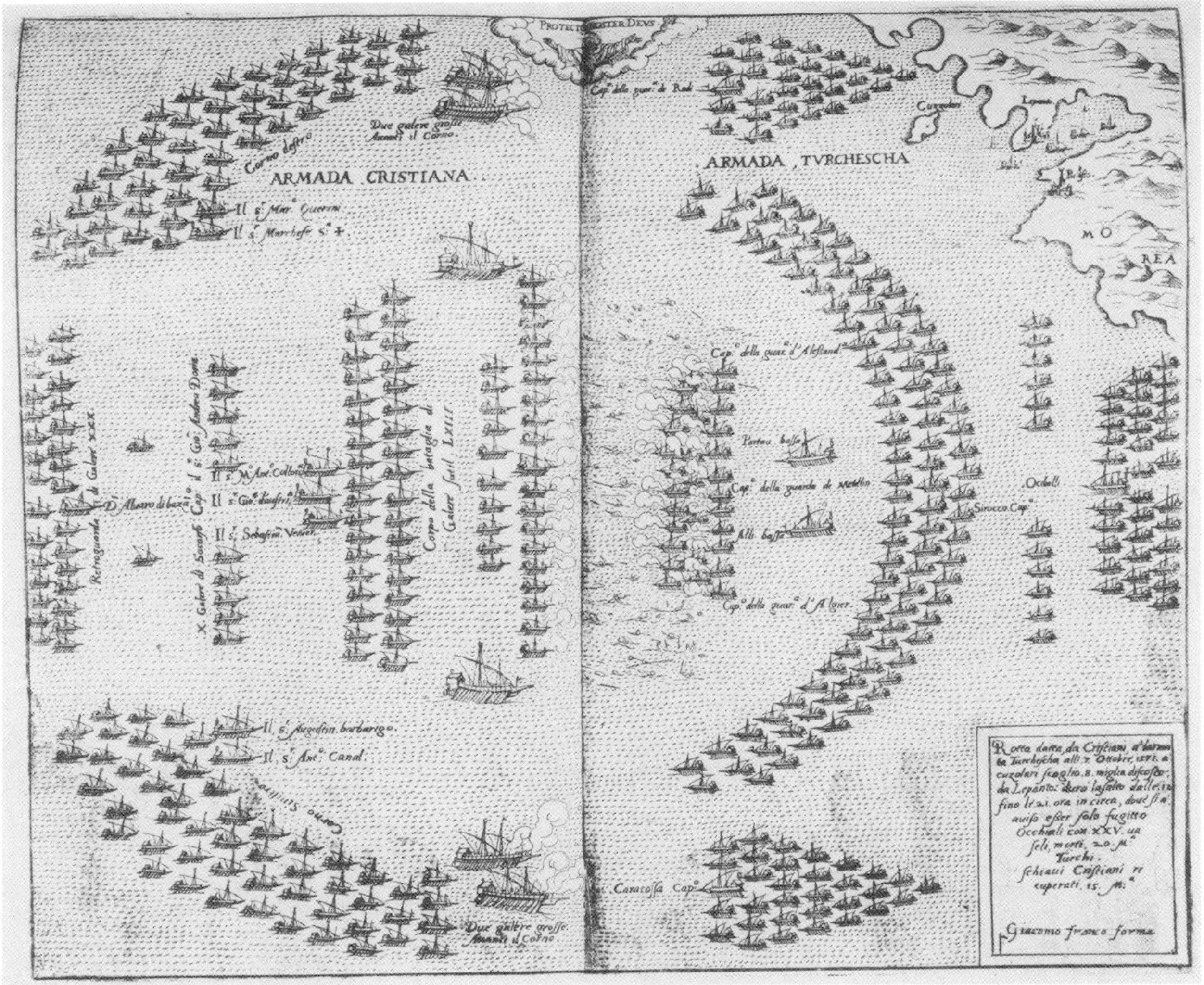

Figure 24.    Giacomo Franco, *Habiti d'huomeni et donne venetiane* (1610). The Christian and Ottoman armadas at the Battle of Lepanto, 1571. By permission of Special Collections, Brotherton Library, University of Leeds.

# 33.   1593–5, 1596 AND 1597 – FYNES MORYSON

**Fynes Moryson (1565/6–1630)** was born at Cadeby, Lincolnshire, the third of five surviving sons of Thomas (d. 1593) and Elizabeth Moryson. His father was a Clerk of the Pipe (registrar of land taxes) and an MP for Great Grimsby. Fynes matriculated on 18 May 1580 from Peterhouse, Cambridge (BA 1584; MA 1587; incorporated Oxford 1591) and was created a fellow of the college by royal mandate, serving as its bursar (1589–90). On 1 May 1591 he left England, 'out of innate desire to gain experience by travelling into forraigne parts',[1] to travel and study for four years on the continent, passing through Germany, Prague and Switzerland (where he enrolled in 1591 at the University of Basle) and the Low Countries. In spring 1593 he travelled via Denmark to Danzig, heading south through Poland, Moravia and Austria before arriving in northern Italy and enrolling at the University of Padua. He stayed at Venice and Padua during the winter of 1593–4. He enrolled at the University of Leiden in January 1594 and in the spring visited Rome (where he made extensive use of the popular guidebook to the city, *Le cose maravigliose della Città di Roma*, which he had probably purchased at Venice where it was often reprinted) and Naples before spending the summer in the state of Florence, mainly at San Casciano. He returned to Padua in December and left there on 3 March 1595. Heading northwards, at Geneva he met Theodore Beza and returned home via France, arriving at Dover on 13 May 1595.

In early December 1595 he left England again, this time with his younger brother Henry, to travel to Jerusalem, Tripoli, Antioch, Aleppo, Constantinople and Crete. They passed through the Low Countries and Germany before crossing the Alps and heading for Venice where on 21 April 1596 they boarded a ship bound for Cyprus and Jerusalem. Henry Moryson (b. 1569) died in the Holy Land on 4 July 1596, probably from dysentery, and Fynes travelled on alone to Crete and Constantinople where he lodged with the English Ambassador, Edward Barton (*c.*1562–98), who had cultivated a close and productive working relationship with Sultan Mehmed III. Moryson left Turkey in late February 1597 and, travelling westwards via Venice (in late April) from where he rode on horseback directly to Stade at the mouth of the River Elbe in north Germany, he arrived back in London in July 1597.

Most of Moryson's later career during the reign of Queen Elizabeth was spent in Ireland through the influence of his brother, Sir Richard Moryson (*c.*1571–1628), a military officer and politician (and later Vice-President of Munster). Fynes served as personal secretary to the Lord Deputy, Charles Blount (1563–1606), Lord Mountjoy, at whose request he began to compile a journal on Irish affairs. Moryson returned to England in 1602, following Mountjoy's appointment as Lord Lieutenant of Ireland and

---

[1] Moryson, *Itinerary*, 1617, I.i, p. 1, Moryson, *Itinerary*, 1907–8, I, p. 2. Peterhouse records contain a memorandum, dated 3 August 1590, granting Moryson 'leave to discontinue' his fellowship for five years, authorized by the Archbishop of Canterbury. Moryson, *Shakespeare's Europe*, pp. iii–xiii.

Master of the Ordnance. Following Blount's death, he devoted much of his energies to writing up records of his extensive travels, culminating in the publication of three folio volumes, *An Itinerary ... Containing his Ten Yeeres Travell Through the Twelve Dominions of Germany, Bohmerland, Sweitzerland, Netherland, Denmarke, Poland, Italy, Turky, France, England, Scotland, and Ireland* (entered in the *Stationers' Register*, 4 April 1617, and published later that year).[1]

Moryson's *Itinerary* comprised three distinct works. The first section, originally compiled in Latin (BL Harleian MS 5133) covered his travels in Europe and the Near East, with his account of Venice in Part I (pp. 74–90). His choice of Latin perhaps indicates his international aspirations for the dissemination of his work. The second (BL Additional MS 36706) focused on the Nine Years' War in Ireland (1593–1603), also known as Tyrone's Rebellion.[2] The third part comprised a series of essays on travel and the geography, cultures, fashions, religions and political institutions of various countries. A fourth part (Corpus Christi, Oxford, MS 94, 344 folios; licensed for the press, 14 June 1626), completed the third part but remained unpublished until 1903 when selections from it were edited by Charles Hughes.[3] Moryson never married and died on 12 February 1630 in St Botolph's parish, London.[4]

While travelling in Italy the Protestant Moryson sought to avoid religious problems by frequently pretending to be German, Dutch or French (although he posed as an English Catholic when staying with French friars at Jerusalem). These stratagems were aided by what seems to have been his reasonable fluency in the German, Italian, Dutch and French languages, as well as being able to converse productively in Latin. His writings also provide an informative perspective on how travel accounts were put together at this period. In his chapter 'Of Precepts for Travellers', he advises that a traveller should make notes twice a day, in the morning and the evening, and then transfer them 'at leasure into a paper booke, that many yeers after he may looke over them at his pleasure'. He recommended discretion in the compilation of these notes because they could arose suspicions and that the traveller 'shall doe well to write such things in Ciphers and unknowne characters, being also ready to give a fained interpretation of them to any Magistrate, if need be'. Finally, he advised that these notes and journals should be forwarded twice a year either to England or to another safe place from where they could be collected later.[5]

Given the wealth of detail provided in Moryson's accounts, it is clear that he often worked from earlier printed (and perhaps manuscript) sources. He drew factual material and ideas from Lewis Lewkenor's 1599 translation of Gasparo Contarini, *The Common-Wealth and Government of Venice*; Francesco Guicciardini, *Storia d'Italia* (probably the 1599 English edition rather than an Italian one) and his *Two Discourses* (1595); Giovanni Botero, *The Traveller's Breviat* (1601); and Richard Knolles' 1606 translation

---

[1] Moryson had earlier worked on his manuscripts between 1596 and 1600 when living with his two married sisters Jane Alington and Faith Mussenden.

[2] Both of these Latin manuscript versions may have been intended for publication.

[3] The fifth chapter of this manuscript was 'Of the Commonwealth of Venice in particular' but was not printed in Hughes's edition. It does not add any material of significance to Moryson's detailed description of Venice included in the 1617 printed edition.

[4] *ODNB*, s.v.

[5] Moryson, *Itinerary*, 1617, III.i, pp. 10–13; Moryson, *Itinerary*, 1907–8, III, p. 375.

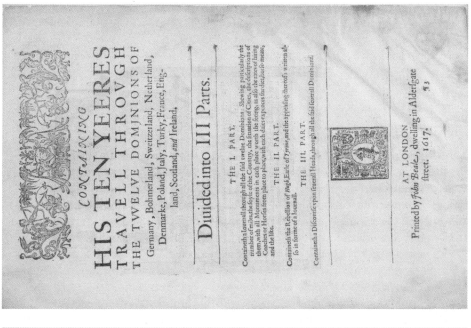

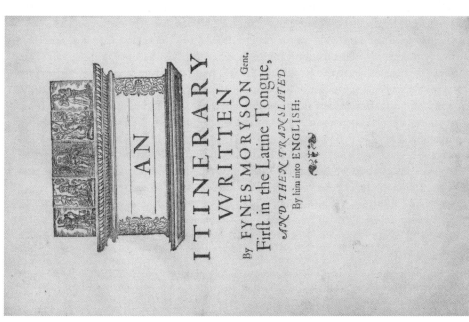

Figure 25.   Fynes Moryson, *An Itinerary*, London,1617, title pages. Special Collections, Brotherton Library, Trv q MOR. By permission of Special Collections, Brotherton Library, University of Leeds.

of Jean Bodin's *Six Books of a Commonweale.*[1] Moryson also had a copy of the authoritative guidebook, *Venetia città nobilissima et singolare* (Venice, 1581) by Francesco Sansovino (1521–83). He was probably consulting the 1604 edition of this encyclopaedic work of 600 pages and he often paraphrased shortened versions of Sansovino's descriptions while adding his personal observations of Venice's churches and secular institutions.[2]

**Text**[3]

All words and passages in italic are as in the original publication.

[p. 74] CHAP. I.

*Of my journey from Paduoa, to Venice, to Ferraria, to Bologna, to Ravenna, and by the shore of the Adriaticke Sea, to Ancona: then crossing the breadth of Italy, to Rome, seated not farre from the Tirrhene Sea.*

Whosoever comes into *Italy,* and from whence soever; but more especially if he come from suspected places, as *Constantinople,* never free from the plague; hee must bring to the Confines a certificate of his health, and in time of any plague, hee must bring the like to any City within land, where he is to passe, which certificates brought from place to place, and necessary to bee carried, they curiously observe and read. This paper is vulgarly called *Bolletino della sanita;*[4] and if any man want it, hee is shut up in the *Lazareto,*[5] or Pest-house forty dayes, till it appeare he is healthfull, and this they call vulgarly *far' la quarantans.*[6] Neither will the Officers of health in any case dispence with him, but there hee shall have convenient[7] lodging, and diet at his pleasure.

In the spring of the yeere, 1594, (the Italians beginning the yeere the first of *January*) I began my journey to see *Italy,* and taking boat at the East gate of *Paduoa,* the same was drawne by horses along the River *Brenta;* & having shot two or three small bridges, and passed twenty miles, we came to the Village *Lizzafusina,*[8] where there is a damme to stop the waters of *Brenta,* lest in processe of time, the passage being open, the Marshes on that side of *Venice* should be filled with sand or earth, and so a passage made on firme ground to the City; which they are carefull to prevent, and not without just cause, having found safety in their Iles, when *Italy* was often overflowed by barbarous people. Besides, they say that this damme was made, lest this fresh water should bee mingled

[1] Kew, 'Shakespeare's Europe Revisited', I, pp. cvii–cxii.

[2] This 1581 edition was published by Francesco's son Jacopo (Jacomo). Sansovino had published two earlier guides to Venice: the twelve-page *Tutte le cose notabili e belle che sono in Venetia,* 1556 (and later editions); and the more substantial *Delle cose notabili che sono in Venetia* (1561). This latter guidebook was designed as a friendly conversation between a Venetian resident and a foreigner (*forestiero,* a non-Venetian stranger of unidentified origin) who was a keen recipient of all available social, political and cultural information about the Republic. Moryson's description of Venice in his *Itinerary* demonstrates him to have been an ideal *forestiero.*

[3] From *Itinerary,* 1617, *STC* 18205.

[4] *Bolletino della sanita*: certificate of health.

[5] *Lazzaretto.

[6] *far' la quarantans*: literally, to do or make quarantine.

[7] *convenient*: printed 'conueuient'.

[8] Fusina.

Within the illustration:

S. *Zorzi*

Il Nobilissimo et gran
uascelo Bucintoro

Il Doge di Venetia con tutta la sig.ia il giorno dell Ascensione à sposare il Mare con questa solenita la quale
et per degnita et per concerto e la piu bella pompa che si uegga in Venetia

8514

Plate 11.　Giacomo Franco, *Habiti d'huomeni et donne venetiane et cerimonie publiche della nobilissima Città di Venetia*, Venice, 1610. Doge and Signoria on Ascension Day, accompanied by other vessels at the Ceremony of the Doge Marrying the Sea. Galleria degli Uffizi, Florence. Bridgeman Images.

Plate 12.   Unknown artist, 'Plan of the Arsenal, Venice'. Watercolour on paper, undated. Museo Correr, Venice, Bridgeman Images.

Plate 13.  Veronese (Paolo Caliari), *Allegory of the Battle of Lepanto, 7 October 1571*. Oil on canvas, *c.*1570s. Gallerie dell'Accademia, Venice. Bridgeman Images.

Plate 14. Veronese (Paolo Caliari), portrait of an unknown woman, known as 'La Bella Nani'. Oil on canvas, *c.*1560s. Louvre, Paris. Bridgeman Images.

Plate 15. Unknown artist, portrait of Thomas Linacre. Line engraving, *c.* late 18th century. © National Portrait Gallery, London.

Plate 16.   Unknown artist, portrait of Sir Thomas Wyatt, based on a portrait by Hans Holbein the Younger. Oil on panel, *c*.1540. © National Portrait Gallery, London.

CÆTERA FAMA~
E D

Plate 17.    Unknown artist, portrait of Sir Philip Sidney. Oil on panel, *c.*1576. © National Portrait
Gallery, London.

Plate 18. Unknown artist, portrait of Sir Thomas Coningsby. Oil on panel, 1572. © National Portrait Gallery, London.

Plate 19.   Tintoretto (Jacopo Comin or Robusti), self-portrait. Oil on pine panel, *c*.1548. © Victoria and Albert Museum, London.

Plate 20. Veronese (Paolo Caliari), self-portrait. Oil on canvas, 1560. State Hermitage Museum, St Petersburg. Bridgeman Images.

Plate 21.    Attributed to Tintoretto (Jacopo Comin or Robusti), portrait of Geronimo Foscarini, Procurator of St Mark's, Venice. Oil on canvas, *c*.1570s. © Victoria and Albert Museum, London.

Plate 22.   Tintoretto (Jacopo Comin or Robusti), portrait of Doge Pasquale Cicogna. Oil on canvas, *c.*1585. © Victoria and Albert Museum, London.

Plate 23.   Unknown Anglo-Netherlandish artist, portrait of Robert Dudley, Earl of Leicester. Oil on panel, *c*.1575. © National Portrait Gallery, London.

Plate 24.    Unknown artist, portrait of Sir Francis Walsingham. Oil on panel, *c.*1585. © National Portrait Gallery, London.

Plate 25.  Unknown artist, English, posthumous narrative portrait of Sir Henry Unton. Oil on panel, c.1596. © National Portrait Gallery, London.

Plate 26.   Unknown artist, portrait, early 17th century, Sir Henry Wotton, oil on canvas.
© National Portrait Gallery, London.

with their salt waters; since all the Gentlemen of *Venice* fetch their fresh water by boats from thence, the poorer sort being content with Well water. Heere whiles our boat was drawne by an Instrument, out of the River *Brenta,* [p. 75] into the Marshes of *Venice,* wee the passengers refreshed our selves with meat and wine, and according to the custome, agreed upon the price of our meat before wee did eat it. Then we entred our boat againe, and passed five miles to *Venice,* upon the marshes thereof; and each man paied for his passage a lire, or twenty sols [*soldi*], and for a horse more then ordinary, that we might be drawne more swiftly from *Paduoa* to *Lizzafusina,* each man paied foure sols, but the ordinary passage is only sixteene sols. We might have had coaches, but since a boat passeth daily too and fro betweene these Cities, most men use this passage as most convenient. For the boat is covered with arched hatches, and there is very pleasant company, so a man beware to give no offence: for otherwise the Lumbards[1] carry shirts of Male,[2] and being armed as if they were in a Camp, are apt to revenge upon shamefull advantages. But commonly there is pleasant discourse, and the proverb saith, that the boat shall bee drowned, when it carries neither Monke, nor Student, nor Curtesan (they love them too well to call them whores,) the passengers being for the most part of these kindes. I remember a yong maide in the boat, crossed her selfe whensoever an old woman looked upon her, fearing she should be a witch, whereat the passengers often smiled, seeing the girle not onely crosse her selfe for feare, but thrust her crucifix towards the old womans eyes. I said formerly that two Rivers *Medoaci,*[3] runne through *Paduoa,* and that the greater by the name of *Brenta,* running to the village *Lizzafusina,* is stopped with a damme, lest it should mingle it selfe with the salt marshes of *Venice,* and that also the lesser River by the name of *Bachilio,*[4] passeth through *Paduoa.* This lesser streame runneth thence into the ditch *Clodia,* and going out of it makes a haven, called *de Chiozza,*[5] which lieth in the way from *Venice* to *Farraria,*[6] and there it divideth it selfe into two streames; and entring the salt marshes, makes the haven of *Venice,* called *Malamocco.*[7] Besides other Rivers falling from the Alpes, through *Frioli,*[8] do increase these marshes, which are salt by the tides of the sea, though the same doth very little ebbe or flow in this Mediterranean, or Inland sea. And this haven *Malamocco* is very large and deep, and is defended with a banke from the waves of the Adriatique sea.

## [*The Description of Venice.*]
Upon the West side of *Venice* beyond the marshes, lies the Territory of *Paduoa.* On the North side beyond the marshes, lies the Province *Frioli.* On the South side [p. 76] beyond the marshes, lies partly the firme land of *Italy,* and partly the Adriatique sea; On the East side beyond the marshes lies the Adriatique sea, and the City consisteth all of Iles, compassed round about with the saide marshes.

---

[1] Lombardy, north-west Italy.
[2] *Male*: chain mail.
[3] *Medoaci*: Rivers Medoacus Maior and Medoacus Minor (*Brenta* and *Bacchiglione*).
[4] River Bacchiglione.
[5] Chioggia.
[6] Ferrara.
[7] Malamocco on the *Lido di Venezia.
[8] Friuli.

*Malamocco.* Beſides other Riuers falling from thé Alpes, through *Frioli,* do increaſe theſe marſhes ; which are ſalt by the tides of the ſea, though the ſame doth very little ebbe or flow in this Mediterranean, or Inland ſea. And this hauen *Malamocco* is very large and deep, and is defended with a banke from the waues of the Adriatique ſea.

## The Deſcription of Venice.

Vpon the Weſt ſide of *venice* beyond the marſhes, lies the Territory of *Paduca.* On the North ſide beyond the marſhes, lies the Prouince *Frioli.* On the South ſide beyond

G 2.

Figure 26. Fynes Moryson, *An Itinerary*, London: 1617, map of Venice. Special Collections, Brotherton Library, Trv q MOR. By permission of Special Collections, Brotherton Library, University of Leeds.

A The great channell.[1]

B The market place of Saint *Marke,* seated in the first Sextary of Saint *Marke.*[2]

C The Cathedrall Church of Saint *Peter,* the seate of the Patriarkes, seated in the second Sextary, called *Caestelli Olivolo.*[3]

D The third Sextary on this side the channell, called di Canarigio.[4]

E The Church of Saint *James* lies neere the bridge *Rialto,* and is seated in the fourth Sextary of Saint *Paul,* being the first of them beyond the channell.[5]

[1] *Grand Canal.

[2] *San Marco, Piazza (St Mark's Square).

[3] *San Pietro di Castello.

[4] Cannaregio.

[5] *San Giacomo di Rialto

The rest of the City is divided into two other Sextaries beyond the channell, namely the fifth *di S^ta Croce,* and the sixth *de Dorso duro.*[1]

F The Church of Saint *George* the greater.[2]

G And the Church of *Santa Maria delle gratie,* both lie in the Sextary *di Santa Croce.*[3]

H The Iland *Giudecca* belongs to the sextary *di Dorso duro.*[4]

K The banke of the sea, vulgarly *Il Lido.*[5]

L The Iland *Murana.*[6]

M The new *Lazaretto.*[7]

N Mazorbo.[8]

| O Buran[9] | P San Franscesco del deserto.[10] | |
|---|---|---|
| Q Torcello. | R Duo Caestelli.[11] | Little Ilands. |
| S La Certosa. | T S^ta. Hellena.[12] | |
| V Lazaretto Vecchio.[13] | | |

W Chioza.[14]

X Malamocco, the haven within the sea banke.[15]

Y Povegia, an Iland.[16]

Z San' Georgio d' Alega, in the way as we come from Paduoa to Venice, a little Iland.[18]

╬ La Concordia:[17] a little Iland.

The Henetians of *Paphlagonia,* their King *Palemon* being dead at the siege of *Troy,* joyned themselves to *Antener,* and possessing these parts, after they had driven out the Euganeans, called the countrey *Venice,* and through their great vertue were made Citizens of *Rome,* and their chiefe men Senators thereof.[19] But when *Attila* King of the *Huns* invaded *Italy,* and the Empire of the West being weakned, did destroy the same, the said Henetians came out of *Histria,* now called *Frioli,* and from the Territory of *Paduoa,* and other Italians came from adjoyning parts, into certaine Ilands compassed with marshes, that they might be safe from those Barbarians; and about the yeere of our Lord, 421, began to build a City, which proving a safe retreat from the tyranny then continually oppressing *Italy,* in processe of time by civill Arts grew incredibly. These Ilands were in number sixty neere adjoyning, and twelve more distant; which being all joyned in one, have made this stately City, and the chiefe of them were called in the vulgar tongue, *Rialto, Grado, Heraclea, & Caestello Olivolo.* The Iland *Grado* was of old the seat of the

[1] Santa Croce and Dorsodoro *sestieri.*

[2] *San Giorgio Maggiore.

[3] Island of *Santa Maria della Grazia (La Grazia)

[4] Island of Giudecca.

[5] *Lido di Venezia.

[6] Island of *Murano.

[7] *Lazzaretto Nuovo.

[8] Island of Mazzorbo.

[9] Island of Burano.

[10] Island of San Francesco del Deserto.

[11] Island of Torcello and *Fortezza di Sant'Andrea.

[12] Islands of La Certosa and Sant'Elena.

[13] Lazzaretto Vecchio.

[14] Chioggia.

[15] Malamocco.

[16] Island of Poveglia, north-west of Malamocco.

[17] Island of San Giorgio in Alga.

[18] *La Concordia*: perhaps near Isola di San Giuliano.

[19] Livy, *History of Rome,* chapter 1, recounted how 'Antenor, being joined by a multitude of the Henetians, who had been driven out of Paphlagonia in a civil war, and having lost their king Pylæmenes at Troy, were at a loss both for a settlement and a leader, came to the innermost bay of the Adriatic sea, and expelling the Euganeans, who then inhabited the tract between the Alps and the sea, settled the Trojans and Henetians in the possession of the country. The place where they first landed is called Troy.' This source was often cited in accounts of the origin of Venice and it is likely that Moryson also consulted William Thomas's account in *The Historie of Italie,* pp. 85–7.

Patriarkes, after that the Patriarchate of *Aquilegia* in *Histria*,[1] was by the Popes authority translated thither: but now the seat of the Patriarkes is removed to *Caestello Olivolo*.[2] At first Consuls governed the City, then Tribunes, chosen out of each Ile one, till the yeere 697, when the Citizens abiding in *Heraclea* chose them a Duke, who dwelt in the same Ile. After forty yeeres they chose a Tribune of souldiers, in stead of a Duke, with like authority as hee had, and at last in the yeere 742, meeting in the Iland *Malamocco*, they chose a Duke againe, and removed his seat from *Heraclea*, to that Iland. Then *Pipin* raigning in *Italy* about the yeere 800,[3] the Venetians demolished *Heraclea* which was built againe, but never recovered the old dignity, being more notable in the seat of the Bishop, then in the number of Citizens. For most of the Gentlemen removed their dwellings into the Iland *Rialto*, otherwise called *Rivo alto;* either of the depth of the marshes, or because it was higher then the other Ilands, and thereupon called *Ripa alta*. Whereupon that Iland getting more dignity then the rest, the Citizens in processe of time joyned the sixty Ilands lying neere one to the other, with [p. 77] some foure hundred bridges; of which Ilands (as is above said) and of the twelve more distant, this stately City consisteth. Then by common counsell, the seat of the Dukes was established in this Iland, who built the stately Pallace which at this day we see.[4] And now a new Dukedome arising out of these salt marshes of the sea, from that time daily grew in dignity. But the City was first called *Rialto*, and after, of the countrey from whence the Citizens came, was called *Venetia*, or in the plurall number *Venetiae*: because many Dukedomes and Provinces, or many Nations were joyned in one, and at this day is vulgarly called *Venegia*. That the City was first called *Rialto*, appeares by old records of Notaries, written in these wordes: After the use of *Venice*. In the name of eternall God, amen: subscribed in such a yeere of *Rivo alto*, and in these wordes after the use of the Empire; In the name of Christ, amen: subscribed, dated at *Venice*. This stately City built in the bottome of the gulfe of the Adriatique sea, in the midst of marshes upon many Ilands, is defended on the East side against the sea, by a banke of earth, which hath five (or some say seven) mouths or passages into the sea; and is vulgarly called *Il Lido*: and being so placed by nature, not made by Art, bendeth like a bowe, and reacheth thirty five miles; and by the aforesaid passages, the ships and the tides of the sea goe in and out, and the deepe marshes whereof I have spoken, are made of these salt waters, and of divers fresh waters falling from the Alpes, and vulgarly called, *il Tagliamonts La livenza, la praac, la Brenta, Il Po, l'Adice,* and *il Bacchiglione*.[5] On the West side, the City is compassed with marshes, and after five miles with the Territory of *Paduoa*. On the North side with marshes, and beyond them partly with the

---

[1] Patriarchate of Aquileia, an episcopal see in north-eastern Italy, centred on the city of Aquileia.

[2] Island of Rialto, linked by the *Rialto Bridge to San Marco Island. Grado (Gravo), in the north-eastern region of Friuli-Venezia Giulia, on an island between Venice and Trieste. As Moryson notes, it was the seat of the patriarch until Pope Nicolas V transferred the patriarchate to Venice in 1451. Eraclea was the capital of the Republic of Venice until 742 when it was transferred to Malamocco. *San Pietro di Castello is an island in the Venetian lagoon.

[3] Pepin (Pippin, Pepin Carloman) of Italy (773–810), a son of Emperor Charlemagne (742–814), was King of the Lombards (781–810) under his father's authority; to be distinguished from Pepin the Short (c.714–68), King of the Franks.

[4] *Palazzo Ducale.

[5] Rivers Tagliamento, Livenza, Brenta, Po, Adige and Bacchilione. Moryson's 'praac' is unclear but may represent the Piave. He fails to mention other rivers which flow, or used to flow, into the Venetian lagoon, including the Rivers Sile, Zero, Marzenego and Muson.

Province *Frioli,* partly with the aforesaid sea banke. And upon the South side with many Ilands, wherein are many Churches and Monasteries, like so many Forts, and beyond them with the firme land of *Italy.* The City is eight miles in circuit, and hath seventy parishes, wherein each Church hath a little market place, for the most part foure square, and a publike Well. For the common sort use well water, and raine water kept in cesternes; but the Gentlemen fetch their water by boat from the land. It hath thirty one cloysters of Monkes, and twenty eight of Nunnes, besides chappels and almes-houses. Channels of water passe through this City (consisting of many Ilands joyned with Bridges) as the bloud passeth through the veines of mans body; so that a man may passe to what place he will both by land and water. The great channell is in length about one thousand three hundred paces, and in breadth forty paces, and hath onely one bridge called *Rialto,*[1] and the passage is very pleasant by this channell; being adorned on both sides with stately Pallaces. And that men may passe speedily, besides this bridge, there be thirteene places called *Traghetti,*[2] where boats attend called *Gondole;* which being of incredible number give ready passage to all men. The rest of the channels running through lesse streets, are more narrow, and in them many bridges are to be passed under. The aforesaid boats are very neat, and covered all save the ends with black cloth, so as the passengers may goe unseene and unknowne, and not bee annoyed at all with the sunne, winde, or raine. And these boats are ready at call any minute of the day or night. And if a stranger know not the way, hee shall not need to aske it, for if hee will follow the presse of people, hee shall be sure to bee brought to the market place of Saint *Marke,* or that of *Rialto*; the streets being very narrow (which they pave with bricke,) and besides if hee onely know his Hosts name, taking a boat, he shall be safely brought thither at any time of the night. Almost all the houses have two gates, one towards the street, the other towards the water; or at least the bankes of the channels are so neere, as the passage by water is as easie as by land. The publike boats, with the private of Gentlemen and Citizens, are some eight hundred, or as others say, a thousand. Though the floud or ebbe of the salt water bee small, yet with that motion it carrieth away the filth of the City, besides that, by the multitude of fiers, and the situation open to all windes, the ayre is made very wholsome, whereof the Venetians bragge, that it agrees with all strangers complexions, by a secret vertue, whether they be brought up in a good or ill ayre, and preserveth them in their former health. And though I dare not say that the Venetians [p. 78] live long, yet except they sooner grow old, and rather seeme then truly be aged: I never in any place observed more old men, or so many Senators venerable for their grey haires and aged gravity. To conclude, the situation of *Venice* is such, as the Citizens abound with all commodities of sea and land; and are not onely most safe from their enemies on the land, being severed from it by waters, and on the sea being hedged in with a strong sea banke, but also give joyfull rest under their power to their subjects on land, though exposed to the assault of their enemies.

The City parted in the middest with the great channell,[3] comming in from the sea banke neere the two Castles, is of old divided into six sextaries, or six parts, vulgarly *sestieri;* three on this side the channell, and three beyond the channell. The first sextary

---

[1] *Rialto Bridge.
[2] *traghetti*, small ferries for crossing the *Grand Canal.
[3] *Grand Canal.

on this side the channell, is that of Saint *Marke*;[1] for howsoever it be not the Cathedrall Church, yet it is preferred before the rest, as well because the Duke resides there, as especially because Saint *Marke* is the protecting Saint of that City. The body of which Saint being brought hither by Merchants from *Alexandria*: this Church was built in the yeere 829. at the charge of the Duke *Justinian*,[2] who dying, gave by his last will great treasure to that use, and charged his brother to finish the building, which was laid upon the ruines of Saint *Theodores* Church, who formerly had beene the protecting Saint of the City. And the same being consumed with fire in the yeere 976. it was more stately rebuilt, according to the narrownes of the place, the Merchants being charged to bring from all places any precious thing they could find fit to adorne the same, whatsoever it cost. The length of the Church containeth two hundred foot of *Venice,* the bredth fifty, the circuit 950. The building is become admirable, for the singular art of the builders and painters, and the most rare peeces of Marble, Porphry, Ophites (stones so called of speckles like a serpent) and like stones; and they cease not still to build it, as if it were unfinished, lest the revenues given by the last wils of dead men to that use, should returne to their heires (as the common report goes.) There were staires of old to mount out of the market place into the Church, till the waters of the channell increasing, they were forced to raise the height of the market place.[3] On the side towards the market place are five doores of brasse, whereof that in the middest is fairest, and the same, with one more, are daily opened, the other three being shut, excepting the dayes of Feasts.[4] Upon the ground neere the great doore, is a stone, painted as if it were engraven: which painting is vulgarly called, *Ala Mosaica,* and upon this stone Pope *Alexander* set his foot upon the necke of the Emperour *Fredericke Barbarossa,* adoring him after his submission.[5] The outward part of the Church is adorned with 148. pillars of marble, whereof some are Ophytes, that is speckled, and eight of them are Porphry neere the great doore, which are highly esteemed. And in all places about the Church, there be some six hundred pillars of marble, besides some three hundred in the caves under ground. Above these pillars on the outside of the Church is an open gallery, borne up with like pillars, from whence the Venetians at times of Feasts, behold any shewes in the market place. And above this gallery, and over the great doore of the Church, be foure horses of brasse, guilded over, very notable for antiquity and beauty; and they are so set, as if at the first step they would leape into the market place. They are said to be made to the similitude of the Horses of *Phoebus,* drawing the Chariot of the Sunne, and to have beene put upon the triumphall Arke of *Nero,* by the people of *Rome,* when he had overcome the Parthians. But others say that they were given to *Nero* by *Tiridates* the King of *Armenia,* and were made by the hands of the famous engraver *Lisippus.* These Horses *Constantine* removed from *Rome* to *Constantinople,* and that City being sacked, the Venetians brought them to *Venice,* but they tooke of the bridles, for a signe

---

[1] *San Marco.

[2] Giustiniano Participazio (d. 829), Doge from 825. His succession had been bitterly contested by his father, Agnello Participazio (Doge, 811–27) and his younger brothers Giovanni and Agnello, appointed by their father as co-doges.

[3] Flooding (*acqua alta*) was a common occurrence in the Piazza San Marco throughout the Middle Ages and continued even after the floor level of the piazza was raised, with especially high water levels in 1550, 1559 and 1599.

[4] The central and southern portal bronze doors had been taken from Constantinople.

[5] See pp. 53 and 334.

that their City had never beene conquered, but enjoyed Virgin liberty. And all the parts of these horses being most like the one to the other, yet by strange art, both in posture of motion, and otherwise, they are most unlike one to the other.[1] Above this gallery the Image of Saint *Marke* of marble, and like images of the other Evangelists, of the Virgin *Mary,* and of the Angell *Gabriell,* are placed, and there is a bell upon which the houres are sounded, for the Church hath his Clocke, though another very faire Clocke in the market place be very neere [p. 79] it. The roofe in forme of a Globe, lies open at the very top, where the light comes in; for the Church hath no windowes, and the Papist Churches being commonly darke, to cause a religious horror, or to make their candles shew better, this is more darke then the rest. I passe over the image of Saint *Marke* of brasse in the forme of a Lion, guilded overouer, and holding a booke of brasse. Likewise the artificiall Images of the Doctors of the Church, and others. I would passe over the Image of the Virgin *Mary,* painted *ala Mosaica,* that is as if it were engraven, but that they attribute great miracles to it, so as weomen desirous to know the state of their absent friends, place a wax candle burning in the open aire before the Image, and beleeue that if their friend be alive, it cannot be put out with any force of wind; but if he be dead, that the least breath of wind puts it out, or rather of it selfe it goes out: and besides for that I would mention that those who are adjudged to death, offer waxe candles to this Image, and as they passe by, fall prostrate to adore the same. To conclude, I would not omit mention thereof, because all shippes comming into the Haven, use to salute this Image, and that of Saint *Marke,* with peeces of Ordinance, as well and more then the Duke. A Merchant of *Venice* saved from shipwracke, by the light of a candle in a darke night, gave by his last will to this Image, that his heires for ever should find a waxe candle to burne before the same. Above the said gallery are little chambers, in which they lay up pieces of stone and glasse, with other materials for the foresaid painting, *ala Mosaica,* which is like to engraving, and Painters having pensions from the state, doe there exercise that Art, highly esteemed in *Italy.* The outward roofe is divided into foure globes, covered with leade. Touching the inside of the Church: In the very porch thereof is the Image of Saint *Marke,* painted with wonderfull art, and the Images of Christ crucified, of him buried, and of the foure Evangelists, highly esteemed; besides many other much commended for the said painting like engraving, and for other workemanship. And there be erected foure great pillars of Ophites, which they say were brought from the Temple of *Salomon.* At the entery of the doore is an old and great sepulcher, in which lies the Duke *Marine Morosini.*[2] Not far thence is the image of Saint *Geminian* in pontificall habit, and another of Saint *Katherine,* both painted with great art. When you enter the body of the Church, there is the great Altar, under which lies Saint *Marke,* in a chest of brasse, decked with Images of silver guilded, and with plates of gold, and Images enamelled, and with the Image of Christ sitting upon a stately throne, adorned with pillars of most white Marble, and many precious stones, and curiously engraven. At the backe of this Altar there is another, which they call the Altar of the most holy Sacrament, made of the best marble, with a little doore of brasse, decked with carved Images, and with foure pillars of Alablaster, transparant as Christall, and highly esteemed; and upon the same hang every day two lampes of Copper: but at the

---

[1] *San Marco, Bronze Horses.
[2] Marino Morosini (1181–1253), Doge 1249–53, was interred in the atrium of Saint Mark's Basilica.

times of feasts there hang two of pure silver. Moreover the Organs are said to be the worke of a most skilfull Artificer. In the higher gallery compassing the Church, is the image of Pope *Pelagius*, under which is a place where the holy relikes are kept, which Pope *Clement* the eight[1] gave to *John Delphin* Knight,[2] one of the Procurators of Saint *Marke*, and Ambassadour at *Rome* for *Venice*, namely a peece of a bone of *Phillip* the Apostle, a peece of the cheeke-bone, and foure teeth of the Martyr Saint *Biagius*: peeces of bones of Saint *Bartholmew*, and Saint *Thomas* (forsooth) of *Canterbury*, and of the Apostles Saint *Matthew*, and Saint *Marke*, (whose body they say is laid in the foresaid chest) and part of the haire of the blessed Virgin, and a peece of a finger of the Evangelist *Luke*, and a peece of a ribbe of Saint *Peter*, with many like, which they shew to the people to be adored certaine daies in the yeere. Aboue the Altar of Saint *Clement*, these verses are written, which shew how they worshipped Images in a more modest though superstitious age.

> *Nam Deus est quod Imago docet, sed non Deus ipse*
> *Hane videas, sed mente colas quod cernis in ipsa:*
> That which the Image shewes, is God, it selfe is none,
> See this, but God heere seene, in mind adore alone.

Likewise these verses of the same Author, be in another place.

> [p. 80] *Effigiem Christi qui transis, pronus honora,*
> *Non tamen effigiem sed quod designat adora.*
> *Esse deum ratione caret, cui contulit esse*
> *Materiale lapis, sicut & manus effigiale.*
> *Nec Deus est naec homo, praesens quam cernis Imago,*
> *Sed Deus est & homo, quem sacra signat Imago.*
> As thou Christs Image passest, fall the same before,
> Yet what this Image signifies, not it adore.
> No reason that it should be God, whose essence stands
> Materiall of stone, formall of workemens hands.
> This Image which thou seest, is neither God nor Man,
> But whom it represents, he is both God and Man.

At the entry of the Chancell, is the throne of the Dukes, made of walnut-tree, all carved above the head, and when the Dukes sit there, it was wont to be covered with carnation satten, but now it is covered with cloth of gold, given by the King of *Persia*. There be two stately pulpits of marble, with Histories carved in brasse, where they sing the Epistles and Gospels. On the left hand by the Altar of Saint *James* is a place, where (if a man may beleeve it) the body of Saint *Marke*, by a crevice suddenly breaking through the marble stone, appeared in the yeere 1094. to certaine Priests who had fasted and prayed to find the same, the memory of the place where it was layed at the building of the Church about 829. being utterly lost. I beleeve that the memory thereof was lost about the yeere 829. when superstition was not yet ripe, but that it was found in the yeere 1094. that age being infected with grosse superstition, let him that list beleeve. They themselves seeme to distrust this miracle, while they confesse that the same body

---

[1] Ippolito Aldobrandini (1536–1605), Pope Clement VIII (1592–1605).
[2] Cardinal Giovanni Delfin (1545–1622). His mausoleum in the Venetian church of San Michele in Isola contains a bust carved (*c*.1621) by Gian Lorenzo Bernini.

was most secretly laid under the great Altar, and never since shewed to any man, but once or twice, and that after a suspicious manner. To the foresaid pulpits another is opposite, where the Musitians sing at solemne Feasts, and from whence the Dukes newly created, are shewed to the people, and likewise the holy relikes (as they tearme them) are shewed twice in the yeere. The wals in the Church are so covered with the best marbles, as the lime and bricke cannot be seene: and these peeces of marble with their spots and brightnes, are very beautifull, whereof two are held for admirable Monuments, which are so joined, as they lively represent the Image of a man. Here *Marino Morosini* first of all the Dukes hung his Armes uppon the wals, whom the other Dukes after him in number forty three have followed, and there hung up their Armes. In the middest of the Church hangs a banner, given by the Citizens of *Verona,* in token of subjection, and two others for the same purpose given by the Citizens of *Crema* and *Cremona.* The Marble pillars set in Caves under the Church, beare up the pavement, which is made of peeces of the best marble, carved and wrought with little stones of checker worke very curiously, especially under the middle globe of the roofe, and neere the great doore. And among the rare stones opposite to the singers pulpit, they shew one of such naturall spots, as it is esteemed a Jewell, which by change of colour (they say) doth shew the change of weather. Moreover they shew certaine Images, carved by the direction of the Abbot *John Joachim* of old time,[1] whereof many shew future events, as that of two cockes carrying a wolfe upon their backe, which they understand to be *Lewis* the twelfth, and *Charles* the eight, French Kings, casting *Lodovico Sfortia* out of his Dukedome,[2] and in like sort, (to omit many other more hidden) that of the Lyons fat in the waters, and leane upon land, which they understand to be the power of *Venice* by sea, and the weakenes by land. Besides they say the same Abbot caused the Images of Saint *Dominicke* and Saint *Francis* to be drawne upon the doore of the Sanctuary, long before they lived; and the title of Saint is added to each of them, but the name is not set upon the pictures, yet they both are painted in the habit of their order. They shew two like pictures drawne by direction of the said Abbot, whereof they understand one to be the last Pope, under whom shall be one shepheard and one fould: but they say it is unknowne what the other signifies. Before the new Chappell of the blessed Virgin, there be two little chambers, whereof one is called the Sanctuary, in which their holy relikes are kept, the [p. 81] other is called the Jewell house, because the treasure of Saint *Marke* (so they appropriate all publike things to Saint *Marke*) is there kept, and it is vulgarly called *Luogo delle gioie,*[3] that is, the place of the Jewels.

The Procurators of Saint *Marke,* keepe this treasure, and make no difficulty to shew it to strangers of the better sort. In this place I saw the Ducall Cap, (vulgarly *ill corne,* or, *Beretta Ducale*) which the Dukes weare at their Creation, being of inestimable value, for the multitude and price of the Jewels, especially of a diamond upon the crowne of the

---

[1] Joachim of Fiore (Flora) (*c.*1135–1202), founder of the monastic order of San Giovanni in Fiore and renowned for his prophecies and his concept of a new age of harmony based upon his interpretation of the Book of Revelation.

[2] Ludovico Maria Sforza (1452–1508), Duke of Milan. When Louis XII became King of France in 1498 he had a hereditary claim to Milan through his paternal grandmother Valentina Visconti. He drove Ludovico out of the city and, after besieging Novara where Ludovico was based, Louis took him prisoner in April 1500. Ludovico was relatively well treated in his confinement but, after an escape attempt in 1508, he was kept in an underground dungeon at Loches and died on 27 May 1508.

[3] *Luogo delle gioie*: place of the jewels (*gioielli*).

Figure 27.   Giacomo Franco, *Habiti d'huomeni et donne venetiane* (1610). The dress of the procurators of San Marco; through the window a view of the Redentore, the Church of the Capuchins. By permission of Special Collections, Brotherton Library, University of Leeds.

Cap, and a chrysolite[1] set in the midst. I saw two crownes of Kings with twelve stomachers of pure gold set with rich Jewels (which the Noblewomen wore at *Constantinople* before the Turkes tooke it) and twelve other Crownes all of pure massy gold; all which the Venetians dividing with the French, had for their part, when they tooke *Constantinople,* in the yeere 1203. I saw a saphyre of extraordinary bignes, and a Diamond which the French King *Henry* the third gave to this state, when he returned that way from *Poland*;[2] and two whole Unicornes hornes,[3] each more then foure foot long, and a third shorter, and a little dish of a huge price, with innumerable vessels, which for price, rarenes, and workemanship, are highly valued. They say that a Candian thiefe tooke away this treasure, which is kept with many doores and barres of iron, but that he restored it, being betrayed by his fellow.

In a Chappell of this Church, is a Font of brasse, with a brasen image of Saint *John* baptizing, and the Altar thereof is of a stone brought out of *Asia,* upon which they say Christ did sit, when he preached at *Tyrus:* but others say it is the stone upon which the Patriarke *Jacob* did sleepe.[4] They shew there the chaire of the blessed Virgin, of stone, and two peeces of marble spotted with the blood of *John Baptist,* and the marble sepulcher of Duke *Andrea Dandoli.* In the Chappell of the Cardinal Zeno, they shew the Rocke strucke by *Moses,* and distilling water, and two precious peeces of porphery. In the upper Vestry they shew the picture of the Virgin, painted by Saint *Lukes* hand,[5] and the ring of Saint *Marke,* and his Gospell written with his owne hand, and a peece of the Crosse of Christ, and of the Pillar to which he was tied, and Bookes covered with massy silver, and candlestickes, chalice, and many vessels of silver guilded, all set with little precious stones, and the Bishops Miter of great price, and many rich vestures for the Priests. The chiefe Priest of this Church must be a gentleman of *Venice,* and though hee be no Bishop, yet the Popes have given him great priviledges, and he is to be chosen by the Duke; because the Dukes built this Church, wherupon it is ever since called the Dukes Chappell. This Church of Saint *Marke,* is not unworthily called the golden Church, for the rich ornaments thereof, especially for the Images thereof, painted *ala mosaita,* like a worke engraven. For the workemen doe incorporate gold with little square peeces of glasse, and guild the same over; then breaking them in very small peeces, they lay them vpon the pictures.

Among the Parish Churches belonging to Saint *Marke,* is the Chappell of Saint Theodore,[6] where the Inquisitors of Religion sit thrice a weeke: namely the Popes Nuntio,

[1] *chrysolite*: green or yellow-green gemstone, often applied to topaz and peridot. Shakespeare refers to this gemstone in *Othello, the Moor of Venice* when Othello laments his jealousy-crazed murder of Desdemona: 'If heaven would make me such another world / Of one entire and perfect chrysolite, I'd not have sold her for it' (V.ii.143–5). Chrysolite is also one of the stones on Aaron's breastplate in Exodus and one of the foundations of the New Jerusalem in Revelation.

[2] Philip Sidney (**item 22**, **Plate 17** and **Figure 17**) witnessed celebrations marking the visit of King Henri III of France to Venice in 1574 (**Plate 9**).

[3] *Unicornes hornes*: usually narwhal 'horn', the extended left canine tooth of the narwhal; much prized for their alleged magical and medicinal properties and as an antidote to poison.

[4] Jacob *did sleepe*: see Gen. 28:10–22.

[5] Cf. accounts of this image and other holy relics by Robert Langton (**item 8**) and Sir Richard Torkington (**item 10**).

[6] St Theodore, 4th-century patron saint of Venice before the arrival of the relics of St Mark. A small chapel dedicated to the saint was built *c.*1486 immediately behind St Mark's and later occupied by the Inquisition at Venice.

and the Patriarke (an Inquisitor by his place, and at this time a Dominican Friar) and three Senators chosen by the Senate. Likewise the little, but most faire Church of Saint *Geminian*,[1] is seated in the market place of Saint *Marke*, whose Priest according to the custome of *Venice*, is chosen by them that have unmoveable goods in the Parish, and is confirmed by the Patriarke, in which Church the most notable things are, three Images graven upon the great Altar, and the sepulcher of *John Peter Stella*,[2] Great Chancellor, and the Altar of *Lodovico Spinello*,[3] and the Monument of *James* and *Francis Sansovine*, famous engravers.[4] In the Church of Saint *Mary Zebenigo*,[5] the Monuments of *Sebastian Foscarini*, a Phylosopher,[6] and of *Jerome Molini*, a Florentine Poet,[7] and the picture of the Lords Supper. In the Church Saint *Vitale*, the artificiall statua of that Saint on horsebacke.[8] In the Church Saint *Angelo*, built by the family of the *Morosini*, the Altar of the holy Sacrament.[9] In the Church of Saint *Fantino*,[10] the Architecture, and among other Images, the head of a Crucifix, and the singular Images of the blessed Virgin, and Saint *John*, painted standing by the Crosse. In the Vestry of Saint *Fantino* (whose Monkes use to accompany and comfort those that are executed)[11] the two [p. 82] Altars, and in the first of them the brasen Images of the blessed Virgin and Saint *John*, and in the second the excellent Marble Image of Saint *Jerome*. In the Parish Church of Saint *Luke*,[12] seated in the middest of the City, a monument of foure most learned men, and another of *Peter Aretine*,[13] Then called the scourge of Princes, are the most remarkable things. The Inquisitors worthily condemned the books of this Aretine, for the filthinesse of them (howsoever they be yet commonly sold) and the common report is, that they also commanded his horrible Epitaph to be blotted out, which was set in this Church of Saint *Luke*, in these words:

[1] *San Geminiano.

[2] Unidentified.

[3] Possibly Ludovico Spinello who was secretary to the Venetian Ambassador to England in 1521 when he witnessed on 17 May the execution of Edward Stafford (1478–1521), 3rd Duke of Buckingham.

[4] Following Jacopo Sansovino's restoration of *San Geminiano, he was buried with his children in one of its chapels. His sepulchre is now in the Baptistry of *San Marco.

[5] *Santa Maria Zobenigo (after its founding family, the Jubanico), also known as Santa Maria del Giglio (of the Lily). The present church dates from the 1680s.

[6] Sebastiano Foscarini was a noted philosopher who lectured at the School of Rialto. He was replaced there in 1521 for two years by Nicolò da Ponte (1491–1585, Doge from 1578) but then resumed his lectureship.

[7] Unidentified but perhaps Girolamo Molino (1500–69).

[8] * San Vidal (San Vitale). Moryson refers to Vittore Carpaccio's painting for its main altarpiece of *San Vidal on Horseback with Eight Saints* (1514) with four saints standing by the saint mounted on a white horse and four in the balconies above. https://commons.wikimedia.org/wiki/File:Vittore_Carpaccio_087.jpg.

[9] Probably *Sant'Angelo in the Campo Sant'Angelo, rather than *Sant'Angelo Raffaele, located in the Dorsoduro *sestiere*, distant from Moryson's area of description at this point in his narrative.

[10] *San Fantin (Fantino). The building viewed by Moryson had been completed by Sansovino in 1564.

[11] The church still contains a Tuscan crucifix which was carried by monks before those condemned to death as they made their way from the prison to the place of execution between the two pillars in Saint Mark's Square.

[12] *San Luca Evangelista.

[13] Pietro Aretino (1492–1556), poet, dramatist, satirist and blackmailer, was renowned for his scurrilous verses. He settled in Venice in 1527 and became a close friend of Titian who painted at least three portraits of him.

*Qui gaice l'Aretin' Poeta Tusco,*
*Chi disse mal' d'ogniun', fuora che di Dio,*
*Scusandosi, dicendo, io nol' conosco,*[1]
Here lies the Aretine, a Poet of Tuscany,
Who spake ill of all but of God,
Excusing himselfe, saying, I know him not.

Of the same *Aretine* saith *Ariosto:*

*Ecco il flagella de'i Principi,* ⎫  ⎧ Behold the scourge of Princes
*Il Divin' Pietro Aretino*    ⎭  ⎩ The Divine *Peter Aretine*

In the stately Church of Saint *Salvatore,*[2] the Marble image of Saint *Jerem,* another of him, and a third of Saint *Laurence,*and the great Altar of pure silver, are curiously ingraven: and in the chappell of the holy Sacrament, the Image of *Mary Magdalen;* and in another chappell, the Image of Saint *Augustine,* praying among his Monkes; and not farre off two Images of the Monument erected to Duke *Francis Venerio:*[3] all painted with great Art, and the Altar of the blessed Virgn equall, or to be preferred to the best in the City: the Altar of S[t] *Antony,* and two Monuments of Dukes, all adorned with rare engraven and painted Images, and a faire paire of Organs. In the Church of Saint *Bartholmew,*[4] the picture of Manna falling from heaven,[5] and the brasen Images of Christ, of the foure Evangelists, and six Angels. In the Church of Saint *Giuliano,*[6] many pictures, but especially that of Christ carrying his Crosse, and neere the doore another of Saint *Jerome,* and two Marble Images upon the Altar. In the Church of Saint *Stephen,*[7] rich with Marble and pillers, the Marble Images of the Apostles, with the pillars whereon they stand, and the Altar ingraven with brasse, and the Monument of *James Suriani,*[8] and another of *Anthony Cornari*[9] with this inscription:

*Antonij ad Cineres viator adsta*
*Hic Cornarins ille, quem solebant,*
*Rerum principia & Deos docentem*
*Olim Antenoriae stupere Athenae,*
*Accitus Patrias subinde ad oras,*
*Ornatus titulis fascibusque,*
*Doctrina venetam beavit urbem.*

[1] In the mid-1650s Sir John Reresby recorded this censored epitaph as: 'Qui jace Aretin, poeta Tusco, qui dice mal d'ogni uno fuora di Dio; scusandosi dicendo, Io no'l cognosco.' It has also been attributed to the bishop, physician and historian Paolo Giovio (1483–1552) who reputedly wrote it while Aretino was alive. This version reads: 'Qui giace l'Aretin, poeta tosco,/ Di tutti disse mal fuorché di Cristo,/ Scusandosi col dir: non lo conosco.'

[2] *San Salvatore.

[3] Francesco Venier, Doge 1554–6.

[4] *San Bartolomeo.

[5] Moryson may be referring to the *Gathering of Manna* by Sante Peranda (1566–1638), near the exit to the sacristy. He does not mention the most important painting in the church, *The Feast of the Rosary* (1506) by Albrecht Dürer (1471–1528), painted during his stay at Venice. It was taken in 1606 by Emperor Rudolf II (1552–1612) to Prague (now in the National Gallery, Prague).

[6] *San Giuliano (Venetian, Zulian).

[7] *Santo Stefano.

[8] Tomb (1493) of Giacomo Surian by Pietro Lombardo.

[9] Tomb in the cloister of the convent of the patrician philosopher Antonio Cornaro (Cornelius) who lectured at the University of Padua and was rector of the Aristotelian School at Rialto (1484–98).

> At the ashes of *Anthony*, passenger stand,
> This is that *Cornarius* whom of old,
> Teaching the principles of Nature and the Gods,
> *Antenors Athens* was wont to admire.
> After called home to his Countrey,
> Graced with Titles and Magistracy,
> With his Learning he made Venice happy.

These things I say are in these Churches most remarkeable.

The second sextary on this side the channell, vulgarly *Il sestiero di Castello*, hath the name of the Castle *Olivolo*,[1] which seated towards the sea, may seeme to be divided from the Citie, yet it is joyned thereto by a long bridge. Of old it was a City by it selfe, and therefore the Dukes Throne being established in the Iland *Realto*, the Bishops seat was made here, who is invested by the Duke, and was consecrated by the Patriarke of *Grado*, till that being extinguished, this was raised to the dignity of a Patriarke, in the yeere 1450. In the Cathedrall Church of Saint *Peter*, this is written upon the Chappell in Latine;

> [f. 83] *Who ere thou be that approachest, worship: Within these grates of Iron the crosse is inclosed, that is adorned with three haires of the beard of Christ, with a naile, the cup in which he drunke to his Disciples, and with a peece of the true Crosse, &c.*

This Patriarcall seat[2] hath two old pulpits of marble, the monuments of the Bishops and Patriarkes, which with the adjoining Pallace of the Patriarkes, are the most remarkeable things thereof. In the Church of *John Baptist* in *Bragola*,[3] many curious pictures, the sepulcher of that Saint guilded over, the Image of Christ, the pictures of the lesse Altar, especially that of Christ baptised, that of Saint *Hellen*, that of Christs resurrection, and the lively picture of Christ sitting with his Apostles at his last supper. In the Church of Saint *Mary Formosa*,[4] this inscription is read; *Vincentius Capellus*[5] *most skilful in Navigation, and Prefect of the Gallies, no lesse praised of old, who received signes of honour from Henry the seventh, King of Britany, &c.* There, upon the great and very faire Altar, the Images of the foure Evangelists, and upon the top, that of Christs resurrection, and of two Angels. In the Church Saint *Marina*,[6] the statua on horsebacke erected by the Senate to *Tadeo della volpe* of *Imola*,[7] and the great Altar, with the pillars of prophry. In the Church of Saint *Leone*,[8] the Images of Saint *Jerome*, of Christ at supper with his Disciples, of *John* the Evangelist, and Saint *Michaell*, all painted by the

---

[1] Island of *San Pietro di Castello.

[2] Basilica di *San Pietro di Castello.

[3] *San Giovanni in Bragora.

[4] *Santa Maria Formosa.

[5] Admiral Vincentius Capellus. On 19 June 1535 it was noted in England that 'The Venetians fear the union of the King [of England], the Emperor and the Almains [Germans]. Antonio Surian, a councillor of Venice, and sometime ambassador in England, and Vincentio Capello, of the most reputation in Venice, have moved the Signoria to send an ambassador to England, and communicate with Harvell, the English ambassador.' *LP*, VIII, item 899.

[6] *Santa Marina.

[7] Taddeo Della Volpe (1474–1534), a mercenary commander who fought under Cesare Borgia and Pope Giulio II. He commanded troops against Padua and the Turks and a (now lost) gilded copper equestrian statue was erected in his memory in the Church of Santa Marina where he was buried.

[8] *San Leone (Venetian, Lio).

hands of most skilfull workemen. In the Church of Saint *Anthony*,[1] foure most faire Altars (in the second whereof the Image of Christ, and in the third rich with excellent pillars, the History of ten thousand Martyres painted, and in the fourth the espousals of the blessed Virgin, areal painted with singular Art) and a foot statua erected by the Senate to *Victor Pisanus*.[2] In the Church of Saint *Dominicke*,[3] the library, and pictures of the Altars. In the Church of Saint *Francis di Paola*,[4] many things given upon vow, and hung upon the wals. In that of Saint *Francis della vigna*,[5] a very faire and stately Church, the Altar of the Chappell belonging to the Family *Grimani,* and the pictures & brasen images of the same: and in the Chappell of the Family *Dandoli,* the picture of Saint *Laurence* martyred, and in the Chappell of the *Justiniani,* being very rich, the Images of the foure Evangelists and twelve Prophets. In the Chappell of our Lady, the monument of *Marke, Anthony, Morosini,* Knight and Procurator (famous in the warre which the French King *Lewis* the twelth, made in *Lombardy,* and thrice Ambassador from the State)[6] also the famous library of this monastery, and the bels (which they say were brought out of *England* after Queene *Maries* death.) In the Church of the Saints, *John* and *Paul,* (being one of the chiefe Churches)[7] the situation, the architecture, the pictures, and the monuments of sixteene Dukes; and another of *Marke, Anthony, Bragadini* (who having defended the Iland *Cyprus* from the Turkes, when they tooke it, had his skinne fleed off, by the command of the tyrant, against his faith, in the yeere 1571.)[8] Also three horsemens statuaes, one to *Leonardo de Prato,* Knight of *Rhodes,*[9] another to *Nichola Orsino* Count of *Pitiglia,*[10] both erected in the Church, the third for greater honour erected in the market place, to *Bartholmeo Coleoni* of *Bergamo,* for his good service to the State in their Warres;[11] all three erected by the Senate. Also a foot

---

[1] *Sant' Antonin in the Castello sestiere.

[2] During the Venetian-Genoese Wars Pietro Doria captured Chioggia and besieged Venice. However, Vittorio Pisano, the commander of the Venetian fleet, blockaded the Genoese galleys and on 23 December 1379 inflicted a major defeat on the Genoese navy. Known as the War of Chioggia, it effectively destroyed Genoese sea power.

[3] *San Domenico. Extensive rebuilding had begun in 1590 which Moryson would have seen.

[4] *San Francesco di Paola in the Castello sestiere.

[5] *San Francesco della Vigna.

[6] Marcantonio Morosini (1434–1509), administrator and diplomat and member of the Council of Ten.

[7] *Santi Giovanni e Paolo.

[8] Marcantonio Bragadin (1523–71), lawyer and soldier, was appointed in 1569 Captain-General of Famagusta, Cyprus. After the Ottomans took the city in August 1571, its Christians were massacred and Bragadin had his ears and nose cut off and was flayed alive. His tanned skin stuffed with straw was taken back to Constantinople as a trophy but in 1580 it was stolen by a Veronese seaman, Girolamo Polidori, and brought back to Venice. It was first kept at the Church of *San Gregorio and then in 1596 interred in a leaden casket with full military honours in a magnificent tomb at *Santi Giovanni e Paolo where it still remains. His death may have inspired Titian's painting the *Flaying of Marsyas.*

[9] Leonardo da Prato (d. 1511), a Knight of Rhodes and *condottiero*, who died during at the defence of Padua during the war with League of Cambrai. His statue is located high on the wall of the left transept.

[10] Niccolò di Pitigliano, Count of Pitigliano (1442–1510), *condottiero* and from 1495 Captain-General of the Venetian forces during conflicts with the League of Cambrai. His equestrian monument in gilded wood is in the right transept of *Santi Giovanni e Paolo.

[11] Bartolomeo Colleoni (1400–75), *condottiero* appointed in 1455 Captain-General of Venice. In his will he left money for an equestrian statue by Andrea del Verrocchio to himself to be erected in the Piazza *San Marco. However, no monuments were permitted there and so it was placed near the *Scuola Grande di San Marco, outside *Santi Giovanni e Paolo.

statua erected by the Senate, to *Deunys Naldo,* a most valiant Commander of their foote, and the stately sepulcher of *James de Cavallis,* and the Chappell of the Rossary (magnificall in the architecture, in rare marbles, in the art of engravers, and excellent pictures, especially that of Christ crucified.) In the Church of Saint *Mary delle Virgini,* (a Cloyster of Nunnes, built by the Dukes, and belonging to them by speciall right)[1] two marble sepulchers. In the Church Saint *Gioseppe,*[2] the admirable monument of the *Germani* (with admirable Images engraven of the Duke *Grimani* created,[3] and his Dutchesse *Morosini,* crowned and the like curiously wrought:) also the Image of Christ transfigured, and another of Christ buried, are the most remarkeable things. And whereas the graven images of this Church, be of rare beauty, they say that the chiefe of them were brought out of *England,* after the death of Queen *Mary.*[4] In the Church of Saint *Justina* (a parish Church, and yet the chiefe cloyster of Nunnes, twice rebuilt by the family *Morosini,*)[5] two curious statuaes of marble of *Paros.* In the Church of the Holy sepulcher, (being a cloyster of Nunnes) the sepulcher of Christ like that at *Jerusalem,* of ophites and like stones.[6] In Saint *Zachary*[7] a cloyster of Nunnes, [p. 84] the pall of the Virgin painted, another like it in the chappell, the sepulcher or Altar under which the said Saint (father to *John* Baptist) is laid, and at the backe of the great Altar, three sepulchers of Porphry and Ophyts, the stones of the great Altar, and the stately architecture of the Church, are the things most remarkeable: and the same cloyster hath great revenues. In generall understand that the Churches are for the most part built of bricke, and some few of free stone, though they be so covered with Marbles and like stones, as the bricke or free stone is scarce seene in the inside. In the Priory of S^t *John,* belonging of old to the Templary Knights, & now to the Knights of *Rhodes* or *Malta,*[8] it is remarkeable that the revenues thereof be great, and that the Priory is given by the Pope, which *Paul* the third gave to the Cardinall Saint *Angelo* his nephew (for so they call their bastards) whom *Alexander* the Cardinall of *Farnese* succeeded, yet not as Cardinall, but as Knight of *Malta,* and after him the Pope gave it to the Cardinall *Ascanio Colonna.* And the most remarkable things in the Church are the pall of the great Altar, the supper of our Lord painted, the picture of Christ speaking with the woman of *Samaria,* and that of *Herods* banquet, when he gave *John* Baptists head to *Herodia.* The Greeke Church belongs to this sextary, built in *Rio di San' Lorenzo.* The almes-house Saint *Lazero,* feeds foure hundred, or five hundred poore people; for all that beg are sent thither, and they have many of these houses. These are the most remarkeable things in the Churches of this sextary.

[1] *Santa Maria delle Vergini.

[2] *San Giuseppe di Castello.

[3] This huge monument by Vincenzo Scamozzi was erected by Marino Grimani (1532–1605), Doge from 25 April 1595. It was begun at this period and so Moryson is likely to have seen it in at least its initial stages rather than adding this detail after Marino Grimani's death on 25 December 1605, prior to the publication of his *Itinerary* in 1617.

[4] Shiploads of discarded Catholic iconography and statuary were shipped to the continent and it is feasible that items in *San Giuseppe di Castello had originally been made in England.

[5] *Santa Giustina.

[6] *San Sepolcro Castello.

[7] *San Zaccaria, a 15th-century former monastic church, located to the south-east of Piazza San Marco. It was dedicated to the father of John the Baptist, St Zacharias.

[8] *San Giovanni di Malta.

The third sextary, or sixth part of the City on this side the channell (meaning towards the gulfe of *Venice*) vulgarly is called *Il sestiero di Canaregio*,[1] of the canes or pipes which they were wont to use in the building of ships. In the Church of the Prophet *Jeremy*[2] (built by three families, *Morosini, Malipieri,* and *Runandi,* the sepulcher of Saint *Magnus* (who built eight Churches when the City was first founded) and the Image of the blessed Virgin much adored. In the Church of Saint *Marciali*,[3] the Images aswel of the great Altar, as of the Altar of *Angelo Raphaeli.* In the Apostles Church[4] (where excellent sermons are made in the Lent,) the carved Image of our Lady upon the Altar, and her picture upon the same painted by Saint *Luke.* In the Church of Saint *John Chrysostome*,[5] the pictures of three Theologicall vertues, & of Saint *Marke,* and the carved Images of the Virgin, and the Apostles. In the Church of Saint *Giob*,[6] the ingraving of the chappell of the *Grimani,* and of the Altar of the *Foscari;* the picture of Christ in the garden, with his Apostles sleeping, and the pictures of the next Altar, namely, that of the Virgin, Saint *Sabastian,* and Saint *Giob.* In the Church of Saint *Mary de servi*,[7] the pictures of the great Altar, especially of the Virgins assumption, and also of the Virgins Altar, and of Saint *Augustins* Altar, especiall that of the wise men adoring Christ, and the carved Images of another Altar, the Marble sepulcher of Duke *Andrea Vendramini,* being the fairest of all other in the City, and the Oratory of the banished men of *Lucea,* who first brought into this City the weaving of silke, and of whom many were made Gentlemen of *Venice.* In the Church of Saint *Mary del' Orto*,[8] the huge Image of Saint *Christopher,* the History of *Moses,* and the prophicies of the last judgement painted, the painting of the arched-roof, rare for perspective Art, and the[9] chiefe of that kinde, the Monument of Jasper, *Contarini* Cardinall, of the Marble of *Paros,* and the pillers of our Ladies Altar, with many Marble stones. In the Church of Saint *Mary de Crostechieri*,[10] the ancient pictures, the notable pall of Saint *Laurence,* worth seven thousand crownes, and the pictures in the chappel of *Lewis Usperi.* In the Church of Saint *Lucia*,[11] the Monument and chappell of the Saints. In the chappell of Saint *Luigi,* the great Altar, fairest of those built of wood. In the Church of Saint *Mary* of the Miracles,[12] the fairest of any Nunnery, for the beauty and rare stones, the walles covered with Marble, two Marble Images of two children under the Organs, (the works of famous *Praxitiles,*) the Images of marble of Paros, the stones of Porphery and Ophytes wonderfully carved, the great Altar of Marble, ingraven with great Art, the brasen Images of Saint *Peter,* Saint *Paul,* and of Angels. These are the things most remarkeable. In the Church of Saint *Mary* of Mercy,[13] *Sansovine*[14] witnesseth this Epitaph, (which I will set downe, lest any should thinke incredible, the like practises of Papists against Emperours, and *John* the King [p. 83][15] of *England,*) in these words: *To* Jerom Savina, a *Citizen* of Venice, *Prior of Saint Maries, notably learned in good Arts;*

---

[1] Cannaregio *sestiere.*

[2] *San Geremia.

[3] *San Marciliano.

[4] *Santi Apostoli.

[5] *San Giovanni Crisostomo.

[6] *San Giobbe.

[7] *Santa Maria dei Servi.

[8] *Madonna dell'Orto.

[9] *the*: misprinted as 'che' in the 1617 text.

[10] *Santa Maria dei Crociferi.

[11] *Santa Lucia. Moryson would have been able to view renovations begun in 1580 by Andrea Palladio.

[12] *Santa Maria dei Miracoli.

[13] *Santa Maria dell'Abbazia della Misericordia.

[14] Since this inscription dates from 1601, it seems that Moryson's copy of Sansovino's guide was the 1604 updated edition.

[15] This should be p. 85 but the 1617 *Itinerary* is mispaginated at this point.

but more renowmed for piety, which hee also shewed at his death towards his enemy, who gave him poyson in the challice at the Lords Supper, by many arguments of his charity. He died in the yeere MDCI. Also in the great schoole, the same is witnessed in these wordes: *To* Jerom Savina *wickedly killed by poyson given, (O horrible villany) in our Lords Supper, &c.*

The fourth sextary or sixth part of the City, and first of those beyond the channell, (meaning towards the Territorie of *Paduoa,*) is vulgarly called of the chiefe Church *Il sestiero di San' Polo.* In which Church of Saint *Paul,*[1] the most remarkeable things are these: the picture of Christ washing his Apostles feet, the pall of silver guilded, and the precious stones upon the great Altar; the pictures of the Altar of the holy Sacrament, and of the blessed Virgin, and the Images of Saint *Andrew* and the Apostles upon pillars. In the very faire market place of the same Church, of old a market was weekely held, and to the yeere 1292, the market was held heere on Wednesday, and in the market place of Saint *Marke,* on the Saturday; but at this day none is held here, but both in the place of Saint *Marke,* for the benefit of those that dwell there, and that the houses may bee more deerely let, which belong to Saint *Marke.* Neere the Church of Saint *Silvestro,*[2] the Patriarkes of *Grado* dwelt, till the Bishop of *Castello Olivolo* was made Patriarke. In the Church of Saint *James* of *Rialto,*[3] narrow, but very faire, the precious stones and the pictures of great Art and antiquitie, and the five Altars. In the Church of Saint *Mary Gloriosa,*[4] faire and great, the Belfrey stately built, the Monument of the most famous Painter *Titiano,*[5] two Images of Marble neere the great doore, the Marble Image of Saint *John,* over against the Florentine chappell, the chancell paved with Marble and adorned with the graven Images of the Prophets, at the charge of the family *Morosini;* the rare pictures of the great Altar, the Epitaph of *Francis Bernardo;* who being imployed into *England* in his yong yeeres, made peace betweene King *Henry,* and the French King *Francis,* which many great men had attempted in vaine, and for this brave act was Knighted by both the Kings.[6] These things in this church are most remarkeable.

The fifth sextary, and the second beyond the channel of the chiefe Church, is called *il Sestiero di Santa Croce:* in which Church,[7] being a cloyster of Nunnes, Duke *Dominick Morosini* lies buried, with this inscription: *Here lies* Dominick Morosini *Duke of* Venice, *with* Sophia *his Dutchesse; hee was a good Duke, and most wise, full of faith and truth; &c. He tooke the City* Tyrus, *and under him* Istria *and* Pola *were subdued with fifty gallies, where of were Captaines his sonne, and* Marino Gradonico. *This glorious Duke died in the yeere* MCLVI.[8] Also the Marble pillers of the great Altar, the brasen Angels, and the brasen Images, of Christ rising from the dead, of Saint *Francis* and Saint *Anthony.* In the Church

[1] *San Polo.

[2] *San Silvestro.

[3] *San Giacomo di Rialto

[4] *Santa Maria Glorioso dei Frari.

[5] Titian had completed several major works for the Frari and was buried there on 27 August 1576. His lavish monument is made of Carrera marble.

[6] The diplomat Francesco Bernardo (d. *c.*1566) contributed to negotiations between Henry VIII and François I and had received pensions from both England and France but was required in 1552 to renounce them by the Senate. *CSP Venice,* 1552, items 730–31.

[7] *Santa Croce.

[8] Domenico Morosini (d. 1156), Doge 1148–56.

of Saint *Simion* Prophet,[1] the picture of Christs supper with his Apostles. In the Church of S[t]. *Giacomo dell' Orio*,[2] a piller esteemed for a Jewell, a Marble pulpit, one of the fairest in the City, and the Images of the chappell for christning. In the Church of Saint *Eustace*,[3] the pictures of Christ whipped, of Christ carrying his crosse, and of Christ praying in the garden, all of great Art. In the Church of Saint *Mary Mater Domini*,[4] the great Altar of most pure silver, and the passion of Christ ingraven, the Altar of the blessed Virgin with her picture; and the Altar of the holy Sacrament with the rich Porphery and Ophyte stones; and the Marble Images of Saint *Marke,* and Saint *John* the Evangelist. In the Church of Saint *Andrew*,[5] the fairest of this sextary, and a cloyster of Nunnes, the pictures of Christ crucified, and of his supper with his Apostles, and the most faire Altars of the Virgin, Saint *Anthony,* and Saint *Nicholas.* In the Church of Saint *George* the greater,[6] (giving name to the Iland in which it is seated, over against the market place of Saint *Marke,* and the chiefe Church next that of Saint *Marke,*) the pall of the great Altar, and the brasen Images; two brasen Images of the Organs, the seats of the walnut tree wonderfully ingraven, another Altar built by *Vincent, Morosini,* the Altar of Saint *Stephen* the first Martyr; the Altar of the blessed Virgin and her Image, the Altar of Saint *Lutia* with her Image, and the wonderfull crucifix of [p. 84][7] another Altar. In the Church of Saint *Mary delle gratie*,[8] the infinite gifts hung up there upon vowes. In the Church of the Holy Ghost, the Pall of the great Altar, and the marble stones and pillars, and the brasen candlestickes, and a skreene of brasse guilded, and the pictures of Saint *Markes* Altar, the candlesticke of the great chappel, curiously carved, the rare Images and arched roofe of the Altar of the Cratch;[9] being all the worke of the famous Painter *Titiano,* whose rare image also the Friars have: and in the publike refectory of the Friars, the admirable pictures of the resurrection, of *Sampson,* and especially of Christ supping with his Apostles. In the monastery of Saint *Hellen,* (giving name to the Iland, and founded by *Alexander Boromeo,* and being one of the fairest in the City)[10] a crosse of inestimable value. In the Church of Saint *Andrew della Certosa*,[11] the monument of *Austine Barbadici,* who hartening the confederates to fight, was chiefe cause of the victory against the Turkes by sea, in the yeere 1571. and while he lived, by faire and rough tearmes, kept the league unbroken, which presently upon his death was dissolved. In the Church of Saint *Nicholas del Liro*,[12] the sepulcher of Duke *Dominicke Contarini,* rich with porphery and ophyte stones, and a well of fresh water, lying very neere the sea, and having so full a spring, as it serveth all the shippes and gallies. The almes-house of Saint *Lazerus,* is built for lepers. The old *Lazereto* is a pest-house, where the Prior and Physitians have yeerely fee to attend the sicke. Not farre from that, is the new

---

[1] *San Simeone Grande.

[2] *San Giacomo dell'Orio.

[3] *San Stae (Eustachio).

[4] *Santa Maria Mater Domini.

[5] *Sant'Andrea della Zirada.

[6] *San Giorgio Maggiore.

[7] This should be p. 86 but the original pagination has been retained (and so on).

[8] *Santa Maria della Grazia.

[9] *Cratch*: a manger or crib to hold fodder for animals; here referring to an altar or chapel containing a representation of the manger at Bethlehem where the infant Jesus was laid.

[10] *Isola di Santa Elena.

[11] *Isola Sant'Andrea della Certosa.

[12] *San Nicolò di Lido.

*Lazareto,* whither they are sent who are suspected to have the plague: but as soone as they begin to be sicke, they are sent thence to the old *Lazareto:* and hither all suspected men are sent to try their health, which if they keepe for forty daies, then they are set free.[1] These things are in this sextary most remarkeable.

The sixth sextary, and the third and last beyond the channell, is of the forme of the Iland, called *Il sestiero di dorso duro.* In the Church of the Saints, *Gervaso* and *Protese,*[2] the graven Images and pictures in the chappell of the holy sacrament. In the cloyster of Saint *Agnes,*[3] the Prioresse bringeth up six Virgins, which being of ripe yeeres, are either married or made Nunnes, and sixe more of good families sent thither in their place. In the Church of Saint *Gregory,*[4] there is a second monument erected to *Anthony Bragadini,* traiterously slaine by the Turkes at the taking of *Cyprus.*[5] The Iland *Giudecca* belongs to this sextary, the chiefe Church whereof is Saint *Eufemia,*[6] it having nine other Churches. The Church of the Jesuites is called Saint *Mary* of *Humblenes,*[7] and it hath pictured with great art the pals[8] of the passion of Christ, of the Apostles *Peter* and *Paul,* of Christ circumcised, and of Saint *Francis,* and the great Altar is one of the fairest in the City. In the Church *Carmini,*[9] a singular paire of Organs; the Images of the blessed virgins, foure Evangelists, and Christ crucified: and upon the altar of Christ crucified, two stones shining like christall, which are esteemed for jewels. In the Church of Saint *Mary* of *Charity,*[10] the rich chappell of *San Salvadore.* In the most faire Church of the Capuchine Friars, seated in the Iland *Giudecca,* the images of brasse, and the faire screene of the great Altar.[11] In the most faire Church of Saint *Mary* the greater, being a Nunnery,[12] the rare pictures of the greater chappell. In the Church of the holy crosse *Della Giudecca,*[13] the monument of the Cardinall *Francis Morosini,* sent Ambassador to the Turke, and *Nuncio* to Pope *Sixtus* the fifth, in the French Court: and here the rest of his Family use to be buried. The Monastery of the converted is for whores repenting.[14] Another is built for Orphan Virgins,[15] the Church whereof hath rich screenes of marble, with brasse images: and in the same live some two hundred and fifty Virgins of almes, and by the worke of their hands, which comming to ripe yeeres, are either married or made Nunnes. These things are in this sextary most remarkeable.

[1] *Isola di San Lazzaro degli Armeni.

[2] *San Trovaso. Moryson makes no reference to the collapse of the nave of this church in 1583 and its extensive restoration (completed in 1657). This brief description implies that he drew much of this section of his description of Venice from secondary sources rather than personal observation.

[3] *Sant'Agnese.

[4] *San Gregorio.

[5] See pp. xxxi and 309 n. 8.

[6] *Sant'Eufemia.

[7] *Santa Maria Assunta (I Gesuiti).

[8] This clearly printed word 'pals'[?] may be a typographical error: the passion of Christ was usually described in its 'stages'.

[9] *Santa Maria del Carmelo.

[10] *Santa Maria della Carità.

[11] Moryson is probably referring here to the church of *Redentore but since it was so recently completed (1592) he only refers to it as a 'most faire Churche' rather than by its now familiar name.

[12] Possibly *Santa Maria della Presentazione (Le Zitelle) in the eastern region of the Giudecca Island. It was designed in the late 1570s and built in the 1580s. It took in young girls without a dowry.

[13] *Santa Croce, Giudecca.

[14] Monastery of Le Convertite, *Santa Maria Maddalena.

[15] Probably the *Ospedale della Pietà.

The Venetians have six fraternities or great schooles, such as be also at *Rome,* and the Gentlemen and Citizens all give their names to one of them, as in *England* at *London,* the Citizens have companies, into which the King, Queene, and Nobles, many times vouchsafe to be admitted. And in these schooles, as it were in Universities, they use to have exercises of religion. The first of them is called Saint *Mary* of *Charity,*[1] after the rule whereof, the rest are framed, and the great Guardian thereof is chosen yeerly, [p. 85] and weares a skarlet gowne with large sleeves, which they call Ducall sleeves, and he hath the title of *Magnifito* by priviledge. These schooles give dowries yeerely to 1500. Virgins, and distribute among the poore much money, meale, and clothes: for besides many gifts by last testaments daily given to those uses, each of the schooles hath some five or sixe thousand duckets in yeerely revenew, and they are governed like common wealthes. In the said schoole, the Images of the Apostles, and the pictures, especially one of the blessed Virgin, and another of the foure Doctors of the Church, are very faire. In the schoole of Saint *John* the Evangelist,[2] the passion of Christ is wonderfully figured, and *Phillip* the second King of *Spaine,* and his sonne *Ferdinand,* and *Don Juan* of *Austria,* and other Princes, have beene of this fraternity. The third is of mercy.[3] The fourth of Saint *Marke.*[4] The fifth of Saint *Rocco,*[5] passing the rest in ceremonies & pompe, and number of brethren. The sixth is of Saint *Theodore,*[6] and each of these hath his Church and Pallace, and precious monuments, and these are subject to the counsell of ten; for there be many lesse schooles, each art having his schoole, and these are subject to the old Justice, and out of them when need is, souldiers are pressed.

It remaines to adde something of the magnificall building of this City. And in the first place, the market place of Saint *Marke*[7] is paved with bricke, and it consists of foure market places, joined in one; whereof two may rather be called the market places of the Dukes Pallace (joining to the Church of Saint *Marke*) the one being on the furthest side from Saint *Marke,* betweene the pallace aud the great channell, the other right before the pallace towards the channell, foure hundred foot in length, and some one hundred and thirty in bredth. The third is before the Church doore of Saint *Mark,* and lies in length five hundred and twenty foot towards the Church of Saint *Geminiano,*[8] and hath one hundred and thirty foot in bredth, which may more properly be called the market place of Saint *Marke.* The fourth is on the other side of the Church, towards the Church of Saint *Basso.*[9] In this market place of foure joined in one, are solemne spectacles or shewes, and all processions made, and there on Ascension day, is the Faire held, and the markets on wednesday and saterday: there they use to muster souldiers; and there the gentlemen and strangers daily meet and walke. Before the doore of Saint *Markes* Church, are three peeces of brasse carved, and for bignesse like the bodies of trees, upon which at festivall daies three rich banners are hung, in signe of liberty, or as others say, for the three Dominions of *Venice, Cypro,* and *Candia.*

[1] *Scuola di Santa Maria della Carità.
[2] *Scuola Grande di San Giovanni Evangelista.
[3] Either *Scuola Vecchia della Misericordia or *Scuola Grande della Misericordia.
[4] *Scuola Grande di San Marco.
[5] *Scuola Grande di San Rocco.
[6] *Scuola Grande di San Teodoro.
[7] * San Marco, Piazza.
[8] *San Geminiano.
[9] *San Basso.

Feste che si sogliono fare per la Città della Caccia del foro, amazzar la Gatta col capo raso, pigliar l'anadre, pigliar l'occa nell'Acqua, et altro.

Iacomo franco forma

Figure 28.  Giacomo Franco, *La Città di Venetia* (1614). Games played in Venice during festivals, including bull and bear baiting, slaying cats and 'Catching the Goose'. By permission of Special Collections, Brotherton Library, University of Leeds.

Under the tower of the Clocke,[1] fifty foot distant from Saint *Markes* Church, is a passage to and from this market place; and this tower all covered with marble, beares a remarkeable Clocke, which sheweth the course of the Sunne and the Moone daily, and the degrees they passe, and when they enter into a new signe of the *Zodiacke,* and above that the guilded Image of our Lady shineth, placed betweene two doores, out of one of which doores, onely at solemne Feasts, an Angell with a Trumpet, and the three Wise Men of the East following, passe before our Ladies Image, and adore her, and so goe in at the other doore. Above that, there is a carved Image of a Lyon with wings, and upon the very top, two brasen Images, called the Mores, which by turnes striking with a hammer upon a great bell, sound the houres.

The houses opposite to the Pallaces of the Procurators of Saint *Marke,* are called the houses of the State, and they belong to the Church of Saint *Marke,* and having some fifty shops under the Arches of the upper roofes (where men may walke dry when it raines) they yeeld great rents to the Church. Opposite to these are the Pallaces of the said Procurators, which are also in the said market place, which I said to be more properly called the market place of Saint *Marke,* and these being stately built, sixty six foot high, and the stones curiously carved, doe not onely adorne the market place, but in summer give a pleasant shade to passengers, besides that under the Arches of them, men may walke drie in the greatest raine, and the shops under these Arches yeeld great rents, and under these Pallaces out of foure little streetes there be so many passages to and from the market place. These Pallaces are built at the charge of the State, the nine Procurators being to have nine Pallaces: for as yet they were not [p. 86] all built; but in the meane time any pallace falling voide, it was given to the eldest of them that had none, yet not according to their age, but according to their election.

The steeple or belfrey of Saint *Marke,*[2] distant some eighty foote from the Church, and set over against it, is to be admired, not onely for the foundation, strangely laid under the earth; but also for many other causes. It is built foure square, each square containing forty foot, and it is three hundred thirty three foot high, of which feet the pinacle containes ninety six, and the woodden Image of an Angell above the pinacle covered with brasse and guilded, and turning with the wind, containes sixteene feete. It is adorned with high pillars of marble, and with a gallery at the bottome of the pinacle, made with many pillars of brasse, and upon the pinacle with great marble Images of Lyons, and from the top in a cleere day, men may see a hundred miles off the ships under sayles; and it beares foure great bels, whereof the greater called *La Trottiera,* is rung every day at noone, and when the Gentlemen meet in *Senate* with like occasions: but when a new Pope or Duke is made, all the bels are rung, and the steeple is set round about with waxe candles burning. I went to the top of this steeple, which hath thirty seven ascents, whereof each hath foureteene lesse ascents, by which the going up is as easie, as if a man walked on plaine ground, at the contriving whereof I much wondered. In the lodge of this steeple, the foure brasen Images of *Pallas, Apollo, Mercury,* and of *Peace,* and above them, the figure of *Venice,* with the Dominion by sea and land, and the Image of *Venus* the Goddesse of *Cyprus,* and of *Jupiter* the King of *Candia,* present themselves, and neere the great gate the Images of the blessed Virgin and of Saint *John Baptist,* are highly valued.

[1] *San Marco, Campanile.

[2] *San Marco, Campanile, contradicting his earlier statement that it was 'fifty foot distant from Saint *Markes* Church'.

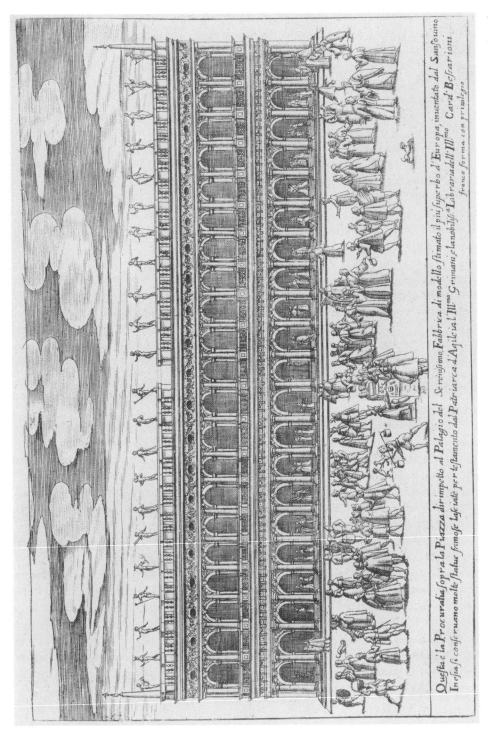

Figure 29.    Giacomo Franco, *Habiti d'huomeni et donne venetiane* (1610). Procurators in the Piazza San Marco, showing the architectural work of Sansovino. By permission of Special Collections, Brotherton Library, University of Leeds.

Right over against the Dukes Pallace, in the foresaid second market place of the pallace, is the library,[1] whose building is remarkable, and the architecture of the corner next the market place of the Bakers,[2] is held by great Artists a rare worke, and divers carved Images of Heathen Gods, and Goddesses in the old habit, are no lesse praised, as done by the hands of most skilfull workemen. On the inside, the arched roofes curiously painted, and the little study of ivory, with pillars of Allablaster, and rare stones, and carved Images (in which an old breviary of written hand, and much esteemed, is kept) are things very remarkeable. The inner chamber is called the study; in which many statuaes and halfe statuaes, twelve heads of Emperors, and other things given to the State by Cardinall *Dominicke Grimani*,[3] are esteemed precious by all antiquaries. And in this Library are laid up the Bookes, which the Patriarke and Cardinall *Bessarione*[4] gave to Saint *Marke* (that is to the State) by his last will, and the most rare books brought from *Constantinople* at the taking thereof, and otherwise gathered from all parts of *Greece*. Out of this Library is a passage, to the chambers of the Procurators of Saint *Marke:* before you enter them most faire statuaes, and on the inside rare pictures, draw your eies to them.

Not farre from thence are two pillars[5] (the third whereof in taking them out of the ship, fell into the sea, and could never be recovered) and they be of huge bignesse; for the erecting whereof, as a most difficult thing, great rewards were given to a *Lumbard,* and immunity was given to him by priviledge, for all that should play at dice under them. Since it is accustomed, that all condemned men are executed betweene these pillars, which of old were put to death neere the Church of Saint *John Bragola*,[6] and upon one of these pillars stands the brasen statua of Saint *Marke,* under the forme of a Lyon, and upon the other stands the marble statua of Saint *Theodor.* The statua of Saint *George*, beares a shield, in token that *Venice* rather defends it selfe, then offends others, since the right hand carries a defensive weapon.

Behind the Library is the Mint house[7] (vulgarly called *La zecca,* whereupon I thinke the gold coyne of the Venetians is called *Zecchino*) in which house it is remarkeable, that there is no wood in any part thereof, but for feare of fire it is all built with stone, bricke, and barres of iron. Here the great statuaes of Gyants, lifting up their massie clubs, as it were forbidding the entrance; and in the court yard the statua of *Apollo,* holding wedges of gold in his hand, to shew that gold is made to grow in the bowels of the earth by the vertue of the sunne, are things remarkeable.

[p. 87] From hence on the left hand is the market place, which I said to be the first of the Pallace, seated betweene the channell the Pallace. And from hence on the right hand is the fish market, in which (as likewise in that of *Rialto*) store of good fish is to bee bought twice in the day.

---

[1] *Biblioteca Nazionale Marciana.

[2] Forni Pubblici (1473), the Republic's bakeries, supplying the city and its ships.

[3] Cardinal Domenico Grimani (1461–1523) whose father, Antonio Grimani (1434–1523), was Doge from 1521 to 1523.

[4] Cardinal Basilios (Basilius) Bessarion (1403–72), Latin Patriarch of Constantinople. See *Biblioteca Nazionale Marciana.

[5] *Piazza San Marco, Columns.

[6] *San Giovanni in Bragora.

[7] *Zecca.

The market place in which the said Bel-frey and Library are built, is also adorned with the stately Pallace of the Duke,[1] all covered with Marble, and most sumptuous in the carved Images and pictures, and in the pillers of the Arched walke on the outside. The first staires towards the second market place of the Pallace, and over against the said Library, are very stately, and are vulgarly called *Scala de Giganti,* that is the staires of the Giants, so called of two huge Marble statuaes of *Mars* and *Neptune,* which the common people call Giants.[2] But the Pallace hath many other staires, whereby men ascend thereunto. Opposite to the aforesaid statuaes, are two other of *Adam* and *Eve,* but not so great as they: and not farre from thence is a stone guilded, with an inscription which the Senate placed there, in memory of the French King *Henry* the third, whom they entertained, passing that way from *Poland* into *France.*[3] On the left hand is the Chappell of Saint *Nicholas,* which is the Dukes private Chappell. Hence you ascend into a large Hall (as they call it) or a large Gallery; in the middest whereof the golden staires shine with gold, and two marble Images and rare pictures. On the left hand of the said staires, is the passage to that part of the Pallace, which is assigned to the Duke for his dwelling, and in the first chamber, called the Dukes Armes, *Sala del seudo,* the pictures of Christs resurrection, and another of him crucified, are much praised, though it hath many other rare pictures. When you have ascended the golden staires, you[4] shall see foure rare pictures. From thence the way on the left hand leads to the Chancery, where many chambers are adjoyning, proper to divers Councels of State, all adorned with graven Images and pictures of the best; namely, the chambers of the Councell rich in the painting of the arched roofe. That of the *Pregadi,* having generall rare painting and carving. That called *La secreta,* in which the secret writings of the State is laied up. The Chappell of the Colledge, where the Duke and the Senators daily heare Masse, and it appeares by an inscription, that the Antiquities were of old laid up there, among the pictures whereof, that of Christs resurrection, and the Map of the Territory of *Venice,* are much praised. That of the Councell of *Tenn,* in which the picture of the Wise-men offering gifts to Christ is much praised, (neere the same are chambers, in which many rich Armors and rare Monuments are laid up.) And that of the great Councell, one hundred fifty foot in length, and seventy foure in breadth, adorned round about with rare pictures, namely on the side towards the foresaid second market place of the Pallace, the History of *Frederlcke* the Emperour, and of Pope *Alexander* the third is cursorily painted. Towards the foresaid first market place, lying betweene the Pallace and the channel, the History of *Constantinople,* taken by the Venetians and French, is painted; and the capitulation of the voyage, made in the Church, and the rest of the Saints in heaven, are reputed rare workes.

The prisons of old were under this Pallace of the Duke, but lately a new house is stately built of the stone of *Istria,* for that use neere the bridge *Della Paglia.*[5]

[1] *Palazzo Ducale.

[2] After a major fire in 1483 the reconstruction of the Scala dei Giganti was completed in 1550. The coronation of new doges had traditionally taken place in the gallery at the top of this staircase. Its two huge statues by Jacopo Sansovino, installed in 1565, represented the Roman gods Mars and Neptune, symbolizing Venice's potency over land and sea.

[3] See pp. 207 and 209–10.

[4] Printed 'your'.

[5] *Ponte della Paglia.

*L'Ecc<sup>mo</sup> Gñale mette à banco le Gallere doue si fa vn beliss<sup>mo</sup> apparato di Tapez-*
*zarie et si mette fuori gran quantita di dinari d'oro et argento et in*
*particolare vna Cattenna di vergle d'oro di valuta d'vn Millione.    I. franco.*
*Com privilegio.*

Figure 30. Giacomo Franco, *La Città di Venetia* (1614). Perspective of San Marco with a procession, merchants of Venice and trading stalls. By permission of Special Collections, Brotherton Library, University of Leeds.

The foure square market place of *Rialto*,[1] is compassed with publike houses, under the arches whereof, and in the middle part lying open, the Merchants meet. And there is also a peculiar place where the Gentlemen meet before noone, as they meet in the place of Saint *Marke* towards evening; and here to nourish acquaintance, they spend an houre in discourses, and because they use not to make feasts one to another, they keepe this meeting as strictly as Merchants, lest their frinship should decay. The Gold-smiths shoppes lie thereby, and over against them the shoppes of Jewellers, in which Art the Venetians are excellent. There is the Pallace of a Gentleman, who proving a Traytor, the State (for his reproch) turned the same into a shambles, and some upper chambers to places of judgement. The fish market lies by this shambles, a great length along the banke of the great channell, and in the same shambles and fish market, as also in the like of Saint *Marke,* great plenty of victuals, especially of fish, is daily to be sold. A publike Pallace stately built lieth neere the bridge of *Rialto.*

[p. 88] This bridge in the judgement of the Venetians, deserves to be reputed the eighth miracle of the world. The old being pulled downe, this new bridge began to bee built in the yeere 1588, and was scarce finished in three yeeres, and is said to have cost two hundred fifty thousand Duckets. It is built of the stone of *Istria, u*pon one arch over the great channell, and the ascent to the toppe hath thirty six staires on each side, and upon each side of these staires, are twelve little shoppes covered with lead: not to speake of the carved Images, of the blessed Virgin, the Angell *Gabriel,* and the two protecting Saints of the City, namely Saint *Marke,* and Saint *Theodore.*

Thereby is a Pallace called *Il Fontico de i Todeschi,*[2] because the Dutch Merchants have it to their use.

The Armory built for all kinde of Armes & Munitions, vulgarly called *l'Arsenale,*[3] as it were the Tower of the Senate, is compassed with walles being in circuit more then two miles, where some foure hundred Artificers are daily set on worke about naval provisions, and they receive weekely for wages about one thousand two hundred duckets. Within the same is a several place to make cables, & within the circuit hereof and no where else in the City, they build Ships and Gallies, and there bee alwayes in the same about two hundred gallies ready for service. To conclude, the State of *Venice,* being not growne to full strength, did in a hundred daies space, arme one hundred gallies against *Emanuel* Emperour of the East,[4] and no doubt their strength hath every day growne greater to this time. In the said compasse of the Armory, lies a great boat called *Il Bucentoro,*[5] because it carries about the number of two hundred; which boat hath upon it a kinde of chamber which useth to be richly hung, and covered over, when in the same the Duke and Senators be carried by water at some times of solemnity, especially at the feast of the Ascension, when of an old custome, they goe forth to espouse the sea, by the ceremony of flinging a

[1] *Rialto.

[2] *Fondaco dei Tedeschi.

[3] *Arsenal (**Plate 12**).

[4] Probably a reference to the Byzantine Emperor Manuel I Komnenos (Comnenus) (1118–80). During the war between Frederick I Barbarossa and the northern Italian states, Manuel I supported the Italians leading up to the Battle of Legnano (1176). However, in 1171 he had broken off diplomatic relations with Venice, arrested Venetian citizens living in imperial territories and confiscated their property. In retaliation, Venice sent a fleet of about 120 galleys and other ships against Byzantium, although its success was limited due to an outbreak of an epidemic and an opposing Byzantine fleet of 150 ships.

[5] *Bucentaur.

ring into the same, and to challenge the command thereof, given them by Pope *Alexander* the third.

The Jewes have a place to dwell in severally, called *Il Ghetto*,[1] where each family hath a little house, and all have one court-yard common, so as they live as it were in a Colledge, or Almes-house, and may not come forth after the gates are locked at night, and in the day they are bound to weare a yellow cap.

Though the City bee seated upon little and narrow Ilands, in the middest of marshes and tides of the sea; yet hath it gardens in great number, and abounding with rare herbes, plants, and fruits, and water conduits, which with the carved Images and pictures, (out of the Gentlemens curtesie) may bee seene by any curious stranger.

The publike Libraries of speciall note are these: *Di S Giovanni & Paolo: di San' Francesco: di San' Stefano: di San' Georgio Maggiore:* and *di Sant' Antonio.* Also private Libraries may be found out by those that be curious, and will bee after the same manner easily shewed them, and are indeede most worthy to bee sought out for the rarenesse of many instruments, pictures, carved Images, Antiquities, and like rare things: For the Venetians being most sparing in diet and apparell, doe exercise their magnificence in these and the like delights, and these precious Monuments, they will with great curtesie shew to any strangers, or to any loving antiquities, which my self-found by experience, more-specially at the hands of *Sig*. *Nicolao vendramini*,[2] a Gentleman dwelling in the Iland *Giuedecca,* who most curteously shewed mee and my friends, though being altogether unknowne to him, some rare clockes, admirable carved Images, and a paire of Organs having strange varieties of sounds.

The Pallaces of Gentlemen were called houses, but are, and worthily deserve to be called Pallaces, some hundred of them being fit to receive Princes. For howsoever this Common-wealth at the first founding, was tied by many lawes to mediocrity, and the equality among the Citizens, yet pride hath by degrees seised upon the same. The said Pallaces have one doore towards the Land, and another towards the water, and most of them have gardens. The foundations are laid of Oake in the waters, and the stone of *Istria* is much esteemed. The flooers of the upper roomes are not boorded, but plastred with lime tempred with tiles beaten to dust. The [p. 89] windowes are for the most part very large, the greater roomes lying almost altogether open to receive aire, but the lodging chambers have glasse windowes, whereof the Venetians brag, glasse being rare in *Italy,* where the windowes are for the most part covered with linnen or paper. And howsoever glasse be common with us on this side the Alpes, yet it is certaine that the glasse makers of *Venice,* dwelling in the Iland *Murano,* have a more noble matter, & thereof make much better glasse then we can. To conclude, as I said the Venetians are most sparing in diet and apparel, so not onely in the building of their houses, but in the furniture thereof, the general sort passeth their degree, and many of the Gentlemen use Princely magnificence. These are accounted the chiefe Pallaces: That belonging to the Procurators office, neere the Church of Saint *Anthony.* The old Pallace which belonged to the Templary Knights. That of the family *Gritti* neere the bridge *Della Madonna.*

[1] *Ghetto.

[2] The Vendramin were one of Venice's most distinguished mercantile families. Andrea Vendramin (1393–1478), whose wealth was based in trade with Alexandria and the Eastern Mediterranean, was Doge 1476–8. Luca Vendramin (d. 1527) founded a bank near the wooden Rialto Bridge (**Plate 2** and **Map 12**). Francesco Vendramin (1555–1619) was Patriarch of Venice (1605) and Cardinal (1615).

That of *Alexander Gritti,* neere the market place of Saint *John Bragora.* That of *Dandoli,* neere the bridge *Della Paglia.* The Pallace neere Saint *Francis* Church, which the Senate bought, and use to assigne it to the dwelling of the Popes *Nuncio.* That of the Dutchesse of *Florence,* built upon the channell of the Dukes Pallace. That of the *Vetturi,* neere the market place of Saint *Mary.* That of the Patriarke *Grimani,* neere the *Malipieri.* That of the family *Georgij,* neere the same. That of *Francis Priuli.* That of *Lodwick Georgij.* That of the *Capelli.* That of *Peter Giustniani.* That of those of *Pesaro,* neere the Church of Sᵗ. *Benedict.* That of the *Loredani* neere Saint *Stephens* Church. That of *Zeni.* That of *Contarini.* That of *Silvester Valierij,* neere the Church of Saint *Job.* That of the *Cornari,* neere Saint *Pauls* Church. That of *James Foscarini,* neere the Church *Carmeni,* That of the *Michaeli,* neere Saint *Lewis* Church. That of *Lewis Theophili,* neere the Church *Della Misericordia.* The chiefe Pallaces upon the channell are these. That of the *Loredani.* That of the *Grimani,* neere Saint *Lucia.* That of *Delphini.* That of the *Cornari,* neere Saint *Maurice* Church, and that of the *Foscarini,* an old building but having the best prospect of all the rest. In which the Venetians entertained the French King *Henry* the third. To conclude, there be two rich Pallaces in the Iland *Giudecca,* one of the *Dandoli,* the other of the *Vendramini.*

In this famous City are twenty thousand families, and three thousand of the Gentlemen, and no age hath beene so barren, which hath not yeelded worthy men for Martiall and civill government and learning. Of this City have beene three Popes, *Gregory* the twelfth, *Eugenius* the fourth, and *Paul* the second,[1] and many Cardinalls of which these are the chiefe: *Peter Morosini, Marke Iandi, Anthony Corari, John Amideus,* and in our age *John* Baptist *Zeni,* and *Dominick Grimani.* Also *Peter Bembus* was a Venetian,[2] whom Pope *Paul* the third made Cardinall. Heere was borne *Pantalean Justinianus,* Patriarke of *Constantinople* when the French ruled there. And *Venice* hath yielded many most learned men, *Andrew Dandoli,* Duke *Francis Barbarigi, Andrew Morosini,* who wrote the History of his time in Heroique Verse. And many famous Civill Lawyers, *Lodwicke Foscarini,* and *Jerom Donati.* And many rare engravers, and painters, *Titiano, Tenterotto,* and *Belino.*[3] And many Commanders in the warre, *John Bolari, Marino Gradinici, Dominick Morosini,* (the first provisors of Military affaires,). *Andrew Morosini,* and *Simion Dandoli,* and many more famous in all kindes of vertue, to the chiefe whereof I have said, that the Senate erected many Statuaes and Monuments. Giue me leaue to adde this of the famly Morosini, namely, that among the most famous men, whose pictures were in the chamber of publike meeting, before it was burnt; there were the pictures of *Barbaro* and *Marco,* and *Antonio, Morosini:* And that the same family hath given three Dukes, *Dominico, Marino,* and *Michaele;* and three Patriarkes, and twelve Procurators of Saint *Marke,* (which number few families have attained, onely that of the *Contarini,* that of the *Justiniani,* and that of the *Grimani,* have a little passed it). And that my selfe being at *Venice,* found there eighty Gentlemen of this name. Let the Reader pardon this observation, which I make for the Consonancy of that name with my owne, onely differing in the placing of a vowell, for more gentle pronuntiation, which the Italian

---

[1] Gregory XII (Pope 1406–15), Eugene IV (1431–47) and Paul II (1464–71).

[2] The humanist scholar and poet Pietro Bembo (1470–1547). See his major history of Venice, *Della historia vinitiana* (Venice, 1551).

[3] Titian, Tintoretto and Bellini.

speech affecteth; yet these Gentlemen being of one family, write their names somewhat [p. 90] diversely, some writing in their owne tongue *Morosini,* others others *Moresini,* and in the Latin tongue, *Morocenus,* and *Maurocenus.*

Of the hiring of chambers, and the manner of diet in *Venice,* I have spoken jointly with that of *Paduoa,* in the discription of that City, onely I will adde, that this City aboundeth with good fish, which are twice each day to be sold in two markets of Saint *Marke & Rialto,* & that it spendeth weekly five hundred Oxen, & two hundred & fifty Calves, besides great numbers of young Goates, Hens, and many kinds of birds, besides that it aboundeth with sea birds, whereof the Venetian writers make two hundred kinds, and likewise aboundeth with savoury fruits, and many salted and dried dainties, and with all manner of victuals, in such sort as they impart them to other Cities. I will also adde that here is great concourse of all nations, as well for the pleasure the City yeeldeth, as for the free conversation; and especially for the commodity of trafficke. That in no place is to be found in one market place such variety of apparell, languages, and manners. That in the publike Innes a chamber may be hired for foure sols a day; but for the cheapenes and good dressing of meat, most men use to hire private chambers, and dresse their owne meat. That in the Dutch Inne each man paies two lires a meale. That no stranger may lie in the City more then a night, without leave of the Magistrates appointed for that purpose; but the next day telling them some pretended causes of your comming to the Towne, they will easily grant you leave to stay longer, and after that you shall be no more troubled, how long soever you stay, onely your Host after certaine daies giveth them account of you. To conclude this most noble City, as well for the situation, freeing them from enemies, as for the freedome of the Common-wealth, preserved from the first founding, and for the freedome which the Citizens and very strangers have, to injoy their goods, and dispose of them, and for manifold other causes, is worthily called in Latine *Venetia,* as it were *Veni etiam,* that is, come againe.

From *Venice* to *Farraria*[1] are eighty five miles by water and land: and upon the third of *February* (after the new stile) and in the yeere 1594. (as the Italians begin the yeere the first of *January*) and upon Wednesday in the evening, my selfe with two Dutchmen, my consorts in this journey, went into the Barke, which weekely passeth betwixt *Venice* and *Ferrara.* The same night we passed twenty five miles upon the marshes, within the sea banke, to *Chioza* or *Chioggia,* or (to speake vulgarly, the better to be understood in asking the way) a *Chioza,* the first village on firme land, or rather seated in an Iland, where the Ditch Clodia maketh a Haven.

### [On route to Jerusalem, *c.* March 1595][2]

After dinner (for I have formerly described *Trevigi*)[3] we rode two Dutch miles, or ten Italian miles, through a like Plaine to *Mestre.* From hence we passed by water to *Venice* being five miles, first in a Ditch, each man paying one soldo for his passage, then in other boats over the Lakes wherewith *Venice* is compassed, each man paying three soldi for his passage. I omit to speake any thing of *Venice,* which I have formerly described.

[1] Ferrara.
[2] Moryson, *Itinerary,* 1617, I, p. 206; Moryson, *Itinerary,* 1907–8, I, p. 444.
[3] Treviso.

**Of the Exchange of Moneys**[1]

Out of *England* to *Venice* in *Italy,* the exchange of foure shillings and six or eight pence English, useth to bee rated at a Venetian Ducket. My selfe tooke no bils of exchange from *England* to *Venice,* but had letters of credit, to receive money of a Venetian Merchant, to be repaid in *London* upon my bill, after the rate of foure shillings three pence for each Venetian ducket. And at first being to take my journey for *Rome* and *Naples,* I tooke up two hundred silver crownes, most fit for that journey, which at *Venice* were rated at two hundred five & twenty duckets, and nineteene grosh, and I gave my bill for three and fifty pound sterling, twelve shillings and sixe pence English, to be repaied by my friend in *London.* Then I retained with my selfe as many of those crownes, as were necessary for my journey, leaving the rest in the hands of a Venetian Merchant, who gave me a bill to receive so many crownes *In specie,* (that is, in kind) at *Florence,* where I purposed to make my aboad for some few moneths.

**Of the Moneys of Italy**[2]

The Venetian zecchine is of the same standard, finenesse, and value as the Hungarian ducket ... the lire of *Venice* being worth about nine pence English, is of a little baser standard ... . All Crownes of gold are currant in *Italy,* and all at one rate, excepting the French Crownes, which at *Venice* and *Naples* are esteemed somewhat higher then other though in all the other Cities of *Italy,* it is more commodious to spend Spanish pistolets or crownes, then French crownes. In generall, the Italian silver crowne, given for seven lires of *Venice,* is worth almost five shillings English, and the Italian gold crowne vulgarly called *d'oro,* given for seven lires, and about fifteene sols of *Venice,* is worth almost five shillings sixe pence English, and the gold crowne, vulgarly called *d'oro in oro del sole,* given for eight lires, and some odde sols of *Venice,* is currant in *England* for sixe shillings. To conclude, greater summes paid in little brasse moneys, are in *Italy* delivered by weight, not by tale [by counting] or number. And more particularly to explaine the values of moneys. At *Venice* a zechine [*zecchino*] of *Venice* is given for ten lires, and ten or twelve sometimes more sols. A double pistolet of *Spaine,* called *Dublon* [doubloon, sp. *doblon*], is there given for seventeene lires. A French crowne is given for eight lires, and eight, or sometimes ten sols. An Italian crowne of gold is there given for eight lires, and some for seven lires sixteene sols (for the weight of *Venice* being heavier then in other parts of *Italy,* the light crownes are lesse esteemed.) The Spanish piastro of silver is given for sixe lires, the silver ducket [*ducato*] for sixe lires and foure sols [*soldi*], the silver crowne for seven lires, the justino [*giustina*][3] for two lires, the mutsenigo for a lire, and foure sols. Besides, the Venetians have silver pieces of 4 lires, of eight soldi (or sols), and of sixe soldi, and a piece of two soldi called Gagetta [*gazzetta*], which are of a baser standard. Touching the brasse moneys, twentie soldi make a lire, two soldi or three susines [*sesino*] make a gagetta, two betsi [*bezzo*] or three quatrines [*quattrino*], make a soldo or Marketta [*marchetto,* a *soldino* with the figure of St Mark blessing the doge], and foure bagatines [*bagattino*] make a quatrine. In the Dukedome of *Ferrara,* the siluer crowne is spent for seven lires of *Venice,* and in the money of the Dukedome twelve bolignei [*bolognino*] make a

---

[1] Moryson, *Itinerary,* 1617, I, p. 279; 1907–8, II, p. 131.

[2] Moryson, *Itinerary,* 1617, II, pp. 290–91; 1907–08, II, pp. 154–5.

[3] *giustina*: silver coins of several denominations first issued by Doge Alvise I Mocenigo in 1572 to mark the first anniversary of the Battle of Lepanto on 7 October, the feast day of St Justina of Padua. The *mutsenigo* was one of the *giustina* coins issued by the Doge.

Venetian lire, three susines make a boligneo, and two bolignei make one amoray,[1] seven make one Saint *Georgio,* foure make one cava lot [*cavallotto*],[2] foure and a halfe make one berlingasso [?], nineteene make one carli [*carlino*], and ten bolignei make one bianco [*bianco*], and two brasse quatrines make a sufine [*sesino*], sixe make a boligneo, seven make a gagetta of *Venice.*

## Of Buildings in General[3]

The Bridge at *London* is worthily to be numbred among the miracles of the world, if men respect the building and foundation, laid artificially and stately over an ebbing and flowing water, upon 21 piles of stone, with 20 arches, under which Barkes may passe, the lowest foundation being (as they say) packs of woll, most durable against the force of the water, and not to be repaired, but upon great fall of the waters, and by artificiall turning or stopping the recourse of them. Or if men respect the houses built upon the bridge, as great and high as those of the firme land, so as a man cannot know that he passeth a bridge, but would judge himselfe to be in the streete, save that the houses on both sides are combined in the top, making the passage somewhat darke, and that in some few open places the River of *Thames* may be seene on both sides. In the second rancke, is the bridge of our Lady at *Paris* in *France.* The next place belongs to the bridge of *Venice,* called *Realto,* consisting of one, but an high Arch, and built partly of marble, partly of freestone, and to be ascended by many staires on both sides, and having low shoppes upon the ascents and on the top, and for the building of the whole bridge, being more stately then that of *Paris.*

## Of the Trade of Turkey[4]

The Venetians bring into *Turkey* woollen clothes, which they call broad, being died Scarlet, Violet, and, of all colours, and they are so strong & well made, as they will last very long, so as the Turks prefer them before our English clothes And because the Venetians furnish them in great quantity, they use few other clothes of that kind. Also the Venetians bring to them Sattins, and Damasks (made in *Italy* of Dalmatian silk) and great quantity of Gold and Silver, to buy the pretious commodittes of *Turkey.* Whence they carry out raw silke. For by reason of the foresaid tyranny, as the Turkes are negligent in Husbandry and trade, so are they in manuall Arts, not drawing their Silke into threads, nor weaving the same into clothes. And howsoever they have infinite numbers of Silke-wormes, especially at *Tripoli,* and in most parts of *Asia,* which make great quantitie of Silke, (as I formerly said in the discourse of *Italy*), yet they sell this Silke raw and unwonen, and buy of the Venetians the foresaid clothes made of their owne silke, so as the silkewormes, may well be said to bee more diligent, and more to promote the publike good, then the inhabitants; for they swarming in all Gardens, diligentlie finish their web, while the idle inhabitants yeeld the commoditie thereof to strangers.

The Venetians also export from *Turkey,* Spices, and Apothecary wares, and great quantitie of the Dye called Indico. They export Galles,[5] Cotten, wooll, Cotton threads,

[1] Possibly *amore* as a colloquial name for a *bezante,* a 'bezant' minted for Venetian Cyprus, which has a cupid on the reverse.

[2] *cavallotto*: silver coin, some with reverse showing St George mounted and slaying a dragon.

[3] Moryson, *Itinerary,* 1617, III, pp. 64–5; 1907–8, III, p. 487.

[4] Moryson, *Itinerary,* 1617, IV, p. 127; 1907–8, IV, pp. 123–4.

[5] Probably 'galls', i.e., oak galls used for dye and ink-making, a known export from Venice and a major trading item of the Levant Company.

Chamlets[1] or Grograms, made of the finest haires of Goates, not sheared but pulled off from their backes, and woven in *Galatia,* a Province of the lesser *Asia.* They export *Turkey* Carpets, Goates skinnes wrought, and died into diuers colours.

The English bring to the Turkes Kersies[2] wrought and dyed of divers colours and kinds, but they bring little Broad-cloth, wherewith they are aboundantlie furnished from *Venice.*

### Of the Apparel of the Italians[3]

Of the Italians it is proverbially said, that the Venetians are gowned, yet by night going to visit their Mistresses, weare short Spanish cloakes ... . The Venetians, by reason of their strict Lawes from all antiquity restraining excesse in apparrell, howsoever many times they weare sumptuous garments, yet are they hidden under their gownes, not to be seene but by their Mistrisses at night. They make woollen cloth of such lasting, as they bequeath their gownes by their last testaments. All the Gentlemen, not one excepted, weare blacke cloth gownes, buttoned close at the necke, with the sleeves put on over their doublets, aswell young as old men, but some under this civill gowne weare rich furres, and imbrodred garments. And the Senators, Doctors, and Knights, weare Scarlet gownes, with large sleeves, lined in winter with rich furres And their Senate is no lesse or more glorious in publike pompes, then the Roman Senate was of old. And the Gentlemen constantly weare these gownes, either in singular pride to be knowne from others, (for no Citizen, nor any Gentlemen of other Cities weare gownes), or for obedience to the Law, or out of an old custome, which the most wise Magistrates permit not to be broken. And for the same cause, all the Gentlemen, none excepted, weare little caps of Freese[4] or Cloth, hardly covering the crowne, or the forepart of the head ... .

The women in generall are delighted with mixed and light colours.[5] The women of *Venice* weare choppines or shoos three or foure hand-bredths high, so as the lowest of them seeme higher then the tallest men, and for this cause they cannot goe in the streetes without leaning upon the shoulder of an old woman. They have another old woman to beare up the traine of their gowne, & they are not attended with any man, but onely with old women. In other parts of *Italy,* they weare lower shooes, yet somewhat raised, and are attended by old women, but goe without any helpe of leading. The women of *Venice* weare gownes, leaving all the necke and brest bare, and they are closed before with a lace, so open, as a man may see the linnen which they lap about their bodies, to make them seeme fat, the Italians most loving fat women. They shew their naked necks and breasts, and likewise their dugges, bound up and swelling with linnen, and all made white by art. They weare large falling bands, and their haire is commonly yellow, made so by the Sunne and art, and they raise up their haire on the forehead in two knotted hornes, and deck their heads & uncouered haire with flowers of silke, and with pearle, in great part counterfeit. And they cast a black vaile from the head to the shoulders, through which the nakednesse of their shoulders, and neckes, and breasts, may easily be seene. For this attire the women of *Venice* are proverbially

---

[1] *Chamlets*: camlets, originally a costly eastern fabric but may denote other fabrics (*OED*, s.v. camlet).

[2] *Kersies*: kersey, a kind of coarse narrow cloth, woven from long wool and usually ribbed (*OED*, s.v. kersey).

[3] Moryson, *Itinerary*, 1617, IV, pp. 171-3; 1907-8, IV, pp. 218-21.

[4] *Freese*: a coarse woollen cloth, with a nap (*OED*, s.v. frieze).

[5] See **Plate 14**.

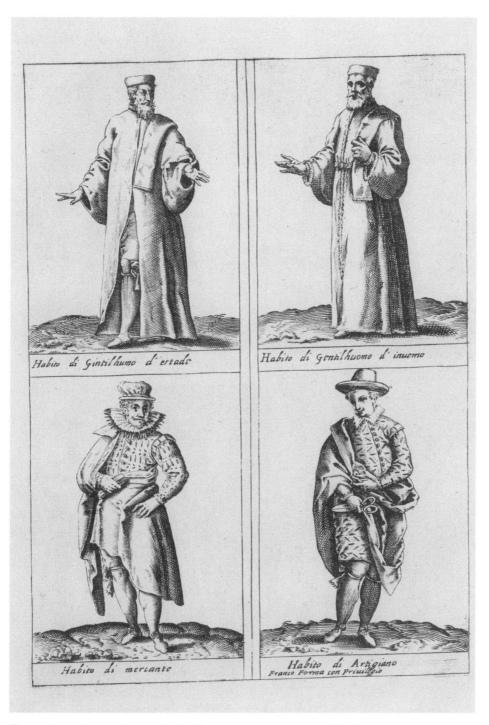

Figure 31. Giacomo Franco, *Habiti d'huomeni et donne venetiane* (1610). The summer and winter dress of a gentleman and the dress of a merchant and an artisan. By permission of Special Collections, Brotherton Library, University of Leeds.

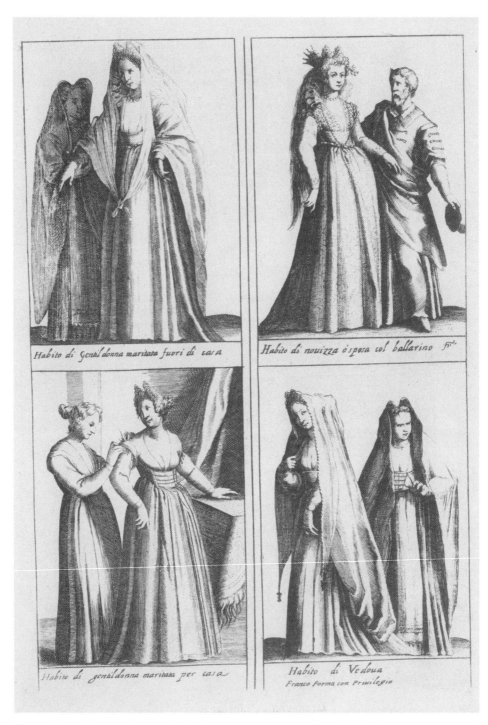

Figure 32.    Giacomo Franco, *Habiti d'huomeni et donne venetiane* (1610). The dress of a married gentlewoman outside the home, a novice or bride, a married gentlewoman at home and widows. By permission of Special Collections, Brotherton Library, University of Leeds.

said to be, *Grande dilegni, Grosse di straci, rosse dibettito, bianche di calcina:* that is tall with wood, fat with ragges, red with painting, and white with chalke ….

In generall the Women of *Italy*, (for divers Cities have some fashions differing from other) most commonly (but especially the wives of shopkeepers) weare gowns of silke and light stuffes, yea, woven with gold, and those close at the brest and necke; with a standing collar, and little ruffes close up to the very chinne, and shewing no part naked. And Gentlewomen in generall, weare gownes loose behind, with a close collar, hiding all nakednesse, and with traines borne up by waiting maides, and sometimes with open hanging sleeves. The married women weare their heads bare, or covered with a fine linnen coyfe, and a hat, and a vaile hanging downe from the hinder part of the head to the backe. The unmarried have their heads bare, with their haire knotted like snakes, and tied with gold and silver laces, or else they are covered with a gold netted cawle, and they weare also gold chaines. The married women weare chaines of pearle about the head and necke, which in some places are forbidden to Virgins; and these pearles are many times (especially at *Venice*) counterfet, and made of glasse, but very beautifull to the eye. Widdowes and Women that mourne, cover all their head and shoulders with a blacke vaile, and upon the forehead they weare a shadow or bongrace, and about their neckes a white vaile, hanging downe before to their feete.) The Countrey wenches weare vpon their heads gold and silver cawles, or at least seeming such, and straw hats, and guilded girdles, and for the rest as other women are delighted with light colours.

The City Virgins, and especially Gentlewomen, cover their heads, face, and backes with a Vaile, that they may not be seene passing the streetes, and in many places weare silke or linnen breeches under their gownes. Also I have seene honourable Women, aswell married as Virgines, ride by the high way in Princes traines, apparrelled like Men, in a doublet close to the body, and large breeches open at the knees, after the Spanish fashion, both of carnation silke or satten, and likewise riding astride like men upon Horses or Muses, but their heads were attired like Women, with bare haires knotted, or else covered with gold netted cawles, and a hat with a feather. And many times in the Cities (as at *Padua*) I have seene Curtizans (in plaine English, whores) in the time of shroving, apparrelled like men, in carnation or light coloured doublets and breeches, and so playing with the racket at Tennis with yong men, at which time of shroving, the Women no lesse then Men, (and that honourable women in honourable company,) goe masked and apparrelled like men all the afternoone about the streetes, even from Christmasse holydaies to the first day in Lent. The Women wearing Mens breeches, have them open all before, and most part behind, onely buttoned with gold or silver buttons: And the Curtizans make all the forepart of their gownes in like manner open, to avoide wrinckling.

## Fynes Moryson's Corpus Christi College, Oxford, Manuscript (completed 1626)[1]

Moryson compiled another voluminous manuscript account of his travels (Corpus Christi College, Oxford, MS 94) which he also intended for publication. This manuscript

[1] There are two printed editions of this manuscript: Moryson, *Shakespeare's Europe*, ed. Hughes, 1903; rpt 1967 (incomplete); and Kew, 'Shakespeare's Europe Revisited: The Unpublished *Itinerary* of Fynes Moryson (1566–1630)', 4 vols, unpublished PhD thesis, University of Birmingham, 1995. I am indebted to Kew's meticulous editorial work on this manuscript which entirely supersedes Hughes's 1903 edition.

Giuoco del Calzo che si fa' nel Brissaglio asᵗ Aluise la Quaresima al quale
non giuocano se non li Gentil' huomini
Giacomo Franco Forma con Priuilegio

Figure 33.    Giacomo Franco, *La Città di Venetia* (1614), Ball game played during Lent in Venice.
By permission of Special Collections, Brotherton Library, University of Leeds.

contained a wide range of material about Venice, some of which repeated information from the 1617 printed edition but other sections provided new or extended materials which are edited here.

## (from) The first Booke. Chap: i. Of the Turkes Commonwealth

[*margin*: The state of Venice.][1] [f. 20] On the Contrary, the Turkes seemed of purpose to provoke the Venetians with continuall injuries, and they taught by experience to be jealous of the Spaniards ayde upon any league, and themselves wanting victualls and soldiers, and equall strength of any forces to make warr without ayde against the great power of the Turkes, were content to stopp their fury by strong fortes, till by peaceable arts and guiftes, they might have tyme to appease the Turkish Emperor, and make their peace with him, in which kinde they had unfaithfull peace with him, troubled with many injuries, and yet were said to pay him the yearely Tribute of 18000 duccatts, for enjoying the Ilands and Townes they possessed in the mediterranean sea, whereof notwithstanding he hath taken many from them at divers breaches of peace. While myselfe was in Turkye, certaine Turkish Pyratts of the Southwest part of Morea or Greece, spoyling the Christians with a few small barques, had the Courage to assaile a Venetian Shipp of 700 Tonns burthen, and well furnished with brasse ordinance, which they tooke and loaded all their Barques with the most precious Commodityes thereof. Uppon Complaint of which hostile act made to the Emperor of Constantinople by the Bayle[2] of Venice for a shewe of Justice he obtayned that a Chiauss[3] was sent thither to apprehend the Pyrats but they withdrawing themselves into other Havens, and using meanes [f. 21] by large presents to make the Chiauss their freind for the present, and after in like sort to make their peace with the Emperor, the cheife Visere and the Admirall they so handled the matter as first the Chiauss returned back with answer, that they could not be found, and after the Venetians were so tyred with delayes of Justice, in that Court, as they were forced in the end to desist from following the cause, without having any restitution.

## (from) Booke. i. The common wealth of Venice Chap: v.[4]

[f. 118] V. Chap: Of the common wealth of Venice in particular touching some of the heads contained in the title of the first Chapter.

The first Chapter.

The free State of Venice, besides the stately Citty of Venice built within Channells of the Sea uppon litle Ilands, hath under it uppon the firme land of Italy, the fayre and well fortified Cittyes of Paduoa, Vicenza, Verona, Bergamo, Udane, and Treviso with their Territories, and the Castle or walled towned of Crema.[5] It hath also under it and adjoying to the forsaid Territories, at the Foote of the German Alps, the Province of Forum Julii vulgarly Friol,[6] the fertile Province of Istriæ being a Peninsul upon the Gulfe of Venice,

---

[1] Corpus Christi MS, ff. 20–21; Moryson, *Shakespeare's Europe*, ed. Hughes, pp. 33–4; Kew, 'Shakespeare's Europe Revisited', II, pp. 78–9. These references retain the Corpus Christi manuscript's use of 'folio' to represent a single page, rather than the usual usage of 'folio' incorporating recto and verso.

[2] *Bayle*: chief officer.

[3] *Chiauss*: chiaus, a Turkish messenger or sergeant.

[4] Corpus Christi MS, ff. 118–135; Moryson, *Shakespeare's Europe*, ed. Hughes [section omitted]; Kew, 'Shakespeare's Europe Revisited', II, pp. 326–73.

[5] Crema, a northern city in the province of Cremona in Lombardy, was under Venetian control from 1449.

[6] Friuli.

diverse Citties uppon the Sea coast of Dalmatia as Cattaro and Zara,[1] and many litle Ilands within the said Gulfe, out of which in the Mediterranean sea it hath subject to it, the Ilands of Corfa, of Cephalonia the greater, and the lesser of Zante, the rich, and goodly Iland of Candia and the litle Iland Serigo.[2] The Pope Alexander supported by the Venetians till in that Citty he trode uppon the neck of the Emperor,[3] for [in?]gratitude gave the Commaund of that Sea (namely the large Gulfe of Venice) to this State, I know not by what right, except it were that by which the divell promised to give the kingdomes of the earth,[4] yet such a title as Princes have in like cases bene content to take from him, for such things as they desired to get and preserve by the sword. From this right they have a Custome yearely uppon Ascention day (as I remember) that the duke and the Senators (with great pompe and solemnity, and with loude instruments of musick tooke boate in the Bucentoro (so called of the Capacity to beare two hundredth men) and rowe to the mouth of the Haven entring the Mayne Gulfe, where the duke casts a gold ring into the Sea, by that Ceremonie espowsing it to the State of Venice.[5] Notwithstanding Pope Julius the second extorted from them priviledge of freedome uppon this Gulfe for all the Popes territories lying there uppon, Of old they had the Island of Cyprus in the bottome of the straights nere Asia, and many Citties uppon the Continent of Grece, all which the Turkish Emperor now possesseth, either won by the sword, or at diverse tymes yielded to him by transactions of peace. This State was in great danger to leese their virgine liberty in the age before this wherein we live, when the Princes of Italy by their growing power, judging them to affect the dominion of all Italy, did jointly combine against them, so as the Pope the Emperor of Germany, the king of Fraunce, and the king of Aragon, Castile, Naples, and Sicily, for diverse ends and provoked by diverse injuries, did all make league,[6] and at one tyme with their forces assaile the Venetians, having none to take their part. In which war Lewes the king of France tooke from them Cremona, and diverse other places which [f. 119] himselfe had graunted them, while they assisted him to conquer the dukedome of Milan, all which the king of Spaine to this day possesseth with the said dukedome taken from the French. Also the Pope making use of the french victoryes, tooke from them Ravenna Faenza Rimini and all the adjoining territories, and as there is no redemption from Hell, so to this day, they have not recovered any thing out of his Pawes, nor ever attempted any recovery. The same victory of the french against the Venetians gave Ferdinand king of Aragon fit opportunity to take from them Monopoli, Brandusio, Trani and Ottranto, Sea bordering Cittyes of the kingdome of Naples formerly ingaged to them for great sommes of mony, all which the king of Spaine his successor holds to this day. In like sort Maximilian the Emperor by the said victory and ayde of the french forces, tooke from the Venetians, Bergamo, Brescia, Verona, Vicenza, and Treviso, all strong and rich Cittyes of Lombardy, with large and rich Territories, lying at the foote of the German Alps, and likewise great part of the Province Frioli and the very City and Territory of Padoua compassing the lakes of Venice, which now had lost all dominions uppon firme land. But the Venetians to stop the Popes mouth, yielded

[1] Kotor and Zadar.
[2] Kíthira.
[3] Pope Alexander III and Frederick Barbarossa. See also pp. 53 and 300.
[4] Comparing the Pope to Satan tempting Christ in the wilderness, Matthew 4:8 and Luke 4:5.
[5] *Marriage of the Sea (**Plate 11**).
[6] The Holy League, see pp. 84, 94 and 150 n. 3.

to him whatsoever he asked, and supported by his friendship and factions, daily growing between the Emperor[s] and the kings, did prevaile against the Emperor, forsaken by both the kings, and soone recovered from him all he had taken from them, with which dominions they rest contented to this day, without attempting to increase the same, by any new Invasion or by recovering that they lost to more powerfull enemynes. This Common wealth of Venice hath lasted more then a thousand two hundredth yeares, and he that shall see the gravity and wisdome of their Senate, and the justness of their government, would judge it likely to last so long as the Sunne and moone indureth; yet may reasons make it unlike to increase and grow much greater; For all Italy being divided into many parts of gree Cities & principalityes every small war threatens ruine, and destruction to the whole Country. And the Venetians are taught by experience of the foresaid Combination against them to prefer a secure peace though dearely bought, to the uncertaine event of war promising gayne. As also the Princes of Italy, so feare their safety in tyme of troubles as they are likely all to joyne their forces against the first disturber of peace. Yea the very Bishopps of Rome, which of old sowed and raysed all dissentions and wars, now since the falling of many kingdoms and Provinces from their obedience finding that they cannot fish in troubled waters as they [were] wont, but rather that the wonted reverence to that Sea is so decayed, as the prevailing party would in all likelihood force them to reformation of the Church, and deprive them of their temporall dominions, have of late applied their Councells to peace, espetially in Italy, where the danger of war [f. 120] would be so neare them to woorke these effects, as no doubt they would oppose themselves against the Rayser of warr in Italy, both by their forces and excommunications. Whereas forrayne kings and Princes under the Popes obedience take it as great favour from them to have their subjects and friends made Cardinalls, the Venetians that their Commonweath may longer last, desire nothing lesse, then that the Pope should preferr any gentleman of Venice to that dignity, being terrified from this ambition by the Examples of the family of Medici in Florence, whereof diverse being made Cardinalls & after Popes utterly overthrew the liberty of their Country, and brought it in hereditary subjection to their owne Family.[1] For they are not ignorant what brave feates the Popes have played in those cases, taught by many examples, but more specially by that of Pope Julius the second, who had the power by the foresaid league to ruine them, and soone after by forsaking that league, and turning his favour towards them, to inable them in short tyme to recover the dominions they now hold upon firme land.

...

[Moryson then supplies accounts of Venice's dealings with other 'bordering Potentates', including the 'house of Austria', 'Turkish Emperor', 'Popes', and 'king of Spaine', along with descriptions of its republican constitution and councils, much of which is drawn from contemporary sources, especially Sansovino's *Venetia città nobilissima e singolare*, Venice, 1581 (using the 1604 edition), Lewis Lewkenor's 1599 translation of Gasparo Contarini's *The Common-Wealth and Government of Venice* and Richard Knolles' 1606 translation of Jean Bodin's *Six Books of a Commonweale*. Although this section of Moryson's manuscript is highly derivative (and, therefore, omitted from this volume), it had a serious purpose. He was clearly seeking to offer from an English perspective a

---

[1] Moryson is referring here to Giovanni di Lorenzo de' Medici, Leo X (Pope 1513–21), and Giulio di Giuliano de' Medici, Clement VII (Pope 1523–34).

judicious reassessment of the city's political structures. In particular, he was aware that while Contarini had presented Venetian republicanism as a mixed constitution dependent for its stability upon the counterbalancing potency of the Senate and its various councils and committees, Bodin viewed Venice's patrician class as essentially aristocratic and closer to a French (and implicitly English) model of traditional hierarchical authority. Some of Moryson's more personal observations on Venice in this section are provided below.]

[f. 123, Council Chamber] The Chamber wherein this Counsell is kept, being in the Dukes publike Palace, is very fayre, large and lightsome, with windows and adorned with most rare woorkes of Paynters, and they say, it is Quadrangular, but I measured the insyde 76. Ordinary paces long, and 32 broade. There is a Tribunall or Throne of wood to be removed at pleasure, much higher then the other seates, and uppon ix double Bankes, and it hath two principall gates. In this Chamber, the great Counsell meetes every Sonday in the afternoon, and upon occasion oftner; As when the Counsell of Pregadi is to be Chosen, and here they chuse all magistrates and the Assembly is called together by the sounds of a great Bell, touling for the space of a whole hower, After which tyme the Chamber is shut, and may not be opened to lett any man enter, except it be one of the Counsellors or one of the Avagadori,[1] or one of the heads of the Councell of the Councell of Tenn, called Capi del consiglio di dieci or one of the Censors. Uppon the dukes left hand sett the six Counsellors the three heades of the Counsell of Quaranta (that is Forty men) then the foresayd three heads of the Councell of Dieci, then the three Avogadori, and the two Censors, all which weare the ducal Robe [?] or gowne of Scarlett with large wyde sleeves, open at the hands, and lined with rich Furres. Neare the dukes throne are two benches uppon which the Chauncelor and his officers sitt. In general, I cann hardly beleeve, that the Roman Senate passed that of Venice in gravity of Countenance or statelynes [of?] ornaments, and all the Gentlemen, aswell as the Senators, weare gownes and litle Caps upon the Crowne of the heads, not only in Councell, but at all tymes, when they goe abroad.

...

[Moryson then describes the drawing of lots, using silver and golden balls, for service as magistrates, the city's various councils and functionaries, procedures following the death of doge. He also recalled his personal sightings of Pasquale Cicogna (1509–95), who was Doge (1585–95) and in his mid-eighties (**Plate 22**) when seen by Moryson.]

[f. 129] While I lived in Venice I did often see the Duke, and once more fully when the french Duke of Nevers came to visit him.[2] The Duke was a very old man for such are comonly chosen. His habit was proper to that dignity of Scarlett and rich Furres, but in the sleeves differing from private men, and under his Ducall Cap he wore a white Coyfe hanging downe from his eares over his neck. The magistrates called the Savii grandi, in blew gownes stood by the Duke, and the six Counsellors in red gownes (for the youngest gentlemen is gowned, all of one fashion and of black Coulor, and aswell young as old weare very litle Capps on the Crowne of the head). At this tyme I observed that one of

---

[1] Avogadori di Commune.

[2] Ludovico Gonzaga (1539–95), Duke of Nevers, was the third son of Federico II Gonzaga, Duke of Mantua and Margherita Paleologo. Venice supported the claim of Henry of Navarre (1553–1610) to the French throne (King Henri IV, from 1589), and persuaded the Pope to support him if he converted to Catholicism.

the Counsellors always stood so neare the Duke, as no word could passe betweene him and the french Duke which was not heard by one or more of them. And indeed it is vulgarly sayd that the Duke may not receive a letter, no not from his sonne or wife, but one of these Counsellors must be at the reading of it, nether can he send any publike or private letters, but uppon the like Condition, yea the Duke may not without leave goe out of the Citty, which Peter Loredon asked,[1] and obtained to goe to his village in the Country, but the like useth seldome or never to be asked or obtained. Many publike Processions are yearely appointed, wherein the Duke betweene two cheife Ambassadors, and accompanied with the grave Senators, with a gentleman carrying a naked sword by his syde, with many banners before him and with Triumpetts, and Bells sounding is carried in a guilded chayre about some parts of the Cittye with a Canopye over his head, and not only all the pompe but the very spaces of tyme, and place in those processions [f. 130] are prescribed by the lawes.[2] Not to speake of the like pompe in going to Sea uppon the Assention day to cast a ring into the Sea as a pledge of marriage betweene it and the State. And I remember that in the market place of St. Marke nere to the Publike Pallace where the Duke resides, there be two stately carved Pillers, uppon which they say that a Duke seeking to oppresse the liberty of the State, was hanged in a tumult.[3] And it was vulgarly sayd that the duke must in all Processions (as myself observed often to be done) passe through these Pillers, I know not whether by law or Custome Sansovine reports, that a Duke making an oration, a gentleman that told him that he spake idly, was severely punished for the same, yet now doubt, excepting those outward pomps the Duke hath no more authority then one of his honourable Senators. Sansovine[?] reports that the Duke hath yearely 3500. Ducats from the State, and that he is tyed to keepe an honourable Family, but the written relations testifye that he hath weekely a hundredth zechines of Gold, and it cannot be imagined, how privately he lives.

...

[This passage illustrates how Moryson was also drawing information from the 1604 edition of Sansovino's guide as he compiled his own account of Venice and provided in the following section a detailed description of the doge's councillors, including how they were elected and for how long they served. He also included information about the Procurators of St Mark (**Plate 21**), mainly drawn from Lewkenor's translation of Contarini, and other officers, including the *Cattaveri who, according to Lewkenor (fol. 133), 'were wont to take the names of Pilgrimes to the holy land, and to judge their differences'. Moryson often tries to update Contarini's advice (even though Lewkenor's translation was only published in 1599) and in this case notes: 'but at this day the names of Pilgrimes are not taken, neither doe any Gallyes (according to the old Custome) transport them yearely from Venice to Palestine'.]

---

[1] Pietro Loredan (1482–1570), Doge 1567–70.

[2] See Cesare Vecellio (c.1521–c.1601), *Procession of the Doge and his Entourage in Piazza San Marco*, 1586 (**Plate 10**). Vecellio, a cousin of Titian, was a painter and engraver. He also published a guide to fashion and dress across the known world, *De gli Habiti Antichi e Modérni di Diversi Parti di Mondo* (Venice, 1590), with numerous woodcuts, many of which may have been those of Christopher Krieger of Nuremberg.

[3] This may be an erroneous verbal report which Moryson had heard while in Venice. Doge Vitale Michiel II (1156–72) was stabbed in the Calle della Rasse during a riot. More famously, Doge Marin Falier (1354–45) was hanged within the inner courtyard of the Doge's Palace, although some of his alleged accomplices were publicly executed before the Doge's Palace.

(from) **Of The common wealth of Italy in General and some of the greater States thereof**

[f. 160] **The tributes in the state of Venice.**[1]

The State of Venice in imitation of the Pope, calling his Rents the Patrimony of St. Peter, doe also call their tributes the Revenues of St. Marke the protecting Saint of the Citty. Of Stable Rents, not such as are Casuall and gotten by industry, each man payes tenn Crownes to St. Marke in the hundredth. Each measure of wyne called Botta vulgarly,[2] payes five Ducates, and each Secchio[3] of wyne payes tenn Soldi. Each measure of Corne called Staio[4] vulgarly payes 48 Soldi. But the shopkeepers pay no such Tributes as are exacted in Florence, exercising their trade freely. The Magazines[5] of Wyne only in the Citty of Venice, were said yearely to yeild three hundredth thousand Ducates, for those that sell wyne by small measures, paid each man some thousand Crownes for his license, after which rate the Inkeepers also paid for their licenses. Many houses kept Chambers to be lett, and suppose the house be hyred for some hundredth Crownes the yeare, or being their owne be valued, at so much, they pay halfe the Rent, namely Fifty Crownes to St. Marke. The very boyes and men wayting in the marketts, like our Porters with basketts to carry home things bought, and vulgarly called Cisterolli,[6] doe pay each moneth Fiftye Soldi each one for his license. In diverse written relations I finde the generall Revenue of this State valued at two millions of gold yearely though Monsr. Villamont attributes so much to the Citty of Venice alone.[7] And for severall tributes of the State, I finde them thus valued in generall. The wyne [f. 161] yearely at one hundredth sixteene thousand Ducates; The oyle at fower Thousand; Marchandize imported at Thirty thousand, and exported asmuch. Corne at fowerteene: Flesh at seventeene thousand. The flatt[8] vulgarly Il Grasso, as butter, suett, and the like, Fourteene thousand. The Iron seaven thousand. The fruites foure thousand: The wood six thousand. And for particular Cittyes, these relations record, that Padoa brings yearely into the Treasure of Venice thirteene thousand Ducates .... My selfe retorning from Padoa towardes England, and having the testimony of the university (vulgarly called Matricola) that I was Student thereof was thereby freed from many small payments in that State, as six Soldi demaunded at the Gate of Padoa, and eight Soldi at the gate of Verona, and some Quatrines for the passing of bridges, and the like, which I mention only to shewe that these payments were due to St. Marke only for my person, since I carried nothing with me but some two or three shirts, and that the same payments being exacted of every Passenger for his head, in such a beaten waye from Fraunce, Germany and many kingdomes to Rome must needs amount to a great somm yearely. I have omitted to speake of the Tribute raysed by Harlotts, called Cortisane, which must needs be great in that State, neither have I spoken

---

[1] Corpus Christi MS, 'Booke .i. The common wealth of Italy. Chap: Viii', ff. 160–161; Moryson, *Shakespeare's Europe*, ed. Hughes, pp. 128–30; Kew, 'Shakespeare's Europe Revisited', II, pp. 433–7.

[2] *Botta*: Venetian wine measure, also used as a ship's measure; one botta equated to *c.*750 litres. Lane, *Venetian Ships*, p. 247.

[3] *Secchio*: bucket.

[4] *Staio*: bushel.

[5] Magazines: from *magazzino*, warehouse.

[6] Cisterolli: probably derived from *cesto, cestino*, basket.

[7] Jacques de Villamont (1558–*c.*1625/8), his *Voyages* (1595 and reprinted thirteen times by 1609) was a popular French travel account, ostensibly recording his pilgrimage to the Holy Land.

[8] *flatt*: probably a slip for 'fat'.

of extraordinary Tributes, as in tyme of warr, wherein the Tenths for Land, and in the like sort the Customes are doubled or trebled, and private men not only with Chearefulnes lend, but also give great sommes of mony and the women have not spared to give their Jewells, so as it may be sayd that the publique treasure is never poore, so long as private men be rich. Neither have I spoken of the depost[1] payd by gentlemen when they are admitted capable to beare office, nor of many like Revenues. Give me leave to add that a late writer hath published in print, that the generall Revenue of Venice amounts yearely to two millions of gold Crownes. That the Townes yeild yearely eight hundredth thousand Crownes, of which sum Bergamo and Brescia yield three hundredth thousand; That thie Imposts of Venice amount to 700 thousand, wyne alone in the State to 130 thousand, and salt alone to 500 thousand Crownes.

...

### [f. 163] of the power of Italy in warr generally[2]

Yet I confesse that the State of Venice being a free State, under the which the people are not so much oppressed as under other Princes of Italy, raise part of their foote of their owne Peasants, but the strength thereof is in straungers, as likewise they imploy some gentlemen of the Cittyes subject to the State to comaund some troopes of men at Armes or Armed horses. But howsoever they make gentlemen of Venice Governors and Generalls of their Navye, yet they never imploy them to command their land forces, having alwayes a Straunger to their Generall. But this they doe, not that they suspect their faith, but lest any gentleman gayning great reputation in Armes, and the love of soldiers, should have power at any tyme to usurpe uppon the Freedome of their State ... . Yet some Princes especially the State of Venice in tyme of peace mantayne some troopes of Armed horse, which I have seene mustered in very brave equipage, the horses being well armed and beautifull, and the horsmen attyred in Coates of blewe velvett or like Coulor ... . The Foote Captaynes especially of the State of Venice, are to be commended that they live not luxuriously and prodigally, but content with their pay of Twentye five Crownes the moneth, live modestly both for diett and apparell, as the Common Soldiers likewise live of the pay of some three or fower Crownes the moneth, the Pioners[3] having only 12 Soldi of Venice by the day. Neither doe the Captaynes make any extraordinary advantages by their Companyes, either in deficiency of numbers or victuals or Apparrell for them, only Guiccardine writes that the Popes use to be much cozened in those kindes.

...

### [f. 167] The power of the State of Venice in warr[4]

The State of Venice is more powerfull in warr then any other State, or Prince of Italy. And this power made them suspected in the last age to affect the subduing of all Italy, where uppon the Pope of that tyme, the Emperor Maximilian, the french King Lewes

---

[1] *depost*: an archaic form of deposit; only two examples (from Wycliffe Bible, 1382) are cited in *OED*, along with an entry in a 1735 dictionary.

[2] Corpus Christi MS, 'Booke .i. The common wealth of Italy. Chap: Viii', ff. 163–164; Moryson, *Shakespeare's Europe*, ed. Hughes, 132–4; Kew, 'Shakespeare's Europe Revisited', II, pp. 440–45.

[3] *Pioners*: pioneers, infantry who dig trenches, repair roads or clear terrain for the main body of troops.

[4] Corpus Christi MS, 'Booke .i. The common wealth of Italy. Chap: Viii', ff. 167–172 (mispaginated as ff. 162–167); Moryson, *Shakespeare's Europe*, ed. Hughes, pp. 138–9; Kew, 'Shakespeare's Europe Revisited', pp. 450–63.

the twelveth, and Ferdinand the king of Arragon made a league at Cameracum[1] to joyne all their forces for suppressing the power of this State, which with great Courage defended it selfe against these strong united forces, and being beaten by the french alone; yet the wise Senators thereof applyed themselves first to appease the Pope by yeilding to his demaunds, who combined the rest of the league in that great action almost to the fatall ruine of this state. And the Pope being onece satisfyed, by this inconstant leaving of his Confederates, and their mutuall jelousyes among themselves, the Venetians having lost all their dominion on firme land[2] soone recovered the same, excepting the Townes yeilding to the Pope (from whose possession as from Hell there is no redemption) and the Townes of the kingdome of Naples which the King of Arragon had ingaged for mony to the State of Venice, and now during this league had by Armes extorted out of that States possession. From which tyme the Venetians have only laboured to preserve their owne, and seeme to have cast of all projects to usurping uppon their neighbours. The written relations of this State taxe the Nobles (so their gentlemen are called) with want of Courage, whereby they abhorr from any Warr, and more spetially against the Turkes daily provoking them with many injuryes, to whose Sultans (or Emperors) they not only pay yearely tribute for the peaceable possession of some Ilands they hold in the Mediterranean Sea, but also uppon all occasions when the Sultanes are incensed against their State, spare not by large bribes, and like meanes to appease them. And indeed the Gentlemen of Venice are trayned upp in pleasure and wantonnes, which must needes abase and effeminate their myndes. Besides that this State is not sufficiently furnished with men and more specially with native Commaunders and Generalls, nor yet with victualls, to undertake (of their owne power without assistance) a war against the Sultane of Turky. This want of Courage, & especially the feare lest any Citizen becoming a great and popular Commaunder in the warrs, might thereby have meanes to usurpe upon the liberty of their State, seeme to be the Causes that for their Land forces they seldome have any native Comaunders, and always use a forrayne Generall. Yet we reade that Gentlemen of Venice have bravely commaunded their Navye even in cheefe.[3] In tyme of peace, they use to give a great yearely stipend to some Prince or great Commaunder to be generall of their land forces in tyme of war.

[f. 168] [*margin*: **The Fortes**] This State hath many and strong Forts well furnished with Artillery, munition and victualls upon all their Confines being many and dangerous as before I have shewed.

[*margin*: **The horse.**] The written Relations of this tyme testifye that in tyme of peace they mantayned in pay 600.th men at Armes, or Armed horse, of their owne Subjects being gentlemen of their Territoryes uppon firme land, each one of these 600.th mustering three horses with their Riders all armed, and each one having yearely 120 Ducates, And that they can rayse 1000 or 1500 uppon necessity. They were divided into twelve Companyes or Troopes, and made a generall Muster every Sommer. Two of these Troopes were of the Citty of Paduoa, which my selfe did see mustered making a glorious shewe, the horse being beautifull and well armed, and the horsemen in like sort armed &

---

[1] War of the League of Cambrai (1508–16).

[2] firme land: i.e., Terra Firma, the mainland territories of Venice.

[3] *cheefe*: in supreme command.

Wearing Coates of blewe velvett, with great plumes aswell for the men as horse. Of old they also mantyned one thousand light horse, but of late had none such in pay using for that purpose the Stradiotti of Dalmatia,[1] whence they say 3000 may be drawne uppon occasion to use them.

[*margin*: **The foote.**] They doe not altogether distrust their owne subjects to whome they are (after the manner of Common wealthes) more milde and gentle in exactions, then the Princes of Italy. So as according to the number of Fyers[2] the Subjects are to mantayne soldiers aswell for land as Sea service, and the Captaynes have the names of all Subjects written for the one, or the other service.

They mustered 25 thousand Foote of their Peasants, serving both in Gallyes and land Armyes, at least for baser uses, but for foote they generally use and have the strength thereof of Grisons and Sweitzers,[3] and to this end some Commaunders among them have stipends even in tyme of peace, but in warr each man hath 3 Crownes for 45 dayes while they were imployed, and in cases of necessity they have given each man 5 Crownes the moneth. The Gentlemen of Venice serve freely without pay.

[*margin*: **The Navye.**] For their Navall power, in the last preceding generall discourse, I have sayd that the Italians or rather Greekes used by them, are neither expert nor bold mariners, and that the great shipps are slowe in sayling, and unfitt for fight at Sea, and that the lesser Barques are unarmed, and that upon the Calme mediterranean Sea, all navall fights use to be made with Gallyes whereof the greatest are called Galeoni the midle sort Galee and the lesser Galeasses and Fregates. And therein I spoke of the miserable Gallyslaves. All this spoken in generall belongs to Venice as a principall part of Italy. The Venetians have a lawe that each marchante shipp of 500 Tonnes, must carry in the voyage it maketh, a young gentleman of Venice, giving him sixe Crownes stipend by the moneth, and must bring upp two boyes of Venice to breede them Mariners. But this wisdom of their Progenitors hath bene made vayne by the sluggish disposition of their posterity, for neither have the gentlemen any skill thereby in navigation or commanding at Sea, since the young gentlemen chuse rather to stay at home, so they may have the stipend and value of their diett for the voyage, neither are the shipps thereby furntished with native mariners, since (as I formerly sayd) the Italians in their nature abhorr from that or any like hard Course of life, tho otherwise they are so proude, as they will doe any service at home rather than basely to begg. They who serve in the Gallies of Venice, are partly Freemen, as the Gondelieri or watermen of Venice which for the Tragetto or passage where they have priviledge to plye, or transport, are bound uppon extraordinary occasions to serve in the Gallyes to rowe, as likewise the Soldiers are free, aswell the native Peasants above mentioned as straungers, and of them that are free some have stipend and victualls from this or that Citty setting them forth, others have the same from the Treasure of St. Marke (so they call the Exchequer) as the Pope calles all he hath St. Peters, and at Genoa the publique Treasure is called the treasure of St. George (their protecting Saint). Others that serve in the Gallyes are slaves, uppon Crimes condemned to the Gallyes for life or

---

[1] *Stradiotti of Dalmatia*: stratioti (stradioti), mercenary soldiers from the Balkans (especially Albania, Bulgaria, Dalmatia), Greece and the southern states of Europe. They were deployed by Venice against the Ottomans and from *c*.1475 as frontier troops in Friuli, often replacing most of the Venetian light cavalry in their militia.

[2] A calculation based upon the number of domestic hearths in the individuals' households.

[3] *Grisons and Sweitzers*: Swiss soldiers and those from the Swiss canton of Grison.

certaine yeares, and St. Marke gives them raggs to cover their shame, and victualls in scant measure, but the victualer gives them Creditt that are condemned for yeares, by which growing debt they are made perpetuall slaves, and both sorts of Condemned slaves are chained by the legg to the place where they rowe, which their Governor unlocks at one end when he sends them forth for fresh water or wood bearing still their Chaynes on their leggs. The Gallyes are commonly called after the names of their Cheefe Governor. Myselfe did enter one of the Gallyes, and the Castle in the Prowe was some twelve of my paces, and the bodye with the Poope fifty of my paces long, and the master commanded from the Castle to the great mast, as the Comito (or mate) commands the rest. In the poope satt the cheefe Governor, under hoopes covered with a fayre Cloath, and beyond the sterne was a litle Gallery, and under the deck his Cabbin, and above the poope hung the cheefe banner of St. Marke, the Gally being graven on all sydes with white lyons for the image of St. Marke. The Gally bore fower great peices in the Castle (where the Trompetters sounde) and Thirty more on the sydes, and in the poope twelve whereof two great lay above directly layd out uppon the sterne, and two of like greatnes under them, and two of like greatnes some 22 spanns[1] long were turned towards the Gallye to shoote sydewayes, the other were lesse, but all of brasse.

The Gallye had 25 oares on each syde, and seaven men to rowe each oare, and when they are in Port two sleepe uppon the benche where they use to sett, two in the place which is under their thighes, and two where they setle their feete, when they rowe, and the seaventh slept uppon the Oare, and uppon a litle boarde betweene each Oare three soldiers use to sleepe. So as their being in the Gallye is nothing commodious, but straight,[2] uneasy and subject to contagion. The State or Citty of Venice continually used to arme Fifty Gallyes, whereof 25 were called of the Schooles or Companyes of Arts, arming and paying them, and 25 Palatines,[3] Armed and payd by St. Marke in which the foresaid watermen are bound to serve when they goe forth. In each Gallye the Cheefe Commaunder is a gentleman of Venice, and the next Commaund is likewise committed to two gentlemen, and they are called Sopracomiti[4] as above the mate, and they which command in the Palatine Gallies are of greater estimation then the other. And I finde in written Relations, that these Commaunders have each of them 1600 Crownes yearely stipend, for which it is expected from them, they should give some releife to the Soldiers, and specially to the slaves, having a slender diett allowed, and so being forced to runn in the victualers debt. They write of twelve Gallies armed by subject Cittyes of the firme land towards the Sea Coast. This Navye they are foced to arme against the Turkish Pyrates using to spoyle their Shipps in the tyme of peace, and in winter tyme, it commonly lyes in the haven of Corfu having a strong Fort, and sometimes in the havens of Candia. And hereof some five Gallyes, and some small Barques armed, lye uppon the Gulfe of Venice to purge the same of Pyrates, more specially the Uscocchi,[5] who living on the Coast of Dalmatia in Signi uppon the Confines of the Empire, Turkey, and the State of Venice,

---

[1] *spanns*: span, measured from the thumb to the little finger, about nine inches.

[2] *straight*: straitened, tight, difficult or constricted.

[3] *Palatines*: administrative areas.

[4] *Sopracomiti*: captains.

[5] Uskoks were mercenary soldiers from the eastern Adriatic coastal areas during the Ottoman wars. They rowed swift boats which were often used for acts of piracy. They fought with Venice and its allies at the Battle of Lepanto (1571) (**Plate 13**).

and being Christians, yet live as outlawes, neither subject to the Turkes nor to any Christian Prince, and robb all men especially the Italian Shipps at Sea.

In the Citty of Venice, they have a fayre and large Arcenall compassed with walls, wherein they keepe all munitions for warr, and have a secure Station for their Gallyes, where likewise they build their shipps and Gallyes, to which purpose they have much timber on the Sea coast of their dominion. The walles are some three myles Compasse, and the officers shewe the same Courteously to straungers. The Maestranza[1] consists of some 2200 woorkemen, weekely paid by St. Marke, whereof 300 are expert men in building of Shipps and Gallyes. They shewed me fower upper Chambers, wherein Sayles were made and layd upp, and therein some 20 or 30 woorke continually, and each of them hath a portion of wyne, Bisquitt and Soldi by the day. In fower low rooms are layd the Cordage and Cables sufficient to furnish more than 300 Gallyes, besides an infinite number of Oares, each woorth five ducates, and Costing the State more then fower ducates. They shewed mee five Magasines upon one syde. In the first were great peeces of Artillery, disposed in 24. Rowes. In the second were peeces for 50 Gallyes, besides 150 peeces, some greater, some lesser. In the third were great peeces for five great Gallyes, Forty for each one, besides 250 other ordinary peeces. In the fourth uppon the right hand were 72 small peeces for the Feilde, and uppon the left hand 356 peeces of battery and some 100th Instruments called Trombi[2] for fyre woorkes. In the fifth were laid upp such peeces, as at diverse tymes were taken from the Turkes, whereof many had bene and were daily melted and newe cast. They told me they had in all some 2000 great peeces, the bulletts whereof were some 70, some 100, some 200, some 300 pounds weight, and myselfe did see one great peece 12400 poundes, and the Bullett 120 pounds. In diverse other roomes they layed musketts and all Armes for Soldiers at Sea. They shewed me many Gallyes newe built, and some 100th old, but strong, lying at Anchor, and together with the Navye they have always abroad, this State can Arme 200th, other say 300th Gallies, and of late in tenn dayes they have armed 30.tye great Gallyes ready for a Sea fight; Besides that they have many litle Barques and fregates. They shewed me a litle Gallye called Bucentoro because it beareth 200th men D. by corruption of speach being changed into B. and therein I had seene the Duke with the Senators goe forth in pompe especially at Whitsontyde when the Duke useth to marry to Sea by casting a Ring into it. Uppon this Gally is a Chamber some 38 of my paces long, which is all guilded and covered with a rich Cloath when the Duke and Senators goe forth in it, and under the Chamber sett 150 mariners to Rowe it, and it is then hung with many banners taken from the Turkes, and the image of Justice is graven at the Prowe.

The Duke of Mantuoa hath the like and so called, to rowe for pleasure, and for journeys uppon the River Po. The keele thereof is flatt bottomed, and the Prowe and sterne are voyde for mariners to rowe, only the sterne is covered as in Gallyes, over the rest of the Gally is a litle house containing fower Chambers belowe, the one of 15 paces the second of 8, the other two each 5 paces, and above them a gallery some 40 paces long, having stayres at each end to ascend it, and all furnished round about with seates.

---

[1] *Maestranza*: a Spanish term, *maestranza de caballería* (cavalry armories), usually applied to militias formed by Spanish noblemen during the 16th century. Here Moryson is probably using a local term to indicate a collection of workers, each a master (*maistrie*) of his trade.

[2] *Trombi*: rocket tubes.

The Arcenall of Venice hath moreover many rooms furnished with all munitions, Armes and necessaryes for an Armye at land, sufficient for 70 thousand Foote, and 2000 horse, Besides many Armes now growne out of use, and layd upp apart from the rest at the gate of the Armorye. To conclude they have aboundance of all necessaryes for warr by land and Sea, so that howsoever this State wants victualls for an Army, and numbers of men answerable to the furniture, and have the defect to use straungers for Soldiers, and even for their Generalls by land; yet since they want not Treasure the sinewe of Warr,[1] and the Sea is open to bring victualls which is commaunded by their Navye, and they have orderly Officers appointed in peace and war, and ever carefull to provide victualls, and since the straungers are so duely paid by them, as they have no cause to mutinye or be discontented, no doubt this State were able to undertake and prevaile in any great attempt in Italy and uppon their neighbors at Sea, had they not the vast power of the Turkish Empire lying heavy on their shoulders.

[*margin*: **Of Venice in particular**][2] In my Journall describing Venice, I have sayd that they numbred 3000 Familyes of Gentlemen in that one Citty, and among the famous men of former ages, I have named the Justiniani, Contarini, Grimani, Morosyni, Dandoli, Barbarigi and others.

The Gentlemen of Venice in singularity wilbe called Nobles, and appropriate to themselves the title of Clarissimo, for which and their general insolencye, they are reproved and condemned, not only by strangers (who may as safely stumble upon a Bull as upon one of these gentlemen, so as when one of them passed by, I have heard men say Guarda il toro, Looke, or take heed to the Bull, as they crye when a Bull is bayted in the streets) but also by other Italian gentlemen who by writings in the vulgar tongue taxe them of unsupportable pride insomuch as (to use their owne words) they dreame themselves to be Dukes and Marquises, while they are indeed covetous, miserable, breakers of faith & hatefull to all men for their pride, vayne glory and ambition, yea in the very Citty they have a Proverbe D'una pietra bianca d'un Nobile Venetiano, et d'una Cortigiana, ch'abbia madre Dio ci guarda, from a white stone (because it is slipperie) from a gentleman of Venice (for their pride) from a Cortisan that hath a mother (to teach her to spoile her lovers), God deliver us. No doubt the Senators are most grave just reverent and comely persons, and generally they are all rich, and many abound in Treasure. In Poduoa, Il signor Pio obici,[3] was sayd to have 12000 Crownes yearely Rent, and I was credibly informed that in Brescia diverse gentlemen had from tenn to thirty thousand Crownes yearely Rent. And the estates of the Gentlemen of Venice must in all probabilitye be much greater.

[f. 183] [*margin*: **The Justice, lawes, and Judgments in the State of Venice.**][4]
The Senate of Venice is most reverent for the gray heads, gravity and Comelynes of their persons, and their stately habitts but for nothing more then their strict observing of

---

[1] *sinewe of Warr*: finance or money, essential for waging war.

[2] Corpus Christi MS, 'Booke .i. The common wealth of Italy. Chap: Viii', f. 176 (mispaginated as f. 166); Moryson, *Shakespeare's Europe*, ed. Hughes, pp. 152–3; Kew, 'Shakespeare's Europe Revisited', II, pp. 474–6.

[3] Pio Enea degli Obizzi (1525–89), a noted *condottiero*, who built the vast Castello del Catajo near Padua and commissioned the poet Giuseppe Betussi to compose a grandiose Obizzi family history.

[4] Corpus Christi MS, 'Booke .i. The common wealth of Italy. Chap: Viii', ff. 183–185; Moryson, *Shakespeare's Europe*, ed. Hughes, pp. 163–6; Kew, 'Shakespeare's Europe Revisited', II pp. 493–8.

Justice. They have a lawe that in tyme of Carnavall or Shrovetyde, no man that is masked may weare a sword, because being unknowne, he might thereby have meanes to kill his enemy on the sodeine, and while I was in Italy a forayne gentleman upon a fancy to mock the officers of Justice, being masked wore a woodden lathe like a sword. The officers apprehended him, and finding it to be a lath, yet carried him to the magistrate, who with a grave Countenance said to him, Non burlar' con la Giustitia, Veh: Jeast not with the Justice, marke me. And he found that he had mocked himselfe more then the officers, for he payd not a few Crownes before he could be freed by mediation of great freinds. But since the Citty of Venice lyes open without any walls, so as malefactors may easily escape, and the Citty lyes uppon Lombardye where murthers are frequent, this Citty especially in the tyme of Carnovall is much subject to murthers, and like outrages. And so is the next Citty Padoa, upon priviledges of the university, whererby murther in schollars is punished only by banishment. And that the rather, because in the State of Venice (for the great Confluence of strangers) it is free for all men to weare Armes by the day, excepting Pistolls, which no man may have without the locks taken of, and also because they who have ill purposes, will adventure and use to weare these Armes by night also, I say for these reasons, murthers (especially in the libertine tyme of Carnovall) are frequent in this Citty, from which also the lesser Cittyes of that State are not free. Murther was punished by hanging till death, till Duke Michele Morosino[1] created in the yeare 1381, made a law that murtherers should be beheaded. But most comonly they escape by flight, and so are banished till they can make peace with the freinds of the murthered, and so obtayne liberty to retorne into their Country. Adulterers are punished (as other like Crymes) according to the Civill and Cannon lawes, but the Italians impatient to bring their honor under publique tryalls dispatch the punishment of all Jelousyes by private revenge killing not only the men so provoking them, but their wives sisters or daughters dishonouring themselves in those kindes. Yea brothers knowing their sisters to be unchast when they are maryed, and out of their owne house, yet will make this offence knowne to their husbands, that they may kill them. Whereof Examples are frequent, as namely of a Florentine gentleman, who understanding from his wives brother that she had dishonoured them by adulterye, tooke her forth in a Coache having only a Preist with them, and when they came to a fitt place gave her a short tyme to confesse her sinnes to the Preist, and then killed her with his own hands. And howsoever in this Case, it is like she confessed the Cryme, yet in this and like Cases the Magistrate useth not to inquire after these revenges, which the Italians nature hath drawne into Custome, besides that many are done secretly without danger to be revealed.

Among other high Crymes it is not rare to heare blasphemous speeches in Italy, and the State of Venice is much to be praysed for the most severe Justice they use against such offendors, having a lawe to cut out their tongues. Yea while I lived there, some roaring boyes[2] one night went out uppon a wager who should do the greatest villany, and when

---

[1] Michele Morosini (1308–82) was briefly Doge in 1382 (10 June–16 October). He died of the plague and was buried in *Santi Giovanni e Paolo. Andrea Contarini was Doge from 1367 until 1382. The fact that Moryson attributes this order to 1381 confirms that he was working from Lewkenor's translation of Contarini which also mistakenly states 1381 (not 1382) as the date.

[2] *roaring boyes*: men or boys given to riotous or drunken behaviour; first recorded usage in *OED* dates from 1611.

they had done most wicked things, at last they came all to the windowe of the Popes Nuntio, where they song horrible blasphemyes against our lord, his blessed mother, and the Apostle St. Peter. The next morning all these Rascalls (so I call them, whereof most notwithstanding were gentlemen) had escaped out of the Citty, only two were taken whome I did see executed in this manner, their hands were cutt of in fower places where they did the greatest villanyes, their tongues were cutt out under the windowe of the Popes Nuntio, and so they were brought into the markett place of St. Marke, where uppon a Scaffold they were beheaded with an axe falling by a Pully, which done the scafford and their bodyes were burnt, and the Ashes throwne into the Sea.

[*margin*: **Civill Judgments. in the State of Venice.**] For Civill Judgments I remember a stone at Paduoa called lapis turpitudinis (that is the stone of filthines because uppon markett dayes such were sett uppon it with naked backsydes, as had runn into debt having no meanes to repay it. The lawes of Venice in general were reputed so just by the Senate of Nurenberg in Germany as in the yeare 1508, by Ambassadors sent to this State they obteyned a Copy of them. Among other Civill Judgments they give singular Justice in the Cases of debt and have particular Judges over Marchants banckrowting, who give the Creditors security to keepe them from prison, and cite such banckrowtes as fly,[1] selling their goods and dividing them equally among the Creditors and preventing all fraudes may be used. So as if they finde other mens goods deposited in their hands they keepe them for the Owners. In which Case myself when I passed from thence into Turkye, and also my brother leaving our Chests with our apparell & bookes in the hands of a marchant, who shortly after proved banckrowte, the magistrate kept our goods safe, and when I returned, did restore to me without any Charge, not only my owne goods, but also my brothers who dyed in the Journey.

I have formerly sayd that all the Venetian lawes are made in the Counsell called Pregadi, for when any Magistrate judgeth it profitable for the Comon wealth to have any new lawe made for any thing concerning his office and Charge, he propounds his reasons in the Colledge of the Savii, and they being there approved, the lawe is propounded, enacted, and published by the Councell di Pregadi. So the Magistrate of the Pomps (or Ceremonies) caused certaine sumptuary Lawes for diett and apparell to be made in this Councell which are in force to this day. Yet sometimes the law is made in the Great Counsell, if the magistrate thinke that it will receive more life and force by being confirmed therein. So the Censors in the last age past desiring a lawe should be made against making any Congratulations with any man that had obteyned an Office or magistracye, the same was first approved in the Counsell of Pregadi, and then with general Consent confirmed in the great Counsell.

[f. 590] **Of the Italyans Nature and Manners, Bodyes and Witts**[2] At Venice the tribute to the State from Cortizans was thought to exceede three hundredth thousand Crownes yearely … . In Venice they are free to dwell in any house they can hyre, and in any streete whatsoever, and to weare what they list. In generall, they are courted and honered of all men, so as Princes in their owne Cittyes disdayne not to visite them privately, to salute

---

[1] *fly*: worthless.
[2] Corpus Christi MS, 'Booke V of Italy Touching nature &c Chapt. I.', f. 590; Moryson, *Shakespeare's Europe*, ed. Hughes, pp. 411–13; Kew, 'Shakespeare's Europe Revisited', IV, pp. 1520–21.

them passing in the streetes, and in the tyme of Carnovall publikely to grace them by flinging egs filled with rosewater at their windowes, where they stand to be seene … . Each Cortizan hath Commonly her lover whome she mantaynes, her Balordo or Gull[1] who principally mantaynes her, besides her Customers at large, and her Bravo to fight her quarrells. If any Cortizan have a Chylde, the father takes the males, but shee keepes the females to mantayne her when shee is olde, for such dwell with and under their mothers. The richer sorte dwell in fayre hired howses, and have their owne servants, but the Common sorte lodge with Baudes called Ruffians, to whome in Venice they pay of their gayne the fifth parte, as four Solz in twenty, paying besydes for their beds, linnen, and feasting, and when they are past gayning much, they are turned out to beg or turne baudes or servants. And for the reliefe of this misery, they have Nonneryes, where many of them are admitted, and called the converted sisters. Both honest and dishonest wemen are Lisciate fin' alla fossa, that is paynted to the very grave. The Italyans love fatt and tall wemen, and for those causes the Venetian wemen are sayd to be Belle di bellito, bianche di calcine, grasse di straccie, alte di legni o zoccole, that is fayre with paynting, white with chalke, fatt with raggs (or stuffed linnen) and high with wood or Pantofles (which many weare a foote or more deepe).

[f. 595] [*margin*: **Bodies and Witts**][2] Touching the Italians bodyes, they are generally of person tall, and leane, and of a browne and pale complection. Only many of the Venetians bordering upon the Germans (the marchants and gentlemen wherof have frequent and great concurse and abode in that Citty), and being borne at the foote of the Alpes, and in the midest of litle lakes made by the Sea (the inhabitants of which mountaynes and borders of the Sea are commonly noted to be more fayre then others) are not so pale as other Italyans, but for great parte of a more sanguine complexion.

…

[f. 597] [*margin*: **Artes sciences Universityes Language**][3]
The Italians, and espetially the Venetians, excell in the Art of setting Jewells, and making Cabinetts, tables and mountaynes,[4] of Christall, corall, Jasper, and other precious stones, and curious worke of Carving. The Italians, and espetially the Venetians excell in making lutes, Organs, and orther Instruments of musicke.

…

[f. 598] And as Italy hath yealded many rare worke men in these Artes of paynting, Carving in stone and brasse, Architecture, setting of Jewells composing these Cabinetts tables and Mountaynes and makeing of Instruments so the Princes and States of Italy are Curious in gathering and preserving the rare peeces of these workemen, but espetially the Venetians, which Citty aboundes with infinite rare Monuments of these kyndes, aswell in publike Pallaces and Churches, as in the private houses of gentlemen, who for Curtesy, or their owne glory, are as willing to shewe them to strangers, as they can be to see them … the Art of weaving silke, wherein the Italyans excell, but espetially the Venetians and Florintines,

---

[1] *Balordo or Gull*: fool or simpleton.

[2] Corpus Christi MS, 'Booke V of Italy Touching nature &c Chapt. I.', f. 595; Moryson, *Shakespeare's Europe*, ed. Hughes, p. 418; Kew, 'Shakespeare's Europe Revisited', IV, pp. 1533–4.

[3] Corpus Christi MS, 'Booke V of Italy Touching nature &c Chapt. I.', ff. 597–599; Moryson, *Shakespeare's Europe*, ed. Hughes, pp. 422–3; Kew, 'Shakespeare's Europe Revisited', IV, pp. 1540–43.

[4] *mountaynes*: mountings.

with whome most of the exiled men lived, and the Florintines also learned of them the Art of making flowers & curious workes like Imbroderies upon silke stuffes, wherein to this day they are most skillfull. The Venetians make the best Treakell,[1] which is transported throughout all Europe, and about the first of November, at which tyme they make it, those Artizans have a Feast, wherein they weare feathers, and have Trumpitts continually sounding, and during the tyme of this worke all the shops about Rialto resounde with the blowing thereof ... [f. 599] To which Studyes I will add the Art of musick, wherein the Italians, and espetially the Venetians, have in all tymes excelled, and most excel at this day, not in light tunnes and hard striking of the stringes, (which they dislike), nor in companies of wandering fidlers, (wherof they have none or very fewe single men of small skill) but in Consortes of grave solemne Musicke, sometymes running so sweetely with softe touching of the stringes, as may seeme to ravish to hearers spiritt from his body, which musike they use at many private and publike meetings, but espetially in their churches, where they joyne with it winde Instruments, and most pleasant voyces of boyes and men, being indeede such excellent Musicke as cannot but stirr up devotion in the hearers.

...

## [f. 609] [*margin*: Ceremonyes Maryages Childbearinges Christninges Funeralls and divers Customes.][2]

...

[f. 612] The Ceremonyes of State and Processions of Religion in the Citty of Venice, are frequent and performed with great pompe, in both which they passe all States not only of Italy, but of the whole worlde (if you except the Popes carying on mens shoulders and his like Adorations, which never any other Potentate by Civill or spirituall power assumed to himselfe, no not the Persion Emperours, more famous for pryde then all other vices and vertues). First for pompes of State, the Duke and the Signory have of old by divers lawes and at divers tymes Instituted publike[3] Andate in Trionfo, that is walkes in triumph, some in memory of victoryes obtayned, or publike dangers escaped, or of publike benefactours, some for rites of the Church, and divers devotians, and some by vowes.[4] They are called walkes, because they are performed on foote by land, and in the triumpfall Barke (called Bucentoro as Capable of 200. Men) when they must passe by water, never riding on horse backe, since the Citty being buylt within lakes upon litle Ilands, distant on all sydes some foure or five myles from firme land, the Importing of horses is troublesome, besides that the streetes are very narrow, so as since the Citty grewe populous and fully built, it is a rare thinge to see a horse brought thether. In these walkes first 8. standers[5] are carryed, then followes six silver Trompitts, then march two by two the Dukes officers, whome the Romans called Cryers, being all 50. in number, attyred in Turchine gownes,[6] with the Cognizance of St. Marke in mettall upon one sleeve, and

---

[1] *Treakell*: Venice treacle, or *Theriaca andromachi*, an electuary containing 64 ingredients used mostly as an antidote to poison. (*OED*, s.v. *treacle*, 1.a. and *Venice*, b.).

[2] Corpus Christi MS, 'Booke V of Italy Touching nature &c Chapt. I.', ff. 609–629; Moryson, *Shakespeare's Europe*, ed. Hughes, pp. 440–62; Kew, 'Shakespeare's Europe Revisited', IV, pp. 1573–614.

[3] *publike*: written 'puplike'.

[4] Much of this section seems to have been derived from Moryson's reading of Sansovino.

[5] *standers*: standards.

[6] *Turchine gownes*: gowns made with dark blue or azure (*turkin*) cloth.

Red Caps upon their heades. Then follow the waytes[1] of the Citty, and the Drumms, attyred in Red, sounding and beating all the way. Then followe the Dukes sheilde bearers two by two, attyred in gownes of black vellvett, then another officer of the Duke bearing in his hand a taper of white wax in a Silver Candlesticke, with six Chanons[2] following and three parish Priests. Then follow the Dukes Castaldi,[3] then the Secretaryes (and the Dukes Chaplayne) attired in Robes of Crimson Vellvitt, then the Dukes two Chancelours, then the great Chan[c]elour of the State, attyred in Crimson with larg ducall sleeves. Then follow two sheilde bearers, the one on the right hand carrying the Dukes Seate, the other on the left hand [f. 613] Carying the Dukes Cushion of Cloth of gold. Then follows the Duke in his Robes, with an hoode of powdred Ermines upon his shoulders, a Scudiero[4] carying his umbrella betweene him and the sunne, and two men beareing up the trayne of his Robe, and upon each syde of the Duke march the legate and Ambassadors, of the Pope, Kings, and Princes. Next after the Duke Followes a gentle man, carying the Dukes Ensigne of State, then the Dukes six Counselors, then the Procuratours of St. Marke two by two, then the three heades of the Counsell of forty, then the three heades of the Counsell of tenne, then the Cusors.[5] And after these Magistrates, followe .60. of the cheefe Senatours, and [60] inferiour (whose turne it is from six to six moneth to attend the Prince in these publike walkes of triumph). These Walkes in triumph are yearely tenn in number. The first is to the Church of our lady Maria Formosa,[6] upon the evening of the Purification of our lady, which feast falls yearely on the second of February. And it was instituted upon this occasion. The Cittizens of old were wont to espouse their virgines, and to pay their dowryes before the Bishop in the Church of St. Peter, upon 31th of January yearely, which Pyratts knowing and hiding themselves in that Iland in the year 943. came Armed upon them, and having killed many, tooke away the spouses, and the dowryes; but the Artizans espetially of this St. Maryes Parish, upon the outcrye taking Armes, and following them in Barques, overtooke them the same day while they were deviding the spoyle, and defeating them, recovered the Virgins and dowryes, for which service being required to demaund what recompence they would have, they required nothing but the establishing by a lawe of this walke in the foresayd triumph, to their said parish Church, at the sayd Feast of our lady yearely, bynding themselves to send to the Duke two hatts for feare it should rayne that day, and to give him and his Company two Flagons of Malmsye to drincke. The second walke is to the Church of St. Zachary[7] upon Easter day, instituted upon holy reliques and great Pardens of sinne sent and graunted by Pope Benidicke the third,[8] to all that should visite the sayd reliques deposed in that Church upon the sayd day. The third walke is upon the 8.th day after Easter, to the Church of St. Geminiano[9] Instituted in memory of a Duke inlarging that part of the markett place of St. Marke or upon pennance imposed by a

---

[1] *waytes*: a small group of wind instrumentalists, maintained at the city's expense.
[2] *Chanons*: canons.
[3] *Castaldi*: stewards or financial managers.
[4] *Scudiero*: squire.
[5] *Cusors*: *cursore*, runner or messenger. Hughes (p. 442) mistakenly transcribes as 'Censors'.
[6] *Santa Maria Formosa.
[7] *San Zaccaria.
[8] Benedict III, Pope 855–8.
[9] *San Geminiano.

349

Pope. The Fourth walke is to the Church of St. Marke[1] upon the 25th of Aprill, the Feast day of that Saynt. whose body being brought to Venice in the moneth of January in the yeare 828, this Church was built where the Church of Saynt Theodor stoode, who till that tyme was the Tutelar Saynt of the State, but now the Senate ordayned St. Marke to be the Protector [f. 614] thereof, and his new built Church to be the Dukes golden Chappell, where the sayde Feast is yearely solemnized, as the greatest of all the rest, and in greatest triumph, the Duke that day Feasting the Senate with great magnificence. The fifth walke is to the two Castles, instituted upon this occasion. Pope Alexander the third[2] chased from Rome by the German Emperour Frederick (nicknamed Barbarossa) after he had lived unregarded in Fraunce, came to Venice about the yeare 1176, and there lived disguised in the habitt of a poore Priest, till he was knowne by a French man, who had seene him in Fraunce, and made him knowne to the Duke and State of Venice, whereupon they came to adore the Pope, and attyre him in Pontificall Robes, and mantayned and supported him for Pope, which caused the Emperour to send his sonne Otho to make warr upon the Venetians by Sea, whome they overcame in a navall fight, and tooke Otho himselfe prisoner, by which accident the Emperour was induced to make peace with Alexander the third, and come to Venice there to Acknowledge and adore him for Pope. Nowe this Pope in thanckfullnes, gave to the Duke and State an hallowed taper of white wax (which useth to be lighted when the Pope himselfe sings Masse) and also a sworde hallowed, and eight Banners of divers Collers, and six silver Trumpitts all to be caryed before the Duke (as I have formerly shewed) in all his pompes of triumph. And because the Venetians obtayned the sayd victory against Otho upon the Ascension daye, the Pope confirmed to that State as wone by sword, the absolute Commande of that Sea, nowe called the Gulfe of Venice, giving the Duke a gold ringe, with which he should espouse the Sea to that State yearely upon the Ascension day,[3] the Senate then by lawe establishing this yearely Walke, which is the greatest solemnity of the yeare, concurring with a great fayer yearely, lasting 15. Dayes, and with a perpetuall Indulgence or Pardon from the Pope, beginning in the Church of St. marke upon Ascension even. Thus the Duke yearely upon the Ascension day marcheth in the foresaid Pompe from his publike Pallace to the great Channell, and at a bridge neere the Arsenall, he with his trayne enters the Ducall Barque called Bucentoro[4] (as Conteyning two hundredth persons, which is a litle Gally rowed with oares, having a large Chamber built over it of wood, with seates rounde about it, all guilded, and for the tyme adorned with rich hangings within, and rich Carpetts, within and without, beside the sayd Banners, Silver trompitts, and other ensignes of State) having two smale Gallyes going before to tow[5] it on if perhaps the Sea or wynde be contrary, and being attended [f. 615] by the exquisite musicke of St. Marke, and with a strange number [of] Gondole wherein the Cittizens and strangers passe to see the pompe, which being thus sett forwarde, the Patriarke meetes the Duke in the midd way, and fastening his Barque to the Bucentoro, they passe to the two Castles, the Patriarke presenting to the Duke and Senatours three silver Basons full of most sweete and rare flowers, and when they come a little beyonde the Castles, the

---

[1] *San Marco.
[2] Pope Alexander III and Frederick Barbarossa. See p. 300.
[3] *Marriage of the Sea (**Plate 11**).
[4] *Bucentaur.
[5] *tow*: written 'towo'.

Duke casts a golde ringe into the Sea, saying wee espowse thee as a signe of our perpetuall dominion over thee, as the husband hath over the wife, or in like wordes to that purpose, according to the sayd Popes institution. Then the Patriarke blesseth the Sea against Shipwrackes, and to be as a Churchyearde hallowed to the bodyes dying therein. And so the Duke retornes to the two Castles, and dismounting heares masse at the Church of St. Nicolas,[1] which done he retornes in like manner to his Pallace, where the Senatours of that trayne dyne with him. The sixth walke is to the Church of St. Vito,[2] upon the .15.th of June, in memory of the States liberty preserved in the yeare 1310, upon the 15th day of June, from the usurping tyranny of Baiamonto Tiepoli,[3] a rich ambitious Cittyzen, the pompe whereof is the greater because it is accompanyed with a solemne Procession of Religion. And in generall the pompe of these Processions consists in Companyes of Prists and Fryers of Religious orders, carrying with them the Crosse and banners of the Images of Saynts, and singing all the way they march, as likewise, in the Attendance of the bretheren of the Schooles, espetially of the six great Schooles, marching in like sorte with their banners and Images. And these Schooles are Fraternityes of gentlemen and cheefe Cittizens, united in one body, and each having their schoole or hall or Pallace proper to them, and not only inriched with lybraryes and precious antiquities, but of old endowed with lands of great yearely Revennues, beside their treasure, daly increasing by legacyes, which the dying bretheren give in their last wills and testaments, all which they imploy in workes of piety and pittye, as in the adorning of Alters, and in freely giving dowryes to poore Virgins (with great magnificence) and in like workes.

The seventh walke is to the Church of St. Marina[4] upon the 17th of July, the feast of that Saynt, instituted to heare masse and give thanckes because on that day and by medeation of that Saynt, they [f. 616][5] recovered Padoa and all their State of firme land, which they had utterly lost by the league of Cambray, (which Pope Julio the second made with the Emperour Maximilian and the King of Fraunce, all Combyned against the State of Venice).

The eighth walke in triumph, is to the Church of our Redeemer,[6] upon the third Sunday in July, instituted in the yeare 1576, when the Citty, being wasted by a fearce pestilence, upon a vowe[7] made by the whole Senate to our Redeemer, was by his goodnes in shorte tyme cleared from this mortall infection, and so this yearely walke was established by lawe for devotion of theire thanckfullnes.

The nynth walke in Triumph, is to the Church of S[ta] Giustina,[8] upon the viith of October the Feast day of that Saynt, and this walke was Instituted by a lawe in the year 1571, for memory of the famous navall victory obtained at that tyme by the Combyned navall

---

[1] *San Nicolò di Lido.

[2] *San Vidal (Vitale).

[3] Bajamonte Tiepolo (d. after 1329), Venetian nobleman who organized an unsuccessful conspiracy on 15 June 1310, the Feast of St Vitus, to overthrow the doge and Council of Venice. He was exiled to Istria and this plot led to the formation of the Council of Ten.

[4] *Santa Marina.

[5] Mispaginated as 'f. 615' by Moryson.

[6] *Redentore.

[7] *vowe*: written 'wowe'.

[8] *Santa Giustina.

forces of the Venetians the Pope and the king of Spayne against the great Turkes powerfull Navye, and to give yearely thanckes to God for the same victory, given them at the intercession of S^ta Giustina.

The tenth and the last walke in Triumph, is to the Church of St. George the greater,[1] on Christmas day after dinner to heare Vesper, and the next morning being the day of St. Stephen to heare masse, instituted some say in the year 1109, others say, 1179, some say in memory of St. Stephens body then brought upon that day to the Citty, others say in memory of a Duke who then left to the State by his last will and testament the inheritance of Certayne landes lying in the same Iland of St. George.

The Duke hath also two walkes in Triumph, but only on the evenings of feasts not on the feasts dayes, both to St. Markes Church, one upon the evening of his feast, the other on the evening of the ascension day.

Also the Duke hath many other walkes but not in Triumph, (that is without the foresayde Pompe and trayne) because most of them are to the Church of St. marke joyning close to the publike Pallice in which the Duke resydes. And hereof foure are principall, as instituted by the Senate.

The first is to our ladyes Church[2] upon our ladyes feast day in march, instituted because the first foundation of the Citty was layde as upon that day of the yeare, when the Goathes came first into Italy.

The second is upon the feast day of St. Isidor[3] being the 16th of Aprill, in the Chappell of that St. within the Church of St. Marke, instituted by the Senate in memory of a Duke executed for conspiring against the liberty of the State in the yeare 1348,[4] [f. 617] wherein the Duke is accompanied with a Religious Procession, of the Clergy, the orders of Fryers, and the foresayd Schooles, and .12. lighted tapers are caryed in memory of that Dukes Funerall. And because the Duke and the Procession passe betweene two marble pillers wanting only timber layd across to make a payre of Gallowes, it is also thought a remembrance to the present Duke, to Contayne himselfe within the boundes of his limited dignity.

The third is to the Church of St. Marke upon the feast of Corpus Domini on the 20th of June. This feast was instituted first by Pope Urban the 4th, in the yeare 1264. upon a Miracle at Bolsena, where a Priest having Consecrated the hostia, and doubting still that it was not the body of Christ, the same shedd forth much blood (if you will beleeve a lye, or at least a lying miracle) and this walke was instituted at Venice in the year 1407, with a Procession as aforesayde, but with greater pompe, the Patriark singing Masse and after carying in Procession the hostia within a Tabernacle, and the Priests weareing their richest vestments, and all men their best attyre, besydes that much plate and many Reliques are caryed about in that Procession, performed as they say with much humility, but it may better be sayd with grosse Idolatry. And of old on this day a Gally was appointed for transporting Pilgrims to Jerusalem, and each Senatour tooke a Pilgrime to

[1] *San Giorgio Maggiore.
[2] Probably *Santa Maria della Carità.
[3] St. Isidore of Seville (c.556–636).
[4] Doge Marin Falier was executed in April 1355.

walke with him in the sayd Procession, but at this day fewe Pilgrimes passing, the sayd Gally is no more provided for them.

The fourth walke without Triumph, is to the Church of St. Marke the 25 of June, Instituted by the Senate in the yeare 1094, upon this occasion. The body of St. marke being of old deposed in this Church, and all memory being lost of the place where it was layd, the Duke and the Senate in the sayde yeare moved by devotion and greefe, required the Patriark that upon the sayde day he would publish a solemne Fast and devote Procession, to pray unto God that he would reveale the place where the blessed Evangelists body was layd, which donne, after the singing of the Masse and publike prayers, the Marbles of a Pillar, in the sight of the Duke and Senatours, Clave asunder, and St. Markes Coffin by litle and litle thrusting out it selfe, at last appeared playnely to the vewe of all the people. It is worth the marking, that in the former ages when the Reliques of dead Saynts were not worshipped, all memory was lost where the bodye of St. Marke was layde, and that this Miracle is written to fall at the tyme when the blynd Ignorance and superstitious devotion to the Roman Religion was highly increased in the Westerne Church.

Moreover the Duke with the Senate makes some .22. publike walkes without Triumph to the Church of St. [f. 618] Marke, whereof that upon Christmas Even is the most solemne, when the Vesper is song with most exquisite musicke both of Instruments and voyses, and also a Masse is song before midnight by old privilege from the Bishops of Rome, for otherwise Masses are not sayd but in the morning and by Priests who are fasting and have not yet either eaten or druncke. And it is most strange to see the Church so full of lights both within and without, from the topp to the botome, as a man would thincke it all on fyer. For they have 1500. small lights, each of a pounde weight, and .60. great lights each of 12. pounds weight, and all these are of wax as white as snowe, the yellowe being not esteemed by them, besides all the ordinary lampes burning, and the waxlights and torches upon the high Alter, and the great number of torches caryed before the Duke and Senatours when they goe from the Church. Nether is it lesse strange to see all these Candles and torches lighted in a moment by foure men at the foure corners of a Crosse, giving light to flax, which conveyeth light by lynes to all the said candles and torches. At which tyme also they have a most solemne Procession with the assistance of the foresayd schooles, Fryers of Religious orders, and parish Priests. And by the way note, that these Priests are to this day chosen by the lay Parishioners, having howses and landes in the Parish, and are only confirmed by the Patriarke of Venice.

The State of Venice useth also great pompe in publike Feasts, some common to the whole Citty, some peculiar to Familyes and Parishes, Some are yearely. As when of olde they defeated and tooke prisonour the Patriarke of Aqualegia,[1] the Senate Instituted by lawe and upon great penalty the yearely feast of Fatt Thursday (being called Giovedi grasso vulgarly, and falling on the thursday before lent). And upon that day the Duke and the Senators sitt in a gallery of the publike Pallice lying uppon the market place of St. Marke, in which a Bull is killed before them, by cutting off his head at one blowe, with a two handed sworde made very sharpe and heavy for that purpose. This done of old they had

---

[1] The Venice Carnival reputedly marked the victory in 1162 of the Republic over Ulrico di Treven (d. 1181), Patriarch of Aquileia (an episcopal see in north-eastern Italy, centred on the city of Aquileia).

*l'giouedi grasso p memoria di certa uittoria ouenuta d.la Rep.ca nel friuli si fa pub.ca festa nella piazza di S.m.co doue'assiste' il Doge et la Sig.ria p non derrogare all'atica istitu[tion]e*

*Giacomo Franco Forma con Priuilegio*

Figure 34.   Giacomo Franco, *La Città di Venetia* (1614). Revelries in Piazza San Marco on 'Giovedì Grasso' ('Fat Thursday'), the last Thursday before Lent. By permission of Special Collections, Brotherton Library, University of Leeds.

a Castle of wood built in a large Chamber of the Pallace, which the Senatours Armed with tronchions did assault and take, but this Ceremony in after ages seeming ridiculous boyes play, hath long beene out of use. Also they used of olde to kill 12. Porkes, and send peeces therof to the Senatours; but this Ceremony also hath long time beene out of use. But to this day they tye Bulls in Ropes helde by men, chasing them through the streetes, which being very narrowe they Cry Guarda il toro, that is [f. 619] take heede of the Bull, lest any passenger[1] whould be gorded by them. Allways understande that the feastes are Celebrated more with outwarde pompe and Ceremony then with larg provisions and proportions of wyne and meate. Some Feasts are Casuall. And thus the State hath many tymes stately intertayned Popes, Kinges, and Princes. Of which kynde the intertaynment of the French king Henry the thirde in the year 1574,[2] is most fresh in memorye and was performed with great pompe and publike expence, when this King retorned that way from Poland into Fraunce, assoone as he came to the Confynes of this State, he was daly mett and attended by the governours of the places wher he passed, and by the troopes of horse and foote Companyes on the firme land, and daly saluted for his welcome by vollyes of small shott, and from all Forts and Castles by peales of great Ordinnance, When he came to the water syde, he was mett by many Senatours coming with great Nomber of Gondole or small boates, which use to be covered with blacke Cloth, but were then richly covered with Cloath of golde and Imbrotheryes,[3] espetially those brought for the king and his trayne. Thus passing, before he came to the Citty he was mett with a guarde of Soldyers in boates, and many young gentlemen of the greatest familyes sent to attend his person, and was saluted with peales of great Ordinance from divers Castles and from many Gallyes and Shipps lying in the Porte. And so he passed with loude soundes of Drumms and trumpitts to the Pallace of Foscarini where he was ledged, b[e]cause it had a fayre prospect both wayes upon the great Channell. Daily he was attended by Senatours and the Duke with the Bucintoro, to invite & conduct him to Banquitts, wherein he was intertayned with some French liberty. For one day at a banquitt in the great Chamber, where the generall Counsell of the Duke['s] Senatours and gentlemen useth to assemble, tw[o] hundredth forty virgins were invited to attend the king, who satt all on one syde, all attyred in white with rich Jewells. The king entring and drawing neere to them bareheaded, they all rose, and as he passed and saluted them, they made lowe Reverence to him, and after the banquitt and tables removed, the Frenchmen and other gentlemen tooke them all to daunse the measures, and after dauncing of some Gallyardes, all departed, the Duke and Senatours in the Bucintoro conducting [f. 620] and attending the king to the Pallace where he lodged. Also the king was conducted to see all the rare things in the City, and intertayned with divers other pastymes, as tw[o] partyes one keeping the other assayling bridges, built within sight of his lodging, which sporte they often use at other tymes with no other weapons then Armes and fists, and sometimes fall from Jeast to earnest, at dry blowes, and flinging one another into the water.[4] In like sorte the king was attended and feasted at his departure till he came to the Confynes of that

---

[1] *passenger*: passer-by (*OED*, s.v. *passenger*, 3.a).

[2] See pp. 207 and 209–10.

[3] *Imbrotheryes*: embroideries.

[4] These fights took place on several bridges, the most famous being Ponte dei Pugni (Bridge of Fists) near Campo San Barnaba, Dorsoduro *sestiere*. It has four footsteps marked in white marble, commemorating the traditional fights between rival factions which took place on it when it did not have a parapet.

State lying towardes Franch, with great magnificence and expence of that State, in testimony of love to France.

[*margin*: **Maryages**] They keepe also soleme Feasts at the maryage of the Duke, which seldome happens, by reason they are olde before they are chosen, but the Duchesse is allwayes Crowned with great solemnity and feasting. At which tyme (as also at the Maryages betweene persons of great familyes) Tylting and like military exercises are proclaimed for many dayes, and to them whome the Judges thincke to have best deserved therin, the cheefe prise Commonly is some rich peece of Cloath or stuffe, with like honorable guifts allotted by the Senate or by the Patrons of the feast.

[*margin*: **Ceremonyes in Generall**] Gentlewemen and others most commonly goe leaning with one hand upon olde wemens shoulders, and the reason why they goe thus Ledd or leaning, is because they weare high Startops or Pantofills[1] of wood, so as they cannot goe without helpe.

[*margin*: **Maryages**] Touching Ceremonyes of maryages. howsoever I have sayd that in Venice persons of great Familyes are marryed with Feasts and tiltings, yet generally the Italians are Jelious, and delight not to shewe the beauty of their brydes. Of olde in the Provinces of the State of Venice, historyes write that they were wont to mary their virgins at the outcrye, namely to him that would give most for them, and by the mony given for the fairest, raysed dowryes for them that were ill favoured, and so deformed as they founde none would give mony for them. After the Citty of Venice was built, and the Cittizens [f. 621] became Christians. I have formerly shewed (upon the first walke of the Duke and the Senate in triumph to the Church of St. mary the faire,[2] instituted in the year .943.) that the virgins upon 31 of January came all to the Church of St. Peter, each bringing her dowry in a portable box (for in those ages the dowryes were small) where the Patriarke after the masse made a Sermon of maryage, which donne and the Patriarkes blessing given to the maryed, the young men there attending with their Parents and neerest kinsmen, tooke the virgins they liked with their dowryes, and caryed them to their houses. In latter ages the maryages of the gentry are concluded betweene the parents before the Virgin is once seene by her husband, then they are brought into the Court of the publike Pallace, where in the presence of many Senatours and gentlemen, the Parents publish the affinity, and the young Cuple having touched handes together the Parents invite the guests against a day appointed, at which day the guests coming to the house of the virgins Parents, and being sett downe, the virgin is brought to them, with her hayre waving loose, but tyed in the Crowne with threds of golde, and being all attired in white, of old custome. There the words and Ceremonyes of the espowsall being performed, she is led about the roome with the sound of Drumms, Trumpitts, and other musicall Instruments, going in a Comely measure of daunsing, and often bending the body to the guests as shee passeth, and so being seene of them all, retyres into her Chamber. Then shee discendes agayne accompanied with many gentlewomen, and enters a Gondala where shee setting in a litle throne adorned, and the rest following her in other Gondale or boates, shee passeth by water to visite the Nunneryes where shee hath any kinswemen.

---

[1] *Startops or Pantofills*: startups were loose shoes made of leather and worn by rural people. The term pantofle was applied to various kinds of outdoor overshoes (rather than slippers).

[2] Probably *Santa Maria della Carità.

Then the feast is Celebrated with great joye, and plentifull provisions, but limited by the lawes according to the nomber of the guists, which many tymes and Commonly are some 100th persons. After few dayes the young maryed wemen visite the Bride. The Bridegrome and bride were wont to visitt the Duke, to make him wittnes of the maryage; but of late tymes that Custome is left, and the maryage with the Indentures of Contract is regestred in a publike office. Through all Italy in generall, the espowsall or betrothinge with the Ring, is made privately, the bride being never seene by the Bridsgrome before that day, and that performed, they lye together in bedd, and some dayes or monthes after at best leasure, the Parents and neerest kindred on both sydes meete together, and going to a masse in pompe, keepe that day among themselves the maryage feast in private manner and with no great expence.

[*margin*: **Childbearing.**] Touching Childebearing. In Venice, the Children of gentlemen, and the tymes of their birth, are registred [f. 622] in the foresayd publike office, in which maryages are regestred, and the howses of gentlewemen brought to bed, and espetially the Chambers wherein they lye, are richly sett forth with costly hangings, with Tables and Cabinetts of mother of pearle, and pearles and Jasper, and other precious stones, and with curious workes of Paynters, and Carving, in brasse, gold, and silver, and like Jewells, in which permanent riches the Italyans and espetially the Venetians greatly delight and abounde. And they were wont to make such large expence in confections to entertayne visitours, as the Senate hath beene forced by lawes to lymitt that excesse ... .

[*margin*: **Christninges**] Touching Christinings: The Citty of Venice differs from all other in Italy upon firme land, in some thinges. They were wont to spend excessively in confections, till that expence was restrayned by lawes. The gentlemen have not two godfathers as other where, but sometymes 150. And because that spirituall kindred (as they call it) hinders maryage in the Roman Church, the lawe forbids them to be gentlemen of venice, and the Priest when he powers water on the Childes head, is bounde to aske and looke that none of them be gentlemen of Venice. And these godfathers are at no charge of guifts, except some at pleasure will cast mony on the Alter for the Priest, but the Chyldes father presents each of them with a marchpane. And this Ceremony is done for boyes, no woman being present, but one that caryes the Chylde.

[*margin*: **Funeralls**] Touching Funeralls. When the Duke of Venice is dead, his body attyred in Ducall habitt is layd forth in a large publike roome of the publike Pallice, and 20. Senatours are chosen to attend and sett about the body in Scarlett Robes, for three dayes; after which he is buryed with solemnity. Assoone as he is dead, the vi Counselors (wherof the eldest is vice duke till another be chosen) and three heades of the Counsell of .40, enter the publike Pallace, and come no more forth till a newe Duke be chosen. At the Dukes death there is no more change in the State then if a private gentleman were dead, only in the Citty all lawe causes cease till a newe Duke be chosen, because the Judges are imployed in the buisines. After the Duke is buiryed, the great generall Counsell the first day chuseth five Counselours, and three Inquisitours to examine the life of the late Duke, and they are bounde to present all errours wherof to the great Counsell, which for great errours sometimes imposeth Fynes upon the hayres. Thus of late Duke loredan,[1] otherwise of singular goodnes and wisdome, being founde to have lived more sparingly

---

[1] Leonardo Loredan (Loredano) (1436–1521), Doge 1501–21 (**Frontispiece**).

then his dignity required, was by the great Counsell Fyned .1500. Ducates, which his hayres payd. The great Counsell upon the second day, after an Oration in prayse or disprayse of the late Duke, begins the Election of a new. In the Church of St. Marke none are buryed, but Cardinalls, the Popes legattes, Forayne Princes and the Generalls of the State for horse and foote, whose Funeralls are attended by the Duke and Senatours, and performed at the publike charge of the State. The evening before the buyriall, the body is brought into the Church, and layd under a Canopy, with many wax lightes burning about it, and so it lyes to be seene of all men till the next day at Vesper, when the service for the dead is songe, and then the body is carryed with a solemne procession, and after buryed. The Dukes are buryed in what churches themselves appoint, and the bodyes are caryed thether by night. In Venice ordinary Funeralls are performed with more Ceremony then upon firme land. The first day the body is layd foorth in the house till two howers within night, when the Priests and frendes of the dead attend the body to the Church, where it is sett downe with two lighted torches at the head, and two at the feete, and the next day the service for the dead is song, and the body carried in procession, [f. 624] and then layd in the grave. The Funerall is not counted honourable in Venice that costs not some 400. Ducates, and the pompe of the foresayd Procession takes up long way in the streetes, and is very great, tho the Duke and Senators be not allwayes present, in regard of the rich vestures, Crosses, and Banners of Images, which are Patron Saynts to the Clergy, the Fryers, and the fraternityes of Schooles. In the midst of this Funerall pompe, the dead body is carried by eight men, and the body is richly apparelled and covered with a Cloth of golde, and followed by the Children and kinsmen and servants of the dead person, all Mourning in black gownes with their heades covered. For the rest of the followers only those of the fraternity to which the dead person belongs, have their heads covered. The wemen mournors, as at venice so through all Italy, weare over their forehead a French bongrace Covered with black Cipres,[1] which also covers the head and hangs over the shoulders, and upon a blacke gowne they weare a peece of white Cloath, one or two handfulls broade, hanging about their neckes and so downe the forepartes to theire feete. As in Venice so through all Italy, they are not buryed in severall graves digged of purpose, as commonly with us, but in Caves or va[u]lts, either private to their Familyes, or common to the people. And they are buryed in their Apparrell, and have their faces open till the Cave be opened, at which tyme theire faces are covered with linen, and the bodyes are cast into the Cave, which is presently made up very close, because as some of the dead bodyes are consumed, so others are more or lesse rotten, as they have beene longer or latter buryed, from the stincke whereof they feare infection.

[*margin*: **Customes**] Touching divers Customes. I have formerly sayde that the Italians are proverbyally taxed with madnes [f. 625] twise in the yeare, namely of devotion in the tyme of lent (whereof I have allready spoken in the discourse of Religion) and of licentious life in the tyme of Carnvall from Christmas feast to Ashwensday (so called of biding farewell to flesh) aswell for eating flesh as for cannall[2] lusts with wemen (since then the old and most devoute leave or at least frequent not much the Company of Curtizans). This Carnavall is a most licentious tyme, wherein men and wemen walke the streetes in

---

[1] *bongrace*: projecting brim attached to the front of a bonnet or headdress, decorated with black cypress (henna-shrub) as a traditional symbol of mourning.

[2] *cannall*: carnal.

Companyes all the afternoones, and sometimes (espetially towardes the end of that tyme) also in the mornings, excepting only fryday in the after noone, having their faces masked, and the men in wemens, wemen in mens apparel at theire p[l]easure. And very matrons towardes the end of the tyme walke the streetes thus masked, but allwayes in wemens apparell and in the Compa[n]y of their husbands. They thus walke up and downe the markett places, and some companyes leade musicke with them and table to place some Instruments in the markett places, where they play excelent musicke. All this tyme, the Curtizans are so taken up as they must hyre them before hande who will have their Company to walke and feast with them. By day they that are masked may weare no weapon, espetially, no pockett weapons, which are forbidden at all tymes, and I remember at Venice a masked gentleman (for sporte as he thought) wearing a wooden sworde, was imprisoned and fyned for mocking the publike Justice. But in the nights of this tyme it is dangrous to walke the streetes, wherein Companyes of swaggerors walke armed, often committing murthers and horrible outrages. All this tyme many houses keepe publike meetinges for dansing, where all that are masked may freely enter, and dance with wemen there assembled and he that danseth at the ende of his danse payes the musitians in ordinary rate of small mony. Yea the very[1] houses of noblemen and gentlemen, upon occasions of meetings to danse with wemen and virgins of honor, are open for any masked persons to enter and beholde them.

[f. 626] The gentlemen seldome feasting one another, except it be upon rare occasions, and those rather particular to some fewe Familyes, then generall to all, as upon affinity contracted by maryage, yet to preserve love and acquaintance among them, daily have generall meetinges in the markett places, and private in gardens, and to the same ende, as also because in many Cittyes they are the cheefe marchants, they kepe the generall meetinges no lesse strictly, then the marchants of our partes keepe their daily meeteinges at the exchange, espetially at Venice, where the gentlemen daly meete, with the marchants, before noone at Rialto, where they stand by themselves, and towardes evening in the markett place of St. marke, where they walke together ... In Venice they may passe to all partes of the Citty by water in commodious boates, aswell as by land.

[f. 628] They are carefull to avoyde infection of the plague, and to that purpose in every Citty have magistrates for health. So as in tymes of danger when any Citty in or neere Italy is infected, travellers cannot passe by land, except they bring a bolletino or certificate of their health from the place whence they came, and otherwise must make la quarantana or tryall of forty dayes for their health, in a lazaretto or hospitall for that purpose. But by Sea generally both the men and all the goods of the shipp, except they can make cleare proofe of health in the partes whence they came, must make the sayd tryall of forty dayes, espetially Shipps comming from Constantinople which is seldome free from infection. And this they use not only for health, but as a mistery[2] of traffique, by which they knowe the quality of all marchants, and of all goodes, before they be admitted to Free traffique in the Cittyes ...

[f. 629] The Italians if they salute neerer, give a light touch in manner of imbracing, but the gentlemen of Venice salute one another with a kisse upon the cheeke. At Venice I

---

[1] *very*: written 'yery'.
[2] *mistery*: ministry or office.

observed that young virgins of the Nobility passing the streetes, and having their Faces covered with a vayle like a Nett, so as they might see and be seene tho not fully, gentlemen for a Curtesy would stop their way, standing still before them as amazed at their beauty, and they tooke pryde to decline asyde with a smyle and light blushing. In the Cittyes upon land the highest place is to goe next the wall, but in Venice most of the streetes are narrow for two to walke, and the kennells[1] are on each syde next the houses, and there the right hand is the highest place, as in larger streetes and Marketplaces raysed in the midst and declining to the kennels on each syde, the greatest man goes in the midst, and the next on the right hand, the third on the left hand of him who goes in the midst, and so for the rest, the right hand being still preferred to the left.

...

[f. 630] [*margin*: **Pastymes Exercises Hawkeing Hunting Fowling Birding and fishing.**][2]

...

[f. 631] In Venice and 25. Myles from the Citty, the lawe forbids dycing, and like games, upon great penaltyes, except it be in publike Innes or at Feasts of great maryages, or under the two great Pillers in the markett place of St. Marke, which pillers being erected by a lombard, the Senate, besides his rewarde in monye, graunted him this privilege for gamsters, to play freely and without penalty under the sayd Pillers. In the publike Inne kept by a German in Venice,[3] whether most strangers of the best quality resorte, I have seene young gentlemen of Italy play franckly with strangers at dyce, but generally in Italy this gamming is forbidden, in some places more strictly then others, and to be a Common gammster is disgracefull, nether are these games used in private houses to wast whole dayes and nights for pastyme, as in our partes.

[f. 633] And it was vulgarly sayde, that when they purposed to builde Tennice Courtes at Venice, the Curtizans paying much tribute made suite to the Contrary, lest it shoulde hinder their trading, which at Venice is insteede of all exercises. For if you call for a boate, and say you will goe a spasso that is for recreation, howsoever you meane to take the ayre upon the water, he will presently carry you to some Curtezans house, who will best pay him for bringing her Customers, as if there were no other recreation but only with wemen. The Venetians seldome or never come on horsbacke, and vulgar Jeasts are raysed on them for ignorance of ryding, as of one who would hyre one horse to carye as many as came with him in his boate, and of another who ready to take horse, asked how the wynde stoode, as thincking he could no more ride then sayle against the wynde, with many like Jeasts ... . At Venice for exercise and sporte the yong men assaul[t]e and defende bridges, and goe to Cuffes at first in Je[a]st, but often proving earnest, yet no further then hand blowes ... . The Venetians say, that in Histria parte of that State lying on the north syde of the Gulfe, [f. 634] The people are much delighted with Hawking, Hunting and Fishing, and that in the lakes neere the City, many delight to persue in

---

[1] *kennells*: gutters (*OED*).

[2] Corpus Christi MS, 'Booke V of Italy Touching nature &c Chapt. I.', ff. 630–634; Moryson, *Shakespeare's Europe*, ed. Hughes, pp. 464, 467–8; Kew, 'Shakespeare's Europe Revisited', IV, pp. 1617–25.

[3] Perhaps the inn of St George, also known as The Flute, close to the Germans' trading centre, the *Fondaco dei Tedeschi.

Per antico essercitio del popolo fu introdotto p decreto pub.co de l'inuerno si facesse p i ponti di Ven.a la
battagliola cobattendosi l'auantaggio del ponte co' legni et l'una delle parti si chiama Castellana et l'altra Nicolotta.

Giacomo Franco Forma con Priuilegio

Figure 35.    Giacomo Franco, *La Città di Venetia* (1614). La Battagliola ('The Battle of the Sticks'),
to secure the bridge between the inhabitants of Castellana and Nicolotta. By permission of Special
Collections, Brotherton Library, University of Leeds.

small boates a kynd of litle fish but delicate to eate, taken by hitting it with a little forked Instrument. They have litle or no Sea fowle, but only at Venice, and there in no great plenty.

[f. 664] [*margin*: **A general and brief discourse of the Jewes and Greekes.**][1]
...

[f. 665] In Italy likewise the Jewes live in no respect no not the most learned or richest of them, but in less contempt of the people, and the Princes who extort upon their own subjectes, doe also for gayne admitt the Jewes into their Cittyes, and permitt them to use horrible extortion upon their subjectes, in the lending of mony, and in selling or letting out by the day or weeke upon use both mens and wemens Apparrell and furnitures for horses, and all kyndes of Fripery wares. Thus at Venice they have a Court yearde closed with gates and capable of great Nombers, wherein they dwell.

[1] Corpus Christi MS, 'Booke V of the Jewes [touching] nature &c Chapt. VI.', ff. 664–665; Moryson, *Shakespeare's Europe*, ed. Hughes, pp. 464, 467–8; Kew, 'Shakespeare's Europe Revisited', IV, pp. 1703–6.

# 34.  1595 – HENRY PIERS

**Henry Piers (1567–1623)**, an Anglo-Irishman, was the son of English parents settled in Elizabethan Ireland and raised in the established church.[1] His soldier father, Captain William Piers, had settled during the mid-sixteenth century at Carrickfergus, north-east Ulster, and was Constable of the castle there.[2] From about 1580 the Piers family lived on the property of a dissolved monastery at Tristernagh, Co. Westmeath. As a youth Henry may have spent some time in England and, back in Ireland, he came under the influence of Christopher Nugent (1544–1602), fourteenth Baron Devlin, a prominent Catholic who had worked closely with the Lord Deputy of Ireland, Sir Henry Sidney, the father of Philip (**item 22**). It is likely that Piers first developed his attraction to the old faith through Devlin's influence. However, soon after Piers's return to Ireland, Devlin fell under suspicion during the Earl of Tyrone's rebellion and was arrested in 1600 on a charge of treason, dying in prison before his trial.

By about 1593 Henry had married Jane, daughter of Thomas Jones (1550–1619), who in 1584 became Church of Ireland Bishop of Meath and a committed anti-recusant. However, Piers's encounters with Catholic laymen, coupled with his doubts over the uniformity of the Protestant faith, prompted during the 1590s his desire to explore continental Catholicism. Piers's sister Mary had also married late in the previous decade an Anglo-Irish Catholic, Thomas Jans, the brother of James Jans (d. 1610), Mayor of Dublin (1593–94). Thomas's household at Dublin became a major centre for Catholicism, welcoming English recusants and returning Irish priests.

The Piers residence at Tristernagh, Brian Mac Cuarta explains, was 'a particularly remote and inaccessible location in the marches area beyond the Pale', which made it a suitable location for recusant visitors to Ireland to be housed. In 1595 a young Englishman from a staunchly Catholic Staffordshire family, Philip Draycott, came to Tristernagh as a servant. Having already studied at the recently founded (1593) English Jesuit College at St Omer in the Spanish Netherlands, Draycott was determined to travel to Rome to become a missionary priest. Draycott and Henry Piers resolved to travel to Rome together, almost certainly with the assistance of the Jans family.[3] This was a life-changing act of spiritual commitment for Piers because it meant leaving behind his wife,

---

[1] This Henry Piers should be distinguished from his namesake Henry Piers (Pierse) (d. 1638), a beneficiary of the Ulster Plantation who served as secretary to Arthur Chichester (1563–1625), 1st Baron Chichester, Lord Deputy of Ireland (1606–16).

[2] Lodge, *Peerage of Ireland*, 1789, II, p. 201, states that William Piers 'had earned the personal gratitude of Princess Elizabeth during her Catholic sister's reign, saving her 'from the rage and fury of her sister Q. Mary' by 'conveying her privately away'. In gratitude, Queen Elizabeth sent him to Ireland in 1566 with a 'considerable post in the army' and the 'grant of several lands of great value'.

[3] Before leaving Ireland Piers sold to James Jans the tithes in corn from several townlands in Westmeath, presumably as a means of financing his continental travels. Piers, *Travels*, ed. Mac Cuarta, p. 11.

family, crown employment as a seneschal (responsible for local defence levies and judicial duties) and even the potential inheritance of his father's estates. They left Dublin on 9 June and arrived at Rome, accompanied by some Italian gentlemen, on 25 September 1595, in clear transgression of 'war-time Elizabethan ordinances against travel to Rome and Spanish-held territories'.[1] During their journey from Dublin to crossing the English Channel, Draycott had posed as Piers's servant and then as his travelling companion when in Catholic territories abroad.

At Rome Piers converted to Catholicism, preceded by an appearance before the Inquisition because of his Anglo-Irish Protestant background and his father's military role in Ireland as a crown agent for over forty years. This procedure was predictable and justified for a new arrival at Rome since Piers could have been a heretic and spy for the English rather than a sincere convert to Catholicism. Soon exonerated of such suspicions, Piers was then drawn via his contacts with the English College at Rome – and especially through his growing friendship with an English priest, Richard Haddock (Haydock) SJ (c.1552–1605) – into the supportive network of English Jesuit exiles on the continent. It is worth noting, however, just how perilous a procedure Piers had undergone by appearing before the Inquisition. His leading inquisitor was Cardinal Domenico Pinelli (1541–1611) who, once satisfied with his sincerity, treated him with warm friendship and provided a letter of recommendation for his brother in Genoa. In contrast, Pinelli was also involved in the Inquisition's interrogation of the renowned Dominican friar, cosmologist and philosopher Giordano Bruno (1548–1600). Bruno was tried for heresy and, when found guilty, burned at the stake in Rome's Campo de' Fiori on 17 February 1600.

Piers's diary, 'A Discourse of HP His Travelles Written By Him Selfe' (Oxford, Bodleian Library, MS Rawlinson D. 83), was probably written sometime between 1604 and his death in 1623. It records his journey in 1595 from Dublin to Rome, via the Low Countries (avoiding France due to the Wars of Religion), Germany and northern Italy. He provides a detailed account of Rome during his time there (1595–7). He left Rome on 15 October 1597 in the company of some English priests returning to their homeland missions. He stayed briefly at the Holy House of Nazareth at Loreto (then the most important Marian shrine in the Catholic world) and went as far as Milan with his travelling companions. At Genoa he met up with a group of English seminarians who were on their way from Rome to Spain. On 22 November 1597 Piers set sail from Genoa with them and other nationals, arriving at Alicante on 11 December 1597 (with the cost of his passage paid for by Cardinal Pinelli). Passing through Valencia he was treated hospitably at the Jesuit College in Madrid and the English College in Valladolid where he stayed until 21 January 1598. On his return journey to Madrid he took the opportunity to visit the royal palace at Escorial and then left Madrid on 9 April for the English College at Seville where he enjoyed a prolonged stay. He left Cadiz on 28 November 1598 on a ship captained by Sebastian Fleming, a merchant from Drogheda. On boarding, he narrowly avoided arrest as an English spy (despite his Irish credentials) and the voyage back to Ireland, which included being pursued by Dunkirk pirates, took four weeks. He finally arrived back at Howth, near Dublin, on 28 December 1598.

[1] Piers, *Travels*, ed. Mac Cuarta, pp. 12–13.

Piers's account offers a rare, and probably unique, example of an Anglo-Irish Catholic, undertaking a primarily spiritual rather than educational, diplomatic or commercial journey, who visited Venice during the last years of Elizabeth's reign.[1] As his editor Brian Mac Cuarta SJ remarks, Piers's manuscript is not only an important account of a late-Elizabethan continental travel itinerary but also 'a Catholic conversion narrative'.[2] His account of Venice includes a description of its geographical situation, the Doge's Palace, St Mark's Basilica, the Arsenal, major churches and nearby islands. Elsewhere in his 'Discourse', Piers also refers to 'a booke called the antiquities and marvellous things of Rome written by Hierom Francis' (f. 162). This work was Girolamo Francini's *Le cose maravigliose dell'alma città di Roma*, one of the most popular guidebooks to Rome during the 1590s. Piers may have purchased his copy at Venice where it was printed in at least ten editions between 1588 and 1595.[3] He also included in his 'Discourse' a detailed account (ff. 121–133) of the Battle of Lepanto (7 October 1571) in which the combined Catholic naval forces of Venice, Spain and the Papacy defeated the Ottoman Sultan Suleiman II (**Plate 13**). He drew extensively on an account of the battle from a history published in London in late 1603, *The General History of the Turks* by Richard Knolles (late 1540s–1610). His account gave particular prominence to the Venetian Admiral Sebastiano Venier (*c.*1496–1578) – whom Piers names as 'Venerius'. In 1570 Venier was a Procurator of St Mark's and in December of the same year was appointed Capitano Generale da Mar of the Venetian fleet. In 1577 he was unanimously elected as Doge of Venice but died on 3 March 1578 soon after a major fire had destroyed several state rooms in the southern section of the Doge's Palace on 22 December 1577.

## Text

[f. 21] [*Lumbardy*] The first daye of September we passed by Preeso[4] here is one who dwellethe in a rock, *which* is in the side of a mightie montayne all the people of that house are cariede up som fortie fadoms in a baskett befor they com to there dwelling; [*The dukedom of Venis begineth at Basania*] and soe to the cittie Basania[5] by *which* runnethe the river Prente,[6] Basania standethe at the fotte of the Alpes, they are of all heights from two myles to xxtie [20] of Englishe measure. The seconde daie through the cittie of Castle francke[7] to mestris,[8] where dothe begine the Italliane miles *which* are skante soe great as the Englishe.

---

[1] The English Catholic priest, Gregory Martin (*c.*1542–82), compiled a detailed description of Rome from his residence there in 1576–8 but he did not visit Venice. Martin, *Roma Sancta*.

[2] Piers, *Travels*, ed. Mac Cuarta, p. 2.

[3] Alternatively, Piers may have acquired a copy of this guidebook at Rome or perhaps possessed a copy before entering Italy.

[4] Piers travelled on the usual route from Trento to Bassano del Grappa but the location of his 'Preeso' is uncertain since much of this route passes through mountainous areas. 'Preeso' perhaps may be a mishearing of Treviso but, if so, Piers would have passed through Treviso after Bassano del Grappa.

[5] Bassano del Grappa.

[6] River Brenta.

[7] Castelfranco Veneto.

[8] Mestre.

[*Venis the ritche*] The theerde ~~daye~~ to the famous and renowned cittie of Venis, which for the situation beinge in the sea, The ritches and stately buildinge thereof is the myrror of the whole worlde, The duke his house[1] is four square builded upon four rankes of stone pillers, xxtie [20] in everie rancke. There are there two chambers of great beautye verie lardge [f. 22] and sumptuously ritchly sett forthe with divers curious (workes gilte with golde) right over against it is the mynte hous builte in licke sorte, betwixt them neighe the sea side stande two pillers of one stone apiece, beinge three fadomes aboute everie of them, and of a great height, before the gatte dothe stande a payere of gallows, upon the which as wee were informed a duke was hanged[2] which woulde have made the dukedome his inheritance by murthering of the Nobilitie, harde by the house is St Marke his churche[3] which is exceedinge ritchly adorned, under the highe altere of the which liethe his body; yt hathe five stately gates at the entrance theof, the rooffe is made in forme licke five half globes of verie strange worckmanshipe. the steeple is framed in suche sorte as a horse maye be riddene to the toppe of it. right against the churche doors stande three tall pillers which signifie as it was toulde me that theie can kepe warr with three kings, [*A Ritche Iueall house*] in the Duks Juell house are said to be two unicornes hornes of ayarde longe, apiece a turkis[4] sett in golde of great bignes, apoynted diamonde of exceedinge muche valewe seven corsletts of golde sett with pearle and precious stone with many other Juells of singular worckmanshipe and unspeakeable worthe, soe as Venis for the inestimable welthe is accounted the ritcheste Cittie in Itallie; There is an exchange called the Rialto verie faire and lardge neighe unto it is a Bridge [*A strange Bridge*] of one arche fortie yards broade, it hathe two courses of shoppes uppon it and is [f. 23] fiftie stepps in the ascending on each side.

[*A worthy armorie*] In the armorye of Venis at the intrance thereof are eight rooms foure score yards longe each of them full of armour, as pycks swordes and other weapons, there are divers rooms full of oares som for five and som for seaven men to rowe withall, beside som other furniture for Gallies. Alsoe wee sawe there three hundred gallies lyinge drye under houses, which doe rowe with twentie five oares aside, more forteene Galliasses which doe use thirtee oares on a side; one Galley ritchly gilte with golde wherein the Duke on St Marckes daie dothe use some sportes upon the water, there are fowre rooms full of Sailes, and fowre roomes full of Cables, alsoe one gallie made in one daie for the receavinge of the kinge of Fraunce,[5] as ther it was toulde us; more over wee viewed five roomes wherein weare contayned twelve hundred caste peeces or more, the greateste peece there was founde in Candie[6] (which is a kingdom subjecte to the Dukedom of Venis) this which is eighteene inches broade in the mouthe and soe passing forwards also

---

[1] *Ducal Palace.

[2] Piers is probably referring to Doge Marin Falier (1274–1355) who was elected Doge in September 1354. He attempted an unsuccessful *coup d'état* to remove power from the Venetian patrician class. Ten of his fellow conspirators were publicly hanged in front of the Doge's Palace but, as befitted his status, Falier was beheaded. His portrait in the Doge's Palace (Sala del Maggior Consiglio) was replaced with a painted black shroud.

[3] *San Marco.

[4] *turkis*: turquoise.

[5] This galley was built for the visit to Venice in 1574 of Henri III of France. Philip Sidney (**item 22**, **Plate 17** and **Figure 17**) delayed his departure from Venice to witness these welcoming celebrations which are depicted in a painting by Andrea Michieli (il Vicentino), 'The Entrance of King Henry III of France at the San Nicolo on the Lido' (Palazzo Ducale) (**Plate 9**). McPherson, *Myth of Venice*, pp. 97–100.

[6] Candia (Crete).

wee might perceive one roome which was full of bulletts for great Ordinance, and (as they which weare there informed us) it had in it noe les then seventeen thowsande soe we went frome thence through seaven rooms which weare full of musketts Callyvers[1] and other furniture, of the which three of them contained armour sufficient for 70 thowsande soldiors; There is armour there in all suffiente to furnishe oute three hundred thowsande men, wee tooke note of one maste there which coste the duke three hundred ducketts. The duke keepethe many men a worcke in that armorie, to his greate cost and chardge he is a peace with all the worlde, and yet dothe [f. 24] dailie make great provision for warre.

In the Nunerie of Saint Sepullcher[2] is a patterne of the Sepullcher of our Saviour Christe, it was wrought at Jerusalem, as is reportede and brought thether. At Morana[3] one myle from Venis is the glasse house, the shipping of Venis come noe further then Mollomocke[4] which is five myle from the Cittie; Venis standethe farr within the straights and therefore the sea dothe not with them ebbe nor flowe. There are in it of parishe churches xxiii and four, and religious howses fortie eight, as also six Synagoges of Jewes, in the which they doe use there Ebrue service, and ancient ceremonies, whoe are in number as good as ten thowsande. I did observe at my beinge there that the noble men of Venis doe use to salute one another with a kisse, but theye doe not accustom (either there or in any parte of Italie) to kisse there wyves or any other women in open presence;

The ixth daye wee wente by water and passed by Lusefesina,[5] where our hoye[6] was cariede upp agreat waye uppon a sledge, with a windeglass,[7] and so let downe againe, and soe came to Padua.

[f. 121] [*The battell of Lepanto*] And for as muche as this batle was verie famous and exceedinge profitable for the whole estate of Christendom, I have thought fitt to make a compendious reporte thereof:

Be it therefore understoode that the firste of the Confederatt Christians which putt into the adriaticke Sea, was Venerius the venetian admirall,[8] and with him fiftie Gallyes whoe attended at Messana for the comminge of Don Juan of [f. 122] Austria,[9] generall of the Spanishe forces and of the whole Fleete, where Marcus Anthonius Collumna[10] whoe was admiral of twelve Gallyes for the Pope, and of twelve more which were sente thether from the great Duke of Florence and three Gallyes of Malta mett him, then came another Anthonius Currynus[11] with three score and twoe venesian Gallyes, and shortly after them

[1] *Callyvers*: calivers, light muskets.
[2] *Nunerie of Saint Sepullcher*: unidentified.
[3] *Murano.
[4] Malamocco.
[5] Fusina on the Venetian lagoon was linked with Padua via the inland waterways of the Naviglio del Brenta and the Piovego canal.
[6] *hoye*: a small vessel used to transport passengers and goods over short distances.
[7] *windeglass*: windlass, a mechanical system utilizing a wheel and axle with a chain or cable to draw the boats along.
[8] Sebastiano Venier (Veniero) (*c*.1496–1578), commander of the Venetian fleet at Lepanto (**Plate 13**) and later elected Doge aged 81 (11 June 1577–3 March 1578).
[9] Don John of Austria (1547–78), half-brother of Philip II of Spain.
[10] Marcantonio Colonna (1535–84), Admiral of the Papal fleet at the Battle of Lepanto.
[11] Probably Marco Antonio Quirini, *provveditore* of the Venetian fleet and commander of their flagship, the galley *Capitana*. Another Venetian galley, the *Cristo Risorto*, was captained by Giovanni Battista Querini.

the Gallyes of Sciscill, Naples, Pisa, and Genua aryved there, and in *the* ende of august Don John whoe then was not above fowre and twentye yeers olde, was verie triumphantly receaved by the Pope and venetian admirals. The venetian Fleete consisted of a hundred and eight Gallyes, six Gallyasses, two tale shipps and agreat number of smale Gallyotts unto them were joyned Colluminus with his forces, and Auria the Spanish admirall[1] with fowre score and one Gallyes, Soe as in all there were two hundred twenty one vessels for fight, In this Fleete were twenty thowsande fighting men of well experienced Soldiors, besides mariners, and agreat number of noble men, namely Alexander fornecio Prince of Parma,[2] franciscus maria Prince of Urbin,[3] Jordanus Ossinus of the honnorable family of the ursinge in Rome,[4] and divers others *which* voluntarily undertooke that voiadge for the defence of the Christian faithe; they beinge thus mett together, [f. 123] called a councell wherein it was debated whether they shoulde presently sett upon the Turckes forces or hover there abouts until suche time as his Fleete shoulde make towards them, [*The Christians resolution for joyninge of battell with the Turcks*] but after alonge consultation wherein there were many different opinions, they resolved to sett forwarde, and putt there Fleetes in order martiallinge the same as if they were readye to joyne battell; passing this by Paxo one Mutius Fortina a Spanishe capten, raysed a quarrel amongeste the venetians *which* grewe to suche a mutinie, as had almoste bene the overthrowe of the whole armye, for Venerius the venetian admyrall sente the capten of his owne Gallye for to patifie them, whoe was ill intreated by Mutius Fortina,[5] And therefor for perventinge of further inconveniences, Venerius caused him to be hanged upon the crosse yarde of a gallie, wherewith Don John being greatly discontented sharply reproved Venerius for the same, so as there had licke to have byne agreat slaghter made between the Spaniards and the venetians, had not Collumnius by his grave councell and good advice, diswaded them from the same … .

[f. 125] [*The battell beginnethe*] Which wordes beinge uttered by these famous commanders soe inflamed the myndes of the captens and Soldiors of bothe the armyes, that *with* cheerefull shoutes (the apparent witnesses of there willing hartes) the Christians courageously gave the onsett, *which* was as resolutely intertained by the Turckes.

Betwene bothe the Fleetes there laye six great Galliasses of the Christiane navie, placed there by the Generall, *which* *with* there great artillery did ecceedingly annoye the Turckes gallies, whoe in respecte of there multitude lay soe thicke that noe shott was spente in vaine.

And nowe the Ordinance began to plaie on either side, the roaring noyse whereof together *with* the warlicke soundes of dromes Trompetts and other martiall instruments, as also the hedious cries of the maimed and wounded Soldiors was suche, that the verie neighboringe hills resounded *with* the echoe thereof, the abundance of arrows and dartes fell licke showers of winters haile, soe thicke as they seemd to dim the Skyeyes, the Sease all neere thereabouts beinge even died *with* the effusion of blode, and spred over *with*

---

[1] Probably the Genoese admiral Gian Andrea Doria (1540–1606).
[2] Alessandro Farnese (1545–92), Duke of Parma.
[3] Francesco Maria della Rovere (1549–1631), Duke of Urbino.
[4] Paolo Giordano Orsini (1541–85).
[5] In Knolles, *Generall Historie*, p. 873, this name is given as 'Mutius Tortona'.

the corpes of slaughtered men, but herein manifestly appeered the mightie and miraculous hande of god, feightinge for his Servants, for where in the beginning of the daye befor the battle, the wynde with a gentle [f. 126] pleasinge gale brought on the Turckishe navie in suche forme and order as they desired ... .

Divers terrible Skirmisses paste between them in sundrie places, here the Turckes overcom, ther the Christians repulsed, either generall carefully observing where any of there partie was destressed, and still releevinge them with freshe supplies, ever presenting there owne persons in places of greatest danger for the hartninge of ther Soldiors. Soe as fortune seemed yet uncertaine on whether side to bestowe the honnor of so great a daye.

[*A crueall incounter betwixt the Generalls gallies*][1] In the middest of which cruell and doubtfull fight, the general gallyes of either side havinge discovered the one the thither, after mutuall [f. 127] dischardge of divers peales of shott, bothe of them eagerly thirsting for the glorie of the victorie, commanded there Gallyes to be grappled together, when as if the battell had even nowe begune a freshe either side coragiously assaulted the other, with eger furie sheathing there Swordes in the bodies of their adversaries, and covering the deckes with the carcasses of the mangled Soldiors, continwinge thus for the space of three houres, oure general Gallye beinge overlaide with the multitude of the Turckes, and having loste many of his beste and approved Soldiors. Begann to fainte, which animated the enemyes, that beinge now confidente of the victories with cheerefull shootes they pressed into the Gallye nothinge doubtinge but that they shoulde easily surprise her, which fell out farr contrarie to there expectation ... .

[*The number of the turckes which were slayne and taken at this battell*] The number of the Turckes slayne and drowned in this battle was 32000 there were taken prisoners 3500, and 12000 Christians prisoners released which weare gallie slaves with the Turckes, and of the turkishe gallies weare taken 162 and suncke or burnte 40 and of galliotts and other small vessels weare taken aboute 60. Prisoners of note taken weare Achamatt and Mohomett the Sonnes of the Haly Bassa,[2] bothe afterwards sente as prisoners to the Pope, there weare divers other principall commaunders of the enemyes forces made captives that daye whom I omitt to name.

---

[1] This account refers to the clash between Don Juan's flagship, *La Real*, and the *Sultana* of the Ottoman Grand Admiral (Kapudan Pasha), Müezzinzade Ali Pasha (d. 7 October 1571) who was slain and his head displayed upon a pike.
[2] Various Ottoman prisoners were sent to Pope Pius V, including the statesman and writer 'Hindi' Mahmud, and incarcerated in the Castel Sant' Angelo.

# 35.   ENGLISH ATTITUDES TO VENICE BY 1600

By 1600 both Venice and London had populations of approximately 150,000.[1] Both were naval and mercantile trading cities with substantial populations of resident and visiting foreigners. A charter of 1592 to London's Venice and Turkey merchants granted a twelve-year monopoly over Venetian and Ottoman trade to fifty-three English merchants; and another charter issued in 1600 granted these rights to eighty-three merchants.[2] Venetian ships still arrived at the London docks, carrying a wide range of goods from Europe, the Middle East and the Levant. However, by 1600 Venice was in decline as a Mediterranean military, naval and commercial power.[3] The Turks had been heavily defeated by a combined Christian navy at the Battle of Lepanto (1571) (**item 34**, **Plate 13**) but the loss of Cyprus (1570–73) to the Turks marked the beginning of a decline in Venetian potency which continued during the seventeenth century as the Turks took control of the eastern Mediterranean. Bronwen Wilson explains:

> At the end of the fifteenth century, Venice was the capital of a vast empire, a mercantile centre, and a departure point for travellers to the East. The city's economy and interests were linked to broad global considerations. By the seventeenth century, however, its dominant trading position was usurped as the centre of European economic gravity shifted toward markets outside of the Mediterranean.[4]

Records of English travellers at Venice during the remainder of the 1590s are scanty, although in July 1593 Polo Paruta, Venetian Ambassador at Rome, reported to the doge and Senate that Pope Clement VIII was concerned about the number of the 'English in Venice, who boasted that they were spreading their false doctrine in that city and making many perverts to Calvinism'. In reply, Paruta assured the Pope that:

> very few English dwelt in Venice; that Venice did not trade with England as much as in times past on account of commercial relations which, for various reasons, had been considerably altered and diminished. And so if by chance some English ships reached that port, as, for

[1] Pezzolo, 'The Venetian Economy', p. 257. Overall population figures are far from certain during the period of this study but Pezzolo offers the following: 1400: 85,000; 1509: 103,500; 1555: 159,467; 1586: 148,097; 1607: 188,970. Major outbreaks of the plague led to significant loss of population. Between 1350 and 1530 there were over twenty outbreaks of plague in Venice, with the 1575–7 outbreak killing *c*.50,000, about one-third of the city's population.

[2] The Venice Company was established in 1583 and merged in 1592 with the Turkey Company (founded 1581) to form the Levant Company. Epstein, *Levant Company*, pp. 1–5, 20–58. Willan, 'English Trade', pp. 401–3, provides examples of Anglo-Venetian naval trade in the latter half of the 16th century, based at London, Southampton and Margate.

[3] Levin and Watkins, *Shakespeare's Foreign Worlds*, p. 114, noting of London's mercantile colony: 'Venetians, and Italians in general, had become conspicuous by their relative absence, and the ones to be found in London were increasingly likely to be intellectuals, artists, and religious refugees rather than merchants engaged in trade.'

[4] Wilson, *World in Venice*, p. 4. See also Iordanou, *Venice's Secret Service*, pp. 1–2, for intelligence reports relating to the loss of Cyprus.

example, had happened this year owing to the importation of grain, they stayed but a short time, and the crews for the most part lived on board, not on shore.[1]

Despite Paruta's assurances, Clement VIII's concerns lingered and in early December 1595 he complained to Giorgio Dolfin, the new Venetian Ambassador at Rome, that 'at Venice there was an open Exchange, full of heretics, who live as they like, to the scandal and danger of all Italy; that the English are freely admitted in Venice, and, in short, that in matters of religion things are managed with indifference'.[2]

In contrast to these concerns, two high-status English parties arrived at Venice in 1595/6. The first was led by the Manners brothers, Roger (1576–1612), fifth Earl of Rutland, and his younger brother Francis (1578–1632), sixth Earl of Rutland. The second was the party of Richard and Edward Cecil, the second and third sons of Sir Thomas Cecil, later first Earl of Exeter, and grandsons of the Lord Treasurer, William Cecil, Lord Bughley (who died on 4 August 1598). It is not clear whether these two groups of young Englishmen and their servants ever met at Venice, even though the Manners and Cecil families were closely linked by both marriage and court affairs. Queen Elizabeth had granted Roger Manners, Earl of Rutland, a licence to travel on the continent in December 1594 but his departure was delayed by the death of his mother in April 1595.[3] He eventually left England in the following October, accompanied on the early stages of his itinerary by Robert Vernon, a cousin of Robert Devereux, Earl of Essex.

Rutland and his party travelled via the Low Countries, Germany and Switzerland and matriculated at Padua University in 1596 where in July he fell seriously ill. He was tended by his servant Thomas Beest and visited by the civil lawyer Dr Henry Hawkins (d. 1646), who served as the Earl of Essex's intelligence agent at Venice during the 1590s, and the astronomer Edmund Bruce, the Consiliarius of the English nation at Padua and also another intelligencer, reporting from Venice and Padua during the late 1590s to the spy Anthony Bacon (1558–1601), the brother of Sir Francis Bacon (1561–1626).[4]

Travelling with Rutland was the Oxford scholar and writer Robert Dallington (1561–1637/8) who in 1592 published *The Strife of Love*, translated and adapted from Francesco Colonna's *Hypnerotomachia Poliphili* (1499). This slim volume was dedicated to the memory of Sir Philip Sidney (**item 22**, **Plate 17** and **Figure 17**) and praised the art and architecture of Italy even though Dallington had not yet travelled abroad. An opportunity to do so came when he was engaged as a tutor and business manager by Rutland for his continental tour and he served Rutland's brother Francis Manners in the same capacity.[5] These experiences led to his guide *A Survey of the Great Duke's State of Tuscany. in 1596* (1605) which, although focused primarily on Florence and other areas of Tuscany, also made passing reference to Dallington's personal knowledge of Venice. He praised Florence's Duomo and its Piazza della Signoria by the Palazzo Vecchio and commented: 'round about it are very faire and high houses. I have not seene a Market-steede,[6] excepting that of *Sancto Marco* in *Venice*, so beautifull' (p. 26). He commended

---

[1] *CSP Venice*, 1593, item 184.

[2] Ibid., item 382, 2 Dec. 1595.

[3] TNA SO3/1, f. 551.

[4] Hawkins travelled from Venice to Padua in July 1596 to assist with drawing up the will of Roger Manners during his illness, although he was recovering by the time Hawkins arrived. Woolfson, Padua, pp. 244–5.

[5] *ODNB*, s.v.

[6] Market-steede: marketstead, market-place (*OED*).

how Venice took care through its election of its doges not to allow any 'great man to deserve too well, and be loved too much' (p. 35)[1] and also noted how the 'Taxations & impositions' on the citizens of Venice were less than those of Florence (p. 46).[2] Dallington was also well aware of the undercurrent of violence which ran through most large Italian cities, including Venice:

> And at my comming hither to *Venice*, (for this is generall through all *Italie*) there were on Shrove-sunday at night seaventeene slaine, and very many wounded: besides that they there reported, there was almost every night one slaine, all that *Carnoval* time. The occasion of most these quarrels and mischiefes arise from the *Burdello*. This is also to be observed, that the party wounded, whereof perhaps in few dayes he dyeth, will never discover by whom he was hurt, except to his Confessor, though he know him very well: neither will the brother or sonne of him slaine, take any acknowledgment of the dooer, though by circumstance and presumptions they be very sure thereof, but rather awaite the good houre to crie quittance. (p. 65)

Roger Manners, fifth Earl of Rutland, returned to England in summer 1597 and served in Essex's ill-fated Azores expedition in July. In early 1599 he married Elizabeth Sidney, the daughter of Sir Philip Sidney and granddaughter of Sir Francis Walsingham. This childless union proved an unhappy one and, according to Ben Jonson, was blighted by a debilitating disease, possibly syphilis, contracted by Rutland during his continental travels. He died on 26 June 1612 and was buried on the Manners's family estate at Bottesford, Leicestershire. His wife Elizabeth died about six weeks later and, pointedly, was buried with her father at St Paul's, London, rather than with her husband.[3]

The fifth Earl of Rutland was succeeded by his brother Francis who had accompanied him to Venice and Padua in 1595/6 and returned there again in 1600.[4] Both Roger and Francis were known for their Catholic sympathies while in Italy. After Francis's marriage in October 1608 to his second wife, Cecily Tufton (the wealthy widow of Sir Edward Hungerford), he, along with his sister Frances and his daughter Katherine, converted to Catholicism. The Manners family were also well connected with earlier travellers to Venice. Roger and Francis Manners were cousins of Gilbert Talbot, the son of the Earl of Shrewsbury, who had accompanied his brother-in-law, Henry Cavendish, to Venice in 1570 (**item 21**). Similarly, Francis associated at Padua with Humphrey Coningsby (*c.*1566–1601), probably a cousin of Thomas Coningsby (**item 22**) who had resided at Venice with Philip Sidney.[5] The presence at Venice and Padua of these individuals between 1570 and the late 1590s confirms how, for a select and high-ranking group of young Englishmen, time spent in Venice and Padua was viewed by their families as a productive training for a future career in politics, diplomacy and international affairs.

---

[1] The text is mispaginated at this point: it runs to p. 40 and then begins again at p. 33. This p. 35 and following page references are in this second sequence.

[2] In his *A Method for Travell*, London, 1605, sig. B3r, Dallington also noted the differences between the Roman, Neapolitan and Venetian dialects and stated that the Tuscan language as spoken at Florence was the most desirable to learn for foreign travellers. Gallagher, *Learning Languages*, p. 165.

[3] *ODNB*, s.v. Woolfson, *Padua*, pp. 211, 215, 244–5, 255–6.

[4] During his time in Italy, some sources refer to Francis Manners as Lord Roos (e.g. Harris, *King's Arcadia*, p. 18). The Roos title had belonged to Edward Manners, 3rd Earl of Rutland, but his daughter Elizabeth had taken it into the Cecil family when she married William Cecil (1566–1640), 2nd Earl of Exeter. At this period his son William (1590–1618) held the title Lord Roos of Helmsley. Francis Manners only reclaimed the title in 1616.

[5] *ODNB*, s.v. Woolfson, *Padua*, pp. 226, 255.

Less is known about the activities at Venice and Padua of Richard Cecil (1570–1633) and Edward Cecil (1572–1638), later Viscount Wimbledon, who had been granted licence to travel abroad in late 1594. It is clear, however, that they had close personal ties with the Manners family and they may even have liaised over their respective plans for visiting northern Italy and the Veneto.[1] Their elder brother William (1566–1640) had married Elizabeth (1574/75–91), daughter of Edward Manners (1549–87), third Earl of Rutland. During his tour of the continent William was at Padua in 1585 when he wrote to both his grandfather Lord Burghley and Sir Francis Walsingham. Furthermore, Edward Cecil was the godson of Francis Manners, later sixth Earl of Rutland. Edward matriculated at Padua University in 1595 on the same day as an English medical student, Nicholas Calwoodley (d. 1621/3), and served as Consiliarius of the English nation (1595–6). He then moved on to Florence where he was received by the Grand Duke, Ferdinando de' Medici (1549–1609), and wrote in Italian to his uncle, Sir Robert Cecil in November 1596.[2]

One intriguing relic of these Englishmen at Venice may have survived in the form of a miniature portrait on a playing card of an unknown young man painted by Isaac Oliver, bearing an inscription on its reverse, 'adv. 13 Magio 1596. In Venetia. Fecit m. Isacq Olivero Francese Ø v.14', recording the date and payment. Edward Chaney has suggested that this may be a portrait of Edward Cecil and also notes that this miniature is the 'only known evidence that Isaac Oliver, the highly talented miniaturist, whose best-known place of work was in the Blackfriars, was ever in Venice'. If this is the case, it may be that Oliver was a member of either the Manners or Cecil brothers' entourage while they were at Venice.[3]

The architect and theatrical designer, Inigo Jones (1573–1652), was employed in 1603 by Roger Manners, fifth Earl of Rutland, as a 'picture maker'. Jones had proved his father's will at London in April 1597 and is thought to have travelled abroad soon afterwards until sometime between 1601 and 1603. Certainly, he became fluent in Italian and it is likely that he spent at least part of his time on the continent in the party of either the Manners or Cecils. He acquired at some later point a copy of Andrea Palladio's *I Quattro libri dell'architettura* (Venice, 1570, rpt 1601) and it is clear from his detailed annotations that he utilized it as one of his key reference books. Even when Palladio refers specifically to Venetian construction problems, Jones's notes indicate that he was intrigued by the challenges of building in such a water-logged area. His annotation: '[R]ules to know whether ye [g]round be fearme' relates to a passage in which Palladio discusses the Venetian technique of driving long wooden piles into the damp ground to create firm foundations for their buildings. Jones's experiences at Venice at this period must have

---

[1] Sustained friendly contacts between the Manners and the Cecils, however, cannot be taken for granted because of the Manners's loyalties to the Earl of Essex who was frequently opposed at court by the Cecils.

[2] Woolfson, *Padua*, pp. 217–20, 236. William Cecil met Samuel Foxe at Padua and later travelled with him through France in 1586. The range of Foxe's own personal contacts at Padua demonstrates the diversity of Englishmen in the Veneto during the 1580s and 1590s about whom very little is now known. These included a Mr Griffin [Griffith or William Grisinus?], Richard Willoughby, Edmund Bruce, [Christopher?] Middleton, John Wroth, William Cecil, John Cecil (alias Snowden), George Talbot, Maneringe, Herson, Cokk [*sic*], Loke, Martin, Vere, William Tedder and Dr Walker.

[3] Chaney, *Jacobean Grand Tour*, pp. 181–2. This portrait has previously been described as of Sir Arundel Talbot. Edward Cecil was also keen to acquire a working knowledge of Italian, as evidenced by his letter in Italian and sent from Florence to his uncle Sir Robert Cecil. 'Edward Cecil', *ODNB*, s.v.

included viewing this construction technique and studying the work of the city's leading artists, including Titian, Veronese and Tintoretto (**Plates 19** and **20**). His contributions to English architecture and theatre design were also fostered by his second extended visit to Italy in 1613–14 in the retinue of Thomas Howard (1585–1646), Earl of Arundel. Approximately fifty books survive from Jones's library, of which forty-eight are in Italian, several with a Venetian imprint. It is possible, of course, that he purchased these copies in London after one or other of his visits but it seems equally likely that Jones frequented the shops of Venetian booksellers while he was in the city.[1] Jones also possessed (or had access to) a 1598 edition of Cesare Vecellio's celebrated book of costumes of the known world, *De gli habiti antichi e modérni di diversi parti di mondo*, first printed at Venice in 1590 and containing over 500 illustrations. He drew inspiration from it as a source book throughout his career as a designer of costumes for court masques, including Ben Jonson's *The Masque of Blackness* (1605) and Aurelian Townshend's *Albion's Triumph* (1632).[2]

It is also important here to mention three individuals who placed Venice firmly in the English imagination but, as far as can be established, never personally visited the city: two of England's leading dramatists, William Shakespeare (1564–1616) and John Marston (1576–1634), and the translator Sir Lewis Lewkenor (*c*.1560–1627). Shakespeare's *Love's Labour's Lost* (staged *c*.1594–5) puts into the mouth of his schoolteacher pedant, Holofernes, the familiar Italian proverb: 'Venetia, Venetia, / Chi non ti vede, non ti pretia' (IV.ii. 95–6, 'Venice, he that does not see thee does not esteem thee') but his plays from the 1590s do not reveal any first-hand knowledge of the Veneto. An entry was made by the stationer James Roberts on 22 July 1598 in the *Stationers' Register* for 'a booke of the Marchaunt of Venyce or otherwise called the Jewe of Venyce'.[3] In September of the same year Francis Meres included Shakespeare's *The Merchant of Venice* in his list of excellent plays. Given that play texts were usually only printed when their commercial value within the theatre had been exhausted, this information makes it likely that Shakespeare's play set in Venice was staged between about 1596 and 1598.[4]

---

[1] *ODNB*. s.v. Jones's copy of Palladio's *I Quattro libri* (Worcester College, Oxford) bears an inscription in the corner of the flyleaf, '1601 doi docati', presumably written by the Italian bookseller. Newman, 'Jones's Architectural Education', pp. 18–19, 22. His library also included copies of Marcus Vitruvius Pollio, *De architectura libri decem* (Venice, 1567), Sebastiano Serlio, *Tutti l'opera d'architettura, et prospetiva*, Venice, *c*.1560/62), Andrea Fulvio, *Delle antichità della città di Roma* (1543), Pietro Cataneo, *L'architettura* (1567), Bernardo Gamucci, *Le antichità della città di Roma* (1569), Cretenis Dictys and Phrygius Dares, *Della guerra troiana* (1570), Alessandro Piccolomini, *Della institution morale* (1575), Francesco Guicciardini, *Dell'historia d'Italia* (1580), Guido Ubaldo, *Le mechaniche* (1581), Andrea Palladio, *Le cose maravigliose dell'alma città di Roma* (1588), Alberti Leandro, *Descrittione di tutta Italia* (1588), Giovanni Rusconi, *Della architettura* (1590), Vincenzo Cartari, *Le imagini de i dei de gli antichi* (1592) and Venetian imprints of Herodotus (1539), Florus (1546), Xenophon (1547), Dio Cassius (1548), Vegetus (1551), Appian (1551), Aristotle (1551), Plato (1554), Quintus Curtius (1559), Ptolemy (1561) and Strabo (1562). Harris, *King's Arcadia*, pp. 64–5, 217–18.

[2] Harris, *King's Arcadia*, pp. 60, 77–8.

[3] This entry probably represents an attempt by Shakespeare's theatrical company to prevent any unauthorized publication of this popular play. Roberts transferred to rights to 'A booke called the booke of the m'chant of Venyce' to Thomas Heyes on 28 Oct. 1600. Shakespeare, *The Merchant of Venice*, ed. Brown, pp. xi–xii.

[4] The first surviving printed edition of *The Merchant of Venice* is a 1600 quarto. Salerio's reference to his ship, the 'wealthy Andrew' (I.i.27) has been interpreted as an allusion to the *St Andrew* or *San Andres*, a large Spanish galleon captured in Cadiz harbour by the Earl of Essex in the summer of 1596 and requisitioned into the English navy. McPherson, *Myth of Venice*, pp. 51–68.

Given the play's sustained preoccupation with Jewry and usury, it seems likely that Shakespeare derived the idea of human flesh used as security for a loan from Ser Giovanni Fiorentino's *Il pecorone* ('The Simpleton' or 'The Big Sheep'), written during the latter half of the fourteenth century and printed in Italian at Milan in 1558, although no English translation is known to have been available to Shakespeare.[1] It has not been established how or from whom Shakespeare may have accessed a copy of *Il pecorone* and it seems possible that either he, or one of his associates, could read enough Italian to extract the key elements of his Bassanio-Portia plot. *The Merchant of Venice* does not show any evidence of first-hand knowledge of the geography or citizens of the city. The play refers only to specifics which would have been well known in England, such as the 'Duke of Venice', gondolas, ducats, links between Venice and Padua and the 'traject' (i.e., '*traghetto*') or 'common ferry / Which trades to Venice' (III.iv.53–4).

Most prominently, Shakespeare makes the Rialto the centre of Venice's mercantile transactions. But all of these details would have been widely known in the London of the 1590s from either written sources, such as William Thomas's *The Historie of Italie*, or from London residents, such as the Anglo-Italian John Florio (1553–1625), who may have been personally acquainted with Shakespeare and whose Italian-English dictionary, *A World of Words* (1598), includes *traghetto*. While the Jew in *The Merchant of Venice* is cynically exploited by the city's Christian citizens, Shakespeare makes no mention of the yellow star which Jews were obliged to wear at Venice; nor does his play reveal any knowledge of the Jewish ghetto. In fact, the term 'ghetto' is only first recorded in an English source in 1611.[2] Similarly, Portia's house at Belmont is a dreamlike, idyllic and fantastic world, perhaps reminiscent of the mainland Palladian villas owned by some of the city's leading families, but never realized in any tangible or identifiable sense. Even the play's preoccupation with usury is more likely to have been informed by such English tracts as Sir Thomas Wilson's *Discourse upon Usury* (1572) than any specifically Venetian source.

A remarkably different presentation of Venice is offered by John Marston's two plays set in the city, his romantic comedy *Antonio and Mellida* (performed c.1599; published 1602) and his tragedy *Antonio's Revenge* (performed c.1600–1; published 1602). Marston was proficient in Italian and seems to have been familiar with William Thomas's *A Historie of Italie*. His mother, Mary, was of Italian origin and her grandfather, Balthasar de Guercis (Guarsi, Guersie) (d.1557), a physician to both Queen Catherine of Aragon and Henry VIII, originated from Milan and had been naturalized in London in 1521/22.[3] However, in these plays Marston pointedly calls his Doge of Venice Duke Piero Sforza,

---

[1] The medieval tales, *Gesta Romanorum*, were translated into English in 1595 and probably supplied the concept of the casket scene in *The Merchant of Venice*. Antony Munday's *Zelauto, or The Fountain of Fame*, printed in 1580 draws on Italian comedy to tell the story of two friends in love with two girls, one of whom is the daughter of a wealthy usurer. Having pledged their right eyes to the usurer as security for loans, the young men are saved by the young women who disguise themselves as lawyers. Shakespeare may also have been influenced by a lost play called 'The Jew' and by Christopher Marlowe's *The Jew of Malta* (performed 1589).

[2] The *Oxford English Dictionary* (on-line edition) cites as the earliest usage of 'ghetto' in English two quotations from Thomas Coryate's *Crudities* (1611), describing his visit to Venice in 1608: 'The place where the whole fraternity of the Jews dwelleth together, which is called the Ghetto' (sig. S4v) and 'Walking in the Court of the Ghetto, I casually met with a ... Jewish Rabbin that spake good Latin' (sig. S6v).

[3] Quarmby, *Disguised Ruler*, pp. 68–9. One of the characters in *Antonio and Mellida* is called Castilio Balthasar.

even though this was the name of the most renowned family of Milan – a city which had often been at enmity with Venice. Also, although the position of doge was always chosen by election, Marston creates a political crisis in his two plays by both the Duke of Venice and the Duke of Genoa being childless. Marston's decision to make Duke Piero both childless and the Doge of Venice (despite his Milanese name) seems to offer an implicit reference to the civic dangers of the Elizabethan succession question. This by 1599–1601 was reaching a crisis, culminating in the failed insurrection in February 1601 of Robert Devereux, Earl of Essex, and resulting in his execution on 25 February on Tower Green at the Tower of London.

Furthermore, it was well known in England when Marston was writing these two plays that the Sforza line as Dukes of Milan had died out in 1535. This offered yet another potent warning to all those concerned by the lack of a clear English succession plan. In May 1534 the last duke, Francesco II Sforza (1495–1535), when aged almost forty had married at Milan, Christina of Denmark (1521–90), the twelve-year-old niece of Emperor Charles V (1500–58). However, Francesco was in bad health, probably because of a poisoning attempt some years earlier, and it was feared that they would not have children to produce a successor to the dynasty. This proved to be the case and Francesco died childless on 24 October 1535, triggering the chaos of the Italian War of 1535–8 between Francis I of France and Charles V over control over northern Italian territories, especially the duchy of Milan. Francesco's half-brother Giovanni Paolo (1497–1535) attempted to claim the duchy of Milan but died at Florence under mysterious circumstances, perhaps poisoned. The war resulted in French troops invading northern Italy and Spanish troops invading France. The Truce of Nice (18 June 1538) left Turin under French rule and greater Spanish control over northern Italy, effectively ending Italian independence. Even after this truce, enmity between Spain and France escalated, as well as between Spain and the Ottomans who had supported Francis I against Charles V. For Marston, therefore, the demise of the Sforzas – transferred in his play to Venice and coupled with his fictionally childless dukes of Venice and Genoa – offered a salutary lesson to late-Elizabethan England over its crisis of monarchic succession.

One of the most important books in English on Venice was published in 1599. Its translator, Lewis Lewkenor, was a recusant whose Catholicism prompted him to take refuge in the Low Countries where he served in the Spanish militia and married Beatrice de Rota, the daughter of a Brabant merchant. Wounded and without an army pension, he obtained in June 1590 safe passage back to England through the influence of Sir Philip Sidney's (**item 22**, **Plate 17** and **Figure 17**) younger brother Robert, then Governor of Flushing. It seems likely that Lewkenor, despite his Catholic sympathies, was being utilized as an intelligence gatherer and he reported directly to Lord Burghley on Englishmen serving the Spanish in the Low Countries. He may also have been the author of an anonymous publication, *A Discourse of the Usage of the English Fugitives, by the Spaniard* (1595). Due to his skill in languages, in 1591 he joined the embassy to France of his cousin Sir Henry Unton (**item 25** and **Plate 25**) and four years later he dedicated to Anne Dudley (1548–1604), Dowager Countess of Warwick, *The Resolved Gentleman* (1595), a translation of H. de Acuña's Spanish version of Olivier de La Marche's *Le Chevalier délibéré*.

This dedication was successful in gaining the Dowager Countess's favour – perhaps through the influence of her nephew Robert Sidney – and in August 1598 Lewkenor completed at her request *The Common-Wealth and Government of Venice*, mainly derived and translated from Gasparo Contarini's *De magistratibus et republica venetorum* (1543).[1] In 1599 he was appointed as a gentleman pensioner and in the following year he became responsible for supervising arrangements for the hosting of foreign ambassadors to the English court. These duties led to his appointment as Master of the Ceremonies after King James I's accession in March 1603, although it seems likely that he also remained in the pay of the Spanish throughout James's reign.[2]

Contarini's expansive work analysed in detail the civic institutions of the Venetian state and provided informative factual information about sixteenth-century Venice. It offered a powerful propagation of the republican 'Myth of Venice' as a harmonious, prosperous and stable mercantile society, characterized by its exemplary justice and religious and racial tolerance. Its appearance in print in 1599 inevitably fuelled an English interest in democratic republicanism, in no small measure exacerbated by the uncertainly over the Elizabethan succession question. Lewkenor's dedication to the Dowager Countess of Warwick was followed by four dedicatory poems. The first, by the administrator and poet Edmund Spenser (1552–99), praises 'Fayre *Venice*, flower of the last worlds delight', renowned for its 'policie of right'; and another by Maurice Kiffin (who, like Spenser, had served in Ireland) expresses the traditional celebration of '*Venice* invincible, the Adriatique wonder, / Admirde of all the world for power and glorie' (sigs. *3v–*4r). Most expansive is Lewkenor's address 'To the Reader' (sigs. *4v–A4r) which offers a panegyrical hymn of praise to the legendary reputation of Venice. He recalls how when speaking with 'Englishmen, French men, Spaniards, Germains, Polonians, yea or Italians borne in the bordering provinces', every person would describe Venice as 'a thing of the greatest worthinesse, and most infinitely remarkable, that they had seen in the whole course of their travels'. Lewkenor continues, while admitting that he had never been able to visit Venice personally:

> Some of the youthfuller sort, would extoll to the skies their humanitie towardes straungers, the delicacie of their entertainments, the beauty, pomp, & daintines of their women, & finally the infinite superflutties of all pleasure and delightes.
>
> Other of a graver humor would dilate of the greatnes of their Empire, the gravitie of their prince, the majesty of their Senate, the unviolablenes of their lawes, their zeale in religion, and lastly their moderation, and equitie, wherewith they governe such subjected provinces as are under their dominion, binding them therby in a faster bonde of obedience then all the cytadels, garrisons, or whatsoever other tyrannicall inventions could ever have brought them unto ... in the person of the Venetian prince, who sitting at the helme of this citie shineth in all exterior ornamentes of royall dignitie; (neverthelesse both he and his authority, being wholy

---

[1] In his address 'To the Reader' Lewkenor notes that Contarini was writing in the early 1540s and he states that he has brought this translation up to date by adding material from 'other learned Authors, as *Donato, Justinian, Munster, Bodin, Ant, Stella, Sansovino, Domenico Francesco, Girolamo Bardi* &c' (sig. A3v). He describes how he had worked from an Italian translation and Contarini's original Latin text. Readers of Lewkenor's volume would also have been interested in Thomas Danett's translation (1596) of the memoirs of Philippe de Commines (1447–1511) which contained information about Venice; and *A Direction for Travellers* (1592), translated by Sir John Stradling from 'Epistola de peregrinatione Italica' by Justus Lipsius (1547–1606). See Hadfield, *Literature*, pp. 49–58, for the complex political implications of Lewkenor's translation.

[2] The Venetian Ambassador Pesaro described Lewkenor to the doge and Senate as 'an utter Spaniard, and a pensioner'. *CSP Venice, 1625–26*, item 55. His son Thomas (1588–1645) became a Jesuit priest who ministered in England from 1625 until his death.

subjected to the lawes) they may see a straunge and unusuall forme of a most excellent Monarchie ... . Then what more perfect and lively pattern of a well ordered Aristocraticall government can there in the worlde bee expressed, then that of their Councell of Pregati or Senators, which being the onely chiefe and principall members of all supreame power; yet have not any power, mean, or possibility at all to tyranize, or to pervert their Country lawes?

Lastly if they desire to see a most rare and matchlesse president of a Democrasie or popular estate, let them beholde their great Councell, consisting at the least of *3000.* Gentlemen, whereupon the highest strength and mightinesse of the estate absolutely relyeth, notwithstanding which number all thinges are ordered with so divine a peaceablenes, and so without all tumult and confusion, that it rather seemeth to bee an assembly of Angels, then of men ... their iustice is pure and uncorrupted: their penall Lawes most unpardonably executed: their encouragements to vertue infinite: especially by their distribution of offices & dignities, which is ordered in such so secrete, strange, and intricate a sort, that it utterly overreacheth the subtiltie of all ambitious practises, never falling upon any but upon such as are by the whole assembly allowed for men of greatest wisedome, vertue and integritie of life

Radically praising Venice's democratic republicanism as an 'unusuall forme of a most excellent Monarchie' – a challenging and potentially dangerous perspective to offer in England during the last years of the 1590s – Lewkenor goes on to describe the astonishing physical location and beauty of the city:

first touching the situation thereof, what ever hath the worlde brought forth more monstrously strange, then that so great & glorious a Citie should bee seated in the middle of the sea, especially to see such pallaces, monasteries, temples, towers, turrets, & pinacles reaching up unto the cloudes, founded upon Quagmires, and planted uppon such unfirme moorish and spungie foundations, there being neyther wood, nor stone, nor matter fit for building within tenne miles thereof, for so farre distant from it was the nearest maine land, at such time as the first foundation was laide?

Besides, what is there that can carrie a greater disproportion with common rules of experience, the*n* that unweaponed men in gownes should with such happinesse of successe give direction & law to many mightie and warlike armies both by sea and land, and that a single Citie unwalled, and alone should command & over toppe mighty kingdomes, and such famous farre extended provinces, remayning ever it selfe invincible, and long robed citizens to bee served, yea and sued unto for entertainment by the greatest princes & peeres of *Italy:* amidst which infinit affluence of glorie, and unmeasurable mightinesse of power, of which there are in soveraignty pertakers aboue 3000. gentlemen, yet is there not one among them to bee found that doth aspire to any greater appellation of honour, or higher tytle of dignitie then to be called a Gentleman of *Venice,* including in the same the height of all imaginable honour, so deare unto this generous people is the name and love of their noble country?

By the first decade of the seventeenth century, Venice had become a frequent point of travel for many Englishmen on the continent. On 27 August 1603 Secretary Scaramelli, who was still residing in England after his audience with Queen Elizabeth in February 1603, noted that 'at the present moment there were no Venetians in London, except the two brothers Federici, people of very moderate pretensions, and only six or seven other Italians ... whereas in Venice there were thousands of English'.[1]

Just over three months later Francesco Vendramin, Venetian Ambassador at Rome, noted that the 'English are in great numbers in Venice, and there is a woman who keeps

---

[1] *CSP Venice,* 1603, item 118.

an English lodging-house'.[1] Such a comment acts as a salutary and concluding reminder that this volume has only been able to study the disparate records of a very small minority of English visitors to Venice between 1450 and 1600. The experiences and observations of the vast majority – numbering countless thousands – are now unknown because either written records were never kept or have been lost. The Venetian historian Marino Sanuto compiled a detailed record on 5 May 1515 of the Council of Ten's discussions of plans for building a major library (Jacopo Sansovino's Biblioteca nazionale Marciana) in the Piazza San Marco. It noted in its senatorial decree drafted in Latin that the preservation of documentary records relating to Venice was of paramount importance because human history and its written records are subject to the *vicissitudo temporum* (vicissitude of the times).[2] Hence, recording the experiences of the individuals included in this volume – pilgrims, scholars, aristocrats, gentlemen, political and religious dissidents, clergymen, diplomats, spies, soldiers, sailors, servants and renegades – can only offer a highly selective and fragmentary insight into Anglo-Venetian relations between 1450 and 1600.

[1] Ibid., 6 Dec. 1603, item 165.
[2] Sanuto, *Diarii*, XX pp. 181–2. Sanudo, *Venice, città excelentissimi*, p. 448.

# APPENDIX

## Venetian Locations, Institutions and Ceremonies[1]

**Arsenal** (*Arsenale*) (**Plate 12**): Large area of shipyards and armouries, traditionally founded 1104; enlarged as the Arsenale Nuovo (1320) and again during 14th–16th centuries to become the largest industrial mass-production complex in Europe. It developed assembly lines with galleys moving down a central canal, enabling the completion in about one day of the construction and basic fitting-out of a galley. It became the central focus of Venice's military and economic power, manufacturing most of the Republic's military and commercial vessels. Its gateway, the Porta Magna, was built in 1460 under Doge Pasquale Malipiero, probably by Antonio Gambello, echoing the design of the Arco dei Sergi at Pola. It owned an exclusive forest of oak and chestnut trees in the Montello hills, in the province of Treviso, from which it obtained timber for shipbuilding. A devastating fire occurred on 10 September 1569 which destroyed huge stockpiles of munitions and several galleys. In 1593 Galileo Galilei (1564–1642) was appointed as one of its engineering advisors.

**Biblioteca nazionale Marciana:** National Library of St Mark, founded 1468 following the donation of 482 Greek and 264 Latin manuscripts by Cardinal Basilios Bessarion (1403–72), Latin Patriarch of Constantinople. Pietro Bembo was appointed librarian (*gubernator*) and official historian of the Republic (1530). His major history of Venice, *Della historia vinitiana* (Venice: 1551) (**Figure 15**) was often consulted by English and other foreign visitors to Venice. Jacopo Sansovino began its construction in 1537 on the Piazza San Marco, facing the *Palazzo Ducale. It was completed by Vincenzo Scamozzi (1548–1616). A law was passed in 1603, requiring the deposit of a copy of all books printed at Venice.

**Bucentaur (Bucintoro):** State barge of the doges of Venice (**Plate 11**), used until 1798 on Festa della Sensa (Ascension Day) to take the doge into the Adriatic Sea to perform the symbolic *Marriage of the Sea. It has been proposed that the name may be a corruption of *ducentorum* ('of two hundred') and the vessel was able to carry about 200 men aboard. The vessels used between 1450 and 1600 were built in 1311, (possibly) 1449 and 1526 (replaced 1606). The earliest known image of the Bucentaur is found in the huge woodcut (1.345 × 2.818 metres) aerial view, *Pianta di Venezia* (Map of Venice) (1500), in the *Arsenal, by Jacopo de' Barbari (1460/70–before 1516) (**Map 14**). The 1526 vessel, with two decks and forty-two oars, transported King Henri III of France during his 1574 visit to Venice (**Plate 9**).

---

[1] This Appendix focuses primarily on the period 1450–1600, providing information on what would have been seen by travellers included in this volume, and does not seek to provide information about post-1600 buildings.

Figure 36.    Giacomo Franco, *Habiti d'huomeni et donne venetiane* (1610). The Porta Magna at the Arsenal where galleys are continuously made by numerous workmen, also showing the grille where they are paid. By permission of Special Collections, Brotherton Library, University of Leeds.

**Cattaveri:** Council established in 1280 to supervise economic matters, financial controls, customs dues, taxation disputes and the control of merchant shipping. It also had jurisdiction over the rights of pilgrims to the Holy Land and financial activities of the Jewish communities at Venice.

**Collegio:** The Republic's executive body and steering committee for the Senate met daily to manage official business and prepare the agenda for voting by either the *Senate or the *Council of Ten. It also read dispatches from its agents and ambassadors and met with foreign envoys. The doge presided and its membership included the *Signoria, and three groups of sages (*savi*): six Savi del Consiglio, (Council), five Savi di Terraferma (mainland territories) and the Savi agli Ordini (maritime matters).

**Council of Ten** (Consiglio dei Dieci)**:** Major Venetian committee from 1310 until 1797, responsible for the security of the city and Venetian dominions. It met in the Palazzo Ducale and comprised seventeen members: ten patrician magistrates elected for one-year terms by the Great Council (Maggior Consiglio) of over 2,000 members including the entire body of male Venetian patricians, the doge as its ceremonial figurehead and his six ducal counsellors who did not have voting rights. Each month three of the ordinary members (Capi) in turn led the council's operations. An additional group (Zonta, Venetian for *aggiunta* or *addizione*, 'addition') of about 15–20 members also served until 1582 and was entrusted with ensuring fair play and to counteract nepotism and cronyism. Only a single member of any Venetian family could be elected at any one time and successive terms were not allowed. It could impose severe punishments, banishments and executions, even on patricians and doges (e.g. Doge Marin Falier was executed in 1355). From 1539 a tribunal of three appointed judges, the Inquisitors of State (Inquisitori di Stato or I tre), with one known as the red inquisitor and two as black inquisitors. Two were selected from the Council of Ten and one was a ducal counsellor, with all three serving for one year. They acted as a counter-intelligence magistracy with responsibilities for state security and treasonable offences. They operated in secrecy, utilizing police powers, spies and secret informers. They required low standards of proof and their decisions were binding, which could include imprisonment, torture, banishment and service in the Venetian galleys.

**Corpus Christi Day and Procession:** Catholic liturgical feast, celebrated on the Thursday after Trinity Sunday, or sixty days after Easter. The feast was abolished in England in 1548 during the Reformation. It was marked at Venice by a grand procession, led by the doge, to *San Marco. It was traditional for pilgrims to participate in this procession and then depart for the Holy Land. Gentile Bellini's painting, *Procession in Saint Mark's Square* (Accademia, Venice) (**Plate 1**), was completed in 1496 but represents this procession in 1444 and depicts St Mark's Square before its 16th-century alterations.

**Doge's Palace:** see **Palazzo Ducale**

**Fondaco dei Tedeschi:** German trading house on the *Grand Canal near the *Rialto Bridge, rebuilt 1505–8 after a fire, and designed for storage and trading with offices and living quarters on its two upper floors. The Venetian Republic received commissions on its business. Its facade was once decorated with frescoes by Giorgione (*c.*1477/8–1510)

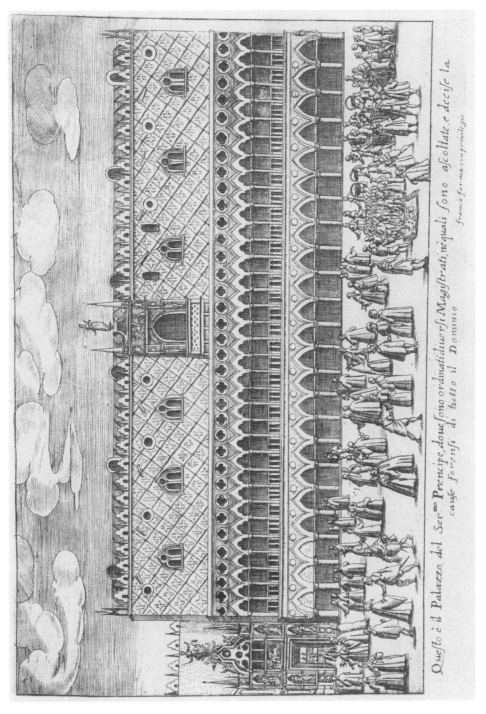

Figure 37.  Giacomo Franco, *Habiti d'huomeni et donne venetiane* (1610). Groups of magistrates meeting near the Doge's Palace. By permission of Special Collections, Brotherton Library, University of Leeds.

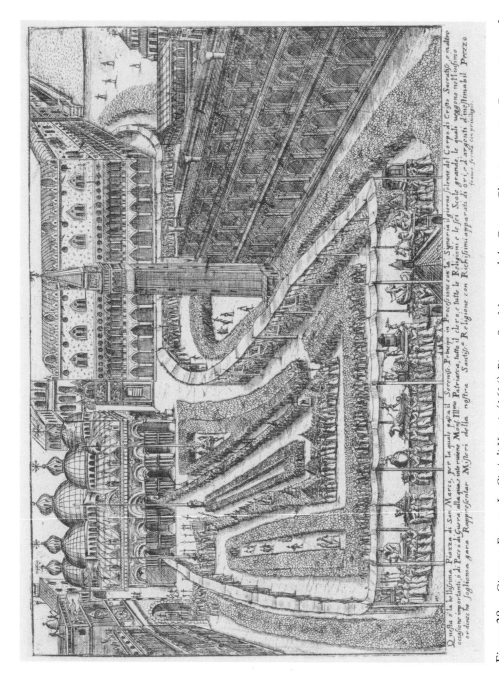

Figure 38.  Giacomo Franco, *La Città di Venetia* (1614). Piazza San Marco and the Corpus Christi procession. By permission of Special Collections, Brotherton Library, University of Leeds.

and Titian and its interior had paintings by Titian, Veronese and Tintoretto (**Plates 19 and 20**), although almost all are now lost.

**Fortezza di Sant'Andrea:** Facing the Lido on the island of Sant'Andrea (at the tip of the island of Vignole). The Veronese military architect and engineer Michele Sanmicheli (1484–1559) was commissioned in 1535 to examine the defences of the lagoon. His new fortification (surrounding an earlier castle on the site built during the reign of Doge Michele Steno, 1400–13), was begun in 1543 and completed by 1549.

**Frari:** see **Santa Maria Gloriosa dei Frari**

**Ghetto:** Following a decree of 29 March 1516 by the Maggior Consiglio, the Jews of Venice were required to live in Cannaregio *sestiere*, an area where the foundries (*geti*) and metal casting (*getto*) had once been situated. The word 'ghetto' is first used in English sources by Thomas Coryate in his description of Venice in *Coryat's Crudities* (1611). There are two sections, Ghetto Nuovo and Ghetto Vecchio, although the former is older. Its synagogues served German, Italian, Spanish and Portuguese, Levantine and Ashkenazi Jews.

**Grand Canal:** Main water thoroughfare of Venice, over 3 km in length and following an old course of the River Brenta as far as the *Rialto. William Thomas (1549) refers to it as the 'Canale grande' (p. 133); and Thomas Hoby uses the same phrase ('Canal grand', p. 161). Fynes Moryson refers to the 'great channell' (pp. 296, 299, 315, 322 and 350). The first recorded English usage of 'Grand Canale' is by Michael Drayton: 'Much is reported of the Graund Canale in Venice' (*England's Heroical Epistles*, 1597, f. 60v (*OED*)).

**Isola di San Lazzaro degli Armeni:** West of the Lido, the island was used from the late 12th century as a leper colony. Its church of San Lazzaro was founded 1348 but, as leprosy declined, the island was abandoned by 1601. Since the early 18th century it has been the home of Armenian Catholics, the Mekhitarists. See also *Lazzaretto Nuovo and *Lazzaretto Vecchio.

**Isola di Sant'Elena:** Located at the eastern end of the main island group, with its church and monastery dedicated to St Helena, the mother of Constantine. Its church was rebuilt in the mid-15th century but abandoned in 1807. It is now linked to Venice by bridges.

**Isola Sant'Andrea della Certosa:** Close to the Venetian Lido, with the 16th-century *Fortezza di Sant'Andrea. The formerly Augustinian (founded 1199) and later Carthusian (from 1422) church and monastery (rebuilt 1490) were allocated to the military in 1810, resulting in the demolition of its monastic buildings.

**Lazzaretto Nuovo:** North of Sant'Erasmo, where shipping arriving at Venice was quarantined. From 1468 it had a plague hospital; occupied by the military in 19th and 20th centuries and abandoned in 1975.

**Lazzaretto Vecchio:** Close to the Lido, founded in 12th century as a pilgrims' hospice with the monastery of Santa Maria di Nazareth. In 1423 the Republic ordered the establishment there of a plague hospital, the first permanent isolation hospital in Europe. Thousands of plague victims were buried on this island; later a military depot but abandoned in 1965 and it now homes stray dogs. Its name 'Lazzaretto' was a corruption of Nazaretum and perhaps derived from the nearby island settlement dedicated to St Lazarus.

**Lido di Venezia:** Formed from an 11 km long sandbar. Its first settlement was Malamocco, once the residence of doges; the site of Hebrew and Protestant cemeteries.

**Madonna dell'Orto:** Late 14th-century church in Cannaregio *sestiere*; restored with main portal added in 15th century. Originally dedicated to St Christopher by the Umiliati order; its name was changed when a discarded statue of the Virgin Mary was acquired which had been originally commissioned for *Santa Maria Formosa.

**Marriage of the Sea** (Sposalizio del Mare): Celebrated the maritime potency of Venice; held during the *Festa della Sensa* on first Sunday after Ascension Day; reputedly established as a *benedictio maris* ('blessing of the sea') to mark Doge Pietro II Orseolo's rescue in 1000 of Dalmatia from the Slavs and the Treaty of Venice (1177) between the Holy Roman Empire and the Pontificate. However, the first public celebration enacted aboard the doge's state barge, the *Bucentaur (Bucintoro), dates from 1311 when the Senate approved the construction of a *navilium ducentorum hominum* (Di Stefano, 'How to be a Time Traveller', pp. 177–9). The vessel sailed to *San Nicolò di Lido where the doge dropped a consecrated ring into the Lagoon, reciting the Latin pledge: 'Desponsamus te, mare, in signum veri perpetuique domini' ('We wed thee, sea, as a sign of true and everlasting domination').

**Murano, Island:** Group of seven islands north of Venice now joined by bridges. It has been the centre of Venetian glass making since 1291 when the city's factories were moved there due to the constant risk of fire from their furnaces. The glass trade was so lucrative that its craftsmen were forbidden to leave Venice, although some did briefly establish factories in England and the Netherlands. Its monastery of San Michele di Murano was suppressed in 1810. It has two renowned churches: Santa Maria e San Donato (rebuilt from 11th century onwards), originally dedicated to the Virgin Mary with San Donato added in 1125 when the saint's relics were brought from Cephalonia; and San Pietro Martire (rebuilt 16th century). Its Palazzo Giustinian now houses the Murano Glass Museum.

**Ospedale della Pietà:** Convent and orphanage, established in 1346 by Venetian nuns (Consorelle di Santa Maria dell'Umiltà) for orphaned and abandoned girls as the earliest of the four major state hospitals (the others being the Incurabili, Mendicanti and Ospedetto). Unwanted children could be left at a window (*scaffetta*) only large enough for infants. It was renowned from the 17th century for its female musical ensembles (*figlie di coro*) and in the 18th century for performances of compositions by Antonio Vivaldi (1678–1741). The current church was begun in 1745 and consecrated in 1760.

**Palazzo Ducale (Doge's Palace):** Originated from 9th–11th century buildings after the doges' seat of government was moved in 810 by Doge Angelo Partecipazio from Malamocco on the *Lido. Its modern appearance owes its gothic qualities, combining Roman, Lombard and Islamic elements, to the 14th-century rebuilding programme (interrupted by an outbreak of the Black Death in 1348). A major fire in 1483 destroyed much of its structure overlooking the canal. The architect Antonio Rizzo (c.1445–99) began the rebuilding work and designed the Stairway of the Giants (Scala dei Giganti) with its statues of Mars and Neptune sculpted by Jacopo Sansovino (1565). Building work was later taken over by Pietro Lombardo and Antonio Abbondi (1465–1549), known as 'Scarpagnino'. William Thomas (**item 16**) witnessed part of this rebuilding programme in 1547/8 (completed 1559). Another fire in 1574 destroyed some of the second-floor rooms and the palace's renovation was not completed until *c.*1559. A third fire in 1577 destroyed the Great Council Chamber (*Sala del Maggior Consiglio*) and other rooms but they were rebuilt and redecorated by Veronese (*The Triumph of Venice*) and Tintoretto (*Paradise*). It is now a museum.

**Palazzo Querini** (**Dubois, Stampalia**): Close to St Mark's Square, south of San Geremia. It was rebuilt in the early 16th century and is now headquarters of the cultural institution, Fondazione Querini Stampalia.

**Ponte della Paglia:** The original was the oldest (1360) stone bridge in Venice. Its name reputedly came from boats mooring to offload straw (*paglia*). The current bridge dates from 1847.

**Procuratie Nuove** and **Procuratie Vecchie:** see **San Marco, Piazza.**

**Redentore** (Chiesa del Santissimo Redentore, Church of Christ the Redeemer): Built (*c.*1577–92) on the Giudecca Island as a votive temple to give thanks for deliverance from a major outbreak of plague (1575–7). It was commissioned by the Senate from the architect Andrea Palladio and echoed the design of the Pantheon of Rome. Its fifteen steps recalled those of the Temple of Jerusalem. It was consecrated in 1592 and placed in the charge of the Friars Minor Capuchin. During the Festa del Redentore a pontoon bridge is constructed between the Zattere and Giudecca for the doge, Senate and choir of San Marco to visit the church on the anniversary of the city's final deliverance from the plague (now third Sunday in July).

**Rialto** (*rivo alto*): Commercial, financial and market centre of Venice in the San Polo *sestiere*. Almost the entire site was destroyed in a disastrous fire during winter 1514, the only major survival being the church of *San Giacomo di Rialto. The area was rebuilt from the plans of a local architect, Antonio Abbondi ('Scarpagnino'), preserving much of its original layout.

**Rialto Bridge:** A pontoon bridge was replaced in the late 14th century by a permanent wooden bridge which collapsed in 1450 under the weight of spectators during the visit of Emperor Frederick III of Austria. The rebuilt wooden bridge had a drawbridge at its centre and was lined with shops, illustrated in Carpaccio's *Miracle of the True Cross* (1494) and Jacopo de' Barbari's map of Venice (1500), but it collapsed in 1524 (**Plate 2 and Map 12**). In 1551 proposals were invited for a stone replacement, leading to the renowned single-span bridge of Antonio da Ponte (1512–97), completed in 1591.

**Sala d'Armi del Consiglio dei Dieci:** Private armoury of the Council of Ten. Gifts from foreign dignitaries were also stored and displayed here.

**Sala del Collegio:** Lavishly decorated room, dominated by Veronese's *Sebastiano Venier Giving Thanks to the Redeemer After the Battle of Lepanto* (1581/2) (**Plate 13**), where foreign delegations or prominent individuals were received and granted an audience by the *Collegio.

Figure 39.   Giacomo Franco, *Habiti d'huomeni et donne venetiane* (1610). View of the Sala del Maggior Consiglio in the Palazzo Ducale with a meeting of the Gran Consiglio of the Republic, showing *Paradiso* by Domenico and Jacopo Tintoretto. By permission of Special Collections, Brotherton Library, University of Leeds.

**Sala del Consiglio dei Dieci:** Seat of the Council of Ten, founded in 1310, with authority over all aspects of public life and for trying political crimes. Its ten members were chosen from the Senate and elected by the Maggior Consiglio, in addition to the doge and six advisors.

**San Bartolomeo:** Near *Rialto Bridge and the *Fondaco dei Tedeschi, San Marco *sestiere*; founded 9th century, rebuilt *c.*1170 and in 18th century; the local church of the German community at Venice.

**San Basso:** Near Piazza *San Marco, close to the clocktower; founded 11th century and rebuilt after fires in 1105 and 1661. Closed by Napoleon in 1806 and granted in 1847 to *San Marco for a marble and sculpture store; now a concert and meeting hall.

**San Domenico:** Near *Arsenal. Dominican church founded early 14th century and restored 1506 and 1536. Following the Arsenal fire of 1569, it was rebuilt (1586–1609). The Court of the Inquisition met there until 1560 when it moved to *Santa Maria Glorioso dei Frari. Prohibited books were burnt there and their ashes thrown into the canal (now Via Garibaldi). In 1806 its friars were moved to *Santi Giovanni e Paolo and its buildings demolished to make way for the Napoleonic Gardens (Giardini Pubblici).

**San Fantin (Fantino):** Located opposite the Fenice Theatre; also known as Santa Maria delle Grazie di San Fantino. Founded 10th century by the Barozzi, Aldicina and Equilia families; later restored by the Pisani family.

**San Francesco della Vigna:** Its name recalls the vineyard bequeathed in 1253 to the austere Observant Franciscans for their convent by Marco Ziani. New church built from 1534 by Jacopo Sansovino with revisions by the friar and scholar Fra Francesco Zorzi. Each of its chapels was sold to patrician donors to raise construction funds and, in return, they could bury their families there. Doge Andrea Gritti (d. 1538) (**Plate 4**) bought the right to be buried in the chancel.

**San Francesco di Paola:** Located in the Via Garibaldi, near the former site of *San Domenico. A 14th-century church, dedicated to St Bartholomew, was granted in 1588 to the Order of Minims of San Francesco di Paola and reconsecrated in 1618 as San Francesco di Paola. Its monastery was suppressed in 1806 and demolished in 1885.

**San Geminiano:** Located in Piazza *San Marco, opposite the Basilica; rebuilt in 1505 and restored by Jacopo Sansovino in 1550s. It was demolished in 1807 to make room for the staircase to Napoleon's Palazzo Reale, scattering major artworks such as an altarpiece by Bartolomeo Vivarini (*c.*1432–*c.*1499); organ doors by Paolo Veronese depicting St Germinianus (reputedly with the face of the church's priest Benedetto Manzini), St Severus, St Menna (reputedly modelled on Veronese's brother Benedetto) and St John the Baptist; and Jacopo Tintoretto's *Angel Foretelling Saint Catherine's Martyrdom*.

**San Geremia:** Facing the *Grand Canal. Originally an 11th-century church, with a reference in 1206 to the relics of St Magnus Oderzo (d. 670) who had taken refuge at Venice from the Lombards. The church seen by William Wey (**item 2**) was built by Sebastiano Ziani (Doge 1172–8), but only finally consecrated in 1292. The current structure dates from mid-18th century with a mid-19th-century facade but the brickwork bell tower possibly dates from much earlier.

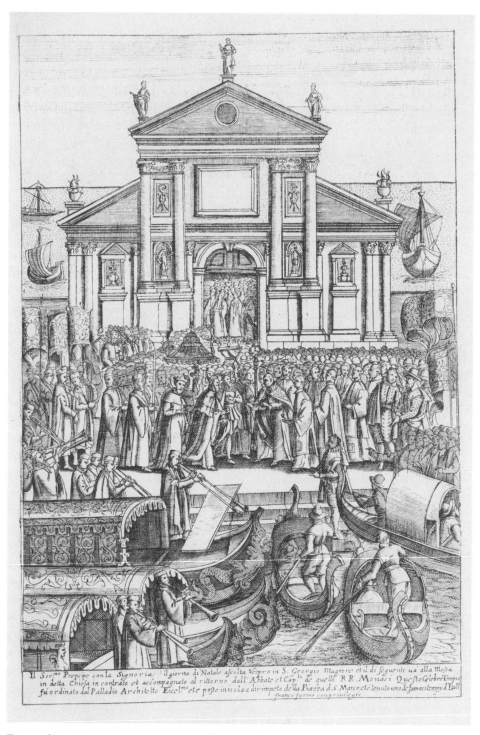

Figure 40.    Giacomo Franco, *La Città di Venetia* (1614). The Doge on Christmas Day at San Giorgio Maggiore. By permission of Special Collections, Brotherton Library, University of Leeds.

**San Giacomo dell'Orio:** Its church was rebuilt in 1220s with major renovations in 1530s. Two of its columns were brought back from the Fourth Crusade (1202–4) after the sacking of Constantinople.

**San Giacomo di Rialto (San Giacometto):** Reputedly the oldest church in Venice; supposedly consecrated in 421, the year when Venice itself was reputedly founded; its Byzantine church, according to Sansovino, was restored in 1071 and chronicles claim that Pope Alexander III consecrated it in 1177 during his renowned meeting with Emperor Frederick Barbarossa. It survived the major fire at Rialto in 1514 and was extensively rebuilt in 1600s. It has a 15th-century clock above its entrance.

**San Giobbe (Job):** 13th-century hospice and oratory was founded on this site by the Contarini family; replaced with a mid-15th-century church with strong Tuscan influences by Doge Cristoforo Moro to mark the visit of San Bernardino of Siena to preach in 1443 (canonized 1450) who also predicted that Moro would become Doge (in 1462; he is buried in the chancel). It was completed by Pietro Lombardo and consecrated in 1493.

**San Giorgio Maggiore, Island:** Situated east of the Giudecca with a Benedictine monastery from at least *c.*10th century. The present Palladian church dates from *c.*1565–1611 (but was largely completed except for its facade by 1576). It required Senate permission for felling 1,000 oak trees for its new foundations. It is the first complete church built by Palladio.

**San Giovanni Crisostomo:** 10th-century foundation but damaged by fire in 1475 and rebuilt (1497–1515) by Mauro Codussi (*c.*1440–1504) on a centralized Veneto-Byzantine Greek-cross plan with a late 16th-century bell tower.

**San Giovanni Evangelista:** 15th-century church (rebuilt mid-17th century), facing the confraternity *Scuola Grande di San Giovanni Evangelista. Renowned for its reputed relic of the True Cross, depicted in Titian's portrait of the Vendramin family (National Gallery, London).

**San Giovanni di Malta:** Palace and grand priory church of the Order of Malta (*Corte San Giovanni di Malta*). Knights of St John of Rhodes (later Knights of Malta) had been resident since 1312. The church was rebuilt 1498–1505. Both the church and monastery were suppressed and their artistic treasures plundered by Napoleon in 1806, with the church becoming a theatre. Knights of Jerusalem were able to retake possession in 1839.

**San Giuseppe di Castello (Sant'Isepo):** Built mainly during first half of 16th century with funds from Grimani family. Closed in 1801 by Napoleon but saved from demolition and later occupied by Salesian nuns. Cloisters now house the Sebastiano Venier Nautical Institute.

**San Gregorio:** Dating from mid-15th century and modelled on the nearby *Santa Maria della Carità. The flayed skin of Marcantonio Bragadin was first kept here before being moved in 1596 to *Santi Giovanni e Paolo. Suppressed by Napoleon in 1806 and used for metal refining as part of the *Zecca (Mint) and as a hotel and warehouse; later restored and used as a centre for art restoration.

**San Leone** (Venetian, **Lio**): Founded in 9th century in honour of St Catherine of Alexandria but rededicated in 1054 to St Leone in honour of Pope Leo IX; extensively rebuilt in late 18th century.

**San Luca Evangelista:** 11th-century foundation, restored during 13th and 14th centuries; rebuilt during early 1600s; reconsecrated 1617.

**San Marciliano (Marziale):** Originally 12th-century building; rebuilt from late 1690s; reconsecrated 1721.

**San Marco, Basilica:** According to legend, St Mark the Evangelist travelled from Aquileia to Rome. Near the Rialto Island he had a vision of an angel who greeted him: 'Pax tibi, Marce evangelista meus. Hic requiescet corpus tuum' (Peace to you, Mark the Evangelist. Here rests your body'). Consequently, Venetians made pilgrimages to St Mark's grave at Alexandria, Egypt, where he had been martyred. Giustiniano Participazio (d. 829, Doge from 825), ordered two merchants, Buono di Malamocco and Rustico di Torcello, accompanied by two monks, to bribe the monks who guarded his tomb, steal the body and bring it back to Venice. Hiding it beneath a shipment of pork, they arrived back at Venice in 828/9. This theft, known as the *translatio*, is commemorated in a 13th-century mosaic on the facade over the Porto Sant'Alipio. Doge Participazio built a private ducal chapel, enlarging the existing Church of St Theodore, to house the saint's remains, as the first Basilica di San Marco (consecrated 832). This church was severely damaged by fire in 976 during a revolt against Doge Pietro IV Candiano (d. 976) who had tried to establish a hereditary monarchy at Venice; rebuilt within two years by Doge Pietro Orseolo (Doge, 976–8). Current building began *c.*1063 by Domenico Contarini (Doge 1043–71); consecrated 1097 under Vitale Falier (Doge 1084–95). This building echoes through its five great domes (encircled in 1527 with iron rings by Sansovino) the Greek-cross plan of churches in Constantinople; domes alternate with barrel vaults over its aisles, supported by numerous columns. The geometrical 12th-century floor is decorated with ornate mosaics of antique marble. It became the cathedral of Venice in 1807.

**San Marco, Bronze Horses:** Copies made in 1980 of the gilded 'bronze' horses now decorate the terrace of the main facade of the basilica. The originals were cast not from bronze but impure (96 per cent) copper to facilitate the gilding process; now displayed in the Museo Marciano; brought to Venice (1204) during the Fourth Crusade after the sack of Constantinople and were displayed at the basilica by the mid-century. They may date from the 2nd century AD and are probably the work of a Roman rather than Greek sculptor. In 1797 they were taken to Paris by Napoleon but returned to Venice in 1815. They were stored at Rome in 1917–19 and again in 1940–45.

**San Marco, Campanile:** Located at the corner of the Procuratie Nuovo; built 9th–12th centuries and extensively restored in 1511–14. It suddenly collapsed on 14 July 1902 but a copy was rebuilt (opened 1912). The Loggetta (1538–49) at the base of the campanile was added by Sansovino, intended as a meeting place for the city's nobles.

**San Marco, Columns:** Two large granite columns located at the open end of the Piazza facing the Lagoon, topped with statues of Saint Theodore with a spear and crocodile and the winged lion of Venice. The columns were erected in the mid-13th century when they

Figure 41. Giacomo Franco, *Habiti d'huomeni et donne venetiane* (1610). The Loggetta del Sansovino at the base of the Bell Tower with Venetian office holders. By permission of Special Collections, Brotherton Library, University of Leeds.

stood on the edge of the Lagoon. Gambling and public executions traditionally took place between them.

**San Marco, Piazza:** On its north side a fire in June 1512 destroyed many of the houses. The Procurators of St Mark (**Plate 21**) ordered a new north wing, Procuratie Vecchie, completed in classical style by mid-1520s. It provided an arcade of shops with two storeys of apartments above with glazed windows. Procuratie Nuove, now the Museo Correr, in the Piazza dates from 1580s–1640s. Biblioteca Nazionale Marciana or Libreria Sansoviniana on the west side was begun in 1537 but not completed until 1580s. The piazza's brick paving was replaced in 1722 with Istrian stone. Napoleon ordered the building of a grand stateroom and staircase for imperial receptions which led in 1807 to the demolition, on the west side of the Piazza, of *San Geminiano and adjoining sections of the Procuratie Nuove and Procuratie Vecchie.

**San Marcuola:** Rebuilt in the mid-14th century; renowned for its relic of St John the Baptist's right hand. Pope Pius II also donated an arm of the Baptist to Siena Cathedral in 1464. The current church dates from the 17th and 18th centuries.

**San Nicolò di Lido:** This monastery houses the relics of St Nicholas, patron saint of sailors. Some of his bones are also preserved at Bari. Due to its strategic position near the main entrance to the Lagoon, the monastery was often used by doges for formal receptions of distinguished visitors. Lavish celebrations were held there in 1574 in honour of Henri III of France (**Plate 9**), attended by Philip Sidney (**item 22, Plate 17** and **Figure 17**).

**San Pietro di Castello:** Located on the island of Olivolo (or Castello) in the Lagoon; founded in 774/5 as the establishment of the bishopric of Rialto; its basilica was the cathedral church of Venice from 11th century until 1807. In mid-15th century the bishopric of Rialto was merged with the patriarchate of Grado, becoming the patriarchate of Venice. The present church dates from 1550s.

**San Polo:** The current church dates mainly from the 15th century but its south doorway from the 9th and its campanile from the 14th. The interior has a *Last Supper* by Tintoretto and a *Marriage of the Virgin* by Veronese.

**San Rocco (Roch):** Built 1489–1508 but substantially altered during mid-18th century; the only Venetian confraternity church specifically designed as a *sacrarium* for the remains of a saint whose body (previously held in *San Silvestro) was brought to Venice in 1485 and preserved within the High Altar.

**San Salvatore (San Salvador, Holy Saviour):** Located in the Campo San Salvador on the Merceria near San Marco. Originally a 12th-century church but rebuilt (1507–34) to the design of three Byzantine crosses placed end to end with a large central dome and four smaller ones. Its now secularized monastery is next to the church.

**San Sepolcro Castello:** Founded in 1409 as a hostel for pilgrims; modernized 1570. Suppressed in 1808 and most of its buildings were demolished.

**San Servilio (Servolo), Island and church:** A Benedictine convent dedicated to Saint Servilio (Servolo), a martyr from Trieste, on an island in the Venetian lagoon, to the south-east of *San Giorgio Maggiore; from 1725 the site of a psychiatric hospital.

Ordine che tiene la Sereniss. República Veneta
nel dare il bastone all' Ecc.mo General di Mare.
Giacomo Franco Forma Con Priuilegio

Figure 42.    Giacomo Franco, *La Città di Venetia* (1614). A procession from San Marco through the Piazza on the appointment of the Capitano del Mare. By permission of Special Collections, Brotherton Library, University of Leeds.

Within the engraving:

A QVESTO MODO VANO LE NOVIZZE
IN GONDOLA
*Per visitar le loro parenti ne' monasterij accompagnate da gran n.º di Gondole*

Figure 43. Giacomo Franco, *Habiti d'huomeni et donne venetiane* (1610). Novices travelling in gondolas to visit their relatives in monasteries, each with two men rowing. By permission of Special Collections, Brotherton Library, University of Leeds.

**San Silvestro:** Located near *Rialto; 12th century but rebuilt 14th–15th centuries; reconsecrated 1422. It partially collapsed in 1820 but was entirely rebuilt 1837–1909 (reconsecrated 1850). Veronese's *Adoration of the Magi* (1573) was painted for the church but sold in 1855 to the National Gallery, London.

**San Simeone Grande (Simeone Profeta):** 10th-century church but rebuilt after a fire in 1150; now an 18th-century neo-classical building. It was so named because it was once bigger than the church of San Simeone Piccolo, although the latter became larger when rebuilt in 1718–38 in imitation of the Pantheon at Rome.

**San Stae (San Eustachio):** Located on the *Grand Canal; founded 11th century and rebuilt 17th century, with early 18th-century facade.

**San Trovaso:** Venetian blending of three saints: the twins Gervase and Protase, Milanese martyrs and the children of the martyrs Vitale and Valeria; and Chrysogonus, a Roman martyred at Aquila. The nave of the church collapsed in 1583 and its restoration was not completed until 1657.

**San Vidal (San Vitale):** Located in Campo Santo Stefano. Its now deconsecrated building dates from late 17th and 18th centuries.

**San Zaccaria:** Located to the south-east of Piazza *San Marco and dedicated to St Zacharias, father of John the Baptist. The church underwent major restructuring between 1444 and 1515; described in 1483 by Fabri, *Book of the Wanderings*, I, pp. 101–2; and in 1494 by Casola, *Pilgrimage*, pp. 136–7. Its magnificent altarpiece, *Madonna Enthroned with Child and Saints*, was completed by Giovanni Bernini in 1505.

**Santa Croce (Giudecca):** Its church and convent were founded in 13th century; rebuilt in early 16th century; suppressed in 1806 under Napoleon's rule; used as a prison and warehouse; now part of the Venetian archives. It should be distinguished from the **Santa Croce (Santa Croce *sestiere*)**, founded in the early 12th century. Its church and convent were redeveloped in late 16th century by Antonio da Ponte after its occupants, the Sisters of the Poor Clares, offered the site for a church to give thanks for Venice's delivery from the plague of 1575–7 (although the *Redentore on Guidecca was eventually built instead). It was reconsecrated in 1600; closed in 1810 with the church used as a warehouse and then demolished in 1813. The site eventually became the public Giardini Papadopoli.

**Santa Giustina:** Benedictine abbey; named after St Justina of Padua; rebuilt from 1514, with two chapels dedicated to St Luke and St Matthew. St Luke, patron saint of artists, was reputed to have created the first Christian icons and painted the Virgin and Child, with devotional images of the latter proliferating from 13th century onwards. Its church and convent were suppressed in 1810; in 1844 the church was converted into a school for sailors. Since 1924 it has housed the Liceo Scientifico Giambattista Benedetti.

**Santa Lucia:** Renovations by Andrea Palladio began 1580; completed *c.*1610. Its nuns were expelled by Napoleon in 1806 and the church was demolished in 1861 to make way for the Venezia Santa Lucia railway station.

**Santa Maria Assunta (later, I Gesuiti):** Original church built 12th century with a monastery and hospital for the order of the Crociferi (Crosechieri, Crocicchieri,

Crossbearers); rebuilt after a fire of 1214. The order was expelled from Venice in 15th century and the estate granted to the Franciscans. After another fire in 1514 it was rebuilt and returned to the Crociferi in 1586. In 1656 Pope Alexander VII granted the property to the Republic of Venice. The Jesuits had been expelled in 1606 from their church and school of Santa Maria dell'Umiltà but were allowed back into Venice in 1657 and purchased this church. They demolished it in 1715 to build their new church (consecrated 1728).

**Santa Maria dei Crociferi:** see **Santa Maria Assunta.**

**Santa Maria dei Miracoli:** Built 1481–9 to the designs of Pietro Lombardo in honour of an icon of the 'Virgin Mary with Child and Two Saints' which had been declared miraculous, following the Immaculate Conception Cult (1476) initiated by Pope Sixtus IV.

**Santa Maria dei Servi:** Originally 14th-century monastery; demolished in 1510 and rebuilt by the Servite friars. Paolo Sarpi (1552–1623), a Servite monk and noted scholar, lived and worked here. Veronese's *Feast at the House of Simon* (1570–73, Château de Versailles) was painted for its refectory.

**Santa Maria del Carmelo (dei Carmini):** Located next to the Scuola dei Carmini (founded 1597). Originally 13th-century foundation of the Carmelite fathers; modernized in early 16th century.

**Santa Maria dell'Abbazia della Misericordia (Santa Maria di Valverde):** Located next to the *Scuola Vecchia della Misericordia. Founded 10th century; present facade dates from mid-17th century and the church was extensively restored in 19th century.

**Santa Maria della Carità:** Founded in 12th century and in 1134 Augustinian monks from Ravenna built a convent next to the church. Pope Alexander III reputedly consecrated the church (5 April 1177), which was celebrated annually on this day until the end of the Venetian Republic with the doge's procession across the Grand Canal on a bridge of boats. Church considerably enlarged between 1441 and the mid-1450s but converted in 1807 into the Academy of Fine Arts (now part of Accademia).

**Santa Maria della Grazia (La Grazia):** On an artificial island in the Lagoon. Its convent was used in 13th century to house pilgrims but was converted to a powder magazine during the Napoleonic period. A huge explosion in 1849 destroyed its former church and convent.

**Santa Maria della Presentazione (Le Zitelle):** Located in eastern part of Giudecca; designed in late 1570s and built in the 1580s. It took in young girls without a dowry.

**Santa Maria delle Vergini:** Augustinian convent; rebuilt (1547–49) but later suppressed and given to the Venetian navy in 1806; converted into a prison (1809) and then demolished (1822–44). A relief from the original convent entrance, depicting God the Father with the Virgin and Saints Mark and Augustine, is embedded in the wall of the *Arsenal.

**Santa Maria Formosa:** Founded in 7th century by St Magnus and rebuilt 1492–*c.*1504 in a Greek-cross plan; seriously damaged during First World War. The square in front of the church was a popular location for public performances of plays and other entertainments.

**Santa Maria Gloriosa dei Frari, Basilica:** Dedicated to the Assumption of the Virgin Mary. The first Franciscan church on this site was begun in 1250 and the second in 1330; campanile completed in 1396, facade in 1440 and High Altar consecrated in 1469. Titian painted two of its altarpieces, the *Assumption of the Virgin* and the *Pesaro Madonna*, and he is buried there, along with several doges.

**Santa Maria Maddalena (La Maddalena, Monastery of Le Convertite):** Located on the Giudecca; founded in 1530s as a convent and hospice for former prostitutes and other women. Its notorious rector, Fra Giovanni Pietro Leon, who sexually exploited its inmates, was condemned in 1561 by the Council of Ten and beheaded (after thirteen attempts with the axe) in the Piazza *San Marco and his remains burnt. It was suppressed in 1806 and became a hospital and under the Austrians a jail in 1857. It should be distinguished from the church of Santa Maddalena (La Maddalena) (14th century, rebuilt from 1780) in Cannaregio *sestiere*.

**Santa Maria Mater Domini:** Founded in 10th century dedicated to St Christina but rededicated to Maria Mater Domini in 12th century; rebuilt in 16th century. Its facade has been attributed to Sansovino.

**Santa Maria Zobenigo:** Located west of Piazza *San Marco and named in 9th century after its founding family, the Jubanico; also known as Santa Maria del Giglio (of the Lily presented by the Angel Gabriel during the Annunciation). The present church dates from 1680s.

**Santa Marina:** Located in the Campo Santa Marina, north of St Mark's Square. It was deconsecrated in 1807 and converted into an inn; demolished in 1820.

**Sant'Agnese:** Located close to *Santa Maria Assunta (I Gesuiti); rebuilt 16th century. Its church was suppressed by Napoleon in 1810 and used as a warehouse for firewood and coal; restored in late 19th century and reopened.

**Sant'Andrea della Zirada:** Founded in 1329 by four noblewomen, Elisabetta Soranzo, Marianna Malipiero, Elisabetta Gradenigo and Francesca Cornaro, for poor and destitute women; rebuilt from the 1470s. The name 'Zirada' may derive from the Venetian for 'bend' because the church stands at the intersection of two canals. Alternatively, it may be so named as the turning point for regattas. It was closed by Napoleon and its convent demolished.

**Sant'Angelo:** Located in Campo Sant'Angelo, close to *Santo Stefano; closed during French occupation and demolished by Austrians in 1837. Some sections of its structure still remain in the Oratory of the Annunciation.

**Sant'Angelo Raffaele:** Traditionally thought to be dedicated to the Archangel Raphael and to have been founded in either 5th or 7th century. The church was rebuilt during the late 1190s and demolished in the early 17th century when a new church was built.

**Sant'Antonin:** Founded by the Badoer family in the 7th century and later sponsored by the Tiepolo family; extensively rebuilt in 13th century and 1680s. Much of its interior dates from after 1600, although the Chapel of San Saba (Sabbas) contains frescoes by Alessandro Vittoria (1525–1608) and an altarpiece by Lazzaro Bastiani (1429–1512), originally from the Church of San Severo.

**Sant'Elena:** Early 13th-century church, rebuilt in 1435. The saint's body had been brought from Constantinople to Venice in 1211. The church was abandoned in 1807 but reopened in 1928.

**Sant'Eufemia (Famia):** Founded in the 9th century on Giudecca Island; originally dedicated to four female saints: Euphemia, Dorothy, Tecla and Erasma.

**Santi Apostoli:** 7th-century foundation, extensively rebuilt from 1575, incorporating the renowned chapel (built 1490s) of the Cornaro family, including Catherine Cornaro, Queen of Cyprus.

**Santi Filippo e Giacomo:** Its church and monastery dated from early 15th century and were entirely rebuilt in 17th century.

**Santi Giovanni e Paolo, Basilica (Zanipolo):** Venice's major Dominican church dedicated to the Roman martyr-saints John and Paul; begun in 1333 and consecrated in 1430. It became a traditional location for the burial of doges and distinguished foreign citizens, including Edmund Harvell (**item 12**) and, in the Chapel of the Crucifixion, Edward, Lord Windsor (**item 22**). His monument is attributed to Alessandro Vittoria, as is the altar of chalcedony black marble (touchstone) and the bronze figures of the Grieving Virgin and St John the Baptist.

**Santissima Trinità:** This church and monastery, dedicated to the Holy Trinity, were located in the Dorsoduro *sestiere* and financed by the Teutonic Knights during mid-13th century (demolished 1631). Baldassare Longhena's classical Santa Maria della Salute (begun 1630s, consecrated 1687) stands on their site.

**Santo Stefano:** Located at north end of Campo Santo Stefano; founded 13th century by Augustinians and rebuilt 14th and 15th centuries. The walls of its nave still preserve 15th-century decorations over its arches; renowned for its ship's-keel ceiling.

**Scuola di Santa Maria della Carità:** Founded in 1343; hospice erected in early 15th century. It was closed in 1807 and is now occupied by the Academy of Fine Arts and Gallerie dell'Accademia.

**Scuola Grande della Misericordia:** Dates from early 14th century (or earlier); rebuilt in 1532 by Sansovino but not finished until 1589.

**Scuola Grande di San Giovanni Evangelista:** Founded in 13th century by flagellants; the second oldest *scuola* in Venice. It possessed a relic of the True Cross and its reliquary is depicted in Titian's painting of the Vendramin family (National Gallery, London). Considerable redevelopment was undertaken during late 15th century. The *scuola* was suppressed by Napoleon in 1797 but reconstituted during 19th century.

**Scuola Grande di San Marco:** Founded in 1260 but its facade was largely rebuilt on the old foundations after a 1485 fire; designed (*c.*1487–90) by Pietro Lombardo and

Giovanni Buora; completed by Mauro Codussi (*c.*1495). The Scuola is now the civic hospital of Venice.

**Scuola Grande di San Rocco:** Founded in 1478 for the lay confraternity of St Roch during an outbreak of the plague; dedicated to San Rocco of Montpellier (d. 1327) who reputedly gave protection from the pestilence. The saint's body had been brought to Venice from Germany in 1485. Its *scuola* was built between 1515 and 1549, with its main facade by Antonio Abbondi ('Scarpagnino'). Tintoretto decorated many of its rooms (1564–88).

**Scuola Grande di San Teodoro:** Reputedly originated from a brotherhood (8th century) dedicated to San Teodoro when he was venerated as the patron saint of Venice. Established 1261 when Teodoro's remains were brought from Venice to Constantinople. It was raised to the status of a *scuola grande* in 1552. It was suppressed by Napoleon in 1807 and its buildings were used for storage; reconstituted in 1960.

**Scuola Vecchia della Misericordia:** Founded *c.*1310 and restored in early 15th -century when its members decided to erect a new *albergo*. The building was further developed in the 1430s, the facade in 1440s and the waterfront arcade added in early 16th century. Bartolomeo Bon (1407–64) carved its great relief, *Madonna della Misericordia*, placed over the doorway (Victoria and Albert Museum, London). Its interior is largely untouched from the 15th century because of its new building opened in 1589. Tintoretto used its upper room as a workshop for his huge painting of *Paradise* for the Palazzo Ducale. The building is now used as a restoration laboratory.

**Senate:** Formerly known as the Consiglio dei Pregadi (Council of the Invited), the main debating and legislative body of the Republic, with a membership of sixty selected by the Great Council. By 15th century the Council of Forty could join the Senate, along with another extraordinary body (Zonta) of citizens, ambassadors and senior military commanders. In 1506 it was decreed that sixty additional members should be elected to the Zonta in perpetuity. References to the 'Senato' often mean the 'Senato e Zonta' rather than two separate bodies. Approximately 300 members, from a nobility of *c.*2,500, had seats in the Senate, although only about 230 could vote. Meetings of the full Senate were presided over by the Full College.

**Signoria (Signory):** Ruling assembly or governing body of Italian republics, especially Venice.

**Zecca (Palazzo della):** Housed the official Mint of Venice; rebuilt (1536–45) by Jacopo Sansovino, as his first major Venetian commission, next to the *Biblioteca nazionale Marciana to replace 13th-century Mint in the *Rialto. It was financed by freeing serfs in Cyprus at 50 ducats per person. In the original designs, gold was to be smelted on the *piano nobile* (first floor) and silver on the ground floor. An additional third storey was begun in 1558.

Figure 44.   Unknown artist, the 1577 fire at the Doge's Palace, Georg Braun and Franz Hogenberg, *Urbium praecipuarum mundi theatrum quintum (Civitates orbis terrarum)*, Cologne, *c.*1600. Special Collections, Brotherton Library, FOR C16 quarto BRA. By permission of Special Collections, Brotherton Library, University of Leeds.

# BIBLIOGRAPHY

## MANUSCRIPT SOURCES

**Arundel Castle, West Sussex**
Archive, Autograph Letters, no. 83: letter of Henry Cavendish

**Baden State Library, Germany**
Cod. St. Peter, pap. 32: pilgrimage of Konrad Grünenberg

**Cambridge University Library**
MS Dd.3.20: letters of introduction for the Earl of Oxford
MS Nn.4.43: Edward Courtenay's translation of the *Beneficio di Cristo*

**Canterbury Cathedral Archives**
dd. MS 68: William Brewyn's account of his pilgrimage to Rome
Hales Papers, MS U. 85, Box 38, 3 vols, I (1578–83): Arthur Throckmorton's diary

**Cheshire Archives and Local Studies**
CR 69, 469: papers of the Aldersey family

**East Sussex Record Office**
RYE/47/20: suit of John Smyth against Sebastian Orlanden

**Essex Record Office**
D/DRG2/25: indentures of the Earl of Oxford

**Hatfield House, Hertfordshire**
Cecil Papers, 7/106: correspondence of Clement Parrett (Clemente Peretti)

**Kew, The National Archives**
C2/Eliz/N3/59: diary of Sir John North
C54/1080: land purchase by Edward de Vere, Earl of Oxford
E157/1/1: documents relating to the travels of Edward de Vere, Earl of Oxford
KB 9/619, m.13: documents relating to death of Thomas Brincknell
PROB 11/17: Sir Richard Guildford's will
PROB 11/32: Andrew Boorde's will
PROB 11/46: Peter Vanne's will
PROB 11/54/109: Sir Nicholas Throckmorton's will
PROB 11/56/512: Antony Bassano's will
PROB 11/57/216–19, 332: Edward, Lord Windsor's wills and estate documents
PROB 11/80/195: Sebastian Bryskett's will
PROB 11/90/25: Sir John North's will

PROB 11/93/10: Thomas Aldersey's will
REQ 2/178/60: land purchase by Edward de Vere, Earl of Oxford
SO3/1: travel licence of Roger Manners, Earl of Rutland
SP 1/90: Thomas Starkey's 'A Dialogue Between Pole and Lupset'
SP 12/29/8/11–12: challenge to legitimacy of Edward de Vere, Earl of Oxford
SP 12/105/105: documents relating to John Hart
SP 70/52/411: documents relating to Edward de Vere, Earl of Oxford
SP 70/133/178–80: documents relating to Edward de Vere, Earl of Oxford
SP 70/133/186: documents relating to Edward de Vere, Earl of Oxford
SP 70/134/238–9: documents relating to Edward de Vere, Earl of Oxford
SP 70/136/113–14: documents relating to Edward de Vere, Earl of Oxford
SP 70/137/322–3: documents relating to Edward de Vere, Earl of Oxford
SP 99/1/28: documents relating to Stephen Powle
SP 101/81: documents relating to Stephen Powle
WARD 8/13: documents relating to Edward de Vere, Earl of Oxford

**Leicestershire Record Office**
26D53/2583: inventory of Sir Henry Unton's property

**London, British Library**
Additional MS 15914: correspondence of Cesare Carrafa
Additional MS 36706: Fynes Moryson, 'Itinerary'
Cotton MS Galba C V: personal goods stolen from the Earl of Oxford
Cotton MS Vespasian D.xviii: William Thomas 'Peregryne'
Egerton MS 1900: Gabriel Muffel, 'Pilgrim Book'
Egerton MS 2148: Thomas Hoby, 'Booke of the Travaile'
Harleian MS 296: papers of Stephen Powle
Harleian MS 2333: anonymous pilgrimage account
Harleian MS 5009: papers of Peter Vannes
Harleian MS 5133: Fynes Moryson, 'Itinerary'
Harleian MS 6994: correspondence of Sir Francis Walsingham
Lansdowne MS 88: correspondence of Stephen Rodway
Royal MS 17 C x: William Thomas's translation of Josaphat Barbaro
Sloane MS 1813: Richard Smith's account of Sir Edward Unton's travels

**London, Lambeth Palace Library**
MS 605: John Hooker's biography of Sir Peter Carew
Talbot Papers, MS 3206: Correspondence of Gilbert Talbot

**Longleat House, Wiltshire**
Talbot MSS, Volume 2, f. 102: letter of Gilbert Talbot

**Manchester, Chetham's Library**
MS Mun. A.4. 107 (formerly MS 6711): Mandeville's travels

**Manchester, John Ryland's Library**
Latin MS 228: pilgrim miscellany

**Oxford, Bodleian Library**
MS 565: 'Itineraries' of William Wey

MS Arch. Seld.B.50: Ognibene da Lonigo's commentary on Juvenal
MS Bodley 646: Basinio de' Basini's 'Astronomicon'
MS Rawlinson D. 83: Henry Piers's diary
MS Tanner 76, 78, 130, 131, 231, 246, 283, 264, 314: documents relating to Stephen Powle

**Oxford, Corpus Christi College Library**
MS 94: Fynes Moryson, 'Itinerary'

**Oxford, New College**
MS 328/2/40: Philip Sidney's travel licence

**Oxford, Queen's College**
MS 357: anonymous account of a pilgrimage to Jerusalem

**Padua, Archivio di Stato**
Notarile, 5007, ff. 26r–27v: doctoral examination of John Hart at Padua

**San Marino, California, Henry E. Huntingdon Library**
MS EL 26.A.13: anonymous travel itinerary, transcribed by John Shirley

**Surrey History Centre, Woking**
LM/COR/3/382–3, ff. 387–8: Blackfriars lease for Rocco Bonetti

**Venice, Archivio di Stato**
Consiglio dei Dieci, Parti Comuni, R. 31, c. 127r: document relating to Philip Sidney
Capi del Consiglio dei Dieci, Lettere. Fil. 75: document relating to Philip Sidney
Consiglio di X, Lettere ai Capi, filza n. 45, 11 October 1543, ff. 204, 214, 217: documents relating to William Brooke
Consiglio di X, Parti Communi, Reg. 17, f. 37: document relating to John Brooke
Consiglio di X, Parti Communi, Reg. 22, July 1555: document relating to William Page
Proprio Mobili, R 16.C.152: inventory of Edmund Harvell's property
Proprio Vadimoni, R.33: Edmund Harvell's marriage to Apollonis Uttinger

**Venice, Biblioteca Nazionale Marciana**
MS 138.c.180.XVIIb: Cristoforo Sabbadino, map of Venice,

**Vienna**
Hofbibliothek, MS 9737.Z.17: correspondence of Henry Wotton

**Wellcome Library, London**
MS 8004: 'The Physician's Handbook' of Richard 'Esty' or Richard 'of Lincoln'

## PRINTED SOURCES

The publisher is not usually cited, except for primary texts edited in this volume and pre-1600 Venetian imprints.

Accarigi (Accarisio), Alberto, *Vocabulario, grammatica, et orthographia de la lingua volgare*, Cento: in casa de l'auttore, 1543; rpt, Venice, 1550.

Adair, E. R., 'William Thomas: A Forgotten Clerk of the Privy Council' [1924], rpt in *Tudor Studies*, ed. R. W. Seton Watson, New York, 1970, pp. 141–4.

Alunno, Francesco, *Le richezze della lingua volgare*, Venice: Aldus Manutius, 1543.

Amelot de La Houssaie, Abraham-Nicolas, Sieur, *The History of the Government of Venice ... written in the year 1675*, London, 1677.

Anon., 'Antiquarius', 'Account of Englishmen Buried at Venice', *The Gentleman's Magazine*, April 1823, pp. 327–8.

Anon., *Entrata del christianissimo Re Henrico III di Francia*, Venice, 1574.

Anon., *Informacon for pylgrymes unto the holy londe*, London: Wynkyn de Worde, *c.*1498/1500, *STC* 14081; rpt 1515, *STC* 14082, 1524, *STC* 14083; facs. rpt ed. E. Gordon Duff, London, 1893.

Ascham, Roger, *The Scholemaster*, London: J. Daye, 1570, *STC* 832.

—, *The Schoolmaster (1570) by Roger Ascham*, ed. Lawrence V. Ryan, Ithaca, NY, 1967.

Bale, Anthony, '"ut legi": Sir John Mandeville's Audience and Three Late Medieval English Travellers to Italy and Jerusalem', *Studies in the Age of Chaucer*, 38, 2016, pp. 201–37.

Bale, Anthony and Sobecki, Sebastian, eds, *Medieval English Travel. A Critical Anthology*, Oxford, 2019.

Barbaro, Giosafat (Giosaphat, Josaphat), *Viaggi fatti da Vinetia, alla Tana, in Persia*, Venice: sons of Aldus Manutius, 1543–5.

—, *Travels to Tana and Persia, by Josafa Barbaro and Ambrogio Contarini*, tr. William Thomas and S. A. Roy, ed. Lord Stanley of Alderley, London: Hakluyt Society, 1873.

Barbaro, Nicolo, *Diary of the Siege of Constantinople*, tr. J. R. Jones, New York, 1969.

Barbatre, Pierre, *Le Voyage de Pierre Barbatre à Jérusalem en 1480: édition critique d'un manuscrit inédit*, ed. Pierre Tucco-Chala and Noël Pinzuti, Paris, 1972/3 [1974], pp. 75–172.

Barrington, Robert, 'Two Houses Both Alike in Dignity: Reginald Pole and Edmund Harvell', *The Historical Journal*, 39:4, 1996, pp. 895–913.

Bartlett, Kenneth R., *The English in Italy 1525–1558. A Study in Culture and Politics*, Geneva, 1991.

Baxter, Nathaniel, *Sir Philip Sidney's Ourania*, London: Edward Allde for Edward White, 1606.

Bell, Gary, M., *A Handlist of British Diplomatic Representatives 1509–1688*, London, 1990.

Bembo, Pietro, *Della historia vinitiana di m. Pietro Bembo card. volgarmente scritta. Libri XII*, Venice: Gualtero Scotto, 1552.

Bennett, M. J., 'Mandeville's Travels and the Anglo-French Moment', *Medium Aevum*, 75, 2006, pp. 273–92.

Blainville, Monsieur de, *The Travels Through Holland, Germany, Switzerland, and ... Especially Italy*, ed. Daniel Soyer and tr. George Turnbull and William Guthrie, 3 vols, London, 1743–5.

Bo(o)rde, Andrew, *The Fyrst Boke of the Introduction of Knowledge*, London: William Copland, 1555, *STC* 3383; 1562, *STC* 3385.

—, *The Fyrst Boke of the Introduction of Knowledge Made by Andrew Borde*, ed. Frederick James Furnivall, London, 1870.

Bourne, Molly, *Francesco II Gonzaga: The Soldier Prince as Patron*, Rome, 2008.

Boyle, Mary, 'William Wey's Itinerary to the Holy Land: Bodleian Library, MS Bodl. 565 (c.1470)', *Bodleian Library Record*, 28, 2015, pp. 22–36.

—, [typescript] 'To Be a Pilgrim: Writing the Jerusalem Pilgrimage in the Late Middle Ages', published as *Writing the Jerusalem Pilgrimage in the Late Middle Ages*, Woodbridge, 2021.

Brefeld, Josephine, 'An Account of a Pilgrimage to Jerusalem', *Zeitschrift des Deutschen Palästina-Vereins*, 101:2, 1985, pp. 134–55.

Brennan, Michael G. and Kinnamon, Noel J., *A Sidney Chronology 1554–1654*, Basingstoke, 2003.

Breydenbach, Bernardus von, *Peregrinatio in Terram Sanctam* (1486); rpt *Picturing Experience in the Early Printed Book. Breydenbach's Peregrinatio from Venice to Jerusalem*, University Park, PA, 2014.

Brigden, Susan and Woolfson, Jonathan, 'Thomas Wyatt in Italy'. *Renaissance Quarterly*, 58:2, 2005, pp. 464–511.

British History Online, Institute of Historical Research, London, 2003 – https://www.british-history.ac.uk/.

Brown, Horatio F., 'The Marriage Contract, Inventory and Funeral Expenses of Edmund Harvel', *English Historical Review*, 20:1, 1905, pp. 70–77.

Brown, Patricia Fortini, *Venice and Antiquity. The Venetian Sense of the Past*, New Haven, CT, and London, 1996.

Brown, Virginia, Hankins, James and Kaster, Robert A., eds, *Catalogus Translationum et Commentariorum: Mediaeval and Renaissance Latin Translations and Commentaries. Annotated Lists and Guides*, VIII, Washington DC, 2003.

Buxton, John, and Juel-Jensen, Bent, 'Sir Philip Sidney's First Passport Rediscovered', *The Library*, 5 ser., 25, 1970, pp. 42–6.

*Calendar of the Cecil Papers in Hatfield House: Volume 2, 1572–1582*, London, 1888.

*Calendar of the Cecil Papers in Hatfield House: Volume 13, Addenda*. London, 1915.

*Calendar of State Papers Foreign: Edward VI 1547–1553*, ed. William B. Turnbull, London, 1861.

*Calendar of State Papers Foreign: Mary 1553–1558*, ed. William B. Turnbull, London, 1861.

*Calendar of State Papers … Rome, Volume 2, 1572–1578*, London, 1926.

*Calendar of State Papers and Manuscripts, Relating to English Affairs, Existing in the Archives and Collections of Venice and in Other Libraries of Northern Italy, Volume 1, 1202–1509*, ed. Rawdon Brown, London, 1864.

*Calendar of State Papers Relating to English Affairs in the Archives of Venice, Volume 2, 1509–1519*, ed. Rawdon Brown, London, 1867.

*Calendar of State Papers Relating to English Affairs in the Archives of Venice, Volume 4, 1527–1533*, ed. Rawdon Brown, London, 1871.

*Calendar of State Papers Relating to English Affairs in the Archives of Venice, Volume 5, 1534–1554*, ed. Rawdon Brown, London, 1873.

*Calendar of State Papers Relating to English Affairs in the Archives of Venice, Volume 6, 1555–1558*, ed. Rawdon Brown, London, 1877.

*Calendar of State Papers Relating to English Affairs in the Archives of Venice, Volume 7, 1558–1580*, ed. Rawdon Brown and G. Cavendish Bentinck, London, 1890.

*Calendar of State Papers Relating to English Affairs in the Archives of Venice, Volume 8, 1581–1591*, ed. Horatio F. Brown, London, 1894.

*Calendar of State Papers Relating to English Affairs in the Archives of Venice, Volume 9, 1592–1603*, ed. Horatio F. Brown, London, 1897.

*Calendar of State Papers Relating to English Affairs in the Archives of Venice, Volume 10, 1603–1607*, ed. Horatio F. Brown, London, 1900.

*Calendar of State Papers Relating to English Affairs in the Archives of Venice, Volume 19, 1625–1626*, ed. Allen B. Hinds, London, 1913.

*Calendar of State Papers Relating to English Affairs Preserved Principally at Rome in the Vatican Archives and Library, Volume 2, 1572–1578*, ed. J. M. Rigg, London, 1926.

*Calendar of State Papers, Spain, Volume 12, 1554*, ed. Royall Tyler, London, 1949.

Cambridge, University of, Alumni Database: http://venn.lib.cam.ac.uk/Documents/acad/2018/search-2018.html.

Casola, Pietro, *Canon Pietro Casola's Pilgrimage to Jerusalem in the Year 1494*, ed. M. M. Newett, Manchester, 1907.

[Cavendish, Henry] *Mr. Harrie Cavendish: His Journey to and From Constantinople, 1589, by Fox, His Servant*, ed. A. C. Wood, *Camden Miscellany*, 3rd series, 64, London, 1940.

Chambers, David, Pullan, Brian and Fletcher, Jennifer, eds, *Venice. A Documentary History 1450–1630*, Toronto, Buffalo, NY, and London, 2001; rpt 2009.

Chaney, Edward, *The Evolution of the Grand Tour. Anglo-Italian Cultural Relations Since the Renaissance*, London and Portland, OR, 1998.

Childs, David, *Tudor Sea Power. The Foundation of Greatness*, Barnsley, 2009.

Cockram, Sarah D. P., *Isabella d'Este and Francesco Gonzaga. Power Sharing at the Italian Renaissance Court*, Farnham and Burlington, VT, 2013.

Contarini, Gasparo, *The Common-Wealth and Government of Venice*, tr. Lewis Lewkenor, London: John Windet for E. Mattes, 1599, *STC* 5642.

Corbett, Julian Stafford, *Fighting Instructions, 1530–1816*, London: Navy Records Society, 1905.

Cosgrove, Denis, 'Mapping New Worlds: Culture and Cartography in Sixteenth-Century Venice', *Imago Mundi*, 44, 1992, pp. 65–89.

Crichton, James, 'In suum ad urbem Venetam appulsum', in *Delitiæ poetarum scotorum huius illustrium*, ed. Sir John Scot and Arthur Johnstone, Amsterdam, 1637.

— [Anon.], *Lo scozzese, detto Giacomo Crionio*, Venice, 1580.

—, *Venice: A Poem in Latin by James Crichton with an English Version by Robert Crawford and Eight Photogravures by Norman McBeath*, Edinburgh, 2013.

Dallington, Sir Robert, *A Survey of the Great Duke's State of Tuscany. in 1596*, London: G. Eld for E. Blount, 1605, *STC* 6201.

—, *A Method for Travell*, London, 1605, *STC* 6203.

Davey, Francis, 'William Wey: the King's Pilgrim', *Confraternity of Pilgrims to Rome, Newsletter*, no. 3, August 2011, pp. 29–35.

Davies, William, *A True Relation of the Travailes and Captivitie of W. Davies, Barber-Surgion of London, under the Duke of Florence*, London, 1614, *STC* 6365.

Day, John, *The Whole Booke of Psalmes*, London, 1562.

De Beer, 'Robert Langton's *Pylgrimage*', *The Library*, 5th series, 10, 1955, pp. 58–9.

D'Este, Isabella, *Selected Letters*, ed. Deanna Shemek, Toronto and Tempe, AZ, Arizona Center for Medieval and Renaissance Studies, 2017.

Di Stefano, Laura Grazia, 'Pilgrims versus Venetians', 2017: http://www.bbk.ac.uk/pilgrimlibraries/2017/03/03/venetians/.

—, 'How to be a Time Traveller: Exploring Venice with a Fifteenth-Century Pilgrimage Guide', in Conor Kostick, Chris Jones and K. Oschema, eds, *Making the Medieval Relevant: How Medievalists are Revolutionising the Present*, Berlin, 2018, pp. 171–90.

Douglas, Francis, *The Life of James Crichton. Of Clunie; Commonly Called The Admirable Crichton*, Aberdeen, 1760.

Dursteler, Eric R., ed., *A Companion to Venetian History, 1400–1797*, Leiden and Boston: Brill, 2013.

Earwaker, J. P. and Bridgeman, C. G. O., *A Genealogical Account of the Family of Aldersey*, London, 1899.

*Elizabeth I's Foreign Correspondence. Letters, Rhetoric and Politics*, ed. Carlo M. Bajetta, Guillaume Coatalen and Jonathan Gibson, New York, 2014.

Epstein, M., *The Early History of the Levant Company*, London, 1908.

Fabri, Felix, *The Book of the Wanderings of Brother Felix Fabri*, ed. and tr. A. Stewart, 2 vols, Palestine Pilgrims' Text Society, London, 1892–3.

Federici, Cesare, *The Voyage and Travaile of M. Cæsar Frederick, Merchant of Venice, into the East India, the Indies, and Beyond the Indies ... Written at Sea in the Hercules of London: comming from Turkie, the 25. of March. 1588*, tr. Thomas Hickock, 1588, *STC* 10746.

Fenlon, Iain, *The Ceremonial City. History, Memory and Myth in Renaissance Venice*, New Haven, CT, and London, 2007.

Foister, Susan, Gibson, Robin, Rogers, Malcolm and Simon, Jacob, *The National Portrait Gallery Collection*, London, 1988.

Fortuna, Stefania, 'The Latin Editions of Galen's *opera omnia* (1490–1625) and Their Prefaces', *Early Science and Medicine*, 17, 2012, pp. 391–412.

Foster, Brett, '"The Goodliest Place in This World": Early Tudor Reactions to Papal Rome', in Mary A. Papazian, ed., *The Sacred and the Profane in English Renaissance Literature*, Newark, NJ, 2008, pp. 36–42.

Franco, Giacomo, *Viaggio da Venetia a Constantinopoli per Mare*, Venice, 1597.

—, *Habiti d'huomeni et donne venetiane con la processione della serma. Signoria et altri particolari, cioè trionfi, feste et cerimonie publiche della nobilissima città di Venetia*, Venice, 1610; Facsimile of Biblioteca Marciana Copy, Venice: F. Ongania, 1876.

Frank, Thomas, 'An edition of A discourse of HP his travelles (MS Rawlinson D. 83), with an introduction on English travellers to Rome during the age of Elizabeth', unpublished BLitt thesis, University of Oxford, 1954.

Freely, John, *The Grand Turk. Sultan Mehmet II – Conqueror of Constantinople, Master of an Empire and Lord of Two Seas*, London and New York, 2009; rpt 2016.

Gallagher, John, 'The Italian London of John North: Cultural Contact and Linguistic Encounter in Early Modern England', *Renaissance Quarterly*, 70, 2017, pp. 88–131.

—, *Learning Languages in Early Modern England*, Oxford, 2019.

Garrett, Christina Hallowell, *The Marian Exiles. A Study in the Origins of Elizabethan Puritanism*, Cambridge, 1936; rpt 1966.

Garton, John, *Grace and Grandeur. The Portraiture of Paolo Veronese*, London and Turnhout, 2008.

—, 'Veronese's Art of Business: Painting, Investment and the Studio as Social Nexus', *Renaissance Quarterly*, 65, 2012, pp. 753–808.

Goldring, Elizabeth, 'A Portrait of Sir Philip Sidney by Veronese at Leicester House, London', *The Burlington Magazine*, 154, August 2012, pp. 548–54.

—, *Robert Dudley, Earl of Leicester, and the World of Elizabethan Art. Painting and Patronage at the Court of Elizabeth I*, New Haven, CT, and London, 2014.

Grünenberg, Konrad, *Konrad Grünenbergs Pilgerreise ins Heilige Land 1486. Untersuchung, Edition und Kommentar*, ed. Andrea Denke, Cologne, Weimar and Vienna, 2011.

Guildford (Gyylforde), Sir Richard, *This is the begynnynge, and contynuance of the Pylgrymage of Sir Richarde Guylforde Knight & controuler unto our late soveraygne lorde kynge Henry the .vii. And howe he went with his servaunts and company towardes Jherusalem, c.1511*, London: R. Pynson, *STC* 12549.

—, *The Pilgrimage of Sir Richard Guylforde to the Holy Land, A.D. 1506*, ed. Sir Henry Ellis, London: Camden Society, 1851.

Hadfield, Andrew, *Literature, Travel, and Colonial Writing in the English Renaissance 1545–1625*, Oxford, 1998.

Hakluyt, Richard, *The Second Volume of the Principal Navigations, Voyages, Traffiques and Discoveries of the English Nation*, London: G. Bishop, R. Newberie and R Barker, 1599, *STC* 12626.

—, *The Principal Navigations, Voyages, Traffiques & Discoveries of the English Nation*, 12 vols, Glasgow, 1903–5.

Hammer, Paul E. J., *The Polarisation of Elizabethan Politics. The Political Career of Robert Devereux, 2nd Earl of Essex, 1585–97*, Cambridge, 1999.

Hammerton, Rachel Joan, 'English Impressions of Venice up to the Early Seventeenth Century: A Documentary Study', unpublished PhD thesis, University of St Andrews, 1987.

Harff, Arnold von, *The Pilgrimage of Arnold von Harff Knight*, ed. Malcolm Letts, London, 1946.

Harris, John, Orgel, Stephen and Strong, Roy, *The King's Arcadia: Inigo Jones and the Stuart Court*, London, 1973.

Harrison, Eric, 'Henry the Eighth's Gangster: The Affair of Ludovico da l'Armi', *The Journal of Modern History*, 15:4, 1943, pp. 265–74.

Historical Manuscripts Commission, *Report on the Manuscripts of Lord De L'Isle & Dudley*, 6 vols, London, 1925–66.

Hoby, Sir Thomas, *The Travels and Life of Sir Thomas Hoby, Kt of Bisham Abbey, Written by Himself, 1547–1564*, ed. Edgar Powell, *Camden Miscellany*, X, 3rd series, London, 1902.

Howard, Deborah, *The Architectural History of Venice*, New Haven, CT, and London, 2005.

Iordanou, Ioanna, *Venice's Secret Service. Organizing Intelligence in the Renaissance*, Oxford, 2019.

Irving, David, *Lives of Scottish Writers*, vol. I, Edinburgh, 1839.

Jones, Deborah, 'Lodowick Bryskett and His Family', in Charles J. Sisson, ed., *Thomas Lodge and Other Elizabethans*, New York, 1933; rpt 1966, pp. 243–362.

Kaminski, Marion, *Art & Architecture in Venice*, Königswinter, 2005.

[Kempe, Margery], *The Book of Margery Kempe*, tr. and ed. Anthony Bale, Oxford, 2015.

Kew, Graham David, 'Shakespeare's Europe Revisited: The Unpublished *Itinerary* of Fynes Moryson (1566–1630)', 4 vols, unpublished PhD thesis, University of Birmingham, 1995.

Knox, John, *The First Blast of the Trumpet Against the Monstrous Regiment of Women*, Geneva, 1558, *STC* 15070.

Kuin, Roger, 'New Light on the Veronese Portrait of Sir Philip Sidney', *Sidney Newsletter and Journal*, 15, 1997, pp. 19–47.

—, 'Languet and the Veronese Portrait of Sidney: Antwerp Findings', *Sidney Journal*, 15, 1997, 42–4.

—, 'The Sidneys and the Continent: The Tudor Period', in Margaret P. Hannay, Michael G. Brennan and Mary Ellen Lamb, eds, *The Ashgate Companion to The Sidneys, 1500–1700*. Volume I: *Lives*, Farnham and Burlington, VT, 2015, pp. 203–22.

[Lancashire and Cheshire], 'Pedigrees Made at the Visitation of Cheshire, 1613', in *The Record Society for the Publication of Original Documents Relating to Lancashire and Cheshire*, n.p., LVIII, 1909, pp. 5–9.

Lane, Frederick Chapin, *Venetian Ships and Shipbuilders of the Renaissance*, Baltimore, MD, and London, 1934; rpt 1992.

Lane, Frederic Chapin and Mueller, Reinhold C., *Money and Banking in Medieval and Renaissance Venice*, vol. I, *Coins and Moneys of Account*, Baltimore, MD, 1985.

Langton, Robert, *The Pylgrimage of M. Robert Langton* [1522], rpt and ed. E. M. Blackie, Cambridge, MA, 1924.

—, [Portrait] https://www.christies.com/lotfinder/Lot/venetian-school-circa-151213-portrait-5813644-details.aspx.

Lasocki, David and Prior, Roger, *The Bassanos: Venetian Musicians and Instrument Makers in England, 1531–1665*, 1995; rpt London, 2016.

Levin, Carole and Watkins, John, *Shakespeare's Foreign Worlds. National and Transnational Identities in the Elizabethan Age*, Ithaca, NY, and London, 2009, Chapter 4, 'Shakespeare and the Decline of the Venetian Republic', pp. 111–40.

*Letters and Papers, Foreign and Domestic, of the Reign of Henry VIII*, ed. J. S. Brewer and J. Gairdner, 21 vols, London, 1862–1910.

Linacre, Thomas, tr., *Iulii Firmici Astronomicorum libri octo ... Procli eiusdem Sphæra, Thoma Linacro Britanno interprete*, Venice: Aldo Manuzio, 1499.

Lodge, John (revised by Mervyn Archdall), *The Peerage of Ireland*, vol. II, Dublin, 1789.

Lowe, K. J. P., *Nuns' Chronicles and Convent Culture in Renaissance and Counter-Reformation Italy*, Cambridge, 2003.

Lutton, Rob, 'Richard Guldeford's Pilgrimage: Piety and Cultural Change in Late Fifteenth- and Early Sixteenth-Century England', *History, The Journal of the Historical Association*, 98, 2013, pp. 41–78.

—, 'Pilgrimage and Travel Writing in Early Sixteenth-Century England: The Pilgrimage Accounts of Thomas Larke and Robert Langton', *Viator, Medieval and Renaissance Studies*, 48:3, 2017, pp. 333–57.

McPherson, David C., *Shakespeare, Jonson and the Myth of Venice*, Newark, NJ, London and Toronto, 1990.

Magri, Noemi, 'Oxford and the Greek Church in Venice', *De Vere Society Newsletter*, September 2003, p. 1.

—, 'Orazio v Nelson' [transcript of the Cuoco Document in Latin/Venetian dialect Italian], *De Vere Society Newsletter*, April 2006, pp. 6–11.

—, 'Edward de Vere Did Not Build Himself a House in Venice', *De Vere Society Newsletter*, June 2008, pp. 11–16.

Mallett, M. E. and Hale, J. R., *The Military Organization of a Renaissance State. Venice c.1400–1617*, Cambridge, 1984.

Manutius, Aldus, the Younger, *Relatione della qualità di Jacomo di Crettone*, Venice, 1581.

—, *In M. Tullii Ciceronis de officiis libros tres*, ed. A. Manutius et al., Venice, 1581.

Martin, Gregory, *Roma Sancta (1581): Now First Edited from the Manuscript*, ed. George Bruner Parks, Rome, 1969.

Martin, John, *A Bibliographical Catalogue of Books Privately Printed; Including Those of the Bannatyne, Maitland and Roxburghe Clubs*, London, 1834.

Masello, Steven J., 'A Booke of the Travaile and Lief of Me Thomas Hoby, with Diverse Thinges Woorth the Notinge, 1547–1564: A Modern Edition with Introduction and Notes', unpublished PhD thesis, Loyola University, Chicago, 1979.

Mattingly, Garrett, *The Defeat of the Spanish Armada*, 1959; rpt London, 1988.

Mayer, Thomas F., *Thomas Starkey and the Commonweal. Humanist Politics and Religion in the Reign of Henry VIII*, Cambridge, 1989.

Mitchell, R. J., 'A Renaissance Library: The Collection of John Tiptoft, Earl of Worcester', *The Library*, 4th series, 18, 1937, 67–83.

—, *John Tiptoft*, London, 1938.

—, 'Robert Langton's *Pylgrimage*', *The Library*, 5th series, 8, 1953, pp. 42–5.

—, 'Antonio Loredan and the Jaffa Voyage', *Italian Studies*, 13, 1958, p. 85.

—, *The Spring Voyage. The Jerusalem Pilgrimage in 1458*, London, 1964; rpt 1965.

Moryson, Fynes, *An Itinerary Written by Fynes Moryson Gent. First in the Latine Tongue, and Then Translated by Him into English*, London: John Beale, 1617, *STC* 18205.

—, *An Itinerary*, 4 vols, Glasgow, 1907–8.

—, *Shakespeare's Europe: A Survey of the Conditions of Europe at the end of the 16th century. Being unpublished chapters of Fynes Moryson's Itinerary (1617)*, ed. Charles Hughes, 1903; New York, 1967.

—, *see also* Kew, Graham David.

Mount, Toni, 'Further Adventures in Historical Research', *Ricardian Bulletin*, Autumn 2007, pp. 30–32.

Nelson, Alan H., *Monstrous Adversary. The Life of Edward de Vere, 17th Earl of Oxford*, Liverpool, 2003.

Newman, John, 'Inigo Jones's Architectural Education Before 1614', *Architectural History*, 35, 1992, pp. 18–50.

Nicolas, Nicholas Harold, *Testamenta Vetusta: being Illustrations from Wills*, vol. II, London, 1826.

Nichols, John Gough, *The Unton Inventories Relating to Wadley and Faringdon, Co. Berks, in the Years 1596 and 1620*, London, 1841.

411

Nichols, Tom, *Titian and the End of the Venetian Renaissance*, London, 2013.

Norwich, John Julius, *A History of Venice*, Harmondsworth, 1983.

—, ed., *A Traveller's Companion to Venice*, London: 1990; rpt 2002.

Ongaro, Giulio M., 'New Documents on the Bassano Family', *Early Music*, 22, 1993, pp. 409–16.

Orliac, Antoine, *Veronese*, tr. Mary Chamot, New York, 1940.

Ormrod, Mark W., 'John Mandeville, Edward III, and the King of Inde', *Chaucer Review*, 46, 2012, pp. 314–39.

Osborn, James, B., *Young Philip Sidney, 1572–1577*, New Haven, CT, and London, 1972.

Overell, M. Anne, *Italian Reform and English Reformations, c.1535–c.1585*, Aldershot and Burlington, VT, 2008.

—, 'Cardinal Pole's Special Agent: Michael Throckmorton, *c.*1503–1558', *History*, 94, 2009, pp. 265–78.

—, *Nicodemites. Faith and Concealment Between Italy and Tudor England*, Leiden and Boston, MA, 2018.

*Oxford Dictionary of National Biography*, ed. H. C. G. Matthew and Brian Harrison, Oxford, 2004– (on-line edition).

*Oxford English Dictionary*, Online Electronic Resource, Oxford, 1989– (on-line edition).

Pächt, Otto and Alexander, J. J. G., *Illuminated Manuscripts in the Bodleian Library Oxford*, vol. II, *Italian School*, Oxford, 1970.

Paine, Lincoln P., *Warships of the World to 1900*, Boston, MA, and New York, 2000.

Partridge, Mary, 'Thomas Hoby's English Translation of Castiglione's *Book of the Courtier*', *The Historical Journal*, 50:4, 2007, pp. 769–86.

Parmenius, Stephanus, *Paean ad psalmum Davidis CIV conformatus*, London, 1582, *STC* 19308.5.

Petrarcha, Francesco, *Il Petrarcha con l'espositione d'Alessandro Vellutelloe con piu utili cose in diversi luoghi di quella novissimamente da lui aggiunte*, Venice: Maestro Bernadino de Vidali Venetiano, 1532.

Pezzolo, Edoardo, 'The Venetian Economy', in Eric R Dursteler, ed., *A Companion to Venetian History, 1400–1797*, Leiden and Boston, MA, 2013, pp. 255–89.

[Piers, Henry], *Henry Piers's Continental Travels, 1595–1598*, ed. Brian Mac Cuarta, SJ, Camden, 5th series, 54, Cambridge: Royal Historical Society, 2018.

Porcacchi, Thomaso, *Le attioni d'Arrigo terzo re di Francia, et quarto di Polonia, descritte in dialogo*, Venice, 1574.

[Poulet, Sir Amias], *Copy-Book of Sir Amias Poulet's Letters, Written During his Embassy to France (A.D. 1577)*, ed. Octavius Ogle, London, 1866.

Quarmby, Kevin A., *The Disguised Ruler in Shakespeare and His Contemporaries*, Farnham and Burlington, VT, 2012.

Rearick, W. R., *The Art of Paolo Veronese 1528–1588*, Exhibition Catalogue, National Gallery of Art, Washington DC and Cambridge, 1988.

*Richard of Lincoln A Medieval Doctor Travels to Jerusalem*, ed. and tr. Francis Davey, Exeter, 2013.

Ridolfi, Carlo, *Life of Titian*, ed. Julia Conaway Bondanella and Peter Bondanella, Bruce Cole and Jody Robin Shiffman; tr. Julia Conaway Bondanella and Peter Bondanella, University Park, PA, 1996.

Rosand, David, *Titian*, New York, 1978.

—, 'Dialogues and Apologies: Sidney and Venice', *Studies in Philology*, 88, 1991, pp. 236–49.

Ross, Elizabeth, *Picturing Experience in the Early Printed Book. Breydenbach's Peregrinatio from Venice to Jerusalem*, University Park, PA, 2014.

Rous, John, *Historia regum Angliae*, ed. Thomas Hearne, Oxford, 1716.

Rowse, A. L., *Ralegh and the Throckmortons*, New York, 1962.

Ruddock, Alwyn A., 'The Merchants of Venice and their Shipping in Southampton in the Fifteenth and Sixteenth Centuries', *Proceedings of the Hampshire Field Club*, 15, 1943, pp. 274–91.

Rutter, Carol Chillington, '"Hear the Ambassadors!" Marking Shakespeare's Venice Connection', *Shakespeare Survey*, 66, 2013, pp. 265–86.

Salomon, Xavier, *Veronese*, London, 2014.

Sansovino, Francesco, *Venetia città nobilissima et singolare*, Venice: Jacomo Sansovino, 1581.

—, *Sansovino's Venice. A Translation of Francesco Tatti da Sansovino's Guidebook to Venice of 1561*, tr. Vaughan Hart and Peter Hicks, New Haven, CT, and London, 2017.

Sanudo, Marin, *Venice Città Excelentissimi. Selections from the Renaissance Diaries of Marin Sanudo*, ed. Patricia H. Labalme and Laura Sanguineri White, tr. Linda L. Caroll, Baltimore, MD, 2008.

Sanuto (Sanudo), Marino (Marin), *I Diarii di Marino Sanuto*, 58 vols, Bologna and Venice, 1969–70.

Schulz, Juergen, 'Jacopo de' Barbari's View of Venice: Map Making, City Views, and Moralized Geography Before the Year 1500, *The Art Bulletin*, 60, 1976, pp. 425–74.

Shakespeare, William, *The Merchant of Venice*, ed. John Russell Brown, The Arden Shakespeare, London and New York, 1981.

Shrank, Cathy, *Writing the Nation in Reformation England, 1530–1580*, Oxford, 2004.

[Sidney, Sir Philip], *The Correspondence of Sir Philip Sidney*, ed. Roger Kuin, 2 vols, Oxford, 2012.

Spenser, Edmund, *Three proper, and wittie, familiar letters*, London, 1580.

[Stationers' Registers], *A Transcript of the Registers of the Company of Stationers of London; 1554–1640 A.D.*, ed. Edward Arber, 3 vols, London, 1876.

Starkey, Thomas, *A Dialogue Between Pole and Lupset*, ed. Thomas F. Mayer, Camden Society, 4th series, 37, London: 1989.

[STC] *A Short-Title Catalogue of Books Printed in England, Scotland, & Ireland ... 1475–1640*, compiled by A. W. Pollard and G. R. Redgrave; 2nd edn, revised and enlarged by W. A. Jackson, F. S. Ferguson and K. F. Pantzer, Volume I, *A–H*, London, 1986; Volume II, *I–Z*, London, 1976.

Steer, John, *Venetian Painting. A Concise History*, London, 1970; rpt 2003.

Stern, Virginia F., *Sir Stephen Powle of Court and Country. Memorabilia of a Government Agent for Queen Elizabeth I, Chancery Official, and English Country Gentleman*, Selinsgrove, PA, London and Toronto, 1992.

Stewart, Alan, *Philip Sidney. A Double Life*, London, 2000.

Strong, Sir Roy, 'Sir Henry Unton and his Portrait: An Elizabethan Memorial Picture and its History', *Archaeologia*, 99, 1965, pp. 53–76.

—, *Tudor & Jacobean Portraits*, 2 vols, London, 1969.

—, *The Cult of Elizabeth. Elizabethan Portraiture and Pageantry*, London, 1977; rpt, 1999.

—, 'Sidney's Appearance Reconsidered', in *The Tudor and Stuart Monarchy. Pageantry, Painting, Iconography*, 3 vols, *Volume II. Elizabethan*, Woodbridge, 1995.

Tait, J., 'Letters of John Tiptoft, Earl of Worcester, and Archbishop Neville to the University of Oxford', *English Historical Review*, 35:150, 1920, pp. 570–74.

Tate, R. B., 'Robert Langton, Pilgrim (1470–1524)', *Nottingham Medieval Studies*, 39, 1995, pp. 182–91.

Tenenti, Alberto, *Piracy and the Decline of Venice 1580–1615*, Berkeley and Los Angeles, CA, 1967 (translated from *Venezia e i corsari, 1580–1615*, Bari, 1961).

Thomas, William, *The Vanitee of this World*, London, 1549, *STC* 24023.

—, *Il pellegrino inglese*, Zurich: Andreas Gessner and Rudolf Wyssenbach, 1552.

—, *The Historie of Italie ... Intreateth of the Estate of Many and Divers Common Weales*, London: Thomas Berthelet, 1549, *STC* 24018, and 1561, *STC* 24019.

—, *Principall Rules of the Italian Grammer, with a Dictionarie for the Better Understandying of Boccace, Petrache and Dante*, London, 1550, *STC* 24040; rpt 1562, 1567.

—, *The History of Italy ... 1549*, ed. G. B. Parks, Ithaca, NY, 1963.

Thompson, J., 'Portrait of Dr. Robert Langton', *Notes & Queries*, 2nd series, 6, 30 October 1858, pp. 347–8.

Thomson, Patricia, 'Wyatt and the Petrarchan Commentators', *Review of English Studies*, new series, 10:39, 1959, pp. 225–33.

Tognotti, Eugenia, 'Prevention Strategies and Changes in Sexual Mores in Response to the Outbreak of Syphilis in Europe in the Early Modern Age', *Journal of Infectious Diseases & Preventive Medicine*, 2, 2014, pp. 1–4.

Tomeo, Niccolò Leonico, *Aristotelis Parva quae vocant Naturalia*, Venice: Bernardino Vitali, 1523.

—, *Opuscula*. Venice: Bernardino Vitali, 1525.

—, *Conversio in Latinum atque explanatio primi libri Aristotelis de partibus animalium*. Venice: G. Farri, 1540.

Torkington, Sir Richard, *Ye Oldest Diarie of Englysshe Travell: being the Hitherto Unpublished Narrative of the Pilgrimage of Sir Richard Torkington to Jerusalem in 1517*, ed. W. J. Loftie, London, 1884.

Ungerer, Gustav, 'Recovering a Black African's Voice in an English Lawsuit: Jacques Francis and the Salvage Operations of the *Mary Rose* and the *Sancta Maria and Sanctus Edwardus*, 1545–ca.1550', *Medieval and Renaissance Drama in England*, 17, 2005, pp. 255–71.

Valcanover, Francesco, *Jacopo Tintoretto and the Scuola Grande of San Rocco*, Venice, c.1983.

Ward, B. M., *The Seventeenth Earl of Oxford 1550–1604 From Contemporary Documents*, London, 1928.

Webbe, Edward, *The Rare and Most Wonderful Thinges Which E. Webbe Hath Seen in the Landes of Jewrie, Egypt, Grecia, Russia, and Prester John*, London: W. Wright, 1590, *STC* 25151.5-25154.

—, *Edward Webbe, Chief Master Gunner, His Travailes. 1590*, ed. Edward Arber, English Reprints, London, 1868.

Weiss, Roberto, 'A Letter-Preface of John Free to John Tiptoft, Earl of Worcester', *Bodleian Quarterly Record*, 8, 1935–37, pp. 101–3.

—, *Humanism in England During the Fifteenth Century*, 3rd edn, Oxford, 1967.

Wey, William, *The Itineraries of William Wey ... From the Original Manuscript in the Bodleian Library*, ed. G. Williams, Roxburghe Club, London, 1857

—, *Map of the Holy Land: illustrating the itineraries of William Wey, fellow of Eton in A.D. 1458 and 1462*, ed. Bulkeley Bandinel, Roxburghe Club, London, 1867. [This fourteenth-century map, Oxford, Bodleian Library, MS Douce 389, was consulted and indexed by Wey; see Bale, 2016, p. 214.]

—, *The Itineraries of William Wey*, ed. Francis Davey, Oxford, 2010.

Willan, T. S., 'Some Aspects of English Trade with the Levant in the Sixteenth Century', *The English Historical Review*, 70, July 1955, pp. 399–410.

Wilson, Bronwen, *The World in Venice. Print, the City, and Early Modern Identity*, Toronto, Buffalo, NY, and London, 2005.

Wing, Donald, *Short-title Catalogue of Books .... 1641–1700*, New York, 1945–51.

Wood, Cameron, '"A commyn wele of true nobylyte": Thomas Starkey and Italian Renaissance Republican Thought in Sixteenth-Century England', unpublished MA by Research thesis, Macquarie University, Sydney, Australia, 2016.

Woodward, David, 'The Italian Map Trade, 1480–1650', in David Woodward, ed., *The History of Cartography, Volume Three (Part I). Cartography in the European Renaissance*, Chicago, IL, 2007, pp. 773–803.

Woolfson, Jonathan, *Padua and the Tudors. English Students in Italy, 1485–1603*, Cambridge, 1998.

Wotton, Sir Henry, *The State of Christendom ... Written by the Renowned Sir Henry Wotton, Knight, Ambassadour in Ordinary to the Most Serene Republick of Venice*, London, 1667, Wing W3655.

—, *The Life and Letters of Sir Henry Wotton*, ed. Logan Pearsall Smith, 2 vols, Oxford, 1907.

Wyatt, Michael, *The Italian Encounter with Tudor England: A Cultural Politics of Translation*, Cambridge, 2009.

Yeames, A. H. S., 'The Grand Tour of an Elizabethan', *Papers of the British School at Rome*, 7:3, 1914, pp. 92–113.

Questa è d'ogni alto ben nido secondo
Vinetia: et tal, che chi lei vede, stima
Veder raccolto in breue spacio il mondo.

Elietypia. C. Jacobi. Venezia.

Figure 45.    Giacomo Franco, *La Città di Venetia* (1614), Giacomo Franco's concluding image of Venice. By permission of Special Collections, Brotherton Library, University of Leeds.

# INDEX

For buildings and locations in Venice, see under individual names, e.g. Arsenal, Fondaco dei Tedeschi, Fortessa di Sant'Andrea and Piazza San Marco. Churches in Venice are also listed under their individual names.